THE
CHICANO
HERITAGE

MEXICAN CALIFORNIA

With an Introduction
by Carlos E. Cortés

ARNO PRESS
A New York Times Company
New York — 1976

Editorial Supervision: LESLIE PARR

———◆———

Reprint Edition 1976 by Arno Press Inc.

Copyright © 1976 by Arno Press Inc.

Notes on Upper California and In California
Before the Gold Rush were reprinted from
copies in the State Historical Society of
Wisconsin Library. The Manifesto to the
Mexican Republic was reprinted from a copy
in the Princeton University Library. Governor
Mariano Chico's Report was reprinted from a
copy in the Bancroft Library. A Description
of California was reprinted from a copy in
the University of California at Riverside
Library.

THE CHICANO HERITAGE
ISBN for complete set: 0-405-09480-9
See last pages of this volume for titles.

Manufactured in the United States of America

———◆———

Library of Congress Cataloging in Publication Data

Main entry under title:

Mexican California.

(The Chicano heritage)
CONTENTS: Smith, F. R. The architectural history of
Mission San Carlos Borromeo, California.--Bandini, J.
A description of California in 1828.--Coulter, T. Notes
on Upper California. [etc.]
1. California--History--To 1846--Sources.
I. Series.
F864.M53   979.4   76-5567
ISBN 0-405-09538-4

MEXICAN CALIFORNIA

Introduction

Mexican California lasted only twenty-five years — from the winning of Mexican independence from Spain in 1821 to the United States conquest of California in 1846. Yet this brief period is rich, complex, and critical for a valid understanding of California history and the Chicano experience since the U.S. occupation. This anthology provides multiple perspectives on this era through first-hand accounts of Mexican Californians, foreign visitors, and early post-conquest Anglo-American occupants as well as through later historical interpretations.

The first work in the anthology, *The Architectural History of Mission San Carlos Borromeo, California* by Frances Rand Smith, takes the story of Mexican California back to its Spanish California roots. The book describes the construction and architectural innovations of the mission following its transfer to the Carmel River Valley in 1771 after a year on Monterey Bay. Numerous photographs, engraving, maps, and architectural diagrams highlight this revealing study of one aspect of the development of the extensive and significant California mission system.

The next two selections are eye-witness descriptions of California in the late 1820's and early 1830's. The first, *A Description of California in 1828,* is by José Bandini, a Spanish-born sailor who settled in California in the 1820's. This report provides a panoramic view of early Mexican California, touching on such topics as government, economics, geography, and types of settlements. Of special interest is the fact that Bandini's son, Juan, became a member of the California legislature and the Mexican Congress and used this report as the basis for one he wrote in 1830. The second eye-witness account, *Notes on Upper California. A Journey from Monterey to the Colorado River in 1832,* is by Thomas Coulter, an Irish botanist. Coulter touches on various aspects of California — its climatic and geographical conditions, its agricultural and livestock development, the mission system, the decline of California's Indian population, and the Mexican government's colonization efforts.

While Bandini and Coulter provide interesting laymen's observations on California, the next two selections present perspectives by two governors of Mexican California. The first document, an 1835 public manifesto by Governor José Figueroa, focuses on the controversial California colony established in the early 1830's by José María Híjar and José María Padrés. Responding to accusations against him concerning his attitude and actions toward the Híjar-Padrés colony, Figueroa issued this manifesto, which includes numerous letters and official documents. Of a more general nature is the 1836 report of Governor Mariano Chico. This report reveals the turbulent conditions of that era, particularly the constancy of revolutionary conspiracies and the continuous depredations from foreign ships along the California coast.

Perspectives by Anglo-Americans comprise the next two selections. Mexican California on the eve of the U.S. conquest is discussed in John Bidwell's *In California before the Gold Rush*. A member of the first Anglo-American wagon train to California, Bidwell arrived in northern California in 1841 and was a participant in and observer of many of the critical events of Mexican California in the 1840's. His recollections cover from the 1841 expedition through the Bear Flag Revolt of 1846 and the final U.S. military victory in California in 1847. Following Bidwell's observations is the 1850 report of William Carey Jones, who in July, 1849, had been appointed as a U.S. government confidential agent to obtain information on California land titles. The report is in the form of a letter from Jones to the U.S. Secretary of the Interior. Of particular importance are the numerous Mexican laws, proclamations, and decrees included in the report.

The last selection provides a retrospective look at the history of one area of Mexican California — the San Bernardino Valley. Written by Father Juan Caballería, the book covers the story of the valley from the time of the early Spanish explorers through the founding of missions, the development of ranchos, the U.S. conquest of California, and the arrival of Mormon settlers immediately after the war. Although limited by its often negative stereotyping of Native Americans, the book nonetheless furnishes a valuable introduction to the area.

The U.S. conquest of California brought to a premature conclusion the remarkable Mexican era in California. While the period was brief in years, its impact on California and on Chicanos is still being felt.

CARLOS E. CORTÉS
Professor of History
Chairman, Chicano Studies
University of California, Riverside
June, 1976

CONTENTS

THE ARCHITECTURAL HISTORY

OF

Mission San Carlos Borromeo

CALIFORNIA

BY

Frances Rand Smith

Published by the

California Historical Survey Commission

BERKELEY, 1921

CALIFORNIA STATE PRINTING OFFICE
SACRAMENTO, 1921

LETTER OF TRANSMITTAL.

To His Excellency, WILLIAM D. STEPHENS, *Governor,*
Sacramento, California.

SIR: Herewith is presented *The Architectural History of Mission San Carlos Borromeo,* the first of a projected series dealing with the architectural history of the Spanish missions of California, the work being undertaken under the statutes prescribing the duties of the Commission.

Respectfully submitted.

CALIFORNIA HISTORICAL SURVEY COMMISSION,

JOHN F. DAVIS, *Chairman,*
HERBERT E. BOLTON,
EDWARD A. DICKSON,
OWEN C. COY, *Director.*

Berkeley, California, August 15, 1921.

FRONTISPIECE. *Ruins of San Carlos about 1865.*

This photo by Johnson is the earliest photograph at hand. This is seen by the remains of the wall against the facade of the church, the condition of the roof over the chapel, and the ruins in the rear to the left.

EDITOR'S PREFACE

This volume is the first of a projected series relating to the architectural history of the Spanish missions of California. The work was undertaken by the Historical Survey Commission under a statute of 1917 (Statutes, 1917, Chap. 410), defining its duties to be among other things "to investigate and acquire information as to the physical characteristics of the several missions which were maintained in the State of California under the charge of the Franciscan fathers."

For many years Mrs. Frances Rand Smith of Palo Alto had been engaged in the study of the old California missions and she already had copious notes, sketches, photographs and models of several of the missions. The commission therefore sought her cooperation in this work and during the summer of 1918 obtained from her the manuscript, sketches and photographs which form the basis for this report. Since that time the author and the commission have been busily engaged in revising, elaborating, and perfecting the original manuscript.

In accordance with the terms of the act a public hearing was held at Carmel, October 31, 1918, at which time the details of this report were carefully gone over by the many persons assembled who represented the Church, historical and landmarks societies, and many others. Many interesting points were developed but no material additions to the information or adverse criticism of the findings of the commission were offered.

Subsequent excavations carried on by Father Raymond M. Mestres, in charge of the parish in which San Carlos Mission is located, brought to light much valuable data and a wealth of detail regarding the mission buildings. These excavations together with continued historical research and the gathering of additional photographs has made it possible for the commission to supplement materially the original text.

In a work of this character, where the official historical records and the archeological remains are not complete but must be supplemented by other less reliable data, it is necessary to keep clearly in mind the varying degrees of reliability of the evidence presented. At least three classes of information have been used in this work. First, the archeological remains as seen in the buildings and ruins now extant. In so far as these remains can be identified as parts of the mission before the time of secularization they are the most valuable data to be obtained as to form, material, and dimension. Second, there are the written records. These vary in reliability from the official contemporary records òf the padres and the detailed descriptions of more or less accurate observations of scientific explorers, as Lapérouse, Vancouver, Du Petit-Thouars and others, to the less definite and unreliable accounts. Third, the pictorial representations of the missions as shown by sketches, survey-plats, and photographs. The relia-bility of these last classes increases in the order named. For San Carlos three sketches made by foreign voyagers antedate the time of the photographs: one by Sykes, made about 1794; one by Wm. Smythe, probably made in 1823; and the other published by Laplace in the account of his voyage along the California coast in 1839. They all possess great value but are merely the artist's description, their accuracy depending directly upon the degree of faithfulness with which he represented the scene before him. It is probable that in some cases merely rude pencil sketches were the only definite record made upon the spot, much of the detail being added during the many leisure hours upon shipboard. It is therefore not remarkable that many points may be found in these sketches which cause difficulty in interpretation. The photographs, which first appear during the sixties, are free from this criticism and preserve for us most valuable information of what still remained of these old landmarks. Of particular value are the views of Johnson, Muybridge, Perkins, Watkins and Fiske.

For aid in the prosecution of this work the commission wishes to express its appreciation to His Grace the Most Reverend Edward J. Hanna, Archbishop of San Francisco, and the Right Reverend J. J. Cantwell, Bishop of Monterey and Los Angeles, for their cordial support and assistance; to Monsignor Joseph M. Gleason of Palo Alto; to Reverend Thomas L. O'Neill of Berkeley, who kindly gave much assistance and valuable advice; and especially does it appreciate the help of Father Raymond M. Mestres of Monterey, whose excavations have enabled the commission to incorporate into this report much valuable material which otherwise would have been inaccessible. Gratitude is due the authorities in charge of the Bancroft Collection for the data contained in the valuable transcripts made by Bancroft from the original archives, many of which have subsequently been destroyed. Mr. C. B. Turrill has furnished copies for several excellent illustrations. From the State Library through Miss Eudora Garroutte and Mr. H. C. Peterson many valuable photographs have been obtained, especially those taken by C. W. J. Johnson, now belonging to the Frances M. Hilby Collection of the State Library. From Mrs. Ivy Perkins Cercle of San Francisco were obtained the views taken by her father, Mr. Perkins, the original negatives subsequently having been placed in the State Library. Valuable criticism and advice regarding architectural features were obtained from Mr. Bernard Maybeck and the School of Architecture of the University of California. Mr. B. S. Hayne assisted in observations at the mission and worked into form for reproduction many of the illustrations contained in this report. It scarcely need be added that all students of the California missions are constantly indebted to Father Zephyrin Engelhardt for his scholarly works.

Much historical data has purposely been eliminated because this study is limited closely to the "physical characteristics" of the mission. On the other hand the architectural study might have been made more elaborate in detail had our resources been less limited. If this data is incomplete in some particular it is believed to be all that may be incorporated with a satisfactory historical basis at present. In view of the fact that the greatest number of readers will be neither technically trained historians nor architects an endeavor has been made to avoid an undue amount of technical language or detail in either field.

The actual restoration of these mission structures is not within the province of this commission. What is here presented is set forth in the hope that it may be of assistance to those so engaged, and with the feeling that it will furnish much useful data to that larger group of general readers interested in studying California mission architecture.

OWEN C. COY.

Berkeley, California, June 15, 1921.

AUTHOR'S PREFACE

For assistance in the prosecution and completion of the present work the writer's thanks are due especially to Professor Herbert E. Bolton, for his personal aid and encouragement; to Dr. Owen C. Coy, for his skillful assistance in investigations at the mission and his unfailing guidance in bibliographic studies and preparation of the text; to the Reverend Monsignor Joseph Gleason, for generous contributions from his library and store of personal knowledge of mission history; to Mr. Chas. B. Turrill, for his contribution of many pictures of historical value; to Mr. L. S. Slevin, for the use of his collections of old pictures and his zeal in securing new ones. The cordial aid of these and many other friends has lightened the labor which has lasted through the years since 1908, when this study was begun. The writer hopes that it may be a modest tribute to the achievements of the pious padres who founded our earliest settlements.

FRANCES RAND SMITH.

TABLE OF CONTENTS

LIST OF ILLUSTRATIONS

HISTORICAL NARRATIVE

HISTORICAL NARRATIVE

Mission San Carlos Borromeo was founded on June 3, 1770, by Father Junípero Serra. The first site was on the shore of Monterey Bay, near the spot where Vizcaíno landed, and where the Carmelite friars said mass "in the shadow of a large oak tree, some of whose branches reached the water." Portolá, who had explored the site the previous year, took formal possession of the port on the date mentioned and was present at the founding of the mission. The historic ceremony is described by Father Serra in a contemporary letter as follows :[1]

"On the holy day of Pentecost, the 3rd of June, after having gathered together all the officers of sea and land and all the rest of the people by the side of the little ravine and oak where the Fathers of that other expedition [Vizcaíno] had held their celebration, an altar was erected, the bells were hung up and rung, the hymn *Veni Creator* was sung and the water blessed, and finally a large cross was erected and the royal standard set up. I then sang the first Mass which we suppose has been celebrated here since that long ago, and then we sang the *Hail to Our Lady* before the image of our Most Illustrious Queen which occupied the altar. After that I preached a sermon to the assembled people. After the service had been concluded with the *Te Deum* the officers performed the ceremony of taking formal possession of the land in the name of the King, our lord (whom may God keep). We afterwards ate our dinner together under a shade on the beach. The whole service had been accompanied with much thunder of powder both on land and from the ship. To God alone be given all the honor and glory."

Father Crespi, who was associated with Serra in the administration of the mission, described its founding in the following words :[2]

"On the same day of Pentecost, June 3rd, . . . the Rev. Fr. Presidente of the missions, Fr. Junípero Serra, in the name of the king and of the Rev. Fr. Guardian and the venerable Discretory of the Apostolic College of the Propagation of the Faith, of San Fernando de Mexico, established the new mission under the title of San Carlos Borromeo. Naming as principal patron of the new church the most holy Patriarch St. Joseph, he took possession of it in the name of the said college, and assigned as his fellow missionary Fr. Juan Crespi, his disciple in philosophy."

Temporary buildings were erected for the presidio. An enclosure made of branches and trees and provided with an altar served temporarily as a church. Soon a small chapel was built, together with the living quarters for the padres and the necessary workshops. All was surrounded by a stockade.[3]

The Question of a New Site. Soon after the founding of the mission Father Serra became dissatisfied with its location. He therefore petitioned the proper authorities to be permitted to remove the mission from the site on Monterey Bay to the valley of the Carmel River about a league distant

---

[1]Palou, *Relacion historica de la vida y apostolicas tareas del venerable padre Fray Junípero Serra* (1787 ed.), 101-102. Hereafter cited as *"Vida."* For translation see James edition, p. 98. See also Engelhardt. *The Missions and Missionaries of California,* II, 74-75, for translation from Crespi's account in Palou, *Noticias de la Neuva California* (San Francisco, 1874), II, 268-269.

[2]Engelhardt, II, 77, 78.

[3]Palou, *Noticias,* II, 271-272; *Vida,* 103.

across the peninsula. As the reason for this request he explained that there was but little arable land in the vicinity of the port and that running water for purposes of irrigation was entirely lacking. Another reason doubtless strong in the mind of Father Serra was to provide a greater distance between the mission Indians and the soldiers of the presidio.[4] The proposed location held all of these advantages over the one already selected, for the valley possessed much fertile land for cultivation and the river could furnish all the water needed for irrigation.

Removal to Carmel Valley, 1771. In response to the petition of Fr. Serra, the Viceroy granted the permit to remove the mission to the Carmel River at such place as Serra might select,[5] and also as a personal donation sent a set of vestments consisting of chasuble and dalmaties, which were to be used on solemn occasions.[6] In June, as soon as the order had been received from the Viceroy granting permission for the removal, Serra set out for Carmel Valley to select the site and make ready for the removal of the mission. Leaving at that place several Lower California Indians under the charge of three marines and five soldiers to cut and prepare timbers, Serra hastened to found a mission later known as San Antonio de Padua.[7] Returning to Carmel Valley he found the work progressing too slowly to suit his desires, so he took up his abode at the new mission site on the first of August, 1771. Since the Indians and soldiers had already provided an amount of wood and timbers, Father Serra set about the construction of the necessary buildings, he himself acting as "engineer and overseer." His first work was to have hewn out a great cross, which after being consecrated was raised and fixed in the ground about the center of the area determined for the mission. Near at hand stood a hut in which he lived and another which served provisionally as a church.[8]

Palou gives the following more detailed account of the removal of the Mission:[9]

"As soon as the Mission of San Antonio had been founded, the reverend padre proceeded to the Royal Presidio of Monterey, and although he eagerly desired to go, and found another mission, San Luis Obispo, it was not possible on account of a lack of soldiers for a guard, and so he assisted in removing the mission as His Excellency had ordered; for this purpose it was arranged that Fray Juan Crespi and the ministers destined for San Luis should remain in the Royal Presidio, and the reverend padre determined to proceed to the place on the Carmel, which had been designated, to plan

[4]Palou, *Noticias,* II, 286; Engelhardt, *Missions and Missionaries,* II, 81; Bancroft, *History of California,* I, 177.

[5]De Croix to Fages, Nov. 12, 1770, in *Archives of California, Provincial State Papers,* I, 70 (Bancroft Collection, ms.)

[6]Engelhardt, II, 84.

[7]*Ibid,* II, 87; Bancroft, I, 177, based on Palou, *Vida,* 121; (James ed.), 115-116; Palou, *Noticias,* II, 289. This was the first use of these extensive forests for construction purposes of which there is at hand any record.

[8]Palou, *Vida,* 128; (James ed.), 124. "La primera obra que mando hacer fué una grande Cruz, que bendita, enarboló (ayudado de los Soldados y Sirvientes) y fixó en la mediania del tramo destinado para compás, que estaba enmediato a la Barraca de su habitacion, y otra que servia de interina Iglesia, siendo su compañia y todas sus delicias aquella sagrada Señal. Adorabala luego que amanecia, y cantaba la Tropa el Alabado, y delante de ella rezaba el Siervo de Dios Maytines y Prima, é inmediatamente celebraba el Santo Sacrificio de la Misa, a que asistian todos los Soldados y Mozos. Despues comenzaban todos su trabajo, cada uno en su destino, siendo Ingeniero y Sobrestante de la obra el V. Padre, quien muchas veces al dia adoraba la Santa Cruz, rezando delante de ella el oficio Divino."

[9]Palou, *Noticias,* II, 291-294. "Luego de concluida la fundacion de la mision de San Antonio de Padua pasó al real presidio de Monterey el reverendo padre presidente, y aunque deseaba con

and promote the work of the church and dwellings. With this purpose in view he journeyed to the banks of the Carmel, the first of August of the said year, 1771, accompanied by the five soldiers.

"The three sailors and four California Indians, assisted by the soldiers, had already cut timbers. Work was begun, and soon a small chapel was erected together with living quarters of four rooms, a large room for a granary, and also a house to be used as a dwelling and kitchen for the boys. All were of wood and had flat roofs and were enclosed in a good stockade. In the corner of the square there was a house, also with a flat roof, for the soldiers, and near, some corrals for the cattle and stock. As the workers were few, and progress could not be rapid because all the tools and utensils were in the old mission joining the Royal Presidio, work was not finished and the removal was not completed until the last of December of the said year of 71, in which year all was moved, the two ministers of the mission remaining to say mass at the Royal Presidio until establishment of the new mission was entirely completed.

"After its removal the mission of San Carlos was in a pleasant location, situated on a hill with a view over an extensive plain, which promises abundant crops. It extends along the Carmel River whose waters flow all the year, for although in dry seasons the water is not very plentiful, in rainy seasons no crossing can be found. The plain has many trees, willow, and other kinds, blackberry bushes, and quantities of Castillian roses. Near by on the left, at the foot of the hill, is a good lake with so much water, especially in rainy seasons, that its banks cannot hold all that it receives from the hills, and at such times the water runs off in a large ditch to the sea, which is at a distance of little more than two gun shots, in a little bay south of the Punta de Pinos; but in dry seasons the lake holds a quantity of good water, and has some springs. In rainy seasons, a dam formed in part by the hill extending across the lake makes it easy to retain enough water for all irrigating purposes on the plain.

"The mission is surrounded by small hills with good pastures for all kinds of cattle; it has an abundance of firewood as well as timber for building purposes, such as pine, white elms, and some redwoods; and at a distance of less than a league there are many cypresses on the point called by the same name, on account of the abundance of the trees; it has a beautiful sky, although after the rains the clouds are thick; the

vivas ansias pasar á fundar la otra de San Luis Obispo, pero no era dable por la falta de soldados para escoltas, y así dió mano á trasladar la mision como le encargaba su escelencia; para ello dispuso que en el real permaneciese su padre compañero fray Juan Crespi, y los ministros destinados para San Luis, y su reverencia determinó pasar á vivir al paraje que habia señalado en el Carmelo para idear la obra de la iglesia y vivienda, como tambien para acalorarlo.

"Con este fin se mudó á las orillas del Carmelo á principio de Agosto de dicho año de 1771, escoltado de los cinco soldados, y habiendo ya cortado alguna madera los tres marineros y cuatro indios Californios, á lo que tambien ayudaban los señores soldados, dió principio á la obra haciendo por de pronto una pieza para capilla y á su continuacion vivienda con cuatro piezas y una mayor para troje como tambien una casa para la vivienda de muchachos y su cocina, todo de madera con su terrado cercado todo de buena estacada. En la esquina del cuadro de elle una casa tambien con su terrado para guardia de los soldados, y á la vista unos corrales para las bestias y ganados. Como eran pocos los trabajadores y no apuraba mucho por tener en la mision vieja contigua al real presidio todas las cargas y trastes pertenecientes á la mision, no se dieron prisa; por cuya razon no se dió por concluida la obra y no se efectuó la total mutacion hasta últimos de Diciembre de dicho año de 71, en que quedaron del todo mudados, quedando en el real los dos ministros de la mision diciendo misa hasta tanto se verificase la fundacion de la mision.

"Quedó la mision de San Carlos con esta traslacion en un ameno sitio, fundada sobre una loma que tiene á la vista un dilatado llano muy á propósito para siembras, que es toda la vega del rio Carmelo cuya agua corre toda el año, aunque en tiempo de secas no es mucha el agua, siendo así que en tiempo de aguas no da vado toda su caja, muy poblada de arboleda, sauces y otros palos con mucha zarzamora é infinidad de rosales de Castilla que están tambien muy poblados los campos; á mano izquierda tiene una buena laguna al pié de la loma de esta mision, con bastante agua, principalmente en tiempo de lluvias que no alcanza á mantener en su caja toda la que recibe de las lomas cercunvecinas, y en dicho tiempo corre por una grande zanja hasta la mar que dista poco mas de dos tiros de fusil, que es la ensenadita de la banda del Sur de la punta de Pinos: pero en tiempo de secas mantiene dicha laguna su porcion de agua buena que en sí tiene unos veneros, y en tiempo de aguas con una presa de unas cien varas que es el tramo de la loma y el ancho de dicha laguna, parece sería fácil retener bastante aqua para regar lo que quisiese del llano que tiene á la vista.

"Está la mision ceracada de lomerias con buenos pastos para toda especie de ganados; tiene abundancia de leña, como tambien de madera para fabricar, como de pinos, álamos blancos y algunos palos colorados; y á una legua poco menos de distancia hay muchos cipreses en la punta llamada de dichos árboles por la abundancia de ellos; tiene hermosa cielo, aunque despues de concluidas las aguas abundan las neblinas; la vista que tiene desde la mision á la mar es de dicha ensenada; en las cercanías de la mision hay varias rancherias de gentiles que desde luego de fundada la mision la empezaron á frecuentar y empezó en breve su reduccion, como diré en su lugar hablando del estado de dicha mision."

view looks out toward the sea upon the bay mentioned above; in the vicinity of the mission there are several rancherias of gentiles who, since the founding of the mission, have begun to frequent it. The mission within a short time began their conversion, as I shall tell in the account of the state of the mission."

Erection of Mission Buildings. In his first report, dated at the mission May 21, 1773, Fr. Serra gives the following description of the mission as it was at that time:[10]

"The first and most northerly, and consequently most remote, from this city, is the Mission of San Carlos de Monterey in the vicinity of the Rio Carmelo. This is the administrative head of the missions. It was founded Sunday, on the Feast of the Holy Ghost, 3d day of June, 1770, but as it was for an entire year incorporated with the Royal Presidio from which it was afterwards transferred to the place it now occupies, it is referred to as being established a year later.

"They first turned their attention to the building of the stockade and dwellings. This mission has a natural advantage over the others on account of its location among an abundance of the woods of various kinds, all easily obtained, and in its situation in a part where the soldiers so earnestly apply themselves to the work. To God praise be given!

"The stockade of rough timbers, thick and high with ravelins in the corners, is something more than seventy varas long and forty-three wide, and is closed at night with a key although it is not secure because of lack of nails. An entrance can easily be forced by the knocking off of timbers. The main house is seven varas wide and fifty long. It is divided into six rooms, all with doors and locks. The walls are made of rough timbers plastered over with mud both inside and out. Those of the principal rooms are whitewashed with lime. One of the rooms serves provisionally as a church.

"Near this building on the outside is the guard-house or barracks of the soldiers, and adjoining it, their kitchen. All are enclosed in the stockade. All of these buildings have flat roofs of clay and mud, and for most of them a kitchen has been made. There are various little houses for the Indians with straw or hay roofs. Attention was later given to a small garden which is near at hand, but for want of a gardener it has made little progress."

During the year 1774 a number of additional structures were built. According to the report of Father Serra, there had been erected during the year a house thirty by seven varas in size, constructed partly of adobe and partly of palisades with thatched roof. This was used as a workshop.

---

[10]Serra, Representacion de 21 de Mayo, 1773, in *Archivo de la Mision de Santa Barbara*, I, 92-93, *Archives of California, Provincial State Papers*, I, 109-111. "La primera y mas avanzada al Norte, y por tanto la mas remota de esta ciudad la de San Carlos de Monterey, en las cercanias del Rio Carmelo, Cabezera de las demas.

"Esta se fundio Domingo, y Pasqua del Espiritu Santo dia 3 de Junio de 1770, pero como estuvo un año entero incorporada al Real Presidio, de donde se transferió despues al lugar hoy tiene, se puede reputar como de un año menos de fundacion. A lo que primer se dió mano en el nuevo sitio, fué como se acostumbra á la Estacada y habitaciones. En uno y otro, ha quedado ventajosa a las demas como que la naturaleza aventajó el sitio en la abundancia de las maderas de varias especies, todas á la mano, y que es la parte en donde se aplicaron mas los soldados al trabajo. Dios se lo pague.

"La cerca ó Estacada de palos gruesos, tupidos, y altos con sus revellines en la Esquinas tiene de largo, algo mas de 70 varas, y de ancho 43 y se cierra de noche con la llave, ahunque por no estar enlatada por falta de clavos, es fácil con tumbor á desviar algun palo la entrada. La casa principal tiene de ancho 7 varas, y de largo 50 dividida en 6 piezas, todas con sus puertas y cerraduras. Las paredes de palos gruesos embarradas por fuera y por dentro, y las piezas principales blanqueadas con cal, una de las que sirve interinamente de **iglesia.**

"Junto a dha, cerca por la parte de afuera está la guardia ó cuartel de los soldados, y junto á **él** su cocina, ceñido uno y otro de su estacada. Todas dhas fabricas son de azotea de barro y tierra; **y** a mas de ellas se hizo nuestra cozina, y varias casitas para los Indios, con techos pajizos, o de zacate; se dio despues mano a una huertecita, que se cerco y por falta de hortelano hizo pocas medras."

Two other houses of about the same size as the one described were built, to be occupied by the families of two married servants. The surgeon and his family had another of similar size with a flat earth roof. It had two rooms together with a bedroom. Similar buildings housed the smith and his family, and the captain of the guard and his family, the latter building being of palisades with roof of straw. In addition to these buildings there had been erected a large oven of adobe for baking bread for the mission, and several smaller ones for the Indians.[11]

During the next twelve years there are but few recorded facts relating to the architectural history of the mission. It is inferred that activities continued without much change, the early structures still serving in large measure the purposes for which they had been erected.

Deaths of Fathers Crespi and Serra. During the years 1783 and 1784 the life of the mission was saddened by the deaths of its beloved founders, Father Crespi and Father Serra. Father Juan Crespi, who had been the faithful companion of Father Serra at Carmel since its first establishment, passed away early in 1783. He was a member of the party which founded San Diego in 1769, and served as chronicler of the Portolá expedition which discovered Monterey and San Francisco bays. He received his last sacrament at the hands of his old friend, companion, and superior, Father Junípero, and was buried within the sanctuary on the gospel side.[12]

The death of Fray Juan was severely felt by Father Serra, whose own health was rapidly failing. In spite of this, however, he again journeyed south by water in 1784, that he might begin his work of confirmation at San Diego, and pass northward through all the missions. His enfeebled condition showed that he was releasing his hold upon life and that his days of labor were nearly over. His deep concern in the success of the missions weighed heavily upon him. Realizing that his life was ebbing, representative priests from nearby missions were requested to gather about him, but Palou was the only one to reach San Carlos in time to be present at the death of the father president.

On the twenty-seventh of August, 1784, Serra stated that he would receive the Most Holy Viaticum in the church, although Palou advised the decoration of Serra's cell, assuring him that His Divine Majesty would come to visit him there. Father Serra replied in the negative, saying that he desired to receive it in the church, and since he was able to walk, there was no reason why his Lord should come to him. He went by himself to the

---

[11]Serra, Informe, 1774, in *Archivo de la Mision de Santa Barbara, Informes y correspondencia,* I, 146,147. (Bancroft Collection, ms.). "Desde el mes de Diciembre de 1773, que fué el primero y ultimo informe á V. Exca del estado, y progressos de estas 5 misiones, hasta ultimos de Diciembre proximo pasado el 74 ha tenido esta mision los augmentos siguientes.
"Primeramente una casa de 30 varas de largo, y 7 de ancho parte de adobes, y parte de palizada, con su techo de zacate para oficina de, ____Otra dha de lo mismo, y del mismo tamaño para un sirviente casado. Otra dha algo mayor tambien de palizada con burrador con techo de zacate para otro sirviente casado con India de la Mision recien christiana. Otro dha de lo mismo con azotea de tierra, con dos piezas de sala y recamara para vivienda del cirujano y su familia. Otra dha de lo mismo y del mismo tamaño con sus 2 piezas para vivienda del herrero y su familia. Otra dha de palizada con techo de zacate en que vive el cabo de la escolta con su familia. Un horno de adobes para hacer pan. Unas hornillas de adoves para cozina de los Indios."
[12]Bancroft, *History of California,* I, 386.

church (a distance of more than one hundred varas) accompanied by the commander of the garrison. All the Indians of the village or mission accompanied the devoted sick father to the church with extreme tenderness and affection. Father Palou received from the lips of the dying padre the request that he be buried in the church, near Crespi.[13] He consequently was also buried within the sanctuary on the gospel side of the altar.[14] For a short time Palou succeeded to the presidency of the missions until the place was taken over by Father Lasuén of San Diego in November, 1785.[15]

San Carlos Visited by Lapérouse, 1786. In September, 1786, Monterey Bay was visited by Jean Francois Galaup de Lapérouse, then making a tour of the world for the purpose of obtaining geographical and other scientific information. For this purpose his expedition had been fitted out by the French government. The record left by Lapérouse gives a vivid and probably fairly accurate picture of the establishment as it was at that date He describes his visit to the mission as follows:[16]

"After traversing a small plain covered with herds of cattle, ... we ascended the hills, and were struck with the sound of several bells which announced our arrival, of which the monks had been apprized by a horseman whom the governor had detached for that purpose.

"We were received like lords of a parish when they make their first appearance on their estate; the president of the missions, clothed in his cope, the holy water sprinkler in his hand, waited for us at the door of the church, which was illuminated the same as on their greatest festivals; he conducted us to the foot of the high altar, where the *Te Deum* was sung in thanksgiving for the happy success of our voyage.

"Before we entered the church, we had passed by a place where the Indians of both sexes were ranged in a row; they expressed no surprise in their countenances, and we were left in doubt whether we were the subject of their conversation during the rest of the day. The parish church is very neat, although covered with straw; it is dedicated to Saint Charles, and ornamented with fairly good paintings, copied from Italian originals. There is a picture of Hell, in which the painter seems to have borrowed a little of the imagination of Callot; but as it is absolutely necessary to strike the senses of these new converts with the most lively impressions, I am persuaded that a similar representation has never done more service in any country, and that it would be impossible for the protestant mode of worship, which forbids images, and nearly all the other ceremonies of our church, to make any progress among this people. I have my doubts, whether the picture of Paradise, which is placed opposite to that of Hell, produces so good an effect on them; the state of quietness which it represents, and that complacent satisfaction of the elect who surround the throne of the Supreme Being, are ideas too sublime for rude unpolished man; but it is necessary to place rewards by the side of punishments, and it was a rigorous duty not to allow the smallest change in the kind of delights promised by the Catholic religion.

"We repassed, on going out of the church, the same row of male and female Indians, who had never quitted their post during the *Te Deum*; the children only had removed a little, and formed groups around the missionary's house, which is in

---

[13]Palou, *Vida*, 271-2, 274. "Deseo que me entierre en la iglesia cerquita del P. Fr. Juan Crespi por ahora, que quando se haga la iglesia de piedra me tiraran donde quisieren."

[14]Palou, *Vida*, 280. "Fué sepultado en el Presbyterio al lado del Evangelio."

[15]Payeras Report, 1818, in *Santa Barbara Archives*, XII, 453, Fages to Palou, 1785, in *Prov. Rec.*, III, 50, (Bancroft Collection, ms.).

[16]Lapérouse, *Voyage autour du monde* (Paris, 1798), II, 293-300.

front of the church, as are also the different storehouses. On the right stands the Indian village, consisting of about fifty cabins, which serve as dwelling places for seven hundred and forty persons of both sexes, including their children, which compose the mission of Saint Charles, or of Monterey.

"These cabins are the most miserable that are to be met with among any people; they are round, six feet in diameter, by four in height; some stakes, of the size of an arm, fixed in the earth, and which approach each other in an arch at the top, compose the timber-work of it; eight or ten bundles of straw, very ill arranged over these stakes, defend the inhabitants, well or ill, from the rain and wind; and more than half of this cabin remains open when the weather is fine; their only precaution is to have each of them two or three bundles of straw at hand by way of reserve.

"All the exhortations of the missionaries have never been able to procure a change of this general architecture of the two Californias; the Indians say that they like plenty of air, that it is convenient to set fire to their houses when they are devoured in them by too great quantity of fleas, and that they can build another in less than two hours. The independent Indians, who as hunters so frequently change their places of abode, have a stronger motive.

"The colour of these Indians, which is that of negroes; the house of the religious; their storehouses, which are built of brick and pointed with mortar; the floor of earth, upon which they press in the grain; the oxen, horses, in a word, everything reminded us of a habitation in Saint Domingo, or any other West India colony. The men and women are assembled by the sound of the bell, one of the religious conducts them to their work, to church, and to all their other exercises. . . . .

"The Indians as well as the missionaries rise with the sun, and go to prayers and mass, which last an hour, and during this time there is cooked in the middle of the square, in three large kettles, barley meal, the grain of which has been roasted previous to being ground; this species of boiled food, which the Indians call *atole*, and of which they are very fond, is seasoned neither with salt nor butter, and to us would prove a very insipid mess.

"Every cabin sends to take the portion for all its inhabitants in a vessel made of bark; there is not the least confusion or disorder, and when the coppers are empty, they distribute that which sticks to the bottom to the children who have best retained their lessons of catechism.

"This meal continues three quarters of an hour, after which they all return to their labours; some go to plough the earth with oxen, others to dig the garden; in a word, every one is employed in different domestic occupations, and always under the superintendence of one or two of the religious.

"The women are charged with little else but the care of their housewifery, their children, and roasting and grinding the several grains; this last operation is very long and laborious, because they have no other means of doing it but by crushing the grain in pieces with a cylinder upon a stone. M. de Langle, being a witness of this operation, made the missionaries a present of his mill, and a greater service could not have been rendered them, as by these means four women would in a day perform the work of a hundred, and time enough will remain to spin the wool of their sheep, and to manufacture coarse stuffs. But at present the religious, more occupied with the interests of heaven than temporal welfare, have greatly neglected the introduction of the common arts; they are themselves so austere, that they have no chimney to their chambers, though winter is frequently very severe there; and even the greater anchorites have never led a more edifying life."

Stone church erected, 1793–97. For more than twenty years temporary structures had served as a place of worship. Under the presidency of Lasuén a determined effort was made to replace the older by a permanent stone structure. During December, 1792, Manuel Estevan Ruíz, master mason and stone worker, took up his work at the Mission San Carlos. He was to instruct the natives in stonework and to supervise the construction of the buildings. As no material was then ready and as the heavy rainy season prevented the gathering of any sufficient amount, it was summer before the construction work upon the new church was actively started, the first stone being laid July 7, 1793.[17] Four years were consumed before the church building was completed. Finally in September, 1797, it was dedicated for service. It was described in the reports as being well built of cut stone (cantería), roofed with tile, and presenting a harmonious and beautiful appearance.[18]

Vancouver at San Carlos. During the time that the new church was under construction Captain George Vancouver of the British navy, while upon this coast, visited the mission in Carmel Valley. The artist of the expedition, J. Sykes, made a sketch of the establishment as it was at that time. This sketch (plate 2) is the first record to illustrate in pictorial form the appearance of the mission. Vancouver records his observations as follows:[19]

". . . . on Sunday the 2nd of December, in consequence of a very polite invitation, I paid my respects to the mission of St. Carlos, accompanied by Senr. Quadra. Senr. Arguella, Senr. Caamano, Mr. Broughton, and several other English and Spanish officers.

"This establishment is situated about a league to the south-eastward of the presidio of Monterey. The road between them lies over some steep hills and hollow vallies, interspersed with many trees; the surface was covered over with an agreeable verdure; the general character of the country was lively, and our journey altogether was very pleasant. . . . .

"The usual ceremonies on introduction being over, our time was pleasantly engaged in the society of the father president and his two companions, the priests regularly belonging to the mission of St. Carlos, who attended us over their premises. These seemed to differ but little from those at St. Francisco, or Sta. Clara; excepting that the buildings were smaller, the plan, architecture, and materials exactly corresponding.

---

[17]Lasuén to Borica, San Carlos, Dec. 10, 1794, in *Archivo de la Mision de Santa Barbara*, VI, 219-220; Lasuén to Arrillaga, June 7, 1794, in *Archivo del Arzobispado*, I, 38. (Bancroft Collection, ms.). It is probable that Serra and Crespi had much to do with the designing of the later stone church. Father Serra made definite reference to the stone church in arranging for his burial (*note* 13). It should be borne in mind that the experiences of both of these men in Sierra Gorda had prepared them for church building as well as religious work. In the valley of Tilaco Crespi had constructed the Mission of San Francisco including a large church of stone "with its vaulted ceiling (bovedas) and tower" (Palou, *Vida*, 237; James edition, 230). Serra had spent seven years in constructing a large church at the Mission of Jalpan. It was more than one hundred forty-seven feet long and thirty feet wide and was built of rubble work. It is described as having a transept and dome and a suitable sacristy with vaulted ceiling. (*Vida*, 34; James edition, 32).

[18]*Archives of California, State Papers Missions*, II, 5; Lasuén Estado General, 1793-4, San Carlos, Mar. 1, 1795, in *Archivo de la Mision de Santa Barbara*, XII, 57. "La iglesia de la Mision de S. Carlos se concluyó en el presente año; es toda de cantería; su techo es de teja y está bien provista de ornamentos y útiles. . . . ." Sal, *Estado*, Monterey, Dec. 31, 1797, in *Archives of California, State Papers Missions*, II, 120. "La iglesia de San Carlos se bendijo y dedico por Sept de 97 y esta buena." *Lasuén Report*, 1797-8, San Carlos, Feb. 20, 1799, in *Archivo de la Mision de Santa Barbara*, XII, 66. (Bancroft Collection, ms.).

[19]Vancouver, *A Voyage of Discovery*, II, 33-36. There appears to be a serious discrepancy between Vancouver and Lasuén in reference to the date when the construction of the mission church was begun. Vancouver gives the date of his visit as Dec. 2, 1792, and proceeds to describe the materials and methods used in building the church which he found in process of construction. On the other hand, Lasuén says the head mason did not arrive at Carmel until after that date and that six months more elapsed before the first stone was laid. It is probable, therefore, that Vancouver may have confused the dates of his visit. He was at Monterey again in November and December, 1794, and it is possible his notes and sketch may belong to that date rather than to the earlier visit, *ibid.*, III, 324-340. This is the opinion of Bancroft.

PLATE 1. *Forest of Monterey Pines.* Moran, photo.

The value of this forest was noted by Vizcaíno and Crespi. From it Serra obtained the timbers for San Carlos Mission.

PLATE 2. *San Carlos Mission, 1794.* Sketch by Sykes.

This is the earliest pictorial representation of the mission. Since it is a sketch it must not be considered as having the same degree of accuracy in detail as a photograph. It will be seen that the church was being constructed, as mentioned by Vancouver, and that there were numerous buildings around an open plaza. Three crosses are shown, one in the plaza to the right, a larger one in the court at the left, and another surmounting a building at the extreme left. The larger cross may have been the one erected by Serra in 1771.

"In their granaries were deposited a pretty large quantity of the different kinds of grain before noticed at the other establishments, to which was added some barley, but the whole was of an inferior quality, and the return from the soil by no means equal to that produced at Sta. Clara. Here also was a small garden on the same confined scale, and cultivated in the same manner as observed at the other stations.

"An Indian village is also in the neighborhood; it appeared to us but small, yet the number of its inhabitants under the immediate direction of this mission was said to amount to eight hundred, governed by the same charitable principles as those we had before visited. Notwithstanding these people are taught and employed from time to time in many of the occupations most useful to civil society, they had not made themselves any more comfortable habitations than those of their forefathers; nor did they seem in any respect to have benefited by the instruction they had received. Some of them were at this time engaged under the direction of the fathers, in building a church with stone and mortar. The former material appeared to be of a very tender friable nature, scarcely more hard than indurated clay; but I was told, that on its being exposed to the air, it soon becomes hardened, and is an excellent stone for the purpose of building. It is of a light straw colour, and presents a rich and elegant appearance, in proportion to the labour that is bestowed upon it. It is found in abundance at no great depth from the surface of the earth; the quarries are easily worked, and it is. I believe the only stone the Spaniards have hitherto made use of in building. At Sta. Clara I was shown a ponderous black stone, that father Thomas said was intended to be so appropriated as soon as persons capable of working it could be procured. The lime they use is made from sea shells, principally from the ear shell, which is of a large size and in great numbers on the shores; not having as yet found any calcareous earth that would answer this essential purpose. The heavy black stone is supposed to be applicable to grinding, and should it be found so to answer, it will be a matter of great importance to their comfort, since their only method of reducing their corn to flour is by two small stones placed in an inclined position on the ground; on the lower one the corn is laid, and ground by hand by rubbing the other stone nearly of the same surface over it. The flour produced by this rude and laborious process makes very white and well tasted, though heavy bread, but this defect is said by the Spaniards to be greatly remedied when mixed with an equal proportion of flour properly ground.

"After we had satisfied our curiosity in these particulars we rode round the neighborhood of the mission. It was pleasantly situated, and the country, agreeably broken by hills and vallies, had a verdant appearance, and was adorned like that in the vicinity of Monterrey, with many clumps and single trees, mostly of the pine tribe, holly-leaved oak and willows; with a few trees of the poplar and maple, and some variety of shrubs, that rather incommoded our travelling, which was chiefly confined to one of the vallies, and within sight of the buildings. Through this valley a small brook of water about knee-deep, called by the Spaniards Rio Carmelo, takes its course, passes the buildings of the mission, and immediately empties itself into the sea.

"In this valley, near the sides of the Carmelo, a few acres of land exhibited a tolerably good plant of wheat; but as the soil here, as well as at Monterrey, is of a light sandy nature, its productions are consequently inferior to the other two missions I had visited; yet I was given to understand, that the interior country here, like that at St. Francisco, improves in point of fertility, as it retires from the ocean.

"On our return to the convent, we found a most excellent repast served with great neatness, in a pleasant bower constructed for that purpose in the garden of the mission."

Elsewhere it is stated that in December, 1793, while in San Diego, Vancouver presented the president of the mission with a "handsome barrelled organ" for the use and ornament of the new church which was being built at the presidency of the missions at San Carlos.[20]

The Quarters of the Neophytes, 1800. In his report for 1800 Father Lasuén, the president of the missions, describes the nature of the dwellings used by the Christianized Indians, criticism of which has been seen in the descriptions by both Lapérouse and Vancouver. He also describes in some detail the dormitory of the girls and unmarried women. The report reads as follows:[21]

"Although the houses of the Neophytes do not differ in material and form from those which the Gentiles use, they are indeed different in cleanliness and good condition. Ordinarily the missionaries and also the Christian Indians continue improving the arrangement of their houses and rarely will one condescend to live in a small hut like he had in his Gentilism. In the channel of Santa Barbara the natives never use similar small huts. They have always, in contrast with the remainder of those in subjection, houses sufficiently roomy. They are built of paling and thatch and because of this exposed to fire. It is well known that for many years neither in missions, nor in pueblos, nor in presidios had there been churches, dwellings nor storerooms of any other material. Of the latter some rooms are still preserved, in many places as in the royal presidio of San Francisco almost all. Accordingly, as they have been able, or as they now find themselves able they construct buildings of adobe or of stone roofed with tile. In this manner are the houses of the Indians (I do not know how this has been reported by the Governor or any of the commandants) of San Francisco and Santa Clara built. Many are furnished with metates, earthen pans, round pots, stewing pans and even little ovens for cooking bread, while others have much more than these.

"The girls and the unmarried women (wrongly called nuns) are gathered together and locked up at night in their quarters. This provision is taken for convenience and it may be said for necessity, for all possible care is taken that nothing may compromise their safety. It has been observed that rarely do those in this rank and station die, nor do they run away and take refuge in the mountains. They have spacious rooms furnished with chairs and with sufficient ventilation. Here in San Carlos (and the same will happen in other missions) they have changed their dormitory many times, seeking each time better accomodation until they have been able to construct the form desired by the missionaries.

---

[20]Vancouver, *A Voyage of Discovery*, II 472. This organ was still in use in 1837, when Du Petit-Thouars visited the mission.

[21]Representation, Nov. 12, 1800, in *Archivo de la Mision de Santa Barbara*, II, 179-181. "Aunque los Alojmtos de los Neofitos no se diferencian en sus materiales, y en su formacion de los que usan los Gentiles, pero si en la limpieza, y buena condicion, de el regularmte andan los Missioneros y aun tambien los Christianos mejorando la disposicion de sus casas, y raro sera el que se acomode ya a vivir en choza estrecha, como la que tenia en su Gentilidad. En el Canal de Sta Barbara nunca usaron los naturales semejtes chozas estrechas, spre tubieron a diferencia de los restantes de esta conquista viviendos suficientemte capaces. Si son ahora como antes de palisada, y zacate, y pr eso expuestas al incendio, es bien sabido que en muchos años, ni en misiones ni en pueblos, ni en presidios tuvo iglesias abitaciones, ni oficianas de otra calidad. Y de esta misma se conserva todabia algunas piezas, en muchas partes que y en el Rl presidio de Sn Franco casi todas. Segun se ha podido, y se va pudiendo se hacen fabricas de adove, o de piedra techadas de teja. Asi estan ya, [no se como no lo ha dho el Sor. Govor. o algo de los Comandtes] las casas de los Indios, de Sn. Franco, y Sta. Clara, surtidas muchas de mas, y se iran surtiendo las otras de metates, comales, ollas cazuelas ye hta de ornitos pa cocer pan. . . . A lo mismo se aspira en las demas misiones.

"Las muchachas y solteras [Monjas pr mal nombre] se recogen, y se encierran de noche en un cuarto. Si esta providencia se toma pr convte y puede decirse pr necesaria, se cuida todo lo que es posibe que no sea en perjuicio de su salud. Efectivamte, se ha observado, que rara de las de este estado, y regimen se mueren, si no es de las que dan en huirse, y retirarse al monte. Se tienen pa eso piezas capaces, asendas, y de correspondte ventilacion. Aqui en Sn. Carlos, [y sucedera lo mismo en otras missiones] se les mudo muches veces el dormitorio, buscando cada vez mejor comodidad hta que llego el tpo de poderlo hacer segun el deceo de los misioneros.

"Es por cierto en el dia la mejor pieza, que fuera de la Iglesia tiene la mission de 17 varas de largo en claro, mas de seis de ancho, y otro tanto de alto: paredes de adobe y medio, enjarradas de mezcla y blanqueadas; un entarimado fuerte, y bien labrado, corrido pr los dos costados y pr una testera, de mas de vara de alto, y mas de dos de ancho, tres ventanas grandes con sus rejas torneadas, pr un lado, y quatro troneras pr otro, su lugar comun es pr separado, y todo con buena vigueria cubierta con tablazon, y techo de teja."

PLATE 3. *San Carlos Mission, 1823.* Sketch by Wm. Smythe.

This sketch appears in various forms. This has been taken from an engaving published by Forbes in his *History of California* in 1839. It gives a much more comprehensive idea of the mission than does the Sykes sketch and if not followed with too slavish attention to detail may be taken as very satisfactory. Several buildings are to be seen upon the hill to the right of the mission church, while to the left is shown a portion of the building enclosing the quadrangle. The road from Monterey is shown in the foreground together with a cross which may have marked the way to the mission.

PLATE 4. *San Carlos Mission, 1839.* From Laplace.

Fortunately the artist in this case chose a point of observation not usually taken and has therefore preserved for us a view of the mission from the hill to the rear of the mission grounds. It shows the enclosed court and indicates that the buildings around the court were more than one story in height. Since it is merely a sketch, care must be taken not to place too much emphasis upon details, especially if these are in conflict with other evidence.

29

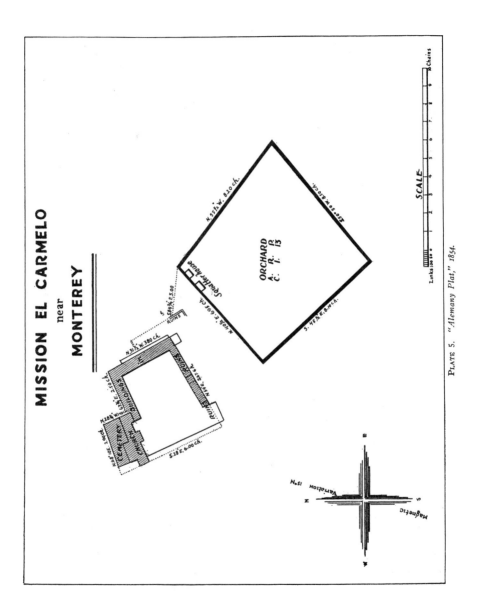

MISSION EL CARMELO
near
MONTEREY

ORCHARD
A. R. P.
C. I. 13

Spatter-house

RUINS

SCALE

Links 100 50 0

10 Chains

Variation 15°N

Magnetic

PLATE 5. "Alemany Plat," 1854.

30

"It is a fact that the best room which the mission has, besides the church, is 17 varas long in the clear, more than 6 wide and as much more in height; walls an adobe and a half in thickness plastered over with mortar and whitewashed; a strong and well-made boarded floor, extended on two sides and on the front, of more than a vara in height and more than two in width, three large windows with round iron gratings, on one side, and four smaller windows on the other, . . . the whole covered with heavy cross beams and planks with a roof of tiles."

The Mission Quadrangle. The report for the year 1815 records that several buildings had been constructed, thus enclosing the quadrangle or court of the mission.[22] In 1818 a small chapel was built adjoining the church. According to the report of Fr. Payeras it was known as "la capilla a la Pasion del Señor," and was built not only as a place of devotion but also to preserve the older building from the fury of the strong south winds. It was provided with an altar and painted wood carvings.[23]

Erection of the "Via Crucis," 1820. For the year 1820 the report mentions several improvements at the mission. Two bells had been provided and several buildings painted. The approach to the church had been adorned with a "Via Crucis."[24] This latter is more fully described by later observers. Capt. F. W. Beechey, who visited Monterey in December, 1827, thus describes the approach to the mission:[25]

"The ride from the presidio to San Carlos on a fine day is most agreeable. The scenery is just sufficiently picturesque to interest, while the hills are not so abrupt as to inconvenience a bold rider. The road leads principally through fine pasture lands, occasionally wooded with tall pine, oak, and birch trees; but without any underwood to give it a wildness, or to rob it of its park-like aspect. Before the valley of San Carmelo opens out, the traveller is apprized of his approach to the mission by three large crosses erected upon Mount Calvary; and further on by smaller ones placed at the side of the road, to each of which some history is attached."

Alvarado says a portion of the road from Monterey to San Carlos was known as that of Calvary, that twelve crosses were planted along the road at equal distances representing the twelve stations of the "Via Crucis," and that on Good Friday appropriate religious services were always celebrated.[26]

Secularization of the Mission. The best days of San Carlos were over. The annual reports make mention of the buildings only to speak of their sad condition. In 1824 the houses and workshops had their roofs renewed.

[22]"Se han hecho 50 varas de fabrica, las que faltaban para cerrar el quadro, y plaza de la mision y se han remendado las fabricas anteriores." Informe de San Carlos, Dec. 31, 1815, in *Archivo de las Misiones,* I, 372.

[23] Informe de San Carlos, Dec. 31, 1818, in *Archivo Misiones, Papeles Originales,* I, 432; and Payeras report of May 4, 1819, "La [mision], de San Carlos ha eregido contigua a la iglesia una capilla a la Pasion del Señor que exista a devocion y preserva de los fuertos sures a la fabrica vieja," in *Archivo de Santa Barbara,* XII, 98. (Bancroft Collection, ms.)

[24]Informe de San Carlos, Dec. 31, 1820, in *Archivo de las Misiones, Papeles Originales,* I, 328 (Bancroft Collection, ms.). "Se han puesto dos campañas la una grande de 36 @, [probably arroba, equivalent to 25 pounds], y la otra mediana de 27 @; se ha adornado a iglesia con una Via Crucis y se han pintado tres colaterales.

[25]Beechey, *Narrative of a Voyage to the Pacific,* 343.

[26]Hittell, *History of California,* I, 639-640. One of these crosses may be seen in the Smythe sketch of 1823. (Plate 3.)

but the walls of the garden were down and other repairs were needed.[27] This decline in the prosperity of the mission was due not only to conditions within the missions themselves but also and in larger measure to the manner in which they were treated by the Mexican government. In January, 1831, a decree of secularization was issued by Echeandía. According to this order San Carlos and San Gabriel were to be organized at once into towns, the surplus property after distribution to the neophytes passing under the control of secular administrators.[28]

A change in administration whereby Echeandía was displaced by Manuel Victoria prevented the putting of this order into effect,[29] and the controversy regarding the secularization of the California missions continued for some years longer. Finally on November 4, 1834, the act of secularization was adopted and announced by Governor Figueroa. By it San Carlos and Monterey were combined as a curacy of the first class.[30] In accordance with the plan of secularization an inventory was made of the property of the various missions. That of San Carlos, dated December 10, 1834, valued the mission property at approximately $46,022. Of this the church itself is estimated at $10,000; the furniture, vestments, library, etc., at $10,217.[31]

San Carlos in Ruins, 1836–41. In October, 1836, the United States ship "Peacock" stopped at Monterey on its way from the Orient where Mr. Edmund Roberts as special agent of the United States government had been engaged in a diplomatic mission. A visit was made to the San Carlos mission which is described as follows:[32]

"At this time there are twenty-one missions in Upper California, all of which are in a state of decay. I visited that at Carmelo, which I found in ruins, and almost abandoned. It is about four miles from Monte-rey. The road to it is easy, and agreeably varied by hill and dale, everywhere covered by pine and other forest trees, and remarkably free from undergrowth.

"The mission building is, perhaps, a hundred yards square, one story high, and roofed with tiles. We rode through the gate, which was just ready to fall from its hinges, into the great central court, round which it is built, where we found eight or ten Indians engaged in repairing the roof. They informed us that the Padre was at the presidio, or garrison, and that there was no one to show us the church, which, exteriorly, was in a dilapidated state. All the windows opened in upon the court, and were heavily barred with iron, with the design of preventing the escape of the christian neophytes, who were locked up at night in apartments to which these windows give light and air. Some of those were open. They were strewed with rubbish and filth, and, altogether, in a worse condition than the commonest stable should be."

[27]Informe de San Carlos, Dec. 31, 1822, in *Archivo de las Misiones, Papeles Originales*, I, 555, 1824, *Ibid*, I, 759 (Bancroft Collection, ms.). "En la iglesia y sacristia existen los [utensilios], de los años anteriores, a excepcion de algunas cosas de poca consideracion que se ha disparecido y se procura de poner y se ha anadido un crucifijo grande cuatro santos de talla grande que son N. S. P. S. Franco, St. Domingo, S. Buenaventura y St. Clara. La casa y demas oficinas se han techado, no se ha hecho fabrica ninguna. Las parades en la huerta se han caido, veremos si se pueden levantar del año. Las herramientas en casa y campo poco mas o menos subsisten como los años anteriores."

[28]Bancroft, III, 305-6.

[29]*Ibid*, III, Chaps. XI, XII; Richman, *California Under Spain and Mexico*, 228 et seq.; Engelhardt, III, 311-360.

[30]Engelhardt, III, 531.

[31]*Ibid*, III, 534.

[32]Ruschenberger, *A Voyage round the world, in 1835, 1836 and 1837* (Philadelphia, 1838), 507.

The next year the French explorer Abel Du Petit-Thouars was along this coast and visited the ruins of the mission in Carmel Valley. His description of the condition of the establishment as seen at that time is as follows :[33]

"Upon our arrival at the mission of San Carlos we were struck by the solitude of the place and by the state of ruin in which the buildings were found. The grounds surrounding this establishment, formerly covered with rich crops, did not offer more to the eye than a picture of the most complete sterility. Through a little door we entered a large court shaped like a parallelogram; this court is enclosed on three sides by the dwellings of the neophytes; the fourth is occupied by the storerooms for the reserve food supply. A large wooden cross still stood in the center of this enclosure. In one of the corners of the court is the church, the principal door of which opens on the field outside of the mission, but one is able to communicate with the establishment by means of a small lateral chapel. We saw no one upon entering the court of the mission: it was deserted! the lodgings were without doors and windows and the roofs, broken in many places, were already giving way under their own weight. On visiting the part at the north of the mission we entered a large room, dark and without furniture, where we met Father *Jose-Maria del Real,* the sole surviving ecclesiastic at the mission: that religious was one of those who had been sent out from the college of Zacatecas. After a reception at first dubious, he recovered from the surprise which our appearance had caused him; he became very polite and with great courtesy showed us about the ruins: we visited with him the ruined buildings in the midst of which he lived without society, and, judging from appearances, very miserably. Two or three families of Indians, fixed by habit, still lived in the ruins which surrounded the mission. . . . The garden of the mission, situated on the ground which stretches out in a gentle slope from the mission to the edge of the river Carmelo, offers scarcely any signs of cultivation. Formerly very fertile, the garden produced in abundance all the vegetables and fruits necessary not only for the establishment, but also for the town of Monterey and for vessels in port. At present it is entirely abandoned, the fence no longer remains, and the few fruit trees which are still to be seen here yield scarcely any produce, and that is always consumed before it attains a suitable degree of maturity.

"Afterwards we went to visit the church, entering through the lateral chapel which gives access to the church through the court of the mission. Upon entering the chapel I noticed several paintings on wood which represented subjects delineated in the holy scriptures; but my attention was particularly attracted by the sight of a large painting of *San Isidro el labrador* [patron of the laborers], which is at the left upon entering the chapel. It was hanging at an angle by one of the upper corners of the frame. In this position the saint and his plough looked upside down. Our reverend guide, after having pointed out to me the painting to the right, made three genuflections and as many signs of the cross and afterwards appeared absorbed in profound meditation from which I could scarcely rouse him. I wished to know the reason for these particular devotions, suspecting that a little of the supernatural might well have become mingled with an event in itself perfectly natural. At last, pressed by me to declare this mystery, the reverend father, in a tone of great sorrow and in a deep voice, informed me that during an earthquake this picture had been thus disarranged and that surely this catastrophe had been the manifestation of the will of God and a definite prediction of the ruin of the missions. After these words the brother, don Jose, crossed himself again and relapsed into his pious reveries! Until recently there could be seen in the church a picture which represented La Perouse arriving at the mission of San Carlos

[33]Du Petit-Thouars. *Voyage autour du monde sur la fregate La Venus, pendant les annees 1836-1839.* II, 116-120. Translated from the French text.

and the brilliant reception which was tendered him by all the mission: this picture disappeared at the time of the departure of the Spanish missionaries. . . .

"We also saw in the church a portable organ given at one time by Captain Vancouver to the president of the missions of California whom he met at the port of San Diego. That organ, of an extreme Gothic type, must have been very beautiful: it was not yet entirely out of service."

The next recorded visit to the mission was made by Laplace, a French traveler in 1839. The author does not discuss the mission but fortunately incorporates a sketch of the establishment as it was seen at that time.[34] This sketch is herewith reproduced (plate 4).

When visited in 1841 by Duflot de Mofras, the ruin of the mission was complete, the padre even having removed to the neighboring town of Monterey. He speaks of the mission as follows:[35]

"The mission of Mount Carmel, situated at the northern extremity of the Sierra de Santa Lucia and hemmed in by the mountains, is no longer a flourishing institution. In 1834 it still assembled five hundred neophytes; it had three thousand horned cattle, seven hundred horses, seven thousand sheep and harvested fifteen hundred fanegas of grain. Today all has gone; under the pretext of forming a pueblo in the vicinity, the mission was allowed to fall in ruins. The Indian population is composed of not more than thirty individuals. This establishment, as also the one at Soledad, lying nearest the seat of government, was one of the first to be despoiled. The missionary in charge of Carmel now resides at Monterey."

Under American Control. In July, 1846, the American flag was raised at Monterey by the forces of the United States Navy. This change in jurisdiction was fully recognized by the treaty of 1848 whereby the territory was definitely ceded by Mexico.

Already a number of American settlers had immigrated to California, but the discovery of gold in 1848 caused an unprecedented rush to the new region. Among these people were many who recorded their observations in articles or books and thus give descriptions of the incidents, scenes and places of interest that attracted their attention. Many of them give accounts of the missions. Unfortunately most of these writings are a mixture of vague historical accounts with indefinite descriptions of the ruined missions, one pleasing exception to this being the account given by J. R. Bartlett of the United States and Mexican Boundary Commission, who visited Monterey in April, 1852. He says:[36]

"The Mission establishment, which consists of a church and the usual accompaniments of a large inclosure with ranges of small buildings, stands upon a little elevation between the hills and the sea, from which it is distant only a few hundred yards. The church which is built of stone, has two towers, containing six bells; its walls are very thick, with an arched roof, and supported by heavy buttresses. The towers, as usual, differ. The adobe buildings near, were all in a state of ruin, and tenantless; not a human being was to be seen near, while the rank grass and weeds which monopo-

---

[34]Laplace, *Campagne de circumnavigation de la fregate l'Artemise, pendant les annees 1837, 1838, 1839 and 1840.* (Paris, 1841-54), vi, 294.

[35]Duflot de Mofras, *Exploration du territoire de l'Oregon, des Californies et de la mer Vermeille, executee pendant les annees 1840, 1841 et 1842.* (Paris, A. Bertrand, 1844). I. 391-2. Translated from the French.

[36]Bartlett, *Personal Narrative,* II, 77.

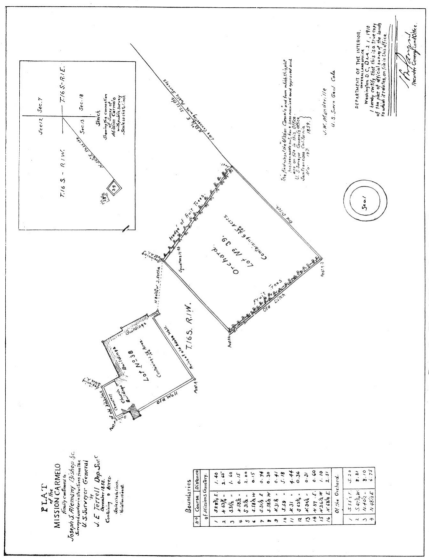

PLATE 6. *Plat of Mission San Carlos Grant.*

PLATE 7. *Ruins of San Carlos, about 1876.*

This photograph by Muybridge is a very early picture of the mission ruins and is of value in that it gives many items of detail regarding the buildings in front of and adjoining the church. The ruined wall in the foreground to the right retained the doorway leading into the court, while it also shows the floor timbers and windows for the rooms of the second floor. The markings upon the front of the church show plainly the height and slant of the roof line.

PLATE 8. *Restoration of San Carlos Mission by Oriana Day, 1884.*

This must not be taken as of the same value as the photographs, or sketches, but merely as an attempt of an artist to reproduce a scene at the mission as it had been described. It is said to represent the ideas of General M. G. Vallejo as he saw the mission before the time of secularization.

lized the ground, showed that even curiosity did not often tempt visitors to its deserted precincts. One corner of the church began to show the ravages of time: its cornice had fallen, and weeds had already taken root among its opening crevices. The remains of an orchard and vineyard, are still seen near, in a decaying state. Small pine trees cover the hills within a short distance of the church; and on its other side, the ocean rolls up its waves with a dull monotonous sound, which adds to the solitary feeling of the place."

Title Confirmed to Church, 1859. Whereas it had been the plan of the Mexican government, under the excuse of secularization, to exploit the missions and place their property for sale, it became the policy of the United States government to confirm to the church authorities full title to those lands that had been used for religious purposes, such as the church site, burial grounds, orchards and gardens. In accordance with this policy the United States Land Commission awarded to Bishop J. S. Alemany, as head of the Catholic Church in California, the title to a tract of land containing nine acres known as Mission Carmelo. The land was first surveyed by the church authorities in 1854 when presenting their claims before the United States District Court (plate 5). This is the first survey extant of the mission buildings and lands. An official survey (plate 6) was made by the United States government in December, 1858, and formed the basis for the issuance of the patent which was granted the church authorities October 19, 1859.[37]

Later Descriptions and Photographs. The ruins of San Carlos, the roof of which fell in during the year 1852,[38] continued to attract people interested in the romantic and picturesque. Mr. H. H. Bancroft, after a visit to the mission in 1874, wrote the following description of the church as it then appeared:[39]

"The church is strong and well built, of irregularly hewn stone with a timbered roof on which had been laid brush or stick and covered with tiles. The building was in a state of ruins, part of the roof was off but most of the walls were standing. It is

---

[37]The "Alemany Plat," so called, is preserved with the plats of the other twenty missions in **the Archives of the United States District Court, San Francisco. Plate 5 is a reproduction of this** document. Since all the other plats accompanying this one indicate the survey as having been made during the fall of 1854, that date is assumed for this also. It is to be noted that this plat gives more definite information regarding the quadrangle buildings than does the United States Survey made four years later.

The second plat is herewith reproduced (plate 6) as preserved in the Surveyor General's Archives, San Francisco. The field notes describing the mission buildings are taken from the Monterey County Archives and read as follows: "Beginning at a stake marked 'A. 1.' at the northeast corner of the cemetery. Thence . . . south 28° 45' east, 95 links [62.7 feet] to the corner of the Church Buildings, 1.40 chains [92.1 feet] to station, at the angle formed by the church and adjoining buildings. Thence, along the line of buildings 63° 45' east 2.65 chains [175 feet] to station at a corner of the buildings. Thence south 31° 30' east, 1.60 chains [105.6 feet] to station, at corner as above. Thence north 58° 30' east, 15 links [9.92 feet] to station at corner as above. Thence south 31° 30' east, 2 chains [132 feet] to station at corner as above. Thence south 58° 30' west, 15 links [9.92 feet] to station at corner as above. Thence south 31° 30' east, 74 links [48.8 feet] to station at corner above. Thence south 58° 30' west, 30 links [19.8 feet] to station at corner as above Thence north 31° 30' west, 41 links [27.1 feet] to station at Old Adobe Wall. Thence along the ruins of an old adobe wall south, 59° west, 5.18 chains [342 feet] to a point marked 'A' station. Thence north 31° west, 4.44 chains [293 feet] to station at point of intersection of the old wall with a row of church buildings. Thence along the line of church buildings south 63° 45' west, 36 links [23.6 feet] to station at corner of buildings. Thence north 30° 30' west 51 links [33.66 feet] to station at corner of buildings. Thence north 57° east, 60 links [39.6 feet] to station at corner of buildings. Thence north 26° 15' west, at 40 links [26.4 feet] leaves the line of church buildings and along the ruins of the old adobe wall of the cemetery, 1.10 chains [72.5 feet] to a point marked 'A' station. Thence along the north boundary of the cemetery, north 68° 15' east, 2.51 chains [165.66 feet] to the point of beginning." *Archives of the Recorder, Patents A,* 435-436.

[38]Hutchings, *California Magazine,* IV (1859-60), 496.

[39]H. H. Bancroft. *Personal observations,* 1874, p. 210-211.

10 by 56 varas, the sacristy 7 by 14 varas. The walls were built without lime with an adobe mortar, except the finer ornamented stone work about the doors and windows which were put together with cement, or lime mortar. Six stone arches two feet wide thrown over head forming part of the ceiling still remained standing, though apparently ready to fall without much warning, threads of tottering stone-work. Bent pieces of timber overlaid the stone arches."

Fortunately new elements now appear which have been found of great value to those now interested in reconstructing the missions. In the place of vague descriptions and sketches whose accuracy is open to serious question, lovers of bygone days began to take a more scientific interest in preserving a true record of the state of the missions as they had been in their prime, the camera also began to come into use with exact photographic reproductions of such ruins as remained. In this manner many important details overlooked by the writers and now long since obliterated have been preserved for all time.

Among the earlier artists and photographers who have shown a special interest in the missions several names should be mentioned. Among these are Eduard Vischer, C. W. J. Johnson, C. E. Watkins, E. J. Muybridge, Perkins, Fiske and Taber, all of whom have made valuable contributions.[40] First in time, if not in importance, is Eduard Vischer, whose mission sketches constitute a most valuable legacy. Three of these sketches are views of San Carlos; unfortunately, however, since they are among his earliest work they do not give as much information as one would desire. Writing in 1872, he says of San Carlos :[41]

"This mission, after an occupation of half a century, was, like others subsequent to the secularization neglected, and finally abandoned—and now only exhibits deserted walls. Besides the natural causes of dilapidation, vandalism was at work, wantonly defacing the interior of the church; more than all, the antiquarian mania and destructive energy of one of the Monterey priests, who, in the fruitless search for Father Junípero's remains, upturning the graves of several generations, removed the altar, and, as a precaution against accident to the workmen there employed, had a great portion of the roof taken off, which was never replaced, and, subsequently, the rafters, tiles, and all serviceable material were carried off for the use of neighboring settlers."

The reference to vandalism is amplified in a note which states that "on the occasion of modern clam and chowder picnics and whisky sprees, more than once bonfires were lighted in the deserted church, using door frames and paneling as convenient fuel." At other times mounted men rode through the buildings amusing themselves firing their revolvers at the images and other objects.

---

[40]Some of Johnson's photographs are reproduced in the frontispiece and by plates 11 and 12. Plate 7 is from a Muybridge photograph, plates 10 and 41 from Fiske, plate 9 from Watkins and plate 21 from Perkins.

[41]Vischer, *Missions of Upper California,* 1872, (San Francisco, 1872), appendix i-ii. He first visited California in 1842. At that time, while many of the missions had been practically abandoned, they still gave evidence of the greatness of earlier days. He again came to California with the gold seekers and in 1861 began the task of preserving by means of carefully executed sketches the record of the missions as they then were. Archives were consulted and ruin heaps carefully examined in order that the work might be done with accuracy. The collection was completed in 1878.

PLATE 9. *San Carlos Church before 1880.*

This enlargement from a stereo by Watkins is valuable not only as showing the condition of the church at the date indicated but also for other features of detail. The most striking feature is probably the exposed arch supporting the roof. Attention is also called to the remains of a wall in the foreground to the left and to the doorway into the dome on the larger tower. This is reproduced from a stereograph in the State Library.

PLATE 10. *San Carlos Church about 1882.*

This is a view similar to the preceding, but taken at a later date, is evidenced by the more ruined condition of the roof. Attention is here called to the cross timbers, the ends of which are visible along the stone walls; to the buttresses, which are also well reproduced; as well as the remains of the high wall around the smaller burial ground. It should also be noted in this as in the preceding photograph that the sacristy had been covered by a roof of shakes at an earlier date. This is a Fiske photograph (No. 601) from a copy made by Mr. C. B. Turrill from his collection.

PLATE 11. *San Carlos Mission Church, about 1883.*
Johnson, photo.

PLATE 12. *San Carlos Mission Church, After the Restoration of 1884.*
Johnson, photo.

More thorough work in photographing the missions was done by C. E. Watkins in the late seventies and early eighties. Eduard Vischer, a contemporary critic, says of his views:

"His fine conception and splendid effects deserve the highest encomium. . . Could views of similar merit and effects have been taken in early times of all the missions as they stood within our recollection, such undertaking, now greatly interferred with by decay as well as many renovations, would have been of inestimable value to the historian or antiquary."

Mission Restoration. No account of the history of San Carlos Mission would be complete that did not consider the various attempts at repair and restoration, some of which has greatly modified the form and appearance of the mission church.

The first recorded action of this character was made by Father Sorentine, the parish priest, in March, 1856. At this time little or no attempt was made to repair or restore the ruined buildings, but only to locate the body of Father Serra among the ruins of the stone church. In writing the results of this investigation, Father Sorentine says:[42]

"The next day, the 11th [of March], the dirt that was in the altar fell on the gospel side and following the traditional directions, we began to excavate and we found in this one a well sealed vault, with a coffin, in which there was a priest with a stole and good vestments. We could see by the stole that it had epaulettes of fine gold, easily recognized. This body of a priest that we found, so luxuriously vested, something that none of the others had, makes me believe that it is one we are looking for."

But little was done until about 1884 when a new interest in the mission was aroused by the opening of the resort at Del Monte. Mrs. Leland Stanford and others became interested in the ruined mission and plans were made to render the church once again suitable for worship. By this time practically the entire roof had fallen in and many of the walls, especially those at the south corner, had crumbled and fallen. As the result of this endeavor, the church was once again habilitated, the walls being rebuilt and a new roof placed upon it.

Unfortunately, however, at this time repair was considered more important than restoration, the result being a repaired church which artistically was far inferior to the original structure. The chief and outstanding fault was that the new roof line was twelve or more feet higher than the older one and consequently at a much greater pitch. The former tile roof was low and with its gentle slope gave the church an appearance of greater length and beauty. The new roof with its exaggerated prominence gives

---

[42]*Letter of Cayetano Sorentine to Bishop Amat,* Monterey, March 12, 1856, in the Delfina de la Guerra Collection, Santa Barbara. Translated by Miss de la Guerra.

the towers a squatty appearance unknown to the padres, and otherwise entirely changes the appearance of the church. This was to some extent made necessary by the substitution of shingles for the old tile roofing, although it is probable that even with this in mind the original line could have been more closely followed. No attempt was made at that time to restore any of the outlying buildings which composed the quadrangle.

ARCHITECTURAL FEATURES

ARCHITECTURAL FEATURES

The First Structures, 1771-1773. The first buildings constructed on the Carmel site were made of wood, easily obtained in abundance from the nearby forest of pines. Both Palou in his *Noticias* and Serra in his report of 1773 describe these temporary buildings and the rude stockade, which during the earlier years served as an additional protection against pilfering and possible hostile attacks of the natives.

This stockade, which Serra says was something more than seventy varas long by forty-three wide, was made of rough palings. It enclosed most of the mission buildings but not all of them, for the soldiers' barracks were just outside. In a prominent place was the cross and near at hand the hut of Father Serra and another crude structure which served in part as the provisional church. Palou says further that this chapel was one of six rooms in a house fifty by seven varas in size, four of the rooms being used as living quarters and another as a store room or granary. These were all built of wood and had flat mud roofs. That they were not permanent buildings may be judged from the nature of the material of which they were constructed, as well as by the fact that they were erected in such a very short time when laborers were scarce. Palou mentions only twelve men as working with Father Serra.[43]

Other Buildings, 1774. Several other buildings were constructed during 1774. As they were built partially of adobe it is probable that they were more permanent in character. Serra mentions five buildings about thirty by seven varas in size, as being constructed that year. One of these served as a work shop, two were for married servants, one was for the surgeon and another for the smith. Another wooden building with thatch roof was built for the captain of the guard. The record does not say that these buildings were within, or a part of, the enclosure mentioned the year before, and from the fact that no enclosure is mentioned thereafter until the completion of the later court in 1815, it is very probable that with the construction of more secure buildings the temporary stockade had been abandoned. These buildings were grouped around the open space spoken of as the mission plaza. The location of these early buildings in relationship to the later court and ruins now extant must be largely a matter of conjecture.[44]

The Adobe Church. It is regretted that reports are not available for the twenty years following 1774, the only evidence at hand being passing references found in the account of the death and burial of Father Serra in 1784, and at the time of the visit of Lapérouse in 1786. From these we gather that Serra was then living in a small room or cell made of adobe, which was

---

[43]See historical statement, *ante*, 18.
[44]For their conjectural location and form see plate 44.

a part of and closely connected with several other rooms; that the church was about one hundred varas from Serra's cell; and that the former was of considerable size since it could accommodate nearly all of the six hundred people present at Serra's funeral. This church had a place for the choir, a side room used as a sacristy, and there were several stations of the cross within the church. Lapérouse in 1786 speaks of this church as being "very neat, although covered with straw," and says that the president of the mission met him at the church door and conducted him to the foot of the "high altar."[45]

From these passages it is certain that the church of 1784 and 1786 was not the same as the temporary structure of 1773 and of course it cannot be the same as the present stone church which was not begun until 1793. There must therefore have been a church erected sometime previous to 1784 of which the records do not make satisfactory statement. Lack of direct evidence makes it very difficult to speak definitely regarding the nature or location of this second church. Many indications however point to its being located upon the site of the present building and that the position of the altar was identical with that of the present altar. If we may assume, as many things indicate, that Serra's room was located at or near the spot now marked by tradition as his death chamber, we have some basis by which to guide us in locating this church. Lapérouse in 1786 says the missionaries' house at that time was in front of the church, and Palou furnished the information that the distance Serra walked from his cell to the altar was "more than one hundred varas."[46] The location of the present church satisfies very well both of these conditions. Furthermore the absence of any record of the removal of bodies of Fathers Crespi and Serra, who were known to be buried in the older church, tends to confirm the belief that such was not necessary because of the fact that the new structure was erected upon ground already made holy not only by the ministration of these men but also as the resting place of their remains, and that the altar of the new was upon the site of the altar of the old church. Upon this point Father J. Adam says:

"Before concluding, it may be proper to answer the question as to what became of that church of stone, of which Fr. Junípero spoke when, just before dying, he requested Fr. Palou to lay his body close by that of Fr. Crespi, remarking: 'When they build the church of stone, let them throw me where they like.' Can we for a moment suspect that his religious friends had so little respect for his memory as to let him be buried outside of the consecrated ground? By no means. Why, then, is no notice taken of the removal of the remains of Fr. Crespi and Fr. Junípero from the old church to the new one? It is the general opinion of the old residents of Monterey that the new stone church, alluded to by Father Junípero, was built on the same spot where the old edifice stood, and according to this supposition the graves of the two first missionaries remained undisturbed and enclosed within the sanctuary of the new church, on the gospel side, as they were in the temporary building."[47]

[45]Serra's quarters are described as "su quartito ó celda que tenia de adoves." Palou, *Vida*, 270. For other references see Historical Narrative, *ante*, 21-22.
[46]Two hundred seventy-eight feet.
[47]Adams translation of Palou, *Life of Serra*, 149.

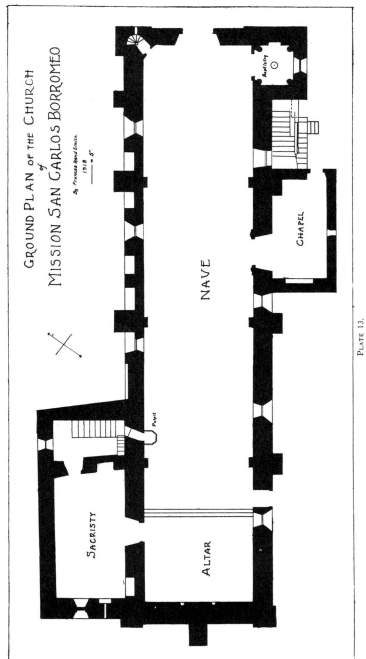

GROUND PLAN of the CHURCH
of
MISSION SAN CARLOS BORROMEO

By Frances Rand Smith.
1918

NAVE

SACRISTY

ALTAR

Pulpit

CHAPEL

Baptistry

PLATE 13.

47

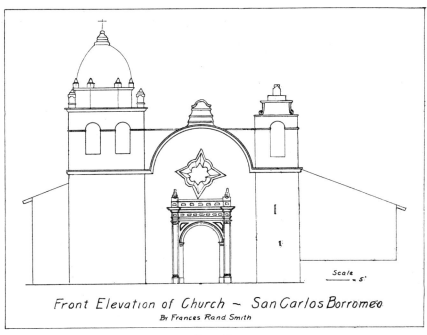

Front Elevation of Church ~ San Carlos Borromeo.
By Frances Rand Smith

Scale
= 5'

PLATE 14.

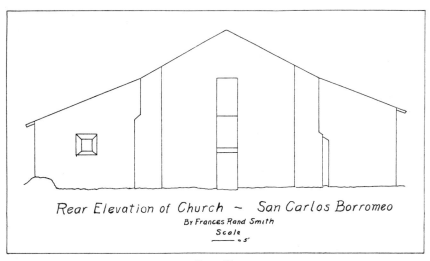

Rear Elevation of Church ~ San Carlos Borromeo
By Frances Rand Smith
Scale
= 5'

PLATE 15.

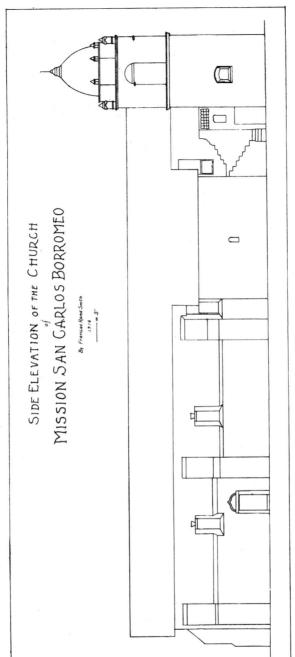

SIDE ELEVATION of the CHURCH
of
MISSION SAN CARLOS BORROMEO

By Frances Rand Smith
1918

PLATE 16.

49

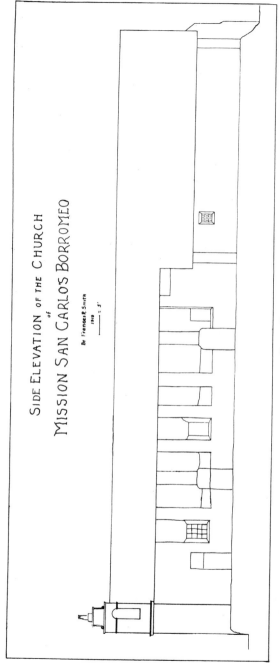

Side Elevation of the Church
of
Mission San Carlos Borromeo

By Frances R. Smith
1918

Plate 17.

50

Using the Sykes sketch of 1794 as a basis for further deduction we must conclude that at least during the construction of the stone church, services were held elsewhere than upon the site just considered as that of the adobe church. It is however extremely probable that at that time a room of some existing building may have served this purpose as had been done during the earlier years. Vancouver in 1794 speaks of the stone church as in the process of construction but makes no mention of the place of worship used at that time. The cross shown upon the building to the left in the Sykes sketch would seem to indicate that for the time being it was used as the church (plate 2).

The Stone Church. Since the mission was primarily a religious institution it is customary to think of the church as the chief if not the only building connected with the establishment. Because also of the fact that at many mission sites the church alone now stands amidst the falling ruins of outbuildings it has to many minds come to be the belief that the church or chapel was the mission. This is untrue to fact. The church was the center of the religious life and around this the whole of the mission activities revolved but it did not alone constitute the mission, for in the days of the Spanish padres church, school, living quarters, workshops, granaries, fields and flocks each occupied an essential part in the make up of a typical California mission. Chief among these buildings was naturally the mission chapel or church.

As has been noted in a preceding paragraph the present church is the third to be built at Carmel. It measures one hundred sixty-seven feet four inches in total length and varies in width from fifty feet four inches at the north end to sixty-two feet at the sanctuary end, the difference in width being due to the baptistry and the sacristy respectively. The church proper is thirty-nine feet wide. The main walls are approximately five feet in thickness. It is constructed of sandstone, obtained near at hand.

As previously stated the present appearance of the church dates from 1884 when an effort was made under Father Casanova to restore it so that religious services could be resumed. A radical modification was made at this time, due to an attempt to give the roof a steeper incline, since shingles were to be substituted for roofing tiles. To accomplish this the peak of the roof was raised some twelve feet, while on the other hand the eaves over the chapel were lowered. The result of all this is to give the roof a prominence never dreamed of by the original builders.

The accompanying elevations show the roof lines and walls as they stood before these changes were made, and when the church had the appearance of greater length and dignity. In this construction was a fitness of proportion characteristic of Spanish architecture. By the use of photographs and traces left upon the building itself many of these points have been determined with a very marked degree of certainty. Through these various means the original height of the roof has been fixed at thirty-seven feet at its peak, and twenty-six feet at the eaves.

When built at these dimensions the main tower stood twenty-six feet above the peak of the roof and the cross even higher, while the smaller tower exceeded the height of the roof by nine feet. Six bells hung in these towers as late as 1852.[48] The larger tower is reached by an outside stairway, and is capped with a hollow dome of stone masonry, to which an entrance could be had from the northwest side (plate 9). There was originally an exterior entrance into the balcony through the larger belfry tower, the ceiled passage way being still noticeable.

Interior of the Church. The interior of the church of San Carlos Borromeo is one of the most picturesque of all the missions of California. The main chapel is twenty-eight feet eight and one-half inches in width and measures one hundred twenty-five feet four inches from the front wall to the first step approaching the sanctuary, from this point to the rear wall there is an additional twenty-five feet ten and one-half inches. This area is separated from the remainder of the church by a low railing as well as being elevated several inches above the floor level.

Subdued light is permitted to penetrate the thick walls through comparatively narrow windows, three on the left of the entrance and four on the right. A most interesting star window over the front entrance furnishes additional light to the church through the balcony.

The beauty of the nave was enhanced by an arched ceiling, the massive tile roof being supported by arches constructed in a most skillful manner. This is shown by photographs taken during the time the mission was in ruins. Of particular value upon this point is the photograph of the interior published by W. Clarence Brown (plate 19). This photograph is remarkable because it includes two of the three stone arches before their destruction, and it is particularly valuable in that it represents the best and most intricate construction in the church. Only at Carmel were stone arches extensively employed. As seen in the photograph the spring of the arch began on a line corresponding to the base of the windows, the curve being gradually met in the massive walls and stone pilasters (plates 19, 20, 21). From the line of the richly ornamented cornice the arch was built strictly for utility and it was the contact with the stone pilasters, the increased proportion of the upper wall, and the buttress against the same section (plate 13) which gave the line of thrust its resistance. In plate 20 the curve is drawn with the original contour showing the slight arch of the three sections. This construction has been referred to as a nave roof of vaulted and ancient con-

---

[48] See note 36, page 34. Two of these were added in 1820, see note 24, page 31. There were in all twenty-four bells located around the mission court. "el numero de las campanas colocadas en distintos puntos del cerco de esa mision, ascendia a veinte y cuatro." Vallejo, *Historia de California,* I, 67-8.

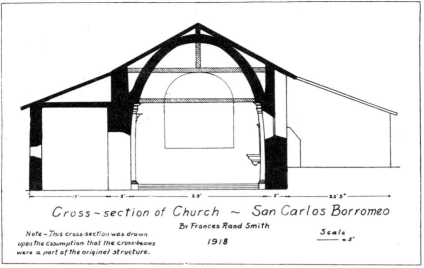

Cross-section of Church ~ San Carlos Borromeo

By Frances Rand Smith

Note – This cross-section was drawn upon the assumption that the cross-beams were a part of the original structure.

1918

Scale ___ = 5'

PLATE 18.

PLATE 19. *Ruined Interior of Church.*
Brown, photo.

PLATE 21. *Ruins of Interior before 1880.* Perkins photo.

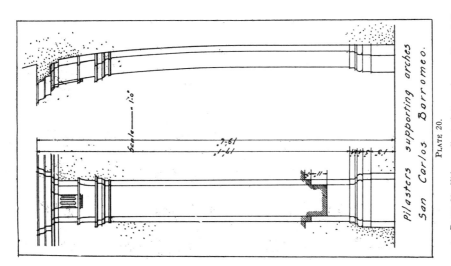

Pilasters supporting arches
San Carlos Borromeo.

PLATE 20.

PLATE 21—This excellent photograph was obtained through the kindness of the family of Mr. Perkins. The original plate with many others is now in the State Library. The most striking feature is the excellent reproduction of one of the three stone arches. The notched rafters are shown resting upon the supporting arch. The star window with its unique irregularity is plainly shown, as is also the stone arch supporting the balcony. In the foreground to the left is to be seen the remains of the stone pulpit and at the extreme left a niche in the wall which did not find a place in the restored church. The original floor tiles had not then been disturbed.

PLATE 23.   *Star Window.*

Note the irregular form of the window, which is here correctly reproduced.

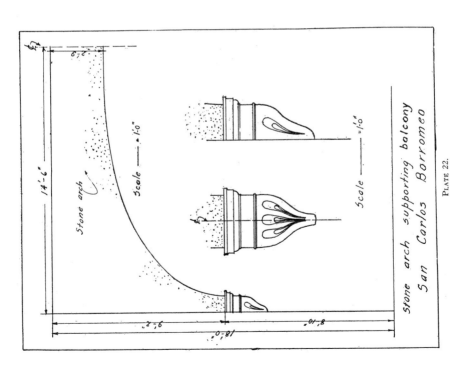

Stone arch supporting balcony
San Carlos Borromeo

PLATE 22.

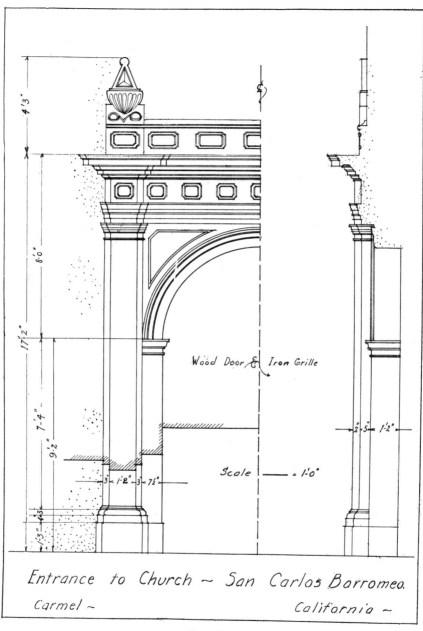

Wood Door & Iron Grille

Scale _____ = 1'-0"

Entrance to Church ~ San Carlos Barromea.

Carmel ~   California ~

PLATE 24.

struction.[49]   So unusual is the construction that it is quite possible the principle of the catenary curve may have been used in these arches.

In addition to the three stone arches supplemental wooden arches also helped to sustain the roof.   Caps, which are still a part of the interior stone cornice, mark, it is said, the places upon which these wooden arches rested. One stone arch has remained and is quite as perfect as the day it was constructed.   Although there is but little spring, it supports the spacious balcony.   In the photographs it appears to be spanning the main entrance.

Upon entering the great doorway (plate 24), one may turn to the right and find a steep and narrow stairway.   Twenty irregular sandstone steps, measuring about two feet six inches in length, one foot two inches in width, and with a nine inch rise, make two complete turns around a column of stone nine inches in diameter.   These steps, worn by the tramp of Indian, priest and tourist, lead to the balcony, which is lighted by the famous star window. (Plate 23.)

The baptistry to the left of the entrance is a memento of workmen skilled in stone-cutting.   For it should be stated that the numerous carvings in the soft sandstone used throughout the great walls of the church, form one of its most interesting features, the granite foundations upon which the edifice is built having provided resistance against earthquake and storm.   Four columns support a Gothic ceiling, the ribs of which are carefully proportioned and are constructed of short lengths of sandstone.   The floor of the baptistry is paved with tiles.   The entrance is an arched doorway of stone (plate 25).   A framework of wood fitted within the stone arch held perpendicular rods which formed an open screen.[50]

The chapel located at the left adjoining the baptistry is reached by the most elaborate doorway in the church (plate 26).   Although the room measures twenty-eight feet by fourteen feet in size it is lighted by one small window whose outer curves are simple and effective.   These outer lines appear to have represented a halo and the window probably held a small statue (plate 28).   Upon the wall of this chapel is a colored decoration including a prayer in Spanish.   This chapel may also be entered by means of an. outside door.[51]

As one approaches further toward the altar another door is found leading to the left into the mission court.   This is also shown in many of the photographs giving an exterior view of the church.   It will be noticed that in the photographs by Johnson and others taken before 1884 that with the exception of the arched top, the doorway is without ornamentation.   During the rebuilding the arched top was made square and it is said that the sandstone carvings from the doorway of the priest's quarters, then in ruin, were

[49]Benton, *The California Mission and its influence upon Pacific Coast Architecture,* in West Coast Magazine, Vol. IX, May, 1911, No. 2.   See also Judson, "*The Architecture of the Missions,*" in Annual Publication of the Historical Society of Southern California, VII (1907-08), 116.

[50]Unfortunately the original baptismal font was badly damaged by vandals.   *Father Sorentine to Bishop Amat,* March 12, 1856.   *Ante,* note 42.   It was later taken to Santa Cruz but subsequently returned to San Carlos.

[51]Paintings in this room were seen as late as 1837.   *Ante,* note 33.   This has been referred to as the chapel of the Crucifixion, *San Francisco Call* Aug. 29, 1884, and may have been the Chapel of the Pasion del Señor, built in 1818.   *Ante,* note 23.

transferred and inserted within this doorway of the church (plates 30 and 31).

The altar of the church is approached by steps of excellent proportion which extend the width of the building, while a spacious arch in the rear wall gives added dignity. A plaque found in the debris of the altar (plate 32) was presented to Mrs. Leland Stanford by Father Casanova and is now in the collection of mission relics in the museum of Stanford University. This is outlined in gold paper and a circle of red pigment, probably ochre. The wood carving shown in plate 33 is a part of the same collection. To the right within the railing is the doorway to the sacristy (plate 34). The irregular shape of certain walls of the sacristy makes it quite probable that this part belonged to a group of buildings erected previous to the building of the stone church. It may have been the one shown in the sketch by Sykes in 1794.

In the sacristy is to be seen one of the well built stairways of the mission. This stairway is the approach to the pulpit, the floor of which is a solid piece of sandstone carving. The door of the pulpit is hand carved and is the same in design as that in the main doorway at San Fernando. It is probable that the designer at San Carlos worked also at San Fernando. The lavabo in the sacristy ranks as one of the finest examples of stone carving in the mission (plate 35).

The Mission Quadrangle. The records do not specify when the buildings composing the quadrangle were erected except that the report of 1815 says that the court was entirely enclosed by the construction of fifty varas of buildings during the preceding year.[52] It is probable that with the building of the stone church the center of mission life was shifted from the early plaza shown by Sykes to the area now seen to have been the mission enclosure.

The exterior limits of this quadrangle as shown in the ground plan herewith produced (plate 45) are based upon actual survey of the extant ruins supplemented by the plat and field notes of the United States engineer who made the survey when the lands were patented to the church. This survey was made by J. E. Terrell in December, 1858, and may be considered as representing the outline of the buildings and ruins as they stood at that date. Unfortunately it is not possible to identify accurately all of the corners in reference to buildings existing at present. It may be probable that the mission was then in such a state of dilapidation that it was impossible for the surveyor to determine the original purpose and relationship of the existing ruins. It is, therefore, to be expected that present ruins may not in all cases be capable of identification upon the surveyor's plat and that in places the survey may not properly represent the external lines of the court. The most noticeable feature to be seen in studying this plat is that the court does not constitute a true rectangle, but was probably built to conform to ground levels.

---

[52] *Ante,* note 22. See plate 44 for conjectural location of these buildings.

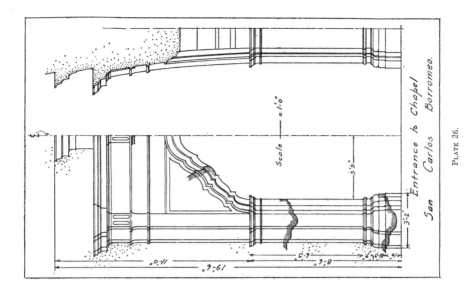

Scale ——— = 1'-0"

Entrance to Chapel
San Carlos Borromeo.

Plate 26.

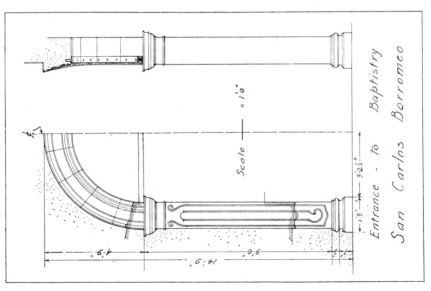

Scale ——— = 1'-0"

Entrance - to Baptistry
San Carlos Borromeo

Plate 25.

59

PLATE 28. *Chapel Window.* Slevin, photo.

PLATE 27. *Baptistry Window.* Slevin, photo.

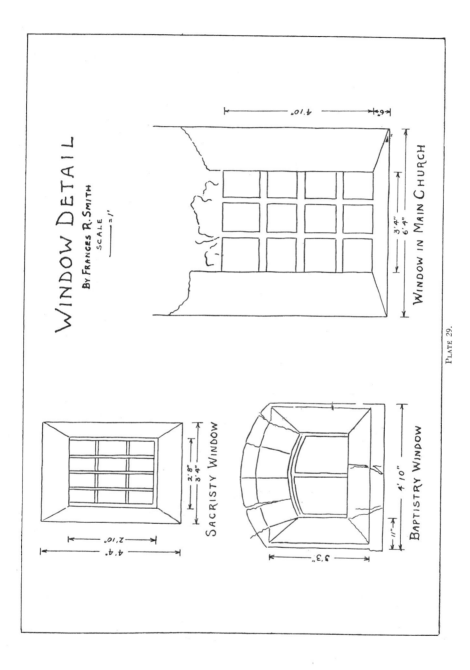

WINDOW DETAIL

BY FRANCES R. SMITH

SCALE
—— = 1'

WINDOW IN MAIN CHURCH

SACRISTY WINDOW

BAPTISTRY WINDOW

PLATE 29.

61

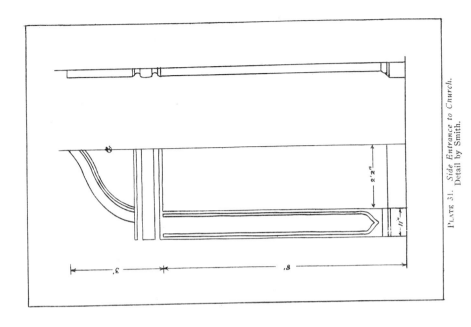

PLATE 31. *Side Entrance to Church.*
Detail by Smith.

PLATE 30. *Side Entrance to Church.*
Slevin, photo.

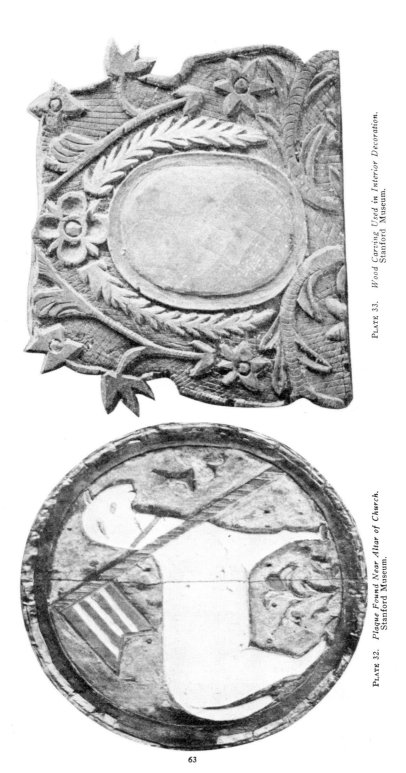

PLATE 33. *Wood Carving Used in Interior Decoration.*
Stanford Museum.

PLATE 32. *Plaque Found Near Altar of Church.*
Stanford Museum.

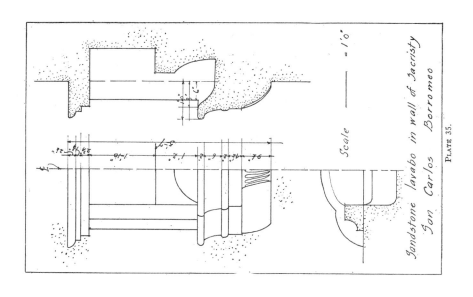

Scale ———— = 1'0"

Sandstone lavabo in wall of Sacristy
San Carlos Borromeo

PLATE 35.

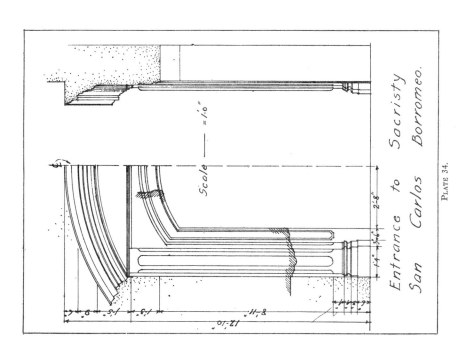

Scale ———— = 1'0"

Entrance to Sacristy
San Carlos Borromeo.

PLATE 34.

Adjoining the church upon its front and eastern corner stood the buildings which began, or rather, continued the enclosure. A recent survey confirms the United States plat when it indicates that they did not join the front of the church at right angles but at an angle of eighty-seven and one-half degrees.[53] That these buildings joined upon the front of the church there can be no question, although at present there are no adobe remains within approximately forty feet of the church, this space having been used for many years as a driveway.

The evidence supporting the claim that the ruins connected with the church is as follows: In the first place, it is stated in the mission report of 1815 that the quadrangle was enclosed and various descriptions after that date mention definitely this enclosure; second, photographs by Muybridge and Johnson show very plainly a wall extending northward from the church for a distance not less than twenty-five feet, while numerous other photographs taken before the restoration of the church show markings upon the facade of the church such as would be made only by adjoining buildings, which had but recently fallen away or had been removed;[54] and third, the remaining adobe ruins and stone foundations indicate a continuation of the buildings which, if extended, would join the church in such manner as to explain the markings in the photographs referred to.

From the data at hand the first section has been restored. The side walls are formed by continuing existing ruined walls. The end is determined from certain foundation stones to be found extending eastward from the corner of the church. This portion was probably used by the mission priests as living quarters, as indicated in the accounts of Lapérouse in 1786 and Du Petit-Thouars in 1837, as well as by present day tradition. On the other hand, an examination of the Sykes sketch made at the time of Vancouver's visit shows upon the right and in front of the stone church, then being constructed, a long building surmounted by a cross, thus indicating that it may then have been the temporary mission church.

The buildings nearer the northern corner of the court are fortunately in a better state of preservation. Existing adobe ruins laid bare by excavations under Father R. M. Mestres show plainly the postion and thickness of these walls (plates 36-40). That this portion of the building at least was more than one story in height is indicated by a Muybridge photograph (plate 7). In it are to be seen the elevation of the wall above the top of the door with projecting floor beams and windows for the upper floor. It is probable that the upper story was a loft which covered the whole of this range of buildings.

The ground plans for the buildings along the northeastern side of the court were worked out from existing ruins, photographic evidence, and from other data gathered several years ago. In the corner is one large room.[55]

---

[53]See note 37.

[54]See any front view of church about 1880 or before.

[55]The author saw this as one large room in 1908 before the excavation made for road work had removed a portion of the above ruins.

Adjoining this room to the east are the adobe remains of three smaller ones. These rooms are about sixteen feet wide inside measurement, and measure respectively twenty-nine, sixteen and eight feet in length.

These three rooms are six feet narrower than the corner room previously described, the extra space being occupied by a portico of that width as shown in the sketch of Wm. Smythe (plate 3). An excellent photograph by Fiske clearly shows that of these three rooms the larger one alone had a door or other exterior opening (plate 41). It may be of interest to note that this door has a striking similarity to the one removed from the adobe ruins during the restoration of 1884, and placed at the side of the stone church.[56] The other openings from these rooms into the court are of necessity largely conjectural, as the ruined walls fail to give satisfactory evidence as to their existence and location.

In the restoration of the building adjoining those just described there is now but little to guide the investigator, for the ruined adobe walls which at one time continued the enclosure have now disappeared. However, knowing from the documents that the court here was enclosed by buildings, and acting upon data obtained in 1908, before these walls had been entirely obliterated to satisfy a temporary demand for road material, this portion has been reconstructed. Acting upon this data these buildings have been indicated as of the same width as the room at the northeast corner. That in their general form and size these buildings have been correctly outlined there seems to be but little ground for doubt.[57]

The United States survey plat shows an extension of nine feet along a portion of the northeast side of the court. Just what these lines represent is not determined in a fully satisfactory manner. It is probable, however, that they represent a projection such as a covered porch, as is suggested by the sketch of Wm. Smythe. Adjoining the corner of the court upon the east is a small rectangular space set off in such a manner as to indicate a building about twenty-six by nineteen feet in size. This was probably built in this manner to serve as a buttress to support the walls of the range of buildings just described, or it may have been a supplemental building added later.

From these buildings the court turned to the southwest at an angle of ninety and one-half degrees. The inner wall of this portion is clearly shown by existing ruins which extend for a distance of about one hundred fifty feet.[58] The outer wall of this portion of the quadrangle has disappeared, but that an adobe wall did exist is indicated by notations upon the plat of the

---

[56]A close examination of the Fiske photograph referred to shows very clearly the characteristics of this doorway. According to the statement of Father R. M. Mestres, this door of the church had been obtained from one of the adobe ruins. *Ante*, 57.

[57]The evidence favoring this conclusion is as follows: First, the line of the United States survey indicates that the buildings here were wider than those previously described, rather than narrower. Second, notwithstanding the many points of conflict between the sketch of San Carlos in 1823 (plate 3), and the archeological evidence now at hand, the former does support strongly the idea of continuous and more or less uniform buildings. This also is borne out in the restoration of Oriana Day (plate 8), which, however, without further evidence, does not stand as an independent source. Third, the Fiske photograph of 1880 (plate 41), shows walls which have now disappeared. Unfortunately, however, from the picture it is impossible to determine definitely the position of these walls with reference to their distance from the court.

[58]The first 30 feet have disappeared, this being used as a roadway.

PLATE 36. *Mound of Ruins, January, 1920.*
Coy, photo.

PLATE 37. *Same Mound After Excavation, April, 1921.*
Coy, photo.

67

PLATE 38.

PLATE 40.

PLATE 39.

Excavated Ruins, April, 1921. Coy, photo.

PLATE 41. *Ruins of San Carlos Mission about 1880.* Photo by Fiske.

This is one of the most valuable photographs here presented, as it shows the whole sweep of mission ruins as they were about 1880. Much of the northeast side of the mission court is well preserved in this photograph. In the foreground is shown what, according to Mr. Muchado, for many years caretaker of the mission, was the foundation of the herder's cabin. We must agree that it was an excellent position as it commanded a view of the valley for many miles. This illustration is reproduced from the collection of Mr. Chas. B. Turrill.

PLATE 42. *Ruins of Mission Quadrangle, January, 1921.*
Slevin, photo.

PLATE 43. *Ruins of Mission Quadrangle, 1908.*
Slevin, photo.

United States surveyor. Its foundations therefore will probably be revealed by future excavations. The windows and doors leading into the court have been restored in the ground plan approximately as shown in these ruins.

At the end of the one hundred fifty feet just described the ruined adobe wall terminates in a well-defined corner, thus indicating the end of a building. Acting upon the following statement by Ruschenberger that there was an entrance to the court on this side, a wagon entrance has been indicated in the ground plan at this point. He says :[59]

"The mission building is, perhaps, a hundred yards square, one story high, and roofed with tiles. We rode through the gate, which was just ready to fall from its hinges, into the great central court, round which it is built, where we found eight or ten Indians engaged in repairing the roof."

In reference to the remainder of the quadrangle there is little evidence now to be found. It is probable that this portion of the quadrangle was constructed in a less substantial manner than the other parts. That the exterior walls were built of adobe is indicated upon the surveyor's plat,[60] but time has obliterated all surface traces of them as well as of the inner walls. It is extremely probable that excavations now in progress will show the exact location of all these walls.

That there were buildings enclosing the whole area of the mission court, however, is well established from documentary sources, and subsoil excavations have brought to light much corroborative data. In the annual report for the year 1815 it is stated that during the year there had been erected several buildings necessary to enclose the court.[61] Ruschenberger in 1836 describes the mission as built around a great central court. Du Petit-Thouars, who visited the mission in 1837, states in his description that the court was enclosed on all four sides by buildings.[62] In addition to these statements there is the sketch of the rear of the mission in 1839 reproduced by Laplace,[63] which shows the greater portion to have been enclosed by buildings, although it is impossible to determine much regarding their form or the material of which they were constructed. It is not improbable that buildings of light adobe had been erected along these two sides of the court either for workshops or neophytes' dwellings. All the walls have now disappeared but at the time of the survey of 1858 the outer and stronger wall of the adobe still remained, although even then in a ruined form.

As the side of the court approaches the church it is noted that the outer wall does not connect with the rear wall of the stone church, but lies some fifteen or more feet to the rear. Furthermore the surveyor's plat seems to show a projection of the church into the rear. When comparison is made with the sketch reproduced by Laplace these irregularities are explained,[64]

[59]Ruschenberger, *Narrative*, 507.

[60]Notations on the plat definitely state that the wall on the southeast side was an adobe. The other is merely described as an "old wall."

[61]*Archivo Misiones, Papeles Originales*, I, 372.

[62]Du Petit-Thouars, *Voyage*, II, 116.

[63]Laplace, *Campagne*, VI, 294 (plate 4).

[64]Plate 4.

for it is seen in the drawing that unless the laws of perspective were entirely disregarded the artist did not intend to show the rear wall of the court as joining directly upon the corner of the church, but rather several feet to the rear. The sketch then shows a lean-to building adjoining the rear of the church. There was probably a door at the corner of the court between the rear wall and the church through which access was had to this outbuilding.[65] From the representation of a corral around this structure it seems that it may have served in 1839 at least as a shelter for the milch cows.

That there were numerous other buildings serving the purpose of the mission outside of the enclosure just described is indicated by the various reports and sketches which have come down from the earlier period. The Smythe sketch of 1823 shows several buildings located outside, in addition to the rude huts of the Indians. Excavations among the ruins surrounding the mission enclosure may disclose the location and form of many of these buildings, but at present there is but little to indicate their number or location. It has been thought best, therefore, to include in this study only those buildings which were a part of, or definitely attached to, the mission court.[66]

The Mission Bells. No description of San Carlos would be complete without reference to its bells, for the bells played an important part in the life of every Spanish mission. They made known the hour of rising and the time of morning worship. At their sound the neophytes went forth to toil and were summoned to food and rest. The bells pealed forth glad welcome to arriving friends and tolled their dolorous lamentation at the death of members of the mission family.

Around the court at San Carlos hung some twenty-four bells of various sizes. At least six of these hung in the two towers of the church. Two of the larger bells were added during the year 1820. Unfortunately the only bell which has remained continuously at the mission has been recast during recent years, and but little is known regarding the history or present location of the other original bells. It is not improbable, however, that further research will disclose many facts still unknown and may make possible the identification of some of the bells which have drifted away from their proper surroundings.[67]

The Burial Ground. On the side of the church opposite the court lies the cemetery. All agree as to its position, but there is as yet no certainty as to its exact extent. This is due to the fact that a well defined wall divided the area described by various authorities as a cemetery into two distinct parts.[68] The wider area is shown upon the plat of the survey of 1858 and would allow for the burial ground space approximately one

---

[65]Vischer represents the walls of the buildings as being very massively built.

[66]For conjectural location of some of these buildings, see plate 44.

[67]For references regarding the bells, see notes 24, 36 and 48. A most valuable study of mission campanology is now being made by Mrs. Alice Harriman of Los Angeles.

[68]This wall is clearly shown in the photographs reproduced herewith. (Plates 5, 9 and 10.)

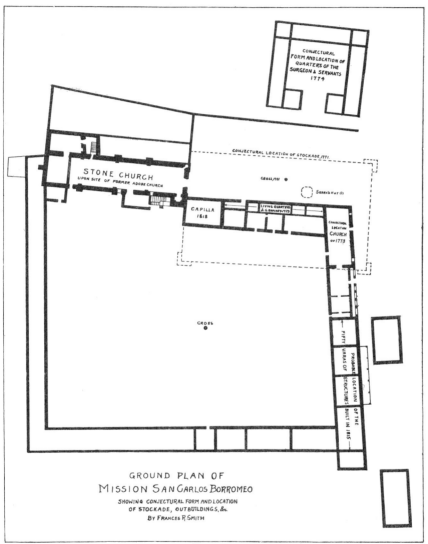

CONJECTURAL
FORM AND LOCATION OF
QUARTERS OF THE
SURGEON & SERVANTS
1774

CONJECTURAL LOCATION OF STOCKADE, 1771.

STONE CHURCH
UPON SITE OF FORMER ADOBE CHURCH

CROSS, 1771

SERRA'S HUT (?)

CAPILLA
1818

LIVING QUARTERS
A. G. BANARY, 1775

CONJECTURAL
LOCATION
CHURCH
OF 1773

CROSS

FIFTY VARAS OF

PROBABLE LOCATION OF THE STRUCTURES BUILT IN 1815

GROUND PLAN OF
MISSION SAN CARLOS BORROMEO

SHOWING CONJECTURAL FORM AND LOCATION
OF STOCKADE, OUTBUILDINGS, &c.
BY FRANCES R. SMITH

PLATE 44.

hundred sixty in length by slightly less than sixty feet in average width. The smaller space lies near the church and is about one hundred long by twenty feet wide. That this latter was the burial ground seems indicated by the Smythe sketch of 1823, as well as that of Laplace of 1839. That this smaller space was inadequate for this purpose would appear very reasonable, but why a substantial wall should divide the grounds is an unsolved question unless the original burial ground had been enlarged, the wall being allowed to remain. Of the existence of this wall there can be no doubt. It is very distinctly reproduced in the Fiske photograph of the ruins of the Mission Church (plate 10), which shows the rear portion of the wall still standing up to a level with the eaves of the sacristy, a height of twelve feet. It is also clearly indicated in the "Alemany Plat," 1854. (Plate 5.)

According to tradition, an unmarked grave is situated in front of the mission church for the bandit Garcia, a member of the band under the leadership of Vasquez, who asked in his deathbed repentance, it is said, that he be buried where the worshipers of the mission might ever tread upon his grave. Before the great door of the church is another grave, that of the weary and worn little Costanoan Indian. This honor was earned when, during the strength of her young womanhood, she helped to bear the burdens in the building of San Carlos.

In the shelter of the great stone walls of the mission of San Carlos Borromeo itself is the last resting place of the priests and Indians who were the builders of the mission. Here, too, rest Serra and Crespi, who conceived the plan of the stone church, and Lasuén, who erected it. Thus, of the little band of four associates, in the convent school of Majorca (*Spanish,* Mallorca), in the Balearic Isles, Serra, Palou, Verger, and Crespi, who in later life set out together on their high-souled missionary adventure to the New World, and all four of whom cooperated to the end in the work of building up the superb chain of California missions, it came to pass that two still sleep side by side.

To the architectural beauty of the ruin at Carmel, the spot where Father Junípero labored and died, Helen Hunt Jackson pays this tribute :[69]

"His grave is under the ruins of the beautiful stone church of his mission,—the church which he saw only in ardent and longing fancy. It was perhaps the most beautiful, though not the grandest of the mission churches; and its ruins have today a charm far exceeding all the others. The fine yellow tint of the stone, the grand and unique contour of the arches, the beautiful star-shaped window in the front, the simple yet effective lines of carving on pilaster and pillar and doorway, the symmetrical Moorish tower and dome, the worn steps leading up to the belfry,—all make a picture whose beauty, apart from hallowing associations, is enough to hold one spell-bound."

[69]Jackson, Helen Hunt, *Glimpses of California and the Missions,* 43.

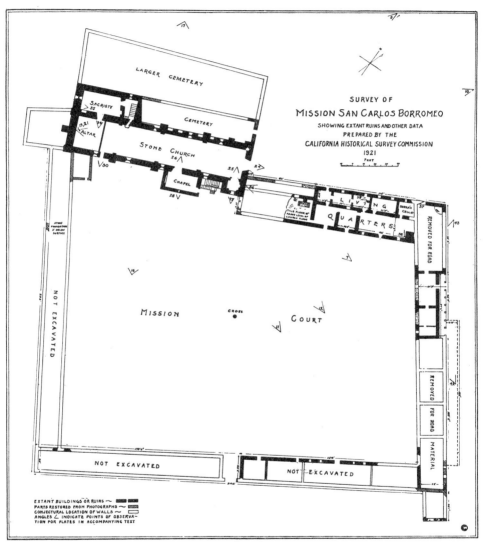

SURVEY OF
MISSION SAN CARLOS BORROMEO
SHOWING EXTANT RUINS AND OTHER DATA
PREPARED BY THE
CALIFORNIA HISTORICAL SURVEY COMMISSION
1921

LARGER CEMETERY

SACRISTY 35

ALTAR

CEMETERY

STONE CHURCH 26

CHAPEL 28

LIVING QUARTERS

REMOVED FOR ROAD

MISSION   CROSS   COURT

NOT EXCAVATED

REMOVED FOR ROAD MATERIAL

NOT EXCAVATED

NOT EXCAVATED

EXTANT BUILDINGS OR RUINS
PARTS RESTORED FROM PHOTOGRAPHS
CONJECTURAL LOCATION OF WALLS
ANGLES ∠ INDICATE POINTS OF OBSERVA-
TION FOR PLATES IN ACCOMPANYING TEXT

PLATE 45.

BIBLIOGRAPHY

PRINTED WORKS

Adam, J. See under Palou.

Bancroft, H. H., *History of California*. San Francisco, 1884-1890.

Bartlett, J. R., *Personal narrative of explorations and incidents, . . . during the years 1850, '51, '52 and '53.* New York, 1854.

Beechey, F. W., *Narrative of a voyage to the Pacific . . . in the years 1825, '26, '27, '28.* Philadelphia, 1832.

Benton, Arthur B., *The California mission and its influence upon Pacific Coast architecture,* in the West Coast Magazine, X, 137-160 (May, 1911).

Cole, G. W., *Missions and mission pictures; a contribution towards an iconography of the Franciscan missions of California,* in California State Library, *News note,* V (1910), 390-412.

Duflot de Mofras, Eugène, *Exploration du territoire de l'Orégon des Californies . . . pendant les années 1840, 1841, et 1842.* Paris, 1844.

Du Petit-Thouars, Abel, *Voyage autour du monde sur la frégate la Vénus pendant les années, 1836-1839.* Paris, 1840.

Engelhardt, C. A. (*in religion* Zephyrin). *The missions and missionaires of California.* San Francisco, 1908-1916.

Hittell, T. H., *History of California.* San Francisco, 1898.

Jackson, Helen Hunt, *Glimpses of California and the missions.* Boston, 1902.

Judson, Wm. L., *Architecture of the missions,* in Historical Society of Southern California, *Annual Publications,* VII, 114-118.

Lapérouse, Jean Francois de Galaup, *Voyage de la Pérouse autour du Monde.* Paris, 1798.

Laplace, [Cyrille Pierre Theodore], *Campagne de Circumnavigation de la frégate l'Artémise pendant les années 1837, 1838, 1839 et 1840.* Paris, 1841-1854.

Palou, Francisco, *Noticias de la Nueva California.* San Francisco, 1874.

   Relacion historica de la vida y apostolicas tereas del Venerable Padre Fray Junípero Serra. Mexico, 1787.

   Francisco Palou's life . . . of the Venerabl Father Junípero Serra. Pasadena (G. W. James), 1913.

   Life of Ven. Padre Junípero Serra. . . . Tr. by Very Rev. J. Adam. San Francisco, 1884.

Richman, Irving B., *California under Spain and Mexico.* New York, 1911.

Ruschenberger, Wm. S. W., *A voyage round the world . . . in 1835, 1836 and 1837.* Philadelphia, 1838.

T. H. S. *The death and burial of Father Junípero Serra,* in Hutching's Illustrated California Magazine, IV (1860), 493-496.

Vancouver, George, *A voyage of discovery . . . in the year 1790, 1791, 1792, 1793, 1794, and 1795.* London, 1798.

Vischer, Eduard, *Missions of upper California, 1872.* San Francisco, 1872.

(Chiefly in the Bancroft Collection)

Bancroft, H. H., *Personal Observations, 1874.*

De Croix to Fages, November 12, 1770, in *Archives of California, Provincial State Papers,* I, 69–71.

Fages to Palou, May 29, 1785, in *Archives of California, Provincial Records,* III, 50.

Informe de San Carlos, December 31, 1810, in *Archivo de las Misiones, Papeles Originales,* I, 328.

Informe de San Carlos, December 31, 1815, in *Archivo de las Misiones, Papeles Originales,* I, 372.

Informe de San Carlos, December 31, 1818, in *Archivo de las Misiones, Papeles Originales,* I, 432.

Informe de San Carlos, December 31, 1820, in *Archivo de las Misiones, Papeles Originales,* I, 328.

Informe de San Carlos, December 31, 1822, in *Archivo de las Misiones, Papeles Originales,* I, 554–556.

Lasuén to Arrillaga, June 7, 1794, in *Archivo del Arzobispado de San Francisco,* I, 38–39.

Lasuén to Borica, December 10, 1794, in *Archivo de la Mision de Santa Barbara, Papeles Miscelaneos,* VI, 219–220.

Lasuén, Estado general bienal 1793-4, Mar. 11, 1795, in *Archivo de la Mision de Santa Barbara, Informes y Correspondencia,* XII, 54–61.

Lasuén, Report, 1797–1798, in *Archivo de la Mision de Santa Barbara Papeles Miscelaneos,* XII, 65–68.

Lasuén, Representacion, November 12, 1800, in *Archivo de la Mision de Santa Barbara, Papeles Miscelaneos,* II, 154–240.

Notas, March 1, 1795, in *Archives of California, State Papers Missions,* II, 4–8.

Payeras, Report, December 31, 1818, in *Archivo de la Mision de Santa Barbara, Informes y Correspondencia,* XII, 451–455.

Payeras, Report, May 4, 1819, *Ibid,* 98–104.

Sal, Estado, December 31, 1797, in *Archives of California, State Papers Missions,* II, 120.

Serra, Representacion de 21 Mayo, 1773, in *Archives of California, Provincial State Papers,* I, 103–137, also in *Archivo de la Mision de Santa Barbara,* I, 83–118.

Serra, Informe, 1774, in *Archivo de la Mision de Santa Barbara, Informes y Correspondencia,* I, 146–154.

Sorentine to Bishop Amat, Monterey, March 12, 1856, in the *Delfine de la Guerra Collection,* Santa Barbara.

Vallejo, Mariano G., *Historia de California,* 5 volumes.

INDEX.

Gentile, Indians, 20.
Gothic ceiling in baptistry, 57.
Granary (1771), 19, 45; well filled (1794), 27.
Grinding flour, method of, 27.
Herder's cabin (plate 41), 69.
Hittell, cited, 31.
Indians, huts of thatch (1773), 20; village described by Lapérouse (1786), 22–23; by Vancouver (1794), 27; quarters of (1800), 28; numbers of, seven hundred and forty (1786), 23; eight hundred (1794), 27; five hundred (1834), 34; eight or ten Indians working (1836), 32; two or three families (1837), 33; not over thirty (1841), 34; tenantless (1852), 34; life of, daily routine, 23; food, 23; grinding meal, 27.
Inventory of property (1834), 32.
Irrigation, possible in Carmel Valley, 18.
Jackson, Helen Hunt, quoted, 74.
James, Geo. Wharton, cited, 17, 18, 24.
Johnson, C. W. J., photographer, 38, 65; photographs by, frontis, (plates 11, 12), 40.
Judson, W. L., cited, 57.
Kitchen (1771), 19.
Lapérouse, 45, 65; visits mission (1786), 22–23; picture, 33.
Laplace, at mission (1839), 34, 71; sketch of mission (plate 4), 29.
Lasuén, 74; president of missions, 22; builds stone church, 23–24; cited, 24; quoted, 28.
Lavabo in sacristy, 58; detail of (plate 35), 64.
Lime made of sea shells, 27.
Living quarters, 45; at the presidio (1770), 17; in 1771, 18–19; in 1837, 33.
Lower California Indians, 18.
Marines, help build mission, 18.
Mestres, Father R. M., 65, 66.
Mill, presented to mission (1786), 23.
Mofras. See Duflot.
Monterey Bay, Spanish occupation of, 17.
Mortar, and whitewash on walls, 31; of adobe, 38; made of shells, 27; wooden wall plastered over, 20.
Mount Calvary, 31.
Muchado (plate 41), 69.
Muybridge, E. J., photographer, 38, 65; photograph by (plate 7), 36.
Neophytes. See Indians.
Orchard. See Garden.
Organ, presented by Vancouver, 27; still in use (1837), 34.
Ovens, 21.
Palou, 21, 22, 45, 74; cited, 17, 18, 22, 24, 46.
Paintings, in church (1786), 22; in chapel (1837), 33, 57.
Patent issued to church (1859), 37.
Payeras quoted, 31.

Perkins, photographer, 38; photograph by (plate 21), 54.
Pilasters, 52; detail of (plate 20), 54.
Pines, 45.
Plaque (plate 32), 58.
Portolá, 17.
Presidio, 18, 24.
Provisional church, at Carmel (1771), 18; in 1773, 20; conjectural location (plate 44), 73. See also Church.
Pulpit, 58.
Punta de Pinos, 19.
Quadrangle, 58, 65–66, 71–72; enclosed (1815), 31, 58; buildings more than one story (plate 7), 36; described by Ruschenberger (1836), 32; described by Du Petit-Thouars (1837), 33.
Quarters. See Living quarters.
Ravelins, 20.
Removal of mission to Carmel, 17, 18, 19.
Repairs on mission (1824), 31.
Restoration of stone church (1884), 41–42; photographs (plates 11, 12), 40.
Richman, cited, 32.
Roof, flat on early building (1771), 19; flat of clay and mud (1773), 20, 45; of thatch (1774), 20, 21, 45; flat earth roof (1774), 21; church roof of straw (1786), 22, 46; stone church roof of tile, 24; arched roof, 34; roof partly fell (1852), 37; in ruins (1874), 37–38; roof removed, 38; shown in photographs (plates 9, 10), 39; height changed during restoration (1884), 41–42; original height determined, 52.
Ruiz, master mason, 24.
Ruschenberger, quoted, 32, 71.
Sacristy, 38, 58; entrance (plate 34), 64; window in (plate 29), 61; lavabo in (plate 35), 64; roof renewed, 39.
Sailors, cut timber, 19.
Sal, quoted, 24.
San Antonio de Padua founded, 18.
Sanctuary, 52.
San Fernando, Mission, carvings similar to, 58; College of, 17.
San Francisco Call, cited, 57.
San Francisco Mission, 24, 28.
San Luís Obispo Mission, 18.
Santa Clara Mission, 24, 27.
Secularization, 31–32.
Serra, 17, 18, 20, 21, 25; as church builder (note 17), 24; death and burial, 21–22; buried in adobe church, 46; remains, 38; hut of, 18, 45; conjectural location of (plate 44), 73; room or cell of, 45.
Servants' quarters (1774), 21.
Slevin, photographs by (plates 42, 43), 70.
Smith's quarters, 21.
Smythe, Wm., 66, 72; sketch by (plate 3), 29.
Soldiers, aid in building, 18, 19.
Soledad secularized, 34.

Sorentine, Father, 41, 57.
Square. *See* Stockade, Quadrangle.
St. Joseph, patron of mission, 17.
Stairway, to tower, 52; to balcony, 57; to pulpit, 58.
Stanford, Mrs. Leland, 41, 58.
Stanford University Museum (plates 32, 33), 63, 58.
Star window, 52; illustration (plate 23), 55, 74.
Stock, at mission (1834), 34.
Stockade, at the presidio (1770), 17; (1771), 19, 20, 45; not mentioned (1774), 45; conjectural location (plate 44), 73.
Stone, church referred to by Serra (note 13), 22; church, 23, 24; church under construction, 27; used in church, 27; arches shown in Perkins photograph (plate 21), 54. *See* Church, Arches.
Surgeon's quarters, 21.
Survey of mission grounds, "Alemany Plat" (1854), 37; reproduced (plate 5), 30; by J. E. Terrell (1858), 37, (plate 6) 35; by Coy (plate 45), 75.
Sykes, 58, 65; artist of Vancouver expedition, 24; sketch (plate 2), 26; 51, 58.
Taber, photographer, 38.
Temporary buildings, at M o n t e r e y (1770), 17; at Carmel (1771), 19.
Terrell, surveyor, 58; plat (plate 6), 35.
Thatch. *See* Roof.
Tile, roof on stone church, 24, 37; carried away, 38; paving in baptistry, 57.

Title confirmed (1859), 37.
Towers, described, 52, 74; contain six bells, 34, 72.
Turrill, Chas. B., 39, 69.
United States, 58, 65, 71, 72; survey plat (plate 6), 35; confirms title to church (1859), 37.
Vallejo, Gen. M. G., 36.
Vancouver, at San Carlos (1794), 24–28, 65; speaks of building of stone church, 27, 51.
Vandalism, 38.
Verger, 74.
Via Crucis (1820), 31.
Viceroy, donation to mission, 18; grants permission for removal, 18.
Victoria, succeeds Echeandía, 32.
Vischer, Eduard, 38, 72.
Vizcaíno, 17, 25.
Wagon entrance to court, 71.
Water, needed for irrigation, 18; plenty at Carmel, 18–19.
Watkins, C. E., photographer, 38, 41; photograph by (plate 9), 39.
Whitewash, used in interior (1773), 20.
Windows, 52; (plates 27, 28), 60, (plate 29), 61; barred with iron (1836), 32.
Women's quarters (1800), 28–31.
Wood carvings in chapel, 31.
Wooden buildings (1771), 19. *See also* Buildings.
Workshop, at Monterey (1770), 17; at Carmel (1774), 20, 45.

O

A Description

of

CALIFORNIA

in 1828

by José Bandini

Translated by
Doris Marion Wright

Friends of the Bancroft Library
Berkeley, California
1951

Contents

Don José Bandini

Introduction

LONG AGO, *when California was very young, a Spanish sea captain named José Bandini visited these shores. He found the country so much to his liking that sometime in the 1820's, when he finally retired from the sea, he decided to make his home in the little village of San Diego. From that point of vantage he surveyed the region with critical eyes, carefully noting down what he observed. His report is worth reading, for a man who faithfully describes his own milieu speaks with authority, and his words have a convincing genuineness. Historians of today may write of that decade with greater accuracy and far less bias, but they cannot possibly say, as Bandini could, "I was there."*

He saw a land so new that its name was still in doubt; some people called it New California, others spoke of Upper California, and a few perverse souls still referred to it as New Albion. The boundaries had not yet been established, and the rich natural resources of this Mexican outpost were for the most part undeveloped or unknown. It would be another twenty years before the Gold Rush would force the sleepy community into the hurrying tempo of a modern state.

Bandini discussed in detail many of the outstanding features of California—the pueblos and presidios; the missions; the mountains and lakes and great tule-covered plains; the inhabitants, particularly the Indians with their strange and wonderful customs; and a host of other things. With commendable foresight he pointed out the enormous potentialities of the territory, suggesting that, since Nature had been so lavish with her gifts, only hard work was needed to make the region amount to something. "But," he remarked bluntly, "unfortunately, industry is unknown in California."

As he looked about, Bandini found other conditions that did not please him. He believed that the government should do more

v

to encourage settlers, so that towns would develop. He noticed
that the missions, with their monopoly of large-scale agriculture
and the hide-and-tallow trade, claimed more land than they
could use, thereby withholding property that might better be in
the hands of private individuals. But his greatest concern was
with the sea trade of this area, which seemed to him to be in obvious and urgent need of reform.

To Bandini the problems were perfectly clear. Most commercial vessels, he explained, visited California for the sole purpose
of collecting hides and tallow. If the captains and the supercar-
goes knew what they were about, they did not attempt to buy
these products with money. Instead, they brought with them a
variety of articles wanted by the Californians—dress materials,
agricultural equipment, and a thousand other things required for
the aid and comfort of the frontier settlers. These goods could be
traded, mainly through the missions, for the hides and tallow
that constituted California's principal exports. The region yielded
one other product, wheat, which was sold to the Russians for use
in their settlements to the north. Now all of this commerce was
being threatened by the unwise regulations imposed by Mexico.
Deeply disturbed, Bandini reasoned that if the strangling of trade
were allowed to continue, vessels would stop coming to these
coasts; supplies needed by the residents would no longer be
brought in; the people would sink back into apathy and indigence; and foreigners, who were the only ones with any business
acumen, would move away. Reforms must be introduced, or
California would be ruined.

Concerning the author of the "Descrision" we know very
little. Unlike his son Juan, José Bandini was in no sense a public
figure, and neither family papers nor government archives have
revealed much about him. Such information as we have indicates
that he was born in 1771 in the city of Cádiz in Andalucía, and
that as a very young man, probably in 1793, he went to South

America, there residing in Lima. Extant church records show that he was married twice, first to Ysidora Blancas, and then, after her death in 1801, to Manuela Mazuelos. He had several children, among them one who became Archbishop of Lima, but only Juan came with his father to California.

The elder Bandini apparently made his first visit to this region in 1819 as captain of the ship Reina de los Angeles, bringing supplies of war from San Blas to California's governor, Pablo de Sola. After a similar voyage two years later, he and all his crew took an oath of allegiance to the revolutionary leader, Iturbide; Bandini claimed that his ship was the first to fly the flag of independent Mexico. In 1822, he was granted military retirement with the rank of capitán de milicias, and soon afterward he and his son came north to San Diego, where, as Richard Henry Dana later reported, "he built a large house with a court-yard in front, kept a great retinue of Indians, and set up for the grandee of that part of the country." He lived there most of the time until his death in 1841.

The original "Descrision" consists of nineteen manuscript pages, in the distinctive handwriting of José Bandini. It is undated, and unsigned except for the initials "J. B." It seems to be an expanded version of a long letter written by Bandini in September, 1828, to Eustace Barron, British vice-consul at Tepic. The latter had requested, almost a year before, a description of the commerce, products, population, etc., of California, and, judging from the rough draft of the reply, Bandini took his assignment seriously. Some of the information he supplied may have been used by Barron's business partner, Alexander Forbes, whose California, published in London in 1839, was the first English book relating exclusively to the territory. Bandini's "Descrision," however, is much more detailed than his letter to Barron, and it contains an additional section dealing with the sad plight of California's commerce.

We do not know Bandini's reason for writing this description of California. It may have been designed for the enlightenment of José María de Echeandía, the Comandante General y Jefe Superior Político, *then in residence in San Diego. Or it may have been intended for the use of Juan Bandini, who, as a member of the California* Diputación, *or legislature, and as a deputy to the Mexican Congress, devoted much time and many speeches to the problems of trade. It is certain that the younger Bandini used it as the basis of a report written by him from the* Comisaría Principal de la Alta California *in 1830, in which he gave an account of California, often in his father's own words, for the benefit of some superior government official. This manuscript is now in the Archivo General de la Nación in Mexico City; a contemporary copy has recently been added to the William Robertson Coe Collection of Western Americana in the Yale University Library. And finally, a few extracts from the original "Descrision" appear in translation in Edwin Bryant's* What I Saw in California, *published in 1848.*

The José Bandini manuscript probably came to the University of California with the Cowan Collection in 1897. It has remained almost unnoticed among the treasures of the Bancroft Library, and we are glad to bring it to the attention of scholars. Both the original version and an English translation are given here.

The editor wishes to thank her colleague, Mrs. Galen Reid Fisher, for aid cheerfully given, and to acknowledge a special indebtedness to Miss Haydée Noya of the Henry E. Huntington Library, Miss Mary Helen Peterson of the Los Angeles Public Library, Señor Alberto Tauro of the Biblioteca Nacional in Lima, and Professor George P. Hammond, Director of the Bancroft Library, University of California.

Doris Marion Wright

The Bancroft Library, 1951

A Description of California
in 1828

A Description of California
in 1828

ALTA CALIFORNIA is the name given to the expanse of coast that lies between 32° N. and 42° and extends, on the west and east, from the shores of the Pacific Ocean to the great Sierra Madre, or perhaps to the western banks of the Colorado River. Some nations improperly call it New Albion, thus trying to obscure the name it acquired when it was first discovered. It is bounded on the south by Antigua California, on the west by the Pacific Ocean, on the north by the Anglo-American possessions, and on the east, where the Government has not yet established the border line, by either the Colorado River or the great Sierra. It is called Alta, as well as Nueva, in order to distinguish it from Baja or Antigua California. If its eastern boundary were fixed in the Sierra, its width would be a little more than fifty leagues. Its length from north to south, as already indicated, is two hundred leagues, counting twenty leagues to the degree.

Between the great Sierra and the Pacific Coast there lies a lower range of mountains whose direction, like that of the former, is almost from north to south. The plains encompassed by these two ranges are known as the *Tulares;* those between the lower mountains and the sea are the ones populated by the presidios, missions, and pueblos that I shall describe.

Government

Since Alta California cannot, because of its small population, be included among the states of the great Mexican Republic, it is classed as a territory. Its government is entrusted to a *comandante general*, who acts also as *jefe superior político*, and who derives his powers directly from the President of the Republic and from the General Congress. In order to supplement the legislation of his office, he has a *Diputación* composed of seven *vocales*. Every two years half of its members retire from office. The jefe superior político presides over its sessions.

The inhabitants of the territory are distributed among the presidios, missions, and pueblos.

Presidios

In order to protect the Apostolic teaching it was necessary to build the presidios, which were established as circumstances required. That of San Diego was the first; Santa Barbara, Monterey, and San Francisco followed. Except for slight differences, the plan is the same for all: a square two hundred or more varas on each side, formed by a weak adobe wall about four varas high. Inside the square, and resting against it, are to be found, arranged all around its circumference, the chapel, the storehouses, and the dwellings of the comandante, officers, and troops. The barracks and guardroom are at the entrance to the presidio.

The presidio buildings were probably suited to their original purpose, since the object was to afford protection against the surprise attacks of the nearby gentiles; but as this need no longer exists I believe they should be demolished, for the buildings are threatening to fall into complete ruin, and the cramped living quarters can only discommode those who dwell in them. Outside the presidios, private individuals have constructed adequate houses, and as more building of this kind may be seen every day it is certain that substantial towns will soon appear in California.

At a distance of one or two *millas* from each presidio and near the entrances to the anchorages, there is a little fort with some

4

pieces of artillery of small caliber. The situation of most of the forts is not the most advantageous for the proper guarding of the port, and, besides, the form of the walls and esplanades, in addition to other defects that may be observed, renders them almost useless. The present comandante general[1] has undertaken to reform them in every respect.

The garrison of each presidio is composed of eighty or more cavalrymen known as *soldados de cuera*,[2] in addition to a number of auxiliary infantry troops and a detachment of artillery. The comandante of each presidio is the captain of the company attached to it, and besides supervising the military and political matters of his district he takes care of its maritime affairs.

Missions

In the territory there are twenty-one missions, which have been established at different times. In the year 1769 the first, San Diego, was founded. It is two leagues distant from the presidio of that name. The rest have been built consecutively, according to circumstances and necessity. The last was founded in 1822,[3] under the name of San Francisco Solano, and is the most northerly of all.

The buildings in some of the missions are more extensive than in others, but they are almost alike in form. The structures are of adobe, with sections of whatever size may be needed. In all of them there are comfortable living quarters for the ministers, warehouses for the storing of goods, granaries large enough for the grain, places for making soap, rooms for weaving, carpenter shops, forges, wine presses, cellars, large patios and corrals, separate apartments for the Indian youth of both sexes, and, finally, as many workrooms as the establishment may require. Adjoining these and connected with them are the churches, which form a part of the mission building; all are of adequate size and are lavishly decorated.

5

The Indians live at a distance of more than two hundred varas from this structure in a village called a *ranchería*. In most of the missions these rancherías consist of some small adobe dwellings built in rows along the street, but in others the Indians have been allowed to keep their primitive customs, and their lodgings are nothing more than cone-shaped huts, at most probably four varas in diameter, with the vertex or point of the cone about two varas above the ground. They are made of rough poles covered with tule or grasses in such a way as to afford complete protection against all inclement weather. It seems to me that these rancherías are well suited to the innate slovenliness of the Indians, since it is easy for them to replace their dwellings frequently, by burning some and putting up others immediately.

Near the mission on the opposite side there is a small barracks with enough rooms for the corporal and five soldiers, with their families. This reduced garrison is sufficient to check any attempted uprising of the Indians, who have been taught, by means of some warning examples, to respect the small force. The picket has the additional duty of carrying the monthly correspondence or any special dispatches that it may occur to the government to send.

All the missions of Alta California are under the care of Franciscan missionaries, of whom there are at present twenty-seven, most of them of advanced age. Each administers one mission and in it has absolute authority. The labor of the fields, the harvest of grain, the slaughter of cattle, the work of the shops, and all of those things that may concern the mission are directed by the Padre; and he alone attends to the sales, purchases, and business agreements, without interference from anyone. Thus if a mission is fortunate enough to have a hard-working and capable minister its neophytes will enjoy an abundance of the necessities of life; but poverty and misery in a mission give palpable evidence of the inactivity of him who directs it.

The missions have extended their holdings from one end of the

6

territory to the other and have had a way of bounding one piece of property by the next, always opposing the private ownership of lands in between. They have unfeelingly appropriated the whole region, although for their planting and for the maintenance of their cattle they do not need all they possess. It is to be hoped that the new system of enlightenment and the need for encouraging the resident *gente de razón* will compel the government to take adequate measures to reconcile the interests of all.

Among all the missions there are recorded from twenty-one to twenty-two thousand Catholic Indians, but these are not equally distributed. Some establishments claim about three thousand souls, while others have scarcely four hundred. This difference accounts for the greater or lesser wealth of a mission. There are also a good many gentiles living in the farms or ranchos annexed to each mission; the number of these is undetermined.

The Indians are by nature[4] slovenly and indolent, and their powers of understanding are greatly limited. In handicrafts they are imitators, never creators. As their true character is one of vengeance and timidity, they are inclined toward treachery. They do not recognize kindness, and ingratitude is common among them. Their present education is not the most suitable one for bringing out their intellectual powers, but even if it were, I doubt that they would ever be capable of responding to good influences.

All of these Indians, because of their continual use of the *temascal* as well as their great slovenliness and the inadequate ventilation of their dwellings, are weak and without vigor. The chills and rheumatism from which they suffer so much are the result of their customs. But that which destroys and retards their propagation more than anything else is the venereal disease with which most of them are so grievously afflicted. It should be noted that their constitutions are very susceptible to this contagion. Thus there is an enormous difference between deaths and births, doubtless exceeding 10 per cent a year. The missionaries try to make up

7

this deficit from among the catechumens who live in the neighborhood.

In general, all the missions produce cattle, sheep, horses, wheat, maize, beans, peas, and other vegetables, and those situated to the south increase their output by means of vineyards and olive groves. Of all these articles the most profitable are the cattle, as they provide hides and tallow for a brisk trade with the vessels that reach these shores. This is the only means that either missions or private individuals have of supplying their needs, and thus they are obliged to do everything possible to stimulate this branch of commerce; most of them undoubtedly fix their whole attention upon it.

Hides have been collected here for the last six years. Before that, only those required by private individuals were turned to account, and the rest were wasted in the fields. But now foreign vessels export between thirty and forty thousand hides annually from the territory, and the *matanzas* produce an almost equal number of arrobas of liquid tallow; and from the way in which this business is being carried on it is certain that within three or four more years the exportation of both products will be doubled. Hemp, flax, wine, olive oil, grains, and other agricultural products would be abundant if the export trade were stimulated, but as this is not done there is only such sowing and reaping as the territory itself requires.

Pueblos

This region contains three Pueblos. The most populous is that of Los Angeles, in which there must be some twelve hundred souls; that of San José Guadalupe contains about six hundred, and the Villa of Branciforte probably not two hundred.[5] In form they are imperfect and without order because the settlers have arbitrarily built their homes wherever has seemed best to them.

8

The first two Pueblos are governed by their respective ayuntamientos, the first composed of an alcalde, two regidores, a síndico and secretario; the second, of an alcalde, two regidores, a síndico and secretario. The third,[6] because of its small population, is subject to the comandancia of Monterey.

The inhabitants of these pueblos are white people, and in order to distinguish them from the Indians they are commonly called gente de razón; there are probably about five thousand of them in the territory. The families are distributed among these pueblos and the presidios. Almost all are the descendants of a small number of individuals who came with their wives from the Mexican mainland, some as settlers and others in the military service. In the short space of a little more than fifty years this generation has been formed.

In general, the white people are robust, healthy, and well-built. Some are occupied in breeding cattle and planting wheat, maize, and beans, but because of the lack of privately owned lands and other benefits their enterprises are limited. Others devote themselves to military service, as all of the presidial companies are reinforced by natives of the country. But most of them live in idleness; it is a rare person who is dedicated to increasing his fortune. They exert themselves only in dancing, horsemanship, and gambling, with which they fill their days. In most cases they ignore the arts, and I doubt if there is to be found anyone who practices a trade. Very few are acquainted with the rudiments of elementary education, and other fields of knowledge are unknown.

The fecundity of the gente de razón is extreme. Married people who fail to have five or six children are rare; an enormous number of them have more than twelve or fifteen. Very few individuals die during adolescence, and those who reach maturity are almost certain to know their grandchildren. In this atmosphere an age of eighty or one hundred has always been quite common. Most illnesses are unknown, and the freshness and hardiness of the

9

people demonstrate the beneficial effect of the climate. The women in particular always have roses in their cheeks. These beautiful creatures are without doubt more active and industrious than the men. The whole of a woman's watchful care is directed toward running her house, keeping her children clean, and waiting upon her husband; her leisure is dedicated to needlework and other occupations useful in providing for her family. The clothing of the women is very clean and always decorous; nakedness is unknown in both sexes.

Ports and Commerce

In the territory there are four principal ports or bays, which take the names of their respective presidios. The most sheltered and safe is that of San Diego, although San Francisco affords other advantages. Monterey is somewhat protected, but the roadstead of Santa Barbara is only seasonal and always bad. In addition, vessels are accustomed to anchor in the small harbors of Santa Cruz, San Luis Obispo, El Cojo, El Refugio, San Pedro, and San Juan Capistrano for the purpose of exporting the products of the nearby missions. But through an order of the Minister of War, which this comandante general has circulated, it is known that Monterey must be the sole port of entry for foreign vessels. However, by disposition of the comandancia general, San Diego, Santa Barbara, and San Francisco remain open provisionally to this commerce,[7] and if this were not so, there is no doubt that all trade with California would be brought to an end, as I shall demonstrate briefly.

Vessels frequent these coasts for the sole purpose of obtaining the hides and tallow they export from the territory. Everybody understands that in this region nothing can be done with money because it does not circulate here, and the vessels bring in merchandise in order to facilitate the purchase of the hides and tallow.

It is well known that the interest of the missions is not in money but in things that the Indians need, so that many who have come with nothing but coin have failed in their expeditions because they were unable to make up a cargo. It may seem extraordinary that money is not prized in a country that recognizes its value, but this fact will be demonstrated if conditions within the territory are kept in mind.

The annual collection of hides is probably from thirty to forty thousand, with an approximately equal number of arrobas of tallow. If we average the value of these articles at two pesos each, it is apparent that every year there are in circulation in California goods having an intrinsic value of one hundred and forty thousand pesos, a sum that, if distributed among the twenty-one missions, would give each one 6,666 pesos. If these products, which are the only marketable ones, were converted into cash, with what would the Indians be clothed? And with what would a thousand other needs be met? Money serves to extend commercial enterprise, but California is not yet ready for this, and her productions scarcely enable her to buy what is essential for her own use. The same thing should be said with respect to those few private individuals who are able to make collections of hides and tallow: the quantity of these articles is so small that the profit from them is negligible. Therefore, if this single source of income, which in its infancy can scarcely provide all the residents with the necessities, is beset by misfortunes just as it is beginning to grow, what will be the result? To me the consequences seem all too apparent, and it may not be superfluous to point them out.

1st. No vessels will visit these coasts, and the nation will lose the duties their merchandise brings in.

2nd. Missions and private individuals will be without those articles needed for the labor of the fields and workrooms as well as for their own comfort and advancement.

3rd. The only profitable industry, and the one in which all put their hopes, is the breeding of cattle; and if exportation is hampered, these people, who for the last five years have taken on new life through this slight commerce, will sink again into their old indigence.

4th. Many foreigners who have been naturalized in the territory, recognizing that in the future they will be unable to find a means of support, will abandon a country that offers only misery and will thus, by their example, retard the system of colonization so strongly recommended by the supreme government.

I ought to explain the misfortunes to which I referred, since not everyone can be aware of all the details about California.

At present the roads of the territory are almost all very good, but at an intermediate point there are two long grades that cannot be traversed by carts and are difficult even for mules. This is undoubtedly enough to prevent most of the missions and the Pueblo of Los Angeles from taking their produce to the Port of Monterey, but it is not the most important consideration. The distance between the wealthiest missions and that port is from eighty to one hundred seventy leagues. Tallow packed in *botas* cannot withstand rough treatment and heat for so great a distance. In the short transits that have been made so far with a load of this kind the shrinkage and loss that continually occur are well known. How, then, can it be carried such a distance as is proposed? The impossibility of so long a transfer is likewise apparent in respect to hides if one takes into account the fact that there is hardly a mule able to carry more than eight of them to a load. An article that in itself has little value should not incur much expense, and if the latter amounts to more than the selling price, how can there be any sale? In view of these disadvantages it is certain that shipments of this kind to the Port of Monterey will always be impossible, yet it is a proved fact that if they are not made, our only commerce will be brought to an end. Very few missions are near enough to transport their goods to that port at a low cost, and

12

they are precisely the poorest and least productive. Those that attract all the attention of navigators are obviously the ones that are going to suffer the disabling of their commerce. In addition, there is the Pueblo of Los Angeles, which, with its various foreign residents and the most influential citizens of California, is worthy of consideration. It is one hundred thirty leagues from Monterey. Its industry and development are dependent upon hides and tallow, and if the transporting of these becomes impossible, its ruin is inevitable.

Thus it is unmistakably clear that if all the ports are closed and only Monterey remains open to foreigners, the territory will inevitably be ruined and will revert to its former state of oppression. It is to be hoped that this comandante general and Diputación will give the supreme government all pertinent information, including some that I have not mentioned and that they have at hand.

Revenue

The administration of revenue at the ports has been, up to the present time, in charge of an authorized official or cadet who himself performs the duties connected with the *Comisaría subalterna* of each presidio. With the administrator, treasurer, auditor, etc., etc., combined in one person, the vices that could exist are obvious; but at present the comandante general is putting the maritime customhouses in the best possible order, and in the Port of San Diego an interim *Administrador* and *Contador*[8] are already carrying out their duties pending approval by the supreme government.

The amount of revenue is so small that it has never been enough to meet one-third of the expenses of the garrison. This is simple to understand if one keeps in mind the value of exports, since the complete absence of coin means that the intrinsic value

13

of what is imported must be equal to the value of the tallow and hides exported. As has been shown, this amounts to one hundred and forty thousand pesos, which is precisely the integral value of the merchandise annually imported into the territory.

The deduction of duties is never made on sales but rather on the basis of the appraisals of the general tariff, which may safely be said to make a difference of at least 20 per cent in the evaluations; therefore, the intrinsic value on which duties must be deducted is probably something like one hundred and twelve thousand pesos.

In the new tariff[9] now in force in the Republic there are set forth the duties to which goods are subject, and those not indicated must pay 40 per cent of their appraised value. However, the supreme government has seen fit to grant this territory the favor of reducing its duties by two-fifths, so that in these customhouses only 24 per cent, or two-fifths less than that indicated by the tariff, is collected.[10] Therefore, of the 112,000 pesos appraised value of imports, only 26,880 pesos will be provided for the treasury annually, and this is practically the only income the territory can have received in late years from the maritime customhouses.

There is also among the national cash receipts another small entry, which comes from tithes. Through a special favor of the Supreme Pontiffs, the tithes have remained in California for the benefit of the public treasury, in order to help meet the expenses of this Apostolic conquest; but as they are levied only upon private citizens they are of little importance, amounting at most to three thousand pesos annually. The missions, which are in charge of the extensive production of cattle and crops, are exempt from this and every other tax; those that are at present supplying the presidios with food do not do it gratuitously but rather as a loan that the nation guarantees along with other debts that the presidios may contract with them.

14

The total municipal revenue of a state depends upon the number of its inhabitants, and since not a single mission is subject to taxation, it must be apparent that income of this sort amounts to almost nothing in the territory. Up to the present no tax has been established except upon the consumption of wines and aguardientes manufactured in this country, but this scarcely suffices to pay the salaries of three elementary teachers, the secretaries of the two ayuntamientos and the secretary of the Diputación (the other members of these organizations do not receive any stipend).

Kingdoms of Nature

Nature has looked with favor upon the territory, and thus in the two most important natural kingdoms, few lands have enjoyed a wider range of her gifts.

In the Animal Kingdom she has been less prodigal than discriminating. She has not permitted insects and worms, as numerous as they are troublesome, to exist in this region, but on the other hand her great care has been responsible for the astonishing rate at which cattle, sheep, and hogs multiply; for the surpassing abundance of horses, which increase so rapidly that it is necessary to slaughter them extensively simply to avoid the damage they would do to the pastures; and for the vehemence with which the fallow deer, reindeer, stags, hares, rabbits, etc., etc., reproduce. And finally, in order to display her power, she has kept in mind the bear, leopard, wolf, wildcat, and coyote. Fowls are abundant, and the sea provides the most delicious fish. Among amphibians one finds the rare otter, and the rivers of the interior offer asylum to the useful beaver. What riches could be supplied by such a variety of valuable animals! But, unfortunately, industry is unknown in California.

The Vegetable Kingdom of this region cannot be surpassed. Rare is the plant that does not attain its full growth. There are all kinds of trees, and most of them supply delicious fruit. Shrubs grow exceptionally well, and so do the useful cotton plant and the delightful grapevine. And the grasses, with their abundance and variety, provide enough material to satisfy the wishes of the naturalist and botanist.

The Mineral Kingdom is unknown in Alta California through lack of investigators. Some persons have seen fairly good quarries, and others maintain that gold, silver, and lesser metals exist, but as there is a lack of data with which to substantiate these opinions, I limit myself to mentioning them.

Rivers

There are eight rivers that constantly spill their waters in Alta California's ten degrees of coast. Some are of great volume and others of little account. A portion of the precious waters of several of them could easily be diverted so as to make fruitful immense plains of dusty land rendered useless by drought, but conditions here are unfavorable to all enterprise. In the winter season the streams that descend from the nearby Sierra are enormous, and while they last their waters are put to use in those places best suited to planting crops. However, the people do not know how to profit by the advantages the nature of the land affords: it would not be at all difficult to hold back a part of these seasonal waters for use during the summers.

Tulares

Within the boundaries of this territory are included the plains that lie between the great Sierra and the low mountain range that is near our establishments. In these plains are situated two great lakes whose waters are connected by a short and narrow canal. The length of both lakes from north to south is probably from ninety to one hundred leagues, and their width from east to west about ten to twenty leagues. In the northern part there is an outlet whose waters form the great Sacramento River; the latter empties into the ocean through one of the inlets of the remarkable Bay of San Francisco. In the interior of these lakes there are various islands, and they as well as the outer shores are covered with tules, for which reason the name of Tulares has been given to these immense plains.

To the west the lakes touch the low mountain range, and on the east they border the plains that terminate in the Sierra Madre. The length of these plains from north to south is very great, but their width is something like ten leagues. The lakes abound with excellent fish, various aquatic birds, and rare beavers, and around their margins, as well as on the islands, some rancherías of the gentiles are to be found.

The plains that lie between these lakes and the great Sierra are undoubtedly the ones that attract attention to these delightful regions. The abundance of pines, live oaks, hazels, and other immense trees, together with the pastures and meadows, make an attractive combination. In this pleasant place there are many rancherías of gentile Indians, of which the number is undetermined. These groups are formed according to tribes, and each one has a chief who inherits the title from his elders. The rancherías do not associate very much with each other. Furthermore, they are in the habit of quarreling, particularly over seeds when the trees are bearing fruit, and most of the time these disputes end with a great number of deaths. Although they are unacquainted with the worship of any cult, they have an incomprehensible respect for their dead. Hair from the head of a deceased person is the most highly esteemed legacy. And in order to perpetuate the memory of the dead, the rancherías are accustomed to unite annually for a general weeping. The chief of the group proposing the celebration invites the friendly rancherías, and at the conclusion of three days of weeping they say good-bye to their guests, giving them presents of feathers, pelts, acorns, pine nuts, and other seeds. They venerate their old people, who are their oracles and healers. Although they practice polygamy, divorce is common among them. Marriage agreements are made with the Indian girl's father, who exacts from the suitor a quantity of beads in proportion to the value he supposes his daughter to possess. Divorce is confirmed by a return of these same beads to the husband. The dress of the women is a short cloak of squirrel pelts pieced together, with the tails left loose at will, but as this is not sufficient to cover them properly they supplement it by four or five thin tule fibers a quarter of a vara long, fastened at only one end to another fiber that encircles the waist. The men wear nothing.

Their life and customs are those of Nature herself, who with a liberal hand supplies them with wild quadrupeds, fowls, fish, and nourishing seeds, with which they meet their only need. Both sexes are of good height, but their features reveal their stupidity. They are of a dark copper color and are extremely agile. Their dancing amounts only to imitating the animals in all their gestures, and their singing is a continual repetition of intolerable howls. If some establishments were made in this region, how useful the site of the Tulares would be!

Islands

There are several islands situated near the coast, from north of Santa Barbara to the parallel of San Diego. The most noteworthy are Santa Cruz and Santa Catalina, each of which is probably more than twenty leagues around. Some are perhaps six, and others as much as twelve, leagues distant from the mainland. The direction of these islands, like that of the coast, is almost north to south, and between them and the mainland there is a navigable stretch called the Santa Barbara Channel. These islands used to be populated, but in our day only Santa Catalina retains a small number of gentiles, probably not as many as twenty souls. The rest have been taken across to the mainland and gathered into the missions.

On most of the islands there are adequate wooded areas, and Santa Cruz supplies some fairly good firs and other trees, which are quite useful in the building that is being done in the Presidio and Mission of Santa Barbara. Santa Catalina, in addition to having some timber and several watering places, as the former does, has the advantage of possessing two good anchorages, sheltered and safe, with good water on shore, and furthermore has in the interior enough pasture and water to support any number of cattle. I believe that when California comes into her own, some of the islands, from which much profit can be derived, will not be forgotten.

Conclusion

Now that the extent of Alta California has been shown, as well as her present circumstances and her potentialities, I shall spend no more time in describing her condition; but her critical situation forces me to make some observations.

All nations are dependent upon one another, since Nature, unable to distribute her riches equally, gives fertile lands to some and sterile ones to others; but the industry of the people and the stabilizing effect of commerce serve to equalize their needs. Thus, in so far as a nation lacks those articles that are essential to a civilized people, it seeks ways of acquiring them, encouraging industry and establishing communication with other nations with only its own maintenance in mind. This mutual exchange is useful to all, for some, in order to facilitate exports and obtain what they need, look for the surest means of accomplishing their purposes, and, as a result, the countries privileged by nature may in their turn enjoy those articles that only the industry of others can provide.

This is the situation in which California finds herself. She has in her land a source of riches with which she can easily sustain many communities, but it is necessary for her to exchange her products for articles that are indispensable to a civilized people. Thus she needs to maintain trade with other nations for her own good. If through a mistaken idea obstacles are imposed so that the exportation of California's products is impeded, the richness of her land will be seen in contrast to the poverty of her people.

The wealth of nations depends less upon the fruitfulness of the country than upon the number of inhabitants. If California had twenty thousand more people her value undoubtedly would be double, so if an effort is made to develop this territory it is essential to increase the population. But how can this be done in view of the miseries that are to be expected? Even the natives will seek a more favorable environment.

A free and honest man, knowing that his efforts are directed toward the general welfare of the nation, should speak frankly, and thus, with all due respect to the dispositions of the supreme laws, I shall explain how I feel about this matter.

It has been determined that only the Port of Monterey should remain open to foreign vessels, and in that event I can assure you that the commerce of California has been brought to a complete close. I believe I have said enough about this in the section on commerce, but I must add that if this law is put into effect, displeasure will be general in California, since it augurs for the future a fate almost as disagreeable as the former epoch.[11] This will be felt even more because there have been six years of happiness; during that time, business affairs had taken on a very different aspect, and the residents had well-founded hopes of making them more extensive. This law can be favorable only to some active and perspicacious foreigner, who, apparently becoming naturalized

20

in the Republic so as to acquire the right to use the national flag on some vessel of his own, thus being authorized to anchor freely all along this coast, will appropriate all the trade of the territory. And what will be the results? These are all too apparent, since, if there were only one exporter, it is clear that the products of the country would become cheaper for lack of buyers, and that imports would increase in price because of being concentrated in one hand alone. All this would contribute to the ruin of the inhabitants. If anyone wants to assume that this course of action is necessary in order to stimulate national maritime activities, I shall say this: that Mexican commerce has paid little attention to seagoing trade, and that it is difficult to find anyone who will engage in this line of speculation; that the articles exported from the territory are useful only to sell to foreigners, since they alone, by means of their great business ability and by their reworking of these articles, are able to make any profit from things of so little value; and, finally, that if it is necessary to wait until the national vessels take an interest in these ventures it means waiting for something uncertain, since it is well known that during all the years they have been visiting California, no national vessel has ever presented itself for the purpose of exporting hides and tallow. Although last year and this a Mexican brig came with this objective, it should be noted that it belongs to a foreigner[12] naturalized in the Republic; the hides it collects are transshipped to another vessel that flies a different flag and that everyone believes to be his also, and by means of which he enlarges his dual purpose. But this expedient is neither open to everyone nor easy for all to undertake. Thus I am confirmed in what I set forth, that if this law is carried into effect it could be favorable only to such an individual and would in general be very harmful to the territory and to the nation.

As I have proposed to express my feeling I should not obscure the course that to me seems most adequate for the safeguarding of the interests of the nation and the well-being of Alta California.

The single port of Monterey has been chosen for foreign vessels, doubtless for the purpose of concentrating all business at one point and in this way avoiding contraband and the double expenditure for treasury employees; but I am of the opinion that everything can very well be remedied without using methods that directly attack the territory. To accomplish this it seems to me that the Port of San Diego also should remain open for the same purpose. This would have no marked ill effect upon its custom-house expenses, since revenue would be increased and there would be a ramification of business interests that would otherwise be impracticable, as has already been noted. Furthermore, the Port of San Diego offers the advantages of a better anchorage and of a safe shelter during the winter season, with opportunity for every kind of repairing and refitting. And this will make it easy for half the territory to enjoy the advantages that have fallen to the lot of the other half because of the impossibility of crossing the two long grades with voluminous loads. It should also be noted that the missions and the pueblo nearest San Diego are the most powerful, and the ones that ought to yield the greatest profits to the treasury; and, in addition, that this presidio needs resources more urgently than Monterey because of having to attend to the frontier establishments, which cannot be given assistance from that port.

If both these ports were authorized, vessels would be able to unload all of their cargo in either; and in whichever this is done there should be a detailed inspection of their holds, after which they should be cleared so that they may anchor freely wherever they did previously, for the purpose of gathering on board the articles they export from the territory.

To my mind it is very unlikely that the vessels would be able to do any smuggling in the anchorages, because their total unloading and careful inspection would have taken place in the two

22

authorized ports; because the missions (which control all the business) would never take part in a fraud of this sort; because in this country there is no capitalist capable of any kind of enterprise; and because the reduced state of the inhabitants makes it certain that in any place whatever, any article brought in, no matter how small, would be conspicuous. But for greater security let the vessels be severely warned of the total confiscation of their interests in case the slightest fraud is discovered in the places where they stop, and I am sure that not one of them will decide to infringe the law; they will be afraid that the deposits and bonds in San Diego and Monterey would answer for their offenses. This method is fairly common among nations that need to encourage production, since by facilitating exports they facilitate also the means of enriching their provinces.

In order to emphasize the need of the territory for vessels (already unloaded) to anchor in the intermediate ports, it is essential to note that every year various Russian barks come to these coasts for the sole purpose of making up cargoes of wheat to supply their establishments of Sitka and Unalaska. This trade stimulates the inhabitants to give every possible impetus to this branch of agriculture, and by means of it a thousand needs are met; but if the vessels are not permitted to come near the ports where these grains are shipped, they will go to the ports of Chile to make up their cargoes, as they have already indicated, since the expense that the difference in the voyage would occasion is always less than the difference in price; in Chile a fanega of wheat is one peso or a little more, while here it brings three pesos in virtue of its proximity. As a result of the withdrawal of these vessels, there will be a loss of the profits that this article yields, and the lands will revert to their ancient sterility because there is no one to guarantee their tilling. All of this will contribute to the deterioration of the populace.

In view of what has been set forth I am of the opinion that, in

23

order to encourage the territory and insure at the same time the interests of the nation, San Diego should be opened, in addition to the Port of Monterey, for the discharge and deposit of imports; and upon the completion of the unloading and other requirements noted, the vessels, no matter which ones they are, should be permitted to stop freely at the places where previously they gathered up hides, tallow, and wheat, which could not be exported in any other way. Otherwise the vessels will take their business to countries that offer more advantages and fewer difficulties, and there will be left for the Californians only the pain of having to lose their one means of support.

J. B.

Notes

1. José María de Echeandía.

2. "These soldiers derived their name from the *cuera,* or cuirass, which in California was a sleeveless jacket made of 7 or 8 thicknesses of deer or sheep skin quilted." Hubert Howe Bancroft, *History of California* (San Francisco, 1884–1890), I, 132, note 12.

3. According to Bancroft, this mission was established in 1823 and was at first known as New San Francisco. On April 4, 1824, its church was dedicated to San Francisco Solano, whose name was then applied to the mission. *Ibid.,* II, 499–505.

4. Here the text has been changed, in different handwriting, to read "education."

5. In this passage we follow an interlinear correction. Bandini's version reads ". . . that of San José de Vitoria contains about 600. and Branciforte not 200." Branciforte no longer exists; present-day Santa Cruz extends over the site it once occupied.

6. Here also we have followed a correction in the text. Bandini's version has "The first two Pueblos are governed by their respective *Ayuntamientos,* each composed of an *alcalde,* four *regidores,* a *síndico* and *secretario.*The third . . ."

7. Echeandía refers to the situation in his letter of July 8, 1828, to the comandantes of presidios and alcaldes. Archives of California, Departmental Records (transcripts, Bancroft Library), VI, 63.

8. The author's son, Juan Bandini, was the provisional *comisario subalterno,* or administrator in charge of the collection of revenues; Antonio Estudillo was *contador,* or a kind of associate collector. Bancroft, *op. cit.,* II, 543; Archives of California, Departmental State Papers, Benicia Military (transcripts, Bancroft Library), LXVI, 1; Archives of California, State Papers, Sacramento (transcripts, Bancroft Library), XIX, 47.

9. *Arancel general para las aduanas marítimas y de frontera de la República Mexicana* (México, 1827). The *arancel* is dated November 16, 1827.

10. "Los géneros, frutos ó efectos extrangeros que se introduzcan por las Aduanas marítimas de Yucatán y territorios de Californias, solo adeudarán tres quintas partes de lo que señala este Arancel." *Op. cit.,* p. 5.

11. Bandini refers to the period of Spanish domination.

12. Probably Henry Edward Virmond.

Glossary of Spanish Words

Alcalde: a kind of mayor, with varying degrees of executive, legislative, and judicial power.

Arroba: a Spanish weight, equal to about 25 pounds.

Ayuntamiento: town council.

Bota: small leather bag.

Comandancia: district under the jurisdiction of the *comandante* of a presidio.

Comandante: commanding officer.

Comandante general: military head of the province.

Comisaría subalterna: office of a subordinate financial agent.

Diputación: legislative assembly.

Fanega: a measure of grain, etc., equal to about 1.6 bushels.

Gente de razón: literally, people of reason. Refers to white persons, as distinct from the Indians.

Jefe superior político: officer in charge of the civil administration of the province.

Matanza: the slaughtering of cattle.

Milla: quarter of a league (terrestrial measure), or about three-fourths of a mile.

Pueblo: in the specific sense, a civilian town that had met certain legal requirements, particularly in regard to population, and had been granted certain privileges.

Ranchería: an Indian settlement.

Regidor: member of the ayuntamiento.

Síndico: officer of the ayuntamiento in charge of accounts.

Temascal: primitive sweat house of the California Indians.

Tulares: places where *tule* grows.

Vara: unit of linear measurement, equal to about 33 inches.

Vocal: voting member.

Angelo Views
Califernios

Doña Ysidora Blancas de Bandini

Descrision
de l'Alta California

LLEVA EL NOMBRE de Alta California la estension de Costa q^e. media entre los 32. g^s. N. y los 42, y el termino del E. y O. es desde las orillas del Oseano Pasifico asta la gran sierra Madre, ó bien asta las orillas osidentales del Rio Colorado. Algunas Nasiones la nombran impropiamente Nueva Albion queriendo obscureser el nombre q^e. adquirió en su primer descubrimiento. Los terminos de ella son por el S. con la Antigua California, por el O. con el Oseano pasifico, por el N. con las posesiones Anglo Americanas, y por el E. no aviendose asta la presente marcado por el Govierno su estension deverá ser, ó bien en el citado Rio Colorado, ó bien asta la gran Sierra: Se llama Alta, como tambien Nueva p^a. distinguirla de la Baja ó Antigua California: Si se prefijase su termino del E en la sitada Sierra, en esse caso su anchor seria poco mas de 50. leguas, quedando ya indicado q^e. su estension de N. a S. es de 200. leg^s. de 20. al grado.

Entre la sitada gran Sierra, y la costa del Pasifico, media otra Sierra menor cuya diresion es igualmente q^e. la primera quasi de N. a S. Los Llanos comprendidos entre ambas Sierras son conosidos bajo el nombre de Tulares, y los Llanos q^e. median entre la baja Sierra, y las orillas del mar, son los poblados por los Presidios, Misiones, y Pueblos q^e. voi a descrivir.

Govierno

Esta California no pudiendo a causa de su corta Poblasion ser uno de los Estados de la gran Republica Mejicana, lleva el caracter de

Teritorio, cuyo Govierno está encargado a un Coman^te. Gene^l. q^e. asimesme ejerse el cargo de Jefe Superior Politico, y sus atribusiones dependen solamente del Presidente de la Republica, y del Congreso Genl.; amas para ampliar la lejislasion de su sentro tiene una Diputasion compuesta de siete vocales cuyos individuos por mitad sesan cada dos años, y el Jefe Sup^r. Pol^o. preside en sus sesiones.

Los abitantes del Teritorio estan repartidos entre los Presidios, Misiones y Pueblos.

Presidios

La nesesidad de protejer la predicasion Apostolica fué la q^e. obligó a la formasion de los Presidios, q^e. se fueron establesiendo segun las sircustansias. El de S^n. Diego fué el primero; Sta Barbara, Monterey, y S^n. Fran^co. fueron posteriores; su forma es igual en todos con corta diferi^a. y esta es de un Cuadro con 200. amas baras por cada frente formado de una debil muralla de Adobes cuya elevasion será como de 4. baras; en el interior del quadro, y apoiado a el se allan colocadas en toda su sircunferiensia la Capilla, Almasenes, y casas del Comandante ofisiales y Tropa, quedando a la entrada del presidio el Cuartel y Cuerpo de Guardia.

La Fabrica de los Presidios en su primera idea seria sufisiente, pues su objeto era estar al abrigo de las sorpresas de la inmediata jentilidad, pero aviendo sesado esta causa, creo q^e. deverian ser demolidos, pues sus fabricas estan amagando una total ruina, y la estreches de sus abitasiones solo pueden prestar incomodidad a los q^e. abitan en ellos. Por la parte esterior de los Presidios an fabricados los vesinos particulares, muy regulares casas, y notandose diariamente una emulasion en estas obras, se puede asegurar q^e. en breve apareseran en California competentes Poblasiones.

A distansia de una, ó mas de dos millas de cada Presidio, y prosimo a las entradas de los fondeaderos se alla un fortin con algunas

30

piesas de Artilleria de poco calibre, la situasion de los mas no es la mas ventajosa para el devido resguardo del puerto, y amas las formas de sus murallas, sus esplanadas, y otras imperfesiones q^e. en ellos se nota, los asen insinificantes; este Com^{te}. Jene^l. a emprendido su reforma en todo sentido.

La Guarnision de cada Presidio se compone de 80. ó mas soldados de Cavalleria llamada de cuera, y amas tiene un numero de tropa ausiliar de infanteria, y un destacamento de artilleros: El Comandante de cada Presidio es el Capi^n. de la respetiva compañía q^e. amas de la intervension Militar y Politica q^e. tiene en su termino, son de su cargo los asuntos relativos a la Marina.

Misiones

Las Misiones q^e. contiene el Téritorio son 21. Sus establesimientos guardan diferentes epocas; el año de 1769 se formó la primera q^e. fué S^n. Diego que dista 2. leg^s. del presidio de su nombre; consecutivamente se han ido establesiendo las demas segun las sircustansias, y nesesidades; la ultima se fundó el ano de 1822. con la advocasion de S^n. Franc^o. Solano, y es la mas N. de todas.

Los edifisios en unas Misiones son mas estensos q^e. en otras, pero en su forma son quasi iguales; las fabricas son de adobes, y sus divisiones son al tamaño de sus nesesidades; en todas se enquentran comodas abitasiones para sus Ministros, Almasenes para guardar efectos, proporsionadas trojes para los granos, ofisinas de javones, talleres de tejidos, Carpinterias, Ererias, lagares, Bodegas, grandes patios, y corrales, departamentos independientes para la juventud Indijena de ambos secsos, y por fin quantas ofisinas son nesesarias para su instituto: Contiguo, y con comunicasion estan situadas las Iglesias formando un cuerpo con el edifisio de la Mision, todas ellas bastante proporsionadas, y adornadas con profusion.

El conjunto de la Indiada vive a distansia de mas de 200. baras

31

de dho edifisio; su poblasion se llama rancheria. Estas en las mas Misiones se componen de unos redusidos cuartos de adobes formando aseras, pero en otras an dejado a la Indiada en su primitiva costumbre, redusiendose sus alojamientos a unos jacales de figura Conica, que quando mas tendran 4. varas de diametro, y el vertise ó punta del cono, se elevará del suelo dos varas, su material es de palos en bruto, q^e. cuvren con tules, ó sacates con tanta proporsion q^e. los pone perfetamente a cuvierto de toda intemperie; a mi entender estas rancherias son las mas adequadas al desaseo nato de la Indiada, pues les fasilita renovar frequentemente sus abitasiones, quemando unas y formando inmediatamente otras con la maior fasilidad.

En el lado opuesto a las Rancherias, y prosimo a la Mision se encuentra un redusido quartel con quartos proporsionados para un Cavo, y cinco soldados con sus familias, esta redusida guarnision es sufisiente a contener qualquier atentado de la Indiada, algunos ejemplares an acreditado el respeto q^e. les impone esta corta fuersa, amas este piquete esta en una Mision con el doble objeto de correr la posta con la correspondiensia mesual ó con los estraordinarios q^e. le ocurra al Goviorno.

Todas las Misiones de esta California se allan al cargo de Relijiosos Fransiscanos de propaganda fide, en la actualidad el numero de ellos son 27, los mas de avansada edad; cada uno administra una Mision, y en ella tiene una autoridad absoluta; el travajo del Campo, el acopio de granos, las matansas de Ganados, el travajo de los talleres, y todo quanto es conserniente a la Mision es dirijido por el Padre, y el solo es el q^e. efetua las ventas compras y negosios q^e. se contraen en una Mision, sin tener q^e. intervenir persona alguna en sus disposisiones; de aqui es q^e. si una Mision tiene la suerte de tener un Ministro lavorioso, y de capasidad en esse caso sus Neofitos disfrutaran de la abundansia en las nesesidades de la vida; pera la desnudes y miseria de una Mision ase palpar con evidensia la inactitud del q^e. la dirije.

32

Las Misiones estienden sus posesiones de estremo a estremo de todo el Teritorio, y an tenido modo para estar limitrofes una de otra aunque no nesesiten para sus siembra, y conservasion de Ganados toda la estension de terreno q^e. poseen, apropiandose insensiblemente todo el partido, y oponiendose siempre a q^e. ningun particular se interponga entre ellas; pero es de esperar q^e. el nuevo sistema de ilustrasion, y la nesesidad de fomentar a los vesinos de razon, aga q^e. el Govierno tome medidas adequadas q^e. consilien los intereses de todos.

Entre todas las Misiones se numeran empadronados de 21. a 22. mil Indijenas Catolicos, pero no todas por igual reune en su congregasion la cantidad proporsionada; unas tendran serca de tres mil almas, y otras apenas llegaran a 400. En esta diferencia dimana la mas ó menos riquesa de una Mision. Amas de los dichos cada Mision tiene un numero considerable de jentiles, q^e. viven en los sitios ó ranchos anecsos a ella cuyo numero es indeterminado.

La Indiada por su naturalesa[1] es desaseada y peresosa, y su entendimiento muy limitado; en los artefatos no carese de idea para la imitasion, pero jamas será inventora; su verdadero caracter es la vengansa, y la timides por lo tanto son propensos a la traision; desconosen el benefisio, y la ingratitud es comun en ellos. Su educasion desde luego no es la mas propia para desenvolver su rason, pero aunq^e. lo fuera creo q^e. jamas será capas de buenas impresiones.

Toda esta Indiada, bien por el continuo uso del Temascal como tambien por su mucho desaseo, y poca vintilasion de sus moradas, es debil, y sin vigor; los pasmos y reumas de q^e. tanto adolesen, es a consequensia de sus costumbres; pero lo q^e. mas aniquila, y entorpese su propagasion es el mal Venereo q^e. la mas de ella fuertemente padese, siendo de notar q^e. su umor es el mas analogo a resivir las impresiones de este contajio; de aqui proviene la enorme diferiensia de muertos á nasidos, q^e. sin duda pasará de un 10. p%

al año, pero los Misioneros procuran cuvrir este defisit con los catecumenos situados en sus inmediasiones.

Las produsiones jeneralmente de todas las Misiones son, la cria de Ganado maior y lanar, la Cavallada, el trigo mais frijol chicharos y demas legumbres, y las Misiones situadas mas al Sur asen mas estensivas sus produsiones con las Viñas y Olivares; de todos estos articulos el mas lucrativo es el Ganado Vacuno, pues les proporsiona con sus queros, y sevos aser un jiro activo con los Buques q^e. recalan a estas costas, siendo este el unico albitrio que tanto las Misiones como los Particulares tienen para cuvrir sus nesesidades; de aqui es la suma presision q^e. tienen de dar todo el impulso posible a este ramo, en el q^e. sin duda se pone jeneralmente toda la atension.

El acopio de Cueros, es de seis años a esta parte. Anteriormente solo se aprovechavan los nesesarios para el servisio particular y el resto quedavan perdidos en el campo, pero en la actualidad asenderá de 30. a 40. mil Cueros los q^e. anualmente esportan los buques Estranjeros del Teritorio, siendo quasi igual las arobas de sevo liquido que produsen las Matansas, y segun el metodo q^e. en ellas se lleva se puede asegurar, q^e. en el termino de tres, a quatro años mas, se duplicará la estrasion de uno y otro articulo. El Cañamo, el Lino, el Vino, el aseite de olivo, los granos, y otras produsiones de agricultura, se isieran estensivas, si uviera estimulo con la estrasion pero por no aver esta, solo se siembra, y benefisia lo nesesario para el consumo del Teritorio.

Pueblos

Los pueblos q^e contiene este distrito son tres; el mas poblado es el de los Anjeles en el q^e avran unas 1200. almas; el de S^n. Jose Guadalupe contendrá 600, y la villa de Bransifort^2 no llegará a 200. La forma de ellos es imperfeta y sin orden por aver los Pobladores fabricado albitrariamente sus casas en donde mejor les á paresido.

34

Los primeros dos Pueblos son Governados por sus coresponds. Ayuntamientos compuesto el primero de un Alcalde quatro rejidores un sindico y secretario; el segundo de un alcalde dos rejidores un sindico i secretario, i el tersero[3] por su corta poblasion está sujeto a la Comanda. de Monterey.

Los abitantes de dhos Pueblos son Blancos, y para distinguirlos de los Indios son vulgarmente llamados *jentes de razon*. El numero de estos qe. contiene el Territorio será serca de sinco mil; estas familias estan repartidas entre los indicados Pueblos, y los Presidios: quasi todos proseden de un corto numero de individuos qe. vinieron del continente Mejicano, unos en clase de pobladores, y otros al servisio de las armas acompañados de sus Mujeres, en el limitado tiempo de poco mas de 50. años se ha formado esta jenerasion.

Los Blancos en jeneral son robustos sanos, y bien formados; algunos se ocupan en criar ganados, y aser algunos sembrios de trigo mais y frijol, pero la falta de terrenos en propiedad, y otros ausilios les limita sus empresas; otros se dedican al servicio de las armas, siendo todas las compañias presidiales cuviertas con los naturales del pais; pero los mas se mantienen en la osiosidad, siendo raro el qe. se dedica a aumentar su fortuna. El baile, el Cavallo, y el juego es todo su connato, y el curso de sus dias: todos en jeneral desconosen las artes, y dudo se enquentre quien ejersa un ofisio; muy pocos son los inisiados en primeras letras, siendo las demas siensias en ellos desconosidas.

La fecundidad en la *jente de rason* es estrema. Raro será el casado qe. deje de tener 5. ó 6. hijos, siendo infinitos los qe. han pasado de 12. y 15. Muy pocos mueren en la adolesensia, y llegando al estado de la Puvertad estan quasi seguros de conoser sus nietos; la edad de 80. y 100. años siempre á sido bien comun en este clima; las mas de las emfermedades son desconosidas, y la frescura y robustes de ellos ase demostrar la benefica influensia de este temperamento; las Mujeres en particular llevan siempre estampadas las rosas en sus mejillas. Esta ermosa espesie es sin duda la mas activa, y lavoriosa; todo su desvelo es el mecanismo de la casa, el aseo de sus hijos, y la atension al marido, dedicando los momentos osiosos en aser lavores, y otras ocupasiones q^e. le sufragen utilidad para mantenerlos; el vestuario de ellas es muy aseado, y siempre onesto, siendo la desnudes desconosida en ambos secsos.

Puertos, y Comersio

Quatro son los Puertos, ó Baias prinsipales del Teritorio, q^e. toman el nombre de sus corespondientes Presidios; el mas resguardado y seguro, es el de S^n. Diego, aunq^e. el de S^n. Franc^{co}. puede proporsionar otras ventajas; Monterey tiene algun resguardo, pero la rada de Sta. Barbara es solamente estasional y siempre mala. Amas de los sitados Surjideros, han solido los Buques fondear en las Caletas de Sta. Crus, S^n. Luis Obispo, el Cojo, el Refujio, S^n. Pedro y S^n. Juan Capistrano con el fin de estraer las produsiones de sus inmediatas Misiones, pero por una orden dirijida por el Ministro de Guerra q^e. há sirculado este Comandante Jeneral se save q^e. el Puerto de Monterey deve ser el unico abilitado para Buques Estranjeros. No ostante por disposision de esta Comandasia jene^l. susisten provisionalmente aviertos para dicho Comersio S^n. Diego, Sta. Barbara, y S^n. Franc^{co}. y si asi no fuera es indudable se concluia enteramente todo el Comersio con California lo q^e. brevemente demostraré.

El unico objeto que mueve a los Buques a frequentar estas costas es por los Cueros, y sevos q^e. del Teritorio estraen, pues es notorio que en estos puntos jamas se podrá realisar cosa alguna a dinero porque aqui no sircula; los efectos q^e. los Buques importan son para fasilitar la compra de dichos articulos, pues bien saven, q^e. el interes de las Misiones, no es el dinero, pero si las espesies nesesarias a la Indiada, de manera q^e. muchos q^e. an venido con solo numerario, an malogrado su espedision por no poder con este articulo completar su cargamento; pareserá estraordinario que no se apresie la plata en un pais q^e. conose bien su merito, pero quedará demostrado este echo si se atiende a las sircustansias del Teritorio.

El acopio anual de Cueros será de 30 a 40. mil, siendo igual con corta diferencia las arobas de Sevo q^e. se junta; graduemos el promedio de ambos articulos a 2. pesos uno y otro, y queda visto q^e. el valor intrinseco q^e. sircula en California anualmente es de ciento quarenta mil pessos, cuya cantidad repartida entre las 21. Misiones, le resulta a cada una 6666. p^s. Si esta unica produsion vendible fuese invertida a dinero, ¿con q^e. se vestia la Indiada? ¿Y con q^e. se cubrian otras mil nesesidades? La Plata sirve p^a. ampliar las especulasiones, pero California no se alla todavia en este caso, y sus produsiones apenas les puede suministrar para comprar lo muy presiso q^e. le es de nesario consumir; la misma comparasion se deve aser con respeto a los pocos Vesinos, q^e pueden aser acopio de cueros y sevos, que siendo en corta cantidad se puede graduar su cambio por insinificante. Aora bien ¿Si a este unico ramo vendible, q^e. en su cuna apenas proporsiona lo nesesario a todo el Vesindario, se les pone travas en el momento q^e. vá tomando incremento q^e. podrá resultar?; Me parese q^e. estan demasiado palpables sus consequensias, y no estará demas demostrarlas.

1º. Ningun Buque recalará a estas costas, y la nasion perderá los drechos que sus mercansias erogan.

2º. Las Misiones, y los Particulares careseran de aquellos Articulos q^e. le son nesesarios para las lavores del Campo, y ofisinas, como para su desensia y sivilisasion.

3º. Que siendo el unico ramo de utilidad el Criadero de Ganado, en el q^e. todos siñen sus esperansas, entorpesiendose su estrasion, volverá nuevamente a sumerjirse esta Poblasion a su antigua indijensia, q^e. de cinco años a esta parte avia tomado otro ser a influensia de este corto Comersio.

4º. Que muchos Estranjeros qᵉ. se han naturalisado en el Teritorio, penetrados de no poder en lo futuro susistir en el, abandonaran un pais que solo podrá proporsionar miserias, entorpesiendose a su ejemplo el sistema de Colonisasion qᵉ. tanto recomienda el Supᵐᵒ. Govᵒ.

Devo esplicar quales son las travas qᵉ. indiqué porqᵉ. no todos pueden estar en el pormenor de las sircustansias de California.

Los caminos del Teritorio desde luego son quasi todos muy buenos, pero en su mediania se allan dos grandes cuestas incapases de transitarse con Caruajes y aun dificultosas para Mulas; este objeto es sin duda bastante poderoso, para impedir qᵉ. las mas Misiones, y el Pueblo de los Anjeles pueda llevar sus produsiones al Pᵗᵒ. de Monterey pero no es el mas esensial; la Distansia qᵉ. intermedia entre las Misiones mas ricas, y el sitado Puerto es desde 80. asta 170. leguas. El sevo en botas no es posible qᵉ. sufra los golpes, y Soles de tanta Distansia, en los cortos transitos qᵉ. asta la presente se ha hecho con esta carga, demasiado notorias son las mermas y perdidas qᵉ. decontinuo se esperimenta, ¿como será pues dable condusilo a la distansia qᵉ. se pretende? : Por lo qᵉ. respeta a los Cueros tambien esta demostrada la imposibilidad de una tan larga traslasion, si se gradua qᵉ. rara será la Mula qᵉ. pueda llevar mas de ocho en carga; un articulo qᵉ. en si tiene poco valor no deve erogar mucho gasto, pero si este asiende a mas del presio a que se puede vender ¿como será dable concurrir a su venta? . En vista de estos inconvenientes se puede asegurar, será siempre caso imposible puedan aserse condusiones de estas espesies al Pᵗᵒ. de Monterey, y no verificandose es cosa demostrada qᵉ. se concluió con este unico Comersio: Las Misiones qᵉ. pueden apoco costo transportar sus esquilmos al sitado Puerto por su inmediasion son muy pocas, y amas son presisamente las mas povres y las qᵉ. menos produsen, pero las qᵉ. llaman toda la atension del Navegante son notoriamente la qᵉ. van a sufrir la incapasidad de su Comersio; Amas no puede echarse al olvido el Pueblo de los

38

Anjeles, q^e. con el concurso de Varios Estranjeros domisiliados en el, y tener el Vesindario mas pudiente de California es digno de Considerasion. Este dista de Monterey 130. leguas, su jiro y fomento es devido a los Cueros, y Sevos, imposibilitandose su enajenasion es inevitable su ruina.

A consequensia delo espuesto se puede asegurar sin riesgo de equivocarse que si se escluian todos los puertos, quedando solamente Monterey abilitado para los Estranjeros, en este caso la ruina del Teritorio era inevitable, asiendo retroseso ala epoca de su opresion; es de esperar q^e. este Com^te. Jenel. y esta Diputasion den al Supremo Govi^o. los informes convenientes con otros q^e. no demarco, y estan asus alcanses.

Rentas

La Administrasion de rentas de los Puertos a estado asta la presente al cargo del ofisial, ó Cadete abilitado, q^e. asimesmo entrava en el sirculo de sus atribusiones la Comisaria subalterna de cada presidio: Señido en un solo individuo la Administrasion, Tesoreria, Contaduria & &. bien claro se demuestra los visios q^e. podria tener, pero en la actualidad este Com^te. Jen^l. está poniendo el mejor areglo posible en las Aduanas Maritimas, y en el P^to. de S^n. Diego ya desempeñan sus cargos un Adminir. y un Contador interinos asta la Aprovasion del Supremo Govierno.

El producto de rentas es de tan poca monta, q^e nunca á podido llegar a cuvrir el tersio del aver de la Guarnision; su calculo es sensillo si se atiende al valor de la esportasion, pues la falta absoluta de numerario ase no dudar q^e. el valor intrinseco de lo q^e. se importa deve ser igual al valor de los sevos y cueros q^e. se estraen, q^e asendiendo este a ciento quarenta mil p^s. como queda demostrado, resulta presisamente ser este el valor integro de las mercansias q^e. anualmente se introdusen en el Teritorio.

Las dedusiones de drechos jamas se asen por las ventas pero si por los aforos del Aransel Jen¹. qᵉ. sin riesgo de equivocarse se les puede graduar quando menos un 20 p% de diferencia, por lo tanto el intrinseco valor sovre qᵉ. deverán dedusirse los dros será como de ciento dose mil pˢ.

En el nuevo Aransel qᵉ. rije en la Republica estan fijados los drechos qᵉ. han de pagar los efectos, y los qᵉ. no se allan indicados deven pagar el 40. p% sobre avaluos qᵉ. se agan, pero el Supremo Govieᵒ. a tenido a bien conseder la grasia a este Teritorio de rebajar 2. quintos a sus drechos, por lo qᵉ. en estas aduanas solamente se covra el 24. p% ó dos quintos menos de lo qᵉ. indica el Aransel; por lo tanto de los Ciento dose mil pˢ. en qᵉ. se puede graduar la introdusion, se apersivirá en Tesoreria 26880. pˢ. anuales; unica entrada poco mas ó menos qᵉ. puede aver tenido en estos ultimos años el Teritorio con respeto a sus Aduanas Maritimas.

Tambien se reconose otro corto ingreso en la Caja Nasional qᵉ. proviene de los diesmos: Por grasia particular de los sumos Pontifises an quedado en Califarnia los diesmos a favor de la asienda publica, con el fin de coaiuvar a los gastos de esta conquista Apostolica, pero gravitando estos solamente en los vesinos particulares resulta de poca considerasion, llegando lo mas a tres mil pˢ. anuales: Las Misiones qᵉ. son las qᵉ. abrasan las grandes produsiones, en Ganados y Siembras, estan esentas de esta pension, y de otra qualquiera, pues las qᵉ. en la actualidad tienen en ausiliar en viveres a los Presidios no es gratuito, pero si un prestamo qᵉ. la Nasion garantisa, igualmente qᵉ. otras deudas qᵉ. pueden los Presidios contraer con ellas.

Las Rentas munisipales de un Estado son siempre al tamaño de su Poblasion; no pudiendo estas recaer en ninguna Mision no será dificultoso conoser la nulidad de este ramo en el Teritorio. Asta la presente no se há fijado mas contribusion qᵉ. al consumo de los Vinos, y Aguardientes manufaturados en el pais, pero esta apenas alcansa a pagar los sueldos de tres Maestros de primeras letras, de los secretarios de los dos Ayuntamientos y del Secretario de la

Diputasion porq^e. los demas individuos de ellas no disfrutan dieta alguna.

Reinos de la Naturalesa

La Naturalesa á mirado con predilesion al Teritorio, y asi es q^e. en sus dos primeros sistemas pocos terrenos avran disfrutado con mas estension de sus dones.

En El Sistema Animal no há sido tan prodiga como preferente pues siendo las familias de insectos, y gusanos tan numero como incomoda no há permitido su esistensia en este punto, pero en cambio se há esmerado en la reprodusion asombrosa de los Ganados Vacuno, lanar y de Serda; en la sovresaliente abundansia de Cavallada cuya propagasion es tan estrema q^e. es nesesario aser grandes matansas por solo evitar el daño q^e. asen alos pastos; en la veemensia con q^e se propaga el Reno, el Gamo, Venado, Lievre Conejo & &. Y ultimame^e. con el objeto de ostentar su poder no há echado en olvido el Oso Leopardo Lobo, Gato monteses y Coiotes. La Volateria es abundante, y las orillas del mar presenta los mas esquisitos peses; Entre los amfibios se distingen la singular Nutria, y los Rios interiores resiven en su seno los utiles Castores. ¿Quantas riquesas pudiera suministrar tanta variedad de animales utiles, pero por desgrasia la industria es desconosida en California.

El Sistema Vejetal de este partido es inmejorable, rara será la planta q^e. deje de tomar todo su incremento; se numeran infinitas espesies de arboles y los mas suministran los mas sasonados frutos; los Arbustos se reprodusen con esmero, sin olvidarse del util Algodon, y del delisioso Viñero. Y las Yerbas prestan con su abundansia y variedad materia bastante para q^e. el Naturalista, y el Botanico sasien sus deseos.

El Reino Mineral es desconosido en esta Alta California por falta de indagadores; algunos an notado regulares canteras, otros sostienen la esistensia de ricos metales, y semi-metales, pero como se carese de datos q^e. acredite la opinion solo me siño con indicarlo.

Rios

Los Rios q^e. costantemente vierten sus aguas en estos 10 grados de Costa q^e. comprende esta California son ocho, algunos son caudalosos, y otros son de poca considerasion; A muchos de ellos con fasilidad se le pudiera dar diferentes diresiones a alguna porsion de sus presiosas aguas con el fin de fertilisar inmensos Llanos de tierras Pulverulentas inutilisadas por la sequedad, pero el sistema de aqui es contrario a toda empresa. En la estasion de Invierno son inmensos los grandes aroyos q^e. desienden de la inmediata Sierra; durante su permanensia, se aprovechan sus aguas en los parajes mas adequados a siembras, pero no saven sacar partido de las ventajas q^e. la naturalesa del terreno les proporsiona, no siendo nada dificultoso poder detener parte de estas aguas estasionales para aprovecharlas en los Veranos.

Tulares

En la demarcasion de este Teritorio son comprendidos los llanos q^e. median entre la gran Sierra, y la Sierra baja q^e. se alla prosima a nuestros establesimientos: En dhos Llanos estan situadas dos grandes Lagunas q^e. se comunican sus aguas por un estrecho canal de corta distansia; la estension de ambas lagunas de N. a S. será de 90. a 100. leguas, y su anchor de E. a O. será desde 10. asta 20. leguas; por la parte del N. tienen el desaguadero cuyas aguas forman el gran Rio del Sacramento q^e. desagua en el Oseano por uno de los senos de la singular Baia de S^n. Fran^{co}. En lo interior de dhas Lagunas se allan diferentes Islas, y tanto estas como tambien las demas orillas estan cubiertas de Tule, por cuyo motivo se le há apropiado el nombre de Tulares a estos inmensos Llanos.

Las Lagunas se apoian por su parte ocidental con la baja Sierra y por la oriental lindan con los Llanos q^e. van a terminar con la Sierra Madre, la estension de N. a S. de estos llanos es inmensa, pero su anchor será como unas 10. leg^s. Las lagunas abundan de esquisitos peses, diversas aves aquatiles y particulares Castores, y tanto en su circunferensia como en sus Islas se allan algunas rancherias de Jentiles.

Los Llanos q^e. median entre dhas legunas, y la gran Sierra son los q^e. sin duda llaman la atension de estos delisiosos terrenos; la abundansia de Pinales, Ensinos, Avellanos, y otras inmensas espesies de arboles forman con los pastales y praderas un conjunto interesante: En este ameno sitio es endonde se allan las muchas Rancherias de Indios jentiles cuyo numero es indefinido; las Reuniones de estos es por Tribus, y cada una tiene un jefe q^e. ereda el titulo de sus maiores. Poco se asosian una rancheria con otra; y tambien suelen tener sus desaveniensias en particular quando frutifican los arboles en defensa de sus semillas, terminando las mas veses estas contiendas con infinitas muertes: No se le conose adorasion a culto alguno, pero el respeto a sus difuntos es misterioso siendo la cavellera de estos la mas apresiada ereensia; anualmente suelen reunirse las rancherias para con un llanto jeneral perpetuar su memoria. El jefe de la orda q^e. propone la celebrasion convida a las rancherias amigas, y concluidos los tres dias de Llanto despiden a los uespedes obsequiandolos con plumas pieles, Vellotas Piñones, y otras Semillas; Veneran a sus Ansianos, y estos son sus oraculos, y curanderos; Usan la Poligamia, pero le es comun el divorsio; los Matrimonios se contratan con el Padre de la joven india q^e. esije del Novio una cantidad de avalorios aproporsion del merito q^e. supone en la ija, el divorsio queda autorisado, con devolver el marido los mismos avalorios: El vestuario de las Mujeres es una capa corta de pieles de ardillas unidas de una en una dejando las colas sueltas a discresion, su anchor no es sufisiente a cuvrir las partes pudendas, en las q^e. solamente tienen quatro ó sinco ilos delgados formados de Tule pendientes una quarta, y asegurado solo un estremo a otro q^e. siñe la sintura; los hombres no tienen obstaculo q^e. se interponga a sus formas.

Su vida y costumbres es de la sola naturalesa, y esta le suministra con mano liberal quadrupedos silvestres, aves, peses, y semillas nutritivas con lo q^e. se ponen a cuvierto de su unica nesesidad: En ambos secsos la estatura es proporcionada pero sus fisonomias denotan su estupides; el color es de covre obscuro, su ajilidad es estrema, sus bailes se redusen a arremedar a los animales en todas sus acsiones, y el canto es una continua repetision con aullidos intolerables. Si se isieran algunos establesimientos en este punto ¿de quanta utilidad fuera el sitio de los Tulares?

Islas

Son varias las Islas situadas en las inmediasiones de la costa desde mas al N. de Sta. Barbara asta el paralelo de S^n. Diego; las mas notables son Sta. Crus y Sta. Catalina q^e. tendran cada una mas de 20. leg^s. de vogeo; su distansia del continente será algunas de 6. y otras asta 12. leguas; la diresion de dhas Islas son quasi de N. a S. como la costa, por lo q^e. dejan un espasio navegable entre esta y ellas al q^e. llaman Canal de Sta. Barbara. Estas Islas anteriormente estavan poblados, pero en el dia solamente en Sta. Catalina permanese un corto numero de jentiles q^e. infiero no llegaran a 20. almas, la demas jentilidad se á pasado al continente y se an congregado en las Misiones.

En las mas de las Islas ay sufisiente arboledas, y Sta. Crus suministra muy regulares pinavetes, y otras espesies, siendo de bastante ausilio para las obras q^e. se asen en el Presidio y Mision de Sta. Barbara; Sta. Catalina amas de tener alguna arboleda, y diferentes aguadas como la anterior, lleva la ventaja de contener dos buenos surjideros resguardados y seguros con agua muy regular en la propia orilla, y amas tiene en el sentro buenos pastos y agua

44

das para mantener un sin numero de ganado: Quando llegue el caso de poder figurar California, creo no quedaran en el olvido unas Islas de las q^e. se pueda sacar mucho partido.

Conclusion

Ya queda demostrada la estension de l'Alta California, sus sircustansias atuales, y de quanto puede ser suseptible, por lo tanto ya no fijare la atension en descrivir su sistema, pero su critica situasion me impusa a q^e. aga algunas reflesiones.

Todos los Pueblos tienen entre si una resiproca dependiensia, pues la Naturalesa no pudiendo repartir con igual mano sus riquesas, proporsiona a los unos tierras fertiles, y a otros esteriles; pero la industria de los Pueblos con la balansa del Comersio ase se igualen sus nesesidades, y asi a proporsion q^e. en una nasion faltan aquellos articulos q^e. a un Pueblo culto le son nesesarios, buscan albilitrios para adquirirlos, fomentando su industria, y poniendose en comunicasion con las demas nasiones solo con el fin de atender a su propria conservasion: Esta mutua correspondiensia ase q^e. a todos se les proporsione utilidad, pues los unos para fasilitar lo q^e. nesesitan estraer, y le es nesesario; indagan los medios mas seguros a fin de realisar sus miras; de aqui resulta q^e. los paises privilejiados por la naturalesa disfruten a su ves de aquellos articulos q^e. solo la industria de otros les puede proporsionar.

Este el caso en q^e. se alla California; ella tiene en su terreno un manantial de riquesas con la q^e. bien puede sostener muchos Pueblos, pero le es de nesesidad cambiar la forma de sus produsiones por articulos q^e. le son indispensables a un Pueblo sivilisado; de aqui es la nesesidad q^e. tienen de conservar un Comersio con otras nasiones por el bien q^e. a ella le resulta; pero si por una equivoca idea, se ponen ostaculos q^e. entorpescan la estrasion de aquellos articulos que produse California, en esse caso se verá la abundansia de su terreno en contraste con la desnudes de sus Vesinos.

45

La riquesa de los Pueblos no es tanto por la ferasidad del pais, como por el numero de su Poblasion; Si California tuviera 20 M. almas mas de la q^e. tiene fuera sin duda duplo su valor, y asi si se pretende fomentar este Teritorio es de nesesidad aumentar su poblasion. ¿Pero como será esto dable a vista de las miserias q^e. se esperan?, los mismos naturales del pais buscaran un clima que le sea mas benefico.

Un hombre de bien y libre, estando penetrado q^e. sus miras estan dirijidas al bien jene^l. de la nasion, deve ablar con franquesa, y asi respetando siempre las disposisiones de la suprema Lejisla- sion espondré mi sentir sovre esta materia.

Se há determinado q^e. solo deve quedar abilitado para los Buques Estranjeros el P^to. de Monterey, y en esse caso yo devo asegurar, q^e. se concluió completamente con el Comersio de Cali- fornia; creo aver dicho lo bastante sovre este particular en el *Capi- tulo de Comersio,* pero aora me resta q^e. desir, q^e si se lleva a efecto esta Ley, será jeneral el disgusto en California, pues le augura en lo futuro una suerte desgrasiada igual con corta diferiensia a la epoca anterior, siendole aun mas sensible por aver ya disfrutado seis años de felisidad, en cuyo tiempo avian tomado muy diferente aspecto sus intereses, y tenia el vesindario fundadas esperansas de aserlos mas estensivos. Esta Ley solo podrá ser favorable a algun Estranjero activo, y prespicas naturalisandose en apariensia en la Republica para adquir el drecho de usar en algun buque de su pro- piedad la bandera nasional, y con ella estar autorisado para poder libremente anclar en todos los puntos de esta costa, y apropiarse todo el jiro del Teritorio ¿Y quales serian los resultados? Estos son demasiado notorios, porq^e. siendo uno solo el esportador es claro se abaratarian las produsiones del pais por falta de compra- dores, y de consiguiente se aumentarian los valores de las impor- tasiones por estar estas señidas a una sola mano, influiendo todo en la ruina de este vesindario. Si se quiere suponer q^e. este medio es nesesario para dar estimulo a q^e. se fomente la Marina Nasio-

46

nal; diré: Que el Comersio Mejicano poco se há dedicado a la Marina, pero amas dificulto se alle quien emprenda este ramo de especulasion: Que los articulos q^e. se estraen del Territorio solamente son utiles para espenderse a los Estranjeros, pues estos con su mucha economia, y con darle nuevo benefisio pueden unicamente sacar partido de una espesie de tan poco valor; Y por fin q^e. si se há de esperar asta tanto los buques Nasionales tomen interes en estas especulasiones, será tener q^e. esperar una cosa insierta, pues es demasiado notorio q^e. en tantos años q^e. estos frequentas California jamas se há presentado un buque nasional con el objeto de estraer cueramenta, pues aunq^e. se há presentado el año anterior, y el presente, un Berg^n. Mejicano con este objeto, se deve avertir q^e. este buque pertenese a un Estranjero naturalisado en la Republica, y q^e. los cueros q^e. acopia los trasborda en otro q^e. arbola diferente bandera, y es asimesmo de su propiedad segun todos opinan, con lo q^e. amplia completamente su doble objeto; pero este medio ni a todos le es permitido, ni es fasil q^e. todos lo puedan emprender, y por lo tanto me confirmo en lo q^e. espuse; q^e si esta Ley se lleva e efecto en esse caso solo podrá ser favorable a tal qual particular, pero en jeneral muy perjudisial al Teritorio y a la Nasion.

Como me hé propuesto manifestar mi sentir, devo no ocultar el medio a mi entender mas adequado, a la seguridad de los intereses de la nasion, y al bien de esta California.

Se há fijado al solo puerto de Monterey para los Buques Estranjeros sin duda con el fin de reconsentrar todas las atensiones en un solo punto, y evitar de este modo el contrabando, y el doble gasto en Empleados de asienda; pero soy de opinion q^e. bien se puede poner remedio a todo, sin q^e. los medios ataquen directamente al Teritorio; para esto me parese q^e. deve tambien quedar abilitado para el mismo efecto el Puerto de S^n. Diego, no resultando de esto perjuisio notable en los gastos de su aduana, pues de este modo se aumentavan los ingresos, y se ramificavan los intereses q^e. de

47

otro modo seria impracticable como ya queda anotado; amas el Puerto de Sⁿ. Diego proporsiona las ventajas de mejor surjidero, y de un resguardo seguro en la estasion de Invierno, con la proporsion de poder emprender qualquier carena, y recorrida; y tambien de este modo se fasilitava q^e. la mitad del Teritorio lograse las ventajas q^e. se les proporsionava a la otra mitad, por la imposibilidad de poder transitar las dos grandes cuestas con cargas volumosas, deviendo tambien prevenir, q^e. las Misiones y Pueblo mas inmediatos a Sⁿ. Diego son las mas pudientes y las q^e. devan produsir al Erario maiores ventajas, y q^e. tambien este Presidio nesesita de recursos mas uljentes q^e. Monterey por tener q^e. atender a los establesimientos de Fronteras, siendo caso imposible poderlos socorrer desde dho Puerto.

Abilitados igualmente estos dos Puertos pueden los Buques desembarcar en ambos el total de su cargamento, y en el q^e. concluya se le deverá aser un reconosimiento prolijo de su Bodega, quedando con esto espedito para poder libremente fondear en los puntos q^e. anteriormente practicavan con el fin de reunir en su bordo los articulos q^e. estraen del Teritorio.

Pensar q^e. los Buques pudieran aser contrabando en los surjideros es a mi entender muy remoto; bien porq^e. avia presedido en los dos Puertos abilitados su total descarga, y su esacto rejistro; bien porq^e. jamas ninguna Mision (q^e. son las q^e. abrasan todos los negosios) pueden intervenir a fraude de esta espesie; bien porq^e. en este pais no se alla capitalista capas de poder aser empresa alguna; y bien porq^e. lo redusido de esta poblasion ase q^e. en qualq^r. punto se aga notable qualquier objeto q^e. se introdusca por nimio q^e. sea; pero para mas seguridad intimesele rigurosamente a los Buques la confiscasion total de sus interes en el caso de averiguarseles el mas leve fraude en sus escalas, y estoi seguro, q^e. ninguno se determinará a infrijir la Ley, pues deven temer q^e. los depositos, y fiansas de Sⁿ. Diego, y Monterey responderian por sus faltas. Este metodo es bien comun en las nasiones q^e. nesesitan dar fomento a sus produsiones, pues fasilitando la estrasion fasilitan lo medios de enriqueser sus provinsias.

Para apoiar mas la nesesidad q^e. tiene el Teritorio de q^e. los Buques (ya descargados) devan fondear en sus puertos Intermedios, es presiso notar q^e. anualmente recalan a estas costas diferentes barcos Rusos con solo el objeto de aser cargamentos de Trigo para surtir sus establesimientos de Sitica y Oonalaska: Este trafico estimula a los Pueblos a dar todo impulso a este ramo de agricultura, y con este su cuvrian mil nesesidades, pero si no se les permite a los Buques aprosimarse a los puertos en donde se asia el embarq^e. de dhos granos, en esse caso iran a aser sus cargamentos a los Puertos de Chile como ya tienan indicado, pues el gasto q^e. les puede erogar la diferiensia de Viaje es siempre inferior a la diferencia de presio, siendo la fanega de trigo en Chile a un peso ó poco mas, lo q^e aqui pagan a tres pessos a virtud de su prosimidad; resultando con la retirada de estos buques perder el producto q^e. rendia este articulo, quedando los terrenos en su antigua esterilidad por no aver quien garantise su travajo, influiendo todo al menoscavo de la Pobla^n.

En vista de lo espuesto soy de sentir q^e. para fomentar el Teritorio y para asegurar al mismo tiempo los intereses de la Nasion se deve abilitar amas del P^{to}. de Monterey, tambien el de S^n. Diego para la descarga y deposito de las introdusiones; y concluida su descarga y demas requisitos anotados, se les deve permitir a los Buques sea qual fuesen, puedan libremente practicar los puntos q^e. anteriormente le era permitido recojer los cueros Sevos y trigos que de otro modo jamas se podrian estraer; y de lo contrario los Buques proiectaran sus negosiasiones en otros paises q^e. les presten mas ventajas, y menos dificultades; quedandole a los Californios el dolor de tener q^e. perder su unico recurso.

J. B.

Notes

1. Here the original text has been altered, in different handwriting, to read "educacion."

2. In this passage we follow an interlinear correction. Bandini's version reads "... el de S^n. José de Vitoria contendrá 600. y el de Bransifort no llegará a 200."

3. This passage has an interlinear correction. Bandini's text reads "Los primeros dos Pueblos son Governados por sus corespond^s. Ayuntamientos cada uno compuesto de un Alcalde quatro rejidores un Sindico y Secretario; el tersero ..."

Index

51

*400 copies printed
for the Friends of the Bancroft Library
by The Westgate Press
December* 1951

NOTES ON
UPPER CALIFORNIA

A JOURNEY FROM MONTEREY
TO THE
COLORADO RIVER IN 1832

BY
DR. THOMAS COULTER

GLEN DAWSON : LOS ANGELES

1951

SAN LUIS REY MISSION, CALIFORNIA

INTRODUCTION

I N THE Early California Travels series the publishers propose to print original accounts of early California. Selections will be limited to obscure and rare texts not generally available.

As an initial venture we reprint the Notes on Upper California *of the Irish botanist, Thomas Coulter.[1] Coulter himself says the work is " desultory and imperfect," but since Coulter's manuscripts were lost and there is no other contemporary account of Coulter's trip we have printed his* Notes *and map without changes or omissions.*

Thomas Coulter was born in 1793. He studied in Dublin, Paris, and Geneva. He sailed from England in 1824, taking a position as physician for the Real del Monte Mining Company in the State of Hidalgo, Mexico. During 1829 and 1830

1. *Originally printed in the* Journal and Proceedings of the Royal Geographical Society, 1835.

he visited Guaymas and was located at Hermosillo, Sonora. Wherever he went he collected plants. In November 1831 he arrived in Monterey, California, apparently by sea from San Blas. In Monterey Coulter met another botanist, David Douglas, who wrote in part:

" . . . Dr. Coulter, from the Central States of the Republic of Mexico, has arrived here with the intention of taking all [specimens] to Geneva to De Candolle. He is a man eminently calculated to work, full of zeal, amiable, and I hope may do much for the great good. As a salmon fisher he is superior to W. F. Campbell, Esq., of Islay, who is the Isaak Walton of Scotland, besides being a beautiful shot with the rifle (nearly as good as me!!) And I do assure you from my heart it is a *terrible pleasure* to me to find a good man who can speak of Plants. . . . Tell Joseph I caught two fine trout yesterday, twenty-seven pounds each." [2]

Coulter undertook a journey which had been considered by Douglas, crossing the Colorado Desert of California to the Colorado River. Coulter re-

2. Quarterly *of the California Historical Society, Volume* II, *page* 227.

turned to California. When he returned to Europe by way of Mexico in 1834 his collection is said to have contained over 50,000 specimens, representing between 1500 and 2000 species. His manuscripts were lost in transit between London and Dublin, apparently including the work mentioned at the end of the Notes. *His collection of plants was placed in the Botanical Museum at Trinity College, Dublin, where he worked as Curator until his death in 1843.*

Frederick V. Colville listed some 57 species which bear Coulter's name, including the large coned Coulter Pine.[3] Coulter's collections were the basis of important contributions to the descriptive botany of Mexico and California. His report on the Geography of California printed here was read at the Royal Geographical Society, March 9, 1835.

Glen Dawson

3. *Article by Frederick V. Colville in the* Botanical Gazette, *December 1895, pages 519 to 531.*

THE TEXT and map of Coulter were supplied by the Department of Special Collections, University of California, Los Angeles. The illustration of Mission San Luis Rey is from the original in the Huntington Library drawn by William Rich Hutton, with color added by Irene Robinson. This plate was made originally for the Title Insurance and Trust Company and is used here with their kind permission.

NOTES ON UPPER CALIFORNIA

NOTES ON
UPPER CALIFORNIA

UPPER CALIFORNIA is usually considered as extending from the coast of the Pacific to the Rio Colorado, and from the boundary with Lower California, a few leagues south of San Diego, to the parallel of 42½° N., which is supposed to run through the middle of the lake Timpanogos (though, with respect to this latter circumstance, I am by no means satisfied, being much inclined to think that Timpanogos, which I believe to be the same as that called by the hunters Black Lake, is wholly within the Mexican territory). But the course of the Rio Colorado is entirely within the Rocky Mountains, which are separated from the inhabited, and indeed habitable, portion of California by a great sand plain, destitute of water. This plain is about 100 miles in breadth at its southern extremity, and about 200 at the northern ; about 700 miles in length, gradually ascending toward the north, and similar in every respect to that on the eastern side of the Rocky Mountains; and we shall have a much better idea of the country by considering it therefore as bounded to the eastward by this plain.

Our view is thus confined, then, to a narrow tract of country of very remarkable features, the general run of its mountain-ridges, continuous with the chain of Lower California, being nearly parallel with the coast, and almost all the minor streams running northwesterly. Of the great rivers falling into the Bay of San Francisco, through the Boca de Carquinas, the Sacramento only has a southern course. The Jesus Maria and the San Joaquin run westerly or north-westerly, as do all the others collected in the Tule Lakes before entering the bay.

This view of the country is somewhat different from that usually entertained, and I am sorry that I am not able to speak to the whole of it on my own authority, not having been to the north of San Francisco, nor east of the Tule Lakes. It is necessary here, to notice the great popular error respecting these lakes. The great object of the earlier Spanish expeditions, under Columbus and his immediate followers, was not the discovery of a new continent, but of a western passage to the islands of the Pacific and to China; and even after a great extent of the coasts of America had been explored, the discovery of this passage continued to be a favorite object, everything that encouraged the hope of its attainment being greedily laid hold of. Hence the endless accounts of deep inlets and inland seas; and the extent to which the imagination was engaged in these may be judged of by the reception given to the fabulous story of a passage said to have been actually made from the northwest coast into Hudson's Bay. This anxiety, then, to find a passage from sea to sea, and the facility some of the earlier travellers had in *creating* what they wished to find, where there was no immediate risk of detection, raised these comparatively insignificant

ponds to the rank of a vast inland sea. The
Tule Lakes are now known not to exceed
100 miles in total length, being fordable in
the dry season in several places; and notwithstanding their many tributaries from
the eastward, they discharge, during a considerable portion of the year, very little, if
any, water into San Francisco. It is only
immediately after the rainy season, which
is usually ended by February, and during
the thaw of the snow on the high range of
hills between the lakes and the great sand
plain, that there is any considerable discharge of water from them in this direction.
Such at least is the account given by the
American hunters. A severe accident prevented my crossing this ground myself in
company with a party of beaver-trappers;
but I afterwards met with their chief, a very
intelligent man, from whose account, compared with that of one of the missionary
priests who had visited the Gentile Indians
(*gentiles*) on the borders of the lakes, I have
ventured to lay them down; and though
there must of course be still some uncer-

tainty respecting them, I hope further observation, whilst it must correct, will confirm
the general view I have taken of the country.
Limited, as I have supposed, to the eastward by the sand plain, the general form
of the country is somewhat triangular, the
ridge of mountains from Lower California
dividing into several others, which slightly
diverge as they advance northward. The
great snowy peak of San Bernardino, east
of San Gabriel, being the point from which
the two principal ranges start; the one, the
great snowy chain, separates the sand plain
from the Tule Lakes; and the other separates
the Tule Lakes from the seaboard, not running farther north than San Francisco. Several minor ridges extend between this latter
and the coast, of which the principal is that
running from Monterey towards Santa
Barbara, separating the Rio San Buenaventura, or the Monterey River, from the
coast, and uniting with the Tule chain
about Santa Ynes. The islands of the
Channel of Santa Barbara also seem like
the summits of a submarine chain, having

its general direction parallel to the others.

It will not be necessary to enter, at present, into much detail of my journeys in the country, of which the principle was that from Monterey to the junction of the Rios Colorado and Gila; but I think it requisite to state the means used for determining the positions laid down in longitude. I had a transit in Monterey; but though set up there, the weather was too unfavourable to allow me to depend much upon the results; which, however, is of the less consequence, as that point has been carefully laid down by Captain Beechey. I have, therefore, assumed the longitude of Monterey as he gives it, and taken departures from it eastward by chronometer. The only point at which I thought it necessary to take lunar distances was the ford on the Rio Colorado, six miles below its junction with the Gila, and that only as a check on my chronometer; for having been then reduced to one serviceable one, I felt it proper to take some precaution lest any accident should happen to it on my return, and so deprive me of the advantage of the returning set of observations for time. I however got it safely back to Monterey, and as I found the differences of meridian made going and returning, as shown by the chronometer only, to correspond very closely, I trusted to it *solely*.

I am the more disposed to insist particularly upon this point, because doubts have been expressed of the possibility of using a chronometer on shore, from the difficulty of transporting it safely, particularly on horseback. I am satisfied, from repeated trials, that this difficulty is not so great as has been imagined. All that appears to be necessary, is to carry the chronometer belted tight against the abdomen, and wear it so day and night. The march of that carried on this voyage affords one proof out of several I could state of what can in this way be accomplished, even under very unfavorable circumstances. The subjoined tables show the rate it kept, and the mode adopted of checking it at different points of the journey. It will be seen by these that time was taken, both going and returning, at several points, and that, had any derangement occurred, it must have been detected.

Observations in the order of their dates. [1832]

			m.	s.
Jan. 22. Monterey.	Chron. by M.T.	+ 22	45.6
Feb. 22. "	"	+ 18	54.3
Mar. 20. "	"	+ 16	06.9
Apr. 6. Sta. Barbara.	"	+ 5	09.1
" 23. San Gabriel.	"	− 2	54.5
" 30. La Pala.	"	− 7	35.4
[Pala, San Diego County]			
May 8. Ford.	"	− 17	48.8
[near present Yuma]			
May 17. Ford.	"	− 18	59.7
" 27. La Pala	"	− 10	40.5
Jun. 15. San Gabriel.	"	− 8	50.3
July 5. Santa Barbara.	"	− 4	39.8
" 7. "	"	− 4	54.9
" 19. Monterey.	"	+ 2	33.4
Aug. 2. "	"	+ 1	07.1

Same observations arranged in sets for rate.

Chron. by M.T. m.   s.

Monterey.	Jan. 22.	+ 22 45.6		s.
"	Feb. 22.	+ 18 53.4	Rate	− 7.5 daily.
"	Mar. 20.	+ 16 06.9	"	− 6.1 "
"	July 19.	+ 2 33.4	"	− 6.7 "
"	Aug. 2.	+ 1 07.1	"	− 6.16 "
S. Barbara.	Apr. 6.	+ 5 09.1		

S. Barbara.	July 5.	−	4 39.8	Rate	−6.56 "
"	" 7.	−	4 54.9	"	−6.7 "
S. Gabriel.	Apr. 23.	−	2 54.5		
"	Jun. 15.	−	8 50.3	"	−6.7 "
La Pala	Apr. 30.	−	7 35.4		
"	May 27.	− 10	40.5	"	−6.8 "
Ford, on R. ⎱	May 8.	− 17	48.8		
Colorado. ⎰	" 17.	− 18	59.7	"	−7.88 "

Results.

				mean
				m. s.
Monterey, ⎱ to Ford. ⎰	diff. made going	= 28 24.4 ⎱		28 31.45
	" returning	= 28 38.5 ⎰		
Monterey, ⎱ to S. Barb. ⎰	" going	= 8 59.4 ⎱		8 54.15
	" returning	= 8 48.9 ⎰		
S. Barbara, ⎱ to S. Gab. ⎰	" going	= 6 19.1 ⎱		6 15.9
	" returning	= 6 12.7 ⎰		
S. Gabriel, ⎱ to Ford. ⎰	" going	= 13 15.5 ⎱		13 20.9
	" returning	= 13 26.3 ⎰		

The sum of the three latter means (28ᵐ 31ˢ.95) corresponding nearly with the result of the first taken singly.

Respecting these tables, there are two circumstances which require some little explanation. One is the change of rate to the amount of about one second daily during my stay at Rio Colorado, attributable perhaps to the excessive heat to which we were

there subjected, the thermometer, exposed
to the radiation of the plain only, standing
frequently at 140° Fahr. (Further on there
will be found some remarks on the causes
of this very high temperature, so unusual in
an extra-tropical latitude, with some other
observations on the climate of Mexico which
may be interesting to the reader.) Perhaps
this degree of heat ought not to affect the
chronometer; but I found it so intolerable,
that I was obliged to to leave off the belt
in which I carried it, and to allow it to lie
horizontally during my stay, which may also
have contributed to produce the disturbance. The effect of this change is got entirely
over by making account only of the time
by chronometer at my arrival and again on
my departing, leaving out of account the ten
days during which I remained stationary.

The other circumstance deserving note is
the difference observable in the easting and
westing in some of the *divisions* of the journey, whilst there is none on the *whole*. This
is not very great, and may be partly ac-
counted for by the want of a barometer,

which, from having frequently broken tubes before, I did not carry on this journey, which I was obliged to make very rapidly. I was consequently obliged to correct the refraction by guess. Whatever error there may have been in my guess would manifestly act in opposite ways, going and returning, and its effect be got rid of by taking the mean of the results, the only evil being the discredit it appears to throw on the chronometer.*

I have laid down the junction of the Rios Colorado and Gila nearly forty miles farther north than Lieutenant Hardy has done, and this also it is necessary to explain. This point, which was the site of the two missions of San Pedro and San Pablo, has long at-

---

*I subjoin also a short table of the chronometrical measurements between Mexico and Zimapan, made in precisely similar circumstances. The chronometer was made by Crossthwaite (1361).

				h. m. s.
Zimapan. [State of Hidalgo]	April 8th, A.M. 8 h.	Chr. by M.T.		1 8 40.7
Zimapan.	" 15th, P.M. 4	"		1 6 31.3
Mexico. [City]	" 22d, P.M. 4	"		1 6 43.2
"	" 29th, A.M. 7½	"		1 5 10
R.D. Monte.	May 1st, P.M. 3½	"		1 6 32.2
"	" 14th, A.M. 8½	"		1 3 4.3

tracted a good deal of attention. Ever since
the unsuccessful attempts of the Jesuits, particularly Padre Kino, to establish a communication over-land between Sonora and
California, this point, near which is the best,
and indeed usually the only practicable ford
on the river below the junction, has been
especially looked to. After Upper California
was partially settled, the two missions above-
mentioned were established, and at first
throve well; but in consequence of the removal of the commander in charge of them,
in whom the Indians had great confidence,
the neophytes rose, destroyed and abandoned
the mission. The remains of that on the
north side are still visible; it was built on
a point of rock projecting a little into the
river, and constituting the extreme southern
point of the Rocky Mountains, towards
which the river has gradually cut its way,
leaving behind a broad plain now pretty
well covered with poplar and brushwood.
The junction of the two rivers is not a mile
above this point, the Colorado coming south
and the Gila nearly west.

When Lieutenant Hardy found himself on the point of the island of Algodones, forty miles south of this, nothing was more easy, unacquainted as he was with the country on either side, than that he should suppose himself at the junction of the two rivers. The two channels of the Colorado at this point run, with respect to each other, exactly as the two rivers do; and if he had known anything of the missions and the point of hill on which one of them was built, he had in view, on his north, a knoll, the only one in the plain, but very remarkable, and close to the river, which would much assist in leading him astray.

It would occupy too much time to go at present into any great detail of my travelling inland. I am tempted, however, to say a few words of the journey of which the principal observations are given above, as it was the most interesting, the longest, and by far the most laborious of those I made in California.

The rainy season of 1832 ended late in February, which is rather after the usual time, and I started so soon as the country was passable, which is not at all during the rains, nor for some time afterwards. The rivers, which in the dry season are mere beds of sand, are quite impassable when swollen; and even for some weeks after they have fallen low, the danger and difficulty of crossing some of them, on horseback, are very considerable. If these streams carried down only sand, they might be passed as soon as the rapidity of the current was so far abated that a horse could stand; but the sand comes down mixed with a vast quantity of mud, which settles together with it; so that even when the stream becomes so low that a small animal can walk across, a horse or a man cannot. It is not until the mud is gradually washed out of the surface of the deposit that this becomes possible. We have then a bed of hard sand resting upon one of semi-fluid mud and sand; and it is very difficult to say when and where it is safe to attempt the passage. On this occasion I had to pass the Guadalupe [Santa Maria River], in this state, between San Luis Obispo and La Purissima; and it was only after long search that I found a place where a bear had passed, and trusting to his sagacity I followed his steps. The stream was broad, very shallow, and the bed of clear sand on the surface of the deposit must have been very thin, for it swagged under foot like the surface of a quagmire. A body of troops which passed this way some days before, though on a most urgent affair, was obliged to wait for ten days to allow the sand to settle.

From Monterey southward the road runs through a series of narrow ravines, as far as San Luis Obispo; but about Santa Ynez, south of San Luis, and again in the neighbourhood of Santa Barbara, it runs on, or close by, the beach; whence, southward, it keeps chiefly along the west foot of the mountains, separated from the sea by low sand-hills, in some places of considerable breadth, as at San Gabriel, where they are almost twelve leagues broad. The best way to the Colorado, in the dry season, is to follow the coast road as far as San Luis Rey, and thence ascend the Pala stream, which runs in a very narrow ravine behind the

maritime ridge, crossing the summit level
between its head and that of the small
stream of San Felipe, which runs south-
eastward till it reaches the border of the
sand plain at Carizal [Carrizo], where it
sinks; though its course across the plain,
when swollen, which it rarely is, is marked
by a dry channel, in many points of which
a little water, usually very bad, is to be had
by deep digging.

There is not much difficulty in any part
of the journey up to this point,—the Carizal;
but from hence across the plain, which is
here about one hundred miles broad, and
totally destitute of pasture, cattle suffer extremely. It is always possible to carry water
enough for a party of men; but horses and
mules must pass the first two days absolutely
without water or food,—and even then get
only brine at the point called the Aqua Sola
[probably lagoons at Alma Mocho], from
its being the only pond on the plain. When
I passed, the water I found at this place
was so strong that it purged both men and
cattle. There is some rush and reed which

mules will eat, though horses generally refuse them.

From hence there is still another day's journey to the Rio Colorado. After passing the river the same difficulties continue for seven days farther, on the Sonora road, as far as Alta; but this part of the journey, from its greater length, it is extremely imprudent to attempt without a proper guide. The only water to be had is found in the ravines, frequently at some distance from the road, in excavations called Tinajas, made by the Indians, who were formerly much more numerous in this neighbourhood than they are at present.

The only settled portion of Upper California lies along the coast; the missions being nearly all within one day's journey from it. The only point where a mission has any settlement farther inland is at San Gabriel, where the Rancho of San Bernardino is at the head of the valley, some thirty leagues from the port of San Pedro. This is indeed the only point of either Californias, south of San Francisco, capable of sustaining a large population. The valley is above thirty leagues long, and of considerable breadth to the westward, where it approaches the coast, and joins on either side the plain of San Fernando and San Luis Rey. It is in many places very fertile, and wheat, where it can be irrigated, yields better here than in any other part of the Mexican territories that I have seen. The vine also thrives better, and is beginning to be extensively cultivated. The mission alone has above a hundred and twenty thousand vines immediately about it; and the inhabitants of the Pueblo [Los Angeles] have many fine vineyards. Here there is room for a great increase of population. The want of a safe port is indeed a great inconvenience; but I have no doubt that it will be got over, and that we shall see the Pueblo rise rapidly to the rank of a considerable town. The anchorage of San Pedro, though very unsafe in bad weather, need be used but for the moment vessels are taking cargo on board or discharging; and the time they are salting hides, or are otherwise detained, may be passed in perfect

safety at the island of Catalina, in front;
which, besides two rather exposed anchorages to the east and south, with good water
at this latter, has a very beautiful little bay
on the west side, perfectly land-locked, where
might be the salting-houses. The present
government does not allow this, from fear
of smuggling, and not without some reason.
San Diego, moreover, where the chief part of
the salting is now performed, is not distant.

I have gone thus far into this subject because the general government is now making
considerable efforts to colonise Upper California from Mexico, under the apprehension
that, if not done, the North Americans will
get in in too great numbers. This apprehension appears to be hardly rational, as the
tierras realengas, or lands still at the disposal
of the state, are in California, as they always
have been in the Spanish colonies, given
gratis, at the discretion of government, and
not sold to the best bidder, as in the United
States. Any efforts made for the purpose of
colonising Upper California should be directed towards the portion of the country

north and east of San Francisco and east
of the Tule lakes, which is fertile, well wooded
and watered, and of sufficient extent to make
its colonisation worth while as a speculation;
the rest of the country south of San Francisco
and west of the Tule lakes, possessing, with
the exception of the valley of San Gabriel,
too little cultivable ground, and of this a
very small portion irrigable—the soil, however, where it is arable, being usually rich.
Wheat, the vine, and all fruit trees that have
been tried, thrive remarkably well, though
the mildew near the coast, about Monterey,
frequently hurts the wheat; and the chapul,
or locust, by which name a great variety of
grasshoppers is known, often destroys the
vine, and indeed everything else. A mild
winter is sure to be followed by this pest,
particularly south of Santa Barbara. They
appear to breed along the coast in the sand-
hills; and as the northwesterly winds prevail, they are carried inland, and destroy
everything they meet.

The great article of produce in Upper
California is black-cattle, and their increase

has been really prodigious. It is not yet seventy years since their first introduction, to the number of twenty-three head. In 1827 the missions possessed 210,000 branded cattle, and it was supposed not less than 100,000 unbranded. It is found necessary to slaughter not less than 60,000 annually, to keep the stock down to its present standard, which it is supposed it could not not much exceed with advantage, until more of the country to the eastward shall have been settled. The young cows usually bear a calf before they are two years old, which, with the rule usually observed not to kill a cow capable of bearing, will account for their rapid increase. Sheep have increased nearly as rapidly, but are as yet of little interest to the trade of the country. I have not heard of any export of wool from California. Sheep are rarely slaughtered for consumption, as their price has been kept up by the priests, either without any definite motive, or what is, I fear, more near the truth, from some mistaken calculation. It is sufficiently strange that where the fattest bullock is worth only eight dollars, and can rarely be sold at all, and where young cows in calf can be bought in droves at about two dollars, and frequently less, a sheep cannot be bought for less than three dollars. This state of things of course cannot last long. The destruction of the missions now in progress will throw into the market a stock of about 200,000 head, which of course must soon fall to its proper value.

The number of the white inhabitants has also increased very rapidly, and I believe is now not under six thousand, though I cannot state their numbers very exactly until I shall have examined the statistical materials which I have collected.

The reverse, however, is the case with the aboriginal inhabitants. They have diminished considerably in number, though, in this case, one would suppose they ought at least not to have lost ground, not having been driven from their homes, as in the United States, nor having had ardent spirits at all within their reach until lately. But they have been compelled to live under a restraint they could not bear, and to labour a little—neither of which they would submit to if they could possibly avoid it. Though the fact is as far as possible dissembled, I believe that a great deal both of force and fraud were used in congregating them together in missions ; and the moment that force shall be altogether withdrawn, I have no doubt that the majority of them will return to the woods. Now that the seaboard is pretty much occupied by whites, the Indians will probably retire to their relations still living free in the interior.

It is a very extraordinary fact that their decrease is greatly hastened by the failure of female offspring,—or the much greater number of deaths amongst the females in early youth than among the males,—I have not been able clearly to determine which, though the latter appears the more probable; the fact, however, of there being a much smaller number of women living than of men, is certain. Infanticide, properly so called, is not common, though very frequent recourse is had to the means of producing abortion, chiefly mechanically; but this will not account for the state of things described, as males and females must be supposed in this way to suffer equally. All the missions of Lower California have perished or are perishing from this cause, or at least with this accompanying circumstance; and in Upper California, in almost all the missions, a great many of the men cannot find wives. The mission of San Luis Rey is the only remarkable exception. In it the Indians are stated to be upon the increase, and the women in numbers equal to the men; but my acquaintance with this mission is too limited to enable me to speak of the causes of their momentary escape from what appears to be the inevitable fate of their race in the neighborhood of white men—a fate from which I fear the Luisenos are not likely to escape. The political reforms now in active operation in California, and of which the first and most important measure is the de- struction of the missions, will enable the white inhabitants to acquire possession of the great bulk of the mission lands; and though agreeably to the spirit of the Spanish laws, which certainly were meant to afford the Indians a degree of protection unknown in our old colonies, they may for a long time retain a portion of their ancient possessions, it is but too probable that the combination of their own vices to which they cling, with those of their intruding neighbours, which they very easily acquire, will insure the ultimate annihilation of a race which exhibits so few traces of moral energy.

I shall not at present go into any examination of the vegetation of California, though this, as well as its fauna, is well worthy of the most attentive consideration. But I am tempted to make a few observations on some circumstances in the general aspect of the country, which appear sufficiently striking. The accompanying map, though very rude, and in many respects certainly not very correct, will serve at least to show that we must consider the whole of the two Californias as one great chain of mountains, with several long but usually narrow valleys dividing it into ridges nearly parallel with the coast, and as a whole, separated by the gulf

of Cortez and the great sand-plain, from
Sonora and the Rocky Mountains; with
which latter, however, the Californian chain
appears ultimately to unite north of the
parallel of 42°, about the great summit-level
dividing the waters of the Columbia from
those falling into the bay of San Francisco.
The neighbourhood of this bay is the only
part of the country likely ever to become of
much interest to Europeans. It is highly
fertile, well-wooded, watered, and perfectly
healthy. The Sacramento is navigable to a
considerable distance, and runs through a
country capable of sustaining an immense
population. Even the Tule lakes, though
navigable for steam-boats only when flooded,
will then afford the means of transport for
timber, hides, and other produce, from a
considerable and valuable tract of country.

Lower California is pretty rich in minerals.
I have seen very rich argentiferous lead ores
from the southern extremity of it, and gold
is also found in several places. But in Upper
California, I know of no place where either
has been found, except to the eastward of

Santa Ynez, where a small silver mine was successfully wrought for some time, till the owners were killed by the Indians; and in one of the streams falling into the southern Tule lake some gold has also been found by the beaver hunters, but as yet in very small quantity.

I shall conclude this paper with a few remarks upon the climate of Mexico. In an early part of my letter I stated that the thermometer had frequently stood at 140° Fahr. This, it is necessary to explain, was the temperature of the atmosphere a few feet above a plain excessively dry and heated by the sun; and something may also be due to the circumstance of the thermometer, although carefully screened from the sun, being exposed to the radiation of the soil, which was very great and frequently oppressive. This very high temperature is not, however, to be considered as of very frequent occurrence, but always owing to some local and temporary causes; one of which, and indeed a necessary condition for its attaining its greatest height, being that there should not

be any wind. Such was the case during the
latter three days of my stay at the ford on
Red River. The wind, after having blown
for many days from the S.W., suddenly
lulled three days before my departure on
my return, and continued dead calm for
the first day of my journey, that is, until
reaching Agua Sola. This was one of the
most painful days I have spent, notwithstanding that the excessive dryness of the
atmosphere necessarily exempted me from
that oppression felt in damp situations even
at very inferior temperatures. To this extreme dryness must also be attributed the
occurrence of severe cold occasionally in
the same situations.

The surface of the country, covered in
almost its whole extent with bare mountains
or sand plains, completely destitute of water,
contributes nothing towards mitigating the
cold of the winds blowing from the elevated
portions of the Rocky Mountains to the N.
and N.E. Hence, when these continue to
blow for any length of time, it freezes even
to the south of Pitis [Hermosillo, Sonora],

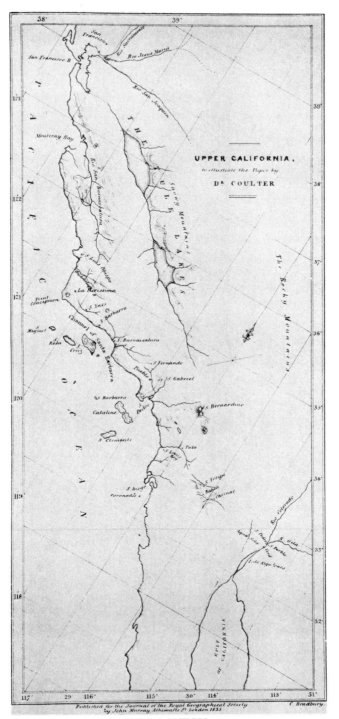

THOMAS COULTER
1835 MAP OF CALIFORNIA

in lat. N. 29°; and in the winter of 1829-30, it froze in Pitis every night for nearly two months. On the 12th December, on arriving at San Jose [probably San Jose de Pimas on the Rio Matare, 60 miles south of Hermosillo], a few leagues from Pitis, I found the thermometer at 18° Fahr., at 8h. P.M. On the 13th, it stood in the shade below 32° all the day, at night sinking even to 18°. This, however, appears to occur very rarely. I understood that for seventy-two years there had not been a frost severe enough to kill the mesquites (a species of acacias), which on this occasion suffered severely.

Though it is not exactly in point, I cannot avoid noting, that, on the table-lands of Mexico, similar cases of cold occur, with the difference of being more frequent, as may be easily conceived from its greater elevation, with the same condition as to the general scarcity of water. At Veta Grande, Zacatecas, during the month of December, 1825, it frequently froze hard. I subjoin here some extracts from my journal.

	Max.	Min.
December 2	53° 5′	20°
,, 3	48° 5′	18°
,, 4	34°	18°
,, 6	59°	41°
,, 12	—	12°

and so on through the remainder of that month and January ensuing.

This was not stated to be unusually severe. It is strange that the agars and many species of cactus should be able to resist this cold. They do not indeed thrive, but they live, only of course in consequence of the extreme dryness of the ground at that season.

A few years before, the water, trickling down the sides of the shaft of Concepcion, froze to the depth of seventy varas (thirty fathom). The shaft is in a very sheltered situation, but as its mouth is far below the level of the general drainage shaft, close by it, the cold air enters by Concepcion, and after circulating through the working, issues warmed through the tiro general as through a chimney.

The condition of countries situate as a

portion of Sonora and California is, between the summer and the winter rains, is worthy of some consideration. Having seen only this one, I shall limit my observations to it.

The whole of the rain in Mexico may be said to fall in the summer months; occasional and usually slight showers fall in winter, but are pretty much limited to particular districts, as Xalapa, &c. In California Alta, on the contrary, it rains only in the winter, with a similar exception in favour of Monterey, where there are sometimes, but rarely, slight showers in summer. The summer rains reach the lower part of Sonora, where, however, they are scanty and irregular; and from Pitis, northward, across the sands, it rarely rains at all; as is also the case in the northern portions of Lower California, where the summer rains scarcely prevail to the north of Loretto, the Capital.

I am sorry to be obliged to content myself with offering the Society so desultory and imperfect a sketch as this; but I have many claims on my time, the most urgent of which is the preparation of a work in some detail on the entire subject of California. Whatever is here defective will there, I hope, be found supplied.

LETTERS FROM THOMAS COULTER
TO SIR W. J. HOOKER

Rosoman House, Islington
London, Mch. 27, 1835

My dear Sir,

I have received your very kind letter of Mch. 12 to which I should have replied sooner——but I have been suffering under a rather severe cold which keeps me even yet pretty much confined to the house. As soon as I shall be able to get my plants into some little order I shall be very happy to exchange duplicates with you——but I fear that I shall not be able to do much at arrangement for this year at least——my hands are so full of other work——

I was not able to visit the neighbourhood of Santa Fe without sacrificing my trip to California which I preferred——Had I known however that poor Douglas was in California I should certainly have taken the other route.——The headwaters of the Gila, between the Colorado and Bravo must be fine ground, but it is now I believe not practicable to visit it, without a force of at least thirty good men——

I should be extremely happy to pay you a visit in Scotland this summer, but I fear I shall not be able——my health is a good deal broken up——and I am much occupied——but I hope I shall have the pleasure of seeing you in Dublin in August at the meeting of the Association——

Ever my dear Sir,
Very faithfully yours
THOMAS COULTER

Dr. Hooker,
Glasgow

[*Letter No.* 17 *from S. American Letters.* 1832-1837. *Royal Botanic Gardens, Kew*].

3 Euston Square, London
July 23, 1840

My Dear Sir,

I have this morning received your favour of the 16th here——where I am on my way to Paris and Geneva——partly on business and in part to pay a long projected visit to De Candolle—— I shall be most happy to exchange with you the duplicate of *what was* my Herbarium——It now belongs to the University on the same arrangement I proposed four years ago——I have however the same discretionary power as before ——I can only guess at what it contains yet, as I have not opened a parcel of it, except a few which had received a little damage——but from all I can see I hope that I shall have my Mexican and Californian collection arranged and the duplicates separated within a year. I have a few pines (cones)——I believe branches of most or all of them in my collection, and I think **Mr. Don** saw all that I could get at, on my return ——I had not any hope of getting them home alive and so generally endeavord to put up un-ripe cones as less likely to gaze——from what I have heard of your collection I am sure you will find it very easy to find wherewith to counter-poise all that I may be able to give you——all I have to give you you shall have——I hope to speak to you on this subject in September as I go to the meeting of the Association chiefly in that hope——My collection of Shells is not likely to make any great progress, for some time at least; tho' I occasionally add a little to it——I have however nothing of the collector in me and indeed must confine myself to types of genera and species without sacrificing much to the beauty or rarity of the specimens——

I expect to meet Mr. Mackay in Edinburg about the 5th or 7th of Septr and accompany him to Glasgow.

I am Dear Sir

Very truly yours

THOMAS COULTER

[*Letter No.* 103 *from English Letters,* A-H, 1840. *Royal Botanic Gardens, Kew*].

Some brief glimpses of Thomas Coulter are found in the Bancroft Library, University of California, Berkeley (Vallejo Documents, XXX, 262 and XXXI, 22). On October 20, 1831 (en route to Monterey) Coulter was "at Santa Barbara catching butterflies." His return to Mexico was by way of San Diego and past Cape San Lucas. On April 27, 1833 he was back in Mexico, as he wrote to William Hartnell, enclosing a printed announcement of a commission business, Coulter y Cia. Coulter was also interested in the reduction of silver ores at that time.

THE MANIFESTO

TO THE

MEXICAN REPUBLIC

DON JOSE FIGUEROA

*Commandant-General and Political Chief
of Upper California*

FOREWORD BY
JOS. A. SULLIVAN

M C M L I I

BIOBOOKS • OAKLAND 10, CALIFORNIA

CALIFORNIA RELATIONS
XXXII

FOREWORD

*Jose Figueroa, Mexican Brigadier General, had been Command-
ing General of Sonora and Sinaloa, and was Governor and Commanding General of California from January 4, 1833, to his death
on September 29, 1835.*

*Figueroa, known as the best of California's Mexican Governors,
in many respects merits his reputation. He was an intelligent man,
of good intentions and liberal views; not a model in respect to private morality, and not always to be fully trusted; well versed in the
arts of making friends and of gaining popularity by overcoming
imaginary obstacles; was fortunate in the circumstances under which
he was called to rule the country and made no serious mistakes.*

*His appointment dated April 17, 1832, his instructions to work
for the perfect restoration of tranquillity, to inspire confidence
in the National Government, to give much attention to the neophytes,
to improve their condition and fit them for a change in the Mission
system, colonization and the distribution of lands to citizens and
foreigners were to be encouraged.*

*Meanwhile at Mexico City the National Congress on August
17, 1833, passed a bill for secularization. This law simply provided
that the Missions should be converted to parishes. Jose Maria Hijar
(pronounced E.R.), appointed Commissioner of Colonization, his
instructions to take possession of all the property belonging to the
Missions of both Californias, his partner, Lt. Colonel Jose Maria
Padres, Ayudante Inspector and aide to Gen. Echeandia, Figueroa's predecessor. The two had devised a project of taking a colony
to California. Hijar was a man of property, influence and reputation. They were greatly assisted by Valentin Gomes Farias, Vice-
President of the Republic, a warm personal and political friend of
Padres, and also by the new deputy from California, Juan Bandini,
who lost no time in identifying himself with the scheme. For several
years prior, California was being used as a penal colony, much to
the discontent of the residents. At Monterey formal resolutions had
been passed against the practice.*

*The colonists left Mexico City, not without some minor problems,
marching to the sea, where some 250 proceeded on the voyage from
San Blas in two ships, the* Natalia *and the* Morelos. *Several passengers died on the way. The ships separated, arriving at San Diego
and Monterey in September, 1834, in both cases receiving a warm
welcome. Shortly during the winter a majority from both ships were*

located at San Francisco Solano, where Mariano G. Vallejo was in charge.

The original project was to this degree fulfilled, that is, to strengthen the northern frontier, adjacent to Fort Ross, its most lasting accomplishment the beginning of the town of Sonoma. The colony contained 19 farmers, 11 painters, 12 seamstresses, 8 carpenters, 8 tailors, 5 shoemakers, 5 tinners, 5 silversmiths, 2 hatters, 2 physicians, 2 barbers, 2 saddlers, 2 blacksmiths, 2 printers, 2 goldsmiths, and also a mathematician, gardener, surgeon, machinist, ribbon maker, rebozo maker, midwife, distiller, candy maker, vermicelli maker, navigator, founder, porkman, musician, vintager, apothecary, boatman, and carriage maker, besides 6 teachers and the officers.

Forbes, quite critical of the group's composition, was proved wrong, for they were of a class far superior to any that had before been sent as settlers to California, many educated, of some property, all had trade or profession. Among those who became very useful citizens were Ignacio Coronel, Augustin Olvera, Jose Abrego, Victor Prudon, Francisco Guerrero, Jesus Noe, Mariano Bonillo, Zenon Fernandez, Auguste Janssens, Florencio Serrano, Jose M. Cavarrubias, Jose de la Rosa, Gumesindo Flores, Francisco Castillo Negrete, Fran. Ocampo, Nicanor Estrada, Juan N. Ayala, Simon O'Donoju and Chas. Baric.

The manifesto was the important book printed in Alta California during the Spanish occupation; is now reaching for the stature of Tamerlane and the Bay Psalm. Geo. Harding, the authority on the printing and the publisher, writes that Augustin Vicente Zamarano, an Army officer, was in 1825 Executive Secretary of the Territory and was Commandant at Monterey, and is best remembered as California's first printer. Harding gives a bibliography of the book and a brief history of the press, saying that Captain John Bradshaw of the ship Lagoda from Boston brought the printing press to Monterey and quotes Kimble that the press was ready to operate about June, 1834. Zamarano was the owner, and assisted the author in preparing his book for printing. The Spanish Edition was dated at Monterey, 1835, the English Edition at San Francisco, 1855. The latter was used for this text. We had several recommendations for having this done in this series of California Relations, including the Librarian at Alma College, Francis L. Sheerin, S.J.

For the chionologist the book has an interesting significance; it is a very pertinent contribution to the literature of the struggle for *the water holes, a struggle that is yet far from finished. The book exposes the forces, even though primitive, that shaped the future of the State, for the Province was in flux; not only were the departments at Mexico interested but the astute and local residents were feeling the expanding influence of the leather economy. Hijar, Padres, Bandini, Vallejo, Santa Anna, Farias, Zamarano, but most definitely Figueroa, did more than any other to foster the Land Grant system of the Mexican Republic.*

We are grateful to George Hammond, Director, and to the Bancroft Library, University of California, for our copy and for research, and to the Oakland Public Library, both of them quite liberal in the facilities placed at our use.

A note for California Relations No. 31, Silverado Squatters, "The California Honeymoon" by Robert Louis Stevenson. The book hand-set and hand-bound, is a very pleasing addition to the Biobook series, in an edition of 900 copies.

For dedication to statesmen we select first,

SAMUEL HOUSTON,

Soldier and Statesman of Texas, born in Virginia, commissioned ensign, saw active service with Jackson and was wounded at Horseshoe Bend in 1814, learned the Indian language, studied law, located at Nashville, in 1823 was elected without opposition to Congress and reelected in 1825, soon a trader in the Indian country, he was adopted by the Cherokees and acted for several years as their agent, with frequent trips to Washington. Attended the Texas Convention of 1833. Shortly, with his commanding presence and capacity to arouse confidence and enthusiasm, was selected Commander of the Army under the Provisional Government of Texas.

On April 12, 1836, at Buffalo Bayou, although outnumbered almost two to one, Houston's Texas troops surprised the Mexicans under Santa Anna and severely defeated them. Houston himself was wounded and Santa Anna captured. Shortly Houston was elected President of the New Texas Republic. His executive ability again noted, was reelected in 1841. In 1846 was at Washington to start fourteen years as Senator from the State of Texas. Outspoken, he said, "I am for the Union, without any 'if' in the case; and my motto is, it shall be preserved." In 1859 he was elected Governor of Texas; he was opposed to secession; the commanding figure in the history of Texas, he was as well the greatest in the history of the West.

Jos. A. Sullivan,
515 Weldon Avenue,
March 17, 1952.   Oakland 10, California.

Remember that only on Paper
has Humanity yet achieved Glory,
Beauty, Truth, Knowledge, Virtue
and abiding Love.

THE DISPLAY which was made throughout the whole of the Republic, in regard to the attempt to colonize the territories of the Californias, and the results which followed the expedition which Señors Don José Maria Hijar and Don José Maria Padres undertook for that purpose, oblige me to lay before the public a brief but exact notice of the facts as they occurred. As the enterprise did not result as the directors intended, it is sought to attribute to me the blame of the miscarriage, when it is exclusively due to their want of calculation, bad combinations, and underhanded management. The public, in view of the facts, will judge of persons.

In the month of April, 1832, the Supreme Government appointed me Political Chief of Upper California, upon which duty I entered in January, 1833. In the month of March I fell seriously ill, for which reason I asked to be relieved. As at that time the territory had just emerged from a dangerous crisis, and as yet I did not consider extinguished the causes of the revolution which had kept the inhabitants divided, I thought that it was not a time to separate the political and military commands in two distinct persons, as had been desired, but that a single individual ought to discharge both functions; so I represented to the Supreme Government when I asked for my relief, because it appeared to me that I might do so with propriety, as I was not then even remotely thinking of remaining in the *command,* for my health was greatly broken, and I was only anxious to return to the bosom of my family.

The Adjutant Inspector, Don José Maria Padres, in the year 1830, manifesting a great interest in bettering the condition of the

Indians, but with no very good intentions, as has been developed, projected the secularization of the Missions in this territory, in conformity with the provisions of the law of the 13th of September, 1813. At that period the Governor of this Territory was Lieut. Col. Don José Maria de Echandeia, whom Padres easily enlisted, presenting him a project which, in the following line, he ordered to be published by proclamation and to be put into execution, just at the moment that Lieut. Col. Victoria arrived to relieve him; and as much from this incident as because the Supreme Government was not consulted, this enterprise, which the said Victoria ordered to be suppressed, was defeated. As Padres had secretly enlisted various patriots who, in good faith, were desirous for the secularization, he had many co-workers, who afterwards, as much from the exaggeration of the principles which he had inculcated in them as from the severity with which it was thought to govern them, were so many opponents of Victoria in the revolution which was formed against his person, headed by Echandeia—a revolution which, whatever may have been its causes, threw this Territory into consternation, because the government was destroyed and the consequences felt, and because the citizens in general were divided and embittered against each other. Thus it is that when I arrived, the Territory was in complete *anarchy*, from which it had not as yet recovered. The Supreme Government highly disapproved of the conduct of Echandeia and Padres, and commanded me, if I found the edict of secularization in operation, that I should order it to be suspended, replacing the Missions in their ancient condition, but not the less to report whether they were or not in a state to be secularized, in order to undertake it with due circumspection; and not the less to go on gradually dividing the lands of the Missions among the neophytes, in order sensibly to convert them into private property. Padres was ejected from this country by Victoria, but he left sowed the germ of the revolution which afterwards appeared, and which owes its origin to the project of secularizing the Missions.

As the distance from here to Mexico is so great, I recovered before learning what course the Government would adopt, and made known to it that I was able to discharge the duties of my office. The Government commanded me then to continue in the discharge of both branches, as I was then doing, notwithstanding that on the receipt of my first communication, it had ordered the Adjutant Inspector, Don José Maria Padres, to proceed to California and take charge of the military command in the event that I continued ill and wished to go to Mexico.

When this despatch was delivered, Señor Gomez Farias was in power, with whom the Adjutant Inspector, Don José Maria Padres, was on terms of great intimacy, as he himself has published, and availing himself of the opportunity, he labored effectively for the passage of the law of the 17th of August, 1833, for the secularization of the Missions of the Californias; for the undertaking of the colonization of both Territories; and that Señor Don José Maria de Hijar should be named Political Chief of Upper California and Director of Colonization. It was easy to persuade one of the utility and suitableness of these projects if they did not embrace other objects, which time has disclosed. But the Government, animated by the best desires for the felicity and progress of the country, took under its protection these magnificent schemes. Padres congratulated himself on seeing the realization of the plans he had meditated since the year 1830, and obtained the appointment of Subdirector of Colonization. Preparations for the voyage were made, and people were engaged in the name of the Government for Colonization. I do not know what aid they received, but it is public that the Government made great *disbursements* down to the embarkation of the expedition in the port of San Blas.

In the month of February, 1834, I received the supreme order which follows:

"OFFICE OF THE FIRST SECRETARY OF STATE,
"DEPARTMENT OF THE INTERIOR.

"The most Excellent Señor Vice President in exercise of the supreme executive power, has been pleased to relieve you from the duties of Political Chief of that Territory and to nominate Don José Maria Hijar for that position, to whom you will immediately surrender the command. At the same time, His Excellency commands me to thank you, as I do, for the zeal with which you have discharged those duties, and His Excellency hopes that you will continue your services in favor of order. The which I communicate to you for your information and fulfilment.

"God and Liberty. Mexico, July 15, 1833.

"GARCIA.

"Señor General Don JOSE FIGUEROA, Political Chief of Upper California."

My answer is of the following tenor:

"POLITICAL GOVERNMENT OF UPPER CALIFORNIA.—No. 7.

"MOST EXCELLENT SENOR:—So soon as Señor Don José Maria Hijar presents himself in this territory, I will deliver to him the command of the Political Government, which has been under my charge, as the Most Excellent Señor Vice President orders, and as your Excellency has been pleased to communicate to me, in your official letters of the 15th of July of the year last past, which after much delay I have received. I am exceedingly grateful to the Most Excellent Señor Vice President for having relieved me of this duty, so much above my small ability, and for the distinguished expressions with which he declares himself satisfied with my conduct in the discharge of my functions; and although I may not be able to boast that I have fulfilled the desires of the Government, I have at least the satisfaction of having reëstablished tranquillity and constitutional order, which, when I entered this territory, I found relaxed in all the branches of the Administration. Fortunately, today we enjoy union and peace, in pursuit of which I have never spared any sacrifice or labor. I pledge myself to continue the same course up to the moment of the arrival of my successor, leaving to results to give proof of my good or bad conduct. In the *meantime,* your Excellency will be pleased to make my sentiments known to the Most Excellent Señor Vice President, to whom I offer respectfully the homage of my gratitude and thanks.

"God and Liberty. Monterey, 18th of May, 1834.

"JOSE FIGUEROA.

"The Most Excellent Señor Secretary of State and Foreign Affairs."

Extraofficially I learned that with Señor Don José Maria de Hijar was coming a multitude of families as colonists, at the expense of the Government, and although neither the Government nor Señor Hijar relied on the local authorities in this enterprise, it appeared to me prudent to make some preparation for their establishment. With this view I made an expedition to the frontier, as far as the Fort of Ross, the establishment of the Russians nearest to us. I examined the country and selected the position which seemed to me best for planting the colony. I established on the same frontier a post for the protection of the said colony, and returned to wait for it at the Capital.

On the 11th of September, one day before my arrival, I received an express from the Supreme Government, coming overland from Mexico, with the following Supreme Order:

"OFFICE OF THE FIRST SECRETARY OF STATE,
　　　　　"DEPARTMENT OF THE INTERIOR.

"The Most Excellent Señor President having been apprised of the contents of your despatch of the 18th of May last, in which you reply to the order which had been transmitted you, relieving you from the duties of Political Chief of that Territory, and say that you will deliver the command to Señor Hijar as soon as he presents himself, his Excellency has ordered me to say to you, in reply, that you must not deliver the said command, and that you must continue in discharge of the Government.

"God and Liberty. Mexico, July 25, 1834.

　　　　　　　　　　　　　　　　　"LOMBARDO.

"Señor Political Chief of Upper California, Don JOSE FIGUEROA."

By the same conveyance I received the first communications which Señor Hijar directed to me from the Port of San Diego, where he disembarked on the 1st of September with part of the colony. On the 25th the corvette-of-war Morelos arrived at the port of Monterey, bringing Don José Maria Padres, several employées, and the rest of the colony.

From this day commenced my difficulties, and it was easy to foretell the consequences. Señor Padres addressed me officially, asking assistance for the colonists which had arrived in his company, and this is the first notice which he gives me of his commission. The Supreme Government advised me nothing in relation to the undertaking of colonization: gave no orders to the officers of the Revenue through any channel that they should make any disbursements on the said colony; nor did it even so much as communicate to me that it had disposed of the person of Don José Maria Padres as a subdirector of the colony, he being of the army and coming to serve in his profession under my orders. Thus it is that in every respect the conduct of Padres appeared to me strange, and though he sought to satisfy me, showing me a despatch directed to him by the Minister of Relations, by which he conferred on him the commission of Subdirector of Colonization, yet that was not the mode in which he ought to have executed it, nor was *Padres* the channel through which a supreme order should have been directed to me; nor ought the Minister of Relations to have disposed of a military person without a previous order from the office of the Secretary of War. Notwithstanding this, it appeared to me prudent to keep silence and to give him to understand that my responsibility was not clear.

No payment ought to be made in the offices, unless a supreme order communicated through the established channels precedes it, and unless determined by some law approved by the Chambers of the Union in the estimate for the fiscal year; yet against all these express prohibitions and in spite of the urgent necessities under which the employées, civil and military, were suffering, I gave orders to succor the colony, in order that it might not be exposed to perish whilst application was being made to superior authority for the proper orders.

This is proof irrefragable of the incapacity, improvidence and want of calculation of the directors, who ought to have provided everything necessary for the people they were bringing under their charge, in order not to expose them to suffer from want: they should have known that it is more than twenty years that the salaries of the few military and civil officers of this territory have not been paid in full for the want of funds, and that besides increasing the necessities of these, they would compromise the officers of the revenue, as they were without orders to make payments to the colony.

As from San Diego to Monterey the distance is one hundred and eighty leagues, Señor Hijar did not arrive at this last mentioned point until the 14th of October.

I received him with public demonstrations of friendship and respect; I treated him with the greatest distinction and attention, and entertained him in the house in which I was residing. The first compliments passed, I showed him the order of the Supreme Government and the necessity I was under to obey it, although with much regret for any injury which it might cause to his feelings or his interests; I offered him with sincerity and good faith my small influence, and that I would engage the good offices of the most Excellent Territorial Deputation in procuring the Supreme Government to invest him with the office of Political Chief, and that in the meantime he should exercise the special commission of Director of the Colony; finally I offered him, that if he could propose any lawful means by which I could deliver him the command without compromising myself, I would do so with pleasure, as I was not ambitious of preserving it.

Señor Hijar, persuaded of my good disposition, convinced, perhaps, that he could not aspire to the command, confined himself to the special commission of Director of the Colony, of which the Government had made no express mention. I, although in doubt whether he should be considered as invested with this, after having been *divested* of the Political Government, saw no danger in his remaining Director of the Colony, and immediately agreed that he should exercise that commission, with the reservation of reporting the fact to superior authority. Then he demands of me to deliver him the property of the Missions, as a thing inherent in his said commission. I answered him that I was ignorant of the foundation of such a pretension, and forthwith he presents me a paper containing the following instructions:

"OFFICE OF THE FIRST SECRETARY OF STATE,
"DEPARTMENT OF THE INTERIOR.

"Instructions by which Don José Maria Hijar will regulate his conduct as Political Chief of Upper California, and as Director of Colonization of Upper and Lower.

"ARTICLE 1. He will begin by taking possession of the property belonging to the Missions of both Californias, and the Military Commandant, on his responsibility, will, whenever required, render the assistance necessary for said possession.

"ART. 2. For the space of one year, counted from the day the colonists arrive at the place in which they are to settle, there shall be furnished to each one of them four rials a day for such as are more than four years old, and two rials for those of lesser age.

"ART. 3. The expense of the journey by sea and land shall be on account of the Federation; the equipment which may have been bought for their transportation, shall be given to the colonists in full property.

"ART. 4. Villages shall be formed, uniting the number of families which may be sufficient for living in safety, choosing situations suitable from the quality of the land, from the abundance and *salubrity* of the waters, and from the mildness of the winds.

"ART. 5. It will be endeavored as soon as possible to make settlements on the frontiers.

"ART. 6. Topographical plans will be drawn, in which shall be designated and marked out the blocks of which the village is to consist. The length of each side of a block shall be one hundred varas, and all the sides shall be equal; the width of the streets shall be twenty varas, and no alley shall be allowed in them. The plazas shall be distributed at every tenth street at least, besides the greater plaza, which shall be situated in the center of the village.

"ART. 7. Care shall be taken to unite the Indians with the villages, mixing them with the other inhabitants, and no village shall be permitted to be composed of them only.

"ART. 8. In each one of the blocks, lots shall be distributed to the families, that they may build their houses, but it shall not be permitted them to do so outside of the line traced for forming the street.

"ART. 9. Outside of these villages there shall be given, in full dominion and property, to each family of colonists, four caballerias of land if it should be irrigable, eight if dependent on the seasons, and sixteen if of pasturage. There shall be given, also, four cows, four yoke of oxen, or two bulls, two broke horses, four colts, four fillies, four head of small cattle (two male and two female), and besides, two ploughs, with their gear.

"ART. 10. Between sowing lot and sowing lot of the land belonging to individuals, there shall remain vacant an extent equal to two sowing lots. The Government shall have the power to dispose of the lands left vacant when it sees fit, and the Director of the Colony shall prefer in that case, and under equal circumstances, the colonists whose lands adjoin.

"ART. 11. The distribution of the movable property belonging to the Missions of California being made, a sale shall be made of one-half of the remainder in the most advantageous manner.

"ART. 12. There shall not be sold to the same *family* more than one hundred head of cattle of one kind.

"ART. 13. The half remaining of the movable or self-moving property shall be preserved as the property of the General Government, and the proceeds thereof shall be used for the expenses of religious worship; the support of the Missionaries; the salaries of the Masters of the Primary Schools, for furnishing the things necessary for children of both sexes in the Schools; and for buying the instruments of husbandry which are to be distributed gratis among the colonists.

"ART. 14. The Political Chief and Director of Colonization will give at this time, and annually thereafter, a circumstantial account of the product of the property of the Missions; of its application; and of that which remains existing after the division of the movable and self-movable property among the colonists has been effected.

"ART. 15. He shall in the same manner give an account, at least once each year, of the condition of the colonists, of the obstacles in their way, if there should be any, and of the means of causing them to progress."

"LOMBARDO.

"Mexico, 23d April, 1834."

I replied that for my part these dispositions would be obeyed, although in my opinion it was an injustice to deprive the neophytes of the effects of the Missions, which they regarded as their property.

With this terminated the private conference which we had on the night of the 15th of October, and at dawn of the 16th I received the following official communication:

"DIRECTION GENERAL OF COLONIZATION IN THE CALIFORNIAS.

"In the orders and instructions of the Supreme General Government, which, as Director of Colonization, I have exhibited to you, there occurs the following article: 'ART. 1. He will begin by taking possession of the property belonging to the Missions of both Californias, and the Military Commandant, on his responsibility, will, whenever required, render the assistance necessary for said possession.'

"It being then of the greatest importance to begin my Commission, as well to avoid the deterioration which the Missions are suffering, as to better the condition of the Indians and establish the families of colonists which accompany me, I beg that you will be pleased to give your orders to the Commissioners whom you have named for the secularization, to the effect that they shall act under my directions, and to the Military Commanders of all the points of the Territory, that they shall furnish me or my agents, respectively, the assistance that may be needed for the object indicated. I repeat to you the protestations of my esteem and distinguished consideration.

"God and Liberty. Monterey, October 16, 1834.

"JOSE MARIA DE HIJAR.

"Señor Commandant General, Don JOSE FIGUEROA."

I answered with this other:

"POLITICAL GOVERNMENT OF UPPER CALIFORNIA.

"I will, as you request, notify the Commissioners of the Missions to act according to the orders which you may direct to them, and the Military Commanders to lend assistance in necessary cases, all in conformity with the dispositions of the Supreme Government, in the first article of the instructions which you have been pleased to transcribe me in your note of this date, to which I have the honor of replying. But you will permit me first to consult the Most Excellent Territorial Deputation, in order to obtain their consent, and to expedite in a better manner your functions in this Commission.

"God and Liberty. Monterey, 16th October, 1834.

"JOSE FIGUEROA.

"Señor Director General of Colonization, Don JOSE MARIA DE HIJAR."

Señor Hijar rejoined with the following:

"Direction General of Colonization in the Californias.

"By your note of yesterday's date I am apprised, with satisfaction, of your favorable disposition to second the orders of the Supreme General Government, first having consulted the Most Excellent Territorial Deputation concerning my Commission of Colonization. I beg of you, if it is possible, that this business may be finished today. The ruinous disorder in which are found many of the Missions where I have passed, the nearness of the time for preparing for wheat, which the Missionaries appear to have forgotten, undoubtedly because they fear to lose the control of the temporalities; the clamors of the Indians, who at the present moment are suffering infinitely; the colony, which I cannot *establish* until this is settled, and the shortness of the time to undertake the labors which must provide their subsistence during the whole year — all, all, Señor General, make it manifest that not a moment is to be lost. Finally, I address myself to you as the Military Authority, to beseech the assistance of which the first article of my instructions speaks, as I transcribed in my former communication, and I would grieve beyond measure that the disturbances and irreparable losses which delay may occasion should rest upon your responsibility.

"God and Liberty. Monterey, October 17, 1834.

"Jose Maria de Hijar.

"Señor Commandant General, Don Jose Figueroa."

The decided and tenacious endeavor to get hold of property whose owners are abject and helpless beings, the intimations which had been divulged by the colonists and Directors themselves, *concerning* the magnificent speculations of the pompous Cosmopolitan Mercantile Company, to which belonged the brigantine Natalia, which the Missions were to have paid for with seven thousand arrobas of tallow; and above all, the Supreme Government having sent an express with the sole purpose that I should not deliver the command, induced me to distrust these demands for the property, and I consulted with the Most Excellent Territorial Deputation, as in the following communications:

"Political Government of Upper California

"Most Excellent Senor:—The law of the 23rd of June, 1813, in its 15th article chapter 3, provides that in marked and grave cases, I shall take counsel of the Deputation, availing myself of their lights. The internal regulation of this body in art. 2, tit. 1, authorizes me to convoke it in extraordinary sessions. In use of this faculty I have ordered its meeting, which I now see with pleasure has taken place.

The cause which has induced this call is exposed; I am now going to lay before you the subjects which will engage your attention. The Supreme Government, under date the 15th of July, 1833, was pleased to relieve me from the duties of Political Chief of this Territory, naming in my place, Señor Don José Maria Hijar: under date the 13th of May of this year I answered that I was ready to deliver him the command as soon as he should present himself, and under date 25th of July last, the said Supreme Government by hurried express, commands me not to surrender to Señor Hijar, and to continue discharging the duties of political chief. All this appears by the documents which I have the honor to present, and pray that they may be read for the better understanding of your body. Señor Hijar was also named director of the colony which has just arrived, as appears from the supreme order which also I have the honor to present for your information. The Supreme Government when notifying me not to deliver the command to Señor Hijar made no mention of the other commission or commissions which it had granted him. Thus it is that, as that of Director of the Colony has a connection, so to speak, with that of Political Chief, I am in doubt whether being deprived of this office he has the authority to exercise that commission, and in what respect, since, although the one is not incompatible with the other, I lack precedents, for the Government has advised me nothing relative to colonization. The Most Excellent Vice-President, in virtue of the law of the sixth of April, 1830, is authorized to appoint commissioners for establishing colonies, and in my view Señor Hijar ought to carry out the undertaking with which he is charged; but desiring to make myself certain and not compromise myself in any respect I have thought it necessary to hear your advice, promising myself from your integrity and intelligence that you will suggest a decorous and conciliatory course. Señor Hijar, under date of 16th inst., has addressed me the note of which I have also the honor to send you the original; it contains inserted an article of the instructions which he received from the Supreme Government, and in conformity with this he prays that the commissioners named in virtue of the 20th article of the Provisional Regulations of secularization may act under his orders. And here arises a doubt for your consideration. Is Señor Hijar Director of Colonization and Secularization, or only of the first? His appointment says that he is Director of Colonies. Are colonization and secularization one and the same thing? No; but the Supreme Government commands him to take *possession* of all the property belonging to the Missions. In what character or capacity is the jurisdiction of these effects to be assumed? I do not understand it. Be pleased to consider this point and advise me what is most proper.

"God and Liberty. Monterey, 17th October, 1834.

"JOSE FIGUEROA.

"'The Most Excellent Territorial Deputation of Upper California."

"POLITICAL GOVERNMENT OF UPPER CALIFORNIA.

"MOST EXCELLENT SENOR:—Since I took into my hands the reins of the Government of this Territory, I have beheld with pleasure the constitutional course which, without obstacles or tumults, these peaceful inhabitants have pursued. I, as the depository of the public confidence, have venerated the laws in which repose the social guaranties; but one of those unforeseen accidents through which the genius of evil exercises its malign influence, seeks to snatch from us that enviable tranquillity which, to Californians alone, it is given to enjoy. Unexpectedly a complication of events has occurred which give rise to a divergence of opinion in the public mind, and it is not unknown to you what means are put in play to affect us with the exaggerated ideas which, unfortunately, are devouring our brothers in the interior of the Republic. The ostensible motive of discontent consists in the supreme order which I have laid before you, to the effect that I should not deliver the political command to Señor Don José Maria Hijar, who had been named to that office. Your Excellencies are apprised of the communications had in this respect, and know that I have had no part in the change, since I neither seek nor desire to continue in the office. I have discharged its duties, and I will continue to do so, so long as the Supreme Government and the dwellers on this soil honor me with their confidence; but if my continuing in command is to produce discord and discontent in the family of Californians with whom I am identified in feeling, I am resolved to renounce it. In proof of my disinterestedness, I have proposed to Your Excellencies that, if the duty of obeying is reconcilable with the public exigency, you should point out the means of which I should avail myself, and no other consideration will withhold me from surrendering the command. In conformity with this *protestation,* I now offer to Your Excellencies to make a voluntary resignation of the command, if at this price is to be preserved the tranquillity of Californians, whose fortunes interest me so much. My resolution is based on the public opinion, energetically manifested in favor of the separation of the political from the military command, and the conviction that the Supreme Government, interested as I am in the progress of this fortunate country, will approve my conduct, and esteem it as prompted by true patriotism and the result of circumstances. No sacrifice, most Excellent Señor—no sacrifice is costly to me for preserving the liberty and tranquillity of the Territory. I desire to be the only victim that shall be immolated on the sacred altars of concord. Let Californians be kept in peace, and upon me fall the consequences and the responsibility. The will of this nascent people is my North—Your Excellency is the organ through which it is to be expressed; may my prayers be fulfilled, and the desires of my compatriots satisfied.

"God and Liberty. Monterey, October 17, 1834.

"JOSE FIGUEROA.

"Most excellent Territorial Deputation."

I knew very well that the Direction of Colonization gave him no power to dispose of or administer the property of the Missions; but I wished to gratify his desires, and only sought to establish guarantees which should secure in his hands the safety of property for which I was responsible as Political Chief; but the subtleties with which it was sought to surprise me caused me to vary my intention, and to place the question in its true point of view.

The followers of Señor Hijar sought to mislead public opinion and to alarm the inhabitants of this Territory in order to expel me ignominiously, and furtively to get the control of the government. Subversive notions were propagated under the pretext of dividing the two commands in two distinct persons, and becoming independent of the Mexican Republic; the abject Indians were sought to be roused; interest and ignoble passions were put in play, and, in a word, it was sought to intimidate me by attempts at revolutions under various and specious pretexts, such as that the Most Excellent President of the Republic had changed the system of Federation, and, with an *armed* hand, destroyed the representation of the national sovereignty. My conduct under such circumstances is manifested in the protestation which I made to the Most Excellent Deputation: to obey the Government and not to oppose the general will. Behold my decision: I am commanded not to deliver the command to Señor Hijar, but I was ready to deposit it in the hands of the First Vocal, who is the person whom the law of the 5th of May, 1822, calls to the government in default of a Political Chief. Nevertheless, I desired to support my resolution with the voice of the representatives of the people.

The Deputation, in order to declare its opinion, referred the papers to a committee of its members, and these were the moments in which were most plied the means of policy, friendship and intrigue to deceive that body. Notwithstanding, it acted with the dignity which belonged to its office, and resolved as follows:

"MOST EXCELLENT SENOR: The Committee of Government report, That the unexpected events which have so justly attracted the public attention were presented in their true point of view, and from the protracted investigation which has been made of them, it results: that having resolved upon the separation of the political and military commands, the Supreme Government appointed Señor Don José Maria Hijar, which personage arrived at San Diego on the first of September last past, bringing also a colony of persons of both sexes, in the capacity of its Director. The same Supreme Government, for causes unexpressed, and in exercise of its authority, ordered that the command should not be turned over to Señor Hijar, and General Don José Figueroa should continue to discharge its duties. This incident has come to the knowledge of the public in an imperfect manner. The intention of the supreme order has been perverted, and it has been attributed to a change of system attempted by the President of th Republic. Such ideas and other invectives have been made use of in public to mislead opinion, a sufficiently long time manifested in favor of the separation of commands; an event of so much importance could but alarm men's minds; the liberties of the country and the fate of the Territory were involved, and no one could be indifferent to the discussion of the exercise of his political rights; but reason and truth make the darkness disappear, and thus Your Excellency ought to rectify public opinion, presenting in the face of the world events as they have occurred. We will not occupy ourselves in discussing whether the commands should be separated or not, because neither has the Supreme Government refused to do this nor are the inhabitants of this Territory deprived of the right of petition, nor will the Deputation, as the immediate representatives of the people, cease to make their voices heard before the Executive of the Union, and even in the sanctuary of the laws itself, demanding for their constituents the *exercise* of their political rights. The inquiry is simply, Who shall exercise the functions of Political Chief? The supreme order of the 25th of last July leaves no room for interpretations. It commands positively that the command shall not be given to Señor Hijar, and that General Figueroa continue to discharge its duties. Then what reason is there to induce us to oppose its mandate? It cannot be said that it was a rebellion or a usurpation of the attributes of the Executive power contrary to the forms of the Constitution. It will be objected that the Republic is in a state of convulsion; and because our brothers are divided by fatal discords, shall we cease to march in the constitutional path? No, most Excellent Señor; liberty subsists while the laws are respected, and unhappy the people who invade them on frivolous pretexts—anarchy is the result, and the consequences the annihilation of the fortunes and existence of the citizens. Let us free ourselves from the poisonous contagion of discord which is devouring our brothers, as nature has freed us by an impregnable wall. If the enemies of liberty and of order provoke them to the combat, we are not in that condition; and if, by misfortune, we should at any time find ourselves involved, we will know how to vindicate our rights. Let, then, for the present, the supreme order in question be fulfilled, and we will have discharged our duty, giving public testimony of our love of order and justice. At the same time, let a representation be made to the Supreme Government, that it may be pleased to decree the separation of the political command, this body proposing to it one or more persons competent to discharge those functions, and we dare to predict the best results.

"Señor Figueroa, impelled by his patriotism, offers spontaneously to surrender the political government, if necessary for the tranquillity of the Territory, taking upon himself the results and whatever responsibility he may incur; but the public tranquillity is secured under his command, and there is no occasion to make that change. The Deputation, who narrowly observe his conduct and watch over the common good, know that he has not failed to deserve the public confidence, and founded in this idea, ought to continue to him their gratitude, with the reservation of recalling him to order if at any time he should go astray. Señor Hijar being invested with the double office of Political Chief and Director of the Colony which he has brought with him, we see that the superior authority *deprives* him of the functions of the first office, and makes no mention of the second. The Committee might consider it as inherent in the first, and that he was deprived of both at the same time, by virtue of the before cited supreme order; but, adhering to its literal sense, is of opinion that he may continue in his special commission of Director of the Colony which he has brought, as his appointment expresses, for which purpose there should be furnished him such aid from the Missions as may be in the power of the Political Chief, without prejudice to the Indians, and the other demands annexed to those foundations, since the expenses of the colonies ought to be borne either by the fund called the Pious Fund of the Californias, according to the decree of the 26th November, 1833, which gave the Government authority for that purpose, or by the Federation, according to the decree of the 6th April, 1830, which we pray may be read; but in no manner by the property of the Missions, which are the exclusive fruit of the immense labors of the neophytes of the Missions, and the only patrimony that awaits them in remuneration for an age of slavery. By what right, then, shall these unfortunates be despoiled of the fruit of their labor and privations? Will they not say, and with justice, that they belong to a leonine partnership? This, Most Excellent Señor, is the occasion when, arising above fine theories and prepossessions, the imperious voice of justice should make itself heard by supreme authority, in order that in vindication of humanity it should cause the property of our unfortunate compatriots to be respected. It is not, Most Excellent Señor, the Government which disposes of this property; it is the courtiers who, adorned with the cloak of patriotism, invoking sacred liberty and the public good, deceive the good faith of the Chief Magistrate of the Republic and draw from him orders which, calculated in their opinion to insure the happiness of men, are the cause of their ruin, and overwhelm them in misery. Let the veil, then, be stripped off, and let us cause the Most Excellent Señor the President, with the respect due to his high position, to see, that if His Excellency believes he is doing good to the Indians, the instructions conferred on Señor Hijar sanction the despoiling them of their property, for the purpose of applying it to objects, which if in other respects they are to be promoted, it should be without detriment to that unfortunate class of our brethren who groan still in the darkness of ignorance, and that to Your Excellency, as one charged to watch over and promote their happiness, it belongs to defend their rights, not with theories and sophisms, but founded in the eternal principles of justice. Men have united in society to secure their lives and property, and it is not possible to despoil them of the least part of their property without violating the pact and common right of nations.

"These incontestible principles being established, the Committee is of opinion that the execution of the instructions given to Señor Hijar should be suspended in that part which commands him to take possession of the effects of the Missions, distribute them, and convert them into money; and that a representation should be made to the Supreme Government, inserting this report, praying that it may be pleased to revoke that order; that the property of the Missions may be distributed among the Indians and in objects for their benefit, they being its only owners; that so far as the colonists may be assisted with a part of that property, it shall be on condition of reimbursing the owners out of the Pious Fund of California or out of the public treasury. From these premises it follows, that the property of the Missions ought not to be placed at the *disposal* of Señor Hijar, because not being entitled to assume the office of Political Chief, neither ought he to take any part in the execution of the law of secularization. The instructions which he presented expressly say in the heading, 'Instructions by which Don José Maria Hijar will regulate his conduct as Political Chief of Upper California and Director of Colonization in Upper and Lower.' The literal sense of these orders leaves no doubt that they empower him as Political Chief, and in no manner as Director of Colonization, which appointment gives him no political authority; it has no functions conferred by any law, and the Supreme Government, acting under the existing laws in relation to colonization, has only delegated to him the authority of conducting the colony, establishing it, and distributing land to it. That appears in the supreme order of the 16th of July, 1833, and in the instructions of which we have made mention; but it is necessary to repeat that the said instructions were given to him as Political Chief, and in this sense the place where the colony should be established was left to his choice; but being deprived of that office, he is subject to the present Chief, and must obtain his assent in all that relates to the place where the families are to be settled. In brief, his special commission is that of Director of the Colony, and this if he can exercise it in accord with the said Political Chief, from whom he is to receive instructions and the necessary assistance, in conformity with the supreme orders relating to this business. The colonists deserve our consideration; they have come under the protection of the Supreme Government; they shall be looked after and distinguished in entire conformity with the promises of superior authority, since the change of the person who exercises the political authority ought not to operate against the lot of these families, who, relying on the public faith, have come to live with us. We will lavish upon them our esteem, and the union of brotherhood, under the protection of peace, will enable them to bear the hardships of solitude. The Californians, Señor, are hospitable, and will divide with pleasure their fortunes among all people who approach their homes. The public awaits the conclusion of this drama, and to guard it against seductions of lamentable excess, the Committee thinks it should be informed of what has happened, causing this report and the resolution of the Most Excellent Deputation to be published, to show distinctly the foundations on which its determination rests, in order to avoid sinister interpretations. Wherefore, it submits to your Excellencies the following propositions:

"1. That the Supreme Order of the 25th July of this year, to the effect that the *command* be not delivered to Señor Don José Maria Hijar, and that Don José Figueroa continue in the discharge of the functions of Political Chief, shall be obeyed.

"2. That Señor Don José Maria Hijar, if he pleases, may exercise the special commission of Director of Colonization, in subjection to the Political Government of the Territory and the bases which the Deputation may prescribe for that purpose.

"3. That Señor Don José Maria Hijar shall not interfere in the secularization of the Missions, nor shall their property be delivered to him, as he solicits.

"4. That until the Supreme Government determines what it may deem proper, the provisional regulation for the secularization of the Missions, adopted by the Deputation, shall be carried into effect, and the *Indians* shall be put in possession of their property and lands.

"5. The Political Chief, out of the stock on hand belonging to the Missions, shall order to be furnished to the colonists the tools and other aids that the instructions call for, as soon as they arrive at the place where they are to be established, drawing the said supplies pro rata, in order not to damage any one Mission. For account of the allowance designated to each person, there shall be furnished to them grain and meat, and whatever is most necessary for their maintenance. The Director of the Colony shall be subject to the Political Chief, and shall give him a circumstantial relation of the number of persons engaged in colonizing, and an estimate of the amount of the payment to be made to them each month, in order that in this respect the supplies may be regulated proportionably. The lands of the Missions belong to the Indians, and no colony shall be established in them.

"6. The Political Chief shall retain in his possession the instructions given by the Supreme Government to Señor Hijar, to whom he will send an authentic copy of them, if he should need them, returning him the Supreme Order of the 23d of April of this year, with which he accompanied them.

"7. That this report, and the resolution which may be adopted, be laid before the Supreme Government for its superior approbation, and that a representation be addressed to it, praying it to revoke the instructions in so much as despoils the Indians of their property, and to approve the Provisional Regulations made by the Deputation; that a reverential petition be addressed to it, praying the separation of the Political and Military Commands, proposing three persons of those who may be considered competent.

"8. That this report, and the resolution which may be adopted by the Deputation, be published and circulated for the information of the public, as early as may be possible.

"JOSE ANTONIO CARILLO,

"PIO PICO,

"JOSE J. ORTEGA.

"Monterey, 21st October, 1834."

The foregoing questions affected the public, and all were occupied in their discussion; various individuals who believed their interests touched, and not being able to conceal their sentiments, divulged in their indiscretion the whole plan, making public matters which for their own honor they ought to have kept secret. Then they allowed to be seen the avarice which agitated their souls and the unmeasured ambition which devoured their hearts; then were disclosed the obligations to which the property of the Missions had been subjected; then were made public the mercantile undertakings of the Cosmopolitan Company, which counted on no other funds for its business than the capital of the Missions; then in fine was made the boast that the Government itself, that is, Gomez Farias, consented that one of the estates of the Pious Funds of the Californias should be encumbered, mortgaging it for the value of fourteen thousand dollars, at which the brigantine *Natalia* was contracted for, and which were to be paid in tallow of the Missions of California; a project truly unjust, as no benefit was to result to these communities; it was said with the same publicity that the Cosmopolitan Company was going to monopolize the interior and exterior commerce of the Territory, placing a house in each mission or pueblo and the necessary vessels on the coast for the transportation of foreign and domestic goods, and for the exportation of the products of the country; here was the true object of the colonial expedition which cost the nation such sacrifices; this was the end to which were directed the efforts of Señor Pades, and which he be praised to us even to disgust, as inspired by the most eminent patriotism. The people knew the attack which was preparing against property and the bankruptcy which threatened the only capital which constituted the public riches and the ruinous monopoly which was in contemplation; thus it is that the pretensions of Señors Hijar and Padres openly conflicted with public opinion, and this is the origin of the censure which was afterwards visited upon them. Blind in their erroneous caprices, they resorted to other means less becoming to attain the result which they desired. Señor Hijar, offended in the highest *degree* by the resolution of the Most Excellent Deputation, answered me with a communication full of gratuitous imputations; he addressed it to me with some insults, which I attributed to an excess of bile or want of reflection, and without noticing them I waited on him in person to assure him of my friendship and to beg him to come into a conference, in order that we might discuss the matters between us, and avoid disagreeable altercations; I offered to show him the laws, orders and regulations on which the Deputation founded the said resolution, and if he proved to me that these laws were repealed, the resolution should be changed; thus it was agreed, and on the 25th and 26th of October we met; Señor Don José Maria Hijar, Don José Maria Padres, Don José Antonio Carillo, Don Pio Pico, Don José Castro, the Judge of the District, Licentiate Don Luis del Castillo Negrete, Licentiate Don Rafael Gomez and I. The discussion was opened by reading the communcation of Señor Hijar, which, as it embraces different points, I will insert, divided into sections, which I will proceed to refute in their order to the conclusion, as it was the moving cause and object of the conference.

"DIRECTION GENERAL OF COLONIZATION OF THE CALIFORNIAS: —I have received your note of yesterday's date; it contains an order of the General Government not to deliver to me the political command of the Territory which had been confided to me, an exposition made by you to the Most Excellent Territorial Deputation, upon the subject of the evils which the execution of the order before referred to might create, because of the desire which exists in the country for the separation of the military and political governments, and finally, eight propositions, approved by the said Most Excellent Deputation, and in which it seems that you concur. I could *desire* that the subjects had been treated with due separation, but since it has not been thought proper to do this, I will answer the propositions in the same order in which they are expressed. In so much as regards the order not to deliver the political command of the Territory, I have nothing to object, as it emanates from the same Government which appointed me; I am a respectful servant of the Government, and will never disregard its orders when these are confined to the orbit of its power, only I am surprised that nothing has been communicated to me that I may know whether my functions have ceased altogether, or whether you are to continue in certain circumstances only; but this is not a question which it concerns us to resolve, and consequently it would be useless to discuss it at this time."

The supreme order of the 25th of July that I should not deliver the Political Government to Señor Hijar is very positive; colonies, according to the regulations of the 4th of February, 1834, article 9, shall be transported under the direction of persons designated by the Government; and according to article 10, "they shall be subject to the political chief or chiefs that the Government shall designate." There can be no doubt then that the functions of Señor Hijar ceased altogether. Nevertheless, the Deputation say that although they might consider him as deprived of both offices, that is, of Political Chief and Director of Colonization, they are of opinion that he may continue in the special commission of Director of Colonization, in subjection to the Political Government of the Territory. It appears that this is very agreeable to the wishes of Señor Hijar, although the title of Director of Colonization is not an office defined by any law.

"I have nothing to say of the *exposition* made by you to the Most Excellent Deputation, since you ought to know what is the situation of the Territory and the opinion of its inhabitants; nor will I add anything on the first proposition which the Most Excellent Deputation approved, as it is in conformity with the principles which I have before laid down. The second proposition is to the effect that, if it pleases me, I may continue directing the colony, in subjection to the Political Government and to the leases which the Deputation may establish. The two conditions with which this proposition concludes are certainly remarkable—the first, from the useless declaration that every man, without any exception of privilege, must be subject to the local authorities; the second is an attack upon the General Government, upon me, and upon the colony. Who has empowered the Most Excellent Deputation to make bases of colonization? How is it that the Most Excellent Deputation pretends that powers are annulled which belong only to the Congress of the Union or the General Executive, when, as in this case, empowered by the Legislature? How many aberrations general, and to what a lamentable extent! If I should continue to direct the colony under other bases than those which the Supreme Government gave me, I would commit treason against the Government which appointed me; I would be false to the confidence with which it honored me, and to the duties of a good citizen, in recognizing the orders of an illegitimate power, such as is that of yourself and the Most Excellent Deputation in the present case. If I submit to the bases of the Most Excellent Deputation, it follows that I will not be Director of Colonization. And who has authorized you, or the Most Excellent Deputation, to deprive me of a special commission, conferred on me by the Supreme General Government? The colony which I have conducted neither can nor ought to be governed by other bases than those which were given me by the Supreme Government. When tearing from their homes the three hundred persons who accompany me, it offered them certain conditions, which must be fulfilled if there is any desire to preserve the honor of the Government. On the other hand, what guaranties could the bases of the Most Excellent Deputation offer, if, as I have said before, they emanated from an illegitimate power? Consider that I am a Director of Colonization, and not only of the colony which has arrived—consequently the natives of the country, and strangers, if they like, have a right to colonize; but if the bases should be changed all will decline, for want of security, and the misfortune will fall upon the Territory, which is so much in want of useful hands."

The Deputation never had the vain pretension to attribute to its determinations the force of law, and for the very reason that it observes the limits of its own authority, it desired that the Director of Colonization should evince a proper dependence on the Government. The Deputation and myself have not pretended to dictate general bases of colonization, but we believed that we ought to establish certain rules for that which was going to be established in this Territory, because the laws have given us sufficient power to do so. If it is doubted, let the Spanish Constitution, which governs in this Territory, and the law of the 13th of June, 1813, titles 2 and 3, be examined. I will not delay to copy these articles, in order not to be too prolix, as Señor Hijar is convinced that "every man, without any exception of privilege, must be subject to the local authorities," and because the Deputation, which never desired to *oppose* the laws and orders of the Government, explained its meaning, expressing the proposition in the following terms:

"That Señor Don José Maria Hijar, if he pleases, may exercise the Special Commission of Director of Colonization, in subjection to the Political Government of the Territory, and to the laws and regulations established on that subject."

And Señor Hijar will see that the proposition which he has combatted is not, as he says, an attack upon the General Government, upon his person and upon the colony; and that although we could lawfully prescribe bases for the establishment of the colony, we refrained from doing so, in order to avoid a merely nominal contest, since Señor Hijar submits to the Territorial Government, and the power which it exercises is not, as he supposes, illegitimate, but emanates from the laws which designate the manner of its transmission to the citizens who hold public office.

And what are the powers of a Director of Colonization? I do not know, but I believe that he has no powers, because it is not an office. The title originated in a project of a law introduced in the Chamber of Deputies of the General Congress, and was taken from thence to be given to Señor Hijar; but as the regulation of the 4th of February, 1834, subjects the colonies which may be established to the Political Chiefs appointed by the Government, and as Señor Hijar ceased to be Political Chief, it is clear that the appointment of Director of Colonization conferred upon him no political authority; yet, notwithstanding this, the Deputation respected him as one commissioned by the Supreme Government, in proof of which I have not attempted to deprive him of that office, as the said Señor Hijar falsely asserts.

Certain it is that the colony ought to be established in conformity with the bases prescribed by the Supreme Government; but this does not prevent it from being in subordination to the Territorial Government, nor can this subjection interfere with the conditions proposed to it—consequently the honor of the Government is preserved and the right of the stranger and native remains intact; and no one has thought of interfering with it.

"The third proposition declares that I shall take no part in the secularization of the Missions, and that their property shall not be put at my disposal. This resolution is scandalous, and like the former, an attack upon the General Government, and is subversive. I have never sought to meddle with the secularization of the Missions, and consequently do not know what is the object of the first part. The Supreme Government, authorized by the decree of the 26th November, 1833, commanded that I should take possession of the property of the Missions, in order to apply it to the purposes which it judged to be proper, and in the proposition under consideration that resolution is absolutely disobeyed. It is certainly a scandal that the persons charged to obey the laws and orders of the Government, and see them executed, should be the first to set the example of disobedience—lamentable example, which tends to the *overthrow* of the whole social order. Where shall we stop, if every one goes on disobeying the laws at his pleasure? To a state of nature, in which the stronger is master of the weak. Reflect that in the act of approving this resolution you have authorized the law of insurrection. If yourself and the Most Excellent Deputation believe that you have a right to attack the laws, every other person may make use of the same right, and the pact terminates. And more: a citizen may do all that the laws do not prohibit, but you and the Most Excellent Deputation can only do that which they prescribe; and your principal duty being to obey them and cause them to be obeyed, your infraction is so much the more remarkable, and your disobedience the more scandalous, as you attack the law which you disregard and those which impose upon you the obligation to see the rest obeyed. How will you punish a soldier for the infraction of a law, if you yourself and the first authorities have given him the scandalous example? I will conclude this branch by asserting that this proposition is subversive, because it tends directly to subvert social order, as I have shown; it is scandalous, because it gives a sad example to inferior persons, and is an attack upon the Supreme Government, for the same reasons which I have given in regard to the former propositions. Neither the Political Chief nor the Most Excellent Deputation can nor ought to set themselves above the orders of the Government. To obey, and to petition if evils are felt—such is the conduct of an upright magistrate and good citizen; but disobedience will always be most disastrous to a people."

Señor Hijar, in his communications of the 16th and 17th of October, which appears on the 12th and 13th* pages of this writing, requests me to command the commissioners whom I had named for the secularization of the Missions to act under his orders; he prays that the effects of the said Missions may be delivered to him, and in effect he asks that the administration of their temporalities may be abolished, and this is not to interfere in the secularization of the Missions? If this is not so, in what respect does he seek to control them, and with what title does he seek to hold their property? Look at his communications referred to, and say whether the administration of the temporalities is or is not annexed to the secularization of the Missions. For this cause I consulted with the Most Excellent Deputation whether Señor Hijar was Director of Colonization and Secularization, or only of the first, and for the same cause the Deputation

---

*Pages 8, 9 and 10 in this edition.

in the argumentative part of their report, to be found at page 20*
of this *writing,* paragraphs four and six, declared with much propriety the grounds upon which it was induced to advise the third
proposition, which caused Señor Hijar such strong sensations. From
that exhibition it is to be understood that there was a very good
reason for saying in the first part of the said proposition, "that Señor
Don José Maria Hijar shall not interfere in the secularization of
the Missions."

Señor Hijar, multiplying the catalogue of sarcasm and invective,
asserts that the Supreme Government is authorized to dispose of
the property of the Missions by the decree of the 26th of November,
1833, and that we have disobeyed its orders; in order to answer this
charge, we will first examine the said decree; it is as follows:

"The Government is empowered to make all necessary orders to
insure the colonization, and render effective the secularization of
the Missions, of Upper and Lower California, and for that purpose
to use, in such manner as may be suitable, the estates of pious works
of said territories in order to furnish resources for the commission
and families now in the Capital with that destination."

I do not understand logic, but it appears to me that Señor Hijar
is in the same condition, for he only has understood that this decree
authorizes the Supreme Government to dispose of the Missions; persons who have thought on it understand that it empowers the Government to render the secularization of the Missions effective, and
that is not to be done by stripping the neophytes of their property.
Secularization, says the Spanish dictionary, is "the act or effect of
secularizing"; "secularization is to make secular that which was ecclesiastical—to withdraw a person or thing from the class of regulars."
Besides, the law of the 17th of August has determined the manner
in which the secularization is to be made, and in none of its articles
does it command that the Government shall take possession of the
property of the neophytes; on the contrary, it exempts it from burdens decreeing that the parish priests, who are to be substituted to
the Missionary Friars, and the expenses of worship are to be provided for out of the estates, capital and revenue of the Pious Fund
of the Missions of California. The consequence which follows from
all that has been said is very clear, and by no forced construction
which may be given to the decree of the 26th November, does there
appear the authority which Señor Hijar supposes in the Supreme
Government to dispose of the property of the Missions, since the
only power which is conferred on it is to dispose of the estates of

*Page 18 in this edition.

pious works to fit out in Mexico the commission and the families destined for these territories, but the *property* of the neophytes was not in Mexico, nor is a part of the estates of pious works. By what has been said it is demonstrated that far from disobeying the laws, we have compelled Señor Hijar to respect them and comply with them.

Certain it is, that the Supreme Government, in the instructions inserted at page 11, commands to take possession of and distribute the property of the Missions. On whom does it impose its execution? On the Political Chief; and as Señor Hijar was deprived of this office by the supreme order of the 25th of July, which appears at page 8, I cannot understand how he ventures to demand the exercise of a power which by no title belongs to him.

The administration of the temporalities, while they remain undivided, pertains only to the Territorial Government, and in no manner to the Director of Colonization. This is the import of the instructions themselves on which Señor Hijar pretends to base his claims, and so the laws, of whose content he shows himself ignorant, expressly determine.

It being sufficiently proved that the Supreme Government has not been empowered to dispose of the property of the neophytes, the imputation that we have disobeyed the laws is refuted; nor do we disobey the order of the Supreme Government, for to petition is not to disobey. The Supreme Government commanded the Political Chief to take possession of the property of the Missions, distribute one portion among the colonists, and realize the other; we are sure that the Government did not calculate on the losses it was going to occasion; it would not have dictated such an order, and this error, which involves an infraction of the fundamental law, was concealed from the Government under the appearance of a benefit. It is easy to understand the false ideas with which it was sought to inspire the Government when it permits and commands the spoliation of property belonging to more than twenty thousand persons. The Territorial Government, in straits between the duty of obeying a supreme order and of preserving the property of the humblest class of their fellow-citizens, sought the means of conciliating both extremes, and adopted the measure of suspending the *occupation* of the temporalities, taking out of them as much as was absolutely necessary to sustain the colony, on condition of reimbursement, and of petitioning the superior authority and praying the revocation of an order as unjust as unconstitutional. In this manner we believed that we would respect and comply with its orders, save its responsibility and ours before the laws, insure their observance, and protect the property of our unfortunate fellow-countrymen. Little or no injury would result from this measure, and, on the contrary, it would be very difficult, and perhaps impossible, to restore the neophytes their property, if the spoliation should be accomplished. Well we knew that this course would not comport with the interest of Señor Hijar, but neither could we prefer the pretensions on an individual to the fate of more than twenty thousand persons, nor should the respect due to the Supreme Government oblige us to consummate the ruin of so many families without making a representation to the superior authority, which perhaps was ignorant of the nature of the case. This was the object of the following note:

"POLITICAL GOVERNMENT OF UPPER CALIFORNIA.—No. 38.

"MOST EXCELLENT SENOR: Since the receipt of the law of the 17th of August, of the year last past, by which the secularization of the Missions of this Territory was sanctioned, we have been waiting with anxiety for the Supreme Government to forward its execution by means of a detailed regulation, which should determine not only what related to the spiritual administration, but should embrace the distribution of the property existing in each one of these communities. After having waited a year for the instructions of the superior authority, and not being able to delay for a longer time the effects of a law so beneficial, so much desired, and so much solicited by the neophytes themselves and by all sensible men: the Territorial Deputation, making use of its powers, with due solemnity, framed the Provisional Regulation, which, under date of the 9th of August last, I addressed to Your Excellency, soliciting the superior approbation of the Government. Then and always the neophytes of the Missions were reputed the owners of the property pertaining to them, because all was acquired by their personal labor in community under the direction of the missionary friars, who, as tutors, have administered and economized the property remaining after maintaining, clothing and supplying the necessities of the subjected natives, as minors, whose education had been committed to them by the Government. Thus it is that the estates, the temples, real and self-moving property, and whatsoever exists in the Missions, has been acquired by the labor and privations of the Indians. The public treasure has never been applied, directly or indirectly, in aid of this property; in the beginning, the first foundations were made at the cost of the missionaries themselves; afterwards they were assisted by the piety of individuals who donated various sums, with which was raised the Pious Fund of the Missions of California. Out of this fund were given, as alms, four hundred dollars a year to each *friar*, with which their wants were supplied, and a thousand dollars, once only, by way of temporal outfit for each Mission and for the cultivation of the soil; the more ancient aided the new with a few things, and this was the only assistance which they received in their origin; all the rest was acquired by the constant labor of the Indians. Thus attests the Regulation of 1781, in title 15, art. 2, and thus thought the Junta for promoting the interests of the Californias, in the exposition which they addressed to the Supreme Government, the 6th of April, 1825, proposing to it a plan for the better regulation of these Missions. For this reason, and because the right of property which the Indians have in the property which they possess under the tutelage of the Government and the immediate administration of the Missionaries, is unquestionable, the Deputation did not hesitate in determining that the half of it should be adjudicated and distributed to them in full ownership, reserving the other half for the disposition of the Supreme Government, in such applications as it might think proper to commend them to make for the benefit of the same Indians—as for paying the teachers who educate them, for funds to support their pueblos, for paying the parish priests who serve them, the expenses of worship, and other expenses which may arise. This is entirely in conformity with justice and in accordance with the directions which the Supreme Government gave to Echandeia, Victoria and myself, in the instructions which were given us on confiding to us the office of Political Chief. Resting upon such strong foundations, and because it considered Señor Hijar without power to dispose of the property of the Missions, to the prejudice of more than twenty thousand Indians, who only are its owners, the Deputation opposed the delivery of it, in the manner which Your Excellency will observe in their resolution of the 22d of October last past, of which I transmit you a copy of this date [No. 5], by which it decided as follows: 'That until the Supreme Government determines what it may deem proper, the Provisional Regulation for the secularization of the Missions shall be carried into effect, and the Indians shall be put in possession of their property and lands; that this *opinion,* and the resolution which may be adopted, be laid before the Supreme

Government for its superior approbation, and that a representation be addressed to it praying it to revoke the instructions insomuch as despoils the Indians of their property, and to approve the provisional regulations made by the Deputation. And I have the honor to enclose it to Your Excellency, together with a copy of the instructions by which it is commanded to take possession of the property of the Missions, give a portion to the colonists, and of the remainder, convert one half into cash, without purpose or rules to insure the safety of the proceeds, and to reserve the other half for the pay of parish priests, teachers, expenses of worship, &c., &c.' No mention is made of the Indians, who are the owners of this property, and it is indeed a violent spoliation. We believe this has happened through forgetfulness in the office of the Secretary, but never from the deliberate intention of the Government to deprive more than twenty thousand indigent persons of the fruit of their toils, the only inheritance which they have received from their forefathers. Señor Hijar, in his communication of the 23d October, maintains that neither are the Indians the owners of this property nor ought the Deputation to command them to be distributed; he thinks that the Indians ought to continue in the same servitude without other difference than paying them hereafter their daily wages. Truly, Most Excellent Señor, in that case, it were better not to change their situation, because it would be to make their evils worse. Señor Hijar says they should be commanded to collect the property which already has been distributed to them, as the most sensible course. Such a proceeding, we believe, has existed only in the head of Señor Hijar. Against principles so erroneous, justice, policy and humanity revolt. All the world knows that the Indians, by their industry and labor, have acquired and preserved the property of the Missions; have subsisted upon it and possessed it since the time when, through choice or force, they were made Christians. Then who shall deprive them of it without attacking the social guaranties? The Federal Constitution [art. 112, restriction 3d] says as follows: 'The President shall have no power to take the property of any individual or corporation, nor disturb him in the possession, use, or enjoyment of it; and if in any case it should be necessary for an object of known general utility to take the property of an individual or corporation, he shall have no power to do so without the previous approbation of the Senate, and in its recess, of the Council of Government, making always such compensation to the person interested as may be determined by arbitrators to be chosen by him and by the Government.' It is thus seen, Most Excellent Señor, that the Supreme Government has not the power (I speak with due respect) to dispose of the smallest part of the property in question. If it does so in the manner prescribed in the Constitution, 'for an object of known general utility,' there ought to have preceded also the approbation of the Senate or of the Council of Government; this requisite failing, it is the duty of the subaltern authorities to represent the unconstitutionality of the order. This is the position to which the Deputation and I find *ourselves* driven, and by reason of which we reverentially declare to Your Excellency that, besides being unconstitutional, the order is unreasonable, since it commands a part of the property, without just reason, to be converted into money, and without determining its application or ordering it to be paid into the Federal Treasury. It is true that part is to be applied to the payment of the colonists, but not the whole. Besides, this expenditure ought to be borne by the Federal revenues, for which purpose the Government is authorized by the laws of the 6th of April, 1830, and 21st November, 1833; but no law authorizes the spoliation of the property of the Indians to apply it to the colonies. Señor Hijar says that the Government is authorized to do this by the law of the 26th November, 1833; but this is a mistake, as the law is literally as follows: 'The Government is empowered to make all necessary orders to insure the colonization and render effective the secularization of the Missions of Upper and Lower California, and, for that purpose, to use in such manner as may be suitable the estates of pious works of said Territories, in order to furnish resources for the commission and families now in the capital with that destination.'

"Will it be inferred that by this law the Government may dispose at pleasure of the property of the Indians? Is spoliation of property the way to make secularization effective? The Deputation has not *understood* it thus, nor believes that the Supreme Government can interpret it as Señor Hijar does. The Deputation deduces from the whole that the instructions referred to were given either under excessive pressure or obtained by surprise, and concludes with praying Your Excellency that you will deign to think carefully on this lengthened exposition, and to obtain from the Most Excellent President the due approbation of the provisional regulation, in which it is commanded to give the Indians possession of their liberty, property and lands, and to declare null and of no force the 1st, 11th, 12th, 13th and 14th articles of the instructions given to Señor Don José Maria

Hijar on the 23d of last April, as well because they are notoriously unjust, as because, being deprived of the political command, neither ought he to exercise the powers in question. Finally, Most Excellent Señor, the Deputation and I are submissively obedient to the laws and the constituted authorities, but, at the same time, we desire to be right, for the sake of our own responsibility, and for the honor of the Supreme Government. This it is which has induced us to discuss so delicate a subject. If we err, it will be for the want of understanding, and in that case we implore the indulgence of the superior authority. And we also pray Your Excellency to assure His Excellency the General President of our respect and subordination, and that at all times we will obey his mandates with pleasure.

"God and Liberty. Monterey, 9th November, 1834.

"JOSE FIGUEROA.

"The Most Excellent Secretary of Internal and External Relations."

I believe that I have sufficiently proven that we have not disobeyed the laws nor the Supreme Government, as Señor Hijar falsely charges us. This admitted, what is the bad example that we have given? What the overthrow of social order? What the disobedience, what the insurrection that I authorize? And what, in fine, the multitude of errors with which he seeks to defame my conduct? Where are the infractions that so scandalize my detractor? Let only one be shown; but by facts, and not by that jargon of words, which signifies nothing. The proposition is subversive, asserts Señor Hijar, because it tends directly to subvert social order; and in what is this calumny founded? In that I would not consent to the usurpation of property of a multitude of citizens; this is my fault.

I leave this business to the judgment of sensible men and of the Supreme Government; but, in the meantime, I may be permitted to ask Señor Hijar by what right he upbraids me? What power has he to reprove me? Is this the duty of a citizen? Is this the manner which the laws prescribe to enforce the responsibility of public functionaries? Can Señor Hijar disobey me with impunity? Who has authorized him to disown my authority and declare me a violator of law? It must be admitted how much more scandalous is the resistance of Señor Hijar to the orders of the Territorial Government, than that of this Government in regard to the delivery of the property of the Missions. Señor Hijar in fact insults and disobeys the authorities lawfully constituted, and this is an offense which ought to be punished. We prevent Señor Hijar from committing, in the name of the

Government, the outrage of plundering the property of citizens, in violation of the Federal Constitution and of the social guaranties, and this is a virtue in the opinion of honorable people. But it was reserved for Señor Hijar to reproach me, because I would not tolerate his robberies and frauds.

Let us make a slight analysis of the application which was to be made of this property which Señor Hijar contends for. One part was to be applied to the maintenance and establishment of the colony; another was to be converted into money, and for what purpose? Señor Hijar only knows, for the instructions do not say. Another part was to go to the expenses of worship and schools and the support of ministers. And in what law is found the authority to plunder one class of citizens to benefit another? In none. What say the laws concerning the foundation of colonies? That of the 18th of August, 1824, established the general bases of colonization; that of the 6th of April, 1830, empowers the Government to colonize such lands as it may deem proper, having first contracted for them and paid for them to the States to which they belong, and to *expend* five hundred thousand dollars in aid of colonization. The same law designates a source of revenue to be applied exclusively to colonization, and gives the Government, in fine, other attributions, which it would be too prolix to refer to. The law of the 21st November, 1833, authorized also the Supreme Government to expend the sums necessary to colonize the Territories and other vacant places where it had the right to do so.

That of the 26th November, 1833, authorized the Supreme Government to take measures to insure colonization.

The Vice-President of the Republic, in exercise of the Supreme Executive power making use of the authority which the law of the 6th April, 1830, confers upon him, framed on the 4th of January, 1834, the regulation for the government of the colonies which should be established; but no law empowers the Supreme Government to convert the property of the Missions to the purposes of colonization.

I will say nothing of the alienation which was required to be made, because this is an unfathomable mystery about which much is to be inferred and nothing can be proved.

In regard to the payment of the salary of ministers, and the expense of worship and schools, no one can be ignorant of its utility and advantage to the owners themselves, and this provision is in force from necessity; but it will be seen that the law of the 17th of of August, 1833, commands that the salaries assigned to the parish priests shall be paid out of the Pious Fund of the Californias; by what right, then, shall we impose burdens upon the property of the most needy class of citizens? I find no provision of law to justify such an act.

"The fourth proposition insists on carrying out the provisional regulation. At every step the violations of law accumulate more and more, and it is inconceivable how so respectable a body should persist in such a manner, not only in disobeying, but in opposing the dispositions of the Supreme Government. By what right can you and the Most Excellent Deputation dispose of property which by no title has been subjected to your inspection? No law, no provision, has authorized you to make an appropriation of funds which do not belong to you, and of which you could not dispose without a Supreme Resolution; how will you and the Most Excellent Deputation respond to the charges which may be made for this arbitrary conduct? What security will the possessors have to whom the effects of the Missions may pass, if neither you nor the Most Excellent Deputation were authorized to transfer them to any corporation or person? If the regulation in *question* should not be approved as solicited, how much confusion is going to be produced! It would be necessary to retake the property out of the hands of the possessors, and then disappointed hope would cause a thousand discontents, and heap up, consequently, an accumulation of evils which would put the territory in consternation. It is insisted on carrying out a regulation, which, if executed, would certainly cause the ruin of the Territory; I pass over, Señor General, the contradictions which it involves and the slavery to which the natives remain subjected; the great difficulty in policy consists in finding the means of withdrawing the Indians from the slavery and nascent state in which they are, to a state of civilization and liberty. Neither you nor the Most Excellent Deputation have appreciated this difficulty. With a facility which is frightful has been decreed the formation of pueblos and institutions of Ayuntamientos in the same manner that you would legislate for civilized people, and with all the necessary elements at hand, what will be the consequence to these new pueblos of a change so novel and sudden? That which has happened in all countries and in all nations where the same course has been attempted; they will be lost, and I appeal to history. Everywhere a people has been violently translated from a state of slavery to one of freedom, it has been wholly unable to follow the flight of its leaders; they have lost sight of them and gone astray. Such is the fate prepared for this Territory by its rulers. I regret infinitely having to touch upon a question which did not concern me, but in view of the persistence to carry into effect a regulation which infallibly must in time produce evil, I have deemed it my duty to make these slight observations upon it."

Various are the charges and accusations which Señor Hijar makes against the Territorial Government, but they are all without foundation, as I shall demonstrate. The first charge is because it is insisted on putting into operation the Provisional Regulation, from which Señor Hijar deduces that the violations of law are accumulating more and more, and that the Deputation is determined to disobey and oppose the dispositions of the General Government.

The Provisional Regulation in question is that which the Territorial Deputation framed to facilitate the execution of the law of August 17th, 1833, in regard to the secularization of the Missions; in it is prescribed the manner of distributing to the neophytes of each Mission the lands which they possess, and also a part of the other property of which they are also in possession, because they are the lawful owners of the whole. The Deputation has done nothing more than obey the law and propose to the Executive the method of putting it into execution; this act is peculiarly within its functions, and it had the legal power to frame the regulation, in order to present it to the approbation of the Supreme Government, as well because local knowledge was wanted, which no one possesses so fully as this body, as because the law of the 23d of June, 1813, and the Spanish Constitution, which *governs* in this territory, impose upon it the obligation to do so; that authorizes it in divers manners, and by art. 14 of chapter 2, commands it to present to the Government the plans and projects which appear to it most suitable for the encouragement of agriculture, the arts and commerce; this, by article 335, attribution 10, empowers it to watch over the economy, order and progress of the Missions.

If this will not suffice, look to the laws of the Indies, from whose pages shine out the wisdom and charity with which that code was dictated in favor of these same Indians, whom, under the free government of Gomez Farias, it has been sought to rob even of the property which they have acquired by their personal labor. The Territorial Government is not ignorant, like Señor Hijar, of the privileges which the Indians have enjoyed under the dominion of the

Spanish Government; it has kept in mind the laws 9, of tit. 3, lib. 6; 14, tit. 4, lib. 6; and 5, 7 and 9, tit. 12, lib. 6, of the Recapilacion of the Indies. By these it is commanded that the Indians shall not be deprived of the lands where they live, nor be molested; that these shall be preserved for them and distributed to them as their own; that their property shall not be converted to other *objects* than their benefit and those for which their pueblos were established; many other directions and provisions are made, but all in favor of the Indians, with heavy penalties against violators. It had in view the laws of the 13th of March, 1811, 9th of November, 1812, 4th of January and 13th of September, 1813, which have provided for the division of their lands among the Indians.

It was intended, my antagonist will say, to confer political importance on the Director of Colonization, and that for this end no means ought to be omitted; for this reason he sought to place his powers in competition with those of the Government, and after the great parade with which they challenged the public attention, there resulted!—what the mountain brought forth!

The laws which governed these establishments from their foundation, subjected them to the Territorial Government, and no one except Señor Hijar has rejected its authority in this respect. He does not know or does not understand what is contained in the laws which I have cited, and this only can serve as an excuse for the audacity with which he abuses the Territorial Government, denying its powers. Let Señor Hijar know, then, that the Government has given its protecting guaranties to preserve this property and adjudicate it to its true owners; that these, not yet having emerged from the abject state in which nature placed them, and being children in civilization, without the use of reason or knowledge of their interests, it is the duty of the Government to discharge the functions of a common father, and afford them every species of protection; this is the obligation of a just Government. And shall it be vituperated because, from miserable pupils it converts them into free proprietors, distributing to them their own lands? Perchance the law of the 17th of August, 1833, is not limited to this single object? It is not to withdraw them from the ecclesiastical estate to which they were subjected, and to redeem them from the servile pupilage in which they have lived? All of us are convinced of these truths.

Admitting that the neophytes are removed from the economical government of the Missionary Friars, they remain unquestionably subject to the Political Government, which is under obligation, by the law of the 23d of June, 1813, to establish its local authority, in accordance with the laws applicable to the subject matter; it ought also to distribute among them the property which they have acquired in community, for this has ceased to exist, and they enter upon the enjoyment of the rights of citizens. These were the grounds upon which the Territorial Deputation acted in projecting the regulation in question and presenting it for the approbation of the General Government—a course which partakes in nothing of the arbitrary, commits no violation or disobedience of law, and opposes no order of the Supreme Government; a course, in fine, worthy of the approved zeal of this body for the *well-being* of its constituents; but notwithstanding the justice with which it undertook the task, it met with the opposition of the Political Chief, who from delicacy, and because he was in hope that his successor would bring the law, as regulated, opposed the opinion of the Deputation, and postponed for more than six months the formation of the said regulation. I was aware that Señor Don José Maria Hijar was coming to relieve me, and I did not wish to anticipate his judgment in regard to carrying out the secularization; neither did I desire to undertake it, because I knew the delicacy and difficulty of its execution, and the afflicting results which it would produce, if carried out simultaneously and with precipitation. My opposition, for these and other reasons, was public and notorious; but as the evil was caused, and it was my duty to obey the laws and see them fulfilled, I was compelled to submit to the force of circumstances, against my own convictions. I make no merit of this incident to vindicate myself, but that it may be judged whether or not I have proceeded with integrity and frankness.

I believe that, after this explanation, Señor Hijar will no longer doubt that the property of the Missions is subject to our control, and that we ought to have regulated the manner of distributing it among its proper owners; the error of supposing that no law authorizes us to make an appropriation of these funds is demonstrated. In this manner we reply to whatever charges may be brought against us for the supposed arbitrary conduct of which he accuses us.

Another of his charges is to the effect that the persons to whom the property of the Missions may be transferred will have no security, because neither I nor the Most Excellent Deputation have the power to transfer it to any corporation or person. Señor Hijar may know, if he is ignorant, that to transfer, is "to cede or pass that which is possessed to another person," and as the fact is, that we only regulate the mode of distributing property among the possessors themselves, it results by necessary consequence that we have not ceded nor passed over anything from one owner to another, and that the possessors of the said property have sufficient guaranties of its enjoyment; because no one but Señor Hijar has disputed their right of property and possession, which they have enjoyed without interruption under the protection of the Government from the foundation of the Missions. And who but Señor Hijar can doubt that the Supreme Government will approve the regulation of secularization? We may be sure that he prophesies falsely that the property will be retaken from the power of the possessors; and that this injustice could be committed only under his *auspices* and never by the assistance of the Supreme Government, which has always respected the property of its subjects, and, with more reason, that of the class of citizens whom its considers minors, and who live under its guardianship. How is it that the regulation will cause the ruin of the Territory, as Señor Hijar asserts? Will it be, perchance, because he will not enjoy at pleasure the fortunes of the neophytes? They alone have the right to enjoy the fruit of their labor, and this it is, exactly, which displeases Señor Hijar.

Señor Hijar says, mysteriously, that he passes over the contradictions which the regulation contains and the servitude to which the natives remain subject. I would be pleased if he would point out the contradictions, and the servitude of the natives, which he condemns, in order to answer his objections; but to suppose, without facts or evidences, argues calumny or bad faith.

Neither the Deputation, nor I, he says, take the trouble to examine the means of withdrawing the natives from slavery to a state of civilization and liberty; that, with a facility which is frightful, has been decreed the formation of pueblos and the institution of Ayuntamientos, as if we were legislating for civilized people. This, to my judgment, evinces an inconceivable contradiction—because he supposes and complains of the servitude of the neophytes, and at the same time objects to the excessive liberty which is granted to them; but, passing by the multitude of redundancies which are not to the purpose, I will limit myself to showing that the Deputation has only taken care to *maintain* the natives in the dependence necessary to preserve among them good order and subordination, so as to avoid the excesses and aberrations to which, from their stupid ignorance, they incline. It has taken care, at the same time, not to attack their liberty or the social guaranties. These facts prove the foresight with which we have endeavored to withdraw them from slavery to a state of freedom, without overlooking the difficulties of the change. Very great obstacles have we had to overcome, and long before the law of secularization we represented its inconveniences, not that it should be suspended, but that it might be determined upon more partially and gradually, because in this way it would be more suitable to the character and circumstances of the natives; but as it has not been cared to listen to the opinion of the local authorities, and as at that time the same Señor Hijar, who now censures us, and the Adjutant Inspector, Don José Maria Padres, were urging in Mexico the passage of the law which was to enrich them, it was not deemed proper to reflect upon what the Political Chief represented. The law was passed, and certainly it is not the Territorial Government that passed it; that granted, neither ought it to be responsible for bad results, for it has done nothing but obey the laws and cause them to be obeyed, avoiding, as much as lay in its power, the aberrations of men translated suddenly from slavery to liberty. Señor Hijar wonders that pueblos should be formed, when the Territorial Government only gives them the name, while they have existed in reality for years under the title of Missions; but, perhaps on this account they ceased to be pueblos? Certainly not. Look at the definition of this word, and it must be confessed that they have always been pueblos. In the same manner he is surprised at the institution of Ayuntamientos, although it is one of the principal duties of the Territorial Government to see that they are established where there are none; thus expressly provides the law of the 23d of June, 1813, chapter 2d, art. 1, and the Constitution, in art. 335. Señor Hijar may also know, that if the laws which regulate the government of pueblos are not appropriate for those of natives, the fault it not with the Territorial Government, because it has no power to change or reform them, but is bound to apply them without restriction. Likewise prophesies Señor Hijar, that the natives will not be able to follow the flight of their leaders, because they have been torn with violence out of a servile condition into that of freedom; that they will be lost, as has happened in all nations where the same course has been adopted. These facts he attests with history, and ends his discourse prognosticating the ruin of the natives due to their rulers; that is to say, to the Territorial Government. I will not trouble myself with proving that the fears of Señor Hijar are panics, because, in his opinion, the neophytes ought not to emerge from pupilage, nor ought property of any kind to be given them, because they are unworthy to possess it, nor could they then be compelled to cultivate the fields of their feudal lords. Such are his philanthropical ideas; on such bases was he projecting to systematize the political government of the neophytes of the Missions, and those to whom he would do a great favor he would consider as colonists, and give them a little piece of land. Señor Hijar will permit me to remind him of these notions, expressed in various conferences which we held, and that I refuted him, contradicting absolutely his opinion. He will remember, very well, that I defended with the same laws the right which the neophytes have to be put on an equal footing as to their possessions with the rest of the citizens, and their preference to have adjudicated to them the lands and property which they possess, acquired by their personal labor and that of their forefathers; neither could I agree that they should be considered as colonists, because they are proprietors established on the land where they were, and for other reasons, which it would be tedious to mention. Grant that all are not able to follow the flight of their leaders on account of the state of ignorance in which they exist, still the beneficent measures which have been dictated in their favor ought not, on this account, to be omitted; some will go astray, but many will succeed, and the result is always a good for society and an advance in civilization; it is proposed not only to convert them from pupils into proprietors, but to educate them and make them industrious; and if this is never begun, they will never issue from the miserable sphere of slaves. It is necessary to suffer them to make this dangerous transit, in order that they may reach the end; and this certainly is not to tear them with violence from the servile state into that of freedom, as Señor Hijar falsely asserts; because they are not abandoned to themselves, but remain under the protection and aid of the Government, subject to peculiar laws and regulations. I know not to what nations Señor Hijar compares them, and for this reason I am unable to answer his argument. He *blames* the Territorial Government, according to his custom, for the bad results which he predicts, without other data than his own assertion, supported by a play of words which signify nothing in substance.

He confesses, finally, that these questions do not pertain to him,

but seeing it was insisted to carry out the regulation, which in time
must produce evil, he felt himself obliged to make those slight observations. Much more honorable to him would it have been to take
no part in the questions, admitting, as he frankly confesses, that
they do not concern him. Indeed, by what power does he object to
the decrees of the Territorial Government, when his authority as
Political Chief has ceased? Why so much acrimony against the Territorial Government because it seeks to distribute property to its
lawful owners, and will not deliver it into the mortmain possession
of Señor Hijar? It is necessary to repeat that the fate of the natives
concerns him little or not at all, and that the only motive for his
ill-digested discourse springs from seeing escape from him the abundant capitals in which he desired to exercise an exclusive brokerage,
under the pretext of colonization, and with notorious injury to those
who accumulated the property. Upon this were calculated those magnificent schemes of happiness which Señor Hijar and his followers
so much lauded, even to launching out upon the arrogant presumption of being called the redeemers of the Californians. If, as he confesses, that it was not his business to discuss these questions, he had
abstained from meddling with them, I would have been spared the
necessity of publishing his ambitious pretensions.

"The fifth proposition is devoted to the regulation of certain of
your proceedings and of mine, and to declaring, with the firmness
of a legislator, that no colony shall be established in the lands of the
Missions, because they belong to the natives. As to what relates to
me, I have nothing to say, since I am resolved to observe no instructions but those which were given me by the Supreme General Government, as they are the only legitimate ones to the present time. I
would make myself contemptible before men, and be an unworthy
son of Jalisco, if I should be so weak as to lower myself to recognize the orders of an erratic authority, which, going out of the orbit
of its own functions, seeks to usurp those committed to the high
powers of the Union. It is not you nor the Most Excellent Deputation who are to regulate my proceedings in respect to my commission. The laws govern me, and not *caprices* nor arbitrary will. If it
is believed that the lands belong to the Indians, how is it that by
your regulation it is only commanded to give them, as a maximum,
a little patch of four hundred varas square and the insignficant portion for pasturage in common? How many contradictions, Señor
General! It appears to be only intended to deceive the miserable

natives—abusing their candor. This is not the place, nor is it for me to investigate the right of property in the soil, with which it is sought to indoctrinate the natives to the total exclusion of the eminent right of the Government; but, if I may be permitted to say so, this doctrine will be disastrous to those who have proclaimed it, and prejudicial to the prosperity of the Territory."

In order to *answer* the different charges of Señor Hijar against the Government, it will be necessary to repeat the contents of the fifth proposition which he has combatted. The language is as follows:

"The Political Chief, out of the stock on hand belonging to the Missions, shall order to be furnished to the colonists the tools and other aids that the instructions call for, as soon as they arrive at the places where they shall be established, drawing the said supplies pro rata, in order not to damage any one mission. For account of the allowance designated for each person, there shall be furnished to him grain and meat, and whatever is most necessary for their maintenance. The Director of the Colony shall be subject to the Political Chief, and shall give him a circumstantial relation of the number of persons engaged in colonizing, and an estimate of the amount of the payment to be made to them each month, in order that, in this respect, the supplies may be regulated proportionably. The lands of the Missions belong to the Indians, and no colony shall be established in them."

I appeal to the judgment of sensible men to say whether the provisions are within the competency of the Territorial Government, and whether they are in conformity with the spirit of the laws. But to avoid mistakes, I will answer briefly to the objections of Señor Hijar.

Says this gentleman, that he is resolved to observe no instructions but those which he received from the Supreme Government, and that he would make himself contemptible if he should be so weak as to lower himself to recognize the orders of an erratic authority which has usurped the powers of the Government of the Union. Already have I demonstrated, and Señor Hijar so confesses, that his office of Political Chief has ceased, and with it all its inherent powers, including those given by the instructions which he received from the Supreme Government. But it is very painful to him to relinquish a power which so much excited his hopes, and he fears not to contradict himself, provided he can wound the respect which he owes to authority. He has said that all men, without any exception of privilege, must be subject to the local authorities, and that it was useless to make that declaration, and thereupon replies that neither I nor the Most Excellent Deputation can regulate his proceedings. I have also demonstrated that by the regulation of the 4th of February, 1834, the colonies are subjected to the Political Chiefs that the Government may appoint, and were so by the civil law. I have proved that the Deputation and I are empowered by the laws to regulate the proceedings of Señor Hijar as Director of the Colony, however disagreeable it may be to him. In the same manner, I have proved the legality of the jurisdiction which we exercise, because it emanates legally from the supreme power, which has confided it to us, with the formalities which the laws prescribe. Thus it is that we do not know in what Señor Hijar makes the illegality and usurpation to consist. But, however against his will, he must be *subject* to the Territorial Government, and obey its mandates without questioning them, because he lacks authority to do so; and even in the hypothesis that we should exceed our powers, he would only have the right to bring us to justice and enforce our responsibility according to law, but never to disobey us. Wherefore, I repeat the question, Who is Señor Hijar—to disown my authority and declare me a violator of the law? Is he, perchance, a jurisconsult, unexceptionable in the present case? He is surely nothing more than a subject, and a subject without jurisdiction, independent of the Government, as he pretends.

Señor Hijar says, ironically, that, with the firmness of a legislator, we declare that no colony shall be established in the lands of the Missions, because they belong to the natives. Before going further, I will prove that it is not a decree of the Territorial Government, but a positive provision of the law of 18th August, 1824, whose second article is as follows:

"The subject of this law are those lands of the nation, which, not being private property nor belonging to any corporation or pueblo, may be colonized."

The Supreme Government regulated this law on the 21st November, 1828, and in the 17th article prescribes the following:

"In the territories in which there are Missions, the lands which they occupy shall not be colonized for the present, and until it may be determined whether they should be considered as the property of the settlements of the neophyte catecumens and the Mexican founders."

What has been said will suffice to convince that it was not the wantonness of the Territorial Government which induced it to dictate that order, but a positive provision of law, which is not repealed, and does not admit of interpretation.

All the laws which I have cited give the neophytes a right of property in the lands which are recognized as pertaining to the Missions, a right which the Spanish Government during its domination respected, and which no one, up to the present time, has disturbed them in; but even if this were not so, is it not certain that they are favored by the natural and civil possession as to which no one can raise a doubt? Will Señor Hijar deny to them that they were born on the land which they have been cultivating under the guardianship of the Government, now more than fifty years? Will they, in spite of their inertia, cease to know and believe that they are the owners of the land which they cultivate, and of the property which they have *acquired* by their labor? This is very certain, notwithstanding all the efforts to render it obscure. Señor Hijar asks, if the lands of the Missions belong to the Indians, "how is it that by your regulation it is only commanded to give them as a maximum a little patch of four hundred varas square, and another insignificant portion for pasturage in common?" The regulation is not mine, but framed by the Territorial Government, and the satire of Señor Hijar comes very ill; this little square was designated to the Indians at first, because they are not considered capable of cultivating a greater quantity, and because it is sought to distribute the superfices of the land in proportion to the number of individuals who are considered entitled to it, leaving the door open to appropriate it to the industrious ones who may devote themselves with most earnestness to its cultivation. It is false that the land designated for pasturage in common of the cattle of the neophytes is so small, as Señor Hijar asserts, and the proof is that no certain quantity was determined, but it was left to the judgment of the commissioners to enlarge or diminish it in proportion to the greater or less number of the cattle, and the extent of the land belonging to each Mission. Besides the land which was to be given to each individual in full ownership and property, it was designed to designate common lands and assign to each pueblo, as municipal lands, a certain quantity of land, for the purpose of employing its products in the common benefit of the pueblo; but Señor Hijar did not fix his consideration upon these points, and his criticism has no other foundation than the unjust gratification of his resentment; his vague exclamations are absolutely without support, and his imputations are so many calumnies. It appears (he says) to be only intended to deceive the miserable natives, abusing their candor. And in what manner will Señor Hijar prove his assertion? With silence, because he has no facts to present, as he has skill in inventing gratuitous calumnies. Señor Hijar may know that the Territorial Government has believed in good faith that it was doing a positive good to the natives in all the provisions which it has dictated in their favor, and in fact, how could it be a deception to give them landed property and liberty to acquire and enjoy whatever goods of fortune their industry might obtain for them? And although they should not attain these positive advantages which have nothing illusory about them, has Señor Hijar forgotten that governments, as the wise Bentham says, have to choose among evils, the least? Señor Hijar confesses, unwillingly, that it is not his business to investigate the right of property in the soil which is taught the natives, with total exclusion of the eminent right of the Government, but that this doctrine will be disastrous to those who proclaim it, and prejudicial to the Territory. If it does not belong to him to inquire into this matter, by what right does he reproach the Territorial Government? Therefore, that scurrilous style is excessively disrespectful, if not criminal. It does not belong to him to inquire, and yet he has the audacity to deny openly to the neophytes not only the right of *property* in the lands which have been ordered to be adjudicated to them, but even in the chattels which they have acquired with their personal labor; this is apparent throughout his discourse, and I refer more expressly to the divers conferences which he had with me on that subject; if Señor Hijar esteems himself a gentleman, he will not deny the truth of this. And what is the eminent right of the Government? I do not know, and I have proved by the Constitution, that the Government has no power to take the property of any individual or corporation. Nor does Señor Hijar say in what consists this eminent right. He holds it very wrong in us to impress the natives with their rights, and a little before accuses us with subjecting them to an ignominious servitude, and that neither the Deputation nor I appreciate the difficulty of withdrawing them from a state of slavery to one of freedom—that we snatch them with violence from that to precipitate them upon this, to their destruction; in the next breath he says that it is only designed to deceive them, abusing their candor, &c., &c. Behold! a lengthened series of inconsistencies which the author himself cannot explain by the rules of reason. And for what reason will it be disastrous to us to impress the natives with their rights? Let us leave to the selfish to lament the progress of our unfortunate natives, while we respect the rights of man, whatever may be his origin. The Territory will by this be prejudiced in the opinion of Señor Hijar, but whence does he deduce such results? I know not; he seeks to be believed upon his assertion, but that is no proof.

"The sixth proposition is devoted to commanding instructions given me by the Supreme Government, to be retained. This resolution has surprised me beyond measure; never did I believe that the good faith with which I sought to comply with the desires of the Most Excellent Deputation, sending them the original instructions, as they requested, with the utmost courtesy, even to proposing to me to show them, if not inconvenient, could be abused to such a degree. By what right am I deprived of that which belongs to me as my property, while the Supreme Government does not relieve me of the Direction of Colonization? I am amazed, Señor General, and never believed that a body so respectable would assail me in a manner which violated its honor and delicacy. For what end are my instructions retained? In truth, I cannot comprehend. If it is to petition against them, I would have given a copy whenever requested. If it is that they may have no effect, it would suffice if the Political Chief had placed at the foot of the order, 'not to be executed in this Territory.' There being no authority then, for retaining a document which belongs to me, and having to execute my commission in other parts beyond the Territory of your command, I hope you will be *pleased* to return me my instructions for consequent ends."

The instructions were retained because they were committed to the Political Chief of Upper California, and not necessarily to Don José Maria Hijar; it is an official document, which belongs only to the Government itself, and not to Señor Hijar, as he improperly pretends; it ought to exist in the archives of the Government, which is the office of the nation; it ought, in fine, to remain in the power of the Political Chief, who alone is charged by the Constitution and laws with their enforcement, and that of the decrees of the Supreme Government. Without pausing to cite all which has been decreed on the subject, I will quote only articles 1 and 17, chapter 3, of the law of the 23d of June, 1813, which are as follows:

"1. The Political Government of each province, according to

art. 324 of the Constitution, being in charge of the Political Chief named by the King in each one of them, in him vests the superior authority within the province to watch over the public tranquillity, good order, security of the persons and property of the inhabitants, the execution of the laws and orders of the Government, and in general all that belongs to the public order and prosperity of the province; and as he will be responsible for the abuse of his authority, he shall likewise be punctually respected and obeyed by all. Not only shall he have power as the Executive to enforce the penalties imposed by the laws of police and decrees of good government, but he shall have the power to impose and exact fines from those who disobey him or treat him with disrespect, and from those who disturb order or the public peace.

"17. The Political Chief only shall circulate through the whole province all the laws and decrees which may be promulgated by the Government, causing them to be published in the capital of the province, and the Territorial Deputation to be made acquainted with them, and taking care to forward them to the interior Political Chiefs, if there should be any, or to the First Alcaldes of the principal towns of the district, for the same purpose. The Political Chief, being responsible for the circulation of the laws and decrees, he will require *receipts* from those authorities to whom he transmits them."

This being so, how shall the Territorial Government execute the orders of the Supreme Government without having knowledge and evidence of them? Or shall Señor Hijar, by himself and before himself, execute them independently of the Political Chief? What kind of authority is it that he exercises? What foundation has he for saying that the instructions are property which belongs to him? If the public employees should in the same way pretend to make themselves owners of the laws, orders and documents which they receive, there would be no archives, and all would be confusion. Besides these reasons, the Territorial Government was apprehensive that he would make a bad use of the instructions, as in fact their fears were afterwards verified, and for that reason commanded them to be retained, with no other object than to endeavor, if possible, to execute them and to avoid the abuses of the Director of Colonization. The Territorial Government was under the necessity of acting in that manner, because neither had it received other orders, which put it in a clear light, because communications had been made to Señor Hijar only while he held the office of Political Chief; but those functions having ceased, no jurisdiction remained to him as Director of Colonization, and to him, as such, it was the duty of the Political Chief to communicate the orders of the Supreme Government contained in the said instructions in relation to his office. In any other manner, how could Señor Hijar comply with those Supreme Orders? Should he act with entire independence of the Political Government? Let him show whence spring those powers which he desired to exercise. But his silence confirms my opinion, and vindicates me from the abuse which has been lavished upon me. In spite of the foregoing, the instructions were delivered to him, to show our deference for all that is compatible with duty. And what has it availed him? Nothing; because of necessity he has applied to the Political Chief to sustain their execution with his authority and orders. This is a fact which Señor Hijar cannot deny.

"The seventh proposition comprises various petitions which the Most Excellent Deputation deems proper to address to the Supreme Government, and I should have nothing to say about them; but as it appears that the revocation of the instructions, in so much as deprives the Indians of their property is prayed for, I believe it my duty to declare that this idea would only originate in some mistake, or in the different conception that we have formed concerning the property of the Missions. The Government, far from depriving the natives, commands me to make them proprietors, and give them possessions which, up to the present time, they have not had; they were going to enjoy a real and true good, as soon as I should be in condition to exercise my commission, but you and the Most Excellent Deputation have not deemed it proper; consequently, not upon me will fall the responsibility."

This is a hallucination, Señor Hijar! So soon have you forgotten that you only desired to get control of the property of the Missions, to distribute part among the colonists, and convert the rest into money? Is it not certain that not one word is said in the instructions in favor of the neophytes? Is it not certain that the first article of the said instructions directs you to take possession of all the property belonging to the Missions, using the military force in aid of said possession? Is it not certain that by this article the neophytes were plundered of the property which they have acquired by their personal labor, and which they enjoy in peaceful possession? Is it not certain that in this act is involved a violent spoliation? Will Señor Hijar deny that on the various occasions that we discussed this business, he maintained, that to insure the happiness of the neophytes, it would suffice to give them their liberty, and pay their daily wages regularly to those who should engage in the labors of the Missions? Is it not certain, that in order to relieve himself from the *remarks* which I made in favor of the property of the neophytes, he answered me that as to anything further, those who solicited land to cultivate, should be regarded as colonists? And he had the boldness to assert with emphasis that he is going to make them proprietors, when he seeks to strip them of the lands and goods which they possess. And is not this to abuse the very meaning of words? Such inconsistencies are the offspring of the heated fancy of the Director of Colonization.

"The eighth proposition is, that the resolution of the Deputation be published. Be it then published, although it is to be regretted that some facts have been misrepresented, and what is more lamentable, to the discredit of the General Government, which we both ought to sustain. Some day the whole of this affair will see the light; all men will be informed of the reasons of both parties. They will compare them and decide."

The day which Señor Hijar predicted has now arrived; the public is about to be informed of these much noised events, and will decide in favor of him who has justice on his side. If to petition the Supreme Government against one of its orders which attacks the Constitution and violates the social guaranties is a discredit to that Government, the fault is not with the inferior authorities who are obliged to make it known, or become themselves accomplices in the violation by executing it without examination. No dishonor can result to the Secretary who signed the order, by revoking it, if he is convinced that it is unconstitutional, because he is not infallible, and may very well have been mistaken.

"I would have desired to know by what accident the decision concerning the delivery of the Political Government came to be mixed up with the special commission of colonization before the Most Excellent Deputation; but you have not thought proper to inform me; I would have considered it a great favor, in order to *correct* mistakes which must have been committed, since in no other manner can I conceive how measures so anarchical, turbulent and widely involving social order could have been adopted."

What does Señor Hijar understand by anarchy? The Spanish dictionary says it is "a condition of things which has no head to govern it." This definition is very badly applied by Señor Hijar in the pres-

ent case, since the measures Señor Hijar calls anarchical are adopted
by the Constitutional Government of the Territory, whose authority
is legitimate, as I have proved; the power which it exercised in adopting those measures is a part of its attributions, and their object is
to call to order Señor Hijar, who seeks to deviate in contravention
of the laws. This Señor Hijar calls anarchical and turbulent measures, which only are so to the extent that the novelty of such strange
pretensions caused commotion in the public. "In view, then, of all
that has been said, I beg you that listening to the voice of your conscience and of reason, you will be pleased to change your opinion,
duty and the laws so requiring, and I hope you will think proper to
return me my instructions without the necessity of a new demand—
this restoration being in every light just."

I have already shown that the instructions, notwithstanding they
belonged to the archives of the Territorial Government, were returned to Señor Hijar, but in nothing else was there any change of
opinion; because far from convincing, his vague exclamations pro-
voked a lengthened examination into the laws by which the Government verified its operations and carried them forward. "I conclude
with begging you to be pleased to make known to me your last
resolution, in order to regulate my ulterior proceedings, and I hope
that you will be pleased to excuse the austere languages of a repub-
lican who demands the fulfillment of the laws."

It is not to demand the fulfillment of the laws, the language that
Señor Hijar has used, for I have proved to him the contrary. The
public shall say whether republicans have the right to violate social
principles and disobey the authorities.

"After *concluding* this communication, I have heard of the publication of the resolution of the Most Excellent Deputation, and according to what I observed in the argumentative part of the report
of the Committee, the whole ground for not complying with the
orders of the General Government consists in considering the instructions with which we are engaged as annexed to the office of
Political Chief. You will allow me, for the sake of moderation, not
to express the idea which I have formed of so remarkable a mistake.
The despatch with which they were transmitted to me, and which
you have returned to me, says literally:

" 'I transmit to you, by order of the Most Excellent Vice-President, the instructions by which you are to be governed in the discharge
of your commission relative to the colonization of California, and

at the same time inform you that the Secretary of the Treasury has given an order to the Commissary General of Jalisco to place at your disposal whatever money he may have received from General Don Joaquin Parres, in order that you may be able to comply with the directions contained in the said instructions.'

"Let the children at school be asked if these instructions are directed to any other than the Director of Colonization! My commission extends equally to Lower California, according to the orders which I have, and in that territory I had no political character. It appears then, beyond a doubt, that the special commission was conferred upon me as Director, and not as Political Chief. I have the honor to reiterate to you the assurances of my esteem and distinguished consideration.

"God and Liberty. Monterey, October 23d, 1834.

"JOSE MARIA HIJAR.

"The Political Chief, General Don JOSE FIGUEROA."

After having filled us with abuse and reproaches, he seeks to make a show of modesty and moderation. In this spirit, he asks that it may be permitted him not to express the idea which he had formed of so remarkable a mistake. If such is his intention, for what purpose does he address us the sarcasm of asking the children at school whether the instructions were given to the Political Chief or to the Director of Colonization? I, on the contrary, appeal to the judgment of sensible men, to say to whom were directed the instructions beginning as follows: "Instructions by which Don José Maria Hijar will regulate his conduct as Political Chief of Upper California and as Director of Colonization in Upper and Lower."

There is nothing peculiar, that in the despatch with which the said instructions were sent, he should be commanded to regulate the discharge of his commission of colonization by them, because this, as I have proved, is inherent in that of Political Chief, with which also he was invested, and by the act of depriving him of that, he was relieved from the other. On this account, the Deputation, advising me that he might go on directing the colony, affixes the condition that he should be subject to the Territorial Government. But the artifice of setting up some authority suited the after views of Señor Hijar, in order to give an appearance of strength to the specious *pretensions* of his partisans. Such is the foreseeing policy of the Director of Colonization.

I have combatted the libel of Señor Hijar with the arms of reason, and although I called upon him to show me the repeal of the laws, ordinances and regulations on which the Territorial Government based its resolutions, I have not obtained the satisfactory answer which I sought. To the truth of this, testify all the persons who were present at the conference. The Señor's Licentiates, Don Luis del Castillo Negrete and Don Rafael Gomez, being requested to state their opinions, both corroborated the view which I had explained, and added arguments, doctrines and laws of much weight, which, coinciding in all things with the conclusion of the Territorial Government, Señors Hijar and Padres were unable to overcome truths so fully demonstrated. Then, feigning to be taken by surprise, or because they really were so, they sought a truce, to reflect and answer satisfactorily, or to admit that they were convinced, and by all means to put an end to controversies so heated and violent. As our object in soliciting the conferences was only to avoid public scandal and animosities, we assured them of our deference in everything compatible with our honor and obligations, and we agreed that we would meet again on the following day, to continue the conference.

So it happened; but before meeting I received from Señor Hijar this billet:

"At home, October 26th, 1834.

"MY GENERAL AND FRIEND: I consider it important that we shall have a secret interview before the meeting. Come, if you can, to this place immediately after breakfast, or designate a point to me. Your most affectionate friend,

"HIJAR."

My answer was to present myself before Señor Hijar in the house of Don José Joaquin Gomez, where, in spite of my prayers and entreaties, he had taken *lodging* two days before—slighting my friendship and habitation in which I had entertained him; but making no mention of these occurrences, I offered to serve him in whatever he might find me useful. Then—Oh, fatal moment, how would I blot you from time!—he proposed to me that if I would deliver him the property of the Missions, he would protect my private interests with that property, with the effects which he could command in Mexico and Guadalajara, and with his credit and connections which he would use in my favor in whatever manner best suited my business, and finally, that he would place at my disposal an account for twenty thousand dollars or more, which he would solicit in Mexico or Jalisco, if I so desired, on condition that the Missions should be delivered to him; that this was accomplished if I was willing to do it, because the Most Excellent Deputation would follow my advice without questioning; that the cause of its opposition was in my person, because that body was governed only by my will; that it was in my power to make the fortunes of all. As he interposed friendship and privacy to propose this arrangement to me, I made use of the same confidence to exact of him that he would convince me with justice, as that only could cause me to abandon the resolution which I had formed, because interest is not a legal and decent consideration, nor that which could induce me to be guilty of the baseness of selling the property of innocent people which I believed myself obliged to defend, and I would only deliver it to his disposition by the express order of the Supreme Government, after representing the injury which would be inflicted on the neophytes. We discussed at length their right of property, and Señor Hijar again declared his opinion, maintaining that the neophytes have no right to the lands and other property of the Missions, and that the Government had the power freely to dispose of all as it should deem most suitable; but all this rests on his word, and nothing more. I maintained the contrary to the best of my ability, and I even dare to assert that I convinced Señor Hijar, but, pledged and highly compromised, he allowed himself to be absorbed in the chimerical projects which Señor Padres suggested to him, and cared not even for his reputation; and as a last resort, he proposed that the property of the *Missions* should be delivered to him under the guarantee not to proceed to convert any part into money until the Supreme Government should resolve the question which should be submitted to it on this point; that he would oblige himself formally to comply with this offer, if his proposition was agreed to. After a discussion sufficiently protracted, I promised the said Señor Hijar that if the Deputation acceded to his proposition, I, out of respect for his honor, would make no opposition, provided the property of the neophytes should not be alienated, but that neither would I support his pretensions, because I should have to incur a most notable inconsistency. Thus we ended our secret conference, of which Señor Padres had knowledge, though he took no part in it; and immediately afterwards, we met, to continue what we left pending the day before.

Señor Hijar commenced by making the proposition which I have just stated, but the Vocals of the Deputation and the Licentiates opposed it with convincing reasons which left no ground for its success. Then, as well Señor Hijar as the Adjutant Inspector, Don José Maria Padres, admitted that they were convinced, declaring that the Deputation had acted within the orbit of its powers, and in entire conformity to the laws and resolutions of the Supreme Government; that the instructions, in which only was the authority of Señor Hijar, were not so explicit as they ought to be to remove all doubt, nor had that force which was necessary in such a case, because of their being contradicted by the supreme order of the 25th of July, by which he was deprived of the political command, and in contradiction to various determinations of the Supreme Government; that therefore he did not insist on his pretensions, but was resolved to carry the colony to Old California, where he thought he could more easily establish it, seeing that there his commission as Director of Colonization remained in force without the opposition which in this Territory he had encountered. Señor Padres was of the same opinion—adding, it was certain that the instructions were defective and in a style which necessarily gave rise to many doubts; but that this resulted from the exceeding confidence which they enjoyed with the Most Excellent Vice-President of the Republic, who verbally gave them further orders and instructions of great interest which they were to put in practice.

The discussion terminated, and we occupied ourselves with persuading Señor Hijar to remain in this Territory, directing the colony; we demonstrated to him the difficulty which there was in transferring it to Old California, for want of resources to sustain it during the return voyage which they must undertake; the very great political injury which must follow from a bad result to an undertaking directed primarily to this country; that neither would he have in Old California lands on which to establish it, owing to the arid nature of the soil, nor resources to sustain it, because there the Missions have only a very few cattle, which do not produce even that which is necessary to support the ministers of religious worship; we made him see that his resolution could only make worse the condition of the colonists, already sufficiently compromised from not having funds to sustain them; that they would fill that country with calumnies by the sudden introduction of so many people, whom it could not maintain without detriment to the inhabitants, who are scarcely able to *subsist,* at the cost of great toil and watchings; that, as well from the sterility of the soil as the want of useful hands, there was a scarcity there even of the articles of first necessity of life—articles which were obtained at much expense from the States of Sonora and Sinaloa, and never in quantity as abundant as needed; that the National Treasury has there less resources to meet the demand upon it than in this Territory, and, in a word, that it was impossible even to move from this point for want of funds and vessels to forward the expedition. We begged him to lay aside his resentment and remain with us in harmony; to establish the colony which he had brought under his care, and that he should enjoy the four thousand dollars assigned by the Supreme Government, which should be consulted, and a recommendation presented, in order to obtain its approbation, and that we would aid him efficiently in carrying out this enterprise, and in his service would do all compatible with our duty.

Convinced that his idea of removing with the colony to Old California was impracticable, he agreed to all that we proposed, and at once we passed to the consideration of the means which we ought to adopt. In consequence of what we agreed to in the conferences, I addressed the Deputation the following note:

"POLITICAL GOVERNMENT OF UPPER CALIFORNIA.

"MOST EXCELLLENT SENOR: — I communicated to Señor Don José Maria Hijar the eight propositions adopted by your Excellency on the 22d inst., and he not assenting to them, answered me, as appears in his note of the 23d, the original of which I have the honor to transmit. The exaggeration of the principles with which he pretends to ridicule the attributions of the Territorial Government might be combatted with the pen victoriously; but, desirous of preserving harmony and reconciling public and private interests, I thought it most prudent to put an end to the discussion by means of conferences, in order to avoid all animosity and public scandal. Consequently, Señor Don José Maria Hijar came into conference, and after conferring at *length* upon the diverse points which his note of the 23d embraces, he being convinced of the just foundations on which the Territorial Government rested its determinations, we agreed on the following: 1. That Señor Don José Maria Hijar should exercise the special commission as Director of Colonization, in subjection to the Political Government of the Territory and the laws and regulations established on that subject; that this should be the true sense of the second proposition approved by the Most Excellent Deputation, because this is the understanding which it had in saying '*the bases which may be adopted for that purpose,*' and therefore authorizes this explanation. 2. That the instructions given by the Supreme Government, which were commanded to be retained, be returned to Señor Hijar, a copy only of them remaining in the archives of the Political Government. That agreeing to all the rest contained in the said eight propositions, he declares his submission, and promises to exercise his special commission until the Supreme Government of the Union determines as it may deem proper. The aforesaid Señor Hijar recommends to the consideration of your Excellency the individuals who have come in his company as teachers, in regard to whom he declares that he received from the Supreme Government a verbal order for their establishment. Be pleased to determine in regard to the foregoing that which you may deem convenient and most just.

"God and Liberty. Monterey, October 29, 1834.

"JOSE FIGUEROA.

"The Most Excellent Deputation of this Territory."

The Deputation, after having heard a committee of its members, approved in session of the 3d November the report and propositions which appear in the following communication:

"POLITICAL GOVERNMENT OF UPPER CALIFORNIA.

"The most Excellent Territorial Deputation was yesterday pleased to approve of the report of the Committee of Government, and to adopt the following propositions:

"MOST EXCELLENT SENOR:—The Committee of Government has examined the communication of the 23d inst., subscribed by José Maria Hijar, in answer to that which the Political Chief addressed him of the same date, communicating to him the eight propositions adopted by your Excellency on that day. Its contents are a tissue of mistaken opinions, unfounded imputations and gratuitous reproaches against the Territorial Government. The Committee, to vindicate the honor of your Excellency, highly offended, might analyze it at length in order to correct the mistakes and refute the calumnies with which your just proceedings are opposed; but resolved to repeat evidences of moderation, politeness and urbanity, it overlooks the acrimony with which this document abounds, and reposes in the testimony of its conscience and honor. Your Excellency, in advising the measures controverted by Señor Hijar, had in view the laws and regulations which govern the subject; it is of no consequence that he may seek to pervert their genuine meaning—

it is necessary to observe them; let those who are offended thereby make use of their right, and the proper authority shall decide in favor of him who has justice; your Excellency being in authority, complies with your duty in carrying out your orders and explaining those which offer any doubt. Señor Hijar, although he sought to disown your authority, has promised to obey it after, in private conferences with the Political Chief, he learned his mistake; this is a tacit confession of his error, and proves his conviction. The disputes which have so much occupied us being terminated in this manner, we ought to make all public scandal cease, and bury in silence all personal resentment. The superior authority will make the proper elucidation, and results will justify our proceedings. The individuals who *compose* this body are republicans as well as Señor Hijar; they use, as well as he, an austere language, but they abstain from insults and abuse; they might use this just reprisal, but they profess principles of liberty, moderation and tolerance; the only rule of their conduct ought to be the laws and the orders of legitimately constituted authorities. It is satisfied that it has not exceeded the limits of its functions, nor usurped powers which the laws do not confer upon it. Thus much being said, the Committee presents to your deliberation the following propositions: 1. To .explain the true meaning of the second proposition approved on the 22d inst., for the words 'and the bases which the Deputation may adopt for that purpose,' shall be substituted the following: 'and to the laws and regulations established on that subject.' 2. That the instructions given by the Supreme Government be returned to Señor Hijar, a copy of them only remaining in the power of the Political Chief. 3. That assuming the acquiescence of Señor Hijar in all the rest resolved by the Deputation on the 22d inst., the present report and the foregoing propositions be inclosed to him, that he may say in writing whether or not he acquiesces in all that has been resolved by the Territorial Government. In the first case the Political Chief will command that his salary of four thousand dollars be allowed him, and will report to the Supreme Government for its approbation.

"The Political Chief is authorized to resolve according to the laws, any doubt referring to this resolution and that of the 22d of October, in all cases in which it belongs to the Deputation to interpose.

"I have the honor to transcribe this report for your information, with the object therein expressed, and as an answer to your note of the 23d of October last past, to enclose you the instructions given by the Supreme Government. I will be obliged to you if any doubt should occur to you, or you have any objection to make, to take the *trouble* to confer with me first upon such point, that we may agree as to the means most prudent to be adopted, or the measures which on my part it may be proper to take. If there should be no further difference in our opinions, be pleased to make it known to me that I may enjoy that pleasure. With these sentiments I repeat to you the assurances of my true esteem and consideration.

"God and Liberty. Monterey, November 4, 1834.

"JOSE FIGUEROA.

"Señor Don JOSE MARIA HIJAR, Director of Colonization."

Señor Hijar answered with the following communication:

"I have noted the contents of your note dated the 4th instant, in which you inclose me the resolution of the most Excellent Territorial Deputation upon my communication of the 23d ultimo, and consider any discussion on the points of which we have treated, useless, seeing that we are not agreed as to the manner of viewing things; only you will permit me to correct one mistake. It is asserted in the argumentative part of the report enclosed me, that I sought to disown the authority of the most Excellent Deputation. Never have I had such a pretension; that which I have done is to deny its power to set itself above the laws, but this is not to deny its authority. I entertain the greatest respect for legitimate authorities and know how to conduct myself when these exceed their bounds. I believe I have fallen into no mistake, as is asserted. In the conferences which are referred to, were only alleged reasons of convenience, philanthropy and humanity towards the natives; but no express power to act in the manner which was resolved on. There is no law, and consequently no right that you and the Deputation should have determined as you have done; this is my opinion; and if some Spanish laws have been cited they are repealed by our own, because repugnant to the system of Government. In the third proposition which is inclosed to me, I am required to say whether or not I acquiesce in the resolution of the Supreme Government, and in the first case that four thousand dollars should be assigned me as salary. It has been a source of regret to me that the most Excellent Deputation should have formed so low an opinion of me, and that perhaps it believes that interest could induce me to give assent to all it has resolved. No, Señor, no; not only do I not acquiesce, but I *protest* against the determinations of yourself and the Deputation in everything, in which the laws and orders of the General Government are attacked, as I have declared in my communication of the 23d. The discussions in which we have been engaged being ended, it only remains for me to declare to you that I am resolved to continue with the colony until its establishment at the point which the Government desires, for the following reasons: 1. The private affections of the families which compose the colony have decided, them, to share my lot and follow me; consequently, if I had desired to abandon them, the colony would have proved a failure, with serious injury to individuals. 2. If the colony should be unfortunate it would be a discredit to the Government, because it would be believed that it is incapable of undertakings of this nature; that it had torn these families from their country to bring them to another and remote, there to abandon them; and finally, it would never be able to induce any man to leave his home and go out to colonize. 3. The desires of the Government would remain unfulfilled, the important frontier of the North, threatened by the Russians and Anglo-Americans, would remain uncovered, and the great expenditures which have been made upon this colony would be lost. All these considerations, Señor General, have decided me to waive my resentments and outraged self-respect to preserve the national honor and interest, and to secure the well-being of the families which were entrusted to me. I have not been able to resist the tears of gratitude which oftentimes the companions of my journey have shed in my presence; I have resolved, and I am decided to sacrifice all, although the ungrateful Government which has so wantonly outraged me, should not recompense me. I go, then, to establish the colony, and if necessary, to take the spade for my subsistence; but there will remain to me the pleasure of having done the duty of a good citizen, sustaining the national honor and striving for the happiness of the families committed to me. I conclude, then, hoping that you will perform your promise, that nothing shall be wanting of what the Government promised the colonists, and I rely upon your probity that all shall be done with due punctuality and fitness, so that no colonist shall have ground to complain. The instructions are in my possession which you sent me with your note, to which I have the honor to reply, with assurances of my regard and distinguished consideration.

"God and Liberty. Monterey, November 6, 1834.

"JOSE MARIA DE HIJAR.

"Señor Political Chief, General Don JOSE FIGUEROA."

Señor Hijar persists in various errors, which I have demonstrated and combatted. I omit, therefore, to answer at length his opinions expressed in this last communication, in which it will be seen that this gentleman always understands things differently from the rest of men. He says that he knows how he should conduct himself when the authorities exceed their powers, and it is useless to point out to him the faults with which his writings abound. Let us leave to time to undeceive him, while we follow the course of events. Observe the importance which he seeks to give to his person, even against the Supreme Government, for having removed him from the office of Political Chief, which it had conferred upon him; he cannot *conceal* his resentment, notwithstanding those solemn protestations of sacrificing himself in the service of the colony and for the national honor. Would that his acts had corresponded with his words!

The Territorial Government, gratified at having amicably arranged this business, was public in its gratulations, and paid to Señor Hijar the suitable attentions of friendship. Animated by the best feelings, it accorded various measures of assistance to Señor Hijar in establishing the colony.

The half of this was at San Gabriel and San Luis Rey, two hundred leagues distant from San Francisco Solano, which is the nearest point to that they were to occupy; its transportation was undertaken, overcoming many obstacles, and at a heavy expense to the nation, caused by its disembarkation at San Diego; but, finally, the orders of the Supreme Government were going on to be fulfilled, and to this end the study of the Territorial Government was devoted.

When it was engaged with most enthusiasm in these objects, it received notice that the First Lieutenant of the National Navy, Don Buenaventura Araujo, had called together an assemblage of the unchristianized savages (the Cahuillas), who attacked the Rancho of San Bernardino, belonging to the Mission of San Gabriel, and committed various robberies and other excesses. For this cause a party of twenty armed men was detached to observe them, and if necessary to bring them to order; but the insolence with which these unfortunate creatures had been inspired gave them the boldness to attack the said party, and it was necessary to beat them. Don Francisco Berdusco, one of the colonists, at the same time sought to induce the neophytes of San Luis Rey to surprise a small detachment stationed there; the project was discovered and frustrated. The Cahuillas repeated their attack upon the same Rancho of San Bernardino, where they committed various assassinations and robberies of importance. A party of fifty men went out in pursuit of them, and chastised their insolence with the death of some who showed front. Don Romualdo Lara, another colonist, who accompanied Señor Hijar in his journey from San Diego to Monterey, endeavored, in the various Missions through which he passed to seduce the neophytes and attach them to his party; this appears from the diary which he wrote himself, and which came to my hands by an accident. All of these attempts inspired the Government with a natural distrust of their authors, but it was content to dictate certain precautionary measures to avoid a disturbance, without even proceeding against the instigators, believing them capable of listening to the voice of reason, and desisting. The contrary happened in everything. They *labored* privately to place Señor Hijar by force at the head of the Political Government, and under his auspices to dispose of the property of the Missions.

From a distance I beheld the storm which must burst upon my head, but could not allay it without exposing myself to the biting censure of my antagonists, who only shelter themselves behind the laws to insult the authorities with impunity.

Don José Maria Padres, who at the moment of his disembarkation desired that I would deliver him the military command, in virtue of the Supreme Order of the 12th of July, 1833: who, on my rejection of this pretension, declared that he would not discharge his office of Adjutant Inspector, because he did not wish to depend on the Military Government, and because it was incompatible with his commission, as Subdirector of the Colony, solicited, after a few days, that I would make him Commandant of the Northern Frontier. This versatility of thoughts so inconsistent, induced me to distrust his person, and I denied his request. This insubordinate officer, from before his arrival, boasted of coming, as he said, at the head of an armed force; all the world knows that he brought two hundred rifles and a considerable stock of munitions of war, and, far from complying with his obligation to give me notice of this armament, whether as Commanding General or Political Chief, he endeavored to conceal it from me; he commanded the colonists that no one should present himself to me, nor confer with me personally about anything, as with him only they were to advise. I had observed that he held a commanding influence over the mind of Señor Hijar, and inclined him to whatever he desired. All this, his known propensity to disorder, the interest which he formerly had in diverting the property of the Missions, the maneuvers and intrigues which he made use of that the Deputation should disobey the order of the Supreme Government, and other considerations, which it would take too long to mention, induced me to believe that Padres was the prime mover of all the conspiracies, and that I ought to observe his conduct with the greatest care. The order which Padres relies on, in order that the Commandancy General should be delivered to him, I will insert in continuation, that the public may see whether or not it is an order as positive as necessary to meet the wishes of the said Padres.

"OFFICE OF THE SECRETARY OF WAR AND MARINE.

"SEC. 9. Under this date I say to the Adjutant Inspector Don José Maria Padres the following:

"MOST EXCELLENT SENOR:—The Vice-President, in exercise of the supreme executive power, has been *pleased* to command you to proceed to the Territory of Upper California for the purpose of taking charge of that Commandancy General, in the event that General Don José Figueroa should continue ill and wish to retire. I communicate this to you by the same superior order for your fulfillment and appropriate ends. I have the honor to transcribe the above for your information and for the object expressed, so that if from your illness it should be agreeable to you to remove to this Capital you may do so.

"God and Liberty. Mexico, July 12th, 1833.

"HERRERA.

"Señor Commandant General, Upper California, GENERAL Don JOSE FIGUEROA."

Notwithstanding what had happened up to that time, I took the utmost pains to unite and establish the colony at the cost of great sacrifices and suffering, because of the Directors having divided it into two parts; but the more I exerted myself in its favor the more the brokers devoted themselves to promoting disorder and preparing a revolution which was to remove me from the Political Government and put Señor Hijar in my place.

To this end were directed all the maneuvers of Don José Maria Padres, Don Francisco Berdusco, Don Francisco Torres, and Don Romualdo Lara, which personages played the principal part in the drama. It is now understood that each one had his satellites and that all were conspiring with the same object. Thus it is that from various points I received information that the colony was attempting a conspiracy against the Government, as was said by many of its members. Under date of the 18th of January and 12th of February of this year, two different persons worthy of credit, communicate to me from the Mission of San Antonio the project of conspiracy as certain. *Various* individuals of the colony itself secretly disclosed to me the disorders, upon which it was desired to precipitate them: others asked to separate from the company, feigning various pretexts. Sedition was attempted in different manners at various points of the Territory, and in the Capital itself, where the most important combinations were made. In this state of affairs Señor Hijar exhibited a passive conduct and a simulated indifference, which repelled suspicion from him; but the principal agents of the revolution made court to him; with them only he consulted about his affairs; they only enjoyed his fullest confidence, and it is almost impossible that he should be ignorant of the projects which they were to execute under his auspices and in his name.

When I could no longer doubt the resolution which they had taken, grounds of vehement suspicions which coincided with the seditious plans, daily presented themselves. Then the winter season, which embarrasses every occupation, conspired against the unfortunate colonists, who, accustomed to a more benignant temperature, were scarcely able to endure the rigor of the season, and under these circumstances they were obliged to travel great distances and double their sufferings without other object than to unite for the purpose of subverting social order, after they had sacrificed the interests of the nation in useless expenses. These results were occasioned by the ignorance or wickedness of the Directors of the colony, because they never considered the comfort of the colony nor the convenience of the nation nor the end of an enterprise worthy of better results. They directed everything without more foresight than the fantastic dreams of Don José Maria Padres and his unbridled avarice to possess himself of the property of the Missions; but such is the blindness of the passions that it appears that all surrendered themselves to the guidance of his inspirations, and this man, infatuated with his arrogant presumption, sought to fill the place of Minerva. Behold! the mentor of the colony whose judgment governed all the rest!

The colonists had arrived; some at San Francisco Solano, and others on the way, occupied different points. A pueblo about to be founded requires strong arms and laborious men accustomed to the labors of the field and to a plain and frugal life; the colony directed by Señors Hijar and Padres is composed in the majority of delicate persons worthy of a better fate. They are families torn suddenly from the court where they were born and educated in the midst of pleasures and opulence. Small as may have been their fortunes in Mexico, they had established a system of life in accordance with their strength, their character, their inclinations, their customs, their disposition and their taste; in proportion to their industry and their connections they enjoyed comfort and pleasures which it would be difficult for them to obtain elsewhere. Many professed some mechanical or liberal art, which in Mexico would produce them some revenue, but in California is useless to them. Witness the tinners, silversmiths, lacemakers, embroiderers, painters, &c., &c.; compare the difference between using the instruments of these arts and handling the plough, the pick, the axe and the other instruments with which the fields are cultivated: the difference between working within doors, sheltered from the sun, the winds and the water, and laboring in the field subject to the exposure and accidents of a life full of privations, discomforts and dangers. Was it *possible* that girls, women, and delicate youths, to whom the roads where they were traveling, was the only country that ever they had beheld—was it possible, I repeat, that these people could overcome the fatigues, the difficulties, the privations, the necessities and the accumulation of difficulties, and accidents incident to attempting new settlements? Let them answer for me themselves, and impartial men will justify the measures of the Territorial Government in preventing the sufferings of the colonists, and delivering them from the painful position to which their Directors were conducting them to make their lot the more unfortunate.

There is no doubt that the colony recruited by Señor Padres lacks the qualities which constitute a good colony, not from any fault of the individuals, but from the ignorance and malice of the Directors, who only sought in the enterprise a pretext to enrich themselves, to the detriment of the neophytes of the Missions of California and of the unfortunate colonists who allowed themselves to be deceived with false promises and fantastic pictures of prosperity, with which they beguiled them in order to induce them to come to this country. Many individuals arrived with the belief that they could freely dispose of the horses and cattle which they needed, without other requisite than to take them in the fields where property was in common; others anxiously inquired for the shores where they could kill with a stick as many otters as they wanted; others looked for the pearl beds where they might fill their pockets; others in fine, believed themselves owners of the estates and most important buildings which had been offered to them. These were the abject means that Señor Padres made use of, to inveigle the families who were to serve as a cover to his iniquitous views. These events have just passed; I speak before the actors themselves; they will contradict me if I do not speak the truth.

Since then the colony by its intrinsic unfitness, was not capable of founding a new pueblo, which was the political object of the Supreme Government, in order to cover the northern frontier from foreign aggressions; as the political faith of the Directors was in open conflict with the wholesome principles of every well-regulated society: as its projects of subversion must cause a positive evil to the generality of the inhabitants; as the Political Chief was blamed for the wants, privations and labors which the colonists suffered: as these could not even suffer with resignation, because they were daily excited to revenge imaginary injuries as indemnity for their sufferings; as for the *purpose* of exciting their anger, the absurd communication with which Señor Hijar replied to me on the 23d of October, was read to them daily in San Francisco Solano, upon whose contents long commentaries were made by the mentor of the colony, who generally concluded by vomiting insults against my person, and invectives worthy of his consequential arrogance. All these elements were so many combustibles prepared for the general conflagration. I saw them plainly and beheld with serenity the approach of the explosion. No one will believe that under such circumstances, I merely kept myself on the defensive, and so remained from the month of September, when the expedition reached the Territory, until the month of March, when they pulled off the mask and compelled me to take the offensive.

As the summer approached, the time in which they were to have consummated the work of regeneration which they had projected, they pretended to be occupied with matters entirely different. Don Francisco Torres held out that he was going to Mexico in the service of Señor Hijar, who did not think proper to communicate to me the object of this journey as he ought to have done, as no colonist ought to be separated from the colony without a full knowledge of the reason by the Political Chief. Notwithstanding this, I gave him his passport without making any objection, knowing that the true object of his journey, was go to Los Angeles on the pretext of seeking passage in some vessel, and there to create a revolution. Accident presented to him a Spaniard, Don Antonio Apalategui, a man naturally restless, without anything to lose, fond of all sorts of revolutions, to whom I had refused an office which he sought, and who was on the lookout for some good fortune. Thus it is that he entered readily into the schemes of Torres, and they travelled together from this capital.

Señor Hijar determined to proceed to San Francisco Solano in company with Berdusco, Lara, and Araujo, to join Padres and the colony, which was still scattered, because of the various obstacles which *opposed* their progress. The true object of this meeting was the revolution; but Señor Hijar pretended to be ignorant of it. I gave him some hints to induce him to avoid the disturbance and the consequences which every revolution brings with it; but he would not understand, and on the contrary, declared to me that he was resolved to return to Mexico, and that so soon as he could arrange with Padres the business and accounts of the colony, he would commence his journey. Under this pretext he set out for San Francisco Solano at the end of February. I proceeded in the same direction without other object than to observe his conduct and discover his plans. We met in San Francisco de Assis, where we had a conference, and I explained to him that his followers and friends sought to involve him, for the purpose of bringing contempt upon the Government, and particularly on me; that I was well informed through various channels of the plans in which they were engaged; that very soon the revolution was to burst out; that I must necessarily defend myself, and perhaps might have to take precautions that would be painful to him. I showed him who were the principal movers and made him see what evils they were going to inflict upon the Territory, and that it was in his power to prevent it all if he so desired, out of regard for the peace and for his own reputation. I assured him that all should remain in silence if they kept quiet, for I was neither in pursuit of them nor afraid of them. But whether he believed the triumph certain, or out of contempt for my offers, he exhibited towards me the same coldness and indifference with which he was accustomed to look upon the most important affairs. Then I saw myself compelled to prevent the union of the colony, in order to restrain it from the revolution to which they invited it; because many individuals had so requested in order to prevent their ruin which was inevitable if they submitted to the caprices of the Directors, who sought even to monopolize their personal labor under the pretext of the Cosmopolitan Company, because they had done nothing useful nor could do, from their physical incapacity as I have shown; and above all because I had no disposable fund to pay their wages as Señor Hijar requested. I adopted the means of leaving them at liberty to establish themselves in the place that might suit them best for undertaking any employment by which to subsist; so it appears from the correspondence which took place and which is as follows:

"I am about to pass to San Francisco Solano for the purpose of fixing the point where the colony is to be established; but you having declared to me in various *private* conferences that it is impossible to make good to the colonists all which the Supreme Government offered them when contracting with them in their country to come to this Territory, I will thank you to be pleased to say to me definitely whether the Government is able or not to comply with its promise, so that I may regulate my proceedings and make the colonists pass to the point in which they are to be established if the Government should furnish the resources offered; or in the event that this cannot be, to tell them so, in order that they may determine as to them seems best, if so be that the Government should fail in the conditions of the contract which it made with the families who were entrusted to me, and which I have the grief to see overwhelmed with want. I think it useless to declare to you the evils which would result from disbanding the colony which has cost the Supreme Government so much expense and toil, the political results which it must cause, and in which the honor of the General Government is interested in so unequivocal a manner. You know as well as I the consequences of this step, and I hope from your prudence that you will decide in the best manner possible, without losing sight of your political influence, the honor of the Supreme Government, the individual interest of the colonists, and the public interest of the Territory."

"God and Liberty. San Francisco de Assis, March 1st, 1835.

"JOSE MARIA DE HIJAR.

"Señor Political Chief, General Don JOSE FIGUEROA."

"POLITICAL GOVERNMENT OF UPPER CALIFORNIA.

"The Supreme Federal Government has given me no directions in regard to the colony. The instructions given to yourself when you were appointed Political Chief are the only documents which evidences the orders issued on this subject; that document is in your possession; true it is that it contains the Supreme order to take the property of the Missions and appropriate it to the colony, but in this order the property of the Indians is attacked, and as I have shown you in various conferences, it is unconstitutional: so I have represented to superior authority, and so, more particularly may be seen in the 112th article, restriction 3d, of the Federal Constitution, which says thus: 'The President shall have no power to take the property of any individual or corporation, nor disturb him in the possession, use, or enjoyment of it, and if in any case it should be necessary for an object of known general utility to take the property of an individual or corporation, he shall have no power to do so without the previous approbation of the Senate, and in its recess, of the Council of Government, making always such compensation to the person interested as may be determined by arbitrators to be chosen by him and by the Government.' This is the foundation on which the Territorial Government has rested the defense of the *property* of the Missions which has always been recognized as belonging to the neophytes in them; but in the face of such serious inconveniences, and under solemn protest to reclaim proper indemnity it adopted a resolution to furnish the colony all the assistance necessary for its establishment and maintenance, since it never believed it just to abandon to their fate so many persons worthy of esteem and respect, nor has it beheld their sufferings with indifference. To you it is known that in conformity with the resolution of the Most Excellent Territorial Deputation of the 22d October last, I commanded to be placed at your disposition, all the articles which you yourself estimated for its establishment and maintenance; it is known to you that some only have been delivered, and that the greater part are still wanting; that as well the season as the scarcity of resources of every kind, hinders or paralyzes the undertaking; that I find myself surrounded with difficulties, and that what with the secularization of the Missions and other complicated affairs, my orders in regard to the colony are frustrated at every step; that the burdens lately imposed upon the property of the Missions and the losses which they suffer in consequence of the innovations which are put in practice, are so many obstacles which cripple the resources on

which I rely. I have shown you the communications which I have
received from the Commissioners of the Missions in relation to the
aids which they ought to furnish the colony, and in them are expressed various irremediable deficiencies. All these embarrassments
I am resolved to overcome as far as I possibly can, and with this
object I have promised you to omit neither labor nor diligence; but
the demands are multiplied to such a degree that it is not possible
to meet them without very great injury to the public; because the
notorious decadence in which the Missions now are; the great debts
which they have contracted and which must be met out of their
effects in hand; the emancipation of the native families, who now
exceed twenty thousand persons, who are to be furnished with property for their establishment and maintenance; the heavy burdens
lately imposed for the support of ministers, and the salaries of
teachers, mayordomos and other employees who formerly did not
exist; payment of the wages of laborers who are employed in the
preservation of their estates: all, all, weigh upon the prosperity of
the natives and conspire to its speedy destruction without the power
of fulfilling completely all demands. Notwithstanding all that I have
here disclosed, I repeat to you that I will make all the efforts which
may be necessary to supply the colony with the means necessary for
its subsistence; but I cannot promise to pay with punctuality its daily
stipend, because there is no money nor is it easy to get it; nor is it
possible to discharge in a short time with any other articles, the
sum of thirty-five thousand dollars or more without bankrupting the
Missions. In consideration of all the foregoing, because many *individuals* of the colony have petitioned me orally and in writing to
permit them to settle wherever was most convenient; because it is
notorious that the majority of the individuals who form the colony,
although very worthy and useful in various occupations, are not so
in the field, to which they have not been accustomed; because more
than six months are passed, and it has not been established nor any
useful labor undertaken; because Señor Don José Maria Padres,
without your knowledge nor that of this Government, is uniting
with the colony persons already established in the country, from
which results only an increase of expense; because the transportation of cattle and other effects to the other side of the Bay of San
Francisco must be very expensive and tedious, besides the losses
which must be occasioned thereby; because it is very difficult to con-
centrate at one point all the appurtenances of the colony; because

there exists among the colonists a general disgust, which may degenerate into disorder if their suffering is aggravated; and above all, because you have declared to me your intention to abandon the direction of the colony, in which view you have already petitioned the Supreme Government, and think of retiring to Lower California to await its orders: all this induced me to study some conciliatory measure and I proposed to you that in my opinion it is suitable to leave the colonists to settle in the place which they find most convenient, in order, that by their industry and trades, united with the assistance which the Government gives them, they might be able to lead a more comfortable life, the most laborious, acquiring advantages which otherwise they are not able to obtain. In this, I not only consult the comfort and taste of the families, but the resources of the public treasury, the general tranquillity of the territory, the greater facility in forwarding aid to the colonists, and the leaving them at liberty so that they can employ themselves usefully in their callings; for in this way only can I contribute to the reduction of their sufferings, fulfilling at the same time, what the Government has promised them. They in my opinion, can thus be more useful and beneficial to society than they could be in the rugged labors of the fields.

"Notwithstanding this, if any or all of the colonists freely and cheerfully desire to establish themselves on the frontier, you are at liberty to choose whatever place may suit you, and I will aid you there with all the resources in my power. National honor, the prosperity of the Government and the public convenience, are satisfied by the measure suggested. The colonists will be furnished with their supplies proportionally, and perhaps with less delay and less burden to the treasury, and more to their satisfaction. I have thought much upon this business, and experience daily convinces me that there is no other *remedy* more adapted to our circumstances or which can better reconcile private interests, with those of the public. This is my opinion, and I would be glad that the colonists should be informed of it that they may choose as they think best, with the assurance, that in their service, I will with pleasure, as I have heretofore proven, give my care and ability to furnishing them with whatever supplies may be at my disposal; since the scarcity from which some have suffered is due to the obstacles of the weather, the exhausted state of the treasury, or some other accident. But you and Señor Padres are satisfied of the frankness and equity with which the national effects have been divided among all, and the cheerfulness with which I have commanded all the petitions which they have addressed me, to be complied with.

"In consequence of your urgency and my offers, I send you of this date, the proper orders to receive and distribute to the colony two thousand dollars, in such effects as may be required, there being no money, all which I have the honor to submit in reply to your note of yesterday, which treats of this subject.

"God and Liberty. San Francisco de Assis, March 2, 1835.

"JOSE FIGUEROA.

"Director of Colonization, D. JOSE MARIA DE HIJAR."

"The expedient which you propose to me of leaving the colonists free to settle wherever may suit them best, will not protect my responsibility; and if the Supreme Government is able to fulfill the promise which it made with them, they must pass to the place which that Government designated in order to accomplish the object which was intended; because merely to leave four or six persons more in one of the settled places of the Territory, it never would have undertaken the heavy expenses which have been incurred. You must be convinced that a policy which tends, among other things, to preserve the integrity of the Territory of the Republic, was the motive which induced the Government to make extraordinary sacrifices in the midst of pressing difficulties. If the Supreme Government is able to comply with its promise, the colonists cannot complain that they have to pass to an unsettled place, because it was contracted to carry them to such point as might be suitable. For this cause and the fate of the colony now depends altogether upon your action, I entreat you to tell me positively, whether the Supreme Government is in condition to carry out its contract, or whether, as you have frequently declared to me, it will be impossible for it to fulfill its promise. With this positive answer, I believe my responsibility will be saved, and then the colonists will remain where they like, and receive their *daily* stipend wherever it may be convenient. You know very well that the assessment made upon the Missions, upon my petition for the colony, has not been satisfied, except to a small amount, and this it will be difficult to collect, on account of the obstacles which are interposed. Although you have issued your orders to aid the colony, it is a fact that they have been obeyed only very partially. In every direction, embarrassments which have impeded the establishment of the colony, present themselves, and difficulties which have obliged you to order the colonists to winter, distributed among the Missions, where being transient persons, they have as yet been unable to undertake any kind of labor. Everything, Señor General, indicates that it is necessary to take a definitive course, and I would desire you to tell me positively, to leave the colonists wherever may suit them, in order that each one may apply himself to that he thinks best, reckoning only on the assistance which may conveniently be furnished them as you propose, and not upon that which by contract is due them. In this way the colonists will be relieved of a distressing uncertainty, and I will save my responsibility. If after some days, it is to be said that there is no means of fulfilling the promise, it is better to do so now, and fewer ills will be caused to the unfortunates who accompanied me. It will be well that you should know that the colonists cannot demand money absolutely, because from Mexico it was told them that it was very scarce here, but that they would be compensated with equivalent values. I will conclude with saying to you, that if Señor Padres has received as colonists, any individuals resident in the country, it is no burden on the public funds, because lands only will be given them, and nothing else of that which was offered to those engaged in the interior. I will also add, that although I may be separated from the colony, as I have solicited of the Supreme Government, this ought to have no influence whatever upon its future fate, and still less upon the objects which the Government proposed in sending it. All which I have believed it proper to say to you in answer to your note of yesterday, without entering into the discussion as to the property of the funds, out of which the colonists should be assisted, because of its not being a matter which concerns me."

"God and Liberty. San Francisco de Assis, March 3, 1835.

"JOSE MARIA DE HIJAR.

"Señor Political Chief, General Don JOSE FIGUEROA."

"POLITICAL GOVERNMENT OF UPPER CALIFORNIA.

"On many occasions I have explained to you the difficulty which exists of meeting in full the expenses which are necessary to be incurred in the establishment of the colony for want of funds, and because the expenses are multiplied daily at the same time that the resources are notably diminished by causes which it is not in my *power* to avoid. For this reason I have believed it necessary to leave the colonists at liberty to establish themselves wherever suited them best, to the end, that aided by their industry and that which may conveniently be furnished them, they may be able to subsist without want. You have experienced the difficulties, and are convinced that it is impossible to carry out the undertaking; but as to cover your responsibility you exact of me in your note of yesterday a positive decision. I announce to you that it is not possible to furnish completely all promised by the Supreme Government to the colony, because the means placed at my disposition do not suffice. I therefore command that the colonists be free to establish themselves within the limits of the Territory in the place which each one may find agreeable, where they shall be assisted in proportion to the means which may be in my power. I have the honor to say this to you in reply to your said note, and to beg you to be pleased to communicate to me any resolution that you may take, for my future guidance.

"God and Liberty. San Francisco de Assis, March 4, 1835.

"JOSE FIGUEROA.

"Señor Director of Colonization, Don JOSE MARIA HIJAR."

In spite of the perfidy with which I was treated I sought to endure my suffering and to aid the colony in every way possible; thus it is that I molested no one nor charged any with his crimes, in the hope that they would recede from their extravagant pretensions. With this resolution I retired after placing two thousand dollars at the disposition of Señor Hijar, for the purpose of securing the colony. I tarried a few days in the Missions of Santa Clara and San Juan Bautista, making investigations in order to complete the discovery of the heads of the revolution. I was making great progress up to the 13th of March, when I received by express information that in the Pueblo of Los Angeles there had been a revolutionary pronunciamiento directed by Juan Gallardo, at the head of fifty adventurers from the State of Sonora—that they were seduced and compromised by Don Francisco Torres and Don Antonio Apalategui under different pretexts and deceptions; but *endeavoring* to exonerate themselves they exposed with what depravity and cunning these had acted, and the insurgents with their own hands delivered them to the Alcalde, that he might judge them according to law, protesting that they were obedient to the Government in whose name they had been called together by Torres and Apalategui; that therefore they delivered them to the authorities before whom they promised to lay down the arms which they had taken up unadvisedly, and not to disturb the public order again under any pretext. The Ayuntamiento of said Pueblo of Los Angeles forwarded me the report and plan, the tenor of which is as follows:

"OFFICE OF THE SECRETARY OF THE ILLUSTRIOUS
AYUNTAMIENTO OF THE PUEBLO OF LOS ANGELES.

"A mob of Sonoranians pronounced at daylight this morning for
the plan, of which I have the honor to send you a copy; considered
in its essence and placed in its true light, it contains nothing but private views, none of which have been foreign to the consideration of
this Illustrious Ayuntamiento. It prudently determined to meet in
extraordinary assembly, of which session likewise I forward you a
copy. It seemed very strange to the generality of this Pueblo that a
multitude of Sonoranians, for private ends, should think of derang-
ing the order of things established in this Territory. It is true that
in the sixth article of the said plan it is seen that the insurgents promise submission and obedience to the laws, whilst they contradict themselves in the same, saying that they will not lay down their arms until
they see their intentions realized; they call themselves protectors of
the laws which they only have infringed; they proclaim order and
have made use of violence even to surprising a Regidor, who had
the key of the Jusgado, for the purpose of taking the arms and accou-
trements which then were in it. Between the critical extremes of
repelling this force without having the means of contending with
it or of yielding to the object of the insurgents, it was necessary to
take means which is that which is seen in the resolution which the
Corporation adopted in their second meeting. In conclusion, the insurgents remained in arms until three in the evening, and the same
person who appeared to be the agent of the party, Don Juan Gallardo, conducted the Spaniard Don Antonio Apalategui and Don
Francisco Torres prisoners to the Jusgado, and presented to Don
Felipe Castillo the statement of which I send you a copy. The said
Apalategui and Torres were placed in safe custody, and proper proceedings are being instituted. I have the honor to assure you in the
name of this Illustrious Corporation, of my sentiments of esteem
and respect.

"God and Liberty. Pueblo of Los Angeles, March 7, 1835.

"FRANCISCO J. ALVARADO.

"MANUEL ARZAGO, Secretary Señor Superior Political Chief of
Upper California."

"In the Pueblo of our Lady of the Angels, on the 7th day of
March, eighteen hundred and thirty-five, a multitude of citizens
having assembled for the purpose of adopting the measures most
suitable for saving the Territory of Upper California from the evils

which it has suffered and is suffering from the administration of General Don José Figueroa, and considering: First, that this Chief has not complied with various orders which the Supreme Government of the Union has directed to him for the purpose of bettering the condition of the inhabitants of this country; that abusing its submissiveness he has exceeded the limits of the powers which the laws grant him, assuming improperly the Political and Military functions, contrary to the system of federation, and contrary to the express laws which prohibit the union of these powers; that with the law of secularization of the Missions, he has made a scandalous monopoly, reducing their products or fruits to an exclusive commerce, and deceiving the good faith of the Territorial Deputation into regulating a general law according to his caprice; that violating the regulation of commissaries, he disposes of the property of the soldier at his pleasure, without the proper permission of the head of that service, and without the formalities which diverse laws and regulations establish for such cases. Second, That the Territorial Deputation, not having the power to regulate or make additions to a general law as it has done with this of secularization of the Missions. Third, That the Missions, going as they are now going, with gigantic steps to their total ruin, through the startling measures which have been adopted for confining the natives and the corresponding division of their property; and, Fourth, That some Commissioners, either through utter ignorance of the management of business of this sort, or a wicked design to enhance their private interests, are ruining the property of the Missions, with very great injury to the natives, who have acquired it by their labor: have agreed and resolved as follows:

"ART 1. General Don José Figueroa is declared unworthy of the public confidence. Consequently the First Constitutional Alcalde of the capital shall take charge provisionally of the political command of the Territory, and Captain Don Pablo de la Portilla as the oldest officer and of the highest rank, of the military, in conformity with the general ordinance of the army. 2. The resolutions of the Territorial Deputation in regard to the regulations which it has adopted for the administration of the Missions are declared null and void, and of no force and effect. 3. The very Reverend Missionary Fathers shall take exclusive charge of the temporalities of the respective Missions as they have heretofore done, and the Commissioners shall deliver the documents relating to their administration to the said fathers, who shall make the proper observations. 4. The foregoing article shall not interfere with the powers of the Director of Colonization in acting in conformity with the instructions which the Supreme Government gave him. 5. The present plan is subject in all respects to the approbation of the General Government. 6. The forces pronouncing will not lay down their arms until they see the foregoing articles realized, and they constitute themselevs protectors of the true administration of justice and its officers. (Here the signatures.)

"Angeles, March 7th, 1835.
[A COPY.]   "JUAN GALLARDO.

"Angeles, March 7th, 1835.
[A COPY.]   "MANUEL ARZAJA, Secretary."

This defamatory libel has no other foundation than calumny. If Torres and Apalategui were not so base and cowardly as to deny the authorship of the plan, I would have sued them for damages as false *calumniators* acting separately from the criminal proceedings against them for conspiracy, disturbance of the public order and sedition. But as I am not able to make use of the means which the law allows me to punish the insolence of these miserable creatures, I will denounce them before the inexorable tribunal of public opinion, contradicting with the language of truth the catalogue of lies which they have stamped on their despicable farago. First they assert that a multitude of citizens assembled for the purpose of adopting measures to save the Territory from the evils which it is suffering under my administration. This is the first political blasphemy of these idiots; the citizens, who, they say, assembled, are a parcel of adventurers just arrived in the country coming from the State of Sonora in search of fortune, for they brought no employment: just so with Torres and Apalategui, they had just arrived in the Territory, and they do not know or understand how it is governed; fools! could they not at least know that the Californians obey me rather from love and pleasure than from the authority which I exercise? Do they not know the contempt and general hatred in which they are held? Is it not plain to them that no Californian took part in their riot notwithstanding they had seduced them for the space of seven months counted from September to March? Do they not see that the very persons whom they had seduced returned to order without the necessity of employing force? Have they not themselves experienced the lenity with which I have treated them, in spite of their crimes? Do they not know that having attacked my military authority it was competent for me to judge them, and that I have renounced this right, not to be obliged, although legally, to pass upon my declared enemies? These perhaps may be the evils which this Territory is suffering under my administration? Infatuates! if they had one trace of integrity they would not lie with such audacity. And what is the right which citizens have to assemble tumultuously to trample upon the laws which regulate society and to attack the public authority? In what publicist has Señor Torres read these *doctrines?* Will he seek to apply in politics the knowledge which he has of drugs and the specifics, laid down in the pharmacopeia? Perhaps he thought that his plan would be as exactly obeyed like prescriptions in the apothecary shops? If so, he deceived himself miserably, and would that this event may be a lesson to him, so that he may betake himself again to relieving suffering humanity, joining anew the multitude of doctors from whose ranks he has deserted.

Following the relation of the celebrated plan, its authors assert that I have not complied with divers orders which the Supreme Government directed for the purpose of bettering the condition of this people. Liars! they speak like parrots. If they would rest their accusation on any foundation, and would designate the orders that I have failed to obey, I could answer them, but in the fact of not showing my fault, they prove their calumny.

The second clause of the first consideration of their plan affirms, that exceeding the limits of the powers which the laws grant me, I improperly assumed the political and military commands, contrary to the system of federation. Barbarians! In what have I transgressed the limits of my powers? Do they not know that the union of the political and military commands was conferred on me by the Supreme Government of the Union, and that it was empowered to do this, without violating any law, because the law of the 23d of June, 1813, art. 5, tit. 3, expressly authorizes it. And in what is this measure opposed to the system of federation? In nothing, or there would also be necessary two Presidents of the Republic, one military and one civil. Do these two commands correspond in intention with any of the three powers into which the national sovereignty is divided? Certainly not, for they both belong to the executive power. We must conclude then that the authors of this invective are idiots, who do not understand what the system of federation is.

The third clause of the first consideration of the plan, is, because I made of the law of secularization a scandalous monopoly, reducing the products of the Missions to an exclusive commerce, and that I deceive the Deputation into regulating a general law according to my caprice. Slanderers. How will they prove these atrocious calumnies? In what consists this monopoly, or what does Señor Torres understand by monopoly? Where is this exclusive commerce? It has only existed in the fantastic plan of Señor Torres, and if he had any shame he would not lie with such audacity in the face of the Republic. In what manner have I deceived the Deputation? I have already shown, that far from desiring the formation of a regulation of secularization, I publicly resisted it, and kept it back more than six months. But against this irreproachable testimony, the apothecary wished to display himself, but he did not desire to venture upon proof, thinking to give credit to his calumny simply by writing it.

The fourth *clause* of the first consideration of the plan asserts that I infringed upon the regulation of commissaries; that I dispose of the supplies of the soldier at my pleasure, without the cognizance of the chief of that service, and without the formalities which the laws and regulations establish. Señor Apothecary! in what and how have I infringed upon the regulation of the commissaries? Is it because I have watched over its exact observance and reduced the sub-commissaryship and the customhouse to the rigid system which the laws prescribe? Is it because I have not left these important offices in the confusion and disorder which prevailed in them from their foundation until I entered upon the command of this territory? Is it, in fine, because I watch over the distribution of the funds, and consent to no malversation? Let then these slanderers say in what manner the regulation of commissaries has been infringed, on my part. Let the chief of that service, the commandants and paymasters of the corps who serve under my orders say, if ever I have interfered with their functions. Let them say if, before I commanded in this Territory, the accounts of the troops were so carefully adjusted as now; let them say if, at any time before I commanded, there has been so much order and method in the equitable distribution of the funds; and above all, let it be observed what the present subcommissary says:

"JOSE MARIA HERRERA, Subcommissary of Upper California.— I certify, that during the time I have been discharging the said office, since the seventh of October, of the year last past up to date, the management and conduct of Brigadier General Don José Figueroa, Commandant General and Political Chief of this Territory, in regard to this office, have been nothing more than the intervention prescribed in the laws and regulations concerning the administration of the public property. And in testimony thereof, and for whatever purpose they may serve, I give these presents at the request of the party concerned in Monterey, June 30th, 1835.

"JOSE MARIA HERRERA."

I defy Torres and Apalategui, and all who may think proper, to prove the slightest fault that I have committed in the management of the Federal property or the supplies of the troops. It would be *sufficient* for me to respond to this atrocious slander, that the responsibility rests with the subcommissary and the paymasters, to whose charge the property is confided; but notwithstanding this, I desire, and it is my will to be held to responsibility whenever anyone shall require it with positive facts.

The second consideration of the plan is to the effect that the Territorial Deputation has not the power to regulate a law as it has done with that of secularization. I have proved that the Deputation could and ought to propose the regulation of secularization, because it is one of its faculties conferred by the law of the 23d of June, 1813, articles 1, 14, and 16, chapter 2. Another of the causes which prompted the plan is the decline of the Missions from the restraint imposed upon the natives, and because their property was being divided among them. This, verily, is a powerful motive for the revolution of Torres; the property being distributed among the owners, they would not permit it to be taken away, and then the Cosmopolitan Company would be without funds to dispose of; for this, the sage Torres, as principal partner, thought to make sure of the property of the Missions by means of a revolution. Excellent thought, but vain because it did not succeed!

Likewise it is asserted, as though casually, that the Commissioners, to forward their private interests, are ruining the property of the Missions, to the injury of the natives, who have acquired it by their labor. Then Señor Torres confesses that the natives are the owners of the property? Yet we will see, nevertheless, how he proposes to strip them of it. And how does he judge of the damage which the Commissioners have done to the Missions? By making use of the terrible weapon of calumny. The Commissioners will justify their conduct by the results, and as yet it is not time to analyze them.

For the *foregoing* reasons, they adopted the plan whose first article was to declare me unworthy, in order to deprive me of the political and military command, transferring the latter to Captain Don Pablo de la Portilla, and the former to the First Alcalde of Monterey. It is certain that the factious Torres and Apalategui, declared me unworthy of the public confidence; but the public—that is to say, all the inhabitants of California except a very few cosmopolitans—honored me with more confidence than I deserved. I would be ridiculous to take the trouble to refute the filthy farrago of Torres. I will only examine the distribution of the commands. The political was destined for the Alcalde, who although not called by law in any case, would serve to disorganize the Government and open the way for Señor Hijar, who was to have been called in after the triumph, under the pretext of having been appointed Political Chief, and being the only person capable of rendering the Territory happy. The oldest Vocal of the Deputation, who in default of the Political Chief, ought to discharge his functions according to the law of the 6th of May, 1822, did not suit the wise foresight of the apothecary, and therefore tacitly he declared him unworthy of the public confidence. The military command was deposited with Captain Portilla to deceive, amuse and commit him, until the Engineer, the Lieutenant, Colonel, Adjutant, Inspector and Subdirector of the Colony, &c., &c., Don José Maria Padres appeared upon the stage, and who ought to have obtained the command by the order of succession, and because General Figueroa ought to have acknowledged himself ill and disposed to go to Mexico. Doubtless the plan was marvelously contrived! Production worthy of Torres!

The second article of the plan declares null and void, and of no force, the resolutions of the Deputation referring to the administration of the Missions. This is to understand the matter, Señor Doctor. What will Señor Hijar say to this mode of legislating? I venture to aver that he will not be so frightened as he was when the Deputation adopted the resolutions which the legislator, Torres, annuls.

The third article commands the restoration of the temporalities to the missionary friars. Who will believe that there is any sinister intention here? Then will I demonstrate it. If Torres knew as I do the probity of these friars, he would not have done them the indignity of stimulating them with the troublesome inducement of administering the temporalities which repeatedly they spontaneously renounced; it is not a sufficient temptation to commit them to a disastrous revolution even though the offer was sincere; but besides the insult to the honor of the friars, he seeks to deceive them like boys, making them the passive instruments of his depredations. Per-

fidious hypocrites! They do not fear to insult sound reason, and
therefore they pretend, and offer that which they least think of performing. How is it that they offer to restore the administration of
the temporalities to the friars, when by the fourth article which
follows in the plan, they are not to obstruct the powers of the
Director of Colonization as contained in the instructions which he
received from the Supreme Government? And these instructions, do
they not direct in the first article to take possession of all the property of the Missions? Then what have the friars to administer?
And is not this deception with the mask off? Do these infatuates
believe that we do not understand their complications? Have I not
proved manifestly that the instructions given to Hijar by the Minister of Relations were drawn from him through imposition, in order
to despoil the Indians of *California* of their property? Have I not
demonstrated to the Supreme Government on the unconstitutionality
of that decree in order that it may be revoked? Have I not demonstrated with facts and evidence that the true object of the colonizing
expedition was to take possession of the effects of the Missions? Is
anyone ignorant of the designs and plans of the Cosmopolitan Company? Is not the exhibition to which the Missions are condemned
to pay for the brigantine Natalia public and notorious? Is it not
certain that the estates of pious works belonging to these Missions
are to pay the value of the said vessel, for such is the desire of the
Director of Colonization and his followers? Is it not certain, that
in addition to this incumbrance, and having used the funds of the
nation to fit out the expedition of the Natalia, the passage and
freight of the colonists and their equipment, who came in her, are
also demanded of the nation? And the Missions and the federation,
have they received, or do they hope to receive any return for so
many exactions? Nothing—absolutely nothing; but with all that,
Torres and Apalategui could say, it costs nothing to deceive and
impose upon the padres if they allow it, offering them the administration of the temporalities; they will contribute to the overthrow
of the Government, and after that, will fall themselves. Such is the
extravagance of their pretensions.

I might make still further observations on the third article of the
plan, but it would be to trouble the public too much. Bear in mind
that the said article offers the missionary friars, the administration
of the temporalities, and in continuation, they contradict themselves
in the following manner:—

"4. The foregoing article shall not interfere with the powers of the Director of Colonization, in acting in conformity with the instructions which the Supreme Government gave him." Ah! villains, here we have uncovered the whole secret of your unbridled avarice. I have said already that it appears in various places of this writing, that the instructions which they seek to make use of are contrary to the Federal Constitution, and that under the *pretext* of fulfilling them in obedience to the Supreme Government, the cosmopolitans seek to enrich themselves upon the ruin of more than twenty thousand persons who are the legitimate owners of the property of the Missions. This is the necessary result whenever the said instructions may be put into practice by Señor Hijar. They are the only object of the revolution, by means of which alone they could get into their hands the property which they covet, after they had found it impossible to get it by honorable means.

By the fifth article they submit their plan to the approbation of the General Government. This is a fiction for the purpose of deceiving the public, because neither have the factionists relied upon the Government, nor would it approve in any case, attacks upon the authorities, whatever may be the pretext proclaimed by the seditious. Where was there ever a Government that approved of its own destruction by a contemptible handful of frenzied demagogues? Who has confided to them the fate and government of the citizen? Who has given to them the power to judge the authorities lawfully constituted, or to require of them an account of their administration?

Nor is the sixth article less nonsensical, in that they vow that they will not lay aside their arms until their plan is realized, and they constitute themselves protectors of the administration of justice and of the authorities. Who shall solve this riddle? Not the most sapient knight of the woeful countenance were capable of so much political prowess, and skill! they declare that they will not lay aside their arms until they see their plan realized, and at the moment of their proclamation they conceal themselves from the view of the profane, leaving the defense of their oaths to the charge of their squires! and so it is that the cowards are to cut their capers and are not to be exposed the public observation! And what is the meaning of this about the protection of justice and the authorities when a mortal blow is given to the body politic, cutting off the head, which is the Government? This, in the language of knights errant, is the reason of unreason—so we have righters of wrongs? There is no doubt, there are, there are! Protectors of justice, imitate Sancho in the government of his island!

I have paused to analyze the abortive plan in the pueblo of Los Angeles because my honor is atrociously attacked; and although the criminals who proclaimed it are at the disposition of the *tribunal* which must judge them, I desire that the public should know the villainy of its authors, who came to the tragical conclusion which is seen in the exposition which follows:

"Señor Constitutional Alcalde—Juan Gallardo and Felipe Castilla, in the name of the armed force which on this day has presented itself before you representing the rights of the people, with due respect appear and say: That having been solicited by the citizens Antonio Apalategui and Francisco Torres to co-operate with our physical force for the good and prosperity of the territory of Upper California as they represent it in the plan which for that purpose they presented to the Illustrious Ayuntamiento, which was not adopted; and satisfied that the illustrious body must have reflected with more judgment and ripeness on that subject; and considering at the same time that it is the best and only means of avoiding a disturbance, we have agreed to surrender, and we do now surrender the instigators of this affair, so that if their undertaking is in accordance with reason, they may justify themselves before the law, and establish their rights in the manner which the laws prescribe. If your authority and public justice should be satisfied that the step taken is criminal, yet let the good intention with which it was done be considered, and its purpose estimated as it deserves. Wherefore we unanimously supplicate you to be pleased to pardon us, decreeing forgiveness, justice which we implore, protesting respect for the laws.

"Pueblo of Los Angeles, March 7, 1835.

"For themselves and those under arms,

"FELIPE CASTILLO.
[A COPY.]   "ALVARADO."

The documents which follow are the answers which I gave to the Ayuntamiento of the Pueblo of Los Angeles, and a proclamation to the public:

"POLITICAL GOVERNMENT OF UPPER CALIFORNIA.

"By your despatch of the seventh inst., I am informed of the disagreeable events which have occurred in that pueblo, and of the audacity of Don Francisco Torres and Don Antonio Apalategui, who, not content to live peacefully under the protection of the laws, are plotting constantly against the society which nourishes them. I have examined their plan, and notwithstanding they have disguised their ambitious views, they are unable to conceal the rage with which they desire to devour the property of the unhappy natives in the Missions. For this reason, and because they see in my person an obstacle to their schemes, they seek my removal from the political and military command; for that reason they annul the resolutions of the Most Excellent Territorial Deputation which prevented the robbery of that property; and, for that in fine, in the fourth article of their plans they resolve to place the Director of Colonization in possession of them, in accordance with the instructions of the Government. This is the *deadly* poison with which those adventurers sought to sacrifice the Territory. The true and only object of their plan is to get into their power the property of the Missions to satiate their avarice at the cost of the sweat of the Californians. I, who have resolutely defended these interests, am the target of all their shots; but it does not matter: I do my duty, even though they may sacrifice me, so that the Californians may not be defrauded. I defend justice, the liberty, security and property of the citizen; my cause is that of the people and the laws; they speak for me; I sustain the Government which has been confided to me; if I abuse my authority or commit any crime, let me be accused before the Government itself, or before the tribunal which should judge me; if I have forfeited the public confidence I am ready to relinquish the command, but to hands of competent authority, and to him whom the laws have empowered for that purpose; but never will I, to the hands of a tumultuous meeting, that only speak of order to subvert it and the laws, to violate them. I have offered to the Californians and am ready to comply, to give up the command; I have renounced it to the General Government, and the Most Excellent Territorial Deputation have interposed their respectable influence to have my successor, as political chief, appointed; the decision will soon come and desires be satisfied; but in the meantime it is the duty of every citizen to respect and sustain my authority. Although you are aware of the monstrosity of the plan and the object to which it is directed, it has been *necessary* for me to make the present suggestions, in order to confirm your judicious opinion, and that you may make it understood by those who were compromised in the pronunciamiento, declaring to them: That their prompt return to order has satisfied me of their good intentions, and that they were only imposed on and deceived by the perfidious Torres and Apalategui, enemies of the people and of all government; that they have given proof which assures me of their good conduct hereafter, by delivering the seducers into the hands of justice, to be judged according to law; that all those engaged in the pronunciamiento, who desisted on the same day, are pardoned in the name of the Supreme Government, to which I will render an account, provided that they do not again mingle in revolution or disturbances which may break the peace; that they retire to live in peace in their houses, under the guaranties of the laws and the securities which are herein extended to them; and that they denounce whatever person, under whatever pretext, who may disturb public order. It remains for me to give to your illustrious body and honored neighborhood, the due homage of my gratitude and respect, for their heroic bearing and the noble firmness with which they refused to take part in the attempts which, in a moment, might have destroyed the public tranquillity. I tender you, therefore, for your eminent service, the most expressive thanks, recommending to you to double your care and vigilance for the public safety, and not to permit order to be disturbed under any pretext which detraction may invent. As to the accused Torres and Apalategui, I recommend you very earnestly to see that their persons are well secured and their cause be prosecuted with all possible brevity, since, although jurisdiction over it belongs to the military department, I suppose that the Alcalde has instituted proceedings and should prosecute them to judgment. If for this purpose, or other objects of the public service, you should need the assistance of armed force, you may demand it of the Lieut. Col. Don Nicholas Gutierrez until the arrival of the division which marches in that direction to complete the assurance of tranquillity. All of which I have the honor to say to you in answer to your note of the seventh inst., with which you transmit me the plan of the insurgents and the correspondence had upon that subject.

"God and Liberty. San Juan Bautista, March 13, 1835.

"JOSE FIGUEROA.

"The Most Illustrious Ayuntamiento of the Pueblo of Los Angeles."

"THE COMMANDANT GENERAL AND POLITICAL CHIEF OF UPPER CALIFORNIA TO THE INHABITANTS OF THE TERRITORY—FELLOW CITIZENS:—The Genius of Evil has appeared among you, scattering the deadly poison of discord. The enemies of order, envious of the felicity which this Territory has enjoyed, and not satisfied with the blood of their fellow countrymen, which they have caused to be shed in the interior of the Republic, brought Californians the sad *present* of anarchy; the repeated proofs which they have received that Californians will not succumb to their iniquitous projects, has irritated their presumptuous pride, and they wish to sacrifice them at whatever cost. This is the sum of all the good which Hijar, Padres, Torres, Berdusco and others brought to California. A country which was progressing under the shadow of peace and confidence, they seek to rob of its repose, and to plunge into the disasters of a civil war. These, fellow citizens, are the magnificent projects which occupy the heated fancy of those men. From the day they put their foot upon the shores of the Territory have they been plotting secretly its ruin, until on the 7th inst. they withdrew the veil from their immeasurable ambition. In the pueblo of Los Angeles certain individuals of Sonora, seduced by Don Francisco Torres, and the Spaniard Don Antonio Apalategui, proclaimed a plan of conspiracy against the Territorial Government. That famous abortion of detraction abounds with artful, atrocious calumnies and falsehoods, with which it is sought to deceive the people, in order to lead them to disobedience, to destroy the prestige of authority, and attack the persons who exercise it. Such is the tissue of abuse with which they honor me, and which I propose to refute with a manifesto so soon as public business will permit; but in the meantime I will state briefly their pretensions: They seek my removal from the command, because I opposed their destruction of the property of the Missions, and because Señor Hijar wishes to be put into my place. They make use of the artifice of choosing the First Alcalde of the Capital for Political Chief, without regarding that in default of this magistrate the law calls the First Vocal of the Deputation in his place; but it is necessary, in order to conceal the ambition of the aspirant, to disorganize the Government entirely, and so to open the way for him. They demand Capt. Portilla as Commandant General, to substitute Señor Padres in his place, who desires it. The annul the resolutions of the Most Excellent Deputation, because they guarantee to the Indians the enjoyment of their property, which they wish to take from them; they demand the suspension of the secularization of the Missions, restoring apparently to the friars the admission of the temporalities, because they sought to deceive them and thereby to interest them in favor of the resolution; and, finally, to put the Director of Colonization in possession of the property of the Missions, to dispose of according to the instructions which the Supreme Government gave him, as if the public were not informed that that order was unconstitutional, because it carries with it the spoliation of the property of more than twenty thousand persons. In a word, all this

is sought by force, which is the law of the highwayman; in this the
Constitution and laws are attacked—all the guaranties of society
are violated, and the social pact is dissolved, leaving the fate of the
people to the will of the hardy usurper, who seeks to rule ever
against the wish of the Supreme Government, which they pretend
to respect, and of the citizens, whom they desire to subjugate. I have
stated succinctly the object of the revolution, which fortunately terminated in its very cradle; the compromised parties themselves, as
soon as they knew the crime they were about to commit—that the
Illustrious Ayuntamiento of Los Angeles disapproved of their conduct, and that no son of California took part in their aberrations—
gave up their attempt and handed over the instigators, and justice
will pass upon their offense, and inflict upon them the punishment
imposed by the laws which they have broken. Tranquillity, which
for a moment might have been disturbed by these events, was immediately re-established; but the advocates of anarchy do not cease to
preach *discord,* nor will I lose sight of their liberticidal plans. This
fellow citizens, is all that has happened. As to myself, the public
will judge of my proceedings, the Government will hold me to any
responsibility which I may have incurred, and the tribunal to whom
it belongs will apply the law, if I have committed any offense. The
office of Political Chief I have renounced, and the Most Excellent
Deputation has interposed its influence to have my successor appointed; the decision will soon come, and you will see me submissively deposit in his hands the powers which the Most Excellent
President of the Republic delegated to me to govern this Territory.
In the meantime, fellow citizens, give no credit to the false suggestions of the enemies of order and of the Government, who, blinded
by ambition and avarice, invoke the sacred name of Justice to profane it, and to waste your blood and property. Continue united and
peaceful in the enjoyment of your social blessings—that is true happiness, and the only reward to which my ambition looks.

"JOSE FIGUEROA.

"Monterey, March 16, 1835."

Although the revolution appeared and expired in a single day in
the pueblo of Los Angeles, it had its ramifications at the head of
which were the principal aspirants. Under the pretext of establishing a colony, they sought to organize an armed force to sustain their
pretensions. In fact, they brought from Mexico a quantity of rifles
and cartridges, which the Government commanded to be furnished
them. These and various other preparations they endeavored to con-

ceal from me. I was acquainted with their designs and only tolerated them, in the hope that they would *exhibit* their crime more publicly, or recede from it. I could not succeed notwithstanding repeated proofs of consideration and forbearance, since the more I strove to convince them and divert them from their tortuous views, or the more I overlooked their designs, so much the more insolent they became, perhaps because they regarded my moderation as weakness or cowardice. Thus it is that animated with that confidence, they daily pressed forward their preparations, and even Señor Hijar himself in spite of his pretended modesty, was not able to conceal his participation in those movements. For that cause he set out for San Francisco Solano, on pretense of assembling the colony, when he had always regarded it with the utmost indifference. For that also he sent under his signature, in the month of February to the Rev. Father, President Fr. Narciso Duran, a copy of the absurd communication which he addressed me on the 23d of October: for that he concealed the maneuvers of Berdusco and Lara, who in his name and under his immediate protection, were exciting to revolution: for that same Señor Hijar without having received the command, was haranguing the Indians in the Missions through which he passed, exhorting them to defend liberty which nobody was attacking; for that he met Torres, Berdusco, Lara and Araujo in secret conferences which they held in the house of Bonifacio; for that, in fine, he looked with so much contempt upon the propositions of peace which I made him at various times, entreating him to restrain his proteges, that I might not be obliged to punish them, since I was aware of their plan and forbore all proceedings from consideration for his person. Whether then Señor Hijar was decidedly the protector of the revolution, or whether he was used as a blind instrument by its authors, the fact is, that his adhesion was felt, and after I observed in friendly intercourse and various other modes, his attachment to my enemies, he could inspire me with no confidence, because even doing him the favor to believe him innocent of that which his creatures were plotting—he has a soul so insensible and apathetic, that his very existence would be indifferent to him. Such being the case, and the revolution breaking out openly, what should I do with Señor Hijar? Is he not the rival that my adversaries set up to cover their crimes and deceive the public? Should I have permitted any longer my condescension to be abused? Should I have longer exposed, than I had exposed, the public tranquillity by an imprudent tolerance? I believed it my duty to remove all motive for disturbance and this could not be done if I left its causes in existence. I was not in condition to wait until proceedings should first be instituted, because, besides that on such occasions it is difficult to prove exactly the secret crimes of the seditious, they were waiting only for a favorable occasion to strike a blow. The small military force which I have under my orders, and the diversified demands which it has to meet throughout an extent of more than two hundred leagues, is another motive which obliged me to act with energy. For all these considerations, I ordered the arrest of Lara and Berdusco; Hijar and Padres I suspended from the Commission of Directors of the Colony, and compelled them to proceed to Mexico for the disposal of the Supreme Government, for which I addressed the former the following note:

"POLITICAL GOVERNMENT OF UPPER CALIFORNIA.

"The revolution has finally occurred, which Señor Torres went to excite, as I announced to you in a friendly manner, informing you that your friends wished to compromise you in order to overthrow the Government. This fact, which was revealed to me beforehand, and other antecedents which I explained to you, directed all to a conspiracy against the public order and the laws, impose upon me the duty to take measures to secure the public tranquillity, constantly threatened: since the prudent deportment which I have observed towards all, and the frank manner with which I have exhibited to you their *erroneous* desires, that you might keep them within the limits of duty, have not proved sufficient to restrain the audacity of your adherents. Notwithstanding I had received in advance, information of the projects they were contriving to attain their ends, I have kept silence in order that in no event I may be chargeable with violence; but now the veil has been removed, and they have very promptly and feelingly been undeceived; the imprudent persons whom Torres succeeded in seducing, discovered their error and themselves delivered him over to justice, a prisoner, and the same with his associate Apalategui. In consequence of these events I have ordered you and the Adjutant Inspector, Don José Maria Padres, to be suspended from the commission which the Government entrusted to you, turning over the arms, munitions, property, and all that you have, to the charge of Ensign Don Mariano G. Vallejo, and that you depart immediately, holding yourself at the disposition of the Supreme Government, before which you will answer the charges which may be brought against you for the conduct which you have observed since your entrance into this Territory. I have the honor to communicate this much for your information and compliance.

"God and Liberty. San Juan Bautista, 13th March, 1835.

"JOSE FIGUEROA.

"Señor Don JOSE MARIA DE HIJAR."

Señor Hijar replied in the communication which follows:

"You say to me in your communication of the 13th inst., that at last the revolution had broken out which Señor Torres went to excite, as you had told me in private; that the instigators are prisoners, and that this obliges you to take measures to secure tranquillity; commanding in fact that I, and the Adjutant Inspector, Don José Maria Padres, be suspended from the commission which the Supreme Government confided to us, turning over to the ensign, Don Mariano G. Vallejo the *arms,* munitions, property and all else in our charge, and concluding that we depart immediately, holding ourselves at the disposal of the Supreme Government in order to answer the charges which may be brought against us for the conduct which we have observed since our entry into this Territory. As to the first you will permit me to say, that the revolution of which you speak appears to me merely imaginary: I will never be able to persuade myself that Señor Torres, who was passing as a traveller bearing important papers for the Supreme Government, should undertake a revolution without object and in a country where he has neither connections nor acquaintance. I see in all this only a mystery which time will disclose. If the veil has been withdrawn for you, for me it still remains sufficiently dense; but I hope that so soon as it shall be rent, things will appear as they are in reality, and all be clear as light itself. It is supposeable that some colonists, heady and justly resentful, might have desired to revolutionize, but I do not know how that could involve me, as if I had instigated or taken part in the revolution. Nevertheless you command me to be suspended, giving me thereby a blow the most terrible, and wounding me in the fibre most delicate. You have endeavored to stain my reputation which I esteem more than existence; it is sought to make me appear guilty of crimes which certainly I have not committed, but I solemnly promise to drag my persecutor, whoever he may be, before the proper tribunals, when I will exact the fullest satisfaction. You know very well that if I remained in this Territory it was only at the repeated and urgent requests of yourself, of a Committee of the Most Excellent Deputation and of others, private persons, whom you are acquainted with; you know likewise that I was going to leave the Territory within a few days, and that consequently I had no interest to continue as Director of the Colony. I make this little digression that you may understand, that the profound regret which devours me, does not spring from the fact that I am suspended from a commission which I was going to give up, but from the injurious manner in which it has been done. I have discharged many delicate and important duties and always with distinction, and the different Governments which have availed themselves of my small capacity have been satisfied with my conduct, never making the least complaint against me; my public conduct, well known in the interior, had never received a stain, and this formed all my glory; but it appears that heaven had reserved it for you to *inflict* upon me the most cruel insult. Yes, Señor General, if I had not hoped to vindicate myself, I would have shot myself that I might not drag out an opprobrious existence and not to appear contemptible in the eyes of my equals. I know no authority which you possess to suspend me, but it is necessary to yield to force; therefore your orders shall be in everything obeyed and I am ready to set out as soon as you furnish me the means (would that it were tomorrow). I will present myself before the Supreme Government with that serenity which a tranquil conscience inspires, and there I hope to confound my accuser. I will terminate this communication, declaring to you that we have suffered unheard-of vexations; that we have been treated in a scandalous manner and such as would not be used with a band of robbers, attacking rudely the imprescriptible rights of man which our charter guarantees. All this would have been avoided, and I would have caused the arms, munitions and everything else to be delivered without the necessity of ill-treating anyone, if Señor Vallejo had presented me your communication, but purposely it has been sought to make us feel all the weight of arbitrary power, treating us rather as outlaws than as Mexicans. Patience, Señor General; perhaps the laws will some day reign. I have transcribed your communication to the Adjutant Inspector for his information, with all which I think I have sufficiently replied to your communication of the 13th inst.

"God and Liberty. San Francisco Solano, March 17, 1835.

"JOSE MARIA DE HIJAR.

"To the Political Chief, General Don JOSE FIGUEROA."

So great is the obfuscation of Señor Hijar that, notwithstanding the public acts of his immediate dependents, who, fed from his hand, he seeks to create a cloud placing them in doubt, as though I were a jester who occupied myself with trifles, or in supposing for the sake of amusement the event which I communicated to him officially. Let it be observed that he says Torres was carrying important papers to Mexico, proof unequivocal of the great confidence which this adventurous Esculapius enjoyed with him; and also he adds that he never will be able to persuade himself that this man would have undertaken this resolution without object, and in a country which is unknown to him. What hypocrisy! I have proved conclusively that Torres was the immediate agent of the rebellion, and that it had its determinate object. Why did it not break out before this same Torres arrived in Los Angeles? For what purpose this untimely friendship with Apalategui, with his gang of Sonoranians? And wherefore did these same Sonoranians, repenting of their guilty attempt, designate Torres and Apalategui as their instigators and the prime movers, and deliver them as prisoners to the authorities?

With all the sophistry and circumlocution that Señor Hijar may use, he will never be able to persuade the Californians that he had no hand in this affair, which I myself announced to him beforehand, from reliable information that I had of its traitorous intent. By throwing the stone and hiding the hand, or sheltering himself behind the names of others, he thinks to avoid the severity of the laws; but he is mistaken. All his steps condemn him, as we have seen.

He vaticinates that he will drag me before the tribunals. All the necessary antecedent facts will be already before them, and I am ready to present myself and to confound him who would trample upon my authority, with reason, with the law, and with justice. The probity of the Judges cannot but be favorable to him who preserved the integrity of the Republic and maintained peace and law in this Territory.

Señor Hijar was never begged to remain in this country. I only interested myself, as did the rest of the gentlemen of the conferences, that he should not carry the wearied colonists to Lower California, as the Directors imprudently desired, or pretended to desire.

If the *services* which Señor Hijar boasts of, have been advantageous in other places, here his apathetic reserve, and his concealed management to take the political command by surprise, have been prejudicial; and if the mind of the Californians had not been so penetrating, and if I had reposed in a vain confidence, the triumph of the cosmopolites is certain—for their chiefs are skillful in the arts of intrigue, and know how to make the best use of their florid and vain loquacity; but their energy and frank and loyal valor are so deficient, that they have not enough even for the cowardly action

of shooting themselves, as Señor Hijar, possessed of his anglo-
mania, says that he would have done, if he had not hoped to vindicate himself.

He denies me the power to suspend him, and he has before asserted that he is submissive to the Political Government and recognizes its authority.

The unheard-of vexations of which he complains were nothing but
the measures absolutely necessary to collect the arms and munitions
that Señor Padres was concealing, and to prevent him from calling
out the colonists and thus render necessary a resort to force. The
truth is, that owing to the skill and military prudence with which
the Ensign Don Mariano G. Vallejo performed this duty, it resulted
in no one's being wounded or even bruised. It is now seen that the
attack upon the imprescriptible rights of man was nothing but the
prevention of an improper use of arms; but it was a sounding phrase,
which ought not to have been omitted. I make no comment.

Received on board the Sardinian frigate, the Rosa, which was in
the Bay of San Francisco, Señors Hijar, Padres, Berdusco, Lara
and others were carried to the roadstead of San Pedro and transferred to the Anglo-American schooner, the Loriot. They sailed in
May last, with Señors Don Bueneventura Araujo, Don Francisco
Torres, and Don Antonio Apalategui, for San Blas, to abide the
decision of the Supreme Government.

The *condition* of the colonists has been improved by the separation from the chiefs, who were enslaving them and leading them
to their total ruin. Established wherever suits them best, aided as
far as possible by the Government, and befriended by the Californians, they do not lack subsistence or employment for the industrious
—already the progress of some of them being a subject of remark.

Peace has been consolidated, and with it its inestimable benefits.
It would be useless to say that the Cosmopolitan Company was dissolved of its own accord, and as it was based on the triple representation of Señors Hijar and Padres, as founders and principal
partners, as Directors of the Colony and Chiefs of the Territory.
The colony and the commands were the basis of the company, and
the most powerful assistance for the magnificent speculation, which
they had planned in idea, setting at nought the laws which prohibit
employees from being traders.

Don José Maria Padres has been the most open and active agent
in this enterprise; I have already mentioned that with his projects
in regard to the Missions, which were in noway connected with his

office, and his tortuous conduct, he disturbed the tranquillity of the Territory in 1830, and was the cause that the lawful government of Lieut. Col. Don Manuel Victoria was resisted by some imprudent citizens, by reason of which he incurred the disapprobation of the Supreme Government; but, nevertheless, he succeeded by the force of artifice to return with the colony and the position of Adjutant Inspector for this Territory, from which he had been expelled. I have touched upon this subject that it may be seen from what date he has been occupied in his mercantile views upon California.

It is presumable that this officious gentleman with the influence which he had over the mind of Señor Hijar and which he prided himself upon enjoying with the Most Excellent Vice-President Gomez Farias, was the same who intrigued in Mexico, to prevent the Supreme Government from seeking information of the Most Excellent Deputation or myself, in regard to the resources which could be reckoned upon here for the settlement and support of the colonists who were coming salaried until the expiration of the full year of their establishment, being to be furnished, as I have said, with grain, *cattle,* and tools; for all which, heavy expenses were necessarily to be incurred, beyond the capacity of the public treasury of this Territory to support, which does not meet even the half of its ordinary demand, and was then, and still is, without a Supreme order for such supplies. But as the report of this Political Government could not be favorable to the object of those who from Mexico were speculating upon the property of these natives, the asking for it was omitted, whilst a pretty plan of destruction was being formed, in substance, to secularize the Missions, in order to deprive the ministering fathers of the tutorship of the neophytes and leave these defenseless, while the Director and Subdirector, in possession of the political and military commands, were disposing at their pleasure, and under the pretext of aiding the establishment of the colonists, of all the property of the Indians; since, the shepherd being removed, it is easy for the wolves to devour the flocks.

But Providence frustrated projects so improper, by a succession of events that the Directors were not capable of foreseeing, who from their departure from Mexico were experiencing the inconveniences of their ill-considered enterprise of colonization as well as of their boastful mercantile Cosmopolitan Company, as destitute of funds, as rich in hopes, and notable for the pedantry of its name; the which had the grief to see their brigantine Natalia stranded upon this coast for the want of cables and through the ignorance and carelessness of those in command, a few days after she anchored in this port.

We have seen that Señor Hijar, under the pretext of his commission, and relying on certain unconstitutional instructions, impolitic and perhaps surreptitious, wished to possess himself of the Missions and attack the unquestionable right of the property of the natives, and that he disowned the legal authority of the Deputation over the common property, and the inspection and vigilance which were *incumbent* upon me as Political Chief, charged with preserving unimpaired the social guaranties, and with observing the laws and causing them to be observed; and I have already related how he sought to make use of my authority as Commandant General, degrading the national arms by making them to subserve his unjust pretensions, and lend their support and sanction to the iniquitous spoliation of property which was meditated against the helpless Indians.

It is wonderful to see the Directors of the colony so bent upon their lamentable undertaking of usurping the property of others that they are compelled to drag in by the hair to their aid, what they call the eminent right of the Government, and to allege that the Missions have no right over their property, being moral persons, and as such, incapable of acquiring property, and still less of holding it. What a sublime philosophy and what delusive theories have these revolutionists, in order to possess themselves of the property of others! More cowardly than bandits, they make use of sophism, and empty and high sounding words; and assuming the mask of patriotism and religion, while they outrage their country and make mockery of religion, opening their schools and making proselytes of the incautious, feeling themselves sufficiently strong, there is no longer any barrier which can restrain them; and with the formalities of law they trample on everything; that only they respect; that only is sacred which pertains to their edict. Do they not see that if moral persons cannot acquire or retain property, as they say, neither can the Government acquire or retain it? Do they not see the conclusion from their principles, that the eminent right of the Government is null in the case which they had alleged, since no one can give that which he does not possess? What contradictions follow from this prurience to pass for learned, and this desire to grow rich by the force of philosophy!

Who will not be struck with Señor Hijar's assertion in his note of the sixth of November, that the Spanish laws which protect the property of the Indians, conflict with our system? Better might he say that they conflict with the system of depredations which they were bringing with them, adopted. He sought to invalidate the wise law of the Recopilacion, which ordains that sovereign orders which tend to deprive anyone of his possessions, shall be *obeyed,* but not executed before he shall have been first heard and cast in a contradictory proceeding. Yet, nevertheless, he pretended that the Indian, ignorant as he is, needy and half wild, was equal, identically and absolutely, in the exercise of political rights, to the rest of the citizens; perhaps the better to deceive him and to surprise him undefended with more facility. According to these principles we should blot from our codes the laws which recognize the paternal power, which regulate the superiority of the husband in marriage, all those which speak of the curatorship and tutorship of minors, idiots, madmen, prodigals and various others.

Legal equality carried to such an extreme would break up society. Such is the fatal attempt to equalize everything in appearance, in order to create inequality in fact, and to destroy, leaving the fanaticism of pretended philosophers to reign alone, intolerant and despotic. This is the direction of our sophists and small politicians; of these gentlemen who deny the Indians the right of property in their Missions; but the plan was to overwhelm them with rights and deprive them of their estate. This is the philanthropy which was going to be applied to the California Indian.

Fortunately the theories and pompous promises of the Directors of the Colony, and their garrulity and spirit of proselytism had no followers among the sensible Californians, and despairing of finding aid among them for their projects of revolution, they resorted, as I have said, by means of their emissaries, to seducing a parcel of emigrants from Sonora, who had come to seek their fortune in this Territory, and chanced to be in the pueblo of Los Angeles. And in truth it was only in the mind of such miserable adventurers that the mission of Señors Torres and Apalategui, who went from this place, and from the very house of Señor Hijar, with this special object, could find a reception. But their seduction and pronunciamiento was but for a moment, and served only to bring upon its authors and instigators, general animadversion, to expose them to the condemnation of the public, and to cause the immediate leaders the degrading humiliation of seeing themselves delivered as prisoners to the inexorable arm of justice by those imprudent Sonoranians themselves, who at once discovered their error and the perfidiousness of those who had abused their situation and compromised their thoughtless confidence.

The Directors of the colony have denied taking part in the criminal insurrection of which I speak, prompted by their satellites, Torres and Apalategui. But who is ignorant in Monterey that Torres was the favorite of Hijar, and one of those who, with Lara, Berdusco and others, composed the staff of the colony? Who doubts that this quack was one of the daily counsellors of Hijar, and for his grand head, medico-political knowledge, his cunning, calm disposition, and his hypocritical and subterranean character, enjoyed the highest esteem of his chief? Hijar himself shows it plainly when in his communication of the 17th of March, he confesses that he had sent him to Mexico with papers of the greatest importance. But there is more proof, in the suit which is pending in the civil tribunal of this city, and which was prosecuted against the Sonoranian, Don Miguel Hidalgo, for bearing certain letters addressed from Los Angeles by Torres to Berdusco and others. It appears, that in the preliminary meetings which were held in the house of Antonio Trujillo, for the purpose of getting up the pronunuciamiento against my authority, it was proposed by Torres himself distinctly, that the principal object of the insurgents was to be the placing of Señor Hijar in the political command, and Señor Padres in the military, and nobody in the Territory has doubted it; the unanimous public opinion attests it; and for the same reason in a very few days after Torres' departure for Los Angeles, Hijar sent out with his satellites to unite with Padres in San Francisco Solano, and to second in the north, with the part of the colonists on which they could rely, the movements of the Sonoranians which occurred in the south.

This was the strategical plan that they considered most advantageous, but it failed them, and they were completely disconcerted and confounded by the public spirit, by my vigilance, and by the zeal and energy that the well-deserving officers who serve under my command, displayed, especially the Ensign Vallejo, commandant of San Francisco Solano. And it is not to be *doubted* that the Supreme Government to whose disposal I have sent them, will bring grave charges against them and the rest of the abettors of the rebellion.

As the greatest question treated of in this Manifesto is not merely of a local, but of a national interest, and on the other hand, it is the flank on which the speculators, my antagonists, attempt to blacken a reputation which I have endeavored to preserve without stain, I could do no less than dwell at length upon the narration of the events and the exposition and refutation of the anti-social doctrines with which it was sought to corrup the virgin California, in order to water with blood her fields of peace and fertility, destroy the riches of her Missions, sow anarchy and upon the ruins of the Territory for the political hypocrites, patriarchs of revolution and disorder to seize upon the abundant wealth of the Indians acquired by their personal labor under the direction and evangelical patience of their venerable missionaries.

My continual duties and my much broken health, ought to excuse me in the eyes of the public, if inadvertently I have failed to touch upon any point necessary to form a decisive opinion. I believe I have omitted nothing essential. There are many witnesses who were on the spot, impartial, and acquainted with the series of these events, who can correct my mistakes and inaccuracies, and combat my errors and omissions, if, involuntarily, I have committed any of these faults.

Above all, my declared rivals, the Señors Director and Subdirector of the colony Don José Maria de Hijar and Don José Maria Padres, have the liberty to answer me and publish their accusation against me substantiated, and their imputations upon the California people whom they have openly vilified; we have the liberty of the press, they pass for literati and superfine politicians; they have their learning and liberty with which to attack this Manifesto rationally and to establish their *doctrines* by lawful means, and clear up their conduct, which in the opinion of many, as is proved by the narration of the facts and the fanciful and ridiculous creation of the Cosmopolitan Company, partakes more of injustice, of trade and monopoly, than of patriotism. How far are these feeble republicans, priding themselves on their austerity, from that virtue, that disinterestedness of the Cincinnati, the Papirii and the Fabii! Their words are belied by their conduct, and servile, despotic and covetous, in the midst of their pretended liberalism, they dissipate by their actions the illusion of their promises, and lose by degrees the prestige which their ominous theories succeeded in introducing in the impressible infancy of our country.

The time has come to be convinced that these men were born to be middling poets, writers of romances and novels, and not to be rulers of a polished and regulated people. Such men have caused Mexican blood to flow in abundance. Their names stain the pages of our history. Anarchy, disorder, confusion, ruin, are the fruit of their toils and the result of their theories—brilliant on the surface, and, beyond measure, corrupt at bottom.

Men dyed in revolutionary scenes, and sectaries of anarchical doctrines, were those who, as leaders, brought to this Territory the unfortunate colonists—causing them to suffer by their wastefulness and stupid management, a thousand unnecessary privations and discomforts, as is notorious.

At their arrival, I found myself at the head of the political and military administration of the country. I think I did my duty in circumstances so critical. I withstood their pretensions, unveiled their designs, exposed their impudence, combatted their doctrines, confounded their presumption, broke up their projects, humbled their arrogance, spoiled their plans, reined in their audacity, extinguished their torch of revolution which they had lighted, and saved the property of the Indians and the riches of the Missions; saved the unfortunate colonists, whom they were conducting to a precipice, and maintained the peace and order and well-being of California : of this important point of the Republic, which needs especial care and exquisite guardianship, lest it should be launched upon the career of disorder by the suggestions of the many *adventurers,* native and foreign, who, like meteors on a tempestuous night, are on every side crossing among us.

From my childhood have I served in the ranks of independence from its earliest days. With my little talent and less instruction, with all my strength, and with my blood, and with my health, have I contributed, to the utmost of my ability, to the glories of the country. The name of my rivals is only known in the anniversaries of fratricidal war, in civil discords, in the farce of anarchists, and in that sect, ominious and abhorred in America and Europe, which constitutes the misfortune of our age. It may be permitted me to draw this parallel in satisfaction of my sense of honor, outraged with equal injustice and calumny. One point there is in this Manifesto so devoid of positive and conclusive proof, that only the individual opinion which each one entertains of Señor Hijar and myself can incline the balance. I speak of the secret conference to which that gentleman invited me by his billet of the 26th of October, and which I have related on page 54.

I have endeavored to express myself in strict conformity with the truth, and without returning insults for insults. If in part there should be observed anything too rough or energetic in my style, let it borne in mind that I am defending myself from calumny, and that I am a soldier who has passed his life in the fatigues of arduous campaigns, and in offices also military, and, consequently, that I am not accustomed to the elegant phraseology and rhetorical flowers with which other writers of more literary merit than I could possibly have, adorn their productions.

But this, my insufficiency, does not intimidate me. I am not a rhetorician or politician. I am a Mexican *soldier,* and do not seek to pass for a scholar. In a martial and simple style, at the same time exact and well considered, I have endeavored to write, in order to present in all their aspects the artful views of the Directors of the Colony and their seditious cosmopolitan satellites.

The malevolence of the refractory does not deter me. I speak before the public, upon the theatre of the events, to my contemporaries, in the face of all the witnesses who were present. Everything is presented to view; I omit nothing essential; I exhibit all the correspondence, and I relate the events with exactness. Let my conduct be judged—let it be compared with that of my adversaries, and let all the circumstances which I have explained be borne in mind. This is what I beg of my readers. In the meantime, reposing on the correctness of my intentions and purity, and absolute legality of my proceedings, I hope that the discerning Mexican People will do me justice, and favor me with their incorruptible opinion.

Port of Monterey, 4th of September, 1835.

JOSE FIGUEROA.

———

NOTE—While this Manifesto was in press, on the 29th of the same month of September, died the General of Brigade, Don José Figueroa: in consequence of this mournful event, the Most Excellent Deputation resolved that the proceedings which follow, should be inserted in this pamphlet.

———

PROCEEDINGS,
TO PERPETUATE THE MEMORY
OF THE
DECEASED GENERAL OF BRIGADE,
DON JOSE FIGUEROA,
Commandant-General and Political Chief of Upper California,
HAD IN THE MOST EXCELLENT DEPUTATION OF THIS TERRITORY

MOST EXCELLENT SENOR :—Our Chief is dead; the protector of the Territory, the father of our California, our friend, our mentor,

General Don José Figueroa is dead: the citizens surround his funeral couch, and with eyes fastened upon the stiffened corpse, are dumb, and with sighs lament the great man whom death snatches from us. The sad, the lamentable news spreads swiftly, *grief* seizes upon all, and the sorrow is general.

The doleful echo of the bells, and the dismal report of the artillery, cause to gush from the heart tears the most compressed; all is bitterness, all is grief. The Californians lament a beneficent father, who has given to their prosperity an incalculable impetus and with an attention without example, and a constant and unequaled industry, has promoted every branch of the public welfare: him who extinguished the torch of discord, and prevented this virgin soil from being drenched in the blood of its sons; him who planted the olive of peace and has cultivated under its shadow every class of virtues which have been successively developed in the loyal breasts of these inhabitants; him to whom our agriculture owes its security and extension, our commerce its protection; him who knew how to repel anarchy when it dared to land upon our peaceful shores; him who consoled the widow, protected the orphan and succored the soldier; him who protected merit and fostered learning; in a word, him who labored to organize our social order.

Strangers even manifest in their grief the affection which they entertained for him, and the lofty conception which they had formed of the *superior* genius who presided over us; the child of the desert, the wild Indian, makes known to us, though in rustic manner, the grief which oppresses him, for so great a loss.

The name of General Figueroa is heard everywhere; his merits are recounted, his political skill is extolled, his zeal and efficiency for the common good, and that habitual skill with which he knew how to captivate the heart. His integrity, his probity, are acknowledged by the public, who declare him an eminent patriot and well-deserving son of the country; all praise and recognize the eminent merit of General Figueroa, and shall not the Most Excellent Deputation of the Territory express how fully it participates in this sentiment? I see in the worthy members of which it is composed, unequivocal marks of the pain which the premature death of our beloved chief inflicts upon them. This feeling is just; yes, it is just, it is laudable; let the whole world know it, and let it be seen that in Upper California they know how to appreciate true merit.

And now that adoring the inscrutable decrees of Providence we have implored at the foot of the altar, divine mercy for the man whom the right hand of the Omnipotent deprives us of; and now that we have rendered him all political and military funeral honors as was his due, let us give, well deserving Deputies, a public and eternal testimony of our gratitude and love for the General Figueroa; let us raise up his memory to the height of our esteem; let us immortalize his glory and our gratitude, and bind his brows with a crown of evergreens. Yes, Most Excellent Señor, hear, your Excellency, and be pleased to approve the following propositions:

1. The portrait of General Don José Figueroa shall be hung in the Hall of the Sessions of this Most Excellent Deputation, in proof of the esteem which it has ever entertained for his distinguished merit.

2. That to perpetuate the pleasing recollection of that distinguished person and the gratitude of this body, there shall be erected a durable monument, with a suitable inscription, in one of the most public and conspicuous places of this capital, and to that end, that the illustrious Ayuntamiento be appealed to, with transmission of these proceedings, in order that all may be done under its care and direction in the manner to be anticipated from its pure patriotism, its noble sentiments, and the love which it has professed for the man whom we deplore.

3. That three copies shall be made of these proceedings; one shall be delivered to the executors of the deceased General and Chief; another shall be sent to his widowed lady and children, and the third to the printer, that it may be printed and published in continuation of his Manifesto, which is now in press.

Monterey, 9th October, 1835.

JUAN B. ALVARADO.

In the session of this day, the Most Excellent Deputation took this proposition under consideration and it was referred to the Committee on Government.

CASTRO, President.

MANUEL JIMENO, Vocal Secretary.

MOST EXCELLENT SENOR:—The Committee on Government has examined the proposition of Señor Alvarado, in which he announces the lamentable news of the death of the General and Political Chief of the Territory, Don José Figueroa, and moves that this Most Excellent Deputation do all in its power for his memory and honor, praying: First—That the portrait of General Don José Figueroa be hung in the hall of sessions of this Most Excellent *Deputation.* Second—That to perpetuate the pleasing recollection of that distinguished person, there be erected a durable monument, with a suitable inscription, in one of the most public and conspicuous places in the capital, appealing to the illustrious Ayuntamiento to see all done under its direction and care. Third—That three copies be made of these proceedings—that one may be delivered to the executors of our deceased General and Chief; another be sent to his widowed lady and children, and the third to the printer, that it may be printed and published in continuation of his Manifesto now in press. The Committee believes that the considerations presented by Señor Alvarado being public and notorious, are liable to no objection, because the name of General José Figueroa is repeated everywhere. All praise and acknowledge his pre-eminent merit, and his distinguished and ancient services rendered to the country. He always observed the laws and caused them to be observed, and sacrificed himself to fulfill the measure of his public duties. It was he who on landing upon the shores of these coasts, planted the olive of peace; it was he who gave security to agriculture; it was he who was vigilant to establish learning and schools for youth; it was he who promoted all the objects which concern the public good of the Territory; it was he who extinguished the torch of discord; it was he, finally, who, by his example and his industry, cultivated the virtues of every kind, earning by such service the name of Father of our Territory. Yes, Most Excellent Señor, the Committee would believe itself *unworthy* in the sight of the citizens if it should attempt to oppose sentiments so natural as those which Señor Alvarado expresses, and therefore concludes, submitting for the deliberation of the Most Excellent Deputation the following propositions:

1. That the three propositions of Señor Alvarado be approved and put in immediate execution.

2. That at the foot of the portrait of Gen. Don José Figueroa there be given him the title of Benefactor of the Territory of Upper California.

Monterey, October 14, 1835.

MANUEL JIMENO.

MONTEREY, October 14, 1835.

In the session of this day the Most Excellent Deputation approved the foregoing report, with its two propositions.

JOSE CASTRO, President.

MANUEL JIMENO, Vocal Secretary.

[A COPY.]   MANUEL JIMENO.

NOTE.—The foregoing proceedings were transmitted to the Illustrious Ayuntamiento, and it appears that it is proposed to place upon the monument in contemplation the following inscriptions:

D. O. M.

DOMINO JOSEPH FIGUEROA,

PRAFECTO ATQUE MILITARI DUCI
SUPERIORIS CALIFORNIÆ,
PATRIÆ PARENTI.

IN PIGNUS OBSERVAMTIAE,
GRATIQUE AMINI SENSUS,
CŒTUS CURATORUM PROVINCIÆ
HUGUSQUE METROPOLIS MUNICESSIUM
SUMPTIBUS DICARANT PUBLICIS
HOC MONUMENTUM.

OBIIT, MONTEREGGIO
III CAL. OCT. A. D. MDCCCXXXV.,
ÆTATIS SUÆ XLIII.

———

T. G. O.

TO THE ETERNAL MEMORY OF THE

GENERAL DON JOSE FIGUEROA,

POLITICAL AND MILITARY CHIEF
OF UPPER CALIFORNIA,
FATHER OF THE COUNTRY.

THE PROVINCIAL DEPUTATION
AND THE AYUNTAMIENTO OF MONTEREY
DEDICATE THIS MONUMENT
AT THE PUBLIC EXPENSE
AS A MARK OF GRATITUDE.

HE DIED IN THIS CAPITAL
ON THE 29TH OF SEPTEMBER A. D. 1835,
AND OF HIS AGE THE 43D.

750 COPIES

Printed by
LEDERER, STREET & ZEUS CO., INC.
BERKELEY, CALIFORNIA

GOVERNOR MARIANO CHICO'S REPORT TO THE MEXICAN GOVERNMENT.

By

George Tays.

Berkeley, Califoraia.   August, 1933.

Monterey, July, 22, 1836.

GOBIERNO SUPERIOR POLITICO DE LA ALTO CALIFORNIA
Archivo General de Guerra y Marina. 52--8-7-1

Colonel Mariano Chico, the third Governor sent from
Mexico to govern California after Independence, has been
perhaps the most reviled and maligned ruler that this pleasant land ever had in any epoch.

From the day on which he first stepped opon the white
sands of the Santa Barbara beach, April 19, 1836, until the
day on which he sailed from Monterey, July 31, 1836, aboard
the Clementina bound for Mexico, he was beset by a series of
difficulties, most of them not entirely of his own making,
whose solution would have baffled a greater man than he. It
is true that he was not a brilliant man, nor even very tact-
ful. He admits as much himself. He was not the man to
govern California at that particular moment; he knew it and
was very desirous to be relieved from office, as he advised
the Supreme Government more than once. That he was quick-
tempered, is also a fact. But he was an educated man, devoted to his duty, and very zealous to see that every one
should obey the laws. That made him somewhat intolerant with
the more or less unlettered Californians who had little respect for those same laws. In that we find his greatest obstacle in gaining their good will which would have preserved
the peace of the country.

Instead we find him in constant conflict with them which was incited by his distrust of them and their enmity for him. In spite of all that, however, he was not the blood-thirsty villain and capricious fool that all historians, except Bancroft, have painted him. As he says, there was rhyme and reason for his clowning. All writers have taken their views from the accounts left by the native Californians. Yet they have never considered that his reputation was fixed by his enemies and can hardly be considered fair. His annoyances were great and his contemporaries all had political or personal motives for attacking him.

That he is entitled to present his side of the case must be admitted; this he does quite ably in several confidential reports made to the Supreme Government and never before published. After reading them I am convinced that all the vituperation heaped upon him is not deserved. The documents follow:

Very Confidential

Excellent Sir:

In order to give the Supreme Government a fair though not an exact idea of the state in which this Department finds itself, I am forced to outline a picture that will improve the knowledge of the Nation's first magistrate by noting all I may happen to disclose in order to fill in what I may omit and to clarify the points that I must leave unexplained due to the haste with which I report, born of the accumulation of work that crowds me in this office and to the absolute lack of helping hands to perform the duties.

On the 19th, of last April I arrived in the port of
Santa Barbara in this Department and on stepping ashore on
that same beach, I met up with several residents from the
Presidio, who informed me of a tumult that had occurred in
the new city of Los Angeles, which probably would actuate the
pretexts to help a revolutionary plan, which beginning by
means of a so-called submissive statement would have ended
with the destruction of the Territorial Government and by
opposing the political change in the republic from which they
hoped to separate. In fact, there being two murderous criminals held as prisoners in said city, the foreigner Don Victor
Prudon, directed by one of the same class, Don Abel Stearns,
gathered a number of the citizens, inculcating in them destructive ideas clad in the guise of sane and patriotic ones.
He in company with Don Manuel Arzaga, called an assembly of
which he made himself president and naming his companion as
secretary they framed a petition demanding from those Judges
the delivery of the criminals to the people aroused to the
point of causing them an untimely and tumultuous death. They
obtained all they desired and this, that should have been
the first step to provoke some action by the Government in
order to charge him with injustice and to compel the accomplices to protect themselves from the punishment that might
threaten them, and due to that incentive thus easily lend
themselves to take up arms against the authority that persecuted them, I was told privately that it was probably

their last step, since my arrival in the Territory was expected. And in view of the flattering picture that I was
painting describing the conditions in Mexico in order to
make sure that they would consider as de facto the business
that it had started, I proposed to go to Los Angeles in person, but I was told by some persons whom I should suppose to
be in touch with the events, to give up my journey, because
it was dangerous for me to go to the city without troops,
and as yet without the authority of the Commander of the Department because Colonel Don Nicolas Gutierrez, who was to
turn over the command to me, was in Monterey at that time.
I was in a country absolutely unknown to me and it was necessary not to rely entirely upon my own judgment so as not to
take any risks, especially since even while in Mazatlan I had
very unfavorable news of the prevailing spirit of this country, which was that of unrest, as I showed Your Excellency in
a personal letter from that port; thus it was that I was forced
to decide to march on to said port of Monterey so as to assume command and afterwards give my instructions concerning
the affair, forstalling its consequences. I set out by land,
in spite of the poor state of my health caused by the ill-
usage of the voyage and on the 2d. of May I entered this
place, where my arrival brought the first news of my appointment, as the despatches from the Supreme Government in which
it gave prior notice of the transfer that was to be made to
me of the Commandancy General and the political magistracy,
had not arrived to date.

Notwithstanding, Lieutenant Colonel Gutierrez, who was
discharging those offices provisionally, and wished to re-
sign the post,did not interpose any difficulty in conforming with the orders that I brought to put me in possession of
the command, which I received on the 2d. During this inter-
val I was able to inform myself about my predecessor, and
about several persons, the first being the judge of this district, Don Luis Castillo Negrete, who without any exaggeration, is the only man upon whom I can rely in all of Alta
California. I was able to learn, I say, that at that particular moment, there was imminent danger of a prematurely conceived revolution which was to have been attempted against
General Figueroa, whose death upset the first projects of the
anarchists, and which had been recently reorganized under the
pretext that the office of political chief did not belong to
the Deputy Don Jose Castro, but were dampened once again by
an order which haply arrived from the Supreme Government so
that the two commands would remain united in one person and
they were reassumed by Señor Gutierrez. Although this order
did not truly fit the case; the lack of common sense of these
inhabitants allowed it to operate with meanings outside its
context, which were quite salutary for the time being, until
it occurred to them to renew their scheme under pretext that
the forementioned Gutierrez was a Spaniard: moreover, without making this opinion public, they began their enterprise
by the Los Angeles affair already indicated, which found a
new obstacle in my arrival. The ease with which the plans of

these intriguing revolutionists are arranged and disrupted, causes no surprise to any man who sees this Territory, more-over sooner or later he will have to admit that ignorance and stupidity are found rooted in its people, and from this cause there springs a cowardly suspicion in the character of the Californians that makes them tractable at times and stubborn at others and always timorous and cruel. The ideas about Mexican Independence inculcated among his countrymen by the Deputy to that General Congress, Don José Antonio Carrillo, (oracle of all this populace who adore him and dread him) ramble through the heads of these people without meditation or examination and that official has actuated from there as much as he can.

Surrounded thus by so many circumstances I took the office, and I resolved to eradicate the cancer of sedition which was already making itself too evident, because the required investigation of the scandalous action of the angelinos having been ordered, their leaders incited them to a new one, making them mob the courtroom demanding an amnesty for the ringleaders or punishment for the whole town, and I saw a plain threat to the public order in that step, so I issued the proclamation of which I have the honor to send Your Excellency some copies, and I began to take measures to place an imposing detachment on the march toward the rebellious place. The condition of all the military forces that I took over led me to believe that I could count upon 100 men of all arms for service, but experience gave the lie to my estimates. Sixteen infantrymen of the Hidalgo Battalion with four rifles without bayonets, eleven artillerymen and fifteen mounted ranchers without arms, this was all of the Monterey Company that I could get ready. The remainder of this company as well as those of Santa Barbara and San Diego, were to be found scattered among the Missions and the rancherias working in order to live, or out on the ranges where they could be idle. The few dragoons of the active squadron from Mazatlan, abandoned some time ago by their commander, Captain Don Pablo de la Portilla, were to be found, some serving as servants to that officer, others lodged with different persons, and still others were sick and in misery, without horses, arms or uniforms. Then I knew that the office with which the Supreme Government had entrusted me is more important and more hazardous than I could imagine.

I was not dismayed by this, but rather I resolved to conquer obstacles on every hand; I exhibited an unconcerned front and in my actions and words I displayed a confidence which I am truly lacking up to this moment; I endeavoured to read the thoughts in the faces of the people and to discover some hidden fear as regards to me, which I nourished, making uses of the assumption that within a few days a warship should arrive bringing me two hundred veteran soldiers and other assistance which the Supreme Government was sending to uphold its authority, and that I among other things would uphold it at all cost. I issued orders to start the march of the available troops upon the city of Los Angeles, and

concerned myself with borrowing money on the duties of the
maritime customs for its administrator, Don Angel Ramirez;
I had cartridges made from the powder which I brought from
Mazatlan, I bought twenty rifles which were for sale at the
store of a foreign merchant and he sold them to me on credit,
I ordered forty lances made; I gathered all the scattered
soldiers that I possibly could and leaving two crippled
artillerymen as the total garrison between San Francisco and
San Fernando, which is a distance of 150 leagues from north
to south, I sent all the troops under the command of the
forementioned Lieutenant Colonel Gutierrez to lay down the
law to the Los Angeles dissenters who were increasing their
petitions asking the Government to consecrate their trans-
gression; and although while sending those petitions they
based them on destructive principles, I hastened my dispositions and on the 6th of the same month of May the detachment
departed.   I had advance notice that at the house of the forementioned Administrator Ramirez they attempted to form a
revolutionary plan to oppose my entry into the Departmental
Government, but that it was abandoned on hearing me tell
that the help, about which I have already spoken to Your
Excellency, was coming, sent by the Commander-in-Chief, and
in order to cut short this fire I took the means of confiding
false secrets to Ramirez, forcing him in that way to reveal
those of his hangers-on and to direct him with respect to
them so that he might gain their sympathy; I obtained everything and now I make him serve effectively.

I did not want to place myself in command of the party
sent to Los Angeles because I did not want to show that I
considered those events of importance, and because I knew
beyond any doubt, that the Lieutenant of the San Francisco
Company, Don Mariano Guadulupe Vallejo, who is stationed at
Sonoma, charged with the command of the northern frontier,
was very much at outs with the new order of political events
accepted over the Republic and had declared that he would
oppose it when its establishment was tried in California;
and I did not want to abandon this capitol, so that it might
become his prey because he would deprive me of all resource.
I remained alone and abandoned to the will of unfriendly
people; there was one who came to tell me to be on guard
against a surprise attack by night; but I answered him
scornfully, daring those who might wish to attempt a crime
against me by leaving the doors to my lodging at the Presidio
open at night and making this custom public.

The foreigners residing here came to me and offered to
serve the Government in whatever way it might employ them, and
I called a meeting of the rest of the inhabitants of the port
to request them to lend themselves to mount the main guard
to keep the criminals in prison and to insure the internal
order, and they were easily convinced, their loyalty having
continued up to the present time. I managed to make some
friends by means of some quixotic strokes, which on account
of being strange to the natives they have a seared singular
and I directed the spirits to the end that they would gradually

accept the change in system against which there had been
instilled in them ideas of stubborn opposition. on account
of which I delayed publishing the organic law until the 20th
of the indicated May when I became certain of public acquiescence, because with the exception of a very few persons (although influential) the remainder got to the point of showing some excitement in wanting to pledge to the new system;
and those others, notwithstanding the vows that they made in
private gatherings to resist even unto death the breaking of
their pledges made to Federalism, were in the end the very
ones who uttered the "I swear", with the greatest enthusiasm on the day in which they were asked to give that answer. I gave the function all the solemnity possible, and I
prepared a table full of everything that is obtainable in
the country, which is only ordinary and above all, dear; but
I gathered the people of all classes in different rooms in
my house and aroused their enthusiasm in order to make them
commit themselves in their opinions to the Government. A
thing I easily accomplished, so that at the same time each
one was ashamed of the others, thus breaking among themselves
the ties that united them and they then formed those ties
with the Government, such that today I live assured of the
happiness of the citizens of Monterey, because they will not
be able to get together again very easily, but nevertheless
I fear the characteristic happiness of the Californians.
Since it is the favorite pretext of the revolutionists in
this country to imagine that the governors do not convene the
respective Legislature, I am encountering difficulties in

making the deputies come because the already mentioned Castro
imbued them with the idea that I intended to convene them
with the sole object of exiling them, and these men schemed,
they feigned sickness and work until I was obliged to resort
to the decree of the Mexican Courts of July 11, 1822, by
which means I installed the body and to whose consideration
I submitted the measures that I had taken some days before in
order to take care of the promotion of local changes and the
arrest of the more turbulent offenders, because the least of
them are so numerous that it would be necessary to apprehend
all the residents of the country, because the most orderly
citizen is a habitual drunkard, which vice and that of thieving
reach such a state in this land so that one finds few good
men among them, and perhaps none among those native to the
country; although the Supreme Government may think I exag-
gerate, nevertheless I am stating the truth without misrep-
resentation in everything I narrate. While I was busy with
these details I had Lieutenant Vallejo come to inform me
about conditions on the frontier which he guards with only
twenty-four men, and he advised me that he was about to enter
into treaties with a great number of tribes of wild Indians
so as to be able to remain in peace with them for some time
to come, and so I sent him back to his post, making him take
the oath to the Constitutional laws before leaving, which he
did without reluctance, but I have been unable to get him to
make the troops under his command take the oath, and I shall
be forced to go and demand it of them myself, as I was forced

to do in Santa Barbara and in Los Angeles, at which places
the Father President Fray Narciso Duran, who although a
Spaniard and publically loyal to his king and hostile to our
Independence was to be found exercising the functions of his
prelacy, delaying by his influence the execution of my orders
on the subject, in accord with the Father, Fray Alejo A-ustin
Bachelot, who cast upon this shore by a vessel coming from
the Sandwich Islands, along with his companion Fray Patricio
Short, have received the most generous hospitality in this
country. Each one of them, both in Santa Barbara and in Los
Angeles, refused to celebrate a solemn mass on the days during
which the ceremonies of taking the oath took place in the two
towns. I repaired to both places, because I was on my way to
the latter with the object of witnessing the first proceedings
in the cases against the mutineers, because their leaders
took the slant of accusing the Alcalder, blaming them as being the principal authors of the act that was being prosecuted, and these officials showed themselves timid and ir-
resolute in their conduct. My presence heartened them, and
some police measures that I dictated then and there and had
carried out along with other energetic acts which they saw
me execute against the malefactors who were overrunning the
town, I made this element realize, that the time had ended,
when the Government submitted to and tolerated offences of all
kinds that were being committed with impunity, the result of
such actions being that the idle have sought to apply themselves
to work and the vagrant have fled to Sonora and New

Mexico, because their sole object in coming to this country
is to steal horses, and they congregate here under the patronage of the deputy to the National Congress, Don José Antonio
Carrillo, and of Don Abel Stearns, who are the two individuals who dominate, and under whose influential leadership
governmental and judicial affairs have turned since the epoch
in which these two persons and Don Juan Bandini overthrew the
Government of Lieutenant Colonel Don Manuel Victoria.

Returning to the causes of the meeting I must state to
Your Excellency, that it has been definitely established by
the proceedings that Prudon and Araujo were the chiefs or
ringleaders who deceived the rest of the accomplices, suggesting to them to act in the way that fitted in with the
secret ends which I have indicated, and for that reason I
have resolved to remove them from here as I have notified the
Supreme Government by my letter to the Secretary of State.
I am doing likewise with Don Abel Stearns, because notwithstanding his tenure of the office as Sindico of the Ayuntamiento of the New City, and as such official making public
opposition to the uprising of w ich I inform Your Excellency,
I am told that secretly he was the most active instigator,
as he has been also the one who had directed all the revolutionary plans for this time, just as he was the partner of the
forementioned Carrillo and Bandini on the occasion of their
revolt in San Diego against Senor Victoria, and the master
mind directing the campaign in wh ch Captain Don Romualdo
Pacheco died, and the former Commanding General and political
chief was wounded.

Such reports, given by a multitude of people of this
Territory, I should have received publicly, were it not for
the blind custom adopted (in this Department), which is that
no person will testify against any other person in any sort
of case of investigation which may come to light; perhaps
because they are all bound up by ties of kinship or those of
god fathers, and when they give any valuable private information, they notify the Government, that in case they are legally questioned they will claim ignorance of all that they
have denounced in private, this with the sole object that
the Government may take only such measures as will not compromise them. I could refer you to thousands and thousands
of cases in proof if the pressure of time would permit me;
but the moments in which I have to write are so short, and
such is the scarcity of helping hands, to carry on governmental work, and such the distrust which I feel even of the
very secretary of this Command who sold out Senor Victoria,
making his measures ineffective and disclosing his resources
to the enemies of that time, so it is impossible for me to
carry on my duties and at the same time give Your Excellency
a detailed account of events. I find it necessary to write
even the first draft of official notes of reference in both
offices under my charge, a thing Your Excellency will no
longer doubt when you deal with the individual sent by the
departmental Deputation and me, to negotiate for assistance
from the Supreme Government, in behalf of this California;
with the understanding that he is the most able person to be

found in all this Territory to perform the duties of secretary to the Governor which he has had in his charge, and for
all other kinds of public affairs, excepting his brother the
District Judge, Don Luis del Castillo Negrete, the only person, I repeat to Your Excellency once more, who deserves the
high regard of the Supreme Magistrate of the nation.

It is evident that the sub-treasurer, Don Jose Maria
Herrera, is also noteworthy for his honesty and his knowledge; but he was once more persecuted by Lieutenant Colonel
Don Jose Maria Echeandia to the point of casting him out of
the Territory because he refused to pay him the different
salaries which he demanded as Commandant General, and as
Political Governor as well as his for his position as engineer,
sending as a prisoner to that Capital in the year 1822, where
he arrived and found no support for his rights and that per-
suades him not to want to leave the compass of his work,
turning away from all other inte meddling out of fear and in
view of the weak state to which this Government is reduced.
But Your Excellency, the pardon granted by the General Con-
ress to the insurrectionists agains Senor Victoria which is
included in the decree of April 25, 1822, and t e compla-
cency of my predeces or, General Don Jose Figueroa, in not
having required the individuals implicated in the crime to
present themselves and ask fo it as the decree demands, and
his tolerating that they should even refuse to accept it when
it was offered to them, answering him that they did not need
it; as well as his pretending that the forementioned Bandini

and Stearns belonged to this number, but who due to not being
born in Mexican territory are excluded by the regulation
which I have mentioned above; all this has given much freedom
to these restless men who are continually quoting this pre-
cedent, and that of the impunity (so they infer) with which
the acts of the Hijares, Pades, Echeandias, Apaláteguis and
others of which they know remained unpunished, thus inspiring
confidence in those whom they make their adherent in their
vain uprisings. Finally Sir, the only officer upon whom this
Commandancy General can count, is Lieutenant Colonel, Don
Nicolas Gutierrez, a person of excellent views and loyal to
the Supreme Government, and very subservient to authority.
Furthermore this officer is a Spaniard by birth and although
a patriot of long standing and a decided enthusiast for Mexican Independence, he is censured at every step by this unjust
stigma. He began his military career as a drummer and from
this Your Excellency may infer his principles of education;
he associates too much with his subordinates and with people of every class; he drinks liquor in company with them
and is wont to lose his reason with some frequency, the result of which is that he is not respected as he should be
when it is necessary, and in spite of all that, he is the
prop, the only resource of the Commandant General, and he
deserves to be recommended for the good services he renders.
Seeing myself in such straits as I have mentioned, I am
forced to make him my second in command in all the branches
of my office and he handles himself in the best possible way.

The aid-de-camp for the Mazatlan cavalry, Don Jose Maria
Cosio is a youth who will be of use to this command and in
spite of the superior orders received so that he may depart
to join his corps, I cannot decide to send him now because
I would have no officer left to whom I could entrust anything
concerning the service, since Lieutenant Don Juan Ybarra of
the same squadron acts as commander of the Presidio of Santa
Barbara which he discharges moderately well and he is not a
man of learning, nevertheles he is a model of subordination.
Neither can I decide to send to said port of Mazatlan the
few soldiers that are here belonging to the foresaid corps
because they are the sum total of the force that I am gathering with laborious efforts in order to insure the peace of
the Department; I hope to assemble twenty-five and recruit
the garrison up to fifty men with the permanent picket of
artillery and the Morales infantry; with this number I must
protect a territory one hundred and twenty leagues in extent,
included between the Presidio of San Franc sco and that of
Santa Barbara, in which are found numerous rancherias, and
ten or eleven missions with three towns. In the first and
in the last places there is a spirit of unrest and predis-
position stirred up against the Government, by the often
mentioned Don Jose Castro, in such a way that several nights
ago there was a small feast in whose drunkedness this Deputy
was the leader and they publicly toasted the restoration of
the federal system, the death of its destroyers, which was
essentially that of the General and President as well as my

own, considering mine as exceedingly important due to the
post I occupy. In the second place, the Indians are likewise incited by the co-workers of that Senor Castro and of
Vallejo, but in the greater portion of said places that I
have visited as I passed on the way to Los Angeles I have
the satisfaction of winning the natives and having replaced
some administrators who after wasting the properties, inspired
the neophytes with hatred against the Government, so that I
now consider myself safe on that side, notwithstanding that,
the peril of my position is not helped by such a small advantage, because there remain just as many settlements in
that southern part between Los Angeles and San Diego as well
as in the north from Monterey to the Sonoma frontier, which
I have been unable to visit personally, where conditions
are the same as they were in those that I have indicated,
and it all results from my not having a large enough force
upon which I can count nor a person capable of discharging
a trust at a time when I so greatly need these aids. In
spite of my poor health I made a journey of one hundred and
thirty leagues in seven days, and before I had rested even
eight days from this hardship, devoting myself to that of
reorganizing the Ayuntamientos and Courts of Santa Barbara
and of Los Angeles, which are like all of those in the Department, in absolute neglect, I was obliged to return over
the same ground in an equal number of days, because I was
advised of a contemplated assult upon this port, which I
have defended to date solely by my presence, and leaning

upon the support of the foreign residents and Mexicans which
comprise the major portion of the citizenry. As for the sons
of California, I count on none to be honest. Along the
northern frontier some eighty ranchers are to be found gathered, whom Vallejo and Castro have offered to arm in order
to curb, so they express it, the despotism of the Government.
Vallejo is daring, has natural talent that is quite evident,
does not drink, and enjoys a prestige in that part greater
than in the rest of the territory, though he does not lack
it elsewhere. If there were four other men like him, I
would not be able to maintain order, but fortunately there
are none, and they are intimidated by my energy and veritable blustering which serve as my arms; when these are found
out they will be useless, as it is, there are only useful to
me now as defensive measures, because if I attack, the weakness of their ranks will be revealed.

The danger that this Government runs is not alone that
of being upset by the dissenters from within the territory,
but also what is done with such disdain for the nation by
the foreign vessels which barter along the whole extent of
the coast hunting the sea-otter almost to extinction and
shielding the smuggling of the rest of the ships that trade
in our ports, as I shall note later. Two brigs and a frigate are now sailing about with the greatest insolence, in
sight of everyone, fishing, and at every step I am informed
that they arrive at any roadstead, some of their crew land
and penetrate into the forest, kill some cattle, and carry

off the flesh without opposition from anyone, even though
they may be seen from the rancherias, because they are armed
with rifles.

If the fishermen of the country go out to fish, the
foreign ships attack their launches, they seize what they
have fished and perhaps they kill them, as it has already
happened before my time. These same vessels carry as many
as fifteen guns and enough men to serve them. I have appointed an able and fearless foreigner to secretly gather
some companions and by some stratagem, such as pretending
that they are bound for some place or other, fall upon and
capture them; it may be difficult to obtain, but any hope of
avenging the outrage, even though vain or ridiculous, will
soothe my rage for a moment. The foreign ships using this
country as a way-station in carrying on their trade bring in
all classes of forbidden goods, which are absolutely necessary; if this trade were not allowed California could not
exist: I have worked a long time over this point in order to
observe the law, and I have been unable to make up my mind
to order other measures than those needed to regulate its
violation. Neither can other legislative measures be effective in this country due to its circumstances and not even the
separation of authorities is feasible; it is necessary that
the governor interfere with the legislative and judicial acts,
or this society will be destroyed. This Department lacks
statutes fitted to its needs, it is wanting in men of common
sense who can apply them to the cases that occur, and finally

this Territory should be considered as a new colony which
requires special institutions, as those common to the Republic do not suit it. A Commandant General in whom the political authority may continue to repose, invested with extraordinary powers to make observations in all the branches of
the administration and to decide on affairs of every nature
that may result; who should be a person of recognized learning, talent, judgment, prudence and energy, is the remedy
that this country requires. Moreover, if this Governor is
in poor health, and does not come accompanied by some individuals who can help him in circumstances which he may have to
meet along military and political lines, he will accomplish
nothing. Your Excellency will perceive that I am not the
man that I require, and I earnestly beg you not to decide to
deny me your influence with His Excellency, the President,
in order that he may relieve me of an office that I cannot
endure, and one in which I have already contracted responsibilities against my will, being forced to yield to the
powerful sway of circumstances, whose charges I shall answer satisfactorily if I am shortly called upon for that
purpose; but if I stay in this government for any length of
time it will be impossible for me to escape from the tribunal that may judge me.

I have told Your Excellency that I saw myself forced to
regulate the violation of the law, prohibiting a certain class
of foreign trade; I now add that I have not enforced the decree of the National Congress, which orders the return of the

Missions to the condition in which they were before secularization, and moreover I have placed administrators of
the properties in some of the establishments still under the
friars' management. I did not carry out the first because
some of the lands once comprised in the properties of those
missions have been allotted among various Indians and white
persons, who have undertaken works and considerable expenses; proportionately as they were judged legitimate owners
of their small endowments and of the cattle which was handed
to them by lawful authority, they made them their properties.
How can I manage to make them give up their possessions at
once without any force? Such an attack upon their properties would incite them to unite to correct their injury, and
this Command has no means of controlling them due to finding
itself in need of troops. I did the second thing because
the departmental government was in need of help from the
missions of Santa Ynez and San Buenaventura, which are
managed by the friars, since these establishments are the
only known recourse of the traveler in this country, in the
form of animals for the troops on the march to Los Angeles,
and for the very person of the Governor, and they refused
them to me with disdain and upon laying my complaint before
the Father President Duran, he answered me assuming an absolute independence for the missionaries and the properties
with respect to the Supreme Government and specially to the
one of this country, and no legal obligation to serve it in
its emergencies. This answer and the one he gave me almost

at the same time of not wanting to take the oath to the
Constitution, nor to say a mass which I requested to celebrate the allegiance of the town, being that he was a loyal
subject of the Spanish Monarchy and that he would not directly
or indirectly contribute to any act that can be interpreted
as a recognition of an unlawful government like our own, forced
me to take possession of the properties on behalf of the
Government in order to avoid the harmful inversion that the
Reverend Fathers might give them, who up to date have not
sworn to observe the fundamental laws already published, and
to elect the President, who has great influence in said Presidio, where they applauded greatly the answers that he gave
me before many of its citizens from the territory. Perhaps
equally compromising circumstances will in the future force
me to commit other offences that the Supreme Government may
be unable to ignore as it will not ignore those that I have
proclaimed, and I can do nothing else but to incur them.
This confession deserves to be heeded, and my plea granted.
I do not ask forgivness for my errors, I solicit the favor
not to be allowed to continue committing them; because I
believe that I will not be able to do any better. The Supreme
Government is very far from this part of the Republic, its
communications are entirely cut off, and its assistance too
remote to be expected.

The danger that public order will be disturbed may be
imminent because there are already signs of disorders, due
to the fact that the resources of the law and the government

do not operate, and if the ruler also weakens, he will be the
gibe of these people, or the shameful victim of a wretched
and comtemptible power. I will not basely yield, I shall
make resources grow out of nothing and I shall uphold the
honor of the Supreme Government to the last point whilst I
turn over to my successor the reigns of a government as small
as it is difficult, because of its lawlessness. Besides
what has been said before regarding the attention req ired
by the events in this country, I must add Your Excellency,
that companies of forty, sixty, and one hundred beaver trappers travel and camp at certain points along the banks of
the Sacramento River, and not only hunt these animals, thus
outraging the weakness of California's Government, but they
shield the horse stealing carried on by the indians in order
to exchange them for beads. Then I have recruited the fifty
men of which I told Your Excellency, I intend to make a very
secret expedition to give those foreigners a surprise, all
of these and the rest of whom I have spoken are of Anglo-
American extraction, except Prudon who is a Frenchman.

The indians from the Tulares valley have gotten into
the habit of turning the fields as harvest time approaches,
so that due to the water shortage of last year on the one
hand, the scarcity of farmers on the other, and finally the
arson by the indians, have left this poor country without
wheat, corn, beans, etc., etc., forced entirely to eat cooked
meat, even in the homes of the well-to-do people, and since
no ships come to trade here from the Republic, there was not

even sugar for our tea until the arrival of the vessel that
brought me, but that supply has been exhausted and is now
worth its weight in gold, and the greater part of the department is without it, as well as without bread, rice, and
even without vegetables, I being one of those who is in
need of what is most essential to life, even though some
people do their best to get it for me.

During this year I have managed up to now to prevent
any general conflagration, by means of announcing to the
indians that troops are being sent to pursue them, so that
the heathen savages will flee from their rancherias; but I
do not know yet whether the crops will escape. By what has
been shown, the Supreme Government will perceive that I have
allowed myself to resolve to charter the vessel in which will
sail the Commissioner with my despatches and the prisoners,
and it should have the condescension to approve this expense
which will be very costly, because making the interests of
the public service coincide with the commercial interests of
of the missions which are under government care I have allowed
its cargo to pay the rent both going and coming to San Blas
and Mazatlan, and it will not be less than half of the cost
(which is that of twenty-five hundred pesos in all) that
will be produced by the freight that the cargo will pay.
Other times it has cost the public treasury four thousand
pesos to send a shipment such as the present one; moreover I
managed to profit by some purely politic offers made by the
owner of the brig, and I was able to save him from paying the

highest charges. Through your influence I also expect the
approval of the highest authorities of sending the secretary
of the political government as commissioner, who enjoys a
salary of fifteen hundred pesos a year, by decree of special
authority, so that they may condescend to order that monthly
payments made on his respective salary at that capital; doing
it with what preference may be just to a person who lends
this service and who has no relations there.

I must now inform Your Excellency that the resources
of this command are very limited, and the nly ones it has
come from the duties paid by the foreign vessels that carry
on their illegal trade here. The custom house hands over
its surplus or what it wants to give up; and were it not for
the help of the missions, the soldiers that are being recruited would not eat, because as political head I order
them to supply the troop with meat, grain and vegetables for
the mess and some blankets to cover them. Notwithstanding
all this, if the Supreme Government, as I expect, decides to
send one of the warships, and two hundred well trained infantrymen with the Commandant General which it may appoint
to replace me and will only assure him an allowance of four
thousand pesos a month for a year, does not take from him the
political control, and gives him some special authority over
the judges and treasury officials of the Department and supporting him in whatever he do with regard to the artillery
corps and the navy, so that he may rightly do what he is
necessarily forced to execute in fact although it may be

prohibited by the Supreme Government, I am sure he needs
nothing else to make this country flourish in a very short
time. I work eagerly to establish some order in all the
branches and I shall accomplish something whilst my successor arrives; he will complete and perfect a labor which I
begin, struggling against obstacles which only he who meets
can appreciate. At this stage of my report I have just received a despatch by special messenger from the provisional
Commander of the port of Santa Barbara, which I copy.

"Today about four o'clock in the afternoon the Brig
Leonidas, property of Don Jose Antonio Aguirre, anchored in
this roadstead, coming from San Blas; and anxious to get some
news its Captain Don Juan Gomez gave me this one, that His
Excellency General Santa Anna had been captured in Texas by
t ose coloni ts, due to having advanced with a vanguard of
700 men leaving the army in the rear, and having been suddenly
attacked from ambush, he was made prisoner along with 61
officers, as a result the republic was found in great activity
in order to increase the army to recapture that worthy chief,
and on the other hand the news has circulated about Tepic
and San Blas that Don Jose Antonio Carrillo has been appointed
as political head of the Territory, which news I have thought
worthy of communicating to Your Honor without loss of time;
pe haps they may be of intere t to Your Excellency."

The lack of communications from the interior lead me to
fear the truth of tho e rumors; on the first part because of
the impo tance of such a misfortune to the nation and to this

Department, and on the second part because of the influence
that the appointment of Carrillo would have upon the complete
disorganization of this society. I have succeeded in dis-
suading those who know both, pretending that I have very
recent news from Mexico that deny those now abroad, and I do
not show my internal uneasiness. It does not seem to have
caused any noticeable stir in Monterey and in order to dis-
pel that which it may have produced in other parts of the
Territory, I intend to force the informer to retract his
words and place him under arrest under the supposition that
he is an imposter, because a story of this sort would influence everything to my detriment and that of public order
particularly at this time. As to the one concerning Carrillo,
I believe none of it because I am in touch with the opinion
that the Supreme Government has of him, and I do not expect
that it could have given him such an office. If it should
have happened by some mischance, I inform Your Excellency
from this moment that far from putting the Government in his
hands, I would place him in prison, and I would make him leave
the Department because I already know what he would be capable
of doing n California and Your Excellency will infer it from
what I have written to you.

With such unexpected news, there comes another one at
the same time to the effect that some Dominican friars that
came overland to San Diego had said that at the time of their
departure for Loreto from the same San Blas, a feast was
being held there in celebration of the victory of the same

Excellent General over those most ungrateful colonists. No
matter how eagerly I try to pacify my spirit I do not obtain
the calm I desire, and now more than ever I am hastening the
departure of the vessel so that it may soon return with better news. I repeat, Your Excellency, that I do not give this
report the scope that I should because I lack the time, as
I find it necessary to write by night since that is the only
time that I am allowed to do so by the affairs of government,
consequently I am not even keeping a copy of all this that
I am writing, but I am sending the very original which should
serve as a first draft, a fact Your Excellency will please
overlook for the sake of all that I disclose; and you will
have the goodness to intercede with the Supreme Magistrate
and with the General Congress, to the end that they cast an
attentive glance towards this Department and extend it their
helping hand with the idea that with very small sacrifices to
the treasury in order to strengthen the dignity of this
country's local government, and placing it in the hands of
a person of the qualities that I have indicated, there would
soon be developed the infinite resources that exist here for
its prosperity, and so that its advantages may redound to
the benefit of all the republic whose shipping will find
here the only port suited to its growth with an abundance of
resources of all kinds. This Department is very attractive,
Excellent Sir, and is beset by different serious perils, if
no endeavour is made to take care of it. The Russian settlement at Ross may mean a risk, and upon seeing that some

extensions had been made last year in the farm towards the
Sonoma frontier, by individuals of that power. I made a
friendly complaint to the Governor and he informed me that
he had received permission for it from General Figueroa, and
also to build a storehouse out of lumber in order to keep
the grain that he buys from this Department; now he has already gathered the quantity that he desires and he will soon
send a vessel to carry it away; in virtue of which it did
not seem politic to me to rebuke the act, because it would
cause the authority of the National Government to fall into
disrepute. This on the one hand and the lack of troops in
this country, which is evident to all the world, forced me
to confirm the permission for the present year and obliged
him to destroy his storehouse at the end of this period. He
agreed to these conditions and I shall see to it that they
are carried out.

Concerning the elements for the development of shipping,
about the Russian advances and upon the danger of falling
prey to foreigners to which the lovely islands of this coast
are exposed, I shall duly dwell upon them at some other time,
although I may as well confess now to Your Excellency that I
shall do it without scientific knowledge and only as my reason may dictate.

After reading this report, an unprejudiced person must
conclude that Mariano Chico, far from being the monster he
has been painted, was a well informed, clear headed, far-
sighted man; zealous in doing his duty and jealously guarding

the onor of his beloved country. Who can blame him for
such qualities? Yet, it seems that it was the exercising of
these very characteristics that brought him into disrepute.
Perhaps, like many other good men, he was too ardent in his
fight for the right. Let us hope that in the future, History
will do him justice.

George Tays

IN CALIFORNIA
BEFORE THE GOLD RUSH

By JOHN BIDWELL *Pioneer of '41*

With a Foreword by Lindley Bynum

PRINTED BY THE WARD RITCHIE PRESS
LOS ANGELES 1948 CALIFORNIA

FOREWORD

JOHN BIDWELL was born at Ripley, New York,
August 5, 1819. During his boyhood his family
moved to Pennsylvania, and later to Ohio. He attended school in Ashtabula County and Greenville,
and finished his education at Kingsburg Academy.
He taught school for at time after graduation and
planned to take further work at a university, but
his tides set westward, and after pioneer experiences
in western Missouri, the Pacific Coast became his
goal.

In 1840, interest in the far West was encouraged
by two early California boosters. The lectures of one
of the Roubideaux brothers and the published letters
of John Marsh did much to quicken the always restless temper of the folk along the western fringe of
American advance. In the spring of 1841, after
some difficulties in getting under way, Bidwell and
a party of emigrants started on their journey across
the continent. They arrived in California in November, completing the first organized emigration
of Americans to this Mexican province.

For several years after his arrival, Bidwell worked
for John A. Sutter, first at Fort Ross, then at Hock
Farm and at Sutter's Fort. He took part as a volun-
teer in the Mexican war, traveling from Sonoma to
San Diego, where he was made quartermaster. After
the hostilities were over he returned to the North,
and when the gold rush was at its height, he mined
at Bidwell's Bar on the Middle Fork of the Feather

River. In 1849 he bought Chino Ranch, originally containing 22,000 acres, which he later increased to 26,000 acres.

John Bidwell became a leading citizen in the new State of California. He was a member of the State's first senate, in 1849, and took an important part in the work of that body. He had a strong interest in the establishment and management of his ranch, and being a progressive and enthusiastic farmer, he had, by 1888, 7000 acres of diversified crops under cultivation. He was elected to Congress November 8, 1864. While in Washington, he met Miss Annie Kennedy, whom he married in 1868. He was three times an unsuccessful candidate for Governor of California, and in 1892 was the Prohibition candidate for President of the United States, again unsuccessful. His interest in education caused him to donate land for the Chico Normal School, and he served as a regent of the University of California. He died April 4, 1900.

The articles printed here appeared first in issues of the *Century Magazine* for November and December 1890 and February 1891. They were later issued, with an additional chapter of reminiscences, by the *Chico Advertiser*, about 1914, with the title *Echoes of the Past*. While written almost fifty years after the events described, the articles give a good account of Bidwell's trip across the plains and his early life in California. In his opinions as to priority in crossing the Sierra Nevada he is occasionally in error. Beginning his second article he says, "The party whose fortunes I have followed was not only the first that went direct to California from the East; we were probably the first white people, except Bonneville's party of 1833, that ever crossed the Sierra Nevada." The Sierra was first crossed by white men in the Spring of 1827, when Jedediah Smith, Robert Evans, and Silas Gobel accomplished this feat, and parties of mountain men had been coming to California for 15 years before the Bidwell party arrived. The Bonneville party referred to was headed by Joseph Reddeford Walker, and a narrative of their crossing, written by Zenas Leonard, records unmistakably their discovery of the *Sequoia gigantea*. This disproves Bidwell's twice-made claim that he was the first white man to see the big trees. The statement, made to Bidwell by Baptiste Ruelle, that he had discovered gold near Los Angeles in 1841 is likewise incorrect. Documentary evidence gives that honor to Francisco Lopez, March 9, 1842. Such incidental errors do not detract, however, from a first-hand narrative of events in California's stirring "forties" by a vigorous and intelligent participant.

LINDLEY BYNUM

IN CALIFORNIA
BEFORE THE GOLD RUSH

Chapter One

THE FIRST EMIGRANT TRAIN
TO CALIFORNIA

IN THE SPRING OF 1839—living at the time in the western part of Ohio—being then in my twentieth year, I conceived a desire to see the great prairies of the West, especially those most frequently spoken of, in Illinois, Iowa, and Missouri. Emigration from the East was tending westward, and settlers had already begun to invade those rich fields.

Starting on foot to Cincinnati, ninety miles distant, I fortunately got a chance to ride most of the way on a wagon loaded with farm produce. My outfit consisted of about $75, the clothes I wore, and a few others in a knapsack which I carried in the usual way strapped upon my shoulders, for in those days travelers did not have valises or trunks.

Though traveling was considered dangerous, I had no weapon more formidable than a pocket-knife. From Cincinnati I went down the Ohio River by steamboat to the Mississippi, up the Mississippi to St. Louis, and thence to Burlington, in what was then the Territory of Iowa. Those were bustling days on the western rivers, which were then the chief highways of travel. The scenes at the wood landings I recall as particularly lively and picturesque. Many passengers would save a little by helping to "wood the boat," i.e., by carrying wood down the bank and throwing it on the boat, a special ticket being issued on that condition. It was very interesting to see the long lines of passengers coming up the gang-plank, each with two or three sticks of wood on his shoulders. An anecdote is told of an Irishman who boarded a western steamer and wanted to know the fare to St. Louis, and, being told, asked, "What do you charge for 150 pounds of freight?" Upon learning the price, a small amount, he announced that he would go as freight. "All right," said the captain; "put him down in the hold and lay some flour barrels on him to keep him down."

In 1839 Burlington had perhaps not over two hundred inhabitants, though it was the capital of Iowa Territory. After consultation with the governor, Robert Lucas of Ohio, I concluded to go into the interior and select a tract of land on the Iowa River. In those days one was permitted to take up 160 acres, and where practicable it was usual to take part timber and part prairie. After working awhile at putting up a log house—until all the people in the neighborhood became ill with fever and ague—I concluded to move on and strike out to the south and southwest into Missouri. I traveled across country, sometimes by the sun, without road or trail. There were houses and settlements, but they were scattered; sometimes one would have to go twenty miles to find a place to stay at night. The principal game seen was the prairie hen (*Tetraonidae cupido*); the prairie wolf (*Canis latrans*) also abounded. Continuing southwest and passing through Huntsville I struck the Missouri River near Keytesville in Chariton County. Thence I continued up the north side of the river till the westernmost settlement in Missouri was reached; this was in Platte County. The Platte Purchase, as it was called, had been recently bought from the Indians, and was newly but thickly settled, on account of its proximity to navigation, its fine timber, good water, and unsurpassed fertility.

On the route I traveled I cannot recall seeing an emigrant wagon in Missouri. The western movement, which subsequently filled Missouri and other Western States and overflowed into the adjoining Territories, had then hardly begun, except as to Platte County. The contest in Congress over the Platte Purchase, which by increasing the area of Missouri gave more territory to slavery, called wide attention to that charming region. The anti-slavery sentiment even at that date ran quite high. This was, I believe, the first addition to slave territory after the Missouri Compromise. But slavery won. The rush that followed in the space of one or two years filled the most desirable part of the purchase to overflowing. The imagination could not conceive a finer country—lovely, rolling, fertile, wonderfully productive, beautifully arranged for settlement, part prairie and part timber. The land was unsurveyed. Every settler had aimed to locate a half-mile from his neighbor, and there was as yet no conflict. Peace and contentment reigned. Nearly every place seemed to have a beautiful spring of clear cold water. The hills and prairies and the level places were alike covered with a black and fertile soil. I cannot recall seeing an acre of poor land in Platte County. Of course there was intense longing on the part of the people of Missouri to have the Indians removed, and a corresponding desire, as soon as the purchase was consummated, to get possession of the beautiful land. It was in some sense perhaps a kind of Oklahoma movement. Another feature was the abundance of wild honeybees. Every tree that had a hollow in it seemed to be a bee-tree, and every hollow was full of rich golden honey. A singular fact which I learned from old hunters was that the honey-bee was never found more than seventy or eighty miles in advance of the white settlements on the frontier. On this attractive land I set my affections, intending to make it my home.

On my arrival, my money being all spent, I was obliged to accept the first thing that offered, and began teaching school in the country about five miles from the town of Weston, which was located on the north side of the Missouri River and about four miles above Fort Leavenworth in Kansas Territory. Possibly some may suppose it did not take much education to teach a country school at that period in Missouri. The rapid settlement of that new region had brought together people of all classes and conditions, and had thrown into juxtaposition almost every phase of intelligence as well as of illiteracy. But there was no lack of self-reliance or native shrewdness in any class, and I must say that I learned to have a high esteem for the people, among whom I found warm and lifelong friends.

But even in Missouri there were drawbacks. Rattlesnakes and copperheads were abundant. One man, it was said, found a place to suit him, but on alighting from his horse heard so many snakes that he concluded to go farther. At his second attempt, finding more snakes instead of fewer, he left the country altogether. I taught school there in all about a year. My arrival was in June, 1839, and in the fall of that year the surveyors came on to lay out the country; the lines ran every way, sometimes through a man's house, sometimes through his barn, so that there was much confusion and trouble about boundaries, etc. By the favor of certain men, and by paying a small amount for a little piece of fence here and a small clearing there, I got a claim, and purposed to make it my home, and to have my father remove there from Ohio.

In the following summer, 1840, the weather was very hot, so that during the vacation I could do but little work on my place, and needing some supplies —books, clothes, etc.—I concluded to take a trip to St. Louis, which I did by way of the Missouri River. The distance was six hundred miles by water; the down trip occupied two days, and was one of the most delightful experiences of my life. But returning, the river being low and full of snags, and the steamboat heavily laden—the boats were generally light going down—we were continually getting on sand bars, and were delayed nearly a month. This trip proved to be the turning-point in my life, for while I was gone a man had jumped my land. Generally in such cases public sentiment was against the jumper, and it was decidedly so in my case. But the scoundrel held on. He was a bully—had killed a man in Callaway County—and everybody seemed afraid of him. Influential friends of mine tried to persuade him to let me have eighty acres, half of the claim. But he was stubborn, and said that all he wanted was just what the law allowed him. Unfortunately for me, he had the legal advantage. I had worked some now and then on the place, but had not actually lived on it. The law required a certain residence, and that the pre-emptor should be twenty-one years of age or a man of family. I was neither, and could do nothing. Nearly all I had earned had been spent upon the land, and when that was taken I lost about everything I had. There being no possibility of getting another claim to suit me, I resolved to go elsewhere when spring should open.

In November or December of 1840, while still teaching school in Platte County, I came across a Frenchman named Roubideaux, who said he had been to California. He had been a trader in New Mexico, and had followed the road traveled by traders from the frontier of Missouri to Santa Fé. He had probably gone through what is now New Mexico and Arizona into California by the Gila River trail used by the Mexicans. His description of California was in the superlative degree favorable, so much so that I resolved if possible to see that wonderful land, and with others helped to get up a meeting at Weston and invited him to make a statement before it in regard to the country. At that time when a man moved out West, as soon as he was fairly settled he wanted to move again, and naturally every question imaginable was asked in regard to this wonderful country. Roubideaux described it as one of perennial spring and boundless fertility, and laid stress on the countless thousands of wild horses and cattle. He told about oranges, and hence must have been at Los Angeles, or the mission of San Gabriel, a few miles from it. Every conceivable question that we could ask him was answered favorably. Generally the first question which a Missourian asked about a country was whether there was any fever and ague. I remember his answer distinctly. He said there was but one man in California that had ever had a chill there, and it was a matter of so much wonderment to the people of Monterey that they went eighteen miles into the country to see him shake. Nothing could have been more satisfactory on the score of health. He said that the Spanish authorities were most friendly, and that the people were the most hospitable on the globe; that you could travel all over California and it would cost you nothing for horses or food. Even the Indians were friendly. His description of the country made it seem like a Paradise.

The result was that we appointed a corresponding secretary, and a committee to report a plan of organization. A pledge was drawn up in which every signer agreed to purchase a suitable outfit, and to rendezvous at Sapling Grove in what is now the State of Kansas, on the 9th of the following May, armed and equipped to cross the Rocky Mountains to California. We called ourselves the Western Emigration Society, and as soon as the pledge was drawn every one who agreed to come signed his name to it, and it took like wildfire. In a short time, I think within a month, we had about five hundred names; we also had correspondence on the subject with people all over Missouri, and even as far east as Illinois and Kentucky, and as far south as Arkansas. As soon as the movement was announced in the papers we had many letters of inquiry, and we expected people in considerable numbers to join us. About that time we heard of a man living in Jackson County, Missouri, who had received a letter from a person in California named Dr. Marsh, speaking favorably of the country, and a copy of this letter was published.

Our ignorance of the route was complete. We knew that California lay west, and that was the extent of our knowledge. Some of the maps consulted, supposed of course to be correct, showed a lake in the vicinity of where Salt Lake now is; it was represented as a long lake, three or four hundred miles in extent, narrow and with two outlets, both running into the Pacific Ocean, either apparently larger than the Mississippi River. An intelligent man with whom I boarded—Elam Brown, who till recently lived in California, dying when over ninety years of age—possessed a map that showed these rivers to be large, and he advised me to take tools along to make canoes, so that if we found the country so rough that we could not get along with our wagons we could descend one of those rivers to the Pacific. Even Frémont knew nothing about Salt Lake until 1843, when for the first time he explored it and mapped it correctly, his report being first printed, I think, in 1845.

9

In California Before the Gold Rush

This being the first movement to cross the Rocky Mountains to California, it is not surprising that it suffered reverses before we were fairly started. One of these was the publication of a letter in a New York newspaper giving a depressing view of the country for which we were all so confidently longing. It seems that in 1837 or 1838 a man by the name of Farnham, a lawyer, went from New York City into the Rocky Mountains for his health. He was an invalid, hopelessly gone with consumption it was thought, and as a last resort he went into the mountains, traveled with the trappers, lived in the open air as the trappers lived, eating only meat as they did, and in two or three years he entirely regained his health; but instead of returning east by way of St. Louis, as he had gone, he went down the Columbia River and took a vessel to Monterey and thence to San Blas, making his way through Mexico to New York. Upon his return—in February or March, 1841—he published the letter mentioned. His bad opinion of California was based wholly on his unfortunate experience in Monterey, which I will recount.

In 1840 there lived in California an old Rocky Mountaineer by the name of Isaac Graham. He was injudicious in his talk, and by boasting that the United States or Texas would some day take California, he excited the hostility and jealousy of the people. In those days Americans were held in disfavor by the native Californians on account of the war made by Americans in Texas to wrest Texas from Mexico. The number of Americans in California at this time was very small. When I went to California in 1841 all the foreigners—and all were foreigners except Indians and Mexicans—did not, I think, exceed one hundred; nor was the character of all of them the most prepossessing. Some had been trappers in the Rocky Mountains who had not seen civilization for a quarter of a century; others were men who had found their way into California, as Roubideaux had done, by way of Mexico; others still had gone down the Columbia River to Oregon and joined trapping parties in the service of the Hudson Bay Company going from Oregon to California—men who would let their beards grow down to their knees, and wear buckskin garments made and fringed like those of the Indians, and who considered it a compliment to be told "I took ye for an Injin." Another class of men from the Rocky Mountains were in the habit of making their way by the Mohave Desert south of the Sierra Nevada into California to steal horses, sometimes driving off four or five hundred at a time. The other Americans, most numerous perhaps, were sailors who had run away from vessels and remained in the country. With few exceptions this was the character of the American population when I came to California, and they were not generally a class calculated to gain much favor with the people. Farnham happened to come into the bay of Monterey when this fellow Graham and his confederates, and all others whom the Californians suspected, were under arrest in irons on board a vessel, ready for transportation to San Blas in Mexico, whither indeed they were taken, and where some of them died in irons. I am not sure that at this time the English had a consul in California; but the United States had none, and there was no one there to take the part of the Americans. Farnham, being a lawyer, doubtless knew that the proceeding was illegal. He went ashore and protested against it, but without effect, as he was only a private individual. Probably he was there on a burning hot day, and saw only the dreary sandhills to the east of the old town of Monterey. On arriving in New York he published the letter referred to, describing how Americans were oppressed by the native Californians, and how dangerous it was for Americans to go there. The merchants of Platte County had all along protested against our going, and had tried from the beginning to discourage and break up the movement, saying it was the most unheard-of, foolish, wild-goose chase that ever entered into the brain of man for five hundred people to pull up stakes, leave that beautiful country, and go away out to a region that we knew nothing of. But they made little headway until this letter of Farnham's appeared. They republished it in a paper in the town of Liberty in Clay County—there being no paper published in Platte County—and sent it broadcast all over the surrounding region. The result was that as the people began to think more seriously about the scheme the membership of the society began dropping off, and so it happened at last that of all the five hundred that signed the pledge I was the only one that got ready; and even I had hard work to do so, for I had barely means to buy a wagon, a gun, and provisions. Indeed, the man who was going with me, and who was to furnish the horses, backed out, and there I was with my wagon!

During the winter, to keep the project alive, I had made two or three trips into Jackson County, Missouri, crossing the Missouri River, always dangerous in winter when ice was running, by the ferry at Westport Landing, now Kansas City. Sometimes I had to go ten miles farther down—sixty miles from Weston—to a safer ferry at Independence Landing in order to get into Jackson County, to see men who were talking of going to California, and to get information.

At the last moment before the time to start for the rendezvous at Sapling Grove—it seemed almost providential—along came a man named George Henshaw, an invalid, from Illinois, I think. He was pretty well dressed, was riding a fine black horse, and had ten or fifteen dollars. I persuaded him to let me take his horse and trade him for a yoke of steers to pull the wagon and a sorry-looking, one-eyed mule for him to ride. We went via Weston to lay in some supplies. One wagon and four or five persons here joined us. On leaving Weston, where there had been so much opposition, we were six or seven in number, and nearly half the town followed us for a mile, and some for five or six miles, to bid us good-by, showing the deep interest felt in our journey. All expressed good wishes and desired to hear from us. When we reached Sapling Grove, the place of rendezvous, in May, 1841, there was but one wagon ahead of us. For the next few days one or two wagons would come each day, and among the recruits were three families from Arkansas. We organized by electing as captain of the company a man named Bartleson from Jackson County, Missouri. He was not the best man for the position, but we were given to understand that if he was not elected captain he would not go; and as he had seven or eight men with him, and we did not want the party diminished, he was chosen. Every one furnished his own supplies. The party consisted of sixty-nine, including men, women, and children. Our teams were of oxen, mules, and horses. We had no cows, as the later emigrants usually had, and the lack of milk was a great deprivation to the children. It was understood that every one should have not less than a barrel of flour with sugar and so forth to suit; but I laid in one hundred pounds of flour more than the usual quantity, besides other things. This I did because we were told that when we got into the mountains we probably would get out of bread and have to live on meat alone, which I thought would kill me even if it did not others. My gun was an old flint-lock rifle, but a good one. Old hunters told me to have nothing to do with cap or percussion locks, that they were unreliable, and that if I got my caps or percussion wet I could not shoot, while if I lost my flint I could pick up another on the plains. I doubt whether there was one hundred dollars in money in the whole party, but all were enthusiastic and anxious to go.

In five days after my arrival we were ready to start, but no one knew where to go, not even the captain. Finally a man came up, one of the last to arrive, and announced that a company of Catholic missionaries were on their way from St. Louis to the Flathead nation of Indians with an old Rocky Mountaineer for a guide, and that if we would wait another day they would be up with us. At first we were independent, and thought we could not afford to wait for a slow missionary party. But when we found that no one knew which way to go, we sobered down and waited for them to come up; and it was well we did, for otherwise probably not one of us would ever have reached California, because of our inexperience. Afterwards when we came in contact with Indians our people were so easily excited that if we had not had with us an old mountaineer the result would certainly have been disastrous. The name of the guide was Captain Fitzpatrick; he had been at the head of trapping parties in the Rocky Mountains for many years. He and the missionary party went with us as far as Soda Springs, now in Idaho Territory, whence they turned north to the Flathead nation. The party consisted of three Roman Catholic priests—Father De Smet, Father Pont, Father Mengarini—and ten or eleven French Canadians, and accompanying them were an old mountaineer named John Gray and a young Englishman named Romaine, and also a man named Baker. They seemed glad to have us with them, and we certainly were glad to have their company. Father De Smet had been to the Flathead nation before. He had gone out with a trapping party, and on his return had traveled with only a guide by another route, farther to the north and through hostile tribes. He was genial, of fine presence, and one of the saintliest men I have ever known, and I cannot wonder that the Indians were made to believe him divinely protected. He was a man of great kindness and great affability under all circumstances; nothing seemed to disturb his temper. The Canadians had mules and Red River carts, instead of wagons and horses—two mules to each cart, five or six of them—and in case of steep hills they would hitch three or four of the animals to one cart, always working them tandem. Sometimes a cart would go over, breaking everything in it to pieces; and at such times Father De Smet would be just the same—beaming with good humor.

In general our route lay from near Westport, where Kansas City now is, northwesterly over the prairie, crossing several streams, till we struck the Platte River. Then we followed along the south side of the Platte to and a day's journey or so along the South Fork. Here the features of the country became more bold and interesting. Then crossing the South Fork of the Platte, and following up the north side for a day or so, we went over to the North Fork and camped at Ash Hollow; thence up the north side of that fork, passing those noted landmarks known as the Court House Rocks, Chimney Rock, Scott's Bluffs, etc., till we came to Fort Laramie, a trading post of the American Fur Company, near which was Lupton's Fort, belonging, as I understood, to some rival company. Thence after several days we came to another noted landmark called Independence Rock, on a branch of the North Platte called the Sweetwater, which we followed up to the head, soon after striking the Little Sandy, and then the Big Sandy, which empties into Green River. Next we crossed Green River to Black Fork, which we followed up till we came to Ham's Fork, at the head of which we crossed the divide between Green and Bear rivers. Then we followed Bear River down to Soda Springs. The waters of Bear Lake discharged through that river, which we continued to follow down on the west side till we came to Salt Lake. Then we went around the north end of the lake and struck out to the west and southwest.

For a time, until we reached the Platte River, one

day was much like another. We set forth every morning and camped every night, detailing men to stand guard. Captain Fitzpatrick and the missionary party would generally take the lead and we would follow. Fitzpatrick knew all about the Indian tribes, and when there was any danger we kept in a more compact body, to protect one another. At other times we would be scattered along, sometimes for half a mile or more. We were generally together, because there was often work to be done to avoid delay. We had to make the road, frequently digging down steep banks, filling gulches, removing stones, etc. In such cases everybody would take a spade or do something to help make the road passable. When we camped at night we usually drew the wagons and carts together in a hollow square and picketed our animals inside in the corral. The wagons were common ones and of no special pattern, and some of them were covered. The tongue of one would be fastened to the back of another. To lessen the danger from Indians, we usually had no fires at night and did our cooking in the daytime.

The first incident was a scare that we had from a party of Cheyenne Indians just before we reached the Platte River, about two weeks after we set out. One of our men who chanced to be out hunting, some distance from the company and behind us, suddenly appeared without mule, gun, or pistol, and lacking most of his clothes, and in great excitement reported that he had been surrounded by thousands of Indians. The company, too, became excited, and Captain Fitzpatrick tried, but with little effect, to control and pacify them. Every man started his team into a run, till the oxen, like the mules and horses, were in a full gallop. Captain Fitzpatrick went ahead and directed them to follow, and as fast as they came to the bank of the river he put the wagons in the form of a hollow square and had all the animals securely picketed within. After a while the Indians came in sight. There were only forty of them, but they were well mounted on horses, and were evidently a war party, for they had no women except one, a medicine woman. They came up and camped within a hundred yards of us on the river below. Fitzpatrick told us that they would not have come in that way if they were hostile. Our hunter in his excitement said that there were thousands of them, and that they had robbed him of his gun, mule, and pistol. When the Indians had put up their lodges Fitzpatrick and John Gray, the old hunter mentioned, went out to them and by signs were made to understand that the Indians did not intend to hurt the man or to take his mule or gun, but that he was so excited when he saw them that they had to disarm him to keep him from shooting them; they did not know what had become of his pistol or of his clothes, which he said they had torn off. They surrendered the mule and the gun, thus showing that they were friendly. They proved to be Cheyenne

Indians. Ever afterwards that man went by the name of Cheyenne Dawson.

As soon as we struck the buffalo country we found a new source of interest. Before reaching the Platte we had seen an abundance of antelope and elk, prairie wolves and villages of prairie dogs, but only an occasional buffalo. We now began to kill buffaloes for food, and at the suggestion of John Gray, and following the practice of Rocky Mountain white hunters, our people began to kill them just to get the tongues and the marrow bones, leaving all the rest of the meat on the plains for the wolves to eat. But the Cheyennes, who traveled ahead of us for two or three days, set us a better example. At their camps we noticed that when they killed buffaloes they took all the meat, everything but the bones. Indians were never wasteful of the buffalo except in winter for the sake of the robes, and then only in order to get the whisky which traders offered them in exchange. There is no better beef in the world than that of the buffalo; it is also very good jerked, i.e., cut into strings and thoroughly dried. It was an easy matter to kill buffaloes after we got to where they were numerous, by keeping out of sight and to the leeward of them. I think I can truly say that I saw in that region in one day more buffaloes than I have seen of cattle in all my life. I have seen the plain black with them for several days' journey as far as the eye could reach. They seemed to be coming northward continually from the distant plains to the Platte to get water, and would plunge in and swim across by thousands—so numerous were they that they changed not only the color of the water, but its taste, until it was unfit to drink; but we had to use it. One night when we were encamped on the South Fork of the Platte they came in such droves that we had to sit up and fire guns and make what fires we could to keep them from running over us and trampling us into the dust. We were obliged to go out some distance from camp to turn them: Captain Fitzpatrick told us that if we did not do this the buffaloes in front could not turn aside for the pressure of those behind. We could hear them thundering all night long; the ground fairly trembled with vast approaching bands; and if they had not been diverted, wagons, animals, and emigrants would have been trodden under their feet. One cannot nowadays describe the rush and wildness of the thing. A strange feature was that when old oxen, tired and foot-sore, got among a buffalo herd, as they sometimes would in the night, they would soon become as wild as the wildest buffalo; and if ever recovered it was because they could not run so fast as the buffaloes or one's horse. The ground over which the herds trampled was left rather barren, but buffalo-grass being short and curling, in traveling over it they did not cut it up as much as they would other kinds.

On the Platte River, on the afternoon of one of

the hottest days we experienced on the plains, we had a taste of a cyclone: first came a terrific shower, followed by a fall of hail to the depth of four inches, some of the stones being as large as turkeys' eggs; and the next day a waterspout—an angry, huge, whirling cloud column, which seemed to draw its water from the Platte River—passed within a quarter of a mile behind us. We stopped and braced ourselves against our wagons to keep them from being overturned. Had it struck us it doubtless would have demolished us.

Above the junction of the forks of the Platte we continued to pass notable natural formations—first O'Fallon's Bluffs, then Court House Rocks, a group of fantastic shapes to which some of our party started to go. After they had gone what seemed fifteen or twenty miles the huge pile looked just as far off as when they started, and so they turned and came back—so deceptive are distances in the clear atmosphere of the Rocky Mountains. A noted landmark on the North Fork, which we sighted fifty miles away, was Chimney Rock. It was then nearly square, and I think it must have been fifty feet higher than now, though after we passed it a portion of it fell off. Scott's Bluffs are known to emigrants for their picturesqueness. These formations, like those first mentioned, are composed of indurated yellow clay or soft sand rock; they are washed and broken into all sorts of fantastic forms by the rains and storms of ages, and have the appearance of an immense city of towers and castles. They are quite difficult to explore, as I learned by experience in an effort to pursue and kill mountain sheep or bighorn. These were seen in great numbers, but we failed to kill any, as they inhabit places almost inaccessible and are exceedingly wild.

As we ascended the Platte buffaloes became scarcer, and on the Sweetwater none were to be seen. Now appeared in the distance to the north of west, gleaming under its mantle of perpetual snow, that lofty range known as the Wind River Mountains. It was the first time I had seen snow in summer; some of the peaks were very precipitous, and the view was altogether most impressive. Guided by Fitzpatrick, we crossed the Rockies at or near the South Pass, where the mountains were apparently low. Some years before a man named William Subletts, an Indian fur trader, went to the Rocky Mountains with goods in wagons, and those were the only wagons that had ever been there before us; sometimes we came across the tracks, but generally they were obliterated, and thus were of no service. Approaching Green River in the Rocky Mountains, it was found that some of the wagons, including Captain Bartleson's, had alcohol on board, and that the owners wanted to find trappers in the Rocky Mountains to whom they might sell it. This was a surprise to many of us, as there had been no drinking on the way. John Gray was sent ahead to see if he could find a trapping party, and he was instructed, if successful, to have them come to a certain place on Green River. He struck a trail, and overtook a party on their way to the buffalo region to lay in provisions, i.e., buffalo meat, and they returned, and came and camped on Green River very soon after our arrival, buying the greater part, if not all, of the alcohol, it first having been diluted so as to make what they called whisky—three or four gallons of water to a gallon of alcohol. Years afterwards we heard of the fate of that party: they were attacked by Indians the very first night after they left us and several of them killed, including the captain of the trapping party, whose name was Frapp. The whisky was probably the cause.

Several years ago when I was going down Weber Cañon, approaching Salt Lake, swiftly borne along on an observation car amid cliffs and over rushing streams, something said that night at the camp-fire on Green River was forcibly recalled to mind. We had in our party an illiterate fellow named Bill Overton, who in the evening at one of the camp-fires loudly declared that nothing in his life had ever surprised him. Of course that raised a dispute. "Never surprised in your life?" "No, I never was surprised." And, moreover, he swore that nothing ever *could* surprise him. "I should not be surprised," said he, "if I were to see a steamboat come plowing over these mountains this minute." In rattling down the cañon of Weber River it occurred to me that the reality was almost equal to Bill Overton's extravaganza, and I could but wonder what he would have said had he suddenly come upon this modern scene.

As I have said, at Soda Springs—at the northernmost bend of Bear River—our party separated. It was a bright and lovely place. The abundance of soda water, including the intermittent gushing so-called Steamboat Spring; the beautiful fir and cedar covered hills; the huge piles of red or brown sinter, the result of fountains once active but then dry—all these, together with the river, lent a charm to its wild beauty and made the spot a notable one. Here the missionary party were to turn north and go into the Flathead nation. Fort Hall, about forty miles distant on Snake River, lay on their route. There was no road; but something like a trail, doubtless used by the trappers, led in that direction. From Fort Hall there was also a trail down Snake River, by which trapping parties reached the Columbia River and Fort Vancouver, the headquarters of the Hudson Bay Company.

Our party, originally sixty-nine, including women and children, had become lessened to sixty-four in number. One had accidentally shot and killed himself at the forks of the Platte. Another of our party, named Simpson, had left us at Fort Laramie. Three had turned back from Green River, intending to make their way to Fort Bridger and await an opportunity to return home. Their names were Peyton, Rodgers, and Amos E. Frye. Thirty-two of our party, becoming discouraged, decided not to venture without path or guide into the unknown and trackless region towards California, but concluded to go with the missionary party to Fort Hall and thence find their way down Snake and Columbia rivers into Oregon.[1] The rest of us—also thirty-two in number, including Benjamin Kelsey, his wife and little daughter—remained firm, refusing to be diverted from our original purpose of going direct to California. After getting all the information we could from Captain Fitzpatrick, we regretfully bade good-by to our fellow emigrants and to Father De Smet and his party.

We were now thrown entirely upon our own resources. All the country beyond was to us a veritable *terra incognita,* and we only knew that California lay to the west. Captain Fitzpatrick was not much better informed, but he had heard that parties had penetrated the country to the southwest and west of Salt Lake to trap for beaver; and by his advice four of our men went with the parties to Fort Hall to consult Captain Grant, who was in charge there, and to gain information. Meanwhile our de-

[1]Of the party leaving us at Soda Springs to go into Oregon I can now, after the lapse of forty-nine years, recall by their names only the following: Mr. Williams and wife; Samuel Kelsey, his wife and five children; Josiah Kelsey and wife; C. W. Flugge; Mr. Carroll; Mr. Fowler; a Methodist Episcopal preacher, whose name I think was also Williams; "Cheyenne Dawson"; and another called "Bear Dawson." Subsequently we heard that the party safely arrived in Oregon, and some of them we saw in California. One (C. W. Flugge) was in time to join a party and come from Oregon to California the same year (1841).

pleted party slowly made its way down the west side of Bear River.

Our separation at Soda Springs recalls an incident. The days were usually very hot, the nights almost freezing. The first day our little company went only about ten miles and camped on Bear River. In company with a man named James John—always called "Jimmy John"—I wandered a mile or two down the river fishing. Seeing snow on a high mountain to the west, we longed to reach it, for the heat where we were was intense. So, without losing time to get our guns or coats or to give notice at the camp, we started direct for the snow, with the impression that we could go and return by sundown. But there intervened a range of lower mountains, a certain peak of which seemed almost to touch the snow. Both of us were fleet of foot and made haste, but we only gained the summit of the peak about sundown. The distance must have been twelve or fifteen miles. A valley intervened, and the snow lay on a higher mountain beyond. I proposed to camp. But Jimmy gave me a disdainful look, as much as to say, "You are afraid to go," and quickened his gait into a run down the mountain towards the snow. I called him to stop, but he would not even look back. A firm resolve seized me—to overtake him, but not again to ask him to return. We crossed the valley in the night, saw many Indian campfires, and gained a sharp ridge leading up to the snow. This was first brushy and then rough and rocky. The brush had no paths except those made by wild animals; the rocks were sharp, and soon cut through our moccasins and made our feet bleed. But up and up we went until long after midnight, and until a cloud covered the mountain. We were above the timber line, excepting a few stunted fir trees, under one of which we crawled to wait for day, for it was too dark to see. Day soon dawned, but we were almost frozen. Our fir-tree nest had been the lair of grizzly bears that had wallowed there and shed quantities of shaggy hair. The snow was still beyond, and we had lost both sight and direction. But in an hour or two we reached it. It was nearly as hard as ice. Filling a large handkerchief, without taking time to admire the scenery we started towards the camp by a new route, for our feet were too sore to go by way of the rocky ridge by which we had come. But the new way led into trouble. There were thickets so dense as to exclude the sun, and roaring little streams in deep, dark chasms; we had to crawl through paths which looked untrodden except by grizzlies; in one place a large bear had passed evidently only a few minutes before, crossing the deep gorge, plunging through the wild, dashing water, and wetting the steep bank as he went up. We carried our drawn butcher knives in our hands, for they were our only weapons. At last we emerged into the valley. Apparently numerous Indians had left that very morning, as shown by the tracks of lodge-poles drawn on the ground. Making haste, we soon gained the hills, and at about 2 P.M. sighted our wagons, already two or three miles on the march. When our friends saw us they stopped, and all who could ran to welcome us. They had given us up for lost, supposing that we had been killed by the hostile Blackfeet, who, as Captain Fitzpatrick had warned us, sometimes roamed through that region. The company had barricaded the camp at night as best they could, and every man had spent a sleepless night on guard. Next morning they passed several hours in scouring the country. Their first questions were: "Where have you been?" I was able to answer triumphantly, *"We have been up to the snow!"* and to demonstrate the fact by showing all the snow I had left, which was now reduced to a ball about the size of my fist.

In about ten days our four men returned from Fort Hall, during which time we had advanced something over one hundred miles toward Salt Lake. They brought the information that we must strike out west of Salt Lake—as it was even then called by the trappers—being careful not to go too far south, lest we should get into a waterless country without grass. They also said we must be careful not to go too far north, lest we should get into a broken country and steep cañons, and wander about, as trapping parties had been known to do, and become bewildered and perish.

September had come before we reached Salt Lake, which we struck at its northern extremity.

Part of the time we had purposely traveled slowly to enable the men from Fort Hall the sooner to overtake us. But unavoidable delays were frequent: daily, often hourly, the road had to be made passable for our wagons by digging down steep banks, filling gulches, etc. Indian fires obscured mountains and valleys in a dense, smoky atmosphere, so that we could not see any considerable distance in order to avoid obstacles. The principal growth, on plain and hill alike, was the interminable sagebrush (*Artemisia*), and often it was difficult, for miles at a time, to break a road through it, and sometimes a lightly laden wagon would be overturned. Its monotonous dull color and scraggy appearance gave a most dreary aspect to the landscape. But it was not wholly useless: where large enough it made excellent fuel, and it was the home and shelter of the hare—generally known as the "jack rabbit"—and of the sage-hen. Trees were almost a sure sign of water in that region. But the mirage was most deceptive, magnifying stunted sage-brush on diminutive hillocks into trees and groves. Thus misled, we traveled all day without water, and at midnight found ourselves in a plain, level as a floor, incrusted with salt, and as white as snow. Crusts of salt broken up by our wagons, and driven by the chilly night wind like ice on the surface of a frozen pond, was to me a most striking counterfeit of a winter scene. This plain became softer and softer until our poor, almost famished, animals could not pull our wagons.

In fact, we were going direct to Salt Lake and did not know it. So, in search of water, we turned from a southerly to an easterly course, and went about ten miles, and soon after daylight arrived at Bear River. So near to Salt Lake were we that the water in the river was too salt for us or our animals to use, but we had to use it; it would not quench thirst, but it did save life. The grass looked most luxuriant, and sparkled as if covered with frost. But it was salt; our hungry, jaded animals refused to eat it, and we had to lie by a whole day to rest them before we could travel.

Leaving this camp and bearing northwest we crossed our tracks on the salt plain, having thus described a triangle of several miles in dimensions. One of the most serious of our troubles was to find water where we could camp at night. So soon came another hot day, and hard travel all day and all night without water! From a westerly course we turned directly north, and, guided by antelope trails, came in a few miles to an abundance of grass and good water. The condition of our animals compelled us to rest here nearly a week. Meanwhile two of the men who had been to Fort Hall went ahead to explore. Provisions were becoming scarce, and we saw that we must avoid unnecessary delay. The two men were gone about five days. Under their lead we set forth, bearing west, then southwest, around Salt Lake, then again west. After two or three fatiguing days—one day and a night without water—the first notice we had of approach to any considerable mountain was the sight of crags, dimly seen through the smoke, many hundred feet above our heads. Here was plenty of good grass and water. Nearly all now said, "Let us leave our wagons, otherwise the snows will overtake us before we get to California." So we stopped one day and threw away everything we could not carry, made pack-saddles and packed the oxen, mules, and horses, and started.

On Green River we had seen the style of pack-saddles used by the trapping party, and had learned a little about how to make them. Packing is an art, and something that only an experienced mountaineer can do well so as to save his animal and keep his pack from falling off. We were unaccustomed to it, and the difficulties we had at first were simply indescribable. It is much more difficult to fasten a pack on an ox than on a mule or a horse. The trouble began the very first day. But we started—most of us on foot, for nearly all the animals, including several of the oxen, had to carry packs. It was but a few minutes before the packs began to turn; horses became scared, mules kicked, oxen jumped and bellowed, and articles were scattered in all directions. We took pains, fixed things, made a new start, and did better, though packs continued occasionally to fall off and delay us.

Those that had better pack-saddles and had tied their loads securely were ahead, while the others were obliged to lag behind, because they had to re-pack, and sometimes things would be strewn all along the route. The first night I happened to be among those that kept pretty well back, because the horses out-traveled the oxen. The foremost came to a place and stopped where there was no water or grass, and built a fire so that we could see it and come up to them. We got there about midnight, but some of our oxen that had packs on had not come up, and among them were my two. So I had to return the next morning and find them, Cheyenne Dawson alone volunteering to go with me. One man had brought along about a quart of water, which he carefully doled out before we started, each receiving a little canister-cover full—less than half a gill; but as Dawson and I had to go for the oxen, we were given a double portion. This was all the water I had until the next day. It was a burning hot day. We could not find the trail of the oxen for a long time, and Dawson refused to go any farther, saying that there were plenty of cattle in California; but I had to do it, for the oxen were carrying our provisions and other things. Afterwards I struck the trail, and found that the oxen instead of going west had gone north, and I followed them until nearly sundown. They had got into a grassy coun-try, which showed that they were nearing water. Seeing Indian tracks on their trail following them, I felt there was imminent danger, and at once ex-amined my gun and pistols to see that they were primed and ready. But soon I found my oxen lying down in tall grass by the side of the trail. Seeing no Indians, I hastened to fasten the packs and make my way to overtake the company. They had promised to stop when they came to water and wait for me. I traveled all night, and at early dawn came to where there was plenty of water and where the company had taken their dinner the day before, but they had failed to stop for me according to promise. I was much perplexed, because I had seen many fires in the night, which I took to be Indian fires, so I fastened my oxen to a scraggy willow and began to make circles around to see which way the company had gone. The ground was so hard that the animals had made no impression, which bewildered me. Finally, while making a circle of about three miles away off to the south, I saw two men coming on horseback. In the glare of the mirage, which distorted everything, I could not tell whether they were Indians or white men, but I supposed them to be Indians, feeling sure our party would go west and not south. In a mirage a man on horseback looks as tall as a tree, and I could only tell by the motion that they were mounted. I made a bee-line to my oxen, to make breastworks of them. In doing this I came to a small stream resembling running water, into which I urged my horse, whereupon he went down into a quagmire, over head and ears, out of sight. My gun also went under the mire. I got hold of something on the bank, threw out my gun, which was full of mud and water, and holding to the rope attached to my horse, by dint of hard pulling I succeeded in getting him out—a sorry sight, his ears and eyes full of mud, and his body covered with it. At last, just in time, I was able to move and get behind the oxen. My gun was in no condition to shoot. However, putting dry powder in the pan I determined to do my best in case the supposed Indians should come up; but lo! they were two of our party coming to meet me, bringing water and provisions. It was a great relief. I felt indignant that the party had not stopped for me—not the less so when I learned that Captain Bartleson had said, when they started back to find me, that they "would be in better business to go ahead and look for a road." He had not forgotten certain comments of mine on his qualities as a student of Indian character. An instance of this I will relate.

One morning, just as we were packing up, a party of about ninety Indians, on horseback, a regular war party, were descried coming up. Some of us begged the captain to send men out to prevent them from coming to us while we were in the confusion of packing. But he said, "Boys, you must not show any sign of hostility; if you go out there with guns the Indians will think us hostile, and may get mad and hurt us." However, five or six of us took our guns and went out, and by signs made them halt. They did not prove to be hostile, but they had carbines, and if we had been careless and had let them come near they might, and probably would, have killed us. At last we got packed up and started, and the Indians traveled along three or four hundred yards one side or the other of us or behind us all day. They appeared anxious to trade, and offered a buckskin, well dressed, worth two or three dollars, for three or four charges of powder and three or four balls. This showed that they were in want of ammunition. The carbines indicated that they had had communication with some trading-post belonging to the Hudson's Bay Company. They had buffalo-robes also, which showed that they were a roving hunting party, as there were no buffaloes within three or four hundred miles. At this time I had spoken my mind pretty freely concerning Captain Bartleson's lack of judgment, as one could scarcely help doing under the circumstances.

We now got into a country where there was no grass nor water, and then we began to catechize the men who had gone to Fort Hall. They repeated, "If you go too far south you will get into a desert country and your animals will perish; there will be no water nor grass." We were evidently too far south. We could not go west, and the formation of the country was such that we had to turn and go north across a range of mountains. Having struck a small stream we camped upon it all night, and next day continued down its banks, crossing from side to side, most of the time following Indian paths or paths made by antelope and deer. In the afternoon we entered a cañon the walls of which were precipitous and several hundred feet high. Finally the pleasant bermy banks gave out entirely, and we could travel only in the dry bed of what in the wet season was a raging river. It became a solid mass of stones and huge boulders, and the animals became tender-footed and sore so that they could hardly stand up, and as we continued the way became worse and worse. There was no place for us to lie down and sleep, nor could our animals lie down; the water had given out, and the prospect was indeed gloomy—the cañon had been leading us directly north. All agreed that the animals were too jaded and worn to go back. Then we called the men: "What did they tell you at Fort Hall about the northern region?" They repeated, "You must not go too for north; if you do you will get into difficult cañons that lead towards the Columbia River, where you may become bewildered and wander about and perish." This cañon was going nearly north; in fact it seemed a little east of north. We sent some men to see if they could reach the top of the mountain by scaling the precipice somewhere and get a view, and they came back about ten or eleven o'clock, saying the country looked better three or four miles farther ahead. So we were encouraged. Even the animals seemed to take courage, and we got along much better than had been thought possible, and by one o'clock that day came out on what is now known as the Humboldt River. It was not until four years later (1845) that General Frémont first saw this river and named it Humboldt.

Our course was first westward and then southward, following this river for many days, till we came to its Sink, near which we saw a solitary horse, an indication that trappers had sometimes been in that vicinity. We tried to catch him but failed; he had been there long enough to become very wild. We saw many Indians on the Humboldt, especially towards the Sink. There were many tule marshes. The tule is a rush, large, but here not very tall. It was generally completely covered with honeydew, and this in turn was wholly covered with a pediculous-looking insect which fed upon it. The Indians gathered quantities of the honey and pressed it into balls about the size of one's fist, having the appearance of wet bran. At first we greatly relished this Indian food, but when we saw what it was made of—that the insects pressed into the mass were the main ingredient—we lost our appetites and bought no more of it.

From the time we left our wagons many had to walk, and more and more as we advanced. Going down the Humboldt at least half were on foot. Provisions had given out; except a little coarse green grass among the willows along the river the country was dry, bare and desolate; we saw no game except antelope, and they were scarce and hard to kill; and walking was very fatiguing. Tobacco lovers would surrender their animals for anyone to ride who would furnish them with an ounce or two to chew during the day. One day one of these devotees lost his tobacco and went back for it, but failed to find it. An Indian in a friendly manner overtook us, bringing the piece of tobacco, which he had found on our trail or at our latest camp, and surrendered it. The owner, instead of being thankful, accused the Indian of having stolen it—an impossibility, as we had seen no Indians or Indian signs for some days. Perhaps the Indian did not know what it was, else he might have kept it for smoking. But I think otherwise, for, patting his breast, he said, "Shoshone, Shoshone," which was the Indian way of showing he was friendly. The Shoshones were known as always friendly to the whites, and it is not difficult to see how other and distant tribes might claim to be Shoshones as a passport to favor.

On the Humboldt we had a further division of our ranks. In going down the river we went sometimes on one side and sometimes on the other, but mostly on the north side, till we were nearing what are now known as the Humboldt Mountains. We were getting tired, and some were in favor of leaving the oxen, of which we then had only about seven or eight, and rushing on into California. They said there was plenty of beef in California. But some of us said: "No; our oxen are now our only supply of food. We are doing well, making eighteen or twenty miles a day." One morning when it was my turn at driving the oxen, the captain traveled so fast that I could not keep up, and was left far behind. When night came I had to leave the trail and go over a rocky declivity for a mile and a half into a gloomy, damp bottom, and un-pack the oxen and turn them out to eat, sleeping myself without blankets. I got up the next morning, hunted the oxen out of the willow thicket, and re-packed them. Not having had supper or breakfast, and having to travel nine miles before I overtook the party, perhaps I was not in the best humor. They were waiting, and for the very good reason that they could have nothing to eat till I came up with the oxen and one could be killed. I felt badly treated, and let the captain know it plainly; but, much to my surprise, he made no reply, and none of his men said a word. We killed an ox, ate our breakfast, and got ready to start about one or two o'clock in the afternoon. When nearly ready to go, the Captain and one or two of his mess came to us and said: "Boys, our animals are better than yours, and we always get out of meat before any of the rest of you. Let us have the most of the meat this time, and we will pay you back the next ox we kill." We gladly let them have all they wished. But as soon as they had taken it, and were mounted ready to start, the captain in a loud voice exclaimed: "Now we have been found fault with long enough, and we are going to California. If you can keep up

with us, all right; if you cannot, you may go to ——";
and away they started, the captain and eight men.
One of the men would not go with the captain; he
said, "The captain is wrong, and I will stay with
you, boys."

In a short time they were out of sight. We followed their trail for two or three days, but after
they had crossed over to the south side of the Humboldt and turned south we came into a sandy waste
where the wind had entirely obliterated their tracks.
We were then thrown entirely upon our own resources. It was our desire to make as great speed as
possible westward, deviating only when obstacles
interposed, and in such case bearing south instead
of north, so as to be found in a lower latitude in the
event that winter should overtake us in the mountains. But, diverted by following our fugitive captain and party across the Humboldt, we thereby
missed the luxuriant Truckee meadows lying but a
short distance to the west, a resting-place well and
favorably known to later emigrants. So, perforce,
we followed down to the Sink of the Humboldt
and were obliged to drink its water, which in the
fall of the year becomes stagnant and of the color
of lye, and not fit to drink or use unless boiled. Here
we camped. Leaving the Sink of the Humboldt, we
crossed a considerable stream which must have been
Carson River, and came to another stream which
must have been Walker River, and followed it up
to where it came out of the mountains, which

proved to be the Sierra Nevada. We did not know the name of the mountains. Neither had these rivers then been named; nor had they been seen by Kit Carson or Joe Walker, for whom they were named, nor were they seen until 1845 by Frémont, who named them.

We were now camped on Walker River, at the very eastern base of the Sierra Nevada, and had only two oxen left. We sent men ahead to see if it would be possible to scale the mountains, while we killed the better of the two oxen and dried the meat in preparation for the ascent. The men returned towards evening and reported that they thought it would be possible to ascend the mountains, though very difficult. We had eaten our supper, and were ready for the climb in the morning. Looking back on the plains we saw something coming, which we decided to be Indians. They traveled very slowly, and it was difficult to understand their movements. To make a long story short, it was the eight men that had left us nine days before. They had gone farther south than we and had come to a lake, probably Carson Lake, and there had found Indians who supplied them plentifully with fish and pine nuts. Fish caught in such water are not fit to eat at any time, much less in the fall of the year. The men had all eaten heartily of fish and pine nuts, and had got something akin to cholera morbus. We were glad to see them although they had deserted us. We ran out to meet them and shook hands, and put our

KIT CARSON

frying-pans on and gave them the best supper we could. Captain Bartleson, who when we started from Missouri was a portly man, was reduced to half his former girth. He said: "Boys, if ever I get back to Missouri I will never leave that country. I would gladly eat out of the troughs with my dogs." He seemed to be heartily sick of his late experience, but that did not prevent him from leaving us twice after that.

We were now in what is at present Nevada, and probably within forty miles of the present boundary of California. We ascended the mountains on the north side of Walker River to the summit, and then struck a stream running west which proved to be the extreme source of the Stanislaus River. We followed it down for several days and finally came to where a branch ran into it, each forming a cañon. The main river flowed in a precipitous gorge in places apparently a mile deep, and the gorge that came into it was but little less formidable. At night we found ourselves on the extreme point of the promontory between the two, very tired, and with neither grass nor water. We had to stay there that night. Early the next morning two men went down to see if it would be possible to get through down the smaller cañon. I was one of them, Jimmy John the other. Benjamin Kelsey, who had shown himself expert in finding the way, was now, without any election, still recognized as leader, as he had been during the absence of Bartleson. A party also went back to see how far we should have to go around before we could pass over the tributary cañon. The understanding was, that when we went down the cañon if it was practicable to get through we were to fire a gun so that all could follow; but if not, we were not to fire, even if we saw game. When Jimmy and I got down about three-quarters of a mile I came to the conclusion that it was impossible to get through, and said to him, "Jimmy, we might as well go back; we can't go here." "Yes, we can," said he; and insisting that we could, he pulled out a pistol and fired. It was an old dragoon pistol, and reverberated like a cannon. I hurried back to tell the company not to come down, but before I reached them the captain and his party had started. I explained, and warned them that they could not get down; but they went on as far as they could go, and then were obliged to stay all day and night to rest the animals, and had to go about among the rocks and pick a little grass for them, and go down to the stream through a terrible place in the cañon to bring water up in cups and camp-kettles, and some of the men in their boots, to pour down the animals' throats in order to keep them from perishing. Finally, four of them pulling and four of them pushing a mule, they managed to get them up one by one, and then carried all the things up again on their backs—not an easy job for exhausted men.

In some way, nobody knows how, Jimmy got through that cañon and into the Sacramento Valley.

45

He had a horse with him—an Indian horse that was bought in the Rocky Mountains, and which could come as near climbing a tree as any horse I ever knew. Jimmy was a character. Of all men I have ever known I think he was the most fearless; he had the bravery of a bulldog. He was not seen for two months—until he was found at Sutter's, afterwards known as Sutter's Fort, now Sacramento City.

We went on, traveling west as near as we could. When we killed our last ox we shot and ate crows or anything we could kill, and one man shot a wildcat. We could eat anything. One day in the morning I went ahead, on foot of course, to see if I could kill something, it being understood that the company would keep on as near west as possible and find a practicable road. I followed an Indian trail down into the cañon, meeting many Indians on the way up. They did not molest me, but I did not quite like their looks. I went about ten miles down the cañon, and then began to think it time to strike north to intersect the trail of the company going west. A most difficult time I had scaling the precipice. Once I threw my gun up ahead of me, being unable to hold it and climb, and then was in despair lest I could not get up where it was, but finally I did barely manage to do so, and made my way north. As the darkness came on I was obliged to look down and feel with my feet lest I should pass over the trail of the party without seeing it. Just at dark I came to an enormous fallen tree and tried to go around the top, but the place was too brushy, so I went around the butt, which seemed to me to be about twenty or twenty-five feet above my head. This I suppose to have been one of the fallen trees in the Calaveras Grove of *Sequoia gigantea* or mammoth trees, as I have since been there, and to my own satisfaction identified the lay of the land and the tree. Hence I concluded that I must have been the first white man who ever saw the *Sequoia gigantea*, of which I told Frémont when he came to California in 1844. Of course sleep was impossible, for I had neither blanket nor coat, and burned or froze alternately as I turned from one side to the other before the small fire which I had built, until morning, when I started eastward to intersect the trail, thinking the company had turned north. But I traveled until noon and found no trail; then striking south, I came to the camp which I had left the previous morning. The party had gone, but not where they had said they would go; for they had taken the same trail I had followed, into the cañon, and had gone up the south side, which they had found so steep that many of the poor animals could not climb it and had to be left. When I arrived the Indians were there cutting the horses to pieces and carrying off the meat. My situation, alone among strange Indians killing our poor horses, was by no means comfortable. Afterward we found that these Indians were always at war with the Californians. They were known as the Horse Thief Indians, and lived chiefly on horse flesh; they had been in the habit of raiding the ranches even to the very coast, driving away horses by the hundreds into the mountains to eat. That night after dark I overtook the party in camp.

A day or two later we came to a place where there was a great quantity of horse bones, and we did not know what it meant; we thought that an army must have perished there. They were of course horses that the Indians had driven in there and slaughtered. A few nights later, fearing depredations, we concluded to stand guard—all but one man, who would not. So we let his two horses roam where they pleased. In the morning they could not be found. A few miles away we came to a village; the Indians had fled, but we found the horses killed and some of the meat roasting on a fire.

We were now on the edge of the San Joaquin Valley, but we did not even know that we were in California. We could see a range of mountains lying to the west—the Coast Range, but we could see no valley. The evening of the day we started down into the valley we were very tired, and when night came our party was strung along for three or four miles, and every man slept right where darkness overtook him. He would take off his saddle for a pillow and turn his horse or mule loose, if he had one. His animal would be too poor to walk away, and in the morning he would find him, usually within fifty feet. The jaded horses nearly perished with hunger and fatigue. When we overtook the foremost of the party the next morning we found they had come to a pond of water, and one of them had killed a fat coyote; when I came up it was all eaten except the lights and the windpipe, on which I made my breakfast. From that camp we saw timber to the north of us, evidently bordering a stream running west. It turned out to be the stream that we had followed down in the mountains—the Stanislaus River. As soon as we came in sight of the bottom land of the stream we saw an abundance of antelopes and sandhill cranes. We killed two of each the first evening. Wild grapes also abounded. The next day we killed thirteen deer and antelopes, jerked the meat and got ready to go on, all except the captain's mess of seven or eight, who decided to stay there and lay in meat enough to last them into California! We were really almost down to tidewater, but did not know it. Some thought it was five hundred miles yet to California. But all thought we had to cross at least that range of mountains in sight to the west before entering the promised land, and how many more beyond no one could tell. Nearly all thought it best to press on lest the snows might overtake us in the mountains before us, as they had already nearly done on the mountains behind us (the Sierra Nevada). It was now about the first of November. Our party set forth bearing northwest, aiming for a seeming gap north of a high mountain in the chain to the west of us. That mountain we found to be Mount Diablo. At night the Indians attacked the captain's camp and stole all their animals, which were the best in the company, and the next day the men had to overtake us with just what they could carry in their hands.

The next day, judging by the timber we saw, we concluded there was a river to the west. So two men went ahead to see if they could find a trail or a crossing. The timber seen proved to be along what is now known as the San Joaquin River. We sent two men on ahead to spy out the country. At night one of them returned, saying they had come across an Indian on horseback without a saddle who wore a cloth jacket but no other clothing. From what they could understand the Indian knew Dr. Marsh and had offered to guide them to his place. He plainly said "Marsh," and of course we supposed it was the Dr. Marsh before referred to who had written the letter to a friend in Jackson County, Missouri, and so it proved. One man went with the Indian to Marsh's ranch and the other came back to tell us what he had done, with the suggestion that we should go on and cross the river (San Joaquin) at the place to which the trail was leading. In that way we found ourselves two days later at Dr. Marsh's ranch, and there we learned that we were really in California and our journey at an end. After six months we had now arrived at the first settlement in California, November 4, 1841.

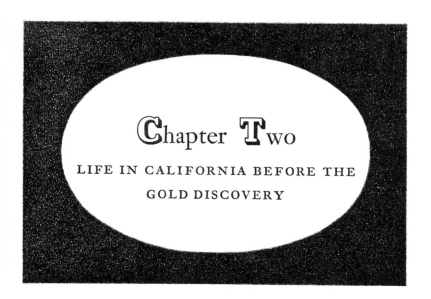

Chapter Two

LIFE IN CALIFORNIA BEFORE THE
GOLD DISCOVERY

THE PARTY whose fortunes I have followed across the plains was not only the first that went direct to California from the East; we were probably the first white people, except Bonneville's party of 1833, that ever crossed the Sierra Nevada. Dr. Marsh's ranch, the first settlement reached by us in California, was located in the eastern foothills of the Coast Range Mountains, near the northwestern extremity of the great San Joaquin Valley and about six miles east of Monte Diablo, which may be called about the geographical center of Contra Costa County. There were no other settlements in the valley; it was, apparently, still just as new as when Columbus discovered America, and roaming over it were countless thousands of wild horses, of elk, and of antelope. It had been one of the driest years ever known in California. The country was brown and parched; throughout the State wheat, beans, everything had failed. Cattle were almost starving for grass, and the people, except perhaps a few of the best families, were without bread, and were eating chiefly meat, and that often of a very poor quality.

Dr. Marsh had come into California four or five years before by way of New Mexico. He was in some respects a remarkable man. In command of the English language I have scarcely ever seen his equal. He had never studied medicine, I believe, but was a great reader: sometimes he would lie in bed all day reading, and he had a memory that stereotyped all he read, and in those days in California such a man could easily assume the rôle of doctor and practise medicine. In fact, with the exception of Dr. Marsh there was then no physician of any kind anywhere in California. We were overjoyed to find an American, and yet when we became acquainted with him we found him one of the most selfish of mortals. The night of our arrival he killed two pigs for us.[1] We felt very grateful, for we had by no means recovered from starving on poor mule meat, and when he set his Indian cook to making tortillas (little cakes) for us, giving one to each—there were thirty-two in our party—we felt even more grateful; and especially when we learned that

[1]Men reduced to living on poor meat, and almost starving, have an intense longing for anything fat.

he had had to use some of his seed wheat, for he had no other. Hearing that there was no such thing as money in the country, and that butcher-knives, guns, ammunition, and everything of that kind were better than money, we expressed our gratitude the first night to the doctor by presents—one giving a can of powder, another a bar of lead or a butcher-knife, and another a cheap but serviceable set of surgical instruments. The next morning I rose early, among the first, in order to learn from our host something about California—what we could do, and where we could go—and strange as it may seem, he would scarcely answer a question. He seemed to be in an ill humor, and among other things he said, "The company has already been over a hundred dollars' expense to me, and God knows whether I will ever get a *real* of it or not." I was at a loss to account for this, and went out and told some of the party, and found that others had been snubbed in a similar manner. We held a consultation and resolved to leave as soon as convenient. Half our party concluded to go back to the San Joaquin River, where there was much game, and spend the winter hunting, chiefly for otter, the skins being worth three dollars apiece. The rest— about fourteen—succeeded in gaining information from Dr. Marsh by which they started to find the town of San José, about forty miles to the south, then known by the name of Pueblo de San José, now the city of San José. More or less of our effects had to be left at Marsh's, and I decided to remain and look out for them, and meantime to make short excursions about the country on my own account. After the others had left I started off traveling south, and came to what is now called Livermore Valley, then known as Livermore's Ranch, belonging to Robert Livermore, a native of England. He had left a vessel when a mere boy, and had married and lived like the native Californians, and, like them, was very expert with the lasso. Livermore's was the frontier ranch, and more exposed than any other to the ravages of the Horse-thief Indians of the Sierra Nevada (before mentioned). That valley was full of wild cattle—thousands of them—and they were more dangerous to one on foot, as I was, than grizzly bears. By dodging into the gulches and behind trees I made my way to a Mexican ranch at the extreme west end of the valley, where I staid all night. This was one of the noted ranches, and belonged to a Californian called Don José Maria Amador—more recently, to a man named Dougherty.[1] Next day, seeing nothing to encourage me, I started to return to Marsh's ranch.

[1]The rancheros marked and branded their stock differently so as to distinguish them. But it was not possible to keep them separate. One would often steal cattle from the other. Livermore in this way lost cattle by his neighbor Amador. In fact it was almost a daily occurrence—a race to see which could get and kill the most of the other's cattle. Cattle in those days were often killed for the hides alone. One day a man saw Amador kill a fine steer belonging to Livermore. When he reached Livermore's—ten or fifteen miles away—and told him what Amador had done, he found Livermore skinning a steer of Amador's!

Dr. Marsh's Passport Scheme

On the way, as I came to where two roads, or rather paths, converged, I fell in with one of the fourteen men, M. C. Nye, who had started for San José. He seemed considerably agitated, and reported that at the Mission of San José, some fifteen miles this side of the town of San José, all the men had been arrested and put in prison by General Vallejo, Mexican commander-in-chief of the military under Governor Alvarado, he alone having been sent back to tell Marsh and to have him come forthwith to explain why this armed force had invaded the country. We reached Marsh's after dark. The next day the doctor started down to the Mission of San José, nearly thirty miles distant, with a list of the company, which I gave him. He was gone about three days. Meanwhile we sent word to the men on the San Joaquin River to let them know what had taken place, and they at once returned to the ranch to await results. When Marsh came back he said ominously, "Now, men, I want you all to come into the house and I will tell you your fate." We all went in, and he announced, "You men that have five dollars can have passports and remain in the country and go where you please." The fact was he had simply obtained passports for the asking; they had cost him nothing. The men who had been arrested at the mission had been liberated as soon as their passports were issued to them, and they had at once proceeded on their way to San José. But five dollars! I don't suppose any one had five dollars; nine-tenths of them probably had not a cent of money. The names were called and each man settled, giving the amount in something, and if unable to make it up in money or effects he would give his note for the rest. All the names were called except my own. There was no passport for me. Marsh had certainly not forgotten me, for I had furnished him with the list of our names myself. Possibly his idea was—as others surmised and afterwards told me—that, lacking a passport, I would stay at his ranch and make a useful hand to work.

The next morning before day found me starting for the Mission of San José to get a passport for myself. Mike Nye, the man who had brought the news of the arrest, went with me. A friend had lent me a poor old horse, fit only to carry my blankets. I arrived in a heavy rain-storm, and was marched into the calaboose and kept there three days with nothing to eat, and the fleas were so numerous as to cover and darken anything of a light color. There were four or five Indians in the prison. They were ironed, and they kept tolling a bell, as a punishment, I suppose, for they were said to have stolen horses; possibly they belonged to the Horse-thief tribes east of the San Joaquin Valley. Sentries were stationed at the door. Through a grated window I made a motion to an Indian boy outside and he brought me a handful of beans and a handful of *manteca*, which is used by Mexicans instead of lard. It seemed as if they were going to starve me to

death. After having been there three days I saw
through the door a man whom, from his light hair,
I took to be an American, although he was clad in
the wild picturesque garb of a native Californian,
including serape and the huge spurs used by the
vaquero. I had the sentry at the door hail him. He
proved to be an American, a resident of the Pueblo
of San José, named Thomas Bowen, and he kindly
went to Vallejo, who was right across the way in
the big Mission building, and procured for me the
passport. I think I have that passport now, signed
by Vallejo and written in Spanish by Victor Prudon, secretary of Vallejo. Every one at the Mission
pronounced Marsh's action an outrage; such a thing
was never known before.

We had already heard that a man by the name of
Sutter was starting a colony a hundred miles away
to the north in the Sacramento Valley. No other
civilized settlements had been attempted anywhere
east of the Coast Range; before Sutter came the Indians had reigned supreme. As the best thing to be
done I now determined to go to Sutter's, afterward
called "Sutter's Fort," or New Helvetia. Dr. Marsh
said we could make the journey in two days, but it
took us eight. Winter had come in earnest, and winter in California then, as now, meant rain. I had three
companions. It was wet when we started, and much
of the time we traveled through a pouring rain.
Streams were out of their banks; gulches were swimming; plains were inundated; indeed, the most of

the country was overflowed. There were no roads, merely paths, trodden only by Indians and wild game. We were compelled to follow the paths, even when they were under water, for the moment our animals stepped to one side down they went into the mire. Most of the way was through the region now lying between Lathrop and Sacramento. We got out of provisions and were about three days without food. Game was plentiful, but hard to shoot in the rain. Besides, it was impossible to keep our old flint-lock guns dry, and especially the powder dry in the pans. On the eighth day we came to Sutter's settlement; the fort had not then been begun. Sutter received us with open arms and in a princely fashion, for he was a man of the most polite address and the most courteous manners, a man who could shine in any society. Moreover, our coming was not unexpected to him. It will be remembered that in the Sierra Nevada one of our men named Jimmy John became separated from the main party. It seems that he came into California, and, diverging into the north, found his way down to Sutter's settlement perhaps a little before we reached Dr. Marsh's. Through this man Sutter heard that our company of thirty men were already somewhere in California. He immediately loaded two mules with provisions taken out of his private stores, and sent two men with them in search of us. But they did not find us, and returned, with the provisions, to Sutter's. Later, after a long search, the same two men, having been

JOHN A. SUTTER

sent out again by Sutter, struck our trail and followed it to Marsh's.

John A. Sutter was born in Baden in 1803 of Swiss parents, and was proud of his connection with the only republic of consequence in Europe. He was a warm admirer of the United States, and some of his friends had persuaded him to come across the Atlantic. He first went to a friend in Indiana with whom he staid awhile, helping to clear land, but it was business that he was not accustomed to. So he made his way to St. Louis and invested what means he had in merchandise, and went out as a New Mexican trader to Santa Fé. Having been unsuccessful at Santa Fé, he returned to St. Louis, joined a party of trappers, went to the Rocky Mountains, and found his way down the Columbia River to Fort Vancouver. There he formed plans for trying to get down to the coast of California to establish a colony. He took a vessel that went to the Sandwich Islands, and there communicated his plans to people who assisted him. But as there was no vessel going direct from the Sandwich Islands to California, he had to take a Russian vessel by way of Sitka. He got such credit and help as he could in the Sandwich Islands and induced five or six natives to accompany him to start the contemplated colony. He expected to send to Europe and the United States for his colonists. When he came to the coast of California, in 1840, he had an interview with the governor, Alvarado, and obtained permission to explore the country and find a place for his colony. He came to the bay of San Francisco, procured a small boat and explored the largest river he could find, and selected the site where the City of Sacramento now stands.

A short time before we arrived Sutter had bought out the Russian-American Fur Company at Fort Ross and Bodega on the Pacific. That company had a charter from Spain to take furs, but had no right to the land. The charter had about expired. Against the protest of the California authorities they had extended their settlement southward some twenty miles farther than they had any right to, and had occupied the country to, and even beyond, the bay of Bodega. The time came when the taking of furs was no longer profitable; the Russians were ordered to vacate and return to Sitka. They wished to sell out all their personal property and whatever remaining right they had to the land. So Sutter bought them out—cattle and horses; a little vessel of about twenty-five tons burden, called a launch; and other property, including forty odd pieces of old rusty cannon and one or two small brass pieces, with a quantity of old French flint-lock muskets pronounced by Sutter to be of those lost by Bonaparte in 1812 in his disastrous retreat from Moscow. This ordnance Sutter conveyed up the Sacramento River on the launch to his colony. As soon as the native Californians heard that he had bought out the Russians and was beginning to fortify himself by taking up the cannon they began to fear him. They were doubtless jealous because Americans and other foreigners had already commenced to make the place their headquarters, and they foresaw that Sutter's fort would be for them, especially for Americans, what it naturally did become in fact, a place of protection and general rendezvous; and so they threatened to break it up. Sutter had not as yet actually received his grant; he had simply taken preliminary steps and had obtained permission to settle and proceed to colonize. These threats were made before he had begun the fort, much less built it, and Sutter felt insecure. He had a good many Indians whom he had collected about him, and a few white men (perhaps fifteen or twenty) and some Sandwich Islanders. When he heard of the coming of our thirty men he inferred at once that we would soon reach him and be an additional protection. With this feeling of security, even before the arrival of our party Sutter was so indiscreet as to write a letter to the governor or to some one in authority, saying that he wanted to hear no more threats of dispossession, for he was now able not only to defend himself but to go and chastise them. That letter having been despatched to the city of Mexico, the authorities there sent a new governor in 1842 with about six hundred troops to subdue Sutter. But the new governor, Manuel Micheltorena, was an intelligent man. He knew the history of California and was aware that nearly all of his predecessors had been expelled by insurrections of the native Californians. Sutter sent a courier to meet the governor before his arrival at Los Angeles, with a letter in French, conveying his greetings to the governor, expressing a most cordial welcome, and submitting cheerfully and entirely to his authority. In this way the governor and Sutter became fast friends, and through Sutter the Americans had a friend in Governor Micheltorena.

The first employment I had in California was in Sutter's service, about two months after our arrival at Marsh's. He engaged me to go to Bodega and Fort Ross and to stay there until he could finish removing the property which he had bought from the Russians. I remained there fourteen months, until everything was removed; then I came up into Sacramento Valley and took charge for Sutter of his Hock Farm (so named from a large Indian village on the place), remaining there a little more than a year—in 1843 and part of 1844.

Nearly everybody who came to California made it a point to reach Sutter's Fort.[1] Sutter was one of

[1]Every year after the arrival of our party, in 1841, immigrant parties came across the plains to California; except in 1842, when they went to Oregon, most of them coming thence to California in 1843. Ours of 1841 being the first, let me add that a later party arrived in California in 1841. It was composed of about twenty-five persons who arrived at Westport, Mo., too late to come with us, and so went with the annual caravan of St. Louis traders to Santa Fé, and thence *via* the Gila River into Southern California.

Among the more noted arrivals on this coast I may mention:

1841—Commodore Wilkes's Exploring Expedition, a party of which came overland from Oregon to California, under Captain Ringgold, I think.

the most liberal and hospitable of men. Everybody was welcome—one man or a hundred, it was all the same. He had peculiar traits: his necessities compelled him to take all he could buy, and he paid all he could pay; but he failed to keep up with his payments. And so he soon found himself immensely—almost hopelessly—involved in debt. His debt to the Russians amounted at first to something near one hundred thousand dollars. Interest increased apace. He had agreed to pay in wheat, but his crops failed. He struggled in every way, sowing large areas to wheat, increasing his cattle and horses, and trying to build a flouring mill. He kept his launch running to and from the bay, carrying down hides, tallow, furs, wheat, etc., returning with lumber sawed by hand in the redwood groves nearest the bay and

---

1842—Commodore Thomas ap Catesby Jones, who raised the American flag in Monterey.

1843—*First*: L. W. Hastings, *via* Oregon. He was ambitious to make California a republic and to be its first president, and wrote an iridescent book to induce immigration—which came in 1846—but found the American flag flying when he returned with the immigration he had gone to meet. Also among the noted arrivals in 1843 was Pierson B. Reading, an accomplished gentleman, the proprietor of Reading's ranch in Shasta County, and from whom Fort Reading took its name. Samuel J. Hensley was also one of the same party. *Second*: Dr. Sandels, a very intelligent man.

1844—*First*: Frémont's first arrival (in March); Mr. Charles Preuss, a scientific man, and Kit Carson with him. *Second*: The Stevens-Townsend-Murphy party, who brought the first wagons into California across the plains.

1845—*First*: James W. Marshall, who, in 1848, discovered the gold. *Second*: Frémont's second arrival, also Hastings's second arrival.

1846—Largest immigration party, the one Hastings went to meet. The Donner party was among the last of these immigrants.

other supplies. On an average it took a month to make a trip. The fare for each person was five dollars, including board. Sutter started many other new enterprises in order to find relief from his embarrassments; but, in spite of all he could do, these increased. Every year found him worse and worse off; but it was partly his own fault. He employed men— not because he always needed and could profitably employ them, but because in the kindness of his heart it simply became a habit to employ everybody who wanted employment. As long as he had anything he trusted any one with everything he wanted—responsible or otherwise, acquaintances and strangers alike. Most of the labor was done by Indians, chiefly wild ones, except a few from the Missions who spoke Spanish. The wild ones learned Spanish so far as they learned anything, that being the language of the country, and everybody had to learn something of it. The number of men employed by Sutter may be stated at from 100 to 500—the latter number at harvest time. Among them were blacksmiths, carpenters, tanners, gunsmiths, vaqueros, farmers, gardeners, weavers (to weave coarse woolen blankets), hunters, sawyers (to saw lumber by hand, a custom known in England), sheep-herders, trappers, and, later, millwrights and a distiller. In a word, Sutter started every business and enterprise possible. He tried to maintain a sort of a military discipline. Cannon were mounted, and pointed in every direction through embrasures in the walls and bastions. The soldiers were Indians, and every evening after coming from work they were drilled under a white officer, generally a German, marching to the music of fife and drum. A sentry was always at the gate, and regular bells called men to and from work.

Harvesting, with the rude implements, was a scene. Imagine three or four hundred wild Indians in a grain field, armed, some with sickles, some with butcher-knives, some with pieces of hoop iron roughly fashioned into shapes like sickles, but many having only their hands with which to gather by small handfuls the dry and brittle grain; and as their hands would soon become sore, they resorted to dry willow sticks, which were split to afford a sharper edge with which to sever the straw. But the wildest part was the threshing. The harvest of weeks, sometimes of a month, was piled up in the straw in the form of a huge mound in the middle of a high, strong, round corral; then three or four hundred wild horses were turned in to thresh it, the Indians whooping to make them run faster. Suddenly they would dash in before the band at full speed, when the motion became reversed, with the effect of plowing up the trampled straw to the very bottom. In an hour the grain would be thoroughly threshed and the dry straw broken almost into chaff. In this manner I have seen two thousand bushels of wheat threshed in a single hour. Next came the winnowing, which would often take another month. It could only be done when the wind was blowing, by throwing high into the air shovelfuls of grain, straw, and chaff, the lighter materials being wafted to one side, while the grain, comparatively clean, would descend and form a heap by itself. In this manner all the grain in California was cleaned. At that day no such thing as a fanning mill had ever been brought to this coast.

The kindness and hospitality of the native Californians have not been overstated. Up to the time the Mexican régime ceased in California they had a custom of never charging for anything; that is to say, for entertainment—food, use of horses, etc. You were supposed, even if invited to visit a friend, to bring your blankets with you, and one would be very thoughtless if he traveled and did not take a knife with him to cut his meat. When you had eaten, the invariable custom was to rise, deliver to the woman or hostess the plate on which you had eaten the meat and beans—for that was about all they had—and say, *"Muchas gracias, Señora"* ("Many thanks, madame"); and the hostess as invariably replied, *"Buen provecho"* ("May it do you much good"). The Missions in California invariably had gardens with grapes, olives, figs, pomegranates, pears, and apples, but the ranches scarcely ever had any fruit.[1] When you wanted a horse to ride, you

[1] With the exception of the tuna, or prickly pear, these were the only cultivated fruits I can recall to mind in California, except oranges, lemons, and limes, in a few places.

would take it to the next ranch—it might be twenty, thirty, or fifty miles—and turn it out there, and sometime or other in reclaiming his stock the owner would get it back. In this way you might travel from one end of California to the other.

The ranch life was not confined to the country, it prevailed in the towns too. There was not a hotel in San Francisco, or Monterey, or anywhere in California, till 1846, when the Americans took the country. The priests at the Missions were glad to entertain strangers without charge. They would give you a room in which to sleep, and perhaps a bedstead with a hide stretched across it, and over that you would spread your blankets.

At this time there was not in California any vehicle except a rude California cart; the wheels were without tires, and were made by felling an oak tree and hewing it down till it made a solid wheel nearly a foot thick on the rim and a little larger where the axle went through. The hole for the axle would be eight or nine inches in diameter, but a few years' use would increase it to a foot. To make the hole, an auger, gouge, or chisel was sometimes used, but the principal tool was an ax. A small tree required but little hewing and shaping to answer for an axle. These carts were always drawn by oxen, the yoke being lashed with rawhide to the horns. To lubricate the axles they used soap (that is one thing the Mexicans could make), carrying along for the purpose a big pail of thick soapsuds which was constantly put in the box or hole; but you could generally tell when a California cart was coming half a mile away by the squeaking. I have seen the families of the wealthiest people go long distances at the rate of thirty miles or more a day, visiting in one of these clumsy two-wheeled vehicles. They had a little framework around it made of round sticks, and a bullock hide was put in for a floor or bottom. Sometimes the better class would have a little calico for curtains and cover. There was no such thing as a spoked wheel in use then. Somebody sent from Boston a wagon as a present to the priest in charge of the Mission of San José, but as soon as summer came the woodwork shrunk, the tires came off, and it all fell to pieces. There was no one in California to set tires. When Governor Micheltorena was sent from Mexico to California he brought with him an ambulance, not much better than a common spring wagon, such as a marketman would now use with one horse. It had shafts, but in California at that time there was no horse broken to work in them, nor was there such a thing known as a harness; so the governor had two mounted vaqueros to pull it, their reatas being fastened to the shafts and to the pommels of their saddles. The first wagons brought into California came across the plains in 1844 with the Townsend or Stevens party. They were left in the mountains and lay buried under the snow till the following spring, when Moses Schallenberger, Elisha Stevens (who was the captain of the party), and others went up and brought some of the wagons down into the Sacramento Valley. No other wagons had ever before reached California across the plains.[1]

Elisha Stevens was from Georgia and had there worked in the gold mines. He started across the plains with the express purpose of finding gold. When he got into the Rocky Mountains, as I was told by his friend Dr. Townsend, Stevens said, "We are in a gold country." One evening (when they camped for the night) he went into a gulch, took some gravel and washed it and got the color of gold, thus unmistakably showing, as he afterwards did in Lower California, that he had considerable knowledge of gold mining. But the strange thing is, that afterwards, when he passed up and down several times over the country between Bear and Yuba rivers, as he did with the party in the spring of 1845 to bring down their wagons, he should have seen no signs of gold where subsequently the whole country was found to contain it.

The early foreign residents of California were largely runaway sailors. Many if not most would change their names. For instance, Gilroy's ranch, where the town of Gilroy is now located, was owned by an old resident under the assumed appel-

[1]Mr. Schallenberger remained a considerable part of the winter alone with the wagons, which were buried under the snow. When the last two men made a desperate effort to escape over the mountains into California, Schallenberger tried to go with them, but was unable to bear the fatigue, and so returned about fifteen miles to the cabin they had left near Donner Lake (as it was afterward called), where he remained, threatened with starvation, till one of the party returned from the Sacramento Valley and rescued him.

lation of Gilroy. Of course vessels touching upon this coast were liable, as they were everywhere, to lose men by desertion, especially if the men were maltreated. Such things have been so common that it is not difficult to believe that those who left their vessels in early days on this then distant coast had cause for so doing. To be known as a runaway sailor was no stain upon a man's character. It was no uncommon thing, after my arrival here, for sailors to be skulking and hiding about from ranch to ranch till the vessel they had left should leave the coast. At Amador's ranch, before mentioned, on my first arrival here, I met a sailor boy, named Harrison Pierce, of eighteen or twenty years, who was concealing himself till his vessel should go to sea. He managed to escape recapture and so remained in the country. He was one of the men who went with me from Marsh's ranch to Sutter's. Californians would catch and return sailors to get the reward which, I believe, captains of vessels invariably offered. After the vessels had sailed and there was no chance of the reward the native Californians gave the fugitives no further trouble.

At that time the only trade, foreign or domestic, was in hides, tallow, and furs; but mostly hides. With few exceptions the vessels that visited the coast were from Boston, fitted out by Hooper to go there and trade for hides.[1] Occasionally vessels would put in for water or in distress. San Francisco

[1]See Dana's "Two Years before the Mast" for a description of the California coast at this period.

was the principal harbor; the next was Monterey. There was an anchorage off San Luis Obispo, the next was Santa Barbara, the next San Buenaventura, then San Pedro, and lastly San Diego. The hides were generally collected and brought to San Diego and there salted, staked out to dry, and folded so that they would lie compactly in the ship, and thence were shipped to Boston. Goods were principally sold on board the vessels: there were very few stores on land; that of Thomas O. Larkin at Monterey was the principal one. The entrance of a vessel into harbor or roadstead was a signal to all the ranchers to come in their little boats and launches laden with hides to trade for goods. Thus vessels went from port to port, remaining few or many days according to the amount of trade. When the people stopped bringing hides, a vessel would leave.[1]

[1]My first visit to the bay of San Francisco was in the first week of January, 1842. I had never before seen salt water. The town was called Yerba Buena, for the peppermint which was plentiful around some springs, located probably a little south of the junction of Pine and Sansome streets. Afterward—in 1847—when through the immigration of 1846 acros the plains, and through arrivals around Cape Horn, the place had become a village of some importance, the citizens changed the name to San Francisco, the name of the bay on which it is situated. With the exception of the Presidio and the Aduana (custom-house), all the buildings could be counted on the fingers and thumbs of one's hands. The most pretentious was a frame building erected by Jacob P. Leese, but then owned and occupied by the Hudson Bay Company, of which a Mr. Ray was agent. The others belonged to Captain Hinckley, Nathan Spear, Captain John J. Vioget, a Mr. Fuller, "Davis the carpenter," and a few others.

Monterey, when I first saw it (in 1844), had possibly 200 people, besides the troops, who numbered about 500. The principal foreigners living there then were: Thomas O. Larkin, David

The Saga of Dr. Meeks

I have said that there was no regular physician in California. Later, in 1843, in a company that came from Oregon, was one Joe Meeks, a noted character in the Rocky Mountains. On the way he said, "Boys, when I get down to California among the Greasers I am going to palm myself off as a doctor"; and from that time they dubbed him Dr. Meeks. He could neither read nor write. As soon as the Californians heard of his arrival at Monterey they be-

---

Spence, W. E. P. Hartnell, James Watson, Charles Walter, A. G. Toomes, R. H. Thomes, Talbot H. Green (Paul Geddes), W. Dickey, James McKinley, Milton Little, and Dr. James Stokes. The principal natives or Mexicans were Governor Micheltorena, Manuel Jimeno, José Castro, Juan Malarine, Francisco Arce, Don José Abrego. Larkin received his commission as American consul for California, at Mazatlan, in 1844. On his return to Monterey the woman who washed his clothes took the small-pox. Larkin's whole family had it; it spread, and the number of deaths was fearful, amounting to over eighty.

When I first saw Santa Barbara, February 5, 1845, the old Mission buildings were the principal ones. The town—probably half a mile to the east—contained possibly one hundred persons, among whom I recall Captain Wilson, Dr. Nicholas Den, Captain Scott, Mr. Sparks, Nibever; and of natives, Pablo de la Guerra, Carlos Antonio, Carrillo, and others.

Los Angeles I first saw in March, 1845. It then had probably two hundred and fifty people, of whom I recall Don Abel Stearns, John Temple, Captain Alexander Bell, William Wolfskill, Lemuel Carpenter, David W. Alexander; also of Mexicans, Pio Pico (governor), Don Juan Bandini, and others. On ranches in the vicinity lived William Workman, B. D. Wilson, and John Roland. At San Pedro, Captain Johnson. At Rancho Chino, Isaac Williams. At San Juan Capistrano, Don Juan Foster.

I went to San Diego, July, 1846, with Frémont's battalion, on the sloop of war *Cyane*, Captain Dupont (afterwards Admiral). The population was about one hundred, among whom I recall Captain Henry D. Fitch, Don Miguel de Pedrorena, Don Santiago Arguello, the Bandini family, J. M. Estudillo, and others. Subsequently, after the revolt of September, 1846, San Diego was the point from which, in January, 1847, the final conquest of California was made.

73

gan to come to him with their different ailments. His first professional service was to a boy who had a toe cut off. Meeks, happening to be near, stuck the toe on, binding it in a poultice of mud, and it grew on again. The new governor, Micheltorena, employed him as surgeon. Meeks had a way of looking and acting very wise, and of being reticent when people talked about things which he did not understand. One day he went into a little shop kept by a man known as Dr. Stokes, who had been a kind of hospital steward on board ship, and who had brought ashore one of those little medicine chests that were usually taken to sea, with apothecary scales, and a pamphlet giving a short synopsis of diseases and a table of weights and medicines, so that almost anybody could administer relief to sick sailors. Meeks went to him and said, "Doctor, I want you to put me up some powders." So Stokes went behind his table and got out his scales and medicines, and asked, "What kind of powders?" "Just common powders—patient not very sick." "If you will tell me what kind of powders, Dr. Meeks—" "Oh, just common powders." That is all he would say. Dr. Stokes told about town that Meeks knew nothing about medicine, but people thought that perhaps Meeks had given the prescription in Latin and that Dr. Stokes could not read it. But Meeks's reign was to have an end. An American man-of-war came into the harbor. Thomas O. Larkin was then the United States consul at Monterey, and the commander and all his officers went up to Larkin's store, among them the surgeon, who was introduced to Dr. Meeks. The conversation turning upon the diseases incident to the country, Meeks became reticent, saying merely that he was going out of practice and intended to leave the country, because he could not get medicines. The surgeon expressed much sympathy and said, "Dr. Meeks, if you will make me out a list I will very cheerfully divide with you such medicines as I can spare." Meeks did not know the names of three kinds of medicine, and tried evasion, but the surgeon cornered him and put the question so direct that he had to answer. He asked him what medicine he needed most. Finally Meeks said he wanted some "draps," and that was all that could be got out of him. When the story came out his career as a doctor was at an end, and he soon after left the country.

In 1841 there was likewise no lawyer in California. In 1843 a lawyer named Hastings arrived *via* Oregon. He was an ambitious man, and desired to wrest the country from Mexico and make it a republic. He disclosed his plan to a man who revealed it to me. His scheme was to go down to Mexico and make friends of the Mexican authorities, if possible get a grant of land, and then go into Texas, consult President Houston, and go East to write a book, praising the country to the skies, which he did, with little regard to accuracy. His object was to start a large immigration, and in this he succeeded. The book was published in 1845, and undoubtedly largely induced what was called the "great immigration" of 1846 across the plains, consisting of about six hundred. Hastings returned to California in the autumn of 1845, preparatory to taking steps to declare the country independent and to establish a republic and make himself president. In 1846 he went back to meet the immigration and to perfect his plans so that the emigrants would know exactly where to go and what to do. But in 1846 the Mexican war intervened, and while Hastings was gone to meet the immigration California was taken possession of by the United States. These doubtless were the first plans ever conceived for the independence of California. Hastings knew there were not enough Americans and foreigners yet in California to do anything. He labored hard to get money to publish his book, and went about lecturing on temperance in Ohio, where he became intimate with a fellow by the name of McDonald, who was acting the Methodist preacher and pretending, with considerable success, to raise funds for missionary purposes. At last they separated, McDonald preceding Hastings to San Francisco, where he became bartender for a man named Vioget, who owned a saloon and a billiard table—the first, I think, on the Pacific coast. Hastings returned later, and, reaching San Francisco in a cold rain, went up to Vioget's and called for brandy. He poured out a glassful and was about to drink it, when McDonald, recognizing him, leaned over the bar, extended his hand, and said, "My good temperance friend, how are you?" Hastings in great surprise looked him in the eyes, recognized him, and said, "My dear Methodist brother, how do you do?"

It is not generally known that in 1841—the year I reached California—gold was discovered in what is now a part of Los Angeles County. The yield was not rich; indeed, it was so small that it made no stir. The discoverer was an old Canadian Frenchman by the name of Baptiste Ruelle, who had been a trapper with the Hudson Bay Company, and, as was not an infrequent case with the trappers, had drifted down into New Mexico, where he had worked in placer mines. The mines discovered by Ruelle in California attracted a few New Mexicans, by whom they were worked for several years. But as they proved too poor, Ruelle himself came up into the Sacramento Valley, five hundred miles away, and engaged to work for Sutter when I was in Sutter's service.[1] Now it so happened that almost every year a party of a dozen men or more would come from or return to Oregon. Of such parties some—perhaps most of them—would be Canadian French, who had trapped all over the country, and these were generally the

[1]New Mexican miners invariably carried their gold (which was generally small, and small in quantity as well) in a large quill— that of a vulture or turkey buzzard. Sometimes these quills would hold three or four ounces, and, being translucent, they were graduated so as to see at any time the quantity in them. The gold was kept in by a stopper. Ruelle had such a quill, which appeared to have been carried for years.

guides. In 1843 it was known to every one that such a party was getting ready to go to Oregon. Baptiste Ruelle had been in Sutter's employ several months, when one day he came to Sutter, showed him a few small particles of gold, and said he had found them on the American River, and he wanted to go far into the mountains on that stream to prospect for gold. For this purpose he desired two mules loaded with provisions, and he selected two notably stupid Indian boys whom he wanted to go into the mountains with him, saying he would have no others. Of course he did not get the outfit. Sutter and I talked about it and queried, What does he want with so much provision—the American River being only a mile and the mountains only twenty miles distant? And why does he want those two stupid boys, since he might be attacked by the Indians? Our conclusion was that he really wanted the outfit so that he could join the party and go to Oregon and remain. Such I believe was Ruelle's intention; though in 1848, after James W. Marshall had discovered the gold at Coloma, Ruelle, who was one of the first to go there and mine, still protested that he had discovered gold on the American River in 1843. The only thing that I can recall to lend the least plausibility to Ruelle's pretensions would be that, so far as I know, he never, after that one time, manifested any desire to go to Oregon, and remained in California till he died. But I should add, neither did he ever show any longing again to go into the mountains to

look for gold during the subsequent years he remained with Sutter, even to the time of Marshall's
discovery.

Early in the spring of 1844, a Mexican working
under me at the Hock Farm for Sutter came to me
and told me there was gold in the Sierra Nevada.
His name was Pablo Gutierrez. The discovery by
Marshall, it will be remembered, was in January,
1848. Pablo told me this at a time when I was calling
him to account because he had absented himself the
day before without permission. I was giving him a
lecture in Spanish, which I could speak quite well
in those days. Like many Mexicans, he had an Indian wife; some time before, he had been in the
mountains and had bought a squaw. She had run
away from him, and he had gone to find and bring
her back. And it was while he was on this trip, he
said, that he had seen signs of gold. After my lecture he said, "Señor, I have made an important discovery; there surely is gold on Bear River in the
mountains." This was in March, 1844. A few days
afterward I arranged to go with him up on Bear
River. We went five or six miles into the mountains,
when he showed me the signs and the place where
he thought the gold was. "Well," I said, "can you
not find some?" No, he said, because he must have
a *batea*. He talked so much about the "batea" that
I concluded it must be a complicated machine.
"Can't Mr. Keiser, our saddle-maker, make the
batea?" I asked. "Oh, no." I did not then know that

a batea is nothing more nor less than a wooden bowl which the Mexicans use for washing gold. I said, "Pablo, where can you get it?" He said, "Down in Mexico." I said, "I will help pay your expenses if you will go down and get one," which he promised to do. I said, "Pablo, say nothing to anybody else about this gold discovery, and we will get the batea and find the gold." As time passed I was afraid to let him go to Mexico, lest when he got among his relatives he might be induced to stay and not come back, so I made a suggestion to him. I said, "Pablo, let us save our earnings and get a vessel and go around to Boston, and there get the batea; I can interpret for you, and the Yankees are very ingenious and can make anything." The idea pleased him, and he promised to go as soon as we could save enough to pay our expenses. He was to keep it a secret, and I believe he faithfully kept his promise. It would have taken us a year or two to get money enough to go. In those days there were every year four or five arrivals, sometimes six, of vessels laden with goods from Boston to trade for hides in California. These vessels brought around all classes of goods needed by the Mexican people. It would have required about six months each way, five months being a quick passage. But, as will be seen, our plans were interrupted. In the autumn of that year, 1844, a revolt took place. The native chiefs of California, José Castro and ex-Governor Alvarado, succeeded in raising an insurrection against the Mexican governor, Micheltorena, to expel him from the country. They accused him of being friendly to Americans and of giving them too much land. The truth was, he had simply shown impartiality. When Americans had been here long enough, had conducted themselves properly, and had complied with the colonization laws of Mexico, he had given them lands as readily as to native-born citizens. He was a fair-minded man and an intelligent and good governor, and wished to develop the country. His friendship for Americans was a mere pretext; for his predecessor, Alvarado, and his successor, Pio Pico, also granted lands freely to foreigners, and among them to Americans. The real cause of the insurrection against Micheltorena, however, was that the native chiefs had become hungry to get hold again of the revenues. The feeling against Americans was easily aroused and became their main excuse. The English and French influence, so far as felt, evidently leaned towards the side of the Californians. It was not open but it was felt, and not a few expressed the hope that England or France would some day seize and hold California. I believe the Gachupines—natives of Spain, of whom there were a few—did not participate in the feeling against the Americans, though few did much, if anything, to allay it. In October Sutter went from Sacramento to Monterey, the capital, to see the governor. I went with him. On our way thither, at San José, we heard the first mutterings of the insurrection.

We hastened to Monterey, and were the first to communicate the fact to the governor. Sutter, alarmed, took the first opportunity to get away by water. There were in those days no mail routes, no public conveyances of any kind, no regular line of travel, no public highways. But a vessel happened to touch at Monterey, and Sutter took passage to the bay of San Francisco, and thence by his own launch reached home. In a few days the first blow was struck, the insurgents taking all the horses belonging to the government at Monterey, setting the governor and all his troops on foot. He raised a few horses as best he could and pursued them, but could not overtake them on foot. However, I understood that a sort of parley took place at or near San José, but no battle, surrender, or settlement. Meanwhile, having started to return by land to Sutter's Fort, two hundred miles distant, I met the governor returning to Monterey. He stopped his forces and talked with me half an hour and confided to me his plans. He desired me to beg the Americans to be loyal to Mexico; to assure them that he was their friend, and in due time would give them all the lands to which they were entitled. He sent particularly friendly word to Sutter. Then I went on to the Mission of San José and there fell in with the insurgents, who had made that place their headquarters; I staid all night, and the leaders, Castro and Alvarado, treated me like a prince. The two insurgents protested their friendship for the Americans, and sent a request to Sutter to support them. On my arrival at the fort the situation was fully considered, and all, with a single exception, concluded to support Micheltorena. He had been our friend; he had granted us land; he promised, and we felt that we could rely upon, his continued friendship; and we felt, indeed we knew, we could not repose the same confidence in the native Californians. This man Pablo Gutierrez, who had told me about the gold in the Sierra Nevada, was a native of Sinaloa in Mexico, and sympathized with the Mexican governor and with us. Sutter sent him with despatches to the governor, stating that we were organizing and preparing to join him. Pablo returned, and was sent again to tell the governor that we were on the march to join him at Monterey. This time he was taken prisoner with our despatches and was hanged to a tree, somewhere near the present town of Gilroy. That of course put an end to our gold discovery; otherwise Pablo Gutierrez might have been the discoverer instead of Marshall.[1]

But I still had it in my mind to find gold; so early in the spring of 1845 I made it a point to visit the mines in the south discovered by Ruelle in 1841.

[1]The insurrection ended in the capitulation—I might call it expulsion—of Micheltorena. The causes which led to this result were various, some of them infamous. Pio Pico, being the oldest member of the Departmental Assembly, became governor, and Castro commander-in-chief of the military. They reigned but one year, and then came the Mexican war. Castro was made governor of Lower California, and died there. Pio Pico was not a vindictive man; he was a mild governor.

They were in the mountains about twenty miles north or northeast of the Mission of San Fernando, or say fifty miles from Los Angeles. I wanted to see the Mexicans working there, and to gain what knowledge I could of gold digging. Dr. John Townsend went with me. Pablo's confidence that there was gold on Bear River was fresh in my mind; and I hoped the same year to find time to return there and explore, and if possible find gold in the Sierra Nevada. But I had no time that busy year to carry out my purpose. The Mexicans' slow and inefficient manner of working the mine was most discouraging. When I returned to Sutter's Fort the same spring Sutter desired me to engage with him for a year as bookkeeper, which meant his general business man as well. His financial matters being in a bad way, I consented. I had a great deal to do besides keeping the books. Among other undertakings we sent men southeast in the Sierra Nevada about forty miles from the fort to saw lumber with a whipsaw. Two men would saw of good timber about one hundred or one hundred and twenty-five feet a day. Early in July I framed an excuse to go into the mountains to give the men some special directions about lumber needed at the fort. The day was one of the hottest I had ever experienced. No place looked favorable for a gold discovery. I even attempted to descend into a deep gorge through which meandered a small stream, but gave it up on account of the brush and the heat. My search was fruitless. The place where Marshall discovered gold in 1848 was about forty miles to the north of the saw-pits at this place. The next spring, 1849, I joined a party to go to the mines on and south of the Cosumne and Mokelumne rivers. The first day we reached a trading post—Digg's, I think, was the name. Several traders had there pitched their tents to sell goods. One of them was Tom Fallon, whom I knew. This post was within a few miles of where Sutter's men sawed the lumber in 1845. I asked Fallon if he had ever seen the old saw-pits where Sicard and Dupas had worked in 1845. He said he had, and knew the place well. Then I told him how I had attempted that year to descend into the deep gorge to the south of it to look for gold.

"My stars!" he said. "Why, that gulch down there was one of the richest placers that have ever been found in this country"; and he told me of men who had taken out a pint cupful of nuggets before breakfast.

Frémont's first visit to California was in the month of March, 1844. He came *via* eastern Oregon, traveling south and passing east of the Sierra Nevada, and crossed the chain about opposite the bay of San Francisco, at the head of the American River, and descended into the Sacramento Valley to Sutter's Fort. It was there I first met him. He staid but a short time, three or four weeks perhaps, to refit with fresh mules and horses and such provisions as he could obtain, and then set out on his return to the United States. Coloma, where Marshall afterward discovered gold, was on one of the branches of the American River. Frémont probably came down that very stream. How strange that he and his scientific corps did not discover signs of gold, as Commodore Wilkes's party had done when coming overland from Oregon in 1841! One morning at the breakfast table at Sutter's, Frémont was urged to remain a while and go to the coast, and among other things which it would be of interest for him to see was mentioned a very large redwood tree (*Sequoia sempervirens*) near Santa Cruz, or rather a cluster of trees, forming apparently a single trunk, which was said to be seventy-two feet in circumference. I then told Frémont of the big tree I had seen in the Sierra Nevada in October, 1841, which I afterwards verified to be one of the fallen big trees of the Calaveras Grove. I therefore believe myself to have been the first white man to see the mammoth trees of California. The Sequoias are found nowhere except in California. The redwood that I speak of is the *Sequoia sempervirens*, and is confined to the sea-coast and the west side of the Coast Range Mountains. The *Sequoia gigantea*, or mammoth tree, is found only on the western slope of the Sierra Nevada—nowhere farther north than latitude 38° 30'.

Sutter's Fort was an important point from the very beginning of the colony. The building of the fort and all subsequent immigrations added to its importance, for that was the first point of destination to those who came by way of Oregon or direct across the plains. The fort was begun in 1842 and finished in 1844. There was no town till after the gold discovery in 1848, when it became the bustling, buzzing center for merchants, traders, miners, etc., and every available room was in demand. In 1849 Sacramento City was laid off on the river two miles west of the fort, and the town grew up there at once into a city. The first town was laid off by Hastings and myself in the month of January, 1846, about three or four miles below the mouth of the American River, and called Sutterville. But first the Mexican war, then the lull which always follows excitement, and then the rush and roar of the gold discovery, prevented its building up till it was too late. Attempts were several times made to revive Sutterville, but Sacramento City had become too strong to be removed. Sutter always called his colony and fort "New Helvetia," in spite of which the name mostly used by others, before the Mexican war, was Sutter's Fort, or Sacramento, and later Sacramento altogether.

Sutter's many enterprises continued to create a growing demand for lumber. Every year, and sometimes more than once, he sent parties into the mountains to explore for an available site to build a sawmill on the Sacramento River or some of its tributaries, by which the lumber could be rafted down to the fort. There was no want of timber or of water power in the mountains, but the cañon features of the streams rendered rafting impracticable. The year after the war (1847) Sutter's needs for lumber were greater than ever, although his embarrassments had increased and his ability to undertake new enterprises became less and less. Yet, never discouraged, nothing daunted, another hunt must be made for a sawmill site. This time Marshall happened to be the man chosen by Sutter to search the mountains. He was gone about a month, and returned with a most favorable report.

James W. Marshall went across the plains to Oregon in 1844, and thence came to California the next year. He was a wheelwright by trade, but, being very ingenious, he could turn his hand to almost anything. So he acted as carpenter for Sutter, and did many other things, among which I may mention making wheels for spinning wool, and looms, reeds, and shuttles for weaving yarn into coarse blankets for the Indians, who did the carding, spinning, weaving, and all other labor. In 1846 Marshall went through the war to its close as a private. Besides his ingenuity as a mechanic, he had most singular traits. Almost every one pronounced him half crazy or hare-brained. He was certainly eccentric, and perhaps somewhat flighty. His insanity, however, if he had any, was of a harmless kind; he was neither vicious nor quarrelsome. He had great, almost overweening, confidence in his ability to do anything as a mechanic. I wrote the contract between Sutter and him to build the mill. Sutter was to furnish the means; Marshall was to build and run the mill, and have a share of the lumber for his compensation. His idea was to haul the lumber part way and raft it down the American River to Sacramento, and thence, his part of it, down the Sacramento River, and through Suisun and San Pablo bays to San Francisco for a market. Marshall's mind, in some respects at least, must have been unbalanced. It is hard to conceive how any sane man could have been so wide of the mark, or how any one could have selected such a site for a sawmill under the circumstances. Surely no other man than Marshall ever entertained so wild a scheme as that of rafting sawed lumber down the cañons of the American River, and no other man than Sutter would have been so confiding and credulous as to patronize him. It is proper to say that, under great difficulties, enhanced by winter rains, Marshall succeeded in building the mill—a very good one, too, of the kind. It had improvements which I had never seen in sawmills, and I had had considerable experience in Ohio. But the mill would not run because the wheel was placed too low. It was an old-fashioned flutter wheel that propelled an upright saw. The gravelly bar below the mill backed the water up, and submerged and stopped the wheel. The remedy was to dig a channel or tail-race through the bar below to conduct away the water. The wild Indians of the mountains were employed to do the digging. Once through the bar there would be plenty of fall. The digging was hard and took some weeks. As soon as the water began to run through the tail-race the wheel was blocked, the gate raised, and the water permitted to gush through all night. It was Marshall's custom to examine the race while the water was running through in the morning, so as to direct the Indians where to deepen it, and then shut off the water for them to work during the day. The water was clear as crystal, and the current was swift enough to sweep away the sand and lighter materials. Marshall made these examinations early in the morning while the Indians were getting their breakfast. It was on one of these occasions, in the clear shallow water, that he saw something bright and yellow. He picked it up—it was a piece of gold. The world has seen and felt the result. The mill sawed little or no lumber; as a lumber enterprise the project was a failure, but as a gold discovery it was a grand success.

There was no excitement at first, nor for three or four months—because the mine was not known to be rich, or to exist anywhere except at the sawmill, or to be available to any one except Sutter, to whom every one conceded that it belonged. Time does not permit me to relate how I carried the news of the discovery to San Francisco; how the same year I discovered gold on Feather River and worked it; how I made the first weights and scales to weigh the first gold for Sam Brannan; how the richness of the mines became known by the Mormons who were employed by Sutter to work at the sawmill, working about on Sundays and finding it in the crevices along the stream and taking it to Brannan's store at the fort, and how Brannan kept the gold a secret as long as he could till the excitement burst out all at once like wildfire.

Among the notable arrivals at Sutter's Fort should be mentioned that of Castro and Castillero, in the fall of 1845. The latter had been in California, sent, as he had been this time, as a peace commissioner from Mexico. Castro was so jealous that it was almost impossible for Sutter to have anything like a private interview with him. Sutter, however, was given to understand that, as he had stood friendly to Governor Micheltorena on the side of Mexico in the late troubles, he might rely on the friendship of Mexico, to which he was enjoined to continue faithful in all emergencies. Within a week Castillero was shown at San José a singular heavy reddish rock, which had long been known to the Indians, who rubbed it on their hands and faces to paint them. The Californians had often tried to smelt this rock in a blacksmith's fire, thinking it to be silver or some other precious metal. But Castillero, who was an intelligent man and a native of Spain, at once recognized it as quicksilver, and noted its resemblance to the cinnabar in the mines of Almaden. A company was immediately formed to work it, of which Castillero, Castro, Alexander Forbes, and others were members. The discovery of quicksilver at this time seems providential in view of its absolute necessity to supplement the imminent discovery of gold, which stirred and waked into new life the industries of the world.

It is a question whether the United States could have stood the shock of the great rebellion of 1861 had the California gold discovery not been made. Bankers and business men of New York in 1864 did not hesitate to admit that but for the gold of California, which monthly poured its five or six millions into that financial center, the bottom would have dropped out of everything. These timely arrivals so strengthened the nerves of trade and stimulated business as to enable the Government to sell its bonds at a time when its credit was its life-blood and the main reliance by which to feed, clothe, and maintain its armies. Once our bonds went down to thirty-eight cents on the dollar. California gold averted a total collapse, and enabled a preserved Union to come forth from the great conflict with only four billions of debt instead of a hundred billions. The hand of Providence so plainly seen in the discovery of gold is no less manifest in the time chosen for its accomplishment.

Chapter Three

FRÉMONT IN THE CONQUEST
OF CALIFORNIA

IN THE AUTUMN OF 1845 Frémont came on his second exploring expedition to California. This time he divided his party east of the Sierra Nevada and sent the greater portion to come in through a gap supposed to exist farther to the south, while he followed substantially what is now the emigrant road, or Truckee route, and came direct to Sutter's Fort with about eight or nine men. At that time I was in charge of Sutter's Fort and of Sutter's business, he being absent at the bay of San Francisco. Frémont camped on the American River about three miles above the fort. The first notice of his return to California was his sudden appearance, with Kit Carson, at the fort. He at once made known to me his wants, namely, sixteen mules, six pack-saddles, some flour and other provisions, and the use of a black-smith's shop to shoe the mules, to enable him to go in haste to meet others of his party. I told him precisely what could and could not be furnished—that we had no mules, but could let him have horses, and could make the pack-saddles; that he might have the use of a blacksmith's shop, but we were entirely out of coal. He became reticent, and, saying something in a low tone to Kit Carson, rose and left without saying good-day, and returned to his camp. As they mounted their horses to leave, Frémont was heard to say that I was unwilling to accommodate him, which greatly pained me; for, of course, we were always glad of the arrival of Americans, and especially of one in authority. Besides, I knew that Captain Sutter would do anything in his power for Frémont. So I took with me Dr. Gildea, a recent arrival from St. Louis, across the plains, and hastened to Frémont's camp and told him what had been reported to me. He stated, in a very formal manner, that he was the officer of one government and Sutter the officer of another; that difficulties existed between those governments; and hence his inference that I, representing Sutter, was not willing to accommodate him. He reminded me that on his first arrival here, in 1844, Sutter had sent out and in half an hour had brought him all the mules he wanted. I protested my willingness to do anything in my power, but was obliged to plead inability to do more than stated, telling him that in 1844 Sutter was

94

in far better circumstances; that on that occasion a man (Peter Lassen) had just arrived with a hundred mules, of which Sutter had brought what Frémont needed. But he had not been able to pay for them, because Frémont's drafts had to go East before Sutter could realize on them the money which had been promised to Lassen. In a few days Sutter returned, but could not furnish anything more than I had offered. Then Frémont concluded to go down to the bay and get supplies. He went with his little party of eight or nine men, including Kit Carson, but without success; so he sent the men back to Sutter's Fort to go, as best they could, to find the main party. Meanwhile he himself had made his way to Monterey to see the American consul, Thomas O. Larkin. After several weeks Frémont and his entire party became united in the San Joaquin Valley.[1] While at Monterey he had obtained permission from José Castro, the commandant-general, to winter in the San Joaquin Valley, away from the settlements, where the men would not be

[1]His men in the mountains had suffered considerably. Frémont had given positive orders for them to wait at a certain gap or low divide till he should meet them with supplies, but the place could not be found. The men got out of provisions and bought from the Indians. The kind they most relished was a sort of brown meal, which was rich and spicy, and came so much into favor that they wanted no other. After a while the Indians became careless in the preparation of this wonderful meal, when it was discovered to be full of the broken wings and legs of grasshoppers! It was simply dried grasshoppers pounded into a meal. The men said it was rich and would stick to the mouth like gingerbread, and that they were becoming sleek and fat. But after the discovery they lost their appetites. How hard it is sometimes to overcome prejudice!

likely to annoy the people. He had in all in the exploring party about sixty well-armed men. He also had permission to extend his explorations in the spring as far south as the Colorado River.

Accordingly early in the spring (1846) Frémont started south with his party. When Castro gave him permission to explore towards the Colorado River he no doubt supposed he would go south or southeast from where he was camped in the San Joaquin Valley, and on through the Tejon Pass and the Mojave Desert; but, instead, Frémont with his sixty armed men started to go west and southwest through the most thickly settled parts of California, namely, the Santa Clara, Pajaro, and Salinas valleys. As he was approaching the last valley Castro sent an official order by an officer warning Frémont that he must leave, as his action was illegal. The order was delivered March 5. Frémont took possession of an eminence called Gavilan Peak, and continued to fortify himself for several days, perhaps a week or more, Castro meantime remaining in sight and evidently increasing his force day by day. Frémont, enraged against Castro, finally abandoned his position in the night of March 9, and, gaining the San Joaquin Valley, made his way rapidly northward up the Sacramento Valley and into Oregon, leaving Sutter's about March 24.

A little over four weeks after Frémont left I happened to be fishing four or five miles down the river, having then left Sutter's service with the view

JOHN C. FRÉMONT

of trying to put up two or three hundred barrels of salmon, thinking the venture would be profitable. An officer of the United States, Lieutenant A. H. Gillespie, of the marines, bearing messages to the explorer, came up the river in a small boat and at once inquired about Frémont. I told him he had gone to Oregon. Said he: "I want to overhaul him. How far is it to the fort?" And receiving my reply, he pushed rapidly on. He overtook Frémont near the Oregon line. Frémont, still indignant against Castro, who had compelled him to abandon his explorations south, returned at once to California. It so happened that Castro had sent Lieutenant Arce to the north side of the bay of San Francisco to collect scattered Government horses. Arce had secured about one hundred and fifty and was taking them to the south side of the bay, *via* Sutter's Fort and the San Joaquin Valley. This was the only way to transfer cattle or horses from one side of the bay to the other, except at the Straits of Carquinez by the slow process of swimming one at a time, or of taking one or two, tied by all four feet, in a small boat or launch. Arce, with the horses and seven or eight soldiers, arrived at Sutter's Fort, staid overnight as the guest of Sutter, and went on his way to the Cosumne River (about sixteen or eighteen miles) and camped for the night.

Frémont hasty departure for Oregon and Gillespie's pursuit of him had been the occasion of many surmises. Frémont's sudden return excited increased curiosity. People flocked to his camp: some were settlers, some hunters; some were good men, and some about as rough specimens of humanity as it would be possible to find anywhere. Frémont, hearing that the horses were passing, sent a party of these promiscuous people and captured them. This of course was done before he had orders or any positive news that war had been declared. When Gillespie left the United States, as the bearer of a despatch to Larkin and Frémont and of letters to the latter, war had not been declared. The letters included one from Senator Benton, who had the confidence and knew the purposes of the Administration. As Gillespie had to make his way through Mexico, he committed the despatch and his orders to memory, destroyed them, and rewrote them on the vessel which took him, *via* the Sandwich Islands, to the coast of California. There had been no later arrival, and therefore no later despatches to Frémont were possible. Though Frémont was reticent, whatever he did was supposed to be done with the sanction of the United States. Thus, without giving the least notice even to Sutter, the great friend of Americans, or to Americans in general, scattered and exposed as they were all over California, he precipitated the war.

Sutter was always outspoken in his wish that some day California should belong to the United States; but when he heard that the horses had been taken from Arce (who made no resistance, but with his men and with insulting messages was permitted to go on his way to Castro at Santa Clara), he expressed surprise that Captain Frémont had committed such an act without his knowledge. What Sutter had said was reported to Frémont, perhaps with some exaggeration.

As soon as the horses arrived at Frémont's camp, the same party—about twenty-five in number—were sent to Sonoma. By this party General Vallejo, the most prominent Californian north of the bay, his brother Salvador, his brother-in-law Jacob P. Leese, and Victor Prudon were surprised at night, taken prisoners, and conveyed to Frémont's camp, over eighty miles distant by the traveled route on the Sacramento River. The prisoners were sent to Sutter's Fort, Frémont arriving at the same time. Then Sutter and Frémont met, face to face, for the first time since Frémont, a month before, had passed on his way towards Oregon. I do not know what words passed between them; I was near, but did not hear. This, however, I know, that Sutter had become elated, as all Americans were, with the idea that what Frémont was doing meant California for the United States. But in a few minutes Sutter came to me greatly agitated, with tears in his eyes, and said that Frémont had told him he was a Mexican, and that if he did not like what he (Frémont) was doing he would set him across the San Joaquin River and he could go and join the Mexicans. But, this flurry over, Sutter was soon himself again, and resumed his normal attitude of friendship towards Frémont, because he thought him to be acting in accordance with instructions from Washington. For want of a suitable prison, the prisoners were placed in Sutter's parlor—a large room in the southwest corner of the second story of the two-story adobe house,[1] which had but one door, and this was now guarded by a sentinel. Frémont gave me special directions about the safety of the prisoners, and I understood him to put them under my special charge. Some of Frémont's men remained at the fort.

Among the men who remained to hold Sonoma was William B. Ide, who assumed to be in command. In some way (perhaps through an unsatisfactory interview with Frémont which he had before the move on Sonoma) Ide got the notion that Frémont's hand in these events was uncertain, and that Americans ought to strike for an independent republic. To this end nearly every day he wrote something in the form of a proclamation and posted it on the old Mexican flagstaff. Another man left at Sonoma was William L. Todd,[2] who painted, on a piece of brown cotton, a yard and a half in length, with old red or brown paint that he happened to

[1]This adobe house is still standing, within the limits of the city of Sacramento, and is the only relic left of Sutter's Fort. It was built in 1841—the first then, the last now.

[2]More than thirty years afterwards I chanced to meet Todd on the train coming up the Sacramento Valley. He had not greatly changed, but appeared considerably broken in health. He informed me that Mrs. Lincoln was his own aunt, and that he had been brought up in the family of Abraham Lincoln.

find, what he intended to be a representation of a grizzly bear. This was raised to the top of the staff, some seventy feet from the ground. Native Californians looking up at it were heard to say "Coche," the common name among them for pig or shoat.

The party at Sonoma now received some accessions from the Americans and other foreigners living on the north side of the bay. Rumors began to reach them of an uprising on the part of the native Californians, which indeed began under Joaquin de la Torre. Henry L. Ford and other Americans to the number of thirty met De la Torre—whose force was said to number from forty to eighty—near the Petaluma Ranch, and four or five of the Californians were said to have been killed or wounded. The repulse of the Californians seems to have been complete, though reports continued alarming, and a man sent from Sonoma to Russian River for powder was killed. A messenger was sent in haste to Sacramento for Frémont, who hurried to Sonoma with nearly all his exploring party and scoured the country far and near, but found no enemy.

I tried to make the prisoners at Sacramento as comfortable as possible, assisting to see that their meals were regularly and properly brought, and sometimes I would sit by while they were eating. One day E. M. Kern, artist to Frémont's exploring expedition, called me out and said it was Frémont's orders that no one was to go in or speak to the prisoners. I told him they were in my charge, and that he had nothing to say about them. He asserted that they were in his charge, and finally convinced me that he had been made an equal, if not the principal custodian. I then told him that, as both of us were not needed, I would go over and join Frémont at Sonoma. Just at this time Lieutenant Washington A. Bartlett of the United States Navy arrived from the bay, inquiring for Frémont. The taking of the horses from Arce, the capture of the prisoners, and the occupation of Sonoma had been heard of, and he was sent to learn what it meant. So he went over to Sonoma with me.

On our arrival Frémont was still absent trying to find the enemy, but that evening he returned. The Bear Flag was still flying, and had been for a week or more. The American flag was nowhere displayed. There was much doubt about the situation. Frémont gave us to understand that we must organize. Lieutenant Gillespie seemed to be his confidential adviser and spokesman, and said that a meeting would be held the next day at which Frémont would make an address. He also said that it would be necessary to have some plan of organization ready to report to the meeting; and that P. B. Reading, W. B. Ide, and myself were requested to act as a committee to report such a plan. We could learn nothing from Frémont or Gillespie to the effect that the United States had anything to do with Frémont's present movements.

In past years rumors of threats against Americans

in California had been rather frequent, several times causing them or other foreigners to hasten in the night from all places within one or two hundred miles to Sutter's Fort, sometimes remaining a week or two, drilling and preparing to resist attack. The first scare of this kind occurred in 1841, when Sutter became somewhat alarmed; the last, in 1845. But in every case such rumors had proved to be groundless, so that Americans had ceased to have apprehensions, especially in the presence of such an accessible refuge as Sutter's Fort. And now, in 1846, after so many accessions by immigration, we felt entirely secure, even without the presence of a United States officer and his exploring force of sixty men, until we found ourselves suddenly plunged into a war. But hostilities having been begun, bringing danger where none before existed, it now became imperative to organize. It was in every one's mouth (and I think must have come from Frémont) that the war was begun in defense of American settlers! This was simply a pretense to justify the premature beginning of the war, which henceforth was to be carried on in the name of the United States.[1]

---

[1]So much has been said and written about the "Bear Flag" that some may conclude it was something of importance. It was not so regarded at the time: it was never adopted at any meeting or by any agreement; it was, I think, never even noticed, perhaps never seen, by Frémont when it was flying. The naked old Mexican flagstaff at Sonoma suggested that something should be put on it. Todd had painted it, and others had helped to put it up, for mere pastime. It had no importance to begin with, none whatever when the Stars

Under these circumstances on the Fourth of July our committee met. We soon found that we could not agree. Ide wished to paste together his long proclamations on the flagstaff, and make them our report. Reading wrote something much shorter, which I thought still too long. I proposed for our report simply this: "The undersigned hereby agree to organize for the purpose of gaining and maintaining the independence of California." Unable to agree upon a report, we decided to submit what we had written to Lieutenant Gillespie, without our names, and ask him to choose. He chose mine. The meeting took place, but Frémont's remarks gave us no light upon any phase of the situation. He neither averred nor denied that he was acting under orders from the United States Government. Some men had been guilty of misconduct in an Indian village, and he reprimanded them—said he wanted nothing to do with the movement unless the men would conduct themselves properly. Gillespie made some remarks, presented the report, and all present signed it.

The organization took place forthwith, by the formation of three companies. The captains elected were Henry L. Ford, Granville P. Swift, and Samuel J. Hensley. Thus organized, we marched into the Sacramento Valley. The men who had not been

---

and Stripes went up, and never would have been thought of again had not an officer of the navy seeen it in Sonoma and written a letter about it.

at Sonoma signed the report at the camp above Sutter's Fort, except a few who soon after signed it at the Mokelumne River on our march to Monterey. This was, so far as I know, the last seen or heard of that document, for Commodore Sloat had raised the American flag at Monterey before our arrival, and soon it waved in all places in California where American influence prevailed.

As yet Frémont had received advices from Washington no later than those brought by Gillespie. His object in going to Monterey must have been to confer with Commodore Sloat and get positive information about the war with Mexico, which proved to be a reality, as we learned even before our arrival there. There was now no longer uncertainty; all were glad. It was a glorious sight to see the Stars and Stripes as we marched into Monterey. Here we found Commodore Sloat. The same evening, or the next, Commodore Stockton, a chivalrous and dashing officer, arrived around Cape Horn to supersede him. Plans were immediately laid to conquer California. A Californian Battalion was to be organized, and Frémont was to be lieutenant-colonel in command. Stockton asked Frémont to nominate his own officers. P. B. Reading was chosen paymaster, Ezekiel Merritt quartermaster, and, I think, King commissary. The captains and lieutenants chosen at Sonoma were also commissioned. Though I did not aspire to office, I received a commission as second lieutenant.

Merritt, the quartermaster, could neither read nor write. He was an old mountaineer and trapper, lived with an Indian squaw, and went clad in buckskin fringed after the style of the Rocky Mountain Indians. He chewed tobacco to a disgusting excess, and stammered badly. He had a reputation for bravery because of his continual boasting of his prowess in killing Indians. The handle of the tomahawk he carried had nearly a hundred notches to record the number of his Indian scalps. He drank deeply whenever he could get liquor. Stockton said to him: "Major Merritt" (for he was now major), "make out a requisition for some money, say two thousand dollars. You will need about that amount at the start. Bring your requisition on board, and I will approve, and direct the purser to honor it." Major Reading wrote the requisition and Merritt got the money, two thousand Mexican silver dollars. That afternoon I met him in Monterey, nearly as drunk as he could be. He said, "Bidwell, I am rich; I have lots of money"; and putting both hands into the deep pockets of his buckskin breeches he brought out two handfuls of Mexican dollars, saying, "Here, take this, and if you can find anything to buy, buy it, and when you want more money come to me, for I have got lots of it."

Merritt was never removed from his office or rank, but simply fell into disuse, and was detailed, like subordinate officers or men, to perform other duties, generally at the head of small scouting parties. Merritt's friends—for he must have had friends to recommend him for quartermaster—in some way managed to fix up the accounts relating to the early administration of his office. In fact, I tried to help them myself, but I believe that all of us together were never able to find, within a thousand dollars, what Merritt had done with the money. How he ever came to be recommended for quartermaster was to every one a mystery. Perhaps some of the current theories that subsequently prevailed might have had in them just a shade of truth, namely, that somebody entertained the idea that quartermaster meant the ability and duty to quarter the beef!

The first conquest of California, in 1846, by the Americans, with the exception of the skirmish at Petaluma and another towards Monterey, was achieved without a battle. We simply marched all over California from Sonoma to San Diego and raised the American Flag without opposition or protest. We tried to find an enemy, but could not. So Kit Carson and Ned Beale were sent East, bearing despatches from Commodore Stockton announcing the entire conquest of California by the United States. Frémont was made governor by Stockton at Los Angeles, but could not enter upon the full discharge of the duties of his office till he had visited the upper part of California and returned. He sent me to take charge of the mission of San Luis Rey, with a commission as magistrate over the larger portion of the country between Los Angeles and

San Diego. Stockton and all his forces retired on board of their vessels. Frémont went north, leaving part of his men at Los Angeles under Gillespie, part at Santa Barbara under Lieutenant Talbot, and some at other points. Pio Pico and José Castro, respectively the last Mexican governor and commander-in-chief, remained concealed a while and then withdrew into Mexico.

Suddenly, in about a month, Frémont being in the north and his troops scattered, the whole country south of Monterey was in a state of revolt. Then for the first time there was something like war. As there were rumors of Mexican troops coming from Sonora, Merritt was sent by Gillespie to reconnoiter towards the Colorado River. Gillespie was surrounded at Los Angeles, and made to capitulate. I fled from San Luis Rey to San Diego. Merritt and his party, hearing of the outbreak, also escaped to San Diego. Meanwhile Frémont enlisted a considerable force (about four hundred), principally from the large Hastings immigration at Sacramento, and marched south. Commodore Stockton had landed and marched to retake Los Angeles, and failed. All the men-of-war, and all the scattered forces, except Frémont's new force, were then concentrated at San Diego, where Commodore Stockton collected and reorganized the forces, composed of sailors, marines, men of Frémont's battalion under Gillespie and Merritt, volunteers at San Diego, including some native Californians and that portion of the regular troops under General S. W. Kearney that had escaped from the field of San Pascual—in all between 700 and 800 men. Of these forces I was commissioned and served as quartermaster. This work of preparation took several months. Finally, on the 29th of December, 1846, the army set out to retake Los Angeles. It fought the battles of San Gabriel and the Mesa, which ended the insurrection. The enemy fled, met Frémont at San Fernando, and surrendered to him the next day. The terms of surrender were so lenient that the native Californians from that time forth became the fast friends of Frémont.

Unfortunate differences regarding rank had arisen between Stockton and Kearney. Frémont was afterwards arrested in California by Kearney for refusing to obey his orders, and was taken to Washington and court-martialed. Stockton, however, was largely to blame. He would not submit to General Kearney, his superior in command on land, and that led Frémont to refuse to obey Kearney, his superior officer. Frémont's disobedience was no doubt owing to the advice of Stockton, who had appointed him governor of California.[1]

The war being over, nearly all the volunteers were discharged from the service in February and March, 1847, at Los Angeles and San Diego. Most of us made our way up the coast by land to our

[1]General Vallejo in one of his letters tells of having received on the same day communications from Commodore Stockton, General Kearney, and Colonel Frémont, each one signing himself "Commander-in-chief of California."

homes. I had eleven horses, which I swam, one at a time, across the Straits of Carquinez at Benicia, which J. M. Hudspeth, the surveyor, was at the time laying out for Dr. Robert Semple, and which was then called "Francisca," after Mrs. Vallejo, whose maiden name was Francisca Benicia Carrillo.

REPORT

ON THE SUBJECT OF

LAND TITLES IN CALIFORNIA,

MADE IN PURSUANCE OF INSTRUCTIONS FROM THE

Secretary of State and the Secretary of the Interior,

BY WILLIAM CAREY JONES:

TOGETHER WITH A TRANSLATION OF THE

PRINCIPAL LAWS ON THAT SUBJECT,

AND SOME OTHER PAPERS RELATING THERETO.

WASHINGTON:
GIDEON & CO., PRINTERS,
1850.

REPORT

ON

LAND TITLES IN CALIFORNIA.

To the Secretary of the Interior:

Sir : On the 12th July last, I received a letter of that date from the Department of State, informing me that I had been appointed a "confidential agent of the Government, to proceed to Mexico and California, for the purpose of procuring information as to the condition of Land Titles in California ;" and at the same time, your letter of instructions, and a letter from the Commissioner of the Land office.

Pursuant to these, I left this city on the 14th of the same month, and embarked from New York on the 17th, on board the steamship Empire City, for Chagres. Arriving at that place on the 29th, I proceeded immediately to Panama, under the expectation of shortly obtaining a passage to California. The first opportunity, however, was by the steamship Oregon the 29th of August. I arrived at Monterey, the then capital of California, and where the territorial archives were deposited, on the 19th of September. I afterward visited the towns San José, the present capital, and San Francisco, and returned to Monterey. I also made arrangements for going by land, so as to visit the principal places on the way, from Monterey to Los Angeles, and thence to San Diego. The early setting in of the rainy season rendered this journey impracticable ; and on the 16th of November I left Monterey on the steamship Panama, and went by sea to San Diego. Thence, I went by land to Los Angeles ; and on the 3d of December returned to San Diego, in order to embark on the steamer which was at that time expected from San Francisco. I embarked from San Diego on the 7th of December, on the steamship Unicorn, and landed the 18th of the same month at Acapulco, in Mexico. I proceeded thence as rapidly as possible to the city of Mexico, where I arrived on the 24th. On the 11th of January I left that city, and on the 18th of the same month embarked from Vera Cruz for Mobile, and thence arrived in this city on the 1st of February. I have been prevented from making my report until the present time, by the unexpected detention of the papers and memoranda which I collected in California, and which I could not, without inconvenience and delay, and some hazard of their loss, bring with me through Mexico, and therefore procured to be brought by way of the isthmus of Panama.

On arriving in California, my attention was immediately directed to the subjects embraced in your letter of instructions.

I. " To the mode of creating titles to land, from the first inception to the perfect title, as practised by Mexico, within the province of California."

All the grants of land made in California (except pueblo or village lots, and except, perhaps, some grants north of the bay of San Francisco, as will be hereafter noticed) subsequent to the independence of Mexico, and after the establishment of that government in California, were made by the different political governors. The great majority of them were made subsequent to January, 1832, and consequently under the Mexican Colonization Law of 18th August, 1824, and the government regulations, adopted in pursuance of the law, dated 21st November, 1828. In January, 1832, General José Figueroa became Governor of the then territory of California, under a commission from the Government at Mexico, replacing Victoria, who, after having the year before, displaced Echandrea, was himself driven out by a revolution. The installation of Figueroa restored quiet, after ten years of civil commotion, and was at a time when Mexico was making vigorous efforts to reduce and populate her distant territories, and consequently granting lands on a liberal scale. In the act of 1824, a league square (being $4,428\frac{402}{1000}$ acres) is the smallest measurement of rural property spoken of ; and of these leagues square, eleven (or nearly 50,000 acres) might be conceded in a grant to one individual. By this law, the *States* composing the federation, were authorized to make special provision for colonization within their respective limits, and the colonization of the *territories,* " conformably to the principles of the law" charged upon the Central Government. California was of the latter description, being designated a Territory in the *Acta Constitutiva* of the Mexican Federation, adopted 31st January, 1824, and by the Constitution, adopted 4th October of the same year.* The colonization of California, and granting of lands therein, was, therefore, subsequent to the law of 18th August, 1824, under the direction and control of the Central Government. That government, as already stated, gave regulations for the same, 21st November, 1828.

The directions were very simple. They gave the governors of the territories the exclusive faculty of making grants, within the terms of the law—that is, to the extent of eleven leagues, or *sitios*, to individuals ; and colonization grants, (more properly, *contracts*)—that is, grants of larger tracts to *empresarios*, or persons who should undertake, for a consideration in land, to bring families to the country for the purpose of colonization. Grants of the first description ; that is, to families or single persons, and not exceeding eleven *sitios*, were " not to be held definitively valid," until sanctioned by the *Territorial Deputation.* Those of the second class, that is, *empresario* or colonization

---

* The political condition of California was changed by the Constitution of 29th December, and act for the division of the Republic into Departments, of the 30th December, 1836. The two Californias then became *a Department*, the confederation being broken up, and the States reduced to Departments. The same colonization system, however, seems to have continued in California.

grants (or contracts) required a like sanction by the *Supreme Government*. In case the concurrence of the Deputation was refused to a grant of the first mentioned class, the governor should appeal, in favor of the grantee, from the assembly to the Supreme Government.

The "*first inception*" of the claim, pursuant to the regulations, and as practised in California, was a petition to the Governor, praying for the grant, specifying usually the quantity of land asked, and designating its position, with some descriptive object or boundary, and also stating the age, country, and vocation of the petitioner. Sometimes, also, (generally, at the commencement of this system,) a rude *map* or *plan* of the required grant, showing its shape, and position with reference to other tracts, or to natural objects, was presented with the petition. This practice, however, was gradually disused, and few of the grants made in late years have any other than a verbal description.

The next step was usually a reference of the petition, made on the margin, by the governor, to the prefect of the district, or other near local officer, where the land petitioned for was situate, to know if it was vacant, and could be granted without injury to third persons or the public, and sometimes to know if the petitioners' account of himself was true. The reply (*informe*) of the prefect, or other officer, was written upon or attached to the petition, and the whole returned to the governor. The reply being satisfactory, the governor then issued the grant in form. On its receipt, or before, (often before the petition even,) the party went into possession. It was not unfrequent, of late years, to omit the formality of sending the petition to the local authorities, and it was never requisite, if the governor already possessed the necessary information concerning the land and the parties. In that case the grant followed immediately on the petition. Again, it sometimes happened that the reply of the local authority was not explicit, or that third persons intervened, and the grant was thus for some time delayed. With these qualifications, and covering the great majority of cases, the practice may be said to have been: 1. The petition; 2. The reference to the prefect or alcalde; 3. His report, or *informe;* 4. The grant from the governor.

" *When filed, and how, and by whom recorded?*"

The *originals* of the petition and *informe*, and any other preliminary papers in the case, were filed, by the secretary, in the government archives, and with them a *copy* (the original being delivered to the grantee) of the grant: the whole attached together so as to form one document (entitled, collectively, an *expediente*.) During the governorship of Figueroa, and some of his successors, that is, from 22d May, 1833, to 9th May, 1836, the grants were likewise *recorded* in a book kept for that purpose (as prescribed in the " regulations" above referred to) in the archives. Subsequent to that time, there was no *record*, but a brief memorandum of the grant: the *expediente*, however, still filed. Grants were also sometimes registered in the office of the prefect of the district where the lands lay; but the practice was not constant, nor the record generally in a permanent form.

The next, and final, step in the title, was the approval of the grant by the Territorial Deputation (that is, the local legislature, afterward, when the territory was created into a Department, called the "Departmental Assembly.") For this purpose, it was the governor's office to communicate the fact of the grant, and all information concerning it, to the assembly. It was here referred to a committee (sometimes called a committee on vacant lands, sometimes on agriculture,) who reported at a subsequent sitting. The approval was seldom refused; but there are many instances where the governor omitted to communicate the grant to the assembly, and it consequently remained unacted on. The approval of the assembly obtained, it was usual for the secretary to deliver to the grantee, on application, a certificate of the fact; but no other record or registration of it was kept than the written proceedings of the assembly. There are, no doubt, instances, therefore, where the approval was in fact obtained, but a certificate not applied for, and as the journals of the assembly, now remaining in the archives, are very imperfect, it can hardly be doubted that many grants have received the approval of the assembly, and no record of the fact now exists. Many grants were passed upon and approved by the assembly in the winter and spring of 1846, as I discovered by loose memoranda, apparently made by the clerk of the assembly for future entry, and referring to the grants by their numbers—sometimes a dozen or more, on a single small piece of paper; but of which I could find no other record.

" *So, also, with the subsequent steps, embracing the proceedings as to survey, up to the perfecting of the title ?*"

There were not, as far as I could learn, any regular surveys made of grants in California, up to the time of the cessation of the former government. There was no public or authorized surveyor in the country. The grants usually contained a direction that the grantee should receive judicial possession of the land " from the proper magistrate (usually the nearest alcalde) in virtue of the grant," and that the boundaries of the tract should then be designated by that functionary with " suitable land marks." But this injunction was usually complied with, only by procuring the attendance of the magistrate, to give judicial possession according to the verbal description contained in the grant. Some of the old grants have been subsequently surveyed, as I was informed, by a surveyor under appointment of Col. Mason, acting as governor of California. I did not see any official record of such surveys, or understand that there was any. The " *perfecting of the title*" I suppose to have been accomplished when the grant received the concurrence of the assembly; all provisions of the law, and of the colonization regulations of the supreme government, pre-requisites to the title being "definitively valid," having been then fulfilled. These, I think, must be counted *complete titles.*

" *And if there be any more books, files, or archives of any kind what-* " *soever, showing the nature, character and extent of these grants ?*"

The following list comprises the books of record and memoranda of grants, which I found existing in the Government archives at Monterey:

1. " 1828. Cuaderno del registro de los sitios, fierras, y señales que posean los habitantes del territorio de la Nueva California."—(Book of registration of the farms, brands, and marks [for marking cattle] possessed by the inhabitants of the territory of New California.)

This book contains information of the situation, boundaries, and appurtenances of several of the missions, as hereafter noticed; of two pueblos, San José and Branciforte, and the records of about twenty grants, made by various Spanish, Mexican, and local authorities, at different times, between 1784 and 1825, and two dated in 1829. This book appears to have been arranged upon information obtained in an endeavor of the Government to procure a registration of all the occupied lands of the territory.

2. Book marked " Titulos."

This book contains records of grants, numbered from 1 to 108, of various dates, from 22d May, 1833, to 9th May, 1836, by the successive governors, Figueroa, José Castro, Nicholas Gutierrez, and Mariano Chico. A part of these grants (probably all) are included in a file of expedientes of grants, hereafter described, marked from No. 1 to No. 579; but the numbers in the book do not correspond with the numbers of the same grants in the expedientes.

3. " Libro donde se asciertan los despachos de terrenos adjudicados en los años de 1839 and 1840."—(Book denoting the concessions of land adjudicated in the years 1839 and 1840.)

This book contains a brief entry, by the secretary of the department, of grants, including their numbers, dates, names of the grantees and of the grants, quantity granted, and situation of the land, usually entered in the book in the order they were conceded. This book contains the grants made from 18th January, 1839, to 8th December, 1843, inclusive.

4. A book similar to the above, and containing like entries of grants issued between 8th January, 1844, and 23d December, 1845.

5. File of expedientes of grants—that is, all the proceedings (except of the Assembly) relating to the respective grants, secured, those of each grant in a separate parcel, and marked and labelled with its number and name. This file is marked from No. 1 to No. 579 inclusive, and embraces the space of time between 13th May, 1833, to July, 1846. The numbers, however, bear little relation to the dates. Some numbers are missing, of some there are duplicates—that is, two distinct grants with the same number. The expedientes are not all complete; in some cases the final grant appears to have been refused; in others it is wanting. The collection, however, is evidently intended to represent estates which have been granted, and it is probable that in many, or most instances, the omission apparent in the archives is supplied by original documents in the hands of the parties, or by long permitted occupation.

8

These embrace all the record books and files belonging to the territorial, or departmental, archives, which I was able to discover. I am assured, however, by Mr. J. C. Frémont, that, according to the best of his recollection, a book for the year 1846, corresponding to those above noted, extending from 1839 to the end of 1845, existed in the archives while he was Governor of California, and was with them when he delivered them, in May, 1847, to the officer appointed by General Kearny to receive them from him at Monterey.

II. "CHIEFLY THE LARGE GRANTS, AS THE MISSIONS, AND WHE-
"THER THE TITLE TO THEM BE IN ASSIGNEES, OR WHETHER THEY
"HAVE REVERTED, AND VESTED IN THE SOVEREIGN?"

I took much pains, both in California and in Mexico, to assure myself of the situation, in a legal and proprietary point of view, of the former great establishments known as the MISSIONS of California. It had been supposed that the lands they occupied were *grants*, held as the property of the church, or of the mission establishments as corporations. Such, however, was not the case. All the missions in Upper California were established under the direction, and mainly at the expense, of the Government, and the missionaries there had never any other rights than to the occupation and use of the lands for the purpose of the missions, and at the pleasure of the Government. This is shown by the history and principles of their foundation, by the laws in relation to them, by the constant practice of the Government toward them, and, in fact, by the rules of the Franciscan order, which forbid its members to possess property.

The establishment of missions in remote provinces was a part of the colonial system of Spain. The Jesuits, by a license from the Viceroy of New Spain, commenced in this manner the reduction of Lower California in the year 1697. They continued in the spiritual charge, and in a considerable degree of the temporal government, of that province until 1767, when the royal decree abolishing the Jesuit order throughout New Spain was there enforced, and the missions taken out of their hands. They had then founded fifteen missions, extending from Cape St. Lucas, nearly to the head of the sea of Cortés, or Californian gulf. Three of the establishments had been suppressed by order of the Viceroy: the remainder were now put in charge of the Franciscan monks of the college of San Fernando, in Mexico, hence sometimes called "*Fernandinos.*" The prefect of that college, the Rev. Father Junipero Serra, proceeded in person to his new charge, and arrived, with a number of monks, at Loreto, the capital of the peninsula, the following year, (1768.) He was there, soon after, joined by Don José Galvez, inspector general *(visitador)* of New Spain, who brought an order from the King, directing the founding of one or more settlements in Upper California. It was therefore agreed that Father Junipero should extend the mission establishments into Upper California, under the protection of *presidios* (armed posts) which the government would establish at San Diego and Monterey. Two expeditions, both accompanied by missionaries, were consequently fitted out, one to proceed by sea the other by land, to the new territory. In June, 1769, they had arrived, and in that month founded the first mission, about two leagues from the port of San Diego. A *presidio* was established, at the same time, near the port. The same year, a *presidio* was established at Monterey, and a mission establishment begun. Subsequently, the Dominican friars obtained leave from the King to take charge of a part of the missions of California, which led to an arrangement between the two societies, whereby the missions of Lower California were committed to the Dominicans, and the entire field of the Upper Province remained to the Franciscans. This arrangement was sanctioned by the political authority, and continues to the present time. The new establishments flourished, and rapidly augmented their numbers, occupying first the space between San Diego and Monterey, and subsequently extending to the northward. A report from the Viceroy to the King, dated at Mexico, 27th December, 1793, gives the following account of the number, time of establishment, and locality of the Missions existing in New California at that time:

Missions.	Situation.	When founded.	
1. San Diego de Alcala,	lat. 32° 42'	16th July,	1769.
2. San Carlos de Monterey,	36 33	3d June,	1170.
3. San Antonio de Padua,	36 34	14th July,	1771.
4. San Gabriel de los Temblores,	34 10	8th Sept.,	1771.
5. San Luis Obispo,	31 38	1st Sept.,	1772.
6. San Francisco, (Dolores,)	37 56	9th Oct.,	1776.
7. San Juan Capistrano,	33 30	1st Nov.,	1776.
8. Santa Clara,	37 00	18th Jan.,	1777.
9. San Buenaventura,	34 36	31st March,	1782.
10. Santa Barbara,	34 28	4th Oct.,	1786.
11. Purisima Conception,	35 32	8th Jan.,	1787.
12. Santa Cruz,	36 58	28th Aug.,	1791.
13. La Soledad,	36 38	9th Oct.,	1791.

At first, the missions nominally occupied the whole territory, except the four small military posts of San Diego, Santa Barbara, Monterey, and San Francisco; that is, the limits of one mission were said to cover the intervening space to the limits of the next; and there were no other occupants except the wild Indians, whose reduction and conversion was the object of the establishments. The Indians, as fast as they were reduced, were trained to labor in the missions, and lived either within its walls, or in small villages near by, under the spiritual and temporal direction of the priests, but the whole under the political control of the governor of the province, who decided contested questions of right or policy, whether between different missions, between missions and individuals, or concerning the Indians. Soon, however, grants of land began to be made to individuals, especially to retired soldiers, who received special favor in the distant colonies of Spain, and became the settlers and founders of the country they had reduced and protected.

Some settlers were also brought from the neighboring provinces of Sonora and Sinaloa, and the towns of *San José*, at the head of the Bay of San Francisco, and of *Los Angeles*, eight leagues from the port of San Pedro, were early founded. The governor exercised the privilege of making concessions of large tracts, and the captains of the presidios were authorized to grant building lots, and small tracts for gardens and farms, within the distance of two leagues from the presidios. By these means, the mission tracts began respectively to have something like known boundaries; though the lands they thus occupied were still not viewed, in any light, as the property of the missionaries, but as the domain of the crown, appropriated to the use of the missions while the state of the country should require it, and at the pleasure of the political authority.

It was the custom throughout New Spain, (and other parts of the Spanish colonies, also,) to secularize, or to subvert, the mission establishments, at the discretion of the ruling political functionary; and this not as an act of arbitrary power, but in the exercise of an acknowledged ownership and authority. The great establishments of Sonora, I have been told, were divided between white settlements and settlements of the Indian pupils, or neophytes of the establishments. In Texas, the missions were broken up, the Indians were dispersed, and the lands have been granted to white settlers. In New Mexico, I am led to suppose, the Indian pupils of the missions, or their descendants, still, in great part, occupy the old establishments; and other parts are occupied by white settlers, in virtue of grants and sales.* The undisputed exercise of this authority over all the mission establishments, and whatever property was pertinent to them, is certain.

The liability of the missions of Upper California, however, to be thus dealt with, at the pleasure of the Government, does not rest only on the argument to be drawn from this constant and uniform practice. It was inherent in their foundation—a condition of their establishment. A belief has prevailed, and it is so stated in all the works I have examined which treat historically of the missions of that country, that the first act which looked to their secularization, and especially the first act by which any authority was conferred on the local government for that purpose, or over their temporalities, was an act of the Mexican Congress of 17th August, 1833. Such, however, was not the case. Their secularization—their subversion—was looked for in their foundation; and I do not perceive that the local authority (certainly not the supreme authority) has ever been without that lawful jurisdiction over them,

---

* Since writing the above, I have learned from the Hon. Mr. Smith, Delegate from the Territory of New Mexico, that the portion of each of the former mission establishments which has been allotted to the Indians is *one league square*. They hold the land, as a general rule, in community, and on condition of supporting a priest and maintaining divine worship. This portion and these conditions are conformable to the principles of the Spanish laws concerning the allotments of Indian villages. Some interesting particulars of the foundation, progress, and plan of the missions of New Mexico are contained in the report, or information, before quoted, of 1793, from the Viceroy to the King of Spain, and in extracts from it given in the papers accompanying this Report.

unless subsequent to the colonization regulations of 21st November, 1828, which temporarily exempted mission lands from colonization. I quote from a letter of " Instructions to the commandant of the new establishments of San Diego and Monterey," given by Viceroy Bucareli, 17th August, 1773:

" Art. 15. When it shall happen that a mission is to be formed into a pueblo (or village) the commandant will proceed to reduce it to the civil and economical government, which, according to the laws, is observed by other villages of this kingdom; then giving it a name, and declaring for its patron the saint under whose memory and protection the mission was founded." (Cuando llegue el caso de que haya de formarse en el pueblo una mision, procederá el comandante á reducirlo al gobierno civil y economico que observan, segun las leyes, los demas de este reyno; poniendole nombre entonces, y declarandole por su titular el santo bajo cuya memoria y venerable proteccion se fundó la mision.)

The right, then, to remodel these establishments at pleasure, and convert them into towns and villages, subject to the known policy and laws which governed settlements of that description,* we see was a principle of their foundation. Articles 7 and 10, of the same letter of Instructions, show us also that it was a part of the *plan* of the missions that their condition should be thus changed ; that they were regarded only as the nucleus and bases of communities to be thereafter emancipated, acquire proprietary rights, and administer their own affairs; and that it was the duty of the governor to choose their sites, and direct the construction and arrangement of their edifices, with a view to their convenient expansion into towns and cities. And not only was this general revolution of the establishments thus early contemplated and provided for, but mean time the governor had authority to reduce their possessions by grants within and without, and to change their condition by detail. The same series of instructions authorized the governor to grant lands, either in community or individually, to the Indians of the missions, in and about their settlements on the mission lands; and also to make grants to settlements of white persons. The governor was likewise authorized at an early day to make grants to soldiers who should marry Indian women trained in the missions; and the first grant, (and only one I found of record,) under this authorization, was of a tract near the mission edifice of Carmel, near Monterey. The authorization given to the captains of *presidios* to grant lands within two leagues of their posts, expressly restrains them within that distance, so as to leave the territory beyond—though all beyond was nominally attached to one or other of the missions—at the disposition of the superior guardians of the royal property. In brief, every fact, every act of government, and

---

* A revolution more than equal to the modern *secularization,* since the latter only necessarily implies the turning over of the temporal concerns of the mission to secular administration. Their conversion into pueblos would take from the missions all semblance in organization to their originals, and include the reduction of the missionary priests from the heads of great establishments and administrators of large temporalities, to parish curates : a change quite inconsistent with the existence in the priests or the church of any proprietory interest or right over the establishment.

principle of law applicable to the case, which I have met in this investigation, go to show that the missions of Upper California were never, from the first, reckoned other than government establishments, or the founding of them to work any change in the ownership of the soil, which continued in and at the disposal of the crown, or its representatives. This position was also confirmed, if had it needed any confirmation, by the opinions of high legal and official authorities in Mexico. The missions—speaking collectively of priests and pupils—had the *usufruct;* the priests the administration of it; the whole resumable, or otherwise disposable, at the will of the crown or its representatives.

The object of the missions was to aid in the settlement and pacification of the country, and to convert the natives to Christianity. This accomplished, settlements of white people established, and the Indians domiciliated in villages, so as to subject them to the ordinary magistrates, and the spiritual care of the ordinary clergy, the *missionary* labor was considered fulfilled, and the establishment subject to be dissolved or removed. This view of their purposes and destiny fully appears in the tenor of the decree of the Spanish Cortes, of 13th September, 1813.* The provisions of that act, and the reason given for it, develope in fact the whole theory of the mission establishments. It was passed "in consequence of a complaint by the Bishop elect of Guiana of the evils that afflicted that province, on account of the Indian settlements in charge of missions not being delivered to the ecclesiastical ordinary, though thirty, forty, and fifty years had passed since the reduction and conversion of the Indians." The Cortes therefore decreed:

1. That all the new *reducciones y doctrinas,* (that is, settlements of Indians newly converted, and not yet formed into parishes,) of the provinces beyond sea, which were in charge of missionary monks, and had been ten years subjected, should be delivered immediately to the respective ecclesiastical ordinaries, (bishops) "without resort to any excuse or pretext, conformably to the laws and cedulas in that respect."

2. That as well these missions, (*doctrinas*) as all others which should be erected into curacies, should be canonically provided by the said ordinaries, (observing the laws and cedulas of the royal right of patronage,) with fit ministers of the secular clergy.

3. That the missionary monks, relieved from the converted settlements, which should be delivered to the ordinary, should apply themselves to the extension of religion in benefit of the inhabitants of other wilderness parts, proceeding in the exercise of their missions conformably to the directions of paragraph 10, article 335, of the Constitution.†

---

* "Collection of Decrees of the Spanish Cortes, reputed in force in Mexico." Mexico, 1829, p. 106.

† The following is the clause referred to, namely, paragraph 10, art. 335, Constitution of the Spanish monarchy, 1812:

" The provincial councils of the provinces beyond sea shall attend to the order, economy, and progress of the missions for the conversion of infidel Indians, and to the prevention of abuses in that branch of administration. The commissioners of such missions shall render their accounts to them, which accounts they shall in their turn forward to the government."

This clause of itself settles the character of these establishments, as a branch of the public administration.

6. That the missionary monks should discontinue immediately the government and administration of the property of the Indians, who should choose by means of their *ayuntamientos*, with intervention of the superior political authority, persons among themselves competent to administer it; the lands being distributed and reduced to private ownership, in accordance with the decree of the 4th January, 1813, on reducing vacant and other lands to private property."*

It has also been supposed, that the act above alluded to of the Mexican Congress, (act of 17th August, 1833,) was the first assertion by the Mexican government of property in the missions, or that they by that act first became (or came to be considered,) national domain. But this is likewise an error. The Mexican government has always asserted the right of property over all the missions of the country, and I do not think that the supposition has ever been raised in Mexico, that they were the property of the missionaries or the Church.

The General Congress of Mexico, in a decree of 4th August, 1824, concerning the public revenue, declares the estates of the inquisition, as well as all temporalities, to be the property of the nation; (that is, no doubt, in contradistinction from property of the States—making no question of their being public property.) This term would include not only the mission establishments, but all rents, profits, and income the monks received from them. A like act of 7th July, 1831, again em-braces the estates of the inquisition and temporalities as national property, and places them with "other rural and suburban estates," under charge of a director general. The executive regulations for colonizing the territories, may raise an idea of territorial and native property in them, but it puts out of the question any proprietary right in the missionaries.

The 17th article of these regulations, (executive regulations for colonization of the territories, adopted 21st November, 1828,) relates to the missions, and directs that, "In those territories where there are missions, the lands which they occupy shall not at present be colonized, nor until it be determined if they ought to be considered as property of the settlements of the neophyte-catechumens and Mexican settlers."

The subsequent acts and measures of the general government of Mexico in direct reference to missions, and affecting those of California, are briefly as follows:

---

* "Collection of Decrees of the Spanish Cortes," &c., p. 56. This decree provides :

1. That "all the vacant or royal lands, and town reservations, (*propios y arbitrios*, lands reserved in and about towns and cities for the municipal revenue,) both in the Peninsula and islands adjacent, and in the provinces beyond sea, except such commons as may be necessary for the villages, shall be converted into private property; provided, that in regard to town reservations, some annual rents shall be reserved.

2. That " in whatever mode these lands were distributed, it should be in full and exclusive ownership, so that their owners may enclose them, (without prejudice of paths, crossings, watering-places, and servitudes,) to enjoy them freely and exclusively, and destine them to such use or cultivation as they may be best adapted to; but without the owners ever being able to entail them, or to transfer them, at any time or by any title, in *mortmain*."

3. In the transfer of these lands shall be preferred the inhabitants of the villages, (or settlements,) in the neighborhood where they exist, and who enjoyed the same in common whilst they were vacant."

A decree of the Mexican Congress of 20th November, 1833, in part analogous to the decree before quoted of the Spanish Cortes of September, 1813, directing their general secularization, and containing these provisions:

1. The government shall proceed to secularize the missions of Upper and Lower California.

2. In each of said missions shall be established a parish, served by a curate of the secular clergy, with a dotation of two thousand to two thousand five hundred dollars, at the discretion of the government.

4. The mission churches, with the sacred vessels and ornaments, shall be devoted to the uses of the parish.

5. For each parish, the government shall direct the construction of a cemetery outside of the village.

7. Of the buildings belonging to each mission, the most fitting shall be selected for the dwelling of the curate, with a lot of ground not exceeding two hundred varas square, and the others appropriated for a municipal house and schools.

On the 2d December, 1833, a decree was published to the following effect:

"The government is authorized to take all measures that may assure the colonization, and make effective the secularization of the missions of Upper and Lower California, being empowered to this effect, to use, in the manner most expedient, the *fincas de obras pias* (property of the piety fund,) of those territories, to aid the transportation of the commission and families who are now in this capital destined thither."

The commission and emigrants, spoken of in this circular, were a colony under the charge of Don José Maria Hijar, who was sent out the following spring, (of 1834,) as director of colonization, with instructions to the following effect: That he should "make beginning by occupying all the property pertinent to the missions of both Californias;" that in the settlements to be formed, special care should be taken to include the indigenous (Indian) population, mixing them with the other inhabitants, and not permitting any settlement of Indians alone; that topographical plans should be made of the squares which were to compose the villages, and in each square building lots be distributed to the colonist families; that outside the villages there should be distributed to each family of colonists, in full dominion and ownership, four *caballerias** of irrigable land, or eight, if dependent on the seasons, or sixteen if adapted to stock raising, and also live stock and agricultural implements; that this distribution made, (out of the moveable property of the mission,) one-half the remainder of said property should be sold, and the other half reserved on account of government, and applied to the expenses of worship, maintenance of the missionaries, support of schools, and the purchase of agricultural implements for gratuitous distribution to the colonists.

On the 16th April, 1834, the Mexican Congress passed an act to the following effect :

* A *caballeria* of land is a rectangular paralelogram of 552 varas by 1,104 varas.

1. That all the missions in the Republic shall be secularized.

2. That the missions shall be converted into curacies, whose limits shall be demarked by the governors of the States where said missions exist.

3. This decree shall take effect within four months from the day of its publication.

The 7th November, 1835, an act of the Mexican Congress directed, that " until the curates mentioned in the second article of the law of 17th August, 1833, (above quoted,) should take possession, the government should suspend the execution of the other articles, and maintain things in the condition they were before said law."

I have, so far, referred to these various legislative and governmental acts in relation to the missions, only to show, beyond equivocation or doubt, the relation in which the government stood toward them, and the rights of ownership which it exercised over them. My attention was next directed to the changes that had taken place in the condition of those establishments, under the various provisions for their secularization and conversion into private property.

Under the act of the Spanish Cortes of September, 1813, all the missions in New Spain were liable to be secularized ; that is, their temporalities delivered to lay administration ; their character as *missions* taken away by their conversion into parishes under charge of the secular clergy ; and the lands pertinent to them to be disposed of as other public domain. The question of putting this law in operation with regard to the missions in California, was at various times agitated in that province, and in 1830 the then Governor, Echandria, published a project for the purpose, but which was defeated by the arrival of a new governor, Victoria, almost at the instant the plan was made public. Victoria revoked the decree of his predecessor, and restored the missionaries to the charge of the establishments, and in their authority over the Indians.

Subsequent to that time, and previous to the act of secularization of August, 1833, nothing further to that end appears to have been done in California. Under that act, the first step taken by the Central Government, was the expedition of Hijar, above noticed. But the instructions delivered to him were not fulfilled. Hijar had been appointed Governor of California, as well as Director of Colonization, with directions to relieve Governor Figueroa. After Hijar's departure from Mexico, however, a revolution in the Supreme Government induced Hijar's appointment as political governor to be revoked ; and an express was sent to California to announce this change, and with directions to Figueroa to continue in the discharge of the governorship. The courier arrived in advance of Hijar, who found himself on landing, (in September, 1834,) deprived of the principal authority he had expected to exercise. Before consenting to coöperate with Hijar in the latter's instructions concerning the missions, Figueroa consulted the Territorial Deputation. That body protested against the delivery of the vast property included in the mission estates—and to a settlement in which the

Indian pupils had undoubtedly an equitable claim—into Hijar's possession, and contended that his authority in the matter of the missions, depended on his commission as Governor, which had been revoked, and not on his appointment (unknown to the law) as Director of Colonization. As a conclusion to the contestation which followed, the Governor and Assembly suspended Hijar from the last mentioned appointment, and returned him to Mexico.*

Figueroa, however, had already adopted (in August, 1834) a project of secularization, which he denominates a " Provisional Regulation." It provided, that the missions should be converted partially into pueblos or villages, with a distribution of lands and moveable property, as follows : to each individual, head of a family, over twenty-five years of age, a lot of ground, not exceeding four hundred nor less than one hundred varas square, in the common lands of the mission, with a sufficient quantity in common for pasturage of the cattle of the village, and also commons and lands for municipal uses ; likewise, among the same individuals, one-half of the live stock, grain, and agricultural implements of the mission ; that the remainder of the lands, immoveable property, stock, and other effects, should be in charge of mayordomos or other persons appointed by the governor, subject to confirmation by the General Government ; that from this common mass should be provided the maintenance of the priest, and expenses of religious service, and the temporal expenses of the mission ; that the minister should choose a place in the mission for his dwelling ; that the emancipated Indians should unite in common labors for the cultivation of the vineyards, gardens, and field lands, which should remain undivided until the determination of the Supreme Government ; that the donees, under the regulation, should not sell, burthen, or transfer, their grants, either of land or cattle, under any pretext ; and any contracts to this effect should be null, the property reverting to the nation, the purchaser losing his money ; that lands, the donee of which might die without leaving heirs, should revert to the nation ; that *rancherias* (hamlets of Indians) situated at a distance from the missions, and which exceeded twenty-five families, might form separate pueblos, under the same rules as the principal one. This regulation was to begin with *ten* of the missions (without specifying them) and successively be applied to the remaining ones.

The Deputation, in session of the 3d of November of the same year (1834,) made provision for dividing the missions and other settlements into parishes or curacies, according to the law of August, 1833; authorized the missionary priests to exercise the functions of curates, until curates of the secular clergy should arrive, and provided for their salaries and expenses of worship. No change was made, in this act, in the regulations established by Gov. Figueroa, for the distribution and management of the property.

---

*Manifiesto á la Republica Mejicana, que hace el General José Figueroa, comandante general y gefe politico de la Alta California. Monterey, 1835.

Accordingly, for most or all of the missions, administrators were appointed by the governor; and in some, but not all, partial distributions of the lands and moveable property were made, according to the tenor of the regulation. From this time, however, all tracts of lands pertinent to the missions, but not directly attached to the mission buildings, were granted, as any other lands of the territory, to the Mexican inhabitants, and to colonists, for stock farms and tillage.

The act of the Mexican Congress of 1835, directing the execution of the decree of 1833 to be suspended until the arrival of curates, did not, as far as I could ascertain, induce any change in the policy already adopted by the territorial authorities.

On the 17th January, 1839, Governor Alvarado issued regulations for the government of the administrators of the missions. These regulations prohibited the administrators from contracting debts on account of the missions; from slaughtering cattle of the missions, except for consumption, and from trading the mission horses or mules for clothing for the Indians; and likewise provided for the appointment of an inspector of the missions, to supervise the accounts of the administrators, and their fulfilment of their trusts. Art. 11 prohibited the settlement of white persons in the establishments, " whilst the Indians should remain in community." The establishments of San Carlos, San Juan Bautista and Sonoma were excepted from these regulations, and to be governed by special rules.

On the first of March, 1840, the same Governor Alvarado suppressed the office of administrators, and replaced them by *mayordomos*, with new and more stringent rules for the management of the establishments; but not making any change in the rules of Governor Figueroa, regarding the lands or other property.

By a proclamation of the 29th of March, 1843, Governor Micheltorrena, " in pursuance (as he states) of an arrangement between the Governor and the prelate of the missions," directed the following named missions to be restored to the priests "as tutors to the Indians, and in the same manner as they formerly held them," namely: the missions of San Diego, San Luis Rey, San Juan Capistrano, San Gabriel, San Fernando, San Buenaventura, Santa Barbara, Santa Ynes, La Purisima, San Antonio, Santa Clara, and San José. The same act set forth, that, " as policy made irrevocable what was already done," the missions should not reclaim any lands thitherto granted; but should collect the cattle and moveable property which had been lent out either by the priests or administrators, and settle in a friendly way with the creditors; and likewise regather the dispersed Indians, except such as had been legally emancipated, or were at private service. That the priests might provide out of the products of the missions for the necessary expenses of converting, subsisting, and clothing the Indians, for a moderate allowance to themselves, economical salaries to the *mayordomos*, and the maintenance of Divine worship; under the condition, that the priests should bind themselves in honor and con-

2

science to deliver to the public treasury one-eighth part of all the annual products of the establishments. That the Departmental government would exert all its power for the protection of the missions, and the same in respect to individuals, and to private property, securing to the owners the possession and preservation of the lands they now hold, but promising not to make any new grants without consultation with the priests, unless where the lands were notoriously unoccupied, or lacked cultivation, or in case of necessity.

Micheltorrena's governorship was shortly after concluded. There had been sent into the Department with him a considerable body of persons, called *presidarios*, that is, criminals condemned to service—usually, as in this case, military service on the frontier—and their presence and conduct gave such offence to the inhabitants, that they revolted, and expelled him and the presidarios from the country. He was succeeded by Don Pio Pico, in virtue of his being the "first vocal" of the Departmental Assembly,* and also by choice of the inhabitants, afterward confirmed by the central government, which, at the same time, gave additional privileges to the Department, in respect to the management of its domestic affairs.

The next public act, which I find, in relation to the missions, is an act of the Departmental Assembly, published in a proclamation of Governor Pico, 5th June, 1845. This act provides: 1. That the governor should call together the neophytes of the following named missions: San Rafael, Dolores, Soledad, San Miguel, and La Purisima; and in case those missions were abandoned by their neophytes, that he should give them one month's notice, by proclamation, to return and cultivate said missions, which if they did not do, the missions should be declared abandoned, and the assembly and governor dispose of them for the good of the Department. 2. That the missions of Carmel, San Juan Bautista, San Juan Capistrano, and San Francisco Solano, should be considered as *pueblos*, or villages, which was their present condition; and that the property which remained to them, the governor, after separating sufficient for the curate's house, for churches and their pertinencies, and for a municipal house, should sell at public auction; the product to be applied, first to paying the debts of the establishments, and the remainder, if any, to the benefit of divine worship. 3. That the remainder of the missions to San Diego, inclusive, should be rented, at the discretion of the governor, with the proviso, that the neophytes should be at liberty to employ themselves at their option on their own grounds, which the governor should designate for them, in the service of the rentee, or of any other person. 4. That the principal edifice of the mission of Santa Barbara should be excepted from the proposed renting, and in it the governor should designate the parts most suitable for the residence of the bishop and his attendants, and of the missionary priests then living there; moreover, that the rents

---

* According to act of the Mexican Congress of 6th of May, 1822, to provide for supplying the place of provincial governors, in default of an incumbent.

arising from the remainder of the property of said mission should be disbursed, one-half for the benefit of the church and its ministry, the other for that of its Indians. 5. That the rents arising from the other missions should be divided, one-third to the maintenance of the minister, one-third to the Indians, one-third to the government.

On the 28th October, of the same year, (1845,) Governor Pico gave public notice for the sale, to the highest bidder, of five missions, to wit: San Rafael, Dolores, Soledad, San Miguel, and La Purisima; likewise, for the sale of the remaining buildings in the pueblos (formerly missions) of San Luis Obispo, Carmel, San Juan Bautista, and San Juan Capistrano, after separating the churches and their appurtenances, and a curate's, municipal, and school houses. The auctions were appointed to take place, those of San Luis Obispo, Purisima, and San Juan Capistrano, the first four days of December following, (1845;) those of San Rafael, Dolores, San Juan Bautista, Carmel, Soledad, and San Miguel, the 23d and 24th of January, 1846; meanwhile, the government would receive and take into consideration proposals in relation to said missions.

In the same proclamation, Pico proposed to rent to the best bidder, for a period of nine years, and under conditions for the return of the property in good order and without waste, the missions of San Fernando, San Buenaventura, Santa Barbara, and Santa Ynes; the rentings to include all the lands, stock, agricultural tools, vineyards, gardens, offices, and whatever, in virtue of the inventories, should be appurtenant to said missions, with "the exception only of those small pieces of "ground which have always been occupied by some Indians of the "missions;" likewise to include the buildings, saving the churches and their appurtenances, and the curate's, municipal and school houses, and except in the mission of Santa Barbara, where the whole of the principal edifice should be reserved for the bishop and the priests residing there. The renting of the missions of San Diego, San Luis Rey, San Gabriel, San Antonio, Santa Clara, and San José, it was further announced, should take place as soon as some arrangement was made concerning their debts. It was also provided that the neophytes should be free from their pupilage, and might establish themselves on convenient parts of the missions, with liberty to serve the rentee, or any other person; that the Indians who possessed pieces of land, in which they had made their houses and gardens, should apply to the government for titles, in order that their lands might be adjudicated to them in ownership; "it being understood that they would not have power to sell their lands, but that they should descend by inheritance."

On the 30th March, 1846, the Assembly passed an act—

1. Authorizing the governor, in order to make effective the object of the decree of 28th May previous, to operate, as he should believe most expedient, to prevent the total ruin of the missions of San Gabriel, San Luis Rey, San Diego, and others found in like circumstances.

2. That as the remains of said establishments had large debts against them, if the existing property was not sufficient to cover the same, they

might be put into bankruptcy. 3. That if, from this authorization, the governor, in order to avoid the destruction to which the said missions were approaching, should determine to sell them to private persons, the sale should be by public auction. 4. That when sold, if, after the debts were satisfied, there should be any remainder, it should be distributed to the Indians of the respective establishment. 5. That, in view of the expenses necessary in the maintenance of the priest, and of Divine worship, the governor might determine a portion of the whole property, whether of cultivable lands, houses, or of any other description, according to his discretion, and by consultation with the respective priests. 6. The property thus determined, should be delivered as by sale, but subject to a perpetual interest of four per cent. for the uses above indicated. 7. That the present act should not affect any thing already done or contracts made in pursuance of the decree of 28th May last, nor prevent any thing being done conformable to that decree. 8. That the governor should provide against all impediments that might not be foreseen by the act, and in six months, at farthest, give an account to the Assembly of the results of its fulfilment.

Previous to several of the last mentioned acts, that is, on the 24th August, 1844, the Departmental Assembly, in anticipation of a war breaking out, passed a law authorizing the governor, on the happening of that contingency, either " to sell, hypothecate, or rent, the houses, landed property, and field lands, of the missions, comprehended in the whole extent of the country from San Diego to Sonoma," except that of Santa Barbara, " reserved for the residence of the bishop."

These comprise all the general acts of the authorities of California which I was able to meet with, on the subject of the missions. Of the extent or manner, in which they were carried into execution, so far as the missions proper—that is, the mission buildings and lands appurtenant —are concerned, but little information is afforded by what I could find in the archives. A very considerable part, however, of the grants made since the act of secularization of 1833, (comprising the bulk of all the grants in the country,) are of lands previously recognised as appurtenances of the missions, and so used as grazing farms, or for other purposes. In some cases, the petitions for such grants, were referred to the principal priest at the mission to which the land petitioned for was attached, and his opinion taken whether the grant could be made without prejudice to the mission. In other cases, and generally, this formality was not observed. This remark relates to the farms and grazing grounds (*ranchos*) occupied by the missions apart from the lands around the mission buildings. There are, however, some grants in the immediate precincts of the missions, and some titles to Indians, pursuant to the regulation of Governor Figueroa, and the proclamation of Governor Pico, of record in the file of *expedientes* of grants before noticed.

What I have been able to gather from the meagre records and memoranda in the archives, and from private information and examination, of the actual state of the missions, is given below. It is necessary to explain, however, still farther than I have, that in speaking of the missions now, we cannot understand the great establishments which they were. Since 1833, and even before, farms of great (many leagues) extent, and many of them, have reduced the limits they enjoyed, in all cases very greatly, and in some instances into a narrow compass; and while their borders have been thus cut off, their planting and other grounds inside are dotted to a greater or less extent by private grants. The extent to which this has been the case, can only be ascertained by the same process that is necessary every where in California, to separate public from private lands—namely, authorized surveys of the grants, according to their calls, which though not definite, will almost always furnish some distinguishable natural object to guide the surveyor.＊ The actual condition of the establishments, understanding them in the reduced sense above shown, was, at the time the Mexican government ceased in California, and according to the best information I could obtain, as follows:

Missions.	Where situated.	
San Diego, -	- 32° 48'	Sold to Santiago Arguello, 8 June, 1846.
San Luis Rey, -	- 33° 03'	Sold to Antonio Cot and Andres Pico, 13 May, 1846.
San Juan Capistrano, -	- 33° 26'	Pueblo, and remainder sold to John Foster and James McKinley, 6 December, 1845.
San Gabriel, -	- 34° 10'	Sold to Julian Workman and Hugo Reid, 18 June, 1846.
San Fernando, -	- 34° 16'	Rented to Andres Pico, for nine years, from December, 1845, and sold to Juan Celis, June, 1846.
San Buenaventura,	- 34° 36'	Sold to Joseph Arnaz.
Santa Barbara, -	- 34° 40'	Rented for nine years, from 8 June, 1846, to Nicholas Den.
Santa Ynes, -	- 34° 52'	Rented to Joaquin Carillo.
La Purisima, -	- 35° 00'	Sold to John Temple, 6 December, 1845.
San Luis Obispo,	- 35° 36'	Pueblo.
San Miguel, -	- 35° 48'	Uncertain.
San Antonio, -	- 36° 30'	Vacant.
Soledad, -	- 36° 38'	House and garden sold to Sobranes, 4 Jan., 1846.
Carmel, -	- 36° 44'	Pueblo.
San Juan Bautista,	- 36° 58'	Pueblo.
Santa Cruz, -	- 37° 00'	Vacant.
Santa Clara, -	- 37° 20'	In charge of priest.
San José, -	- 37° 30'	In charge of priest.
Dolores, -	- 37° 58'	Pueblo.
San Rafael, -	- 38° 00'	Mission in charge of priest.
San Francisco Solano, -	- 38° 30'	Mission in charge of priest.

The information above given concerning the condition of the missions, at the time of the cessation of the former Government, is partly obtained from documents in the archives, and partly from private sources. What is to be traced in the archives is on loose sheets of paper, liable to be lost; and parts quite likely have been lost; there may also be some papers concerning them which, in the mass of documents, escaped my examination. I have no doubt, however, of the exactness of the statement above given, as far as it goes.

＊I was told by Major J. R. Snyder, the gentleman appointed territorial surveyor by Col. Mason, and who made surveys of a number of grants in the central part of the country, that he had little difficulty in following the calls, and ascertaining the bounds of the grants.

It will be seen, then, that the missions—the principal part of their lands cut off by private grants, but still, no doubt, each embracing a considerable tract—perhaps from one to ten leagues—have, some of them, been sold or granted under the former Government, and become private property; some converted into villages, and consequently granted in the usual form in lots to individuals and heads of families; a part are in the hands of rentees, and at the disposal of the Government when these contracts expire; and the remainder at its present disposal.

If it were within my province to suggest what would be an equitable disposition of such of the missions as remain the property of the Government, I should say, that the churches, with all the church property and ornaments; a portion of the principal building, for the residence of the priest, with a piece of land equal to that designated in the original act of the Mexican Congress for their secularization, (to wit, two hundred varas square,) with another piece for a cemetery, should be granted to the respective Catholic parishes, for the uses specified; and the remainder of the buildings, with portions of land attached, for schools and municipal or county purposes; and for the residence of the bishop, the same allotment at the mission of Santa Barbara that was made in the last proclamation of Governor Pico. The churches, certainly, ought not to be appropriated to any other use; and less than I have suggested would, I think, be less than equity and justice, and less than the inhabitants have always considered and enjoyed as their right.

To conclude the inquiry in the last portion of your letter of instructions, namely, concerning "*large grants*," other than the supposed ecclesiastical grants.

I did not find in the archives of California any record of large grants, in the sense I suppose the term to be here used. There are a number of grants to the full extent of the privilege accorded by law to individual concessions, and of the authority of the local government to make, independent of the Central Government—to wit, of eleven *sitios*, or leagues square.

There are understood, in the country, however, to be large claims, reputed to be founded on grants direct from the Mexican Government—one held by Captain Sutter; another by General Vallejo. The archives (as far as I could discover) only show that Captain Sutter received, on the 18th July, 1841, from Governor Alverado, the usual grant of *eleven sitios*, on the river Sacramento, and this is all I ascertained. The archives likewise show than Gen. Vallejo received from Governor Micheltorrena, on the 22d October, 1823, a grant of ten sitios, called "Petaluma," in the district of Sonoma; and I was informed by a respectable gentleman in California, that Gen. V. had likewise a grant, from the Mexican Government, given for a valuable consideration, of a large tract, known by the name of "Soscol," and including the site of the present town of Benicia, founded by Messrs. Vallejo and Semple, in the straits of Carquinez. It is also reputed that the same gentleman has extensive claims in the valley of Sonoma, and on Suisun bay. It appears from documents which Gen. Vallejo caused to be published in the newspapers of California in 1847, that he was deputed, in the year 1835, by Gen. Figueroa, to found a settlement in the valley of Sonoma, "with the object of arresting the progress of the Russian settlements of Bodega and Ross." Gen. Vallejo was at that time (1835) military commander of the northern frontier. He afterwards, (in 1836,) by virtue of a revolution which occurred in that year in California, became military commandant of the department—the civil and military government being by the same act divided—to which office he was confirmed in 1838 by the Supreme Government.

The following extract from Gov. Figueroa's instructions to him, will show the extent of Gen. Vallejo's powers, as agent for colonizing the north :

" You are empowered to solicit families in all the territory and other States of the Mexican Republic, in order to colonize the northern frontiers, granting lands to all persons who may wish to establish themselves there, and those grants shall be confirmed to them by the Territorial Government, whenever the grantees shall apply therefor; the title which they obtain from you serving them in the mean time as a sufficient guarantee, as you are the only individual authorized by the superior authority to concede lands in the frontier under your charge. The Supreme Government of the territory is convinced that you are the only officer to whom so great an enterprize can be entrusted; and in order that it may be accomplished in a certain manner, it is willing to defray the necessary expenses to that end."

An official letter to Gen. Vallejo from the Department of War and Marine, dated at Mexico, 5th August, 1839, expresses approbation of what had thitherto been done in establishing the colony, and the desire that the settlements should continue to increase "until they should be so strong as to be respected not only by the Indian tribes, but also by the establishments of the foreigners who should attempt to invade that valuable region."

I did not find any trace of these documents, or of any thing concerning Gen. Vallejo's appointment or operations, in the government archives. But there is no reason to doubt the genuineness of the papers. They do not, however, convey any title to lands, beyond authority to grant, during the time his appointment continued, to actual colonizers. The appointment of Gen. V. seems to have been made by direction of the Supreme (National) Government. I had no means of ascertaining how long the appointment lasted, nor to what extent its powers were used; but infer from Vallejo himself taking a grant of his rancho of Peteluma, in 1843, that his own authority, in that respect, had then ceased. As there are other grants, also, of considerable extent, in the same neighborhood, embraced in the government archives, I apprehend that most, if not all, of the grants made by him, exclusive of what may be embraced in the town privileges of Sonoma, (and which will be noticed hereafter,) were confirmed, or re-granted to the parties, by the departmental government. In this view, however, I may be mistaken. And I desire to be distinctly understood as not intending to throw any doubt or discredit on the titles or claims of either of the gentlemen I have mentioned. I had no opportunity of inspecting any grants they may possess, beyond what I have stated ; and I imagine their lands can only be separated from the domain by the process universally requisite—the registration of outstanding grants, and their survey.

III. " GRANTS OF ISLANDS, KEYS, AND PROMONTORIES, POINTS OF IMPORTANCE TO THE PUBLIC," &c.

The only points of special public importance which I learned were granted prior to the cessation of the former government, are the site of the old fort of San Joaquin, near the outlet of the bay of San Francisco, and Alcatras (or Bird,) Island, commanding its entrance: the Key to the Golden Gates. The date of the first named grant is 25th June, 1846; it was made to Benito Diaz, and by him transferred to Mr. T. O. Larkin, of Monterey. I understand a portion of the land embraced in the grant is in occupation of the United States troops, or has property of the United States upon it, and a part in possession of Mr. Larkin.

Alcatras island was granted in June, 1846, to Mr. Francis P. Temple, of Los Angeles. The indispensableness of this point to the government, both for the purpose of fortification, and as a proper position for a light-house, induced Lt. Col. Frémont, when governor of California, to contract for the purchase of it on behalf of the United States. The government, it is believed, has never confirmed the purchase, or paid the consideration. This island is a solid rock, of about half a mile in circumference, rising out of the sea just in front of the inner extremity of the throat or narrows, which forms the entrance to the bay, and perfectly commands both front and sides. It is also in the line of the sailing directions for entering the bay,* and consequently a light-house upon it is indispensable.

The local government had special authority and instructions from the general government, under date of 12th July, 1838, to grant and distribute lands in "the desert islands adjacent to that department."

Whether the grants *"purport to be inchoate or perfect?"* The grants made in that department under the Mexican law, all, I believe, purport to be perfect, except in the respect of requiring "confirmation by the departmental assembly." The difficulties of determining what grants have not received this confirmation have been above explained.

IV. "IF THERE BE ANY ALLEGED GRANTS OF LANDS COVERING A PORTION OF THE GOLD MINES, AND WHETHER IN ALL GRANTS IN GENERAL [UNDER THE MEXICAN GOVERNMENT,] OR IN CALIFORNIA IN PARTICULAR, THERE ARE NOT CONDITIONS AND LIMITATIONS, AND WHETHER THERE IS NOT A RESERVATION OF MINES OF GOLD AND SILVER, AND A SIMILAR RESERVATION AS TO QUICKSILVER AND OTHER MINERALS?"

There is but one grant that I could learn of, which covers any por-

---

* Beechy's Narrative of a Voyage to the Pacific: London, 1831: Appendix, p. 562.

tion of the gold mines. Previous to the occupation of the country by the Americans, the parts now known as *The Gold Region*, were infested with the wild Indians, and no attempts made to settle there. The grant that I refer to, was made by Governor Micheltorrena, to Don Juan B. Alvarado, in February, 1844, and is called the *Mariposas*, being situated on the Mariposas creek, and between the Sierra Nevada and the river Joaquin, and comprises ten *sitios*, or leagues square, conceded, as the grant expresses, "in consideration of the public services" of the grantee. It was purchased from the grantee (Alvarado,) in February, 1847, by Thomas O. Larkin, esq., for Mr. J. C. Frémont, and is now owned by that gentleman.

The only "*conditions or limitations*" contained in the grants in California, which could affect the validity of the title, are, that in the grants made by some of the governors, a period of time (one year,) was fixed, within which the grantee should commence improvements on the grant. In case of failure, however, the grant was not thereby void, but open to denouncement by other persons. This limitation was not contained in such of the grants made in the time of Micheltorrena, as I have examined, nor is it prescribed in the law. No doubt, however, the condition was fulfilled in most instances where it was inserted, unless in a few cases where the lands conceded were in parts of the country infested by the wild Indians, and its fulfilment consequently impossible. In fact, as far as I understood, it was more customary to occupy the land in anticipation of the grant. The grants were generally for actual (immediate) occupation and use.

I cannot find in the Mexican laws or regulations for colonization, or for the granting of lands, any thing that looks to a reservation of the mines of gold, or silver, quicksilver, or other metal or mineral; and there is not any such thing expressed in any of the many grants that came under my inspection. I inquired and examined, also, while in Mexico, to this point, and could not learn that such reservations were the practice, either in general, or in California in particular.

V. " IN ALL LARGE GRANTS, OR GRANTS OF IMPORTANT OR VALU-
" ABLE SITES, OR OF MINES, WHETHER OR NOT THEY WERE SURVEY-
" ED AND OCCUPIED UNDER THE GOVERNMENT OF SPAIN OR MEXICO,
" AND WHEN PUBLICITY WAS FIRST GIVEN TO SUCH GRANTS?"

The first part of this inquiry is already answered, in the statement that, as far I am aware, there were never any *surveys* made in the country, during its occupation by either of the former governments. Most of the grants, however, were *occupied* before, or shortly after they were made, and all, as far as I am informed, except where the hostile Indian occupation prevented. In respect of the grants to which I have made any reference, I did not learn that there had been any delay in giving publicity to them.

Having met, sir, as far as in my power, the several inquiries set forth in the letter of instructions you were pleased to honor me with, my attention was turned, as far as they were not already answered, to the more detailed points of examination furnished me, with your approbation, by the Commissioner of Public Lands. The very minute information contemplated by those instructions, it would have been impossible, as you justly anticipated, to obtain in the brief time proposed for my absence, even had it been accessible in systematic archives and records. My examination, moreover, was sufficient to show me that such minute and exact information, on many of the various heads proposed, is not attainable at all ; and that the only mode of *approximating* it must be through such measures as will produce a general registration of written titles, and verbal proof of possession where written titles are wanting, followed or accompanied by a general *su·vcy*. By such means only can an *approximation* be made to the minute information sought, of the character, extent, position, and date, particularly of the old grants in California.

The first branch of the inquiries proposed by the instructions from the Land Office. relate to " Grants or claims derived from the Government of *Spain*."

The chief local authority to *grant* lands in the province of California was, *ex officio*, the military commandant, who was likewise governor of the province; and the principal *recipients* of grants, officers and soldiers as they retired from service. The grants to the soldiers were principally of lots in and about the *presidios* (military posts) or the *pueblos* (villages) ; to the officers, farms and grazing lands, in addition to such lots.

There were also, at different times, settlers brought from Sonora, and other provinces of New Spain, (single men and families,) and grants made to them ; usually of village lots, and to the principal men, ranchos in addition. The first settlement at San Francisco was thus made ; that is, settlers accompanied the expeditions thither, and combined with the military post. The pueblos of San José and Los Angeles were thus formed. The governor made grants to the retired officers, under the general colonization laws of Spain, but, as in all the remote provinces, much at his own discretion. He had likewise special authority to encourage the population of the country, by making grants of farming lots to soldiers who should marry the native women bred at the missions. The captains of the *presidios* were likewise authorized to make grants within the distance of two leagues, measuring to the cardinal points, from their respective posts. Hence, the presidios became, in fact, villages. The Viceroy of New Spain had also of course authority to make grants in California, and sometimes exercised it. It was pursuant to his order that presidios, missions, and pueblos were severally established, and the places for them indicated by the local authority. Under all these authorities, grants were made ; strictness of written law required that they should have been made by exact measurements, with written titles, and a record of them kept. In the rude and uncultivated state of the country that then existed, and lands possessing so little value, these formalities were to a great extent disregarded; and if not then altogether disregarded, the evidence of their observance in many cases now lost. It is certain, that the measurements even of the grants of village lots, were very unexact and imperfect ; and of larger tracts, such as were granted to the principal men, no measurement at all attempted, and even the quantity not always expressed, the sole description often being by a name, descriptive, in fact or by repute, of the place granted. The law of custom, with the acquiescence of the highest authorities, overcame, in these respects, the written law. Written permits and grants were no doubt usually given, but if any systematic records or memoranda of them were kept, they have now disappeared, or I was not able to meet with them. In some cases, but not in all, the originals no doubt still exist, in the possession of the descendants of the grantees ; indeed, I have been assured there are many old written titles in the country, of which the archives do not contain any trace. But, in other cases, no doubt, the titles rested originally only on *verbal* permits. It was very customary, in the Spanish colonies, for the principal neighborhood authorities to give permission to occupy and cultivate lands, with the understanding that the party interested would afterward at a convenient occasion obtain his grant from the functionary above. Under these circumstances, the grant was seldom refused, but the application for it was very often neglected ; the title by permission being entirely good for the purposes of occupation and use, and never questioned by the neighbors. All these titles, whatever their original character, have been respected during the twenty-six or twenty-seven years of Mexican and local government. And whether evidenced now or ever by any written title, they constitute as meritorious and just claims as property is held by in any part of the world. They were, in the first place, the meagre rewards for expatriation, and arduous and hazardous public service in a remote and savage country ; they are now the inheritance of the descendants of the first settlers of the country, and who redeemed it from (almost the lowest stage of) barbarism. Abstractly considered, there cannot be any higher title to the soil.

Many of the holders of old grants have taken the precaution to have them renewed, with a designation of boundary and quantity, under the forms of the Mexican law ; and of these the proper record exists in the archives. To what extent old titles have been thus renewed, could not be ascertained, for the reason that there is no record of the old titles by which to make the comparison.

The principal difficulty that must attend the separation of the old grants from the public lands, or rather, to ascertain what is public domain and what private property, in the parts where those old grants are situate, is in the loose designation of their limits and extent. The only way that presents itself of avoiding this difficulty, and of doing justice both to the claimant and the government, would seem to be in receiving, with respect to the old grants, verbal testimony of occupation and of commonly reputed boundaries, and thereby, with due consideration of the laws and principles on which the grants were made, governing the surveys.

The military commandant or governor had authority, by virtue of his office, to make grants. He had, also, special authority and direction to do so, in a letter of instructions from the Viceroy, 17th August, 1773, and entitled "Instructions to be observed by the commandant appointed to the new establishments of San Diego and Monterey." These instructions authorized (as already noticed) the allotment of lands to Indians, either in community or individually; but it is to be understood only of Indians who should be in charge of the missions, and of the parcels of land within the mission settlements. Article 13 gave the commandant "equal authority, likewise, to distribute lands to other settlers, according to their merit, and conformably to the compilations of laws concerning new conquests and settlements." That is, according to the compilation of the "Laws of the Indias," which we know make certain provisions of the most liberal character for the founding and encouragement of new populations.

Subsequently, without abrogating the general colonial laws, a special Regulation was adopted, with the royal assent, for the government of the Californias, and making special provision for the settlement of that province, and the encouragement of colonizers. This regulation was drawn in Monterey, by Governor Don Felipe Neve, in 1779, and confirmed by a Royal Cedula of 14th October, 1781. Its character and objects are shown in its title, namely: "Rules and directions for the Presidios of the Peninsula of Californias, erection of new Missions, and encouragement of the Population, and extension of the establishments of Monterey." The first thirteen articles relate to the presidios and military. Title fourteen relates to the " Political Government and directions for Peopling." After providing liberal *bonuses* to new settlers, in respect of money, cattle, and exemptions from various duties and burthens, this Regulation prescribes: That the *solares* (house lots) which shall be granted to the new settlers, shall be designated by the governor, in the places, and with the extent that the tract chosen for the new settlement will allow, and in such manner that they shall form a square, with streets, conformably to the laws of the kingdom; and by the same rule shall be designated common lands for the pueblos, with pasturage and fields for municipal purposes *(pro-pios.)* That each *suerte* (out-lot,) both of irrigable and unirrigable land, shall be two hundred varas square; and of these *suertes*, four (two watered and two dry) shall be given, with the *solar,* or house lot, in the name of the king, to each settler.

These rules relate to the formation of villages and farming settlements, and are exclusive of the extensive ranchos—farms and grazing lands—allotted to persons of larger claims or means; sometimes direct from the viceroy, usually by the local governor.

The acts of the Spanish Cortes, in 1813, heretofore quoted, may also be referred to as a part of the authority under which grants might be made in California, during the continuance of the Spanish government, and prior to the colonization laws of Mexico, and afterwards, indeed, as far as not superceded by those laws.

The second point of inquiry in the instructions furnished me from the Land Office, relating to grants made under the *Mexican* Government, is already met in most respects, as far as was in my power to meet it, in the early part of this report. The *" authority of the granting officers, and their powers for alienating the national domain,"* were derived from appointment by the Central Government, and from the general colonization laws and regulations of the Republic. There is little room for discrimination "between such as are perfect titles, and such as are inceptive or inchoate." A grant by the territorial (or departmental) governors within the extent of eleven *sitios*, constituted a *valid* title, and with the approbation of the departmental assembly, a *perfect* one. After the governor's concession, however, it could not with propriety be termed merely *inceptive;* for, in fact, it was complete until the legislature should *refuse* its approbation, and then it would be the duty of the governor to appeal for the claimant to the Supreme Government. I am not aware that a case of this kind arose. The difficulties, already explained, of ascertaining to what grants the legislative approbation was accorded, and from what it was withheld; the impossibility, in fact, of ascertaining in many cases, coupled with the fact that that approbation was so seldom refused, and that the party had still an appeal in case of refusal, would seem to render that provision of the law of those grants nugatory as a test of their merits.

The third inquiry, touching " grants made about the time of the *revolutionary* movements in California, say in the months of June and July, 1846," is chiefly answered in what is said concerning the actual condition of the missions, and the grants of Fort Joaquin at the mouth, and Alcatras island inside the entrance, of the bay of San Francisco. In addition to these, the large island of *San Clemente*, I understood, was granted about that time, say in May, 1846. I found nothing in the archives concerning it. I do not think there were other grants to attract particular attention, except the proposed great Macnamara grant or contract, of which the principal papers are on file in the State Department, and have been printed in the Congressional documents.

In the second branch of the last mentioned inquiry, namely, concerning any "grants made *subsequent to the war,*" I suppose the intent is, grants, if any, made after the reduction of the country by the arms of the United States. There are, of course, no Mexican grants, or grants by the Mexican authorities, which *purport* to have been issued subsequent to that time. The inquiry must relate, therefore, either to supposed *simulated grants,* by persons formerly in authority there, or to whatever may have been done, in respect of the domain, by or under the American authorities. It is believed in the country that there are some simulated grants in existence; that is, some papers purporting to be grants which have been issued since the cessation of the Mexican Government, by persons who formerly, at different times, had the faculty of making grants in that country. It would be impossible, however, to make a list of them, with the particulars enumerated in the instructions; for, if there be any such, they would of course not be submitted for public inspection, or in any way seek the light. But I believe it would not be difficult for a person skilled in the grants in that country, and acquainted with the archives, and the various facts to be gathered from them, to detect any simulated paper that might be thus issued after the person issuing it had ceased from his office. The test, however, would necessarily have to be applied to each case as it rose. No general rule, I believe, can be laid down.

Recurring, then, to the other point which I suppose the inquiry to relate to. The most considerable act, affecting the domain, had subsequent to the accession of the American authorities in California, was a " decree " made by Gen. Kearny, as governor, under date of 10th March, 1847, as follows:

" I, Brigadier General S. W. Kearny, Governor of California, by virtue of authority in me vested, by the President of the United States of America, do hereby *grant, convey,* and *release* unto the town of San Francisco, the people, or corporate authorities thereof, all the right, title, and interest of the *Government of the United States,* and of the *territory of California,* in and to the beach and water lots on the east front of said town of San Francisco, included between the points known as the Rincon and Fort Montgomery, excepting such lots as may be selected for the use of the United States Government by the senior officers of the army and navy now there; provided the said ground hereby ceded, shall be divided into lots, and sold by public auction to the highest bidder, after three months notice previously given; the proceeds of said sale to be for the benefit of the town of San Francisco.''

Pursuant to the terms of this paper, what are termed "government reservations" were made, both within and outside the limits specified, and the remainder of the lots designated have been since in great part sold by the town of San Francisco. These lots extend into the shallow water along the beach of San Francisco, and are very suitable and requisite for the business purposes of that growing city. The number of four hundred and forty-four of them were sold in the summer ensuing the "Decree," and in December last, I have learned since my return, the remainder, or a large portion of them, were disposed of by the corporation. But little public use has been made of what are denominated the "government reservations." Portions of them are reputed to be covered by old grants; portions have been settled on and occupied by way of preëmption, and other portions, particularly "Rincon Point," have been rented out, as I am informed, to individuals, by the late military government.

Under the above "decree" of General Kearny, and the consequent acts of the authorities of San Francisco, such multiplied, diversified, and important private interests have arisen, that, at this late day, no good, but immense mischief, would result from disturbing them. The city has derived a large amount of revenue from the sale of the lots; the lots have been resold, and transferred in every variety of way, and passed through many hands, and on many of them costly and permanent improvements have been made; improvements required by the business and wants of the community, and which ought to give the makers of them an equitable interest in the land, even without the faith of the Government implied by leaving the act of its agent so long unquestioned. An act of Congress, relinquishing thus in the lawful mode, the interest of the United States in those beach and water lots, would seem to be only an act of justice to the city and to the lot holders, and to be necessary to give that validity and confidence that ought to attach to property of such great value and commercial importance.

In regard to the "government reservations," so called, where they may be in private hands, whether under a former grant, or by occupancy and improvement, the same equity would seem to call for at least a *pre-emption right* to be allowed the holders, except for such small parts as may be actually required for public uses. In regard to the places known as "Clark's Point," and the "Rincon Point," which are outside of the land embraced in Gen. Kearny's decree, and portions of which it is understood have been put in the hands of rentees, perhaps the most equitable use that could be made of them, (except, as before, the parts needed for public uses,) would be to relinquish them to the city, to be sold as the beach and water lots have been; with due regard, at the same time, to rights accruing from valuable improvements that may have been made upon them, but repressing a monopoly of property so extensive and valuable, and so necessary to the improvement, business, and growth of the city.

Other operations in lands which had not been reduced to private property at the time of the cessation of the former government, have taken place in and about different towns and villages, by the alcaldes and other municipal authorities continuing to make grants of lots and outlots, more or less according to the mode of the former government. This, I understand, has been done, under the supposition of a right to the lands granted, existing in the respective towns as corporations. Transactions of this nature have been to a very large extent at San Francisco; several hundred inlots of fifty varas square, and outlots of one hundred varas square, have been thus disposed of, by the successive alcaldes of the place since the occupation of it by the American forces, both those appointed by the naval and military commanders, and those subsequently chosen by the inhabitants.

It is undoubtedly conformable to the Spanish colonial laws, that, when villages were to be established, there should be liberal allotments to the first settlers, with commons for general use, and municipal lands (*propios*) for the support and extension of the place—that is, to be rented, or otherwise transferred, subject to a tax; and that the principal magistrate, in conjunction with the *ayuntamiento*, or town council, should have the disposal of those town liberties, under the restrictions of law, for the benefit of the place; and the same was the practice in California, under the Mexican government. It is not always so easy to determine within what limits this authority might be exercised; but in new communities, whether the settlement was founded by an *empresario* (contractor,) or by the government, the allotments were always on a liberal scale, both for the individuals and the village. A very early law (law 6, tit. 5, lib. 4, Recop. de Indias) fixes " four leagues of limits and land (*de termino y territorio*,) in square or prolonged, according to the nature of the tract," for a settlement of thirty families; and I suppose this is as small a tract as has usually been set apart for village uses and liberties, under the Spanish or Mexican government in New Spain; sometimes much more extensive privileges have no doubt been granted. The Instructions of 1773 to the commandant of the new posts, authorizes pueblos to be formed, without specifying their limits, which would of course bring them under the general law of four leagues.

The royal Regulation of 1781, for the Californias, directs suitable municipal allotments to be made, " conformable to the law;" and this likewise must refer to the law specifying four leagues square.

The letter of instructions of 1791, authorizing the captains of presidios to make grants, in the neighborhood of their respective posts, specifies the same quantity, to wit, "the extent of four common leagues, measured from the centre of the Presidio square, two leagues in each direction, as sufficient for the new pueblos to be formed under the protection of the presidios."

The Mexican laws, as far as I am aware, make no change in this rule; and the colonization regulations of 1828, provide (art. 13,) that " the reunion of many families into a town shall follow in its formation, policy, &c., the rule established by the existing laws for the other towns of the Republic."

From all these, and other acts which might be quoted, it would seem that where no special grant has been made, or limits assigned to a village, the common extent of four leagues would apply to it; it being understood, however, as the same law expresses, that the allotment should not interfere with the rights of other parties. The Presidio settlements, under the order of 1791, were certainly entitled to their four leagues; the right of making grants within the same only transferred from the presidio captain to the municipal authorities who succeeded him, as is conformable to Spanish and Mexican law and custom. This was the case under the Spanish government; and I am not aware that the principle has been changed; though no doubt grants have been made to individuals which infringed on such village limits. The Territorial Deputation of California, however, by an act of 6th August, 1834, directed that the ayuntamientos of the pueblos should " make application for common and municipal lands (*ejidos y propios*) to be assigned them." Wherever it shall appear that this was done, the town, I suppose, could only now claim what was then set apart for it. Where it was omitted or neglected, custom, reputed limits, and the old law, would seem to be a safe rule.

As to the point now under consideration, that of *San Francisco*, I find that in the acts of the Departmental authorities the settlements in and about the presidio were styled " *the pueblo of San Francisco*," and the particular place where the village principally was and the

city now is, "*the point of Yerba Buena.*" The local authorites,
as its alcalde, or justice of the peace, were termed those of the pueblo of
San Francisco. Its privileges were not, therefore, at any time limited
to the point of Yerba Buena. Originally, probably, it had boundaries
in common with the mission of Dolores, which would restrict it in its
four leagues; but after the conversion of the mission into a pueblo, the
jurisdiction of the authorities of San Francisco was extended, and special
license given to its principal magistrate to grant lots *at the mission.*
San Francisco is situated on a tongue or neck of land, lying between
the bay and the sea, increasing in breadth, in a southerly direction. A
measurement of four leagues south from the presidio would give the
city, in the present advanced value of property, a magnificent corporate
domain, but not so much as was fairly assignable to the precincts of
the presidio under the order of 1791, nor so much as all new pueblos are
entitled to under the general laws of the Indias. There are private rights,
however, existing within those limits, apart from any grants of the
village authorities, which ought to be respected: some through grants
from the former government; some by location and improvement, a
claim both under our own law and custom, and under the Spanish law,
entitled to respect. To avoid the confusion—the destruction—that
would grow out of disturbing the multiplied and vast interests that have
arisen under the acts of the American authorities at San Francisco; to
give the city what she would certainly have been entitled to by the
terms of the old law, what she will need for the public improvements
and adornments that her future population will require, and what is
well due to the enterprise which has founded in so brief a space a great
metropolis in that remote region, perhaps no better or juster measure could
be suggested, than a confirmation of past acts, a release of government
claims to the extent of four leagues, measuring south from the presidio,
and including all between sea and bay, with suitable provision for
protecting private rights, whether under old grants or by recent improvements, and reserving such sites as the government uses may require.

By the authorities of the village of *San José*, there have been still
larger operations in the lands belonging or supposed to belong to the
liberties of that town. The outlands there, as I learned, have been
distributed in tracts of three to five hundred acres.

The pueblo of San José was founded 7th November, 1777, by order
of Felipe de Neve, then military commandant and governor. The
first settlers were nine soldiers and five laboring men or farmers, who
went thither, with cattle, tools, &c., from San Francisco, where had
been established the year before, by order of the Viceroy, the presidio
and the mission of Dolores. Those persons took possession, and
made their settlement, " in the name of his Majesty, marking out the
square for the erection of the houses, distributing the *solares* (house lots)
and measuring to each settler a piece of ground for the sowing of a
fanega of maize, (two hundred varas by four hundred,) and for beans
and other vegetables."* Subsequently, the Regulation of 1781, al-

---

*Noticias de Nueva California, by the Rev. Father Palou: MSS. Archives of Mexico.
3

lowing to the new settlers each four lots of two hundred varas square, beside their house lots, was no doubt applied to this village. It was designed for an agricultural settlement, and, together with the pueblo of the south (Los Angeles) received constantly the favor and encouragement of the government, with the view of having sufficient agricultural produce raised for the supply of the military posts. Both villages are situated in fertile plains, selected for their sites with that object. In a report, or information, made by the Governor Don Pedro Fages, in February, 1791, to his successor Governor Romeu, the encouragement of the two pueblos is the first topic referred to:

" 1. Being (says Governor Fages) one of the objects of greatest consideration, the encouragement of the two pueblos, of civilized people, which have been established, the superior government has determined to encourage them with all possible aids, domiciliating in them the soldiers who retire from the presidios, and by this means enlarging the settlement.

" 2. By the superior order of 27th April, 1784, it is ordered that the grains and other produce, which the presidios receive from the inhabitants of the two pueblos, shall be paid for in money, or such goods and effects as the inhabitants have need of.

" 3. The distribution of lots of land, and house lots, made with all possible requisite formalities, with designation of town liberties, and other lands for the common advantage, as likewise titles of ownership given to the inhabitants, were approved by the Señor Commandante General, the 6th February of the present year of 1784."

There are also records of families being brought at the government expense, from the province of Sonora, specially to people the two pueblos. Both these villages—being thus objects of government favor and encouragement—claim to have been founded with more extensive privileges than the ordinary village limits; and I have no doubt, from the information I received, that such was the case.

The village of *San José* had a dispute of boundary as early as the year 1800, with the adjoining mission of Santa Clara, and which was referred the following year to the government at Mexico. The fact is noted in the index to California papers in the Mexican archives, but I did not find the corresponding record. There is likewise in the book of records, marked " 1828," in the archives at Monterey, an outline of the boundaries claimed by the pueblo at that time. But at a later period, (in 1834, I believe,) there was a legislative action upon the subject, in which, as I understand, the boundaries were fully agreed upon. Some documents relating to this settlement are in the archives at San José, and also in the territorial archives. My time did not permit me to make a full investigation of the question of those boundaries, nor did I think it necessary, because, at all events, they can only be definitively settled by a survey, the same as private estates. My instructions, however, call for a discrimination between acts done "with legal formalities," and such as are "without legal sanction." It is therefore proper for me to say, that I do not know of any law which would authorize the distribution of town property in California in lots measured by hundreds of acres; such distribution, in fact, would seem rather to defeat the ends for which town grants are authorized by the Spanish law. Perhaps an act to authorize the limits of the town to be ascertained by survey, and to leave the question of the validity of those recent large grants within the limits of the same, to be determined between the holders, and the town in its corporate capacity, would be as just and expedient as any other mode.

In and about the town of *Monterey*, likewise, there were large concessions, as I understood, and some including the sites of forts and public places, made by the magistrate appointed there after the accession of the American authority. The limits of this town, also, I think, depend on an act of the territorial legislature, and may be ascertained by an authorized survey.

The city of *Los Angeles* is one of the oldest establishments of California, and its prosperity was, in the same manner as that of San José, an object of Government interest and encouragement. An act of the Mexican Congress, of 23d May, 1835, erected it into a city, and established it as the capital of the territory. The limits which, I understood, are claimed as its town privileges, are quite large, but probably no more than it has enjoyed for sixty years, or ever since its foundation. The grants made by this corporation since the cessation of the former Government, have been, as far as I learned, quite in conformity with the Spanish law, in tracts such as were always granted for house lots in the village, and vineyards and gardens without, and in no greater number than the increase of population, and the municipal wants required.

The only provision that seems to be wanting for the puebla of Los Angeles, is for the survey and definition of its extent, according to its ancient recognised limits. The same remark, as far as I have learned, will apply to the remaining towns of the country established under either of the former Governments

The remarks made in a previous part of this report in relation to the *Missions*, cover, to a good degree, the substance of that branch of the inquiries proposed by the Commissioner of the Land Bureau. I have already stated that, originally, the "mission lands" may be said to have been coëxtensive with the province, since, nominally, at least, they occupied the whole extent, except the small localities of the *Presidies*, and the part inhabited by the wild Indians, whom and whose territory it was their privilege to enter and reduce. Among the papers accompanying this report is included a transcript of their recorded boundaries, as stated in a record book heretofore noticed. It will be seen from the fact first mentioned, of their original occupation of the whole province, and from the vast territories accorded to their occupation, as late as the year 1828, how inconsistent with any considerable peopling of the country, would have been any notion of *proprietorship* in the missionaries.

I am also instructed to "make an inquiry into the nature of the *Indian Rights* [in the soil,] under the Spanish and Mexican governments."

36

It is a principle constantly laid down in the Spanish colonial laws, that the Indians shall have a *right* to as much land as they need for their habitations, for tillage, and for pasturage. Where they were already partially settled in communities, sufficient of the land which they occupied was secured them for those purposes.* If they were wild, and scattered in the mountains and wildernesses, the policy of the law, and of the instructions impressed on the authorities of the distant provinces, was to reduce them, establish them in villages, convert them to Christianity, and instruct them in useful employments.† The province of California was not excepted from the operation of this rule. It was for this purpose especially, that the missions were founded and encouraged. The instructions heretofore quoted, given to the commandant of Upper California in August, 1773, enjoin on that functionary, that "the reduction of the Indians, in proportion as the spiritual conquests advance, shall be one of his principal cares;" that the reduction made, "and as rapidly as it proceeds, it is important for their preservation and augmentation, to congregate them in mission settlements, in order that they may be civilized and led to a rational life;" which, (adds the instructions,) "is impossible, if they be left to live dispersed in the mountains."

The early laws were so tender of these rights of the Indians, that they forbade the allotment of lands to the Spaniards, and especially the rearing of stock, where it might interfere with the tillage of the Indians. Special directions were also given for the selection of lands for the Indian villages, in places suitable for agriculture, and having the necessary wood and water.‡ The lands set apart to them were likewise inalienable, except by the advice and consent of officers of the government, whose duty it was to protect the natives as minors or pupils.||

Agreeably to the theory and spirit of these laws, the Indians in California were always supposed to have a certain property or interest in the missions. The instructions of 1773 authorized, as we have already seen, the commandant of the province to make grants to the mission Indians of lands of the missions, either in community or individually. But apart from any direct grant, they have been always reckoned to have a right of settlement; and we shall find that all the plans that have been adopted for the secularization of the missions, have contemplated, recognised, and provided for this right. That the plan of Hijar did not recognise or provide for the settlements of Indians was one of the main objections to it, urged by Gov. Figueroa and the territorial deputation. That plan was entirely discomfitted; all the successive ones that were carried into partial execution, placed the Indian right of settlement amongst the first objects to be provided for. We may say, therefore, that, however mal-administration of the law may have de-

* Recopilacion de Indias: laws 7 to 20, tit. 12, bk. 4.
† Ib., laws 1 and 9, tit. 3, bk. 6.
‡ Law 7, tit. 12, Recop. Indias; ib., laws 8 and 20, tit. 3, bk. 6.
|| Ib., law 27, tit. 6, bk. 1. Peña y Peña, 1 Practica Forense Mejicana, 248, &c. Alaman, 1 Historia de Mejico, 23–25.

stroyed its intent, the law itself has constantly asserted the rights of the Indians to habitations, and sufficient fields for their support. The law always intended the Indians of the missions—all of them who remained there—to have homes upon the mission grounds. The same, I think, may be said of the large ranchos—most, or all of which, were formerly mission ranchos—and of the Indian settlements or *rancherias* upon them. I understand the law to be, that wherever Indian settlements are established, and they till the ground, they have a right of occupancy in the land which they need and use; and whenever a grant is made which includes such settlements, the grant is subject to such occupancy. This right of occupancy, however—at least when on private estates—is not transferable; but whenever the Indians abandon it, the title of the owner becomes perfect. Where there is no private ownership over the settlement, as where the lands it occupies have been assigned it by a functionary of the country thereto authorized, there is a process, as before shown, by which the natives may alien their title. I believe these remarks cover the principles of the Spanish law, in regard to Indian settlements, as far as they have been applied in California, and are conformable to the customary law that has prevailed there.*

The continued observance of this law, and the exercise of the public authority to protect the Indians in their rights under it, cannot, I think, produce any great inconvenience; while a proper regard for long recognised rights, and a proper sympathy for an unfortunate and unhappy race, would seem to forbid that it should be abrogated, unless for a better. The number of subjugated Indians is now too small, and the lands they occupy too insignificant in amount, for their protection, to the extent of the law, to cause any considerable molestation. Besides, there are causes at work by which even the present small number is rapidly diminishing; so that any question concerning them can be but temporary. In 1834, there were employed in the mission establishments alone the number 30,650.† In 1842, only about eight years after the restraining and compelling hand of the missionaries had been taken off, their number on the missions had dwindled to 4,450; and the process of reduction has been going on as rapidly since.

In the wild or wandering tribes, the Spanish law does not recognise any title whatever to the soil.

It is a common opinion, that nearly all of what may be called the coast country—that is, the country west of the Sacramento and Joaquin valleys—which lies south of, and including, the Sonoma district, has been ceded, and is covered with private grants. If this were the case,

---

* Of course, what is here said of the nature of Indian rights, does not refer to titles to lots and farming tracts, which have been granted in ownership to individual Indians by the government. These, I suppose, to be entitled to the same protection as other private property.

† This is not an *estimate*, it is an exact statement. The records of the missions were kept with system and exactness; every birth, marriage, and death was recorded, and the name of every pupil or *neophyte*, which is the name by which the mission Indians were known; and from this record, an annual return was made to the government of the precise number of Indians connected with the establishment.

it would still leave the extensive valleys of those large rivers and their lateral tributaries, almost intact, and a large extent of territory—from three to four degrees of latitude—at the north, attached to the public domain, within the State of California, beside the gold region, of unknown extent, along the foothills of the Sierra Nevada. But while it may be nominally the case, that the greater part of the coast country referred to is covered with grants, my observation and information convince me, that when the country shall be surveyed, after leaving to every grantee all that his grant calls for, there will be extensive and valuable tracts remaining. This is explained by the fact that the grants were not made by measurement, but by a loose designation of boundaries, often including a considerably greater extent of land than the quantity expressed in the title; but the grant usually provides that the overplus shall remain to the government. Although, therefore, the surveys, cutting off all above the quantity expressed in the grant, would often interfere with nominal occupation, I think justice would generally be done by that mode to all the interests concerned—the holders of the grants, the Government, and the wants of the population crowding thither. To avoid the possibility of an injustice, however, and to provide for cases where long occupation or peculiar circumstances may have given parties a title to the extent of their nominal boundaries, and above the quantity expressed in their grants, it would be proper to authorize any one who should feel himself aggrieved by this operation of the survey, to bring a suit for the remainder.

The grants in California, I am bound to say, are mostly *perfect titles;* that is, the holders possess their property by titles, that, under the law which created them, were equivalent to patents from our Government; and those which are not perfect—that is, which lack some formality, or some *evidence* of completeness—have the same *equity*, as those which are perfect, and were and would have been equally respected under the government which has passed away. Of course, I allude to grants made in good faith, and not to simulated grants, if there be any such, issued since the persons who make them ceased from their functions in that respect.

I think the state of land titles in that country will allow the public lands to be ascertained, and the private lands set apart, by judicious measures, with little difficulty. Any measure calculated to discredit, or cause to be distrusted, the general character of the titles there, besides the alarm and anxiety which it would create among the ancient population, and among all present holders of property, would, I believe, also retard the substantial improvement of the country: a title discredited is not destroyed, but every one is afraid to touch it, or at all events to invest labor and money in improvements that rest on a suspected tenure. The holder is afraid to improve; others are afraid to purchase, or if they do purchase at its discredited value, willing only to make inconsiderable investments upon it. The titles not called in question, (as they certainly, for any reason which I could discover, do not deserve to be,) the pressure of population, and the force of circumstances, will soon operate to break up the existing large tracts into farms of such extent as the nature of the country will allow of, and the wants of the community require; and this under circumstances, and with such assurance of tenure, as will warrant those substantial improvements that the thrift and prosperity of the country in other respects invite.

I think the rights of the Government will be fully secured, and the interests and permanent prosperity of all classes in that country best consulted, by no other general measure in relation to private property, than an authorized survey, according to the grants, where the grants are modern, or since the accession of the Mexican government, reserving the overplus; or, according to ancient possession, where it dates from the time of the Spanish government, and the written evidence of the grant is lost, or does not afford data for the survey. But providing that in any case where, from the opinion of the proper law officer or agent of the Government in the State, or from information in any way received, there may be reason to suppose a grant invalid, the Government (or a proper officer of it) may direct a suit to be instituted for its annulment.

It is proper for me to say, that at Monterey, Gen. Riley, then in charge of the government, promptly directed the archives to be open to my inspection ; and that in Mexico, my application, made by Mr. Walsh, chargé d'affaires of the United States, to be allowed to examine the Mexican archives, was courteously received and acceded to by Mr. de Lacunza, the Minister of the Interior and Foreign Relations. I received, also, from Col. Geary, principal magistrate of San Francisco, unusual facilities for acquainting myself with the papers in his office, relating to that city.

Very respectfully, sir, your obedient servant,

WM. CAREY JONES.

WASHINGTON, 9th March, 1850.

SOME OF THE PRINCIPAL LAWS AND ORDERS RELATING TO THE SUBJECT OF THE FOREGOING REPORT.

TREATY PROVISIONS RESPECTING PRIVATE PROPERTY IN CALIFORNIA.

Portions of the treaty of 2d February, 1848, which relate to PRIVATE PROPERTY, *existing in the territories thereby acquired by the United States.*

Art. VIII. Mexicans now established in territories previously belonging to Mexico, and which remain for the future within the limits of the United States, as defined by the present treaty, shall be free to continue where they now reside, or to remove at any time to the Mexican Republic, retaining the property which they possess in the said territories, or disposing thereof, and removing the proceeds wherever they please, without their being subjected, on this account, to any contribution, tax or charge whatsoever. * * * * * * *

In the said territories, property of every kind, now belonging to Mexicans not established there, shall be inviolably respected. The present owners, the heirs of these, and all Mexicans who may hereafter acquire said property by contract, shall enjoy, with respect to it, guaranties equally ample as if the same belonged to citizens of the United States.

Art. IX. Mexicans who, in the territories aforesaid, shall not preserve the character of citizens of the Mexican republic, conformably with what is stipulated in the preceding article, shall be incorporated into the Union of the United States, and be admitted at the proper time (to be judged of by the Congress of the United States) to the enjoyment of all the rights of citizens of the United States, according to the principles of the Constitution; and in the mean time shall be maintained and protected in the free enjoyment of their liberty and property, and secured in the free exercise of their religion without restriction.

MEXICAN COLONIZATION LAWS AND RULES.

Act of the Mexican government, 4th January, 1823.

Art. 1. The government of the Mexican nation will protect the liberty, property, and civil rights of all foreigners, who profess the Roman Catholic apostolic religion, the established religion of the empire.

Art. 2. To facilitate their establishment, the executive will distribute lands to them, under the conditions and terms herein expressed.

Art. 3. The empresarios, by whom is understood those who introduced at least two hundred families, shall previously contract with the executive, and inform it what branch of industry they propose to follow, the property or resources they intend to introduce for that purpose, and any other particulars they may deem necessary, in order that with this necessary information, the executive may designate the province to which they must direct themselves, the lands which they can occupy with the right of property, and the other circumstances which may be considered necessary.

Art. 4. Families who emigrate, not included in a contract, shall immediately present themselves to the ayuntamiento of the place where they wish to settle, in order that that body, in conformity with the instructions of the executive, may designate the lands corresponding to them, agreeably to the industry which they may establish.

Art. 5. The measurement of land shall be the following: establishing the *vara* at three geometrical feet; a straight line of five thousand *varas* shall be a league; a square, each of whose sides shall be one league, shall be called a sitio; and this shall be the unit of counting one, two, or more sitios; five sitios shall compose one hacienda.

Art. 6. In the distribution made by government of lands to the colonists, for the formation of villages, towns, cities, and provinces, a distinction shall be made between the grazing lands destined for the raising of stock, and lands suitable for farming or planting, on account of the facility of irrigation.

Art. 7. One *labor* shall be composed of one million square varas, that is to say, one thousand varas on each side, which measurement shall be the unit for counting one, two, or more labors. These labors can be divided into halves and quarters, but not less.

Art. 8. To the colonists, whose occupation is farming, there cannot be given less than one labor, and those whose occupation is stock raising, there cannot be given less than one sitio.

Art. 9. The government of itself, or by means of the authorities authorized for that purpose, can augment said portions of land as may be deemed proper, agreeably to the conditions and circumstances of the colonists.

Art. 10. Establishments made under the former government shall be regulated by this law in all matters that may arise, and that are now pending; but those that are finished shall remain in that state.

Art. 11. As one of the principal objects of laws in free governments, ought to be to approximate, so far as possible, to an equal distribution of property, the government, taking into consideration the provisions of this law, will adopt measures for dividing out the lands, which may have accumulated in large portions in the hands of individuals or corporations, and which are not cultivated, indemnifying the proprietors for the just price of such lands, to be fixed by appraisers.

Art. 12. The union of many families at one place shall be called a village, town, or city, agreeably to the number of its inhabitants, its extension, locality, and other circumstances which may characterise it, in conformity with the law on that subject. The same regulations for its internal government and police, shall be observed as in the others of the same class in the empire.

Art. 13. Care shall be taken in the formation of said new town, that, so far as the situation of the ground will permit, the streets shall be laid off straight, running north and south, east and west.

Art. 14. Provinces shall be formed, whose superficie shall be six thousand square leagues.

Art. 15. As soon as sufficient number of families may be united to form one or more towns, their local government shall be regulated, and the constitutional ayuntamientos and other local establishments formed in conformity with the laws.

Art. 16. The government shall take care, in accord with the respective ecclesiastical authority, that these new towns are provided with a sufficient number of spiritual pastors, and in like manner, it will propose to Congress a plan for their decent support.

Art. 17. In the distribution of lands for settlement among the different provinces, the government shall take care that the colonists shall be located in those which it may consider the most important to settle. As a general rule, the colonists who arrive first, shall have the preference in the selection of land.

Art. 18. Natives of the country shall have a preference in the distribution of land, and particularly the military of the army of the three guarantees, in conformity with the decree of the 27th of March, 1821; and also those who served in the first epoch of the insurrection.

Art. 19. To each empresario who introduces and establishes families in any of the provinces designated for colonization, there shall be granted at the rate of three haciendas and two labors, for each two hundred families so introduced by him, but he will lose the right of property over said lands, should he not have populated and cultivated them in twelve years from the date of the concession. The premium cannot exceed nine haciendas, and six labors, whatever may be the number of families he introduces.

Art. 20. At the end of twenty years the proprietors of the lands, acquired in virtue of the foregoing article, must alienate two thirds part of said lands, either by sale, donation, or in any other manner he pleases. The law authorizes him to hold in full property and dominion one third part.

Art. 21. The two foregoing articles are to be understood as governing the contracts made within six months, as after that time, counting from the day of the promulgation of this law, the executive can diminish the premium as it may deem proper, giving an account thereof to Congress, with such information as may be deemed necessary.

Art. 22. The date of the concession for lands constitutes an inviolable law, for the right of property and legal ownership; should any one through error, or by subsequent concession, occupy land belonging to another, he shall have no right to it, further than a preference in case of sale, at the current price.

Art. 23. If after two years from the date of the concession, the colonist should not have cultivated his land, the right of property shall be considered as renounced; in which case, the respective ayuntamiento can grant it to another.

Art. 24. During the first six years from the date of the concession, the colonists shall not pay tithes duties on their produce, nor any contribution under whatever name it may be called.

Art. 25. The next six years from the same date, they shall pay half tithes, and the half of the contributions, whether direct or indirect, that are paid by the other citizens of the empire. After this time, they shall in all things, relating to taxes and contributions, be placed on the same footing with other citizens.

Art. 26. All the instruments of husbandry, machinery, and other utensils, that are introduced by the colonists for their use, at the time of their coming to the empire, shall be free, as also the merchandise introduced by each family, to the amount of two thousand dollars.

Art. 27. All foreigners who come to establish themselves in the empire, shall be considered as naturalized, should they exercise any useful profession or industry, by which, at the end of three years, they have a capital to support themselves with decency, and are married. Those who, with the foregoing qualifications, marry Mexicans, will acquire special merit, for the obtaining letters of citizenship.

Art. 28. Congress will grant letters of citizenship to those who solicit them, in conformity with the constitution of the empire.

Art. 29. Every individual shall be free to leave the empire, and can alienate the lands over which he may have acquired the right of property, agreeably to the tenor of this law, and he can likewise take away from the country all his property, by paying the duties established by law.

Art. 30. After the publication of this law, there can be no sale or purchase of slaves which may be introduced into the empire. The children of slaves born in the empire shall be free at fourteen years of age.

Art. 31. All foreigners who may have established themselves in any of the provinces of the empire, under a permission of the former government, will remain on the lands which they may have occupied, being governed by the tenor of this law, in the distribution of said lands.

Art. 32. The executive, as it may conceive necessary, will sell or lease the lands, which, on account of their local situation, may be the most important, being governed with respect to all others by the provisions of this law.

[The above law was suspended by an order of 11th April, 1823, in the following words: "Is suspended until a new resolution, the colonization law enacted by the *Junta Instituente*." It had previously, however, been forwarded to California, where it was officially published, 14th July, 1823.]

Decree of the Mexican Congress, of 18*th August,* 1824, *on Colonization.*

The sovereign general constituent Congress of the United Mexican States has held it proper to decree:

1. The Mexican nation offers to foreigners, who shall come to establish themselves in its territory, security in their persons and in their pro-

perty; provided, that they subject themselves to the laws of the country.

2. Constitute the object of this law, those lands of the nation, which, not being private property, nor belonging to any corporation or town, may be colonized.

3. To this effect, the Congress of the States shall form, with the least delay, laws or rules of colonization for their respective limits, conforming themselves in all respects to the constitutive act,* the general constitution, and the rules established in this law.

4. Shall not be colonized those territories comprehended within twenty leagues of the boundaries with any foreign nation, nor within ten leagues of the seacoast, (*literales*,) without the previous approbation of the supreme general executive power.

5. If for the defence or security of the nation the government of the federation should find it expedient to make use of any portion of those lands to construct warehouses, arsenals, or other public edifices, it may do so with the approbation of the general Congress, or in its recess with that of the government council.

6. There shall not, before the expiration of four years from the publication of this law, be imposed any duty on the entrance of the persons of foreigners who shall come to establish themselves for the first time in the nation.

7. Prior to the year 1840, the general Congress shall not prohibit the entrance of foreigners to colonize, except imperious circumstances oblige it so to do with respect to the individuals of some (particular) nation.

8. The government, without prejudicing the objects of this law, shall take the measures of precaution which it may judge proper for the security of the federation with respect to foreigners who come to colonize.

9. In the distribution of lands, Mexican citizens are to be preferred, and between them no distinction shall be made, except such only as is due to special merit and services rendered to the country, or, in equality of circumstances, residence in the place to which the lands to be distributed are pertinent.

10. Military persons who, agreeably to the proffer of 27th March, 1821, may be entitled to lands, shall be attended to in the States, on exhibiting the diplomas which to this effect the supreme executive authority shall deliver to them.

11. If by the decrees of *capitalization*† according to the probabilities of life, the supreme executive power should think proper to alienate some portions of land in favor of any officers of the federation, either civil or military, it may do so of the vacant lands in the territories.

12. It shall not be permitted to unite in one hand as property more than one league square of five thousand varas of irrigable land, four in superficies of farming land not irrigable (*de temporal*,) and six in superficies for stock raising (*de abrevadero*.)

---

*Acta Constitutiva de la Federacion, adopted 31st January, 1824.

† *Capitalizacion* signifies the turning of an income, rent or annuity, into a capital.

13. The new settlers shall not transfer their property in *mortmain*.

14. This law guaranties the contracts which empresarios shall make with families whom they bring at their own expense, provided that they be not contrary to the laws.

15. No one who by virtue of this law shall acquire lands in ownership, shall be able to preserve them, being domiciliated without the territory of the Republic.

16. The government, conformably to the principles established in this law, shall proceed to the colonization of the territories of the Republic.

Government Regulations for the Colonization of the Territories, pursuant to the preceding law, adopted 21st *November,* 1828.

It being provided in the 16th article of the general colonization law of the 18th August, 1824, that the Government, in conformity with the principles established in said law, shall proceed to the colonization of the territories of the Republic; and it being desirable, in order to give to said article the most punctual and exact fulfilment, to dictate some general rules for facilitating its execution in such cases as may occur, his Excellency has seen fit to determine on the following articles:

1st. The Governors (gefes politicos) of the territories are authorized, (in compliance with the law of the general congress of the 18th of August, 1824, and under the conditions hereafter specified,) to grant vacant lands in their respective territories, to contractors, (*empresarios*,) families, or private persons, whether Mexicans or foreigners, who may ask for them for the purpose of cultivating or inhabiting them.

2d. Every person soliciting lands, whether he be an *empresario*, head of a family, or private person, shall address to the Governor of the respective territory a petition, setting forth his name, country, profession, the number, description, religion, and other circumstances of the families, or persons with whom he wishes to colonize, describing, as distinctly as possible, by means of a map, the land asked for.

3d. The Governor shall proceed immediately to obtain the necessary information whether the petition embraces the conditions required by said law of the 18th August, both as regards the land and the candidate, in order that the petitioner may at once be attended to, or if it be preferred, the respective municipal authority may be consulted, whether there be any objection to making the grant.

4th. This being done, the Governor will accede or not to said petition, in exact conformity to the laws on the subject, and especially to the before mentioned one of the 18th of August, 1824.

5th. The grants made to families, or private persons, shall not be held to be definitively valid without the previous consent of the territorial deputation; to which end the respective documents (expedientes) shall be forwarded to it.

6th. When the Governor shall not obtain the approbation of the territorial deputation, he shall report to the Supreme Government, forwarding the necessary documents for its decision.

7th. The grants made to *empresarios* for them to colonize with many families, shall not be held to be definitively valid until the approval of the Supreme Government be obtained, to which the necessary documents must be forwarded, along with the report of the territorial deputation.

8th. The definitive grant asked for being made, a document, signed by the Governor, shall be given to serve as a title to the party interested, wherein it must be stated, that said grant is made in exact conformity with the provisions of the laws, in virtue whereof possession shall be given.

9th. The necessary record shall be kept in a book prepared for the purpose, of all the petitions presented, and grants made, with the maps of the land granted, and a circumstantial report shall be forwarded quarterly to the Supreme Government.

10th. No stipulation shall be admitted for a new town, except the contractor bind himself to present as colonists at least twelve families.

11th. The Governor shall designate to the new colonist a proportionate time within which he shall be bound to cultivate or occupy the land, on the terms, and with the number of persons or families, which he may have stipulated for; it being understood that, if he does not comply, the grant of the land shall remain void. Nevertheless, the Governor may revalidate it in proportion to the part which the party may have fulfilled.

12th. Every new colonist, after having cultivated or occupied the land agreeably to his stipulation, will take care to prove the same before the municipal authority, in order that the necessary record being made, he may consolidate and secure his right of ownership, so that he may dispose freely thereof.

13th. The union of many families into one town shall follow in its formation, interior government and policy, the rules established by the existing laws of the other towns of the republic, special care being taken that the new ones shall be built with all possible regularity.

14th. The *minimum* of irrigable land to be given to one person for colonization, shall be two hundred varas square. The *minimum* of land called *de temporal*, (that is, dependent on the seasons, or not irrigable,) shall be eight hundred varas square; and the *minimum* for breeding cattle (*de abrevadero*) shall be twelve hundred varas square.

15th. The land given for a house lot shall be one hundred varas.

16th. The spaces which may remain between the colonized lands may be distributed among the adjoining proprietors, who shall have cultivated theirs with the greatest application, and have not received the whole extent of land allowed by the law; or to the children of said proprietors, who may ask for them to combine the possessions of their families; but in this respect particular attention must be paid to the morality and industry of the parties.

17th. In those territories where there are missions, the lands occupied by them cannot be colonized by them at present, nor until it is determined whether they are to be considered as the property of the establishments of the neophytes-catechumens, and Mexican colonists.

Decree of 4 November, 1833.

Art. 1. Shall be repealed in all its parts, the 11th article of the law of 6th April, 1830.*

Art. 2. The Government is authorized to expend the sums that may be necessary in the colonization of the territories of the Federation, and other vacant places which it has the right to colonize.

Art. 3. It is also authorized, that with respect to colonizable lands, it may take such measures as it believes conducent to the safety, better progress, and stability of the colonies which shall be established.

Art. 4. The repeal spoken of in article 1 of this decree, shall not take effect until six months have expired after its publication.

Art. 5. In the authorization conceded in article 2, is comprehended that of raising fortresses at those points of the frontiers where the executive may think them useful and expedient.

DECREE OF THE SPANISH CORTES OF FOURTH JANUARY, 1813.

On reducing vacant and other common lands to private ownership, lots conceded to the defenders of the country, and to citizens not proprietors.

The general and extraordinary Cortes, considering that the reduction of common lands to private ownership is one of the measures most imperiously required for the weal of the pueblos, and the encouragement of agriculture and industry, and wishing at the same time to provide, with that class of lands, some help to the public necessities, a reward to well-meriting defenders of the country, and succor to citizens who are not proprietors, decree:

I. All vacant or royal lands, and lands for municipal uses *(terrenos baldios ó realengos, y de propiòs y arbitrios,†)* both in the peninsula

---

* The act of 6th April, 1830, relates principally to the admission of cotton fabrics into Texas, and the colonization of that State. The 11th article above repealed is as follows:

"11. In exercise of the power which is reserved to the General Congress in article 7 of the law of 18th August, 1824, the colonization of foreigners of adjacent countries in those States and Territories of the Federation which are coterminant with their nations, is prohibited. In consequence, the contracts which have not been fulfilled, and which are opposed to this law, are suspended.

† " *Propios* are the hereditaments, meadows, houses, or other possessions whatsoever, which a city, town, or place has for its public expenses; and *arbitrios* signify those duties or taxes which, in default of *propios*, a place imposes, with competent authorization, on certain products or industry."—*Escriche: 2 Diccionario de Leyes,* 770.

and adjacent islands, and in the provinces beyond sea, except the commons necessary to villages, shall be reduced to private property; provided that, in the lands for municipal uses, their annual rents shall be supplied by the most proper means, which, proposed by the respective provincial deputations, shall be approved by the Cortes.

II. In whatever mode those lands shall be distributed, it shall be in full and separate ownership, (*plena propiedad, y en clase acotados,*) so that their owners may enclose them, (without prejudice to the paths, crossings, watering places, and servitudes,) enjoy them freely and exclusively, and appropriate them to the use or cultivation they are adapted to; but they shall not be able to entail them, nor to transfer them, at any time, or in any manner, in *mortmain*.

III. In the alienation of said lands, shall be preferred the inhabitants of the villages within the limits of which they exist, and who enjoyed them in common while vacant.

IV. The provincial deputations shall propose to the Cortes, by medium of the regency, the time and manner most suitable to carry this provision into effect in their respective provinces, according to the circumstances of the country, and the tracts which may be indispensable to preserve to the pueblos, in order that the Cortes may determine that which shall be most fitting to each territory.

V. This point is recommended to the zeal of the regency of the kingdom, and to the two secretaries of government, in order that they may advise and enlighten the Cortes when presenting to them the propositions of the provincial deputations.

[Articles 6, 7, 8, 9, 10, 11, 12, 13, 14, relate to a reservation of one-half the lands of the monarchy to be hypothecated for the national debt, and to the making of concessions to the military and others who should assist, in the existing war, in the defence of the nation.]

XV. Of the said remaining vacant and royal lands, shall be assigned the most fitting for cultivation, and to each inhabitant of the respective pueblos who ask it, and has not other land of his own, shall be given gratuitously, by lot, a parcel proportioned to the extent of the tract; provided that all that may be thus distributed shall not exceed one-fourth part of said vacant and royal lands ; and if there shall not be sufficient, the lot shall be given in the sowing grounds of the municipal lands, imposing on it, in such case, a redeemable tax equivalent to the rent of the same for the period of five years, unto the end of 1817, so that the municipal funds shall not fail.

XVI. If any grantee under the preceding article fail for two years to pay the tax, (his lot being of the municipal lands,) or to put his lot to use, it shall be given to another more industrious inhabitant, who may lack land of his own.

XVII. The measures necessary for these concessions shall be made, likewise without any charges, by the ayuntamientos, and the provincial deputations shall approve them.

XVIII. All the lots which shall be conceded conformably to articles IX, X, XII, XIII, and XV, shall likewise be in full ownership to the

4

grantees and their successors, in the terms and with the powers expressed in article II; but the owners of these lots shall not have power to alienate them within four years from the time they are conceded, nor subject them ever to entail, nor transfer them at any time or by any title, in *mortmain*.

XIX. The said grantees, or their successors, who shall establish their permanent habitations on the said lots, shall be exempt for eight years from any contribution or impost on that ground or its products.

ACTS GOVERNING THE EARLY SETTLEMENT OF CALIFORNIA.

Extracts from the " Instructions to be observed by the commandant of the new establishments of San Diego and Monterey," given by the Viceroy, 17th August, 1773.

Art. 5. The reduction of the Indians in proportion as the spiritual conquest may advance, is one of the principal cares of the commandant, and in which the missionaries ought to make the greatest efforts, the commandant giving the necessary assistance.

Art. 6. The reduction of the Indians accomplished, and in proportion as it may be accomplished, it is important for their preservation and increase that they should be congregated in mission pueblos, in order that they may be civilized and led to a rational life, which experience has shown can scarcely be done if they be left to live dispersed in the mountains.

Art. 7. The place in which the mission settlement is to be made, ought to be selected, if possible, where it will not be exposed to inundations, but have sufficient of water to drink and for irrigation of the fields, with hills and woods near by to furnish fire-wood and house timbers.

Art. 8. In the construction of the houses the Indians shall be taught, in order that they may know how to build them, whether of adobe, or of stone and mortar, conformably to the proportions which the tract of land offers, and that the whole shall have capacity for a garden, where the Indians shall sow some seeds and herbs, and plant trees, that, at the proper time, will reward their owners with their fruits; thus holding them with constancy to the place, and restraining their propensity to wander.

Art. 9. All settlements begin with few families, and afterwards increase to contain large cities; and in those where defects are not remidied from the beginning, they grow disproportioned, and without suitable symmetry.

Art. 10. As the mission settlements are hereafter to become cities, care should be taken in their foundation that the houses should be built in line, with wide streets and good market squares; by this means will not only be obtained symmetry, but the desire of the Indians will be excited not to withdraw; and even those not reduced may be reclaimed and drawn to establish themselves, and adopt a rational life.

Art. 11. For the preservation of the new mission settlements, it is very essential that near them should be encouraged the raising of cattle, cultivation and the planting of trees, and for this purpose to choose suitable lands, and on all to bestow strict attention.

Art. 12. With the desire that population may be more speedily assured in the new establishments, I, for the present, grant the commandant power to designate common lands, and also even to make individual concessions to such Indians as may most dedicate themselves to agriculture, and the raising of cattle, for, having property of their own, the love of it will cause them to plant themselves more firmly; but the commandant must bear it in mind, that it is very adviseable not to allow them to live dispersed, each on the land given him, but that they must have their house and habitation in the town or mission where they have been gathered or settled.

Art. 13. I grant the same faculty to the commandant with respect to distributing lands to the other settlers, (*pobladores,*) according to their merit and ability to improve; they also living in the town, and not dispersed; declaring, that in the exercise of what is prescribed in this article and the preceding, he must act in every respect in conformity with the provisions made in the collection of laws respecting new reductions and settlements, granting them legal titles for the owner's protection without exacting any remuneration therefor, or for the act of possession.

Art. 15. When it becomes expedient to change any mission into a pueblo, the commandant will proceed to reduce it to the civil and ecocomical government which, according to the laws, is observed in the other pueblos of this kingdom, giving it a name, and declaring for its patron the saint under whose auspices and venerable protection the mission was founded.

Extract from the " Regulation and Instruction for the Presidios of the Peninsula of Californias, the erection of New Missions, and encouragement of the Population and extension of the Establishments of Monterey." Drawn by Governor Felipe de Neve, 1st June, 1779, and approved by a royal cedula of 14th October, 1781.

TITLE XIV.—*Political government and instructions for Peopling.*

[Art. 1. Relates to the importance of encouraging the reduction and conversion of the Indians, and the establishment of settlements of civilized persons, in order to retain the dominion of the country and render it useful to the State. 2. Prescribes a different mode of payment of the premiums theretofore granted to settlers in money and rations. 3. Provides for supplying the new settlers with stock and with agricultural implements.]

4th. The house lots to be granted to the new settlers shall be designated by the governor in the places and of the extent correspondent to the tract where the new pueblos are to be established, in such manner that streets and a square shall be formed, according to the provisions of the laws of the kingdom, and agreeably to the same, competent common lands (*egidos*) shall be designated for the pueblos, and pasture grounds with suitable sowing lands, for municipal purposes (*propios.*)

5th. Each *suerte* of land (out-lot) whether capable of irrigation (*de riego*) or dependent on the seasons, (*de temporal,*) shall consist of two hundred varas in length by two hundred in breadth, this being the area generally occupied in the sowing of one fanega of Indian corn ; the distribution of these house lots and pieces of land to the new settlers shall be made in the name of the King our master by the government, with equity, and in proportion to the ground which admits of irrigation, so that after making the necessary demarcation, and reserving vacant the fourth part of the number which may result, counting with the number of settlers, should there be sufficient, each one shall have two suertes of irrigable land, and other two of dry ground, delivered to him; and of the royal lands (*realengos*) as much as may be considered necessary shall be separated for the *propios* of the pueblo; and of the remainder, as well as of the house lots, shall be granted in the name of H. M. by the governor, to those who may hereafter come to colonize, and particularly to soldiers, who having fulfiled the term of their engagement, or on account of advanced age may retire from service, and likewise to the families of those who may die; but these persons must make their improvements at their own expense, out of the funds which each possesses, and will not be entitled to receive from the royal revenue either salary, rations, or cattle, this privilege being limited to those who leave their own country for the purpose of peopling this.

6th. The houses built on lots granted and designated to the new settlers, and the parcels of land comprehended in their respective concessions, shall be perpetually hereditary to their sons and descendants, or to their daughters, who marry useful colonists who have received no grants of land for themselves;provided they all comply with the obligations expressed in these instructions; and in order that the sons of the possessors of these concessions, observe the obedience and respect which they owe to their parents, the latter shall be freely authorized, in case of having two or more sons, to choose which of them, being a layman, shall succeed to the house and lots, and they may likewise dispose of them among their children, but not so as to divide a single lot, because each and all of these are to remain indivisible and inalienable forever.

7th. Neither can the pobladores, nor their heirs, impose on the house or parcels of land granted to them, either tax, entail, reversion, mortgage, (*censo, vinculo, fianza, hipoteca,*) or any other burthen, although it be for pious uses; and should any one do so in violation of this just prohibition, he shall be deprived of his property, and his grant shall by said act be given to another colonist who may be serviceable and obedient.

8th. The new colonists shall enjoy for the maintenance of their cattle, the common use of the water and pasturage, firewood and timber of the commons, forest, and meadows, to be designated according to the laws to each new pueblo, and besides each one shall separately enjoy the pasture of his own lands.

9th. The new colonists shall be exempt for a term of four years from tithes, or any other tax on the fruits and produce of the lands and cattle given to them, provided that within a year from the day on which the house lots and parcels of land be designated to them, they build a house in the best way they can, and live therein; open the necessary trenches for watering their land, placing at the boundaries, instead of land marks, some fruit trees, or wild ones of some use, at the rate of ten to each out-lot, and likewise open the principal drain or trench, construct a dam, and the other necessary public works for the benefit of tillage, which the community is bound particularly to attend to; and said community shall see that the government buildings (casas reales) be completed within the fourth year, and during the third a storehouse for a public granary, in which must be kept the produce of the public sowing which at the rate of one almud (the twelfth of a fanega) of maize per inhabitant, must be made from said third year to the fifth inclusive, in the lands designated for municipal purposes (*propios.*)

10th. After the expiration of the five years they will pay the tithes to H. M. for him to dispose of agreeably to his royal pleasure, as belonging solely to him not only on account of the absolute royal patronage which he possesses in those dominions, but also because they are new, (*novales*) being the produce of lands hitherto uncultivated and waste, which are about to become fruitful at the cost of the large outlays and expenses of the royal treasury. At the expiration of the said term of five years, the new settlers and their descendants will pay, in acknowledgment of the direct and supreme dominion which belongs to the sovereign, one-half of a fanega of Indian corn for each irrigable suerte of land for their own benefit; they shall be collectively under the direct obligation of attending to the repair of the principal trench, dam, auxiliary drains, and other public works of their pueblos, including that of the church.

GRANTS BY THE CAPTAINS OF PRESIDIOS.

Instruction from the Commandant General of the Internal Provinces of the West to the Commandant of California.

In conformity with the opinion of the solicitor of this *Commandancia General,* I have determined, in a decree of this date, that notwithstanding the provisions made in the 18th article of the ordinance of

*Intendants,** the captains of presidios are authorized to grant and distribute house lots and lands to the soldiers and citizens, who may solicit them to fix their residences on. And considering the extent of four common leagues, measured from the centre of the presidio square, viz., two leagues in every direction, to be sufficient for the new pueblos, to be formed under the protection of said presidios, I have likewise determined, in order to avoid doubts and disputes in future, that said captains restrict themselves henceforward to the quantity of house lots and lands within the said four leagues, without exceeding, in any manner, said limits, leaving free and open the exclusive jurisdiction belonging to the managers of the royal hacienda respecting the sale, composition, and distribution of the remainder of the lands in the respective district. And that this order may be punctually observed and carried into effect, you will circulate it to the captains and commandants of the presidios of your province, informing me of having done so.

God preserve you many years.

Chihuahua, *March* 22, 1791.

PEDRO DE NAVA.

Senor DON JOSEPH ANTONIO ROMAN, *Monterey.*

SECULARIZATION OF MISSIONS.

Decree of the Spanish Cortes, 13th September, 1813.

That the settlements of Indians converted to Christianity by the monks in the provinces beyond sea, shall be delivered to and remain at the disposition of the ordinaries (bishops.)

I. All the new reductions and *doctrimas* (missions) of ultramar, which are in charge of missionary monks, and shall have been ten years reduced, shall be immediately delivered to the respective ecclesiastical ordinaries, without any excuse or pretext, according to the laws in that respect.

---

* The following is the article referred to, to wit, Art. 81, of the *Ordinanza de Intendentes,* of 4th December, 1786. (The preamble to this ordinance divides the kingdom of New Spain into twelve intendencies, expressly excluding, however, the Californias.)

"The intendants shall also be the exclusive judges of the causes and questions that may arise in the district of their provinces, about the sale, composition, and granting of royal lands, and of seigniory, it being required of their possessors and of those who pretend to new grants of them, to produce their rights and institute their claims before the said intendants, so that these matters, being legally prepared in conjunction with a promoter of my royal treasury whom they may appoint, may be decided upon, the opinion of the ordinary assessor being heard, and they may admit appeals to the superior junta de hacienda ; or, if the parties interested do not appeal, they shall communicate to said junta, for its information, the original proceedings, when they shall judge these proceedings ready for the issuing of the title; which, after examination by the junta, shall be returned, and the title issued, unless some difficulty occur ; and then, before executing it, the measures found to be neglected by the junta shall be observed. The proper confirmations shall, in consequence, be furnished by the same superior junta, in due time, which shall proceed in the case, as also the intendants, their sub-delegates, and others, in conformity with the royal regulation of the 15th of October, 1754, as far as it may not be opposed to the requirements of this ordinance, without losing sight of the wise dispositions of the laws cited therein, and of law 9th, title 12, lib. 4."

II. Both these *doctrinas*, and all others that shall be erected into curacies, shall be provided canonically by the said ordinaries, observing the laws and cedulas of the royal advowson, with fit ministers of the secular clergy.

III. The missionary monks, relieved from the reduced pueblos, thus delivered to the ordinary, shall apply themselves to extend religion in other unreduced places, for the advantage of their inhabitants, proceeding in the exercise of their missions conformably to the direction in paragraph 10, art. 335, of the Constitution.

IV. The reverend bishops and ecclesiastical prelates, in virtue of the ordinary jurisdiction which belongs to them, shall have power, as they may judge proper, to appoint capable monks temporarily to fill the curacies of the secular parishes, where it may be necessary; but provided that they shall never aspire to the possession of the parish, nor continue in its service longer than the ordinary may require, conformably to the laws.

V. [Provides that, until otherwise ordered, the monks then in charge of curacies should continue the same.]

VII. The missionary monks shall cease immediately from the government and administration of the property of those Indians, leaving to their charge and election to dispose of it through the medium of their ayuntamientos, and with intervention of the superior political authority, to name among themselves persons to their satisfaction, and who shall have most intelligence to administer it; the lands being distributed and reduced to private property, conformably to the decree of 4th January, 1813, on reducing vacant and other lands to private ownership.

Decree of the Mexican Congress, of 17*th August,* 1833.

On the Secularization of the Missions of Upper and Lower California.

ART. 1. The Government will proceed to secularize the missions of Upper and Lower California.

Art. 2. In each of said missions a parish shall be established under the charge of a parish priest of the secular clergy, with a salary of from $2,000 to $2,500 per annum, at the discretion of the Government.

Art. 3. These parish curates shall not exact any emolument for marriages, baptisms, burials, or any other religious functions. With respect to fees of ceremony, they may receive such as shall be expressly stipulated in the tariff to be formed for that object, with as little delay as possible, by the reverend bishop of the diocess, and approved by the Supreme Government.

Art. 4. The churches which have hitherto served the different missions, and the sacred vessels, ornaments, and other appurtenances now belonging to them, shall be assigned to those new parishes, and also such buildings annexed to the said churches as the Government may deem necessary for the use of said parish.

Art. 5. The Government will order a burial ground to be erected outside of each parish.

Art. 6. There shall be $500 per annum assigned to each parish as a donation for religious worship and servants.

Art. 7. Of the buildings belonging to each mission the most appropriate shall be designated for the habitation of the curate, with the addition of a lot of ground, not exceeding two hundred varas square, and the remaining edifices shall be specially adjudicated for a court-house, preparatory schools, public establishments and workshops.

Art. 8. In order to provide quickly and efficaciously for the spiritual necessities of both Californias, a vicar-generalship shall be established in the capital of Upper California, the jurisdiction of which shall extend to both territories; and the reverend diocesan shall confer upon its incumbent the necessary faculties as fully as possible.

Art. 9. For the dotation of this vicar-generalship $3,000 per annum shall be assigned, but the vicar shall be at all the expenses of his office, and not exact, under any title or pretext, any fee whatever.

Art. 10. If for any reason this vicar-generalship shall be filled by the parish curate of the capital of any other parish in those districts, said curate shall receive $1,500 yearly, in addition to the donation of his curacy.

Art. 11. No custom obliging the inhabitants of California to make oblations, for whatever pious uses, although they may be called necessary ones, can be introduced.

Art. 12. The Government will procure that the reverend diocesan himself concur in carrying into effect the object of this law.

Art. 13. When those new curates are named, the Supreme Government will gratuitously furnish a passage by sea for them and their families, and besides that may give to each one from $400 to $800 for their journey by land, according to the distance and the family they take with them.

Art. 14. Government will pay the passage of the missionary priests who return to Mexico; and in order that they may comfortably reach their convents by land, it may give to each one from two hundred to three hundred dollars, and, at its discretion, what may be considered necessary for those to leave the Republic who have not sworn to the independence.

Art. 15. The Supreme Government will provide, for the expenses comprehended in this law, out of the product of the estates, capitals, and revenues at present recognised as the piety fund of the missions of California.

Decree of 26th *November,* 1833, *to make effective the secularization of the missions in Californias.*

The Government is authorized to take all measures that may assure the colonization and make effective the secularization of the missions of Upper and Lower California, and to this effect to use, in the manner most convenient, the estates for pious uses *(fincas de obras pias**) of said territories, for the purpose of facilitating the resources of the commission and families who find themselves in this capital destined to the Californias.

Extract from a "Letter in relation to Missions," sent by the Viceroy, the Conde de Revilla Gigeda, to the King, and dated at Mexico, 27th December, 1793.

MISSIONS OF CALIFORNIA.

7. Their establishment commenced in the year 1697, by the monks of the extinguished company of Jesuits, and at the time of the expulsion of that Order there were existing fifteen missions.

8. Three were suppressed by order of the Señor Marquis de Sonora; the remainder were delivered in the year 1767 to the Franciscans, of the apostolical college of San Fernando, of this capital; and in the year 1772 the Dominicans, who came from Spain for that purpose, received them and continue to administer them.

9. In their time they have added five, and the Franciscans or Fernandinos have founded those of New California, and occupied the posts of San Diego, Monterey, and San Francisco.

10. According to the preceding notes it will be found that there are established in the peninsula of Californias thirty-one missions; twelve founded by the extinguished order; five by the Dominicans, and the remaining fourteen by the Franciscans of San Fernando.

11. Those of the old establishment were reduced in 1767 to the territories which measure from the Cape of San Lucas, in latitude 22° 48″, to latitude 30° 30″, where is found the mission of All Saints; but those of the new erection have extended to latitude 37° 56′, where is that of San Francisco, and covering the whole coast for the space of more than one hundred leagues.

12. It does not appear that any judicial formality has been observed for the designation of limits or boundaries of each mission; the extinguished order established them arbitrarily, without any other rule than that of a prudent consideration to the distance from one mission to another, in proportion as the spiritual conquests went forward; and this mode has continued the practice unto the present time in all the peninsula.

26. The income, revenue, or stock of such mission settlement is confined to the tillage of the field, and raising of cattle, the harvest and increase of which the Indians enjoy in community, under the adminis-

---

*The "*piety fund of the Californias*," consisting of large estates in different provinces of New Spain, originally donated by their owners to the Jesuits for the conversion of the natives of the peninsula of Californias.

5

tration of the missionaries, (who truly constitute their spiritual and temporal fathers,) in such manner that the Indian labors when so directed, and the product of his toil is returned in the abstemious sustenance and humble clothing of those families, and the overplus applied to the divine worship and encouragement of the said pueblos.

27. The missionary fathers keep their accounts in formal books; the prelate or father president examines them in his visits, and at the end of a year remits extracts from them to the governor of the province, to be forwarded to the viceroy, who approves them if they be correct, or otherwise makes the proper order upon them.

31. It is already stated that in all the ancient California they are in community, and that consequently there have not been made any distribution of lands to the Indians; nor is it possible, for neither do they desire property, nor would they preserve or improve it, if not compelled to labor by the missionaries.

34. As to the missions of the new or Upper California, they are of modern creation, the oldest scarcely counting twenty-four years, and their Indians still find themselves in the rank of *neophytes*, but well trained in a rational and christian life.

37. In each one reside two Franciscan monks, of the college of San Fernando, and named by its guardian and council, giving notice to the viceroy of those who are sent thither, and asking his permission for those who wish to retire and return to the college for any cause.

38. They do not receive any perquisites or duties; but each missionary is assisted with a salary of four hundred dollars a year from the piety fund, out of which is likewise paid the sum of one thousand dollars to the Franciscans, and the same to the Dominicans, for each new mission they respectively establish.

39. With this assistance, and that which the missions already established are able to afford, together with the pains and apostolical care of the missionaries, and the personal labor of the Indians, the churches and houses of the settlement are built, the ornaments and sacred vessels bought, with agricultural utensils, and, finally, the seed for sowing, and a small stock of cattle.

44. Hitherto there has not been made, nor is it now time to make, any allotments of lands in the missions; the sowings are in community, and the harvests and increase of the cattle are expended in the maintenance of the said Indians, in the encouragement of the pueblos, and in divine worship.

MISSIONS OF NEW MEXICO.

119. This province was discovered and conquered in the year 1600, and the monks of San Francisco began the establishment of the missions.

120. Their progress was so happy and rapid, that in the year 1628 was founded the *custodia*,* which still exists with the name of the con-

---

* *Custodia*—among the Franciscans, the union of a number of convents not sufficient to form a *province*.

version of St. Paul, and in the year 1630, it was proposed to his Majesty to establish a bishoprick, as there had already been reduced 86,000 Indians of different nations.

121. Afterward, according to the confused accounts of those times, the Indians revolted, scandalous disagreements arose between the missionaries and the royal judges, and the Governor, Don Luis de Rosas, was assassinated, which painful news was related to the King by the viceroy, in the year 1640.

122. Whether from that bad example, or from the vexations suffered by the Indians, they were again excited in the year 1650, to the extent that the reduced nations united hostilities with those who had remained heathens, and the province was entirely lost in the year 1680; the Spaniards retiring to the village of Paso del Norte with some Christian Indians, and with the Governor Don Antonio Otermin.

123. The successor of the last named, Don Domingo Girona Petris de Cruzat commenced the restoration of New Mexico, and the Marquis de las Navas, who relieved Girona from the governorship of the province, accomplished it entirely.

124. This province extends, according to the latest, and least doubtful observations, from latitude 34° to 37½°, and by a prudent computation from 268° to 272° of longitude, counting from the meridian of Teneriffe; its confines being at the south the province of New Biscay and Sonora; at the north, the mountains of Taos and *rancherias* of the *Vistas;* at the east, by the plains of Cubo (*llanos del Cubo,*) which extend many leagues, until they terminate in the territories of Texas and Louisiana; and at the west, with the Indian tribes, Comines, Moquis, Navajos, Yumas, Painchis and Moachis.

125. The Rio Grande del Norte, whose source is still unknown, traverses the whole of this province, fertilizing its best settlements, as far as the Paso del Norte, where it runs to the southeast by the frontiers of New Biscay and Coahuila, emptying into the sea in the colony of New Santander, with the name of the Rio Bravo.

126. In the year 1780, there were registered 20,810 persons in the eighteen jurisdictions which compose the province, the capital of which is the town and presidio of Santa Fé.

139. In the province of New Mexico, the pueblos of Indians are governed by alcaldes of their own nation, whom they call governors, and by other subordinate officers.

142. Those of each pueblo have in their charge the matters of police, regimen and justice, exercising their functions very often arbitrarily.

143. There are neither goods of community in the missions, nor formal allotment of lands. Each family counts for its own that which its ancestors possessed, occupying it and cultivating it according to their necessities or their foresight.

GRANTING OF ISLANDS ON THE COAST OF CALIFORNIA.

Letter from the minister of the Interior to the Governor of California, respecting the granting of certain islands to Mexican citizens.

"His excellency, the President, being desirous on the one hand to advance the population of the desert islands adjacent to that department, which form a part of the national territory, and on the other to hinder the many foreign adventurers from benefiting themselves with these considerable portions, whereby they may do great injury to our fisheries, commerce, and other interests, has been pleased to resolve that your Excellency, in conjunction with the departmental junta, shall proceed with activity and prudence to grant and distribute lands on said islands, to the Mexicans who may solicit them, recommending to you in particular the citizens Antonio and Carlos Carrillo, for their useful and patriotic services, in order that you may attend to them in preference, and grant them exclusively one of said islands which they themselves may select."

Extract from an act of the Territorial Deputation of California, 6 August, 1834.

"Art. 1. The ayuntamientos shall make application, through the usual channels, requesting lands to be assigned to each pueblo for *egidos*, (common lands) and *propios*, (municipal lands.)

"Art. 2. The lands assigned to each pueblo for *propios* shall be subdivided into middling sized and small portions, and may be rented out or sold at public auction, subject to an emphiteutic rent, or tax, (*en senso enfiteutico*,) the present possessors of lands belonging to the *propios* will pay an annual tax, to be imposed by the ayuntamiento, the opinion of three intelligent and honest men being first taken.

"Art. 3. For the grant of a house lot for building on, the parties interested shall pay six dollars and two rials for each lot of one hundred varas quare, and in the same manner for a larger or smaller quantity, at the rate of two rials for each vara front."

HISTORY

❋ OF ❋

San Bernardino Valley

FROM THE PADRES
TO THE PIONEERS

❋1810--1851❋

❋ BY ❋

REV. FATHER JUAN CABALLERIA

ILLUSTRATED BY CONSTANCE FARRIS

TIMES-INDEX PRESS
SAN BERNARDINO, CAL.
1992

Table of Contents.

REV. FATHER JUAN CABALLERIA.

INTRODUCTORY.

History may be compared to a skein of tangled threads, gathered here and there. After a time, often many years, these strands are taken up, straightened and woven into a fabric that may satisfy the weaver—for the story is not of his day. So, as the present weaves the story of the past, it prepares the web of its own story, for the future to weave. The shears of Atropos never rust.

These brief chapters of the history of San Bernardino Valley have been prepared by Father Caballeria with the sole purpose of preserving some historical facts that are in danger of being overlooked and forgotten. The later days have many chroniclers, but of events prior to American colonization nothing has been written. These events form an important link in the historical chain; they provide a starting point, beyond which there is no record, no tradition.

As the early history of San Bernardino Valley is interwoven with mission history, it is well to outline the principal events preceding the first settlement of the valley. This will cover briefly the Spanish occupation of California and what is known as the missionary era.

No person is more competent to write of mission history than Father Caballeria. Endowed with a love for ancient historical lore, and the spirit that impels men to search for knowledge, he deems no effort or labor too great if knowledge may be gained. He found in the Indian and mission history of California an interesting field to which he has devoted much time, study and research. His profession is the "open sesame" to doors sealed to the average student. The faded, musty old records of a by-gone age and generation written in the seclusion of cloistered missions, need no translation to tell to him their story; for the language in which they are written is his mother tongue; the men who made the early history of California, by faith, race and land of birth, his kindred.

Father Caballeria is already well known as the author of several philosophic works in Spanish. He has written a history of Santa Barbara Mission which has been translated into English. All this gives value to the work of his pen and is assurance of a thorough comprehension of the subject upon which he now writes.

AMY DUDLEY.

San Bernardino, Cal., January, 1902.

CHAPTER I.
THE EARLY SPANISH EXPLORERS—CABRILLO.

Long before the caravel of the first explorer touched the western coast of North America, marvelous stories had reached the ears of the Spaniards of a wonderful island lying afar off in unknown seas, called California. In these stories nothing was lacking to excite the imagination and appeal to the cupidity of man. It was said to be a land of enchantment, inhabited by a race of people unlike the Europeans, who lived in wonderful cities and were garbed in raiment glittering with gold and precious stones. It was a dream of oriental splendor rivaled only by the tales of the Arabian Nights.

These fables at last bore fruit. In them is found the lure that beckoned the early explorers to California. In this respect the history of the world reads the same today as yesterday; and though men follow the ignis fatuus of personal ambition to bitter disappointment and death, it has ever served its purpose as a beacon light of civilization. Through the selfishness of a few, in time, comes the betterment of many. In this may be traced the master hand of human destiny— the Will of God.

Among the Spaniards, the true pioneers of the New World, the names of Cortez, Nuno de Guzman, Hurtado, Manzuela, Ximenes, Alarcon and Coronado are interwoven with the annals of the earliest explorations of the western coast, and to the northwest of Mexico. The colonization of Baja-California was begun as early as 1530. But, passing over the history of the Spanish conquest and settlements in North America, that of California begins with the expedition under command of Admiral Juan Rodriguez Cabrillo.

On the 27th of June, 1542, Cabrillo sailed from Navidad, for the purpose of discovering "a shorter route, in a westerly direction, from New Spain, or Mexico, between the North and the South Sea." He was in command of two sailing vessels, the Victoria and the San Salvador. After leaving the coast of Lower California he entered the unexplored waters of the then called Mar del Sur. On the 28th of September he sailed into a harbor, to which he gave the name of San Miguel, but now known as San Diego Bay. These were the first vessels to enter the waters of that bay; and these the first white men to set foot on the land which Cabrillo named Alta-California.

An account of this voyage, published by Juan Paez, is the source from which writers of history have drawn their information. It abounds in errors and inaccuracies which make it difficult to determine the extent of the voyage. However, Cabrillo remained at San Miguel six days. They landed, made explorations and give a very good description of the country, with some mention of the Indians inhabiting that section of the coast. These Indians are described as well formed and clothed in the skins of animals. They appeared suspicious of the white men and could only be approached with difficulty.

About the 10th of October they anchored in a small bay, now believed to be San Pedro. From there a party proceeded inland some distance, where they obtained a view of high mountains and again saw the Indians. On the 17th of November, Cabrillo discovered the Bay of Monterey, but was unable to make a landing on account of the roughness of the sea. He continued the voyage as far as 44 degrees latitude, but owing to the inclemency of the weather and the unsafe condition of his vessels, he decided to return to the Santa Barbara Islands and remain for the winter.

The latter part of this voyage was accomplished under serious difficulties. The brave commander was suffering from severe injuries, the result of a fall received during the month of October, and constant exposure and lack of proper attention caused inflamation which resulted in his death January 3, 1543. This occurred on the island now known as San Miguel, where his remains received burial. The command of the expedition devolved upon Lieut. Bartolome Ferrer, who, not daring to continue the explorations, returned to New Spain.

Cabrillo sleeps in an unknown grave, but history has buiit for him an enduring monument, and while the record of the deeds of brave men adorn its pages, the name of Cabrillo will not be forgotten. He was a man of sterling qualities, a fearless navigator and the discoverer of Alta-California.

CHAPTER II.
VISCAINO.

Sixty years elapsed before Spain made any attempt to proceed with the work of discovery and exploration which the untimely death of Cabrillo postponed.

On May 1, 1603, a fleet sailed from Acapulco for the purpose of establishing a harbor on the coast of California, where vessels engaged in the Philippine trade could, in case of necessity, find shelter and supplies. This fleet of three frigates, the San Diego, Santo Tomas and Los Tres Reyes, was under command of Admiral Don Sebastien Viscaino. On November 10, they anchored in the bay where Cabrillo first landed, and which Viscaino named San Diego de Alcala, although Cabrillo had given to it the name of San Miguel.

Accompanying this expedition was a party of learned scientists sent purposely from Madrid to take part in the explorations. They were under direction of Fray Antonio de la Ascencion, of the Order of Carmelite Brothers. He had as assistants Fray Andreas de la Asuncion and Fray Tomas de Aquino. They were the first to make maps of the coast and of the islands lying off the coast of California.

A knowledge of the progress of this expedition may be gained by following the Roman Calendar of Saints. These pious fathers not only made the maps but named each place visited by the expedition with the name of the saint whose anniversary occurred on the day of their arrival at the place. California owes a debt of gratitude to these devout padres for the beautiful names bestowed upon many of her now popular pleasure resorts and islands, these names having been retained to this day.

The expedition visited San Clements Island November 23, and on the 25th, Santa Catalina Island; on the 26th they landed at San Pedro; thence northward to Santa Barbara, arriving December 4, the anniversary of Santa Barbara day. On the 8th of the month they doubled Point Concepcion; and on the 16th dropped anchor in an excellent harbor which Viscaino named Monte Rey—king's mountain. Here they landed, and beneath the spreading boughs of a large oak tree near the shore, beside which bubbled a spring of clear, cool water, a solemn mass was offered by Fray Ascencion. The rough, bearded sailors from the ships knelt in silent devotion while the three priests, in their sacred vestments, chanted the mass "In Gratiarum Actione," their voices uniting and ascending in the devout prayer of thankfulness to God, who had so preserved and cared for them amidst the many perils that constantly surrounded them. It was an impressive scene. On one side the unbroken solitude of mountain and the vastness of trackless wilderness; on the other side the immensity of an unknown ocean. The moment was worthy of immortalization and one destined to live in the history of the land.

This expedition did not go beyond 42 degrees latitude. The maps, records and descriptions of the coast, climate and general condition of California were accepted as authority, and thus the expedition added to knowledge of the country; but aside from this there was no benefit derived and no practical use was made of the knowledge gained. Although Viscaino solicited the opportunity of returning to California, desiring to make a permanent settlement in the country, no provision was made for that purpose and he died with the hope unfulfilled. Spain seemed content to rest until the trend of events far in the future, awoke her to a realization of the value and importance of the rich possessions which for so many years suffered neglect at her hands.

CHAPTER III.
THE COMING OF THE MISSIONARIES.

In the Seventeenth century Spain was mistress of the world. Her diplomats were a power at every European court; her ships sailed every sea; she was foremost of nations. Her many interests had so absorbed her attention elewhere that the vast territory of California, which she claimed, was apparently overlooked or forgotten. This forgetfulness, however, was only apparent. When the Russians, coming down from their possessions in the north, seemed about to invade the territory, Spain awoke to the necessity for immediate action and there was no hesitancy in asserting her right of sovereignty. Carlos III., then king of Spain, issued a royal mandate commanding Jose de Galvez, viceroy of New Spain, to make preparation for the immediate occupation of the country. They were to establish military stations at San Diego and Monterey—these points, according to Viscaino's maps being the opposite extremities of California.

The object of this expedition was two-fold: the occupation and colonization of the country by Spain, and the conversion to Christianity of the native inhabitants.

The latter undertaking was given to the Brotherhood of the Order of Franciscans. They were to have entire control of the religious movement, and the protection and co-operation of the military in furtherance of the important mission entrusted to them.

It was deemed prudent to have this expedition consist of four divisions—two to go by land and two by sea—the objective point of all being San Diego.

On the 9th of January, 1769, the San Carlos sailed from La Paz. Solemn religious services preceded the voyage. St. Joseph was named as patron saint of the expedition. Mass was celebrated by Father Junipero Serra and divine blessing invoked for protection and guidance to the ultimate success of their undertaking. Fifteen days later, after similar services, the San Antonio followed the San Carlos. Another ship, the San Jose, was fitted out and set sail on the 16th of June, but this vessel was probably lost at sea. It was never heard from again.

In the meantime, the land expeditions were well under way. The first division, under command of Rivera y Moncada, captain of "soldados de cuera," was composed of soldiers, muleteers and neophytes of the Lower California Missions. They took with them cattle, horses, mules, sheep, and a supply of garden seeds. Padre Juan Crespi, whose diary of this and later expeditions has been a valuable and fertile source of information to historians, accompanied this expedition.

The second land division was commanded by Gaspar de Portala, a captain of dragoons, who had been appointed governor of Alta California. At Vellicata he was joined by the Venerable Fray Junipero Serra, the Missionary President, who made the journey with them to the field of his future labors.

After great physical hardships, difficulties and delays, the four divisions comprising the expedition met at San Diego, July 1, 1769. The last to arrive was that of Governor Portola.

On the 16th of July, 1769, the mission San Diego de Alcala was founded. This day was selected as most appropriate, it being commemorative of the Triumph of the Most Holy Cross over the crescent in 1212, and also the feast day of Our Lady Mount Carmel. This was the beginning of the missionary work in California.

After resting a few days an expedition started to discover the harbor of Monterey, but failing to recognize the place returned to San Diego disappointed and disheartened. A second expedition was more fortunate and the desired harbor located, all unchanged as described by Viscaino. Here was the mountain, the ravine, the spring of sparkling water, the oak tree under which so many years before Fray Ascension had offered his mass of thanksgiving, and the hearts of the pilgrims leaped with joy as their voices shouted the glad tidings of recognition and discovery. The words of the beloved Father Junipero can best tell the story. In a letter to his life-long friend, Father Francis Palou, he writes: "On the great feast of Pentecost, June 3rd, close by the same shore, and under the same oak tree where the Fathers of Viscaino's expedition had celebrated, we built an altar, and the bell having been rung, and the hymn Veni Creator intoned, we erected and consecrated a large cross, and unfurled the royal standard, after which I sang the first mass which is known to have been sung at this point since 1603. I preached during the mass, and at its conclusion we sang the "Salve Regina.' Our celebration terminated with the singing of the Te Deum; after which the officers took possession of the land in the name of the King of Spain. During the celebration a salute of many cannons was fired from the ship. To God alone be honor and glory."

Thus was founded, on June 3, 1770, the Mission of San Carlos Borromeo, the second of the missions of California.

Messengers were at once dispatched to carry the glad tidings to the City of Mexico. The occupation of California by Spain was considered complete.

CHAPTER IV.
THE FRANCISCANS.

The history of the world can show no nobler efforts in the work of civilizing savage races than that put forth by the Roman Catholic Church in North America. Perfection is not of earth. Living up to a high ideal, and entire and unfailing devotion to duty may so purify and strengthen the soul of man as to enable him to overcome many inherent tendencies and weaknesses, but it will not immediately eradicate them. The missionaries may oftentimes have erred through a mistaken sense of duty, but their mistakes were rather those of the time in which they lived, and were brought about by conditions from which they themselves suffered. In the main, their lives were heroic in devotion to duty and sacrifice of self. No hardship was too great and no personal discomfort ever considered or permitted to stand in the way of the work to which their lives were consecrated. They penetrated the wilds of the great Northwest; they tramped barefooted and alone over the barren waste of desert in the South; no tribe of Indians too remote or too savage for their ministry; even though in going they knew they were facing almost certain death, and death in its most horrible form. Such were the men who planted the cross on the Western Continent; such the men selected to Christianize Alta-California.

The Franciscans held high place among the religious orders of that time. Their founder, St. Francis, was born in the village of Assissi, Italy, in 1182. In early manhood, after prolonged meditation on the evil and sins of life, he sold all his possessions, gave the proceeds to the church and, renouncing the world, became a religious devotee. Clad in the roughest clothing, he went about performing acts of charity and mercy, literally following in the footsteps of his Divine Master. Soon his devotion attracted the attention of ohers, who, joining him, endeavored to emulate him in his good works. In 1209 the religious order of Franciscans was organized, and though the regulations and discipline of this order were most severe and trying, they rapidly increased in numbers. The death of St. Francis occurred in 1226, and his canonization in 1228. In less than fifty years the order numbered over two hundred thousand members, and had established many schools and colleges.

Spain reposed the fullest confidence in the Order of Franciscans. Their work in California started under most favorable auspices. They had figured in every conquest Spain had made and were active in promoting the Catholic faith in the new lands. Among their numbers were men of high ecclesiastical and political standing, and in beginning their work in California they brought to bear a direct influence with the Spanish crown, and a power was given them granted to no other religious order of that period.

The Franciscan Missions in Mexico had prospered in every way. The Franciscan missionaries were men of marked executive ability. They were experienced in the work and well able to cope with any difficulty that might confront them in the new field of labor about to be opened.

In taking up the work in Alta-California, these missionaries brought minds single to one purpose, and that purpose the sowing of the seed of Christianity. If they succeeded in their undertaking the wealth and honors were always for the order; the individual reaped neither material gain nor glory. The life of every missionary was one of toil, privation and danger; his hopes were not for earthly riches; his reward, that which surely comes to all who labor unselfishly for the good of humanity.

FATHER JUNIPERO SERRA.

CHAPTER V.

FATHER JUNIPERO SERRA.

Father Junipero Serra, the first Apostle of Christianity to Alta-California, was born in the village of Petra, in the island of Mallorica, November 24, 1713. His parents were of the poorer class of people, but mindful of the advantages of religious training, early instilled in the mind of their son the principles which governed his after life. His quickness of perception attracted the attention of the priests of his native city, who encouraged the lad by teaching him Latin and to sing. ¡Later, he entered the college of San Bernardo de Palma, where he advanced rapidly in all his studies. At the age of seventeen years he donned the habit and took the vows of the Franciscan Brotherhood, determined even then to become a missionary and devote his life to the saving of savage souls.

In the meantime, in obedience to the desires of his superiors, he took up the study of theology and philosophy and became an instructor in those branches, his learning obtaining for him the degree of Doctor of Divinity. His discourses attracted much comment and large audiences greeted him whenever he spoke publicly; but in spite of the flattering attention of his numerous admirers, his desire to devote himself to missionary work did not lessen. His faith and patience was at last rewarded. On the 28th of August, 1749, in company with his lifelong friend and brother priest, Father Francisco Palou, he set sail from Cadiz, Spain, for America. After a long, tempestuous voyage, and much suffering from sickness, they arrived at Vera Cruz, and from there went to the mission of Sierr a Gorda, in the north of Mexico, where he had been assigned for duty, arriving January 1, 1750. There he lived and taught nine years. His mission work prospered and he was soon able, with the help of his Indian neophytes, to build a new church, which was the admiration of the whole country. He learned the language of the Indians; taught them to build houses, sow grain, prepare clothing, and in all ways advanced them far on the road to civilization.

Leaving the peaceful mission he went to the city of Mexico and while there learned of the need of a missionary to go among the treacherous Apache Indians in the Northwest. Though going meant almost certain death, he volunteered his services. Circumstances, however, prevented the sacrifice on his part, and the next seven years were passed in the City of Mexico preaching the gospel and converting many sinners to Christianity.

His energy, zeal and untiring devotion to the faith eminently fitted him for the great work to which he was chosen —that of President in charge of the mission of Alta-California.

All unsolicited the call came to him and though it found him miles away in the interior of the country, he was ready for it and made immediate preparation for his journey. Owing to a badly ulcerated leg he was not able to start until March 28, 1769, eighteen days behind the expedition under the command of Governor Portola, whom he overtook at the frontier. Traveling so aggravated the swelling on his leg that he could proceed only through great suffering. He was repeatedly urged to abandon the journey, but insisted on going forward with the expedition, saying that he "had put his faith in God and if He willed that he should die among savages he was content." Father Junipero's abiding faith in, and trust in Divine guidance, brought him through the difficult journey, and his faith and trust was amply rewarded.

Combined with his faith was a belief that he was the

instrument chosen by God, and under Divine direction, for the prosecution of the work in Alta-California. Though physically weak and suffering in health, this belief filled his soul with sublime inspiration and he entered upon his labors fully alive to their importa nce, with a spirit imbued with energy and determination to bravely meet all difficulties, and, with the help of God, to overcome all obstacles in the path to success. He lived to see the mission system well established and many natives converted to Chritianity. He fell asleep in the Lord, passing from life peacefully at his mission of San Carlos, August 28, 1784, at the age of seventy-one years.

CHAPTER VI.
THE MISSIONS.

When the Franciscans, under the able leadership of Junipero Serra, arrived in California, their first work was to select locations for the missions which they were instructed to establish. To this en d, expeditions were formed for the purpose of exploring the country between San Diego and Monterey. It was their plan to have these missions situated not more than one day's journey from each other. This was in order to afford mutual protection in case of attack from Indians, and also to lessen the fatigue to travelers on the long journey between missions situated at a considerable distance from each other.

The missions were usually located in close proximity to some of the numerous Indian rancherias where there was to be found an abundance of water. The consent of the Indians would first be obtained and then the work of building the mission begun. First, an enramada of green boughs was prepared as a place for holding temporary religious services. After arranging an improvised altar the bells would be swung from the branches of some near-by tree, and then ringing them to call the soldiers, the ceremony of consecration took place. The soldiers formed themselves into a square about the padres and waited the raising of the cross. The wondering natives, in the background, gazed in awe on the strange proceedings and watched until their close. The padre, in snowy alb and stole, advanced and invoked the blessing of God on the work about to commence, and with the chanting of the hymn the cross was raised. After this ceremony, mass was celebrated at the altar, and with the singing of the "Te Deum Laudamus," the services ended. The military ceremonies then followed and consisted in unfurling the royal standard and formally taking possession of the country in the name of the king of Spain.

Temporary shelter was next prepared and the work of erecting permanent buildings begun. The church, naturally, was considered of principal importance and received the greatest attention. It usually occupied a commanding positon. Then came the buildings for the padres, soldiers and Indian neophytes. Whatever material was conveniently at hand was used for the buildings, consequently some were of stone and others of sun-baked brick or adobe. They were built around a hollow square, inclosing the court-yard, into which all the buildings opened. (New buildings were added from time to time as work-shops for the different trades established at the missions.

The missions were conducted on the patriarchal plan. The inmates lived as one large family, their interests general and identical. Separation of the sexes was rigidly enforced from the beginning. A "majordomo," usually a soldier, was appointed to take charge of the men. The women occupied a portion of the building called the "monjerio" and were carefully watched over by "la maestra," the wife of a soldier, or some old Indian woman, who guarded her charges with the utmost vigilance. After arriving at a proper age they were permitted to marry. The padres endeavored to teach the Indians of both sexes the sanctity of the marriage relation, and to thus lay the foundation of the family among them. After marriage provision was made for them outside of the mission buildings, and villages of natives governing themselves soon became a part of the mission system.

While in the missions the Indians were taught the various domestic arts. The men learned trades and to plant and harvest crops of grain and vegetables. As vaqueros they have never been excelled. The women were taught to weave, sew and spin. The Indians had some natural skill at dyeing and were taught to weave blankets from native wool, on looms set up at the missions. So skilled did they become in this art that the missions furnished all the blankets used in the country after 1797. Hemp was also raised and used.

Mission life was one of industry. At day-break the whole place was awake and preparing for labor. After attending mass, the first meal of the day was served. This usually consisted of "atole," or ground barley, a staple article of food at the missions. The noonday meal consisted of atole accompanied with mutton in some form and an occasional addition of frijoles. At five o'clock the evening meal was served. The Indians were always allowed to bring to their tables nuts and wild berries. At sunset the Angelus called to prayers and benediction, after which all retired to their respective quarters. The working hours at the missions were from four to six hours for a day's labor. Not more than half the Indians were employed at the same time.

The mission Indian was naturally docile and submissive. After a few years of training at the mission, the unclothed, degraded savage, living a life of sloth and immorality was transformed into an industrious Christian with fair ideas of religion and morality .

CHAPTER VII.
FOUNDING OF THE MISSION SAN GABRIEL ARCANGEL.

San Gabriel was the fourth mission to be built in Alta-California—the others, San Diego, Monterey and San Antonio. This mission was founded on the 8th of September, 1771. It is still in a very good state of preservation. It is one of the oldest of the mission buildings now existing. In material prosperity it was second only to San Luis Rey mission.

Many romantic tales are told of the mission of San Gabriel—most of them having little or no foundation in fact, and therefore without historical value.

On the 6th of August, 1771, Fathers Pedro Cambon and Angel Somera, with an escort of ten soldiers, left San Diego for the purpose of founding a mission to be dedicated to San Gabriel Arcangel. After traveling forty leagues and making several explorations they selected a place about ten miles east of where the city of Los Angeles was afterwards built. The Indians in the vicinity were inclined to resent the coming of the Spaniards and made some warlike demonstrations; whereupon one of the padres unfurling a banner bearing a representation of the Blessed Virgin, held it up before the natives. Upon beholding this picture, the Indians fell upon their knees, laid down their weapons and brought gifts of beads and shells which they laid before the banner in token of submission.

After the customary ceremonies of the raising of the cross, work was commenced on the temporary buildings. The natives seemed anxious to take part in the work and rendered material assistance to the soldiers in preparing shelter. The location of the mission however, did not prove satisfactory, and a new

site was selected, about one mile from the original location,
After making arrangements with the natives occupying the
place, the mission was removed to the site it now occupies.

The material progress of the mission of San Gabriel was
assured from the beginning, and after the first few years, the
spiritual progress was equally marked.   From 1771 to 1831,
the mission records show the baptism of 7,709 persons; 5,494
burials, and 1,877 marriages.   In 1817 the mission had a population of 1701 souls.

Important industries were established in this mission to
teach the Indians useful trades.   A shoe-shop, soap factory,
and carpenter shop gave constant employment to the natives
while others operated a saw-mill and a grist-mill.   The remains of the latter building, "el Molino," are still visible
There was an extensive vineyard planted, and the San Gabriel
wines and brandies were famous throughout the territory.
Vast herds of cattle and horses roamed the plains, and a tan-
nery converted the hides into leather from which was made
shoes, saddles and other articles, besides exporting large quantities of tallow and many hides.   A most wonderful cactus
hedge was planted by Father Jose Maria Zalvidea in 1809, a
portion of which still remains and excites the wonder of the
tourist visiting the mission.

The mission is an imposing structure.   In dimensions it is
about 138 feet in length and 30 feet in height.   The walls
and foundation of masonry, are five feet thick and as firm as
solid rock. The interior has been somewhat changed from the
original by enlarging the windows and replacing the arched
roof with timbers heavy enough to assist in preserving the
building and rendering it secure from possible damage through
earthquake, from which it once suffered severely.

Many articles of interest still remain in this mission. The
ancient pictures of the Apostles and saints have been restored
and are now in an excellent state of preservation.   A very
ancient baptismal font brought from Spain still serves the

needs of the present generation, while censers and other vessels of copper of the same age claim the attention of the visitor to the historic place.

One of the most familiar of the pictured mission representations is the belfry of San Gabriel. It was originally intended for six bells, though but four remain. Two of these bells are much older than the others; one dedicated to the Blessed Virgin is without date; another bears date of 1828; that of a third, "A. D., '95," and the other 1830.

San Gabriel Mission.

CHAPTER VIII.

THE FIRST CHRISTIAN SETTLEMENT IN THE VALLEY-POLITANA.

The missionaries not only contemplated the conversion and civilization of the Indians in the immediate vicinity of the missions, but aimed to reach out into the surrounding country and enlarge the radius of work until the whole territory came within the boundaries of some one or other of the missions.

As soon as a mission was established, expeditions were sent out into the adjoining territory to make surveys and to ascertain the names of the different tribes, or rancherias, and the number of Indians inhabiting that section of the country. As rapidly thereafter as possible the padres founded "asistencias," or branch chapels, at locations not too far distant from the mission, making them dependencies of the different missions. Los Angeles, Puente, San Antonio de Santa Ana and San Bernardino all came within the jurisdiction of San Gabriel mission.

The history of San Bernardino Valley begins with the coming of the missionary priests into the valley.

In 1774, Juan Batista de Anza, Captain of the Presidio of Tubac, was directed by the viceroy to open a road between Sonora in Mexico and Monterey in California. He came from the Colorado River to San Gabriel across the desert from southeast to northwest, by a route practically the same as that afterwards followed by the Southern Pacific Railway—by the way of Yuma, San Gorgonio Pass and through San Bernardino Valley.

The Anza expedition was an extensive outfit—240 persons, men, women and Indians, and 1050 beasts. They entered the valley on the 15th of March. Tney gave to San Gorgonia Pass and San Timeto Canon the name Puerto de San Carlos or St. Charles Pass. San Bernardino valley was called valle de San Joseph, and Cucuamunga, Arroyo de los Osos or Bear Gulch.

San Gabriel mission became an important stopping place on the road, and the first place where supplies could be pro_ cured after crossing the desert. In the course of time, as travel over this road increased, it was arranged to establish a supply station at some intermediate point between the mission and the Sierras on the north, in order to lessen the hardship of this journey by providing travelers with a place where they could rest and obtain food.

With this object in view, a party of missionaries, soldiers and Indian neophytes of San Gabriel mission, under the leadership of Padre Dumetz, were sent out to select a location. On the 20th of May, 1810, they came into the San Bernardino Valley. This, according to the Roman Calendar of Saints, was the feast day of San Bernardino of Sienna and they named the valley in his honor.

They found here an ideal location. The valley was well watered and luxuriant with spring-time verdure. It might become to the weary traveler a perfect haven of rest. The Indian name of the valley, Guachama, when translated, signified "a place of plenty to eat." The Indians inhabiting this section of the valley were known as Guachama Indians and had here a populous rancheria. A number of other rancherias were scattered throughout the valley, each bearing a name sig_ nificant of the place where it was situated. Many of the names were retained by settlers of a later day and applied to ranchos granted by the government. These Indian names make a very interesting study. Those near San Bernardino Valley, are as follows:

San Bernardino—Guachama—A place of plenty to eat.

Cucamonga—Cucamungabit—Sand place.

Riverside—Jurumpa—Water place.

San Timoteo (Redlands)—Tolocabit—Place of the big head.

Homoa—Homhoabit—Hilly place.

Yucaipa—Yucaipa—Wet lands.

Muscupiabe—Muscupiabit—Pinon place.

The supply station was located at the Guachama rancheria, which was near the place now known as Bunker Hill, between Urbita Springs and Colton. The location was chosen on account of an abundance of water in that vicinity. Here a "capilla" was built, which was dedicated to San Bernardino, the patron saint of the valley. After completing the building of the station the padres returned to San Gabriel leaving the chapel, station and a large quantity of supplies in charge of neophyte soldiers, under command of a trustworthy Indian named Hipolito. The settlement, or rancheria of mission Indians, taking its name from this chief became known as Politana.

During the next two years the padres made frequent visits to the capilla; the Guachama Indians were friendly; grain was planted and the settlement seemed in a fair way to permanent prosperity.

The year 1812, known in history as "el ano de los temblores," (the year of earthquakes), found the valley peaceful and prosperous—it closed upon the ruins of Politana. The presence of the padres and Christian neophytes among the gentile Indians of the valley had been productive of good re_sults and many of them became converted to Christianity. When the strange rumblings beneath the earth commenced and frequent shocks of earthquake were felt, the effect was to rouse the superstitious fears of the Indians. The hot springs of the valley increased in temperature to an alarming ex-

tent; a new "cienegata" or hot mud spring, appeared near
Politana, (now called Urbita.)   This so excited the Indians
that by direction of the padres the spring was covered with
earth, hoping to thus allay their fears.   These hot springs
were regarded by the Indians with superstitious veneration.
They were associated with their religious ceremonies and
were known to them as medicine springs. When these changes
became so apparent they were filled with   apprehension of
danger bordering on terror.   This, accompanied by the frequent shocks of "temblor," so worked upon their superstitious
natures that, looking for a cause, they came to believe it was
the manifestation of anger of some powerful spirit displeased
at the presence of the Christians among them.   Desiring to
appease this malevolent deity and avert further expression of
his displeasure, they fell upon the settlement of Politana,
massacred most of the mission Indians and converts and destroyed the buildings.

The Guachamas rebuilt the rancheria and inhabited it
until long after the decree of secularization.   A few Indians
remained there at date of American colonization, and older
settlers of the country retain a recollection of the rancheria
of Politana.   As the country settled the Indians decreased
in numbers and dispersed; the few miserable habitations fell
into decay, and there is now no trace of the rancheria, except as the plow of the rancher may occasionally bring to
the surface a piece of tile, sole relic of the first Christian settlement in San Bernardino Valley.

Very few descendants of the early Guachama Indians remain.   Here and there may be found one understanding the
language and somewhat familiar with the history of the tribe.
The Indians now living in the valley are principally of the
Cahuillas—originally belonging to San Luis Rey mission—
and of the Serranos, or mountain tribes.   These Indians have
intermarried and the language spoken is a mixture of dialects.

The burial place of the Christian Indians of San Bernardino Valley was at Politana. Until brought under the influence of the missionaries they cremated their dead, burning not only the body but all of the belongings of the deceased.   The padres taught them the rites of Christian burial.   This cemetery was to them a sacred spot, a place of veneration.   It was used by the Indians of the whole valley until comparatively recent years.   The place where it was situated is now on the left side of the new electric railway as it turns north from Colton on Mt. Vernon Avenue, but no trace of this cemetery remains.   As settlers came into the valley their greed for possession of land did not spare the Indian burial place; the graves were leveled and the land placed under cultivation.   A thriving orange grove now blossoms and bears its treasure of golden fruit over the crumbling bones of a dead and forgotten generation.   But they sleep none the less peacefully, even through the land where their forefathers roamed free and untramelled, and of which they were the sole and original owners, denies them a place of undisturbed sepulchre.   Los muertos con la corrupcion de sus cuerpos alimentan ahora los arboles que dan fruto para los vivos; solo su espiritu se halla elevado sobre la materia y goza de la immortalidad.   "Quia Dominus dedit eis lumen ut viderent eum."

THE PATRON SAINT OF THE VALLEY.
CHAPTER IX.

From the earliest dawn of civilization men and women who have devoted their lives to the betterment of humanity have been awarded the respect and gratitude of the whole world. The pages of history are filled with names of men who have been potent factors in the advancement of the world through the different branches of learning, of arts and of science. These names are immortalized because the men who bore them bequeathed something of worth to the race, something which left imprint upon the history of the world. Their words and deeds are imperishable and will endure as long as the human race endures. Who studies philosophy and forgets the names of Cicero, Seneca, Socrates and Plato? Who reads of war and conquest and sees not the names of Hannibal, Alexander, Caesar, Napoleon, Washington and Bolivar? Who studies the masterpieces of poetry and fails to find Homer, Anacreon, Virgil, Dante, Milton? Who opens the pages of the history of early Christianity and reads not of St. Augustine, St. Anselm, St. Thomas and Santa Teresa, and other zealous workers, who constituted the bulwark of the Christian religion.

It is the custom of the Roman Catholic church, from early times, to canonize those men and women, who, through sublime acts of faith, devotion and self-sacrifice, performed valuable and heroic service for the cause of Christianity. It is not for the commendation of the world. It is a recognition of the worth and work of the noble sons and daughters of the church who, having passed to their eternal reward, need not the praise of the multitude; but the church, desiring to perpetuate the memory of their deeds, inscribes their names upon her calendar of saints that they may be kept before the world as examples worthy of emulation and remembrance.

San Bernardino was born at Sienna, Italy, on the 20th of May, 1382. It was a time of severe affliction. Bigotry and infidelity had corrupted the minds of men; and blasphemy was carried even to the extent of denying the divinity of Jesus Christ, the Saviour of mankind. France, Spain, Italy and other countries suffered from persecution directed against the church. Sacred buildings were desecrated and destroyed; political factions were arrayed against each other in bitterest dissension, and the whole of Europe on the verge of warfare.

When San Bernardino arrived at manhood he warmly espoused the cause of the church and dedicated his life to the service of Christianity. He was a man of superior intellectual ability, a powerful speaker and a logical and forceful writer of theological works. His sermons, still preserved, are considered among the treasures of church literature. Gifted with the power of eloquence, like St. Paul, he went from town to town throughout the land preaching in the name of the Lord Jesus. He was instrumental in overcoming the spirit of blasphemy and in bringing peace to the church. Three times he was offered a bishop's mitre as a reward for his services, but, deeming it better to serve the cause through evangelical labors, he declined all honors that he might continue his efforts without the responsibilities attached to so high an office. San Bernardino died at the city of Aquila in 1448, at the age of sixty-six years, and his name was afterwards placed on the calendar of the Roman Catholic church as a Saint of God.

It is not to be marveled at that the padres coming into this beautiful valley in the month of May—when Nature, reveling in luxuriance of vegetation had clothed the foothills and plain with gorgeous vegetation and bloom—should rejoice and find pleasure in bestowing upon the earthly paradise the name of San Bernardino.   It is small wonder if they saw in the smiling heavens the beautiful azure skies of Italy; or if the balmy air reminded them of the caressing breezes of the sunny land across distant seas. And so the name San Bernardino of Sienna has a peculiar fitness to the place and remains as a happy inspiration of the padres—the first white men to set foot within the beautiful valley.

CHAPTER X.
THE INDIANS.

Writers of early California history generally characterize the type of Indian inhabiting the country at the coming of the Spaniards as stupid, brutish and utterly lacking in intelligence. Father Venegas, one of the earliest writers, says of them: "Even in the least frequented corners of the globe there is not a nation so stupid, of such contracted ideas, and weak both in body and mind, as the unhappy Californians. Their characteristics are stupidity and insensibility, want of knowledge and reflection, inconstancy, impetuosity, and blindness to appetite; an excessive sloth and abhorrence of fatigue of every kind, however trifling; in fine, a most wretched want of everything which constitutes the real man and renders him rational, inventive, tractable, and useful to himself and society."

Notwithstanding all this, the fifty years following the advent of the missionaries demonstrated the fact that these Indians were capable of civilization. Under the tutelage of the padres they developed wonderfully. Without the help of the Indians the material progress of the missions would have been impossible. The padres were the directing minds; but the unskilled hands of the Indians built the mission structures, the ruins of which are still the wonder and admiration of all who visit them. With their help, vast tracts of land were brought under cultivation; they constructed a system of irrigation; planted orchards and vineyards; manufactured many articles of domestic use, and accomplished much that would have been considered extremely difficult among races farther advanced in civilization.

But it cannot be denied that the native Indians were low in the scale of humanity. They were wholly unlike the Eastern Indians. They lacked the social organization of the Pueblos. There were no powerful tribes among them, as the Sioux of the north and the Apache of the southwest. Their settlements, or rancherias, were independent of each other. Each rancheria had a name of its own, and a different language was spoken, the inhabitants of one rancheria many times being unable to understand the language of another.

The Indians of San Bernardino Valley differed in no respect from those of other portions of California. The early missionaries found in the valley six Indian rancherias. After the Indians had become converted to Christianity, and the padres were able to estimate their numbers, they found each rancheria contained from two to three hundred people. This estimate would show about fifteen hundred people inhabiting San Bernardino Valley.

Their dwellings were circular in form. They were built from poles stuck in the earth and bending over at the top to form the roof. This was covered with brush, tules and mud, leaving at the top an aperture to allow the smoke to escape. They were similar in construction and appearance to the Navajo "tehogane" of the present day.

The early Indians did not cultivate the soil. They subsisted upon wild roots, herbs, nuts, field mice, worms, lizards, grasshoppers and other insects, birds, fish, geese, ducks and small game. The flesh foods were consumed raw or only slightly cooked. They were very fond of acorns, which, during their season, were gathered in large quantities. These were often prepared by grinding in mortars or on stone slabs similar to the Mexican "metate." They were sometimes placed in woven baskets of reeds, and boiled in water heated with hot stones, then kneaded into a dough and baked on hot stones in front of a fire. A small, round seed, called "chia," was also used. This was prepared by drying and making into a flour called "atole." Their subsistence was often very precarious and their habits somewhat migratory, going from place to place in search of their food supply, which varied with the season of the year.

In personal appearance the California Indians were not prepossessing. There was little physical beauty among them. They were undersized, broad-nosed, with high cheek bones, wide mouths and coarse black hair. Their personal habits were uncleanly. Their clothing extremely scanty; that of the men "in naturalibus," but the women partially covered themselves with skirts of woven grass reaching from the waist to the knees. They were fond of ornaments of various kinds and decorated their faces and bodies with paint, often in a most grotesque manner.

Upon the coming of the Americans they were classed without distinction under the term "Diggers."

CHAPTER XI.
THE RELIGIOUS BELIEF OF THE INDIANS.

In studying the history of a people the point first taken into consideration is their religion.   By that standard the intellectual development of the race, nation or tribe is measured and determined.   This will apply to the higher forms of civilization as well as to the lowest   fetish   worshipers. With the first light of intelligence the savage, conscious of the unknown which surrounds him, builds a shrine to some vaguely comprehended power which he personifies in his imagination and clothes with attributes which seem to him superior.   This he calls his God.   His mind can comprehend nothing better or more powerful than this deity.   It is the summit of his intellectual capacity.

The Indians of San Bernardino Valley had a crude form of religious belief.   It was similar to that of other native tribes of Southern California.   Their beliefs differed somewhat according to locality. They were never thoroughly un derstood.   The   Padres   were   so   zealously   engaged in teaching the natives the Christian religion that they gave practically little attention to beliefs previously existing among them; and as the Indians had neither writings, pictured representations or records of any description, the origin and growth of their religious ideas is lost in obscurity.

This much, however, is known: The early Indians were not idolators.   Their religion might properly be termed a form of Manicheism.   They worshiped both the good and the evil principle.   The latter, typified by the coyote, was evidently considered the more powerful, as their dances and religious ceremonies were generally propitiatory and usually in honor of the evil one, the object being to placate him and avert the consequences of his displeasure.

According to the belief of the Indians of San Bernardino Valley, the god Mutcat created the earth, the sea and all the animals, birds, fishes, trees, and lastly man. Then, desiring to view the work of his hands, he descended from his heavenly abode of Tucupac, to visit Ojor, the earthly creation. Wishing to express his satisfaction and still further beautify the earth he gave to man the various seeds, plants and flowers. Knowing that in employment man finds happiness, he taught them to build their houses and the many arts whereby they might pass their time in contentment and usefuiness.

For a period of time all was peace and serenity. Men lived together in brotherly love and harmony and no discord came among them in their relations with one another. The earth yielded fruit in abundance to supply all their needs, and no want of man was unsatisfied. Earth was itself a paradise inferior only to the abode of the god Mutcat, and death had never entered to bring sorrow and separation to mankind.

Unfortunately the peace was broken. Isel, the evil god, became envious of the happiness of men and set about devising means to accomplish their downfall and destruction. He caused death to come into the world, brought famine and pestilence and sowed the seed of discord among men. But as Isel was moved solely by envy, it was believed his anger could be appeased and favor obtained through gifts of food, chanting, dances and feasts in his honor.

On the other hand, Mutcat, the spirit of good, was ever solicitous for the welfare of his earthly children. Observing the faithfulness of men, and their affliction, he directed them to increase their number, and promised that, though they must first die, after death they should be admitted into his paradise of Tucupac where the dominion of the wicked Isel would cease and he could not follow and could no longer work their harm.

This was the foundation of the Indian religious belief. The whole fabric was woven around these incidents.

Each tribe had its sorcerers or medicine men. They were the guardians of the traditions of the tribe, directed all ceremonies and were regarded with superstitious awe on account of the mysterious supernatural powers that they claimed to possess. Every rancheria had a place for religious ceremonies where incantations and secret rites were performed. The sorcerers were more powerful than the chiefs, who yielded obedience to them. They claimed to cure disease, bring rain. ward off misfortune and were called upon to decide all matters of importance pertaining to the tribe or rancheria.

The missionaries experienced the greatest difficulty in overcoming the evil influence of the sorcerers. They were usually vicious men steeped in vileness, wickedness and duplicity. They naturally resented the interference of the padres and exerted all their influence to keep the Indians under their own control. Thus, the teaching of Christianity while working great moral good to the Indians, could not immediately overcome and eradicate this superstitious fear of the medicine man. Their influence was everywhere apparent and came to be dreaded by the Indians as well as disliked by the padres. In hidden recesses of the mountains. far away from the missions, the padres often discovered shrines erected for the worship of the coyote, and evidence of their continued use. The poor, weak nature of the Indian, while honestly embracing the new belief, could not rise above a feeling of timidity, and this prompted him to secretly steal away with some propitiary gift to the evil deity whose vengeance he still feared. Though in time Christianity predominated among them and most of the old rites passed away and were forgotten, the Indian was never completely free from superstition. Even to this day, whoever can gain the confidence of the Indian sufficiently to study his characteristics and learn his true nature, finds—in spite of Christianizing influences and the years of contact with civilization—there still remains curiously intermixed with their modern religious belief some of the ancient superstitions of their savage ancestors of generations long past.   Et sic quia quod non venit ex natura "turarura."

CHAPTER XII.

THE PRIMITIVE INDIAN LANGUAGE OF SAN BERNAR-
DINO VALLEY.

The grammatical construction and peculiarities of the
Indian language, as preserved by the padres, cannot fail to
be interesting to students of philology. The Smithsonian Institute has attempted to gather up, classify and preserve these
early records, but the work is one of Herculean proportions.

Father Lasuen, successor to Father Junipero Sierra as
missionary President, states in a letter that there were no
less than seventeen different languages spoken by the natives
between San Diego and San Francisco. This does not take
into account the various dialects. Every rancheria had an
idiomatic language of its own, which was frequently unintelli-
gible to the neighboring rancherias, perhaps separated only
by a few miles. These dialects could hardly be dignified by
the name of language.

One of the first tasks of the missionaries was to familiarize themselves with the native language and to teach to the
Indians the Spanish language. Until this was accomplished
the work of Christianizing them could not begin. The var-
iance in the language of the Indians added in no small degree
to the difficulties encountered, and to overcome them required
minds schooled to the mastery of patience, with an abiding
faith that the end, however remote, would fully justify the day
of small beginnings. This was the spirit that animated the
padres and gave such marvelous success to their enterprise.

For example, three distinctly separate languages were

spoken in the neighborhood of San Gabriel Mission. The Qulchi language was spoken by the Indians of Los Angeles, San Gabriel and as far east as Cucamonga. Another language was spoken all along the Santa Ana River and in Orange County, while the language of the Guachama was spoken by the Serrano tribes, among whom were the San Bernardino Indians.

The Guachama language was gutteral and principally mon-osyllabic. The orthography, recorded by the padres, is, of course, phonetic. In analogy the nouns formed plural by pre-fixing the word "nitchel." The conjugation of the Guachama verbs is exactly the same as in other Indian languages of Southern California. Pronouns, and the different tenses of the verb are also expressed by prefixes.

The system of numeration, like other mission Indian lan-guages, counts only to five. The number with the prefix one (con) is repeaed to express six, seven, etc.

Vocabulary of the Guachama, the language of the tribe of Indians located in the San Bernardino Valley:

NOUNS.

Man—nejanis.
Father—jana.
Daughter—pullen.
Brother—iua.
Enemy—panajanucan.
Eyes—japus.
Hand—jamma.
Sun—tamit.
Mountain—temas.
Tree—paus.
Fire—cut.
Night—tuporit.
Bow—yujal.
Rabbit—tabut.
Name—esen.

Woman—nitchul.
Son—mailloa.
Sister—nau.
Friend—niquiliuj.
Head—toloea.
Mouth—tama.
Foot—jai.
Moon—mannuil.
River—uanish.
Water—pal.
Stone—cauix.
House—jaqui.
Arrow—penyugal. „
Cold—yuima.

ADJECTIVES.

Good—utcha.
Small—cum.

Bad—elecuix.
Large—lul.

NUMERALS.

One—supli.

Three—pa.

Five—namacuana.

Seven—conuil.

Nine—conuitchu.

Two—uil.

Four—uitchu.

Six—consupli.

Eight—conpa.

Ten—namachuma.

PRONOUNS.

I—nehe.

He—pe.

You—eheh.

Thou—eh.

We—chem.

They—pehem.

VERBS.

To eat—gua.

To cook—culcu.

To walk—nacaix.

To wish—nacocan.

To rain—nenix.

To fight—nucan.

To cure—tinaich.

To be—yanash.

To drink—paca.

To sleep—culca.

To wash—paixjanx.

To have—nauca.

To be sick—mucal.

To paint—piecuaquis.

To give—anaixgam.

ADVERBS.

Nearer—sunchi.

Tomorrow—paix.

Not—quihi.

Plenty—chama.

Today—iach.

Yesterday—tacu.

Many—meta.

PRESENT.

Example of conjugation: Tculcu (to cook).

I cook—neheculcu.

He cooks—peculcu.

We cook—chemculcu.

They cook—pempemculcu.

Conjugation of the verb

Thou cookest or you cook—ehculcu.

You cook—ehehculcu.

PAST.

I cooked—tocu neheculcu. cooked—tocu ehculcu.

He cooked—tocu peculcu.

You cooked—tocu ehehculcu. 'ulcu.

Thou cookest, or you

We cooked—tocu chemculcu.

They cooked—tocu pempemc

FUTURE.

I shall cook—paix neheculcu.   Thou wilt cook, or you will cook— paix ehculcu.

He will cook—paix peculcu.   You will cook—paix ehehculcu. They will cook—paix pempemculcu.   We will cook—paix chemculcu.

The Lord's Prayer in the Guachama language is used as a specimen of the work performed by the padres.   Having no word in Indian to express God, the Spanish Dios is used.   The same applies to the word pan (bread).   The staple article of food among the Indians was acorns.   Not wishing to ask for acorns the Spanish word is substituted to give the idea of the article asked for.

THE LORD'S PRAYER IN INDIAN.

Dios Janna penyanash Tucupac santificado ut cha et en pennacash toco jahi cocan najanis Tubuc aix.

Guacha pan meta tamepic penaixjan chemyanaix ut cha panajanucan quihi elecui suyu Amen.

C. F.

CHAPTER XIII.

THE SOCIAL AND DOMESTIC CONDITION OF THE EARLY INDIANS OF SAN BERNARDINO VALLEY.

After the coming of the padres the tribes of Indians all over California were given Spanish names; these names generally applying to the part of the country which they inhabited. The Guachama and other Indians living in San Bernardino Valley, became known as Serrano Indians, the name Serrano signifying of the mountains. The Indians known as the Cahuillas came into the valley at a later date, having originally belonged to the country around San Luis Rey Mission. Other tribes contiguous to the valley were the Piutes, Chimehuevas, Mohave and Yumas; the first frequenting the desert north of the Sierras, and the other tribes inhabiting the desert and country all along the Colorado River. The Yuma and Mohave Indians are of a race superior in many ways to the California Indians. They are more intelligent and more warlike, and were ever a menace to the peace of the valley and in their frequent raids a constant source of disturbance to the natives of the valley.

The Indians of California were not united either socially or politically. Their rancherias were independent of each other, they spoke different idioms, though often related, and sometimes banding together for the purpose of making a raid on or defending themselves against some other tribe. They were sometimes friendly, sometimes hostile to each other, but could never be relied upon.

The Indians were not endowed with personal courage.

They were cowardly in battle, and consequently a few soldados
de cuera were able to control a large community and could
easily bring them into subjection in case of an uprising. Their
weapons were bows and arrows, spears and a rude kind of stone
knife.   This further placed them at   a disadvantage in attempting to cope with the white men.

Each community was governed by a chief, called by the
Spaniards, "el capitan."   The office of chief was usually hereditary.   The chief was generally respected and his commands obeyed without question.   When war against a neighboring rancheria was contemplated the tribe, and their allies,
if there was combination, gathered together, when the chiefs
would state the grievance, and after certain ceremonies and
incantations the matter would be decided according as the
sorcerers found in favor or otherwise.   In battle there was
no concerted action.   Each chief assumed leadership of his
own band and fought or ran away as the impulse moved him

The Indians soon learned their independent rights according to the ideas of the white men.   Several instances are related where the Indians demanded certain things of the government and the justice of their demands conceded, by their
requests being granted.

The marriage customs of the Indians were similar to that
of uncivilized people all over the world—that is to say, they
had no ceremony of marriage, though marriage was recognized. Sometimes, if the parties were of sufficient importance,
a feast was prepared.   In all cases the daughter was subject
to the command of the father and was usually bought and sold
without regard to her own preferences or desire.   The price
paid varied according to the desirability of the girl and the
ability of the purchaser to pay.   There were occasions when
marriage by capture was resorted to.   This was   when   the
woman belonged to some other tribe, or when obstacles were
in the way to other possession.

The birth of the first child was made occasion for rejoicing.   Sterility was deplored as a great misfortune.   The maternal instinct was very strong in the Indian mother and the children were invariably treated with much affection.   The infant was carried in a rude basket "cuna" strapped upon the back of the mother, and thus encumbered she attended to the usual labor of gathering and preparing food for the family. The life of the Indian woman was one of toil and privation, and she received little consideration at the hands of her savage lord.   The men were notoriously idle and lazy, their only occupation that of hunting small game and fishing.   Their food supply of acorns, when gathered, was prepared by crushing in stone mortars, or on flat stones, after the manner now in vogue among the Mexicans.   This converted the nuts into a meal from which was made "atole."   It was sometimes prepared by boiling in water heated with hot stones. The women were expert in the making of cunningly woven baskets. These were of different shapes and were used for all domestic purposes.

Polygamy was common among many of the tribes, but there were exceptions to the practice. Adultery was sometimes punished, but gross immoralties and vices were prevalent among them and their moral condition was unaccountably degraded.

These marriage ties were not considered binding and separation or divorce was easily obtained by consent of parties interested.

This, in brief, covers the social and domestic condition of the Indians of San Bernardino Valley, and of California. Morally, intellectually and physically they were the inferiors of any race of natives on the North American continent.   That the missionaries accomplished their work with these Indians and brought them to a degree of civilization is little less than marvelous.

CHAPTER XIV.
INDIAN CEREMONIES AND SUPERSTITIONS.

The subject of Indian ceremonies and superstitions, when approached in a spirit of honest investigation and not of mere curiosity, is one of great interest.

No race or people can be declared entirely free from superstitious beliefs, and a very little inquiry will show that superstitious beliefs are not so exclusively confined to the ignorant as many suppose. If verification of this statement is needed it can be readily found in any community, and the seeker will further discover that superstitious beliefs are surprisingly prevalent among educated men and women. The spirit which moves the untutored savage to seek the sorcerer, prompts members of the higher civilized race to invest in "charms," "fortune-telling" and divination of various kinds, while "signs" and omens innumerable are observed to the ultimate of "reductio ad absurdum." In view of these facts it is not becoming to treat the subject of Indian ceremonials and superstitions with contempt.

Whatever may be said of Indian dances it is certain that the Indians never did, and do not, indulge in their dances for the mere pleasure of dancing. Their dances always signify something, though the meaning is often too obscure and difficult for white men to determine. Survivals of ancient ceremonial dances are still common among certain tribes of semi-civilized Indians. In some instances the government has attempted to suppress the dances, but with indifferent results. The so-called ghost-dance of the Northern Indians is looked upon by white men as premonitory of approaching trouble, and as indicating a state of unrest and dissatisfaction among the Indians. The Indian tribes living along the Columbia River indulge in a wierd kind of dance with the idea of propitiating the spirit believed by them to rule the winter. This dance is called the Chinook-dance and is exceedingly barbarous and revolting on account of self-inflicted torture. The Moki Indians of the Arizona desert have several interesting tribal dances. Their periodical Snake dance has received much attention and is a religious ceremonial which the Moki Indians firmly believe produces rain. In early times the Indians of Northern California indulged in a very grotesque dance called the Dance of Death, which has been graphically described by the missionaries.

The time set for ceremonial dances and feasts was always fixed by the sorcerers, in whom the Indians placed the most implicit confidence. Seldom an undertaking of any kind was entered into without first invoking the aid of supernatural powers, and this was always done by feasting and dancing. The ceremonies often lasted a number of days and nights. Those taking part in the dances made elaborate preparations by decorating their bodies with different colored paints and donning ceremonial costumes. In some tribes the women and men danced together, in others only the men danced, while the women would form a circle outside by themselves. Some of the old men and women of the tribe, seating themselves in a circle accompanied the dancers with a peculiar chant, others at the same time, playing on bone flutes and beating rude drums. The dancing was often indulged in to the point of extreme exhaustion, the dancer falling to the ground insensible.

Among the principal dances of the Indians of San Bernardino Valley were those known as the Hawk-Feast, the Dance of Peace, the Dance of Plenty, the Dance of Victory, and the Dance of Deprecation. Another of their peculiar ceremonial dances was designated by the padres as "tatamar ninas" or "roasting young girls." This custom filled the padres with great horror and they made every effort to induce the Indians to abandon the practice. The ceremony of "tatema" took place upon the first evidence of maturity. A hole was dug in the ground and filled with stones previously heated in the fire until very hot. Over this was spread a covering of leaves and branches and the girl laid upon it and then nearly covered with heated earth. The result was a profuse perspiration which was kept up for twenty-four hours and sometimes longer. At intervals the girl was taken out, bathed and again imbedded in the earth. During the whole time constant dancing and chanting was kept up by young girls, attended by hideously painted old women who had charge of the ceremonies. At the close, a great feast was prepared in which all joined and which lasted several days and nights. The girl was then considered ready for marriage, which usually took place soon after.

The Dance of Deprecation took place when a member of the tribe fell sick with some unusual disease. The disease was always attributed to the influence of an evil spirit. The whole tribe would assemble each person bringing a food offering, and all the gifts were placed in a large basket. The dancing would then begin. Significant words were chanted by the women, children and old men, while the younger men kept up the dance in the ordinary way beating time with arrows. After awhile the sorcerer would arise and present the offering to the supposed offended spirit. In making the offering he moved from left to right, and then in a circle, all the time mumbling mysterious words. During the time the sorcerer was engaged the people observed complete silence. At the close of the ceremony the dance broke up. The offerings would be cooked and left until the following day. This act was believed to appease the evil spirit whose baneful influence would then be removed and the sick person allowed to recover in the usual way.

The Indians looked upon their medicine men as beings endowed with superior knowledge and skill in the art of healing. The medicine men practiced their art through mystical incantations and also used various herbs, balsams and healing leaves, to effect their cures.   When a person was taken sick the medicine men were always called.   They approached the patient with an air of solemn mystery, and after diagnosing the case and locating the pain proceeded to work a cure.   The principal point was to first impress the patient, and those around him, with their importance, and in order to do this incantations, passes, contortions and gesticulations were made by the medicine men, after which it would sometimes be announced that the disease was due to some extraneous matter, whereupon one of the medicine men would apply his lips to the affected part and soon produce the alleged cause of the disease.   This cause was usually a stick, stone, thorn, flint or piece of bone.   The patient often experienced immediate relief and a marvelous cure followed.   There is no doubt but some very wonderful cures were effected in this way. Modern materia medica admits the potency of the imagination as a factor in both the cause and cure of diseases.

The Indians of San Bernardino Valley were fully aware of the medicinal properties of the hot springs in the vicinity of the valley.   They regarded these springs with much veneration and believed them to be a cure for many diseases. The springs were also visited frequently by Indians from a distance.

The "temescal" or sweat-house was another mode of curing diseases among the Indians, and it was also used by Indians in good health.   These sweat-houses were built by first excavating the earth to some depths for a foundation, then building above it a hut and covering the exterior with mud until it resembled a huge mound.   A hole was left at the bottom barely sufficient to allow a person to crawl in and out of the hut. Light and air was almost entirely excluded. In the center a great fire would be built, around which the Indians would sit or lie stretched upon the ground. Here they would stay until nearly suffocated and in a profuse perspiration, when they would climb out, make a wild dash to the nearest stream of cold water and plunge into it. In many instances this heroic treatment was very successful, but in some sickness, like small-pox, it was quite likely to prove fatal.

The Indians of San Bernardino Valley burned their dead. Their method of cremating was similar to that employed by the desert Indians of the present day. As soon as death occurred, material was collected and a funeral pyre built. Around this the family of the deceased and members of the rancheria gathered, the body was brought forth and placed on the pile and the fire would be lighted by one of the sorcerers. All clothing, utensils and other articles used by the deceased was burned with the body. Oftentimes the house where the deceased had lived and the domestic animals belonging to him were burned in the same way. The women were especially demonstrative on these occasions, their mournful wails and lamentations, continuing for several days and nights, could be heard a long distance away.

The early Indians did not eat the flesh of large game. This came from a superstitious belief that the bodies of the larger animals contained the souls of departed ancestors. This same superstitious belief was held among the Mission Indians even after they had learned to use some of the larger domestic animals for food, and they could seldom be induced to eat pork. If a wild animal devoured a dead body it was believed the soul of the deceased was then compelled to take up its habitation in the body of the animal. This belief was not that of palingenesis as held by ancient races, but rather an idea arising among themselves without theory or rational reason to give for the belief.

XV.

THE BUILDING OF SAN BERNARDINO BRANCH MISSION

A feeling of tender reverence unconsciously associates it-self with thoughts of the old Missions of California. Imagination rehabilitates the ruined walls and recalls from the vanished past the brown-robed padres—most of them saintly souls —who, offering their lives on the altar of their faith, firmly planted the cross of Christianity in the new land. Again the fertile fields are tilled by dark-skinned natives, and as the vesper bells chime softly the evening call to prayer, they flock to the mission to receive the paternal priestly blessing, then the benediction and to sleep and silence—a silence now long unbroken. The hands that laboriously toiled day by day to upbuild the walls, the hearts that beat high with hopes and aspirations for the future, have long been dust. That which they builded in the fulness of their faith outlasted the hands of the builders, but only to fall at last into decay and ruin; and amidst the desolation again may be read the world-old lesson of the mutability of earthly things; the passing of all human hopes, ambitions, loves and fears.

Something of this same spirit hovers around the ruins of "Old San Benardino Mission." Its place in mission history is unimportant, yet it is a point of especial interest in the history of San Bernardino Valley. It has been occupied in turn by the padres and Mission Indians; Mexican rancheros; Mormons, and then for many years as a homestead by one of the later American families. Its ancient walls, blessed and made sacred for holy use, first heard the chant of the Gloria in Excelsis and the prayers of priest and penitent. It has been baptized in blood and twice crumbled in the flames set by the hands of infuriated savages, and lastly echoed the gleeful voices and the laughter of happy children.

As a habitation it has long been abandoned and used only as a corral for cattle. A portion of the walls are standing, but not sufficient to give any idea of the original building. The ruins are surrounded by beautiful orange groves, watered from the old zanja built by the Indians, under direction of the padres, and which has been used constantly for irrigating purposes from the time it was built to the present. This old zanja was bordered by two rows of cottonwood trees, which, upon the coming of the American colonists, gave to the place the name of "Cottonwood Row," by which it was commonly known for many years.

After the destruction of the mission station and "capilla" at Politana the missionaries withdrew from the valley and several years elapsed before any special effort was made toward resuming missionary work in the valley. In the meantime, the Indians became accustomed to the presence of white men and through the ministrations of the padres a number of them were converted to Christianity at San Gabriel mission.

The Indians of San Bernardino Valley had ever manifested a friendship for the missionaries and gave them very little trouble. On the other hand the Indians of the desert were of a turbulent, warlike nature, constantly making incursion into the valley, killing the peacefully disposed Indians and disturbing the whole country. As the padres were unable from their small garrison of soldiers at San Gabriel to provide protection for the missionaries in outlying districts, they were compelled to await the time when missionaries could be sent among the Indians with some assurance of personal safety. It was due to this reason and not to any neglect on the part of the missionaries that work in San Bernardino Valley was temporarily abandoned at the time of the burning of the station at Politana.

SAN BERNARDINO MISSION

In 1819 the Guachama Indians requested the padres to again establish themselves in the valley. The request was favorably received and immediate steps were taken by the padres to build another and larger branch mission. They selected a location about eight miles from Politana and in 1820 the new chapel and mission buildings were ready for occupancy. Again the chapel was dedicated to San Bernardino of Sienna and the buildings occupied by a priest and several neophytes from San Gabriel. A community of Indians settled around the mission, a zanja was built, land brought under cultivation and grain planted. A vineyard and olive trees were planted, and as the valley furnished excellent grazing grounds for cattle and horses, stock was brought from San Gabriel Under the thrifty management of the padres the mission rancho not only raised sufficient grain for its own use and that of the Indians, but also furnished large quantities to the mother mission. The herds increased rapidly until in 1830 five thousand head of cattle were slaughtered in the valley and their hides taken to San Gabriel to be sold from that mission.

The same system was employed at this branch mission as at the larger establishments. One of the padres from San Gabriel had general supervision. The first mayordomo at Old San Bernardino Mission was Casius Garcia. He carried out the work in detail and looked after the material welfare of the Indians engaged in agricultural labors and as vaqueros on the rancho. The hours of labor were short, the Indians contented, and no serious disturbance occurred until 1831. In that year the old enemies of the valley, the desert Indians, made a raid on the mission. The usual devastation marked their trail. The missionaries were surprised and unable to resist the attack. The buildings were destroyed and the stock scattered and driven away. The padres, accustomed to seeing the work of their hands time and again ruthlessly destroyed and time and again renewing their efforts, immediately set about rebuilding the mission, making it more substantial than before.

The new mission was built on a cobble stone foundation. The walls of adobe were three feet thick. The building, in dimensions, was about 250 feet in length, 125 feet in width and 20 feet in height. A corral extending nearly 100 feet beyond the main building and the full width of the building, the outside wall of which was very near the center of the road now passing the ruin. Another rectangular inclosure was surrounded on three sides by the building itself, and inclosed on the north side by a high wall of adobe, through the center of which a huge gateway was cut. The whole inclosure formed a fort well nigh impregnable to attack of desert Indians. Across the south end of the building a porch was built, the roof of which was supported by posts instead of the usual adobe pillars common to mission architecture. Another porch extended along the outer wall on the north side of the building.

CHAPTER XVI.
SECULARIZATION.

For over two hundred years Mexico was a colony of Spain. The work of civilization and development of the territory was carried on by the mother country until her destiny, under Divine Providence, was fulfilled. In 1821 Mexico revolted and declared her independence. But the cry "Viva la Independencia" had scarcely ceased to echo ere it was followed by "Viva el Emperador," in 1832, and Iturbide set up a monarchy. In 1824 the Mexicans declared a Republic, without even comprehending what the word Republic signified. Then followed a succession of "pronunciamentos," revolutions and restorations, each having its brief day of authority and vanishing to be succeeded by another as ephemeral and unstable. There was a procession of Generals, Dictators and Presidents.

As Mexico suffered from this condition of affairs so did California. The government was considered a prize to be used for personal gain, and the territory of California was called upon to contribute her proportion to the spoils. It was an era of almost general maladministration. A stream cannot rise above its source; a government can be no better than the people. Under Mexican rule, California had thirteen governors of varying degrees of good, bad and indifferent, the latter qualities largely predominating. They began with Pablo Vicente de Sola in 1822 and ended with Pio Pico in 1846.

The Missions of California could not escape the universal spoliation. They were known to be rich, and the fertile imagination of envious and covetous officials added ten-fold to the amount of possession. For years the missions were threatened with despoliment and escaped only because no political party had been bold enough, or in power long enough, to attack the property of the church in California without warrant for their act.

In 1833 Antonio Lopez de Santa Ana proclaimed himself Dictator of Mexico. He was an unscrupulous man, devoid of sentiment or principle. He took pride in styling himself "El Napoleon del Oeste." He knew well the value of the Mission holdings in California and needed no urging to any act tending towards the enrichment of himself or of his followers and favorites. But fearing that the masses were not so wholly deadened to the sense of justice as to permit so unwarranted an outrage as the despoliment of the church without authority of excuse, the Mexican government set about preparing the excuse. The work of the missionaries was discredited; they were accused of enslaving the Indians, keeping them in bondage and maltreating them; and furthermore,—the greatest sin of all—of conspiring against the republic in the interests of Spain.

This was sufficient. On the 17th of August, 1833, a decree of secularization was issued by the Mexican Congress against all mission property in California. This was virtually confiscation. It provided that the management of the missions should be taken from the control of the padres, and mission property placed in charge of "Administradores" selected by the government. It was the beginning of the end of the missionary era in California. The downfall of the missions dates from that day. The magnificent structures, representing years of toil, were doomed; orchards and vineyards fell into decay, the Indian neophytes were turned out to provide for themselves as best they could, and in a few short years the work of despoliation was complete.

This is the darkest page in the history of California. On one side injustice and insatiable greed; on the other side error committed while suffering from a sense of grievious wrongs.

As secularization marked an epoch in the history of California, so it also marked an epoch in the history of San Bernardino Valley. It was the cause of the final abandonment of the branch mission and the distribution of mission lands to individuals, under the Mexican land grant system.

In 1833 San Gabriel Mission embraced within its boundaries a princely domain. The ranchos belonging to the mission were those of San Bernardino, San Gorgonio, Cucamunga, Yucaipa, Jurupa, Rincon, Chino, Azusa, Guapa, San Antonio, San Pasqual, San Francisquito, Santa Anita, Puenta, San Jose, Ybarras, Serranos, Coyotes, Serritos, Rosa Castilla, Las Bolsas, Alamitos, Jaboneria and Mission Viejo.

August 9, 1834, Jose Figuroa, then governor of California, issued an edict putting into effect the decree of secularization. He ordered the immediate release of all Indians under control of the padres at the various missions; and also that ten of the missions should be changed into pueblos for the use of the Indians, the latter order to take effect the year following. Certain lands were set aside for the use of the Indians residing at the missions.

The result of this order was anything but satisfactory. The Indians, removed from all restraining influences, rapidly degenerated to their primitive condition. They refused to work, became dissipated, lawless, and abandoned themselves to all kinds of vices and excesses. Their later condition became immeasurably worse than that from which they were rescued by the padres. Lack of restraint, and contact with the white race, brought to them nothing but absolute degredation, disease and death.

Many of the twenty-one missions eventually became private property. In later years the Supreme Court of the United States declared the transfer of much of the mission property illegal and void and ordered its return to the church; but the ruin had been wrought and passed beyond remedy.   Mientras dure la historia, se recitaran para su eterna verguenza y condenaciou las maldades de los despotas que sacrilegamente arruinaron las monumentales missiones de California; y mientras que los nombres de sus fundadores seran venerados con los immarcibles laureles de la gloria y de la immortalidad.

DISPOSAL OF MISSIONS UNDER MEXICAN GOVERNMENT

San Diego—Sold to Santiago Arguello, June 8, 1846.

Carmelo-Monterey.—Pueblo.

San Antonio.—Abandoned.

San Gabriel—Juan   Bandini, Comisionado   1838-40; sold to Julian Workman and Hugo Ried 1846.

San Luis Obispo—Pueblo.

San Francisco Dolores—Pueblo.

San Juan Capistrano—Pueblo.   A portion sold to McKinley and Foster, 1845.

Santa Clara.—1834-5, Ignacio del Valle, Comisionado appointed to carry out decree of secularization.   The property at this mission was valued   at $47,000, exclusive of church lands.   Of this amount $10,000 was distributed among the Indians of the mission, but where the money went to has ever been a mystery.   In 1839, it is related that the Indians of this mission were absolutely destitute, their condition bordering on starvation.

San Buena Ventura—Sold to Joseph Arnaz.

Santa Barbara—Leased and then sold to Nicholas Den, June 8, 1846.

La Purisima Concepcion.—Sold to John Temple, December 6, 1845.   In 1856 the·U. S. Land Commission restored the buildings to the "inalienable possession of the Catholic church."

Santa Cruz.—Abandoned.

La Soledad.—Sold January, 1846.

San Jose.—Don Jose Jesus Vallejo appointed Comisionado. Whe nhe took charge there were at this mission about 1800

When he took charge there were at this mission about 1,800 Christian Indians.   There were 8,000 head of cattle, 3,000 horses and 10,000 sheep.

San Juan Batista.—Pueblo.

San Miguel.—Disposition of this mission uncertain.

San Fernando.—Leased to Andreas Pico and sold in 1846 by Pio Pico to Eulogio Celis for $14,000.   It is related that this mission was sold to raise funds to prosecute the war with the United States.

San Luis Rey.—Sold to Antoine Cot and Andreas Pico, 1846.

Santa Inez.—Leased to Jose Carillo.

San Rafael.—In charge of a padre.

San Francisco Solano.   In charge of a padre.

CHAPTER XVII.
THE ABANDONMENT OF SAN BERNARDINO MISSION.

The enforcement of the decree of secularization completed the downfall of the mission system. For several year prior to the decree a state of general unrest had prevailed. It was a time of turbulence and excitement. In the nature of things it could scarcely be otherwise. So radical a change could not be made without friction and discord.

Many of the padres left the country; others staid on and contested step by step the infringement on their unquestionable rights. It was a hopeless contest for the padres The missions were doomed and the padres who remained saw with bitterness of spirit, born only of despair, the destruction wrought by the new order; saw the tearing down and obliteration of all they had toiled, hoped and prayed for during so many years.

The process of the destruction of the missions was swift That of San Gabriel Mission is a fair example. It was, at the date of the decree of secularization, one of the wealthiest of the missions. Beside vast landed property it possessed 100,000 head of cattle. In two years they had all disappeared The plains for miles were literally covered with decaying animal bodies and the whole country threatened with pestilence Rage, hate, and vengeance held unrestrained sway throughout the land.

It was the avowed intent of the government to distribute the mission lands among the Indians in an endeavor to make the Indians self-supporting. The plan was a failure from the very beginning. The Indians had been treated as chil-

dren by the padres and as children they must still be cared
for and controlled.   To meet this condition the government,
through its appointed comisionados, attempted to manage the
mission properties.   This plan also proved a dismal and dis-
heartening failure.   The men appointed were so often incapable and corrupt that under their management the mission properties rapidly dwindled away, decreased in value
and soon fell into decay.   The whole system tended only to
individual enrichment.   The condition of the Indians became
wretched in the extreme.   They decreased rapidly in numbers.   They were treated as outcasts, enslaved, beaten, and
starved until in sheer desperation many of them ran away
into the mountains and, banding together in lawlessness, began a series of raids and depredations which kept the country in a state of terror for many years and retarded its settlement and development.

The restlessness of the Indians was a constant source of
trouble to the occupants of San Bernardino Mission.   The
rancho afforded grazing ground for a large number of cattle
and this attracted predatory Indians to the vicinity and frequent raids were made for the purpose of running off the
mission stock.   However, excepting the loss of cattle, no
serious disturbance occurred until October, 1834, when a band
of Piute Indians, coming from the desert into the valley, attacked San Bernardino Mission.   A furious battle was waged
in which a number of Indians were killed, both sides sustaining loss.   At last, when further resistance seemed futile,
it was decided to attempt an escape from the mission and retreat to San Gabriel Mission.   The Indians defending San
Bernardino—under command of a neophyte chief named Per-
fecto—advanced upon the hostile Indians and succeeded in
driving them back from the mission buildings.   The sacred
vessels and vestments used in church ceremonies, together
with some other valuable property, were collected and loaded into three carretas and the party started for San Gabriel.

The Piutes followed, but so well did the mission Indians cover and guard the retreating party that the hostile Indians abandoned the pursuit at Cucamunga and returned across the mountains from whence they came.

Order having been apparently restored, the padres returned to San Bernardino, but only to face fresh disaster from another quarter. In the latter part of December of the same year an uprising of Indians took place. A war party of two hundred Indians, under the leadership of two chiefs, ex-neophytes of San Gabriel, en route to attack the mission San Gabriel, stopped and laid siege to San Bernardino. After repeated attacks entrance to the mission was gained through the corral. The mission Indians, few in number, unable to continue further resistance, surrendered. This time the mission buildings were sacked and set on fire in several places. The priest in charge, Padre Estenaga, was made captive and carried away to the mountains. He, however, suffered no serious harm at their hands. Believing him to be a powerful medicine man the Indians feared to put him to death. He was held prisoner for some time until finally the mission Indians were able to negotiate his ransom and by payment of a quantity of provisions obtained his release. Padre Tomas Ellutario Estenaga was the last priest in charge of the mission of San Bernardino. He was a native of Spain, a man of education and refinement. He came to California in 1820, and died at San Gabriel in 1847. The last of the mayordomos of San Bernardino mission was Epomuceno Alvarado.

Tales of buried treasure are associated with every one of the California Missions; and there are people still living who, with all seriousness, relate the story of treasure buried by the padres at San Bernardino at the time of their hasty flight from the mission. There is no foundation in fact for these stories. San Bernardino was tributary to San Gabriel. Its material wealth was poured into the lap of the mother mission and whatever gain there might have been went to fill the coffers of that mission.   But so long as the mind of man retains its imaginative faculty so long will fertile fancy revel in visions of hoarded treasure, green and moldy with age, deep buried in the bosom of earth, where by some lucky chance it may yet be discovered.

This closes the mission history of San Bernardino. It was never again occupied by the missionaries.

Owing to the non-inflamable character of materials used in constructing the last building, the fire set by Indians did very little damage to the main structure; but that which escaped the hands of vandal Indians was destined to fall prey to the later agent of destruction which outrageously and wantonly wrought the partial demolition of many of the missions of California.   They were destroyed for the sake of obtaining the building material in them.

A portion of the last mission had been roofed with hewn timbers, brought from the mountains, and this was too valuable to long escape notice.   Two well known citizens of Los Angeles, with characteristic American foresight, saw the opportunity to make some money and did not hesitate to grasp it.   Mission property was anybody's property and the chance of getting something for nothing appealed as forcibly to the mind in those days as at present, while the opportunities offered were vastly· in advance of today.   Eleven   carretas of material from San Bernardino mission were taken into Los Angeles and used in the construction of Los Angeles buildings.   But, however slow the mills of the gods grind, it is unfailingly true they in time do measure, to a degree, with exactness.   The day came when some form of restitution was demanded for many acts of vandalism committed   against mission property.   The two estimable Los Angelenos eventually paid for that timber at the rate of $3.00 per vara.   As for the adobes, no accounting seems to have been made.   The native Californian was not particularly energetic, unless in the avoidance of labor, and as mission-made adobes were superior articles, after the lapse of a few years San Bernardino Mission was nothing but a dismantled, crumbling ruin.

"So fleet the works of men back to the earth again,
Ancient and holy things fade like a dream."

CHAPTER XVIII.
EARLY LAND TITLES—MEXICAN LAND GRANTS.

The subject of land titles is an interesting one.   Their history may be said to show the advancement of races through various periods, patriarchial, feudal, mediaeval and modern; communal, vassal, tenant and owner.   They represent the growth of the individual; the development of man from savagery to civilization.

The history of land titles in California shows the influence of two races, widely divergent in character—the Latin and the Anglo-Saxon.

The early Spanish and Mexican inhabitants of California did not look upon the possession of land as did the later occupants.   It was a pastoral age and they were a pastoral people.   They regarded land as of little value and were supremely indifferent to certainty of boundaries. Land was used principally for grazing cattle and a description accurate enough to obtain a grant was sufficient for all practical purposes.   If boundaries overlapped the possessions of a neighbor here and there, it did not matter. There was land enough for everyone.

All this changed with the coming of the Americans.   After the mad excitement over the discovery of gold had abated somewhat, clear-headed men saw the value of the land for agricultural purposes.   The ranchers succeeded the Argonauts.   A sweeping tide of immigration set in from the older Eastern States and from Europe.   They were an alien race and brought with them new manners, new customs and a new language.   With the new comers, possession of land amounted almost to a passion.   There must be no uncertainty of description.   The title to the land must be absolute, and fixed by metes and bounds, must be determined with exactness, and when once determined no encroachment was tolerated.

The Americans found nearly all the desirable land claimed under Spanish or Mexican grants.   The treaty of Guadalupe-Hidalgo, between the United States and Mexico, provided security for the inhabitants of the ceded territory and that they should "be maintained and protected in the full enjoyment of their liberty and property."   This, in itself, was clear and the Americans were bound to respect and abide by it. Therefore title to these lands could only be secured by right of purchase.   Then came the important question of validity of title under these Spanish and Mexican grants.   In order to give a good title to land a valid title must be shown.   In many cases this was impossible.   In some instances as many as five different grants had been issued to certain lands.

The first Spanish land grant in California was made in 1775.   The first two large grants of land were made in 1784. These were the ranchos of Santa Gertrudis and San Rafael, in what afterwards became Los Angeles county.

After Mexican independence a number of new laws were passed and land grants made, but these were comparatively few in number   until   after the   act of secularization in 1833. Under this act the vast tracts of land held by the missions became public domain and were opened   to settlement under Mexican colonization laws.

To obtain a grant of land, under the laws of Mexico, a petition was drawn up, giving, as near as possible, a description of the land desired; and also   stating the age, nativity, and occupation of the petitioner.   This   petition was then forwarded to some local officer who would report upon the matter.   If the report was favorable a grant would be issued. Memoranda of such action was sometimes recorded in a book kept for the purpose, but as often as otherwise it was simply filed away. Final proceedings to secure the grant consisted in obtaining the approval of the territorial deputation, and after California had become a department of the territorial assembly, this was not difficult. Upon presentation of the matter to the assembly it would be referred to a committee, and the report of the committee having been made, upon application to the secretary, a certificate was given to the grantee. No formal record or registration was made outside of the journals of the legislative body. Many of these journals became lost or were mislaid and when wanted could not be found. This carelessness laid the foundation for litigation which later occupied the courts of the country for many years and cost claimants immense sums of money.

No regular surveys were made under either the Spanish or Mexican governments. Juridical possession was given the grantee by the nearest alcalda or other magistrate, but the title was considered complete without juridical possession. The description and boundaries were designated by certain landmarks. This was all the law and usage of Spain or Mexico required. It made a perfect title to all intents and purposes.

There were instances where attempt was made to fix boundaries by survey, but nothing like accuracy could be arrived at through the methods employed. In such a case a reata of about fifty varas would be procured and this was used as a chain. Stakes would be prepared and placed in position and the surveyor, after setting his instruments, would take bearings, with some far distant mountain, hill, rock, tree or river as a landmark. He would then give command to his assistants who would start in the directions indicated, urging their horses at a rapid pace. Without pausing the stakes would be set in the ground here and there, until the line had been drawn. It was, however, only in exceptional cases that even this crude attempt at survey was made. The maps made would indicate a tree, a mountain, a river, with the number of leagues distant from each other.   This method of surveying was purely Mexican.   It was not the system used in Spain.

After the departure of the padres from San Bernardino Mission in 1834, the valley was in possession of the Indians who roamed at will over the country.   A rancheria of Indians continued to make use of the mission buildings, but many of the Indians formerly living at the mission removed to San Gabriel and the different ranches in the south.   There was no attempt made to settle the country.   It was impossible. No inducement offered to settlers could overcome the lack of security.

No land grants were made in this section of the State until 1838.   In that year the Jurupa Rancho was granted to Juan Bandini.   This rancho was then in Los Angeles County, afterward in San Bernardino County and now in Riverside County.   I^t consisted of 7 (or 14) leagues. It was sold to D. B. Wilson in 1841 for $1,000 per league.

The Cajon de Muscupiabe was granted to Juan Bandini in 1839, but his claim to this grant was afterwards rejected by the Land Commission.

In 1843, one league of land at the mouth of the Cajon de Muscupiabe was granted to Michael White (Miguel Blanco.) The boundaries of this grant, in later years, became the subject of extensive litigation.

Cucamonga, 3 leagues, granted Tiburcio Tapia in 1839.

Chino, or Santa Ana del Chino, was granted to Antonio Maria Lugo in 1841.   It consisted of 5 and 3 leagues of land. Later it became the property of Colonel Isaac Williams. This rancho received its name from a half-breed Indian vaquero who had charge of the mission cattle at that place in early days.   This Indian was named Jose Maria, but by reason of his curly hair was called "el Chino."   The place became known by that name and has retained it.

In 1841, Don Antonio Maria Lugo, of the Rancho San Antonio, petitioned the Mexican government for a grant of the Rancho de San Bernardino.   The grant was obtained in the name of his three sons, Jose del Carmen Lugo, Jose Maria Lugo, Vicente Lugo and Diego Sepulveda, a nephew of Don Antonio.   Formal grant was made on the 21st day of June, 1842, and signed by Governor Juan B. Alvarado, then Constitutional Governor of both Californias. Juridical possession was given by Manuel Dominguez, Juez de Primera Instancia. The rancho is described as containing nine leagues or 37,000 acres of land.   "It is bounded on the east by the 'Sierra del Yucaipe' and on the west by the 'Arroyo del Cajon' and the 'Serrita Solo,' and on the south by the 'Lomerias,' and on the north by the brow of the 'Sierra' (falda de la Sierra.)" This grant included the entire valley of San Bernardino.

These Mexican land grants afterwards came within the boundaries of San Bernardino County.   They were all mission ranchos, once the property of San Gabriel Mission.

CHAPTER XIX.
THE EARLY MEXICAN PIONEERS.

The early Mexican pioneers of California were of Spanish blood. They were proud of their descent, proud of their
birth and of the traditions of the race from which they
sprung. This pride of race is one of the strongest sentiments
of the human mind. It is not an unworthy sentiment for
it tends to uphold the ideals of a nation and of the family,
and, in striving to emulate the traditional virtues the individual is uplifted and the general tendency is toward the
elevation of all. Were it not for this feeling of national and
genealogical pride, men would scarcely know who they were
or where they came from.

This pride was one of the distinguishing characteristics
of the early Californians. It may be said to have been measured in the individual by the degree of pure Castilian blood
possessed. In any case it dominated their actions and was
the fuel which fed the fire of their ambitions. Generous and
hospitable to a fault; passionate and excitable in temperament; careless with money; abhorring labor, still, they never
forgot for an instant what was due their birth. As time
passed the blood became fused with that of other races; the
language deteriorated and lost its original purity; the customs of old Spain, though lingering long, at last gave way,
but the pride remained.

The resources of the early Californians were limited.
They lacked teachers and were without schools. They had
little conception of anything outside of their own circum-
scribed sphere. Spain, Mexico and California was their world.
It is slight wonder that they viewed the approach of the

Americans with distrust and showed little desire to encourage American trade or American occupancy of the territory.   It was an instinctive fear and, all unconsciously, they followed that immutable law of nature which, if heeded, points the danger-signal to nations and to individuals, and endeavors to shield the weaker from the stronger.   They   acted in the light of what seemed best to them.   They were forced, at last, to succumb to the inevitable.   The present understands the past as little as the future will understand the present. These early Californians were of a type that has passed away. Let their virtues, and they had many, be remembered; their faults be forgotten.

A name well known in the early history of California is that of Juan Bandini, grantee of the Jurupa rancho.   Though the Jurupa rancho was never, strictly speaking, any part of San Bernardino Valley, it was once entirely within the boundaries of San Bernardino county and has a place in the early history of the valley.   A small portion of the original Jurupa grant still remains within the line of San Bernardino county— Agua Mansa.   The Jurupa rancho was the first of the Mexican land grants in the vicinity of the valley. Of the   grantee, Juan Bandini, Bancroft's Pioneer Register gives the following condensed account:

"Bandini (Juan) son of Jose, born at Lima in 1800.   The exact day of his arrival in California is not known.   It is possible that he came with his father in '19 or '21.   His public life began in '27-8 as member of   the   diputacion; '28-'32 sub-comisario of revenues at San Diego; suplente congressman '31-2.   In '31 he took a leading   part in   fomenting the revolution against Gov. Victoria, and in opposing Zamorano's counter-revolt of '32.   In '33 he went to Mexico as member of congress, but came back in '34 as vice-president of Hijar and Padres' grand colonization and   commercial   company; supercargo of the company's vessel, the Natalia, and inspector of customs for California.   The disastrous failure of the col-

ory scheme, and the refusal of California to recognize his
authority as inspector, were regarded by Don Juan as the most
serious misfortunes of his whole life and of his adopted
country's history, his failure being rendered the more humil-
iating by the detection of certain smuggling operations in
which he was engaged. In '36-8 Bandini was in several respects the leading spirit of the southern opposition to Alvarado's government; at each triumph of the arribenos he was
lucky to escape arrest, and lost no time in fomenting new re-
volts. His position was a most unwise one, productive of great
harm to California; his motive was chiefly personal feeling
against Angel Ramirez, whom he regarded as influential in the
new administration, for he had been a personal friend of the
northern leaders and supporters of their general views; and
his record as a politician throughout the sectional troubles
was neither dignified, patriotic, nor in any way creditable. Under Carillo he was nominally in charge of the San Diego custom house. He was owner of the Tecate rancho on the frontier, which was sacked by the Indians in '37-8, Bandini and
his family being reduced to poverty and serious want; but
Governor Alvarado made him administrator of San Gabriel
mission '38-40, granting him also in '38 Jurupa, in '39 Rincon
and Cajon de Muscupiabe, and land at San Juan Capistrano
'41.   He was appointed fiscal of the tribunal superior '40-42,
was comisionado at the new pueblo of San Juan de Arguello
in '41, and sindico at L. Angeles '44, taking but slight part
in the troubles with Gov. Micheltorena. In '45-6 Don Juan
was Gov. Pico's secretary, and a zealous supporter of his administration, particularly in mission affairs and opposition to
Castro, being also a member of the assembyl and originator
of the projected consejo general.   Later, however, he espoused the U. S. cause, furnished supplies for Stockton's
battalion, was offered the collectorship, and named as member of the legislative council in '47, and alcade of San Diego
in '48.   In '49 he declined a judgeship; is said to have im-

paired his fortune by erecting a costly building in '50 at San Diego, where he kept a store; and subsequently appears to have gone across the frontier, where the estate of Guadalupe had been granted him in '46, resuming his Mexican citizenship and serving as juez in '52. He still dabbled to some extent in revolutionary politics, and as a supporter of Melendres had to quit the country with all his live stock in '55. He died at Los Angeles in 1859. It is evident from the preceding resume of what is for the most part more fully told elsewhere that Juan Bandini must be regarded as one of the most prominent men of his time in California. He was a man of fair abilities and education, of generous impulses, of jovial temperament, a most interesting man socially, famous for his gentlemanly manners, of good courage in the midst of personal misfortunes, and always well liked and respected; indeed his record as a citizen was an excellent one. He also performed honestly and efficiently the duties of his various official positions. In his grander attempts as a would-be statesman, Don Juan was less fotunate. His ideas were good enough, never absurd if never brilliant; but when once an idea became fixed in his brain, he never could understand the failure of Californian affairs to revolve around that idea as a center; and in his struggles against fate and the stupidity of his compatriots he became absurdly diplomatic and tricky as a politician. He was an eloquent speaker and fluent writer, though always disposed to use a good many long words when a few short ones would serve the better purpose. Bandini's first wife was Dolores, daughter of Capt. Jose M. Estudillo, whose children were Arcadia—Mrs. Abel Stearns and later Mrs. Robert S. Baker; Isadora, who married Col. Cave J. Coutts; Josefa, the wife of Pedro C. Carillo; Jose Maria, whose wife was Terese Arguelio: and Juanito. His second wife was Refugio, daughter of Santiago Arguello, whose children were Juan de la Cruz, Alfredo, Arturo and two daughtes, who married Charles R. Johnson and Dr. James B. Wins-

ton.   Bandini's daughters were famous for their beauty; all
or most of his children live in Southern California in '85,
some wealthy, all in comfortable circumstances and of respectable family connections."

The name of Lugo, however, properly heads the list of
Mexican pioneers of San Bernardino Valley. They were
grantees of the rancho de San Bernardino and this rancho
practically took in the whole valley.

In the time intervening between the passing of the friars
and the coming of the Lugos there seems to have been an oc-
cupant of the rancho de San Bernardino in the person of Jose
Bermudas, who, with his family, came from Los Angeles
County about 1836 and "squatted" on the property afterwards
granted the Lugos.   He built the historic "old adobe" dwelling, afterwards the site of "the Mormon fort," and now the
property of Wozencraft, on C street.   Bermudas occupied the
property until dispossessed by the grant to the Lugos.   It
is doubtful if he ever made any regular claim to or application for this property.   At all events, the matter of his re-
linquishment was amicably settled and he removed to the
Yucaipe, having been promised a grant of land in that locality.   This promise was never fulfilled. Later, land was promised him in Canade de San Timoteo and he removed from
Yucaipe to the property now owned by his son.   This son,
Miguel Bermudas, was born at San Gabriel, and was a child
of five years of age when his father moved into the valley. He
claims to be the oldest settler, in point of residence, of San
Bernardino Valley.

Juan Nepomuceno Alvarado may be said to have been an
almost continuous resident of the rancho San Benardino from
1830, when appointed by the padres moyor domo of the mission, until the lands came into possession of the Lugos.   He
was the last mayordomo, honest, industrious, faithful in the
performance of his duties, and implicitly trusted by the padres.
After the Lugos came he removed to Cucamonga and after-

wards settled on land near North Ontario, naming his place San Antonio. He abandoned this property and removed to Los Angeles, where he died in 1869.

Don Antonio Maria Lugo, grantee of the Santa Ana del Chino, or Chino rancho, and father of Jose del Carmen Lugo, Jose Maria Lugo and Vicente Lugo, grantees of the rancho de San Bernardino, was born at the Mission of San Antonio de Padua, in 1775. He was owner of the San Antonio rancho, one of the earliest and richest of the Alta-California land grants, given him in 1810, while serving as a soldier of Spain. Don Antonio was a picturesque character. He was uneducated, but a man of great energy, decision and strength of mind. He was of commanding figure, fully six feet in height, spare and sinewy. His face was of the purely Spanish type with square-cut features and closely shaven; the naturally stern expression relieved by an appearance of grim humor. He was a superb horseman and retained his erect carriage to the date of his death, at eighty-five years. This occurred in 1860.

Bancroft's Pioneer Register states that he was "alcalde of Los Angeles in 1816 to 1819; juez del campo 1833-34; a member of the ayuntamiento and took part in the troubles between the north and south."

Juez del campo, or judge of the plains, was an important position in the early days. The person holding the office was, in a way, an autocrat. There was no appeal from his decisions. His duties consisted in settling disputes between rancheros relative to the ownership of cattle, etc.

H. D. Barrows, of Los Angeles, in one of the annual publications of the Historical Society of Southern California, writes entertainingly of Don Antonio, and as he had the benefit of a personal acquaintance is well able to estimate the character of this early pioneer:

"Don Antonio Maria Lugo was, in most respects as thoroughly a Spaniard as if he had been born and reared in Spain. With "Los Yankees," as a race, he, and the old Californians generally, had little sympathy, although individual members of the race whom from long association he came to know intimately, and who spoke his language, he learned to esteem and respect most highly, as they in turn, learned most highly to esteem and respect him, albeit, his civilization differed in some respects radically from theirs.

It is related of him that on seeing for the first time an American mowing-machine in operation, he looked on with astonishment, and holding up one long, bony finger, he exclaimed: "Los Yankees faltan un dedo de ser el Diablo!" The Yankee only lacks one finger of being the Devil!

To rightly estimate the character of Senor Lugo, it is necessary for Americans to remember these differences of race and environment. Although he lived under three regimes, to-wit: Spanish, Mexican and Anglo-American, he retained to the last the essential characteristics which he inherited from his Spanish ancestors; and although, as I have intimated, he had as was very natural, no liking for Americans themselves, as a rule, or for their ways, nevertheless, he and all the better class of native Californians of the older generations did have a genial liking for individual Americans and other foreigners, who, in long and intimate social and business intercourse, proved themselves worthy of their friendship and confidence."

Jose del Carmen Lugo, son of Antonio Maria Lugo, according to Bancroft's Pioneer Register, "was born at Los Angeles 1813; regidor at Los Angeles '38-9; grantee San Bernardino 1842; juez del campo 1844; prominent in Chino fight and several Indian expeditions '46-7; alcalde Los Angeles '49. After selling his ranch to the Mormons in 1851 he lived in Los Angeles, in good circumstances until about 1865, when he lost his property. He had a wife and four daughters.

"Jose Maria Lugo, son of Antonio Maria Lugo." Bancroft's Pioneer Register fails to give date of birth, but says: "juez del campo at Los Angeles '36-8; one of the grantees of San Bernardino."

"Vincente Lugo; one of the grantees of San Bernardino 1842; justice at San Gabriel 1850; supervisor Los Angeles County '62-3."

"Diego Sepulveda," one of the grantees of San Bernardino 1842; was somewhat prominent in the Flores revolt at Los Angeles '46-7." Sepulveda appears to have taken part in the battle of the Chino and to have figured in political disturbances of the time.

Of the younger Lugos very little can be said. They came into San Bernardino Valley in 1841 and secured a grant of the San Bernardino rancho in 1842. They lived the life of the average ranchero and, passing on, left very little impress on the history of the valley. The valley, in their time, was simply a vast tract of land, magnificently beautiful, but the future possibilities, all undreamed of, waited the coming of another race.

Jose del Carmen Lugo occupied the old adobe house, built by Jose Bermudas. He afterwards removed to the old mission. Jose Maria Lugo built for himself a house at Homoa, about four and one-half miles south of the present city of San Bernardino. It was at the base of the foot-hills, then, and for many years after, the site of an Indian rancheria. Vicente Lugo lived at the rancheria of Politana and Diego Sepulveda at Yucaipe.

A large number of cattle were brought from the Lugo rancho San Antonio to San Bernardino. Stock-raising was conducted on an extensive scale. The animals increased rapidly in number and it is said the Lugos never knew how many head of cattle they owned. The work of caring for them was, at first, principally performed by Indian vaqueros.

Throughout the whole period of the Lugo occupancy they suffered much from Indian depredations which, however, were confined to running off the stock. Horse and cattle stealing was a recognized industry in those days and it was not until after the advent of the Americans that it received a set-back.

CHAPTER XX.

MEXICAN   PIONEERS—ISAAC   WILLAMS—BATTLE   AT
CHINO.

The Americans who came into California in the early days were not ordinary men.   As a rule they were men endowed with unusual characteristics.   It was not love of gold that led them to face the perils of a journey across mountain, desert, plain or ocean, for gold had not yet been discovered in California.   It was rather a restlessness of spirit that could not brook the restraints of an older civilization and found in the freer life of the frontier that which appealed strongest to their adventure-loving natures.   Such men have ever been of the vanguard in the progress of civilization.   From out of the old lands of a weary old world they crossed the stormy Atlantic to the new lands of a newer world; then, step by step across a continent until the calm, smiling waters of the Pacific seemed to set a boundary beyond which they could not further go.   But the wheels of Progress will not stay their resistless course and men must advance, always to some far-off ideal the end of which is beyond vision.   So these Americans came to California and found here what appeared to them limitless possibilities—wealth without labor, life without toil.   These big, strong, virile American men were favored by the dark-eyed senoritas of the sunny land and with their love went dower of rich lands and herds of fat cattle.   Those that came in search of adventure stayed.   Here was wealth, beauty, pleasure, love, and the spell of it all soon bound them in a thrall they did not care to break.   It was lotus-land and the cooler northern blood was not proof against the languor of the southern sun, and the desire to bask forever in the soft, warm rays grew upon them until the wild spirit of adventure which had thrilled their pulses and led them from afar slumbered under the spell and no longer beckoned. Then they took to themselves wives, the beautiful daughters of the best families in the land . All that was required of them was some slight formality in the way of change of faith—and their religious prejudices were not strong—and an allegiance to another government than their own.   This did not weigh heavily upon them, so they embraced the new faith and the new customs—and yet they became not so much a part of the latter, for in return they infused into the new life that which the native Californians lacked—a spirit of enterprise and the energy of the colder-blooded race.

Isaac Williams of the Rancho del Chino, was a typical American pioneer of that period.   He was the first American to settle in this section of the State.   His was a spirit born to command.   Whole-souled, generous, hospitable, he kept open house for every American passing his door.   A hearty greeting awaited every comer; the best the rancho afforded was at their disposal and they were invited to regard it as their own, and when at last the time came for departure, it was with sincere expressions of regret that the genial owner of the place bade them God-speed.   Many a party of exhausted emigrants halted at the Chino rancho, and many a weary, footsore wanderer found here a resting place.   Not one among his countrymen, if in need, left the home of Isaac Williams empty handed .   Indeed, it is stated that Colonel Williams, in his desire to aid his countrymen, sometimes came very near to embarrassing himself.   However, if he erred at all in this respect it was on the right side, and if the blessings and remembrance of the weary, home-sick, heart-sick travelers in a strange land may count to his credit, Colonel Williams needs no other monument.

Isaac Williams, generally known in California as Julian

Williams, was born in Wyoming Valley, Penn., Sept. 19, 1799 He came to Los Angeles in 1832 with Ewing Young's party of thirty men who had been engaged in hunting and trapping on the Gila River, in New Mexico.   With this party also came Moses Carson, a brother of the celebrated Kit Carson.   Mr. Williams appears to have become prominent in local affairs very soon atfer his arrival, as his name is mentioned in connection with several matters.   He was a member of the vigilance committee in 1835.   In 1839 he took the oath of allegiance and became a naturalized citizen of Mexico.   Immediately following he married Senorita Maria de Jesus Lugo, daughter of Don Antonio Maria Lugo, and in 1841 became cwner of the Chino rancho, of which Don Antonio was the original grantee.   In 1843 he obtained an additional grant of land adjoining his Chino property and settled down   as a rancher and stock breeder, devoting himself to the management of his large estate.   In 1846 he proposed to build a fort at the Cajon, on condition that he be allowed to bring goods to the value of $25,000 into California, free of import duty, as at that time there was a tax of $600 on every vessel.

At the time of the American invasion of California the Americans living in the territory were looked upon by the Californians with more or less suspicion.   While nominally citizens of Mexico, the Americans saw the advantage which would accrue to California if brought under the government of the United States, and many of them were pronounced in advocating the change.   This, naturally, was not pleasing to the native Californians who were Mexican in their sympathies, and more or less coldness and friction resulted in consequence.

Open hostilities between the Californians and the Americans began at Los Angeles, September, 1846, when Cervol Varela attacked the Americans under A. H. Gillespie, a Lieutenant of Marines, left in charge as Military Commandant at Los Angeles, by Commodore Stockton.   D. B. Wilson, owner of the Jurupa rancho, was then in command of a force of twenty men stationed at Jurupa for the purpose of protecting the inhabitants and property on the San Bernardino frontier from Indian raids.   Wilson, ordered by Gillespie to come to his aid, was en route to Los Angeles and stopped at the Chino rancho, the property of Colonel Williams . The party was nearly out of powder and found Williams in the same condition.   In the afternoon of the day of their arrival, while deliberating as to future movements, Isaac Callaghan, a scout sent out to reconnoitre, returned to the house with a bullet in his arm and reported the approach of a party of Californians.   After consultation it was decided   that, taking all things into consideration, the Americans were more than equal to the Californians and they   decided, notwithstanding their lack of ammunition to withstand a siege.

The Californians under Varela, Diego Sepulveda and Ramon Carillo, with fifty men, made up the attacking party. They were later reinforced with twenty men from San Bernardino rancho   under command of Jose del Carmen Lugo. The Californians were also short of weapons and ammunition.

The Chino ranch house was an adobe building fashioned in the usual California manner, surrounding a courtyard. The roof was of asphaltum.   There were few doors and windows, but the walls were plentifully supplied with loop-holes.   The entire building was surrounded with an adobe wall and a ditch.

Early in the morning of the 27th of September, an attack was made on the rancho.   The Californians, on   horseback, made a fierce onslaught firing as they approached the house. to which the Americans responded.   The horses of the Californians became frightened and in attempting to leap the ditch threw several of their riders who received injuries, and one man, Carlos Ballestros, was killed.   Three men inside the ranch house were wounded.   The attacking party succeeded in reaching a secure position under the shelter of the walls and from there set fire to the roof of the building.   The

Americans finding themselves trapped   and   in danger of a scorching concluded to surrender, and in order to make as good terms as possible induced Col. Williams, whose brother-in-law was one of the captains in command of the assailants, to take his children and presenting himself outside, make an appeal to Lugo.   The Americans surrendered.   The Califor- nians then set about extinguishing the flames and afterwards proceeded to loot the building.   Enraged   at the death of Ballestros, who was a general favorite among them, the in- furiated men insisted on putting the prisoners to death, but milder counsel prevailed and they were taken to Los Angeles, where the more prominent of them were held by Flores until January, 1847. It is related that these men were promised their liberty on condition that they agreed not to bear arms or use their influence in favor of the United States, but to their cred- it they refused to secure freedom on such terms. Among those captured at the battle of Chino were D. B. Wilson, Isaac Wil- liams, David W. Alexander, John Rowland, Louis Robidoux, Joseph Perdue, William Skene, Isaac Callaghan, Evan Calla- ghan, Michael White, Matt Harbin, George Walters.

Colonel Williams returned to the Chino rancho where he resided until his death, Sept. 13, 1856.   He sleeps in the old cemetery at Los Angeles.   He left two daughters, Maria Mer- ced, wife of John Rains, and Francesca, wife of Robert Car- lisle.

Don Tiburcio Tapia, of Cucamonga rancho was a man of considerable importance in his day and time.   His name ap- pears frequently in the history of the city of Los Angeles. He is credited with being a man of "good sense, good char- acter and some wealth."   It is a very desirable combination though possibly a trifle rare.

Tiburcio Tapia was born at San Luis Obispo in 1789. He served his country as a soldier and was a corporal at the Presidio of Santa Barbara.   He was a member of the Purisma Guards in 1824, and a member of the diputaciou **from** 1827 to 1833. After Mexico had adopted the centralized **form** of government the seat of Prefecture for the Southern District of California was established at Los Angeles, and Tiburcio Tapia was first Prefect, holding the office from 1839 **to** 1841. He received a grant of the Cucumonga rancho in 1839.

Stories of buried treasure become slightly wearisome **in** the history of California. San Bernardino valley has **its** share and Cucamunga is one of the hiding places of money. It is reported that a small portion of this treasure was discovered a few years ago, but the larger portion still remains within the bosom of earth. Men have resorted to all **sorts** of methods to unearth the old Don's treasure. Magic **wands** and electrical "gold finders" have been brought into use; **and** not content with the inventions of mere mortal men, the habitants of the realms of space in the upper and nether **worlds** have been called to assist in the search for treasure. **But** still the treasure eludes the hand of the seeker, and the seekers still hope to find the treasure.

As the story runs, Don Tapia was believed to possess **fabulous** wealth. In those turbulent days when government **was** on the move and continually shifting from one side to the other, with undreamed of possibilities in the way of change, a man's best and safest place for the deposit of money **was** not far removed from his hand. Don Tapia shared the general distrust. He had money and he wanted to keep it. **At** first some adobes were removed from the walls of his house and the money hidden within a cavity prepared for it. Time passed until in 1846 the Americans, under General Fremont, were dangerously near, too close to be interesting. The old Don was in deep distress and at a loss to know exactly what to do with his money. Night after night he tossed restlessly on his bed and his sleep, when it came, was disturbed by frightful dreams in which he saw the invaders ferreting out the hiding place of his treasure.   At last he conceived the idea of burying it in some spot far enough removed from the house to be secure from suspicion.   One night, taking with him two Indian servants, he loaded the treasure in a cart and set out for the place selected.   The distance from the house can only be surmised.   The treasure was buried and as the morning light dawned the Don and his servants returned to the rancho.   In some way the Don was able to work upon the superstitious fears of the Indians sufficiently to insure their silence, for, though Don Tapia passed away with the secret untold, no amount of persuasion could induce the Indians to divulge the hiding place.   They were afraid to do so.   It is said the old Don's restless spirit still guards the treasure and for many years the house was pointed out as a "haunted house," the place of strange sights and mysterious sounds.

After the death of Don Tapia the property passed into the possession of his daughter, the wife of Leon V. Prudhomme.

Michael White, known also as Miguel Blanco, was one of the first English-speaking settlers of Los Angeles.   He was a native of England, born February 10, 1801.   At the age of fourteen he shipped on a whaler and came out to the Pacific ocean.   He came to California in 1817.   He landed at Cape St. Lucas, in Lower California, and for a number of years was engaged as seaman on vessels along the Mexican coast.   In 1828 he was Captain of his own vessel, the "Dolly," engaged in the coasting trade between San Francisco, Monterey, Santa Barbara, San Pedro, and San Diego. Some people are unkind enough to intimate that his marine operations were in the line of smuggling.   If so, it was not considered much of a crime in those days.

Miguel Blanco received a grant of the Cajon de Muscupiabe rancho in 1843. He obtained this grant on condition that he reside on the land and endeavor to keep the Indian raiders out of the valley. The grant originally consisted of one league of land, but it must have been of an expanding nature, for it "grew and it grew" until it covered some eleven leagues and caused considerable trouble.

In 1831 Miguel Blanco married Maria del Rosario Guillen. She was a daughter of Eulalia Perez, who was famous as being a woman of advanced years, "the oldest woman in the world," supposed to be many years over one hundred years of age at date of death.

Mr. White owned considerable property near San Gabriel mission, where he resided during the latter years of his life, but finally losing his property, removed to Los Angeles, where he died February 28, 1855. He left a large family of children and grandchildren.

CHAPTER XXI.

THE NEW MEXICAN PIONEERS—LA PLACITA DE LOS
TRUJILLOS—AGUA MANSA.

Foreigners visited California prior to 1825, but the highway over which they journeyed was the Pacific Ocean, and whether from norcn, south, east or west it was always the same. The mountains and desert appeared to put an impassable inland barrier between California and the territory on the east, and the land beyond the Sierras was terra incognita which the feet of white men had not trodden.

Jedediah S. Smith of the Rocky Mountain Fur Company was the first white man to enter California overland. He started from the Yellowstone River, August, 1826, with a party of fifteen men, intent on a hunting and exploring expedition. Their course was down the Colorado River to the Mojave villages, where they found two wandering neophyte Indians, who guided them across the desert to San Gabriel Mission. They were not welcome visitors, and though the Californians furnished them with supplies, of which the Smith party were sorely in need, they were not invited to remain.

Smith appears to have camped in the vicinity of San Bernardino, for from this place he sent a letter to Padre Sanchez, of San Gabriel, begging for relief as they were in a destitute condition. As they were supposed to have left the country this fact aroused suspicion in the minds of the Californians and orders were issued for the detention of the whole party, but before the orders could be carried out Smith had left San Bernardino and was moving northward. In this party were a number of New Mexican hunters and trappers and through these men reports of California were carried into New Mexico.

In 1830 a trapping party was organized at Taos, under William Wolfskill and Ewing Young, to come into California and hunt the waters of the San Joaquin and Sacramento Valleys. The party failed to cross the mountains between Virgin River and the rivers diverging into the Bay of San Francisco, and the men becoming discouraged, through their sufferings with the cold, the line of travel was changed and the party went to Los Angeles, where they arrived February, 1831.

They had brought with them a quantity of "serapes" and "frasadas" (woolen blankets) for the purpose of trading with the Indians, planning to exchange them for beaver skins. They disposed of these blankets to the California rancheros, exchanging for mules, and with them returned to New Mexico. The mules were fine, large animals, superior to those of New Mexico, and when their destination was reached, caused much favorable comment. From this began a trade between the two sections of country which flourished for ten or twelve years. Caravans crossed the desert yearly bringing woolen goods from New Mexico and exchanging them for mules, silks and Chinese goods obtained in California.

Los Angeles was the central point for this New Mexican trade. It came by the way of the Green and Virgin River routes, through the Cajon Pass to Los Angeles. From there it distributed over the country from San Diego to San Jose and across the bay to Sonoma and San Rafael. After disposing of the goods brought, the traders made purchase of what they wished to carry back and what mules they could drive, and again concentrated at Los Angeles for their yearly return.

Between 1831 and 1844 a number of native New Mexicans, and some foreigners, came through with these trading parties in search of homes in this country.   It was at a time when owners of the large ranchos were experiencing much trouble from the depredations of Indians and they were very glad to make allotments of lands to colonists, asking only in return the help of settlers in protecting the stock on the ranches from the Indians.

In 1842 Don Lorenzo Trujillo brought the first colony of settlers from New Mexico to this section of the country. The Lugos made them a donation of land about one-half mile south of the Indian village of La Politana.   Among these colonists were William Walker, Julian Rowland and Benito Wilson. Walker and Rowland had married Mexican women; and later, Wilson married a daughter of Don Bernardo Yorba.   Wilson was at one time half owner of the rancho belonging to M. Louis Rubidoux, on which the city of Riverside is now located. Walker and Rowland removed to Los Angeles and afterwards owned La Puente rancho.

After remaining about two years on the Lugo donation, Don Lorenzo, and four other families of colonists were induced to remove to a donation of land made them by Don Juan Bandini of the Jurupa rancho.   This donation consisted of a large tract of land extending along the Santa Ana river bottoms for a considerable distance and which was fertile and well watered.   Here they founded the early settlement known as "La Placita de los Trujillos,"—the Little Town of the Trujillos.   The original settlers of the Placita were: Don Lorenzo Trujillo; Jose Antonio Martinez; Juan Jaramillo; Hipolito Espinosa and Dona Feliciana Valdez de Jaramillo.   The Placita was located on the west corner of Loma district in San Bernardino county.

The Placita was built in a semi-circle around a small plaza.   As soon as the houses were completed a church was built in the center of the plaza.   It was a rude structure with neither doors ,windows or benches.   An altar was erected and services conducted by Padre Francisco Sanchez, a priest from San Gabriel. Don Lorenzo Trujillo was appointed, by Don Bandini, commissioner to distribute the lands. Miguel Ochoa taught the children of La Placita for many years, and has the honor of being the first school teacher in San Bernardino county.

In 1843 a second party of colonists, commanded by Don Jose Tomas Salazar, arrived at La Politana. In 1845 these colonists removed one mile northeast of La Placita and there founded the village known as Agua Mansa. The name Agua Mansa, meaning gentle water, was descriptive of the smoothly flowing, limpid waters of the Santa Ana river, along the banks of which the settlement was located. Among the settlers of this second colony were Louis Rubidoux and Christobal Slover. Both had married Mexican women. Rubidoux afterwards removed to the Jurupa rancho, and Slover lived in the neighborhood of the mountain bearing his name, near Colton, and there continued to reside until on a hunting trip, he met his death from the claws of a bear. Slover Mountain was originally known by the Indain name of Tahualtapa— meaning Raven Hill ,and which in the early days was nesting place for large flocks of ravens.

Ignacio Moya was appointed first Alcalde of Agua Mansa, but he resigned and the people appointed Don Louis Rubidoux to succeed him. His jurisdiction was La Placita and Agua Mansa.

The colonists were employed not only as vaqueros on the ranchos, but also acted in the capacity of soldiers. The famous Ute Indian chief Cuaka--best known as Walker—was very active about this time and his repeated depredations on the stock of the settlers were very annoying. It was Walker's boast that the rancheros were only allowed to remain in the valley as stock raisers for his especial benefit. Nearly every full moon he came down from the mountains with his band of Indians and these incursions generally resulted in loss to the settlers. The Indians were in the habit of running the stock into the canyons, and there departing from the trails, drive them up over the mountain and down the other side of the range into the desert. When they had accumulated a sufficient number of horses they were taken across the desert and they found no difficulty in disposing of the animals at Salt Lake City, which was their usual destination. The settlers were armed with rifles and were expert in their use. In protecting the Bandini stock they had many fierce battles with the Indians. They usually fought on horseback, but sometimes it was necessary to follow the Indians into the mountains and there dismounting, continue the pusuit on foot until the Indians were overtaken and the stock recovered; but they were not always successful in recovering the stock. One of their fights took place in the mountains southeast of where the town of Highgrove is now situated. The Indians, after capturing sixty head of horses, escaped through a path between the mountains. In this battle Doroteo Trujillo was shot in the back with an arrow; Esquipula Trujillo was shot through the nose, and Teodoro Trujillo was shot in the right foot. They succeeded in recapturing the stock.

The church of La Placita, being only a temporary affair, did not long withstand the action of the elements, and the people, recognizing the necessity of a more substantial building, were called together in a public meeting to take steps for building a new church. It was a community affair and the settlers of La Placita and Agua Mansa responded to the call. They chose as commissioners, for the purpose of raising funds and selecting a site: Don Ignacio Palomares, Don Ricardo Bejar and Ramon Ybarra. After going up and down the river the commissioners decided to build the new church at Agua Mansa. As money was not plentiful, all the settlers turned out and assisted in the work of building. Some made adobes, others prepared cement, and others hauled timbers and lumber from the mountains. Joaquin Moya owned twelve or fourteen yoke of oxen and hauled most of the lumber from Aliso's mill; Pablo Velarde, a mason ,laid the adobes; Miguel Bustamente roofed the building. They began the building in 1851 and completed it in 1852. When finished ,the church was dedicated to San Salvador, but it became better known as the "Little Church of Agua Mansa." Padre Amable was first to officiate, and from that date to the present an unbroken record of the marriages, births, and deaths of the parish has been preserved. These records are now in keeping of the church at San Bernardino.

The year 1862 was a year to be remembered by the settlers of San Bernardino valley. This was the year of the great flood, which culminated on the night of January 22, and wrought great destruction and desolation. It rained continuously for fifteen days and nights. The gentle Santa Ana river became a raging torrent, which rushing, swirling and seething, swept everything from its path. The settlers awoke in alarm. The inhabitants of La Placita rushed to the Cerro de Harpero—the hill west of Loma district; those of Agua Mansa took refuge in the little church which seemed to offer a place of safety. The church and the house of Cornelius Jensen, opposite the church, were the only buildings on high ground and the only ones that escaped destruction in the flood.

When the morning dawned it showed a scene of desolation. The village of Agua Mansa was completely washed away, and where flowers bloomed and trees had been planted, a waste or muddy, turbulent water met the gaze. Nothing remained of the little village but the church, which stood upon higher ground, some distance from the river. The settlers were left entirely destitute and some assistance was sent

them from Los Angeles to enable them to build their homes
upon higher ground far enough from the river to escape future
danger from its overflow.   The settlement again flourished,
but never did the people   trust the river which had twice
treacherously deceived them and wrought destruction to the
work of their hands.

A local poet, Don Antonio Prieto, wrote of this flood as:

El veinte y dos de Enero
Que desgracia tan atroz
Bajo una grande corriente,
Por la voluntad de dios.

The Little Church of Agua Mansa remained standing for
many years, but at last, yielding to the ruthless hand of time,
t too passed away.   Barely a trace of it remains.   The bell,
cast in the sands of the hillside near Agua Mansa, was dedicated to "Nuestra Senora de Guadalupe"—Our Lady of Guadalupe—stood for a long time outside of the church of the Holy
Rosary at Colton, but was at last elevated to the little church
belfry, where, old, cracked, and badly defaced, it still calls
the people to worship.

CHAPTER XXII.

MEXICAN PIONEERS—RELIGIOUS, SOCIAL AND DO-
MESTIC CUSTOMS.

The law of life is change. Impermanency marks the pathway of progress. Inanition is stagnation and stagnation is death. So it is found in the customs of a people. Every new influence, however slight, leaves an impress and all tend toward the fulfillment of the immutable law.

The social and domestic customs of the early Mexican pioneers of California were those of Spain, and yet not entirely Spanish. To conform with life in the newer world and to meet new surroundings and conditions, innovations were necessary, and these, becoming engrafted upon older customs, individualized themselves and became a part of Mexican life, with usages distinctly foreign to those of the people from which they sprang. These customs in turn were supplanted by others and have in their turn passed away, until, becoming traditional, they remain only in the memory of a few surviving Mexican pioneers ,of whose life they were once a part. This chapter on the religious, social and domestic customs of the early Mexican pioneers is compiled from manuscript furnished by Mr. M. M. Alvarado, a descendant of one of the early Mexican pioneer families, and F. V. Archuleta, whose kindness and genuine courtesy is hereby gratefully acknowledged.

There is much error prevailing with regard to the number of Mexican families in California in the early days. When compared to the Americans, and other foreigners they, of course, outnumbered them, but not to the extent generally imagined.

At the coming of the Americans into the country there were in San Bernardino valley four Lugo families: Diego Sepulveda in Yucaipa; the Bermudas family in La Canada de San Timeteo, and some twenty-five families of new Mexicans on the Santa Ana river, from near Slover mountain to about three miles below.   There were a few families at San Jose (Pomona and Spadra), San Gabriel, La Mission Vieja, Los Nietos, and quite a town at Los Angeles, Santa Barbara and Monterey; the other hamlets consisted of from one to three dozen families, and such communities did not reach twenty in number.   Another fact, which will give some idea of the Mexican population, is that at the outbreak of the war between the United States and Mexico, the whole number of men that could possibly be pressed into service did not reach six hundred.

It was quite natural that the Mexican families should be intimately acquainted with each other.   They were almost entirely dependent upon themselves and their intercourse with one another extended from San Diego to Santa Barbara and from Santa Barbara to Vallejo.   A family would decide to make a visit to some relative, or to attend a fiesta, at one of the mentioned places.   When preparations for the journey were completed the inevitable carreta, drawn by oxen, was made ready for the women.   The men always traveled on horseback.   The carreta was a rude conveyance, but the only kind of wheeled vehicle in the country.   It was constructed entirely of wood and consisted of two wooden wheels, a wooden axle and a wooden rack.   It was manufactured mainly with an axe, an adze and coyundas (hide straps). Travel in this conveyance was necessarily slow; but on the other hand it had its advantages in the benefit derived from the pure air and magnificent scenery spread out before the travelers like a panorama. The virgin land blossomed with a profusion of brilliant hued flowers and luxuriant grasses, varied here and there with wood-bordered rivers, barren mesas, and deep arroyas. Large herds of cattle grazed amidst the vegetation and for diversion to relieve the monotony of the journey the men of the party occasionally engaged in a dart on a coleada of cows or steers. A coleada consisted in running at full speed, grasping a cow by its tail and throwing her head-over-heels. It was considered great sport and the participants enjoyed it immensely. When evening came the party would stop at some house where they were acquainted and remain for the night. They were always heartily welcomed and hospitably entertained. All ate at the same table and slept beneath one roof. Sometimes, when circumstances favored, the evening was made merry with music, dancing and singing. Care and attention were lavished on the guests in unstinted measure, and the whole effort of the host was to make the visitors feel at home. To offer to pay for accommodation of this kind was considered by the host as an insult.

While intercourse between families, whether near neighbors or not, was much the same all over the country, it was the invariable custom to keep the young people of both sexes separate. In mixed company and at social and religious gatherings the young ladies were seated by themselves, and the young men were instructed that it was ungentlemanly to approach the young ladies except when social right and privilege warranted. Opinion will always differ as to the wisdom of this custom of restriction, but by avoiding unnecessary freedom it certainly avoided immorality. In those days young people arrived at manhood and womanhood with all the pure, unsullied innocence of childhood coupled with the vigor of ripening maturity.

Notwithstanding the restrictions surrounding the young

men and women, love found its way much in the same manner as it does today. A young man wishing to get married would notify his parents of his choice, and if they were favorable to the match they would give their consent. If they considered his choice unsuitable they endeavored to dissuade him from the match. Similar proceedings were taken in the case of a young girl and an unworthy suitor, and so well were children trained to obedience that they submitted to the decisiion of the parents and the affair ended. Exceptions to this course were of rare occurrence. In case no objection existed on either side, the parents of the young man would write a courteous letter to the parents of the young lady requesting the hand of their daughter in marriage for their son. The father of the young man would then take this letter personally to the father of the young lady. After waiting eight days the father of the young lady would bring a written reply. After this, as soon as consistent with good manners, the whole family of the young man's father would visit the family of the young lady, taking with them the "donas"—gifts, consisting of jewelry and money, which were given to the parents of the bride-elect. After a sumptuous repast all the details of the marriage would be arranged by the contracting parties. Relatives and friends from far and near were invited to the wedding fiesta which was given. On the day of the marriage a large crowd was on hand, some of the people coming from a distance of fifty, one hundred and more miles. The marriage would sometimes take place at the church, sometimes at the house of the bride or the groom. As soon as the ceremony was completed the guests manifested their joy and congratulations by firing guns and by music prepared for the occasion. The newly married couple would next repair to their parents and, kneeling, ask the parental blessings. The wedding fiesta lasted from three to eight days and during that time the guests gave themselves up to pleasure and enjoyment. The fiesta entertainment consisted in singing, music, dancing and occasionally a horse race, bull fight or a toreada, and plenty to eat all the time.

Three religious holidays were especially observed by the early Mexican pioneers of this vicinity—Corpus Christi, San Juan and Noche Buena.

Corpus Christi, according to the established rules of the church, comes on Thursday, sometimes in the month of May and sometimes in June. Several altars were erected, a short distance from the church, and in commencing the religious ceremony the priest, robed in vestments proper for this celebration, would form a procession, which he headed ,carrying a reliquary, or the Blessed Sacrament, and assisted by two boys with the incensory, and other articles used in the ceremony, and these were followed by a number of girls, dressed in white. After them came the people of the church congregation. The Reliquary or Blessed Sacrament was placed on each altar in succession, prayers were said, accompanied by singing and the procession ended at the church where a high mass was said. This ceremony was simple but most beautiful and full of meaning, as are all the ceremonies of the Roman Catholic church.

San Juan day was celebrated on the 24th of June each year. After high mass the day was devoted to sports of some kind.

Noche Buena, or Christmas, was especially important. Three masses, with appropriate ceremonies, were held during the first twelve hours of the day; the first at 1 a. m., another at 6 a. m., and the last, a high mass, at 10 a. m.

The people were possessed of a deep religious feeling and veneration for things holy. They had many religious observances aside from these mentioned. Each Friday during Lent the people met, either at some house or at the church, where the prayers of the Via Crucis (Way of the Cross) were recited. From Wednesday to Friday night of Holy Week special religious services and ceremonies were observed.

The early Spanish and Mexican pioneers were a sociable people and indulged in several characteristic sports. Pelia de gallos, or cock fights, were very popular. Some person in nearly every hamlet or rancho was possessor of fighting cocks. When two roosters were to meet in combat the owners prepared them by special training. The trainers were men who understood the business—which was in itself as much of a science as horse racing, and required of the trainer knowledge, tact and judgment. A person without experience could not hope for success. Much care was taken, especially in tying the deadly "navaja" (a blade) just above the spur of the rooster. This blade was four or five inches long, pointed and sharp as a razor. When everything was in readiness those who had the roosters in charge would take them in their arms, pique them against each other, and finally place them on the ground two or three feet apart. In the fight which followed one of the roosters, perhaps slightly wounded, might run away, while at other times both roosters would be killed on the spot. It is needless to say that bets of more or less value were staked as a result of such fights.

"Corrida de gallos" was another popular sport. On the afternoon of San Juan's day a large crowd would assemble in some place where the ground was level and suitable for running at full speed. One or more roosters would be furnished by some person with the given name of Juan or Juana. The fowl was buried alive leaving only the head above the ground. Men riding at full speed on horseback, as they approached the rooster would lower themselves by the side of the horse and make an attempt to pull the rooster out of the ground by grasping its head. This was not an easy task and required skill and daring horsemanship, for the cock would dodge its head whenever any one tried to grasp it. Whoever succeeded in pulling it out of the ground would start on a full run, followed by all the others who had taken part in the coursing. If overtaken by one or more of the party, he had to look out for himself as the competitor would, either by force or strategy, take the rooster away. In retaining possession of the rooster and defending himself from attack the captor was considered justified in striking his opponents right and left with the yet living rooster. The cock being taken away from the first man ,the scene was repeated, until the fowl being dead, was severed into pieces in the affray. Then another cock would be furnished, and yet another, if they wanted it, until wearied of the sport all were ready to quit. Sometimes a purse was buried in the ground with the rooster and the money went to the man who pulled it out. If anyone showed anger during the course of the sport he was considered disgraced. It was understood that those taking part in the sport should not give way to exhibition of temper.

A bull fight and a toreada or capateada were two different sports. A bull fight was an encounter between a bull and a bear. Don Jose del Carmen Lugo, when living at Old San Bernardino, had a plaza de toros (an amphitheatre for bull fights) where they engaged in that kind of sport on the 15th of August for some years. That amphitheatre was simply a place walled in by large adobes with seats built on the top of the wall. Bears were numerous, and when they were wanted they were usually procured in the neighborhood where the insane Asylum now stands at Highland. The bear would be lassoed by some daring horseman and brought to the place of the fight a few days previous to the day of the event. As ferocious a bull as could be found would be brought in the same way, and when the hour of the fight arrived both beasts were turned loose together in the amphitheatre. It did not take long for a genuine and terrible fight to begin in which the bull was always killed, but the bear was also left in a deplorable condition, gored almost to death.

In the sport called "torear," or "toreada," no bull was killed. A wild bull would be turned loose in the corral, or plaza de toros, and a daring vaquero on a well-trained horse would ride in and tantalize the bull, until, goaded to desperation ,the bull would attack them. The men being expert, and on well trained horses, would easily evade the horns of the bull, and though horses were sometimes gored it was seldom fatally. Torear was a sport indulged in, not only in inclosed places, but anywhere.

Horse races were the most common and the most popular of all the Mexican sports. Large sums of money were staked on these races and numbers of stock were bet, and men frequently traveled hundreds of miles to see or to make a race. A place in open, level country was chosen, and the race track laid out and prepared in straight lines. When the day for the race arrived, men, women and children came, all attired in their finest clothing and riding their gayest horses bedecked with silver mounted bridles and saddles. If the race was one on which large sums of money had been staked nearly all the people in the neighborhood attended and it was considered no disgrace to bet with friends or neighbors. People won or lost without permitting it to make any difference in regard to their friendly and social relations. After the races passed. all things went on as smoothly as before. It was the only sport that brought on a shade of rivalry, but in that, only so far as to stimulate a desire of raising or owning the swiftest horse. Races in those days were not as detrimental to the morals of the people as they seem to be today. The money staked was usually deposited with some disinterested person who had made no bet on the result of the races. If horses were staked in the race they would be tied together in couples. Other stock might have been bet in advance, but as stated, some disinterested person always acted as stakeholder.

There were two ways of starting the horses in a race. One called Santiago parado and the other Santiago andando. By the first method both horses would be standing side by side; by the second method both horses would be on a walk, or a short trot, and at the word "Santiago" would have to go. If at the given word, one of the horses failed to start, no excuse was accepted, the race was lost. Men who made a business of caring for race horses were called "magnates" and indeed they were magnates in their line of work, for it took brains, patience and a certain knowledge to take care of and properly train a race horse.

The rodeo, or round-up, was a regular and needed institution of the country. There were many wealthy men who owned cattle by the thousands, others had a few hundred, and still others only a few head. As there were no large pastures fenced in the stock roamed at large all over the country and the cattle of different owners became mixed. When branding, marking and gelding time approached, after the calving season, the rodeos would be in order. For example, if one was decided upon near Slover mountain on a certain day, all the rancheros and their vaqueros of the surrounding country were notified of the fact by the Juez de Campo. On that day, early in the morning, all the men, in small squads, from all around the objective point, would drive the cattle to the rodeo where it would all be centered by nine or ten o'clock in the morning. If there were any cattle belonging to other than the owner of the ranch where the rodeo was held, it was separated from the balance and driven home by its owner until ready to brand. If there were only a few head this branding was occasionally done at the rodeo. Usually though, the process of branding, marking, and gelding followed the rodeo.   The stock was driven to the corral where a few expert "lazadores" (men who throw the riata) would lasso the cows, steers or calves by their feet, throw them down; another man would come with the hot fierro (branding-iron) and apply it to the left hip of the fallen animal, and after that would cut off a small piece, in some particular shape, or split the ear, and finally geld it.   There were men so expert in this kind of work that it was not uncommon for one man to do it all, with no assistance but his horse.   There was   a   great   deal   of work attached to cattle raising through all its different stages, but no intricacies, and most any common horseman or vaquero could attend to all branches.   Rodeos were held at all the large ranches on different dates, and men attending always found their missing cattle.

This was not a farming community, but the people raised nearly everything they used to eat.   It was necessary to raise grain and other foood products.   Corn, wheat, barley, potatoes, lentils, chic peas, sweet peas, a very large bean called haba, vegetables and garden products for seasoning were cultivated.   Among the last mentioned the principal were the traditional chile verde (green pepper) onions, garlic, tomatoes, coriander, majoram and saffron.   Wheat and barley were cut with sickles and made into small sheaves.   Beans and peas were pulled out and bunched and taken to the "era."   The era was a place cleaned out and irrigated, and then sheep and other stock driven over it to harden the surface, and which was finally inclosed with a strong fence.   The grain, peas or beans once in the era, a large band of horses were driven in and around until it was threshed.   The time taken to thresh would depend on the size of the pile of grain.   After threshing, when the wind began to blow, the men would take their forks and toss the straw up into the air and the wind would carry the straw away leaving the grain.   This work was continued until very little straw remained, when the "pala" was used to finish up.   The pala was a piece of board a foot and a half long by a foot wide attached to a long handle. The time used for threshing and cleaning in this way was several days and a few weeks of it amounted to a great deal and required the use of several eras.   Corn was piled up in the ear and beaten with a heavy stick having the effect of shelling most of it.   This was slow work, but it was the only way it could be done in those days.

Mission grapes were abundant; the making of wine was common and understood by many.   The grapes were picked and spread out in the sun about long enough to wither them. After this they were placed in tinas and trod thoroughly by foot.   The tinas were made from hides cleansed and prepared specially for the purpose, and hung and arranged between four posts so as to hold the grapes and juice without spilling.   To crush the grapes at times a "trapiche" was used. The trapiche was a simple contrivance of a roller with a handle and worked by hand.   When fermentation began the juice was strained, placed in barrels and left for a certain length of time.   It was examined now and then and cared for to prevent turning into vinegar.   At the end of a few months the wine was ready to use, but the longer it was kept the better it grew with age.

It has been said that the Mexicans did not know how to cook. Such assertions were made by people who did not know them and had never associated with them. While they do not cook the so-called fancy dishes, their food, especially in days past, was nourishing, wholesome and digestible.   Indigestion, dyspepsia and kindred ailments were unknown, while today they are as subject to these diseases as are other people.

There were no stoves in the early days, but in their stead fireplaces of mud and stones.   They were built in a semicircular form, varying from a foot and a half to three feet long ,and from one to two feet wide, and about one foot high, with bars across the top to hold the pots.   To bake bread "hornos" (ovens) were built of bricks and mud, on the same principle as bakers' ovens are built at present. Tortillas were oaked on large pieces of iron called "comales."

Everyone is familiar with the making of tortillas, tamales and enchilades, but there were other foods prepared which are not so well known, namely, puchero, estofado, albondigas and colache.

To make puchero select pieces of meat were placed to boil until it made froth, when that was thrown out.   Then to the meat and broth were added green corn, string beans, garlic, onions, cabbage, squash, carrots and a few of the spicy weeds, and all boiled until the vegetables were well cooked. To prepare estofado, some pieces of meat with   lard   were placed on the fire, and after a short time dry grapes were added and left until well cooked.   Then slices of bread, sugar and some spice were added and again placed on the fire for a short while.   Albondigas were made from the sirloin of the beef. The meat was well ground on a metate, or otherwise; to it were added onions, black pepper, coriander and yerba buena (a species of mint).   All   these   were made into a dough or paste, and from this little balls were shaped and cooked in boiling water.   Colache was a common dish, wholesome and easily cooked.   Some lard was thoroughly heated, and in that squash cut up fine, green corn, also cut up, some cheese and meat, all being cooked together.

The dress of the men was very much the same as shown in the pictured representations.   California was a stock country, and as nearly all were engaged in the occupation of stock raising they wore what was called "botas de haya."   These were large pieces of leather, some of common and some of fancy workmanship, wrapped and secured around the legs below the knee.   They were worn by men when chasing cattle, to protect their limbs from trees or chaparral.

The dress of the women was not vastly different from that worn at present, except in the articles of apparel known as enaguas or tunicos, rebosos and tapalos.   It was a common thing, before the coming of the Americans, for the women to wear enaguas or tunicos (gowns) of pure silk, which, of course, differed in color and pattern.   The material from which such garments were made was brought from Spain directly to Mexico; thence to New Mexico, California and other places.   Such garments were high priced and frequently handed down as heirlooms from one generation to another. The reboso was a long shawl of different colors with fringes at the borders; some of pure silk and some mixed with other material.   The tapalo was also a shawl, but a square one with fringes on its four sides and plenty of fancy embroidery all over it.   These were of pure silk, very costly and only a few women could afford them.   The rebosos and tapalos were gracefully used by women so as to cover the head and then thrown over or around the shoulders and chest.   A beautiful woman wearing one of these fancy tapalos presented a most charming and elegant picture.

The early Mexicans had so much respect for their word that it was not lightly given and when once given it was sacredly kept.   In business affairs of all kinds, in social intercourse or particular doings a man's word once pledged was held binding.   Written documents were not considered necessary.   Sometimes writing was used, but not generally.   If a contract between two or more parties was entered into it was done by verbal agreement, observed and adhered to strictly. A person might make a deal, trade or purchase from another about stock, land, money or any other matter, and their word was their document, binding and kept sacred until death.

These methods no doubt seem lax and unbusinesslike, viewed in the light of today; and yet such was the native virtue of these people that pecuniary loss was welcomed sooner than soil or tarnish their honor. As an example it is worthy of emulation and practice.

Unfortunately a change came, and that change, under such circumstances, was ruinous to their welfare. Take for example holders of land. There were large numbers of families who could not present a better title to ownership than possession and the word of another, perhaps dead, or bought out. Such facts could not avail or help them against established or newly enacted laws which clearly defined matters regarding ownership or acquisition of land. It was not strange then to see individuals or corporations take advantage of such state of affairs in order to acquire either small or large tracts of land, frequently lawfully, but many times unjustly. These doings gave rise to endless litigation and despoiled many Mexican families of their land all over the State.

Much could be written illustrative of their filial love and courage. Children, whether grown or not, for the sake of their love to their parents, would make any sacrifice, however great, if it would save them from a tear or sorrow. Young men, on the point of leaving home for a short or prolonged absence, on their knees would ask for the parental blessing; they would depart carrying engraved in their memory, always bearing in their heart, the advice and undying love of the dear ones left behind.

Two short anecdotes will be sufficient to illustrate their courage. On one occasion, Don Antonio Maria Lugo and his son Jose Maria, when on one of their rounds after cattle, lassoed a bear. The old gentleman handed his son a machete (a short sword) and told him to get down and kill the beast, which the young man did without hesitation. Francisco Alvarado, son of the Mayor-domo at San Bernardino, Viejo, once lassoed a half grown bear, tied him to a juniper tree from one end of the riata, then cut a stick of wood about a yard long and approached the animal as though he would allow himself to get hugged. The bear would rise on his hind legs and reaching out with his fore feet would try to reach Alvarado. Quick as lightening Alvarado would give him a blow on his paws, when the brute would draw them back and howl. Again the act would be repeated, until Alvarado, tired of the fun, killed the bear with his knife, taking the skin home as a trophy.

This is a brief description of a few of the religious, social and domestic customs of the early Mexican pioneers. In honor, honesty and true manliness the men of that day will stand comparison with the men of any nation; the women were marvels of love, purity and devotion unsurpassed by those of any nation or clime. The time was one of primitive simplicity and social equality. The people as a whole were happy and contented.

The passing years have wrought many changes to the people and to the State. Most of the old pioneer settlers have passed away. Their descendants are scattered, some of them having fallen on evil days, are the victims of distressing poverty; but many of them, in spite of the disadvantages under which they labor, still maintain the traditional virtues of their fathers.

Those now residing near the old La Placita, which they founded, are: Antonio Atencio, born in 1838; Esquipula Garcia, born 1818; Tomas Archuleta, born 1834; Jose Antonio Martinez, born 1842; Mrs. Teodoro Trujillo (Miss Peregrine Gonzalez), born 1828; Mrs. Jose Antonio Martinez (Miss Florentine Garcia), born 1828; Mrs. Miguel Alvarado (Miss Ascencion Martinez), who was born at La Politana a few months before her parents removed to La Placita.

In the county remain three other Mexican pioneers who

should receive mention in these pages. Miguel Bermudaz of San Timeteo canyon, who, despite his years, is active in mind and body, is doubtless the oldest settler in the valley. Ignacio Reyes of Reche canyon, born at Los Angeles in 1816, is a marvel of physical activity and considers it as little of a hardship to mount his horse for a ride to Los Angeles as he did in the years before steam had lessened the distance between the Rancho San Bernardino, and ere the city bearing that name had been founded. His wife was Francisco Lugo, a granddaughter of Don Antonio Maria Lugo. Reyes had charge of the vaqueros in the removal of cattle from the rancho after its purchase by the Americans. They drove 11,000 head of cattle from the valley at one time; then returned and drove a herd of 500 bulls and a large number of horses to the San Antonio rancho of Don Antonio. He is a remarkable type of the old-time Mexican, and sits on his horse with the grace and vigor of the days when men and horses were inseparable companions and fighting wild Indians or wild animals their daily task.

Miguel Bustamente came to California in 1849 and settled in Agua Mansa in 1852, taking a prominent part in the affairs of the colony until, mindful of advancing years, he declined further honors. For thirteen years, from 1867, he served as Justice of the Peace of San Salvador township. He was first Postmaster of Agua Mansa and a school trustee and road supervisor for many years. Though physically infirm his mentality is unimpaired and as keen and bright as in the days of his active life.

These pioneers serve to link the past with the present; they are still a part of the one and had their share in making possible the other; for as tomorrow is dependent on today, so today is dependent on yesterday. Each generation has its part in the sum of the whole; each must bear its proportion in the making of history; for nations, like individuals, are dependent upon each other.

CHAPTER XXIII.

AMERICAN COLONIZATION—THE MORMON PIONEERS.

The presence of gold in California was known to the padres long years before the Americans came into the country. It was on land belonging to the Mission San Fernando, in the Sierras north of the mission, that gold was first discovered. But it was on the 19th day of January, 1848, that the great discovery was made. Two weeks later the treaty of Guadalupe Hidalgo, whereby a vast territory came into the possession of the United States, was signed. California, languid in the golden sunshine, awoke from eons of dreaming. The pastoral era was at an end.

Then it was the name of California echoed and re-echoed to the outermost parts of the civilized world. Men, mad with excitement, fevered with the wild thirst for quickly acquired riches, rushed through the gateways of the mountains and over the vast expanse of ocean to the new "el dorado," where gold could be had for the picking up Never in the history of the world had there been such an excitement. But the Argonauts cared nothing for California. They saw not the glory of her sunshine, the beauty of her mountains, the fertility of her valleys. It was for the golden treasure hidden in the bosom of earth, and for that alone they came. To all the rich possibilities of the marvelous land they were blind. The story is old and worn threadbare in telling. The years filled with excitement and terror, the bitterness of disappointment and the heart-aches have left their record, and the successes also. In the history of the golden garnerings of the few the woes of the many have been forgotten. It is material success in life which appeals strongest to men. But time, always kind, has soothed the wounds and smoothed the roughness the years wrought, and "the days of gold, the days of '49" are paged in the annals of romantic history of the Golden State.

San Bernardino Valley was far removed from the scene of early gold excitement. Now and then tales were brought to the Mexican settlers herding their flocks in the valley; now and then some of the young men would wander forth to find how true the tale. But, as a rule, the Mexicans of the valley were not disturbed by the stories. They pursued the even tenor of existence, content with the life they lived, and having contentment desired naught else—had naught else to gain.

The causes which led to the colonization of San Bernardino Valley by Americans antedated the war with Mexico and might even be said to have remote origin in the exodus of the Mormons from Nauvoo.

The dominating minds, or mind, which governed the interests of the Mormon people fully recognized the great possibilities of the whole Western Territory. Mormon missionaries were actively engaged in the work of proselyting, not only throughout Europe, but in Asia, South America, Australia and the Islands of the Pacific. They were numbering their converts by hundreds. Brigham Young's fondest hope was to colonize the whole Pacific coast and to extend the dominion of the Mormon church even to the City of Mexico   It was another dream of empire with its capitol at Salt Lake City. California was especially desirable and important to the carrying out of his plan, which anticipated the planting of colonies of immigrants throughout the territory and these, forming a chain of settlements, would provide resting places for "saints" en route from the coast to Salt Lake City, the Mecca of their faith. It was a brilliant conception, well worthy the master-mind that conceived it, and but for the war between the United States and Mexico might have developed into more than an iridescent dream.

It was toward the close of the war between the United States and Mexico that a regiment was recruited from among the Mormons for service in the U. S. army. This regiment was known as the Mormon Battalion. After their return from Mexico they were quartered for some time in Southern California and while here received final discharge from service. They were law-abiding, God-fearing men and gained the respect of the people of California. Indeed, the citizens of San Diego found them so useful and desirable as neighbors that a general petition was circulated and signed by every inhabitant of the town requesting them to make a permanent settlement among them, and many of them remained in that part of California.

Captain Jefferson Hunt was the first of the Mormons to come into San Bernardino Valley and it was chiefly through his efforts that the Mormons colonized here. He was a man of more than average energy and ability and whose honesty and integrity of character was unquestioned. He was instrumental in organizing the Mormon Battalion and was commissioned Captain of Company "A." This company was stationed for some time at Los Angeles, and while there Captain Hunt became acquainted with many of the Spanish rancheros and made it a point to familiarize himself with the whole surrounding country. After the regiment mustered out of service, Captain Hunt, with his two sons, went into theh northern part of the State to the gold mines. He returned to Salt Loke Cityy in the fall of the same year by the Humboldt route which was then only a trail between Utah and California. In the spring of 1850 he made a trip to California, coming through by way of Southern Utah, the Mojave Desert and Cajon Pass, the first white man to enter California by this route, which was afterwards known as the Mormon Trail, or southern route to California.   He stopped in San Bernardino Valley and purchased 300 nead of cattle and 150 horses of the Lugos, and packing the latter with provisions, which he purchased of Rowland and Workman, he engaged 20 Indian vaqueros to take care of the stock and returned over the same route to Utah.

In 1850 Captain Hunt engaged to pilot a party of emigrants, en route to Sutter's Fort, as far as San Bernardino Valley.   After they were well on their way some dissention as to the advisability of the route chosen caused a division of the party, the dissenting members taking an old Spanish trail which they believed was a more direct route to their destination.   This was the party of emigrants who met so tragic a fate in Death Valley.   Those under Captain Hunt reached their destination with no mishap other than incident to overland travel of the time.   Returning to Salt Lake City Captain Hunt began agitating the question of the formation of a colony of Mormons to locate in San Bernardino Valley.   This coincided with the plans of Brigham Young, who encouraged the move and used his influence in furtherence of the plan.

In March, 1851, a large party of emigrants, consisting of about 500 persons, with cattle, horses, etc., left Salt Lake for San Bernardino Valley.   This train was under command of Captain Hunt who was to   take the lead and pilot them through to their destination.   As it was impossible for them to travel as one company, on account of scarcity of forage and water in crossing the desert, the train was divided into three sections.   The first section, under Captain Hunt, came into San Bernardino Valley and encamped at Sycamore Grove, at the mouth of Cajon Pass, on St. John's day, the 24th of June, 1851.

Amasa Lyman and Charles C. Rich, two of the original Twelve Apostles of Brigham Young, were with this party of colonists. They at once opened negotiations with the Lugos for the purchase of the Rancho de San Bernardino. During the summer the transfer was effected and they took possession of the property. The purchase price was $7,500.00. The colonists did not have the money to pay for the property and Elders Lyman and Rich, with Captain Hunt as agent, went to San Francisco, where they negotiated a loan for the amount. The money was borrowed of Haywood and Morley and was paid in three installments.

It is not within the province of this chapter to criticize or discuss doctrinal points, tenets of faith or the circumstances which brought the Mormon church into conflict with the government of the United States. It is sufficient to say that the Mormons who first came to San Bernardino Valley were ideal colonists. They were farmers, mechanics and artizans of the various crafts. So far as material advantages went there was perfect equality. There was no wealth and no poverty among them. The system upon which the government of the Mormon church was based was purely patriarchial and it was carried out in the religious, domestic and social life of the Morhon people. They were the extreme of conservatives, and sufficient unto themselves did not desire or tolerate outside influence or interference. As a community they were honest, industrious, law-abiding, peaceful citizens, and under their thrifty management the beautiful valley blossomed into marvelous productiveness. The church laws were sufficient to regulate all public matters until state laws were established. All minor dissensions among themselve s were carried into the church council and there submitted to arbitration. There was no appeal to other tribunal. Their moral conduct was beyond reproach. Idleness, drunkenness, gambling and vice was unknown among them until a later day when another class of people came to mingle with them.

Such were the people who colonized San Bernardino Valley.   Let credit and honor be given where credit and honor are due.

When the colonists came into the valley there was a rancheria of about 500 Cohuilla Indians, under Chief Juan Antonio, near the old mission.   During the summer Indians from Potrero came in and together they committed some depredations and in a few instances drove the settlers on the outskirts into the camp.   Anticipating further disturbance it was decided to build a stockade fort.   This fort was located in the vicinity of the block between Third and Fourth streets and C and D streets.   Houses for the settlers were constructed inside the palisades which furnished a good protection. Most of the settlers moved into the fort, only a few families remaining outside.   Though the Indians quieted down without any serious disturbance many of the colonists continued to reside in the fort, which they occupied for about four years, when it was demolished.

Bishop Tinney was the first to occupy the old mission. The mission building was used as a tithing house.   Charles C. Rich occupied an adobe house on the site of the homestead property of Joseph Brown, on E street.   Captain Hunt was President of the High Council of the Mormon Church of San Bernardino.

In 1855 San Bernardino Valley was a part of Los Angeles county. Captain Hunt was one of the two representatives of the county in the State Legislature.   In 1853 he presented a petition to that body asking the segregation of a portion of the county, the part set aside to be known as San Bernardino county.   An Act was passed and approved April 26, 1853 authorizing the segregation and providing for an election to locate a county seat.   Isaac Williams, David Seeley, H. G. Sherwood and John Brown were appointed commissioners to designate election precincts and to appoint inspectors of election. At this election the town of San Bernardino was chosen county seat of the new county. In the first years of the settlement the town was commonly known as "The Camp" and to the Mexicans as "El Campo de los Mormones." Old San Bernardino was called San Bernardino, or Cottonwood Row, taking the name from the rows of cottonwood trees bordering the mission zanja.

During the first two or three years the land was used as a whole by the community. Each settler was allotted the amount of land he wished to cultivate, and planted whatever he desired. After the county was established and the town platted the land was surveyed, subdivided into tracts and sold to individual purchasers.

The town plat of San Bernardino was filed for record at the request of Amasa Lyman and Charles C. Rich, on July 20 1854, R. R. Hopkins, Recorder. The streets were laid out due north and south, east and west, and numbered as they stand at present, but the lettering of the streets is of more recent date. On the original plat A street was Kirtland street, B street Camel street, C street Grafton street, D street Salt Lake street, E street Utah street, F street California street, G street Nauvoo street, H street Independence street, I street Far West street.

The town was controlled by the Mormons until 1857 when Brigham Young, desiring to centralize the church interests in Utah, issued the recall to Zion. Many obeyed the mandate and sacrificed their property to do so; others elected to abide in the land they had colonized.

Thus was founded the Imperial county of the United States. Its history since that date has been varied. Though far removed from the scene of civil strife the citizens, keenly alive to all the issues at stake, were agitated with the momentous question of loyalty or secession until internecine war threatened to develop. The city of San Bernardino has known its reign of terror and lawlessness incident to frontier towns of the far west; but the better element prevailed and from disorder came peace and prosperity. It has had its periods of depression and its periods of prosperity; but always looking to the future it has ever kept abreast with the chariot of progress.

What the future may have in store for the beautiful valley no man may know, for no man can know the scheme of human destiny.   Sublimely grand and ever watchful tower the mountain peaks of San Bernardino, San Gorgonio and San Jacinto, "Sentinels of the Valley," where grim and silent as now they saw it emerge from the primeval ocean; saw it lie for centuries desolate and barren of life saw it gradually emerge from its desolation until, reveling in a wilderness of verdure, it laughed up to the cloudless skies as though intoxicated with the exuberance of living.   Civilized man followed savage man and harnessed Nature to the plough of his needs. From the tangled wilderness of untamed beauty he developed an earthly paradise, for here Nature and Art combined touch perfection.   And the work of man in the valley is within the memory of men still living.   They have cultivated the land until it teems with blossom and fruitage; they have dotted the valley with thriving cities and villages.   The mountains, patient and silent can afford to wait for they know the possibilities of Time; but man, ever conscious of the briefness of his day, grows impatient, and looks toward the ever elusive Future for the fruition of his happiness.

But here Contentment should reign, for they who dwell within the shadow of her mountains, beneath the sunlight of her skies can say in truth, there is no fairer spot on earth than San Bernardlino Valley.

"Finis coronat opus"
"Los bons talls no se los menjan los dropus."

THE CHICANO HERITAGE

An Arno Press Collection

Adams, Emma H. **To and Fro in Southern California.** 1887

Anderson, Henry P. **The Bracero Program in California.** 1961

Aviña, Rose Hollenbaugh. **Spanish and Mexican Land Grants in California.** 1976

Barker, Ruth Laughlin. **Caballeros.** 1932

Bell, Horace. **On the Old West Coast.** 1930

Biberman, Herbert. **Salt of the Earth.** 1965

Casteñeda, Carlos E., trans. **The Mexican Side of the Texas Revolution (1836).** 1928

Casteñeda, Carlos E. **Our Catholic Heritage in Texas, 1519-1936.** Seven volumes. 1936-1958

Colton, Walter. **Three Years in California.** 1850

Cooke, Philip St. George. **The Conquest of New Mexico and California.** 1878

Cue Canovas, Agustin. **Los Estados Unidos Y El Mexico Olvidado.** 1970

Curtin, L. S. M. **Healing Herbs of the Upper Rio Grande.** 1947

Fergusson, Harvey. **The Blood of the Conquerors.** 1921

Fernandez, Jose. **Cuarenta Años de Legislador:** Biografia del Senador Casimiro Barela. 1911

Francis, Jessie Davies. **An Economic and Social History of Mexican California** (1822-1846). Volume I: Chiefly Economic. Two vols. in one. 1976

Getty, Harry T. **Interethnic Relationships in the Community of Tucson.** 1976

Guzman, Ralph C. **The Political Socialization of the Mexican American People.** 1976

Harding, George L. **Don Agustin V. Zamorano.** 1934

Hayes, Benjamin. **Pioneer Notes from the Diaries of Judge Benjamin Hayes, 1849-1875.** 1929

Herrick, Robert. **Waste.** 1924

Jamieson, Stuart. **Labor Unionism in American Agriculture.** 1945

Landolt, Robert Garland. **The Mexican-American Workers of San Antonio, Texas.** 1976

Lane, Jr., John Hart. **Voluntary Associations Among Mexican Americans in San Antonio, Texas.** 1976

Livermore, Abiel Abbot. **The War with Mexico Reviewed.** 1850

Loyola, Mary. **The American Occupation of New Mexico, 1821-1852.** 1939

Macklin, Barbara June. **Structural Stability and Culture Change in a Mexican-American Community.** 1976

McWilliams, Carey. **Ill Fares the Land:** Migrants and Migratory Labor in the United States. 1942

Murray, Winifred. **A Socio-Cultural Study of 118 Mexican Families Living in a Low-Rent Public Housing Project in San Antonio, Texas.** 1954

Niggli, Josephina. **Mexican Folk Plays.** 1938

Parigi, Sam Frank. **A Case Study of Latin American Unionization in Austin, Texas.** 1976

Poldervaart, Arie W. **Black-Robed Justice.** 1948

Rayburn, John C. and Virginia Kemp Rayburn, eds. **Century of Conflict, 1821-1913.** Incidents in the Lives of William Neale and William A. Neale, Early Settlers in South Texas. 1966

Read, Benjamin. **Illustrated History of New Mexico.** 1912

Rodriguez, Jr., Eugene. **Henry B. Gonzalez.** 1976

Sanchez, Nellie Van de Grift. **Spanish and Indian Place Names of California.** 1930

Sanchez, Nellie Van de Grift. **Spanish Arcadia.** 1929

Shulman, Irving. **The Square Trap.** 1953

Tireman, L. S. **Teaching Spanish-Speaking Children.** 1948

Tireman, L. S. and Mary Watson. **A Community School in a Spanish-Speaking Village.** 1948

Twitchell, Ralph Emerson. **The History of the Military Occupation of the Territory of New Mexico.** 1909

Twitchell, Ralph Emerson. **The Spanish Archives of New Mexico.** Two vols. 1914

U. S. House of Representatives. **California and New Mexico:** Message from the President of the United States, January 21, 1850. 1850

Valdes y Tapia, Daniel. **Hispanos and American Politics.** 1976

West, Stanley A. **The Mexican Aztec Society.** 1976

Woods, Frances Jerome. **Mexican Ethnic Leadership in San Antonio, Texas.** 1949